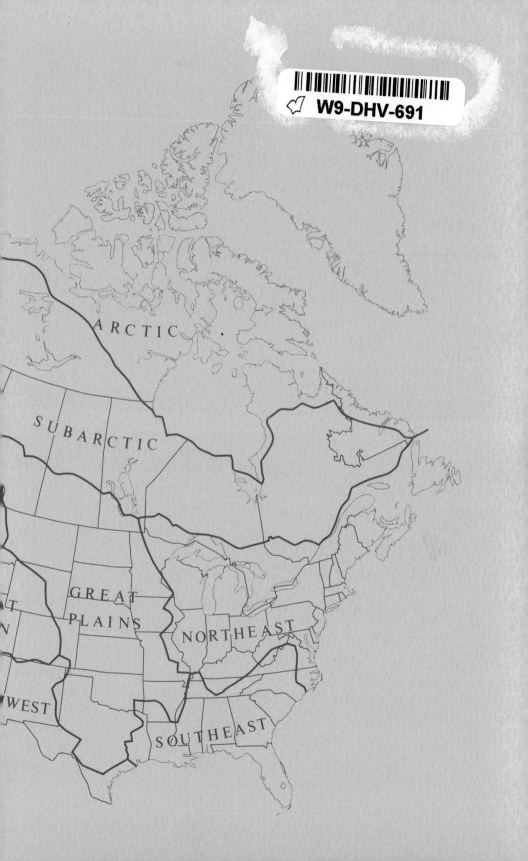

ARCTIC

SUBARCTIC

GREAT
PLAINS

NORTHEAST

WEST

SOUTHEAST

INDIANS
OF THE
UNITED STATES AND CANADA

Clio Bibliography Series

Abstracts from the periodicals data base of the
American Bibliographical Center

Eric H. Boehm, Editor

Users of the Clio Bibliography Series may refer to current issues of
America: History and Life *and* Historical Abstracts
*for continuous bibliographic coverage of the subject areas
treated by each individual volume in the series.*

1.
The American Political Process
Dwight L. Smith and Lloyd W. Garrison
1972   LC 72-77549   ISBN 0-87436-090-0

2.
Afro-American History
Dwight L. Smith
1974   LC 73-87155   ISBN 0-87436-123-0

3.
Indians of the United States and Canada
Dwight L. Smith
1974   LC 73-87156   ISBN 0-87436-124-9

Indians

of the

United States and Canada

A Bibliography

Dwight L. Smith

EDITOR

John C. Ewers

INTRODUCTION

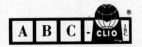

A B C - CLIO ®

SANTA BARBARA, CALIFORNIA
OXFORD, ENGLAND

Library of Congress Catalog Card Number 73-87156
ISBN Clothbound Edition 0-87436-124-9

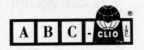

American Bibliographical Center–Clio Press, Inc.
2040 Alameda Padre Serra
Santa Barbara, California

European Bibliographical Center–Clio Press
Woodside House, Hinksey Hill
Oxford OX1 5BE, England

Design by Barbara Monahan
Cartography by Bill Rinaldo
Printed and bound in the United States of America

Second printing, 1976

CONTENTS

PREFACE

Indians of the United States and Canada is addressed to the renewed and contemporary public interest in the subject. It is the latest contribution to the *Clio Bibliography Series,* an open-ended series of special reference works published by the American Bibliographical Center. Its entries are taken from the data bank of the abstracts publication *America: History and Life.*

The 1,687 annotated citations constitute a bibliographic report on the great bulk of scholarship on the Indian which has appeared in the historical and social sciences periodical literature of the world from 1954 through 1972. The publication date of any bibliography limits the imprint date coverage of its entries. In this series, however, the researcher and scholar can update that coverage simply by using subsequent volumes of *America: History and Life.* In this instance, such updating can be achieved by commencing with Volume X (1973).

I assumed editorial responsibility for this Indian bibliography while on summer assignments in 1972 and 1973 as consultant to the American Bibliographical Center. Lloyd W. Garrison, managing editor of *America: History and Life,* was my editorial mentor and advisor for the project. Terry A. Simmerman, assistant editor of the *Clio Bibliography Series,* classified, edited, and indexed the abstract entries and coordinated production. She was especially aided by Lillian Kurosaka Anderson, Daniel J. Engler, and James R. Crane. Joan Haugh, Rachel Hayes, Marcia Katz, Barbara Monahan, William S. Rinaldo, Nancy J. Sandstrom, Cathy Schroeder, and David Trumbo enthusiastically supported the project with their special skills and expertise.

We are pleased that John C. Ewers, senior ethnologist, Smithsonian Institution, has written the introductory essay for *Indians of the United States and Canada.* He enhances the utility of the volume with a meaningful context and surveys and evaluates the recent scholarship as reflected in the periodical literature.

Finally, I am indebted to the hundreds of volunteer abstracters whose descriptive annotations of the periodical literature of the last several years are the sum and substance of this bibliography.

DWIGHT L. SMITH

Miami University
Oxford, Ohio

INTRODUCTION

John C. Ewers, Smithsonian Institution

Historians are increasingly aware of the roles of minorities in American history. Paradoxically, one of the fastest-growing "new" fields of research deals with America's oldest inhabitants and their descendants—the Indians. Researchers recognize that the Indians, the original ingredients in the American melting pot, have not been assimilated. They know that the Indians occupied the forests, plains, deserts, and mountains during the colonial period and were a major concern to European explorers and settlers. The descendants of those Indians should be a major concern of American and Canadian society today, especially since a growing proportion of the Indian population is urban.

Indians on isolated reservations and in great urban centers are increasingly aware of their own identities: their cultural backgrounds, tribal histories, the achievements of their past leaders, and their relations with non-Indians and their national governments. Increasingly Indians seek college educations. Courses in Indian history and Indian Studies Programs have been established in institutions of higher learning.

Teachers, students, and other scholars who want to keep abreast of new findings in this active field need to know what has been written of Indian history in recent years. This bibliography of 1,687 articles published in hundreds of serial publications in the United States, Canada, and abroad during the years 1954 through 1972 fills an important part of that need. The bibliography is systematized, annotated, and indexed analytically to help the user select writings most pertinent to his interests—whether a particular tribe or region, a particular aspect of Indian culture, or Indian-white relations. Those who sample these entries will become aware that there is a great variety of sources which can increase our general knowledge of Indian cultures and history. The archaeologist's spade and the folklorist's tape recorder yield data quite as important to an understanding of Indian history as the archivist's shelves of manuscripts. Dated artifacts, maps, drawings, paintings, and photographs are as revealing as written words. Just as the writings of explorers, traders, missionaries, natural scientists, settlers, and government officials have furnished valuable first-hand observations of Indians in the past, so have more recent studies by educators, geographers, lawyers, linguists, and physicians.

The evidence literally uncovered by archaeologists in field excavations is uniquely valuable to historians. It provides the background necessary for an appreciation of antiquity, especially the dynamics of Indian experience in the various environments of North America before the coming of Europeans. The broader application of radiocarbon dating by archaeologists provides more precise chronologies of cultural trends and sequences. Significantly, historians now know that Indian communities grew, developed, declined, and disappeared on this continent *before* the incursion of white men. Knowledge of prehistoric Indian life should help historians to understand the characteristics of Indian communities that persisted into the historic period. The variety of prehistoric cultures—such as the Paleo-Indian hunters of large and now extinct mammals, the complex agricul- turally-based cultures of the Classic Pueblo Period in the Southwest, and the Mound Builders of the Eastern Woodlands—is sufficient to warn historians of the pitfalls inherent in generalizing about "the Indians." The agricultural, architectural, and artistic achievements of some prehistoric Indian cultures rivaled or surpassed those of their Old World contemporaries. Archaeologists also provide a greater awareness of intertribal relations in prehistoric North America. Their evidence documents the influence of Meso-America upon the Indian cultures of the Eastern Woodlands and our own Southwest; it reveals that intertribal trade, even in luxury items, extended over trade routes from seacoast to the remote interior long before the initiation of the white man's fur trade on this continent. The remains of fortified villages suggest there was intertribal warfare in prehistoric times.

Archaeologists have found metal tools and weapons, glass beads, and other objects of European manufacture in protohistoric village sites, unnamed on historic maps. These findings clearly indicate that some distant tribes gained some of the advantages of the fur trade, through Indian intermediaries, *before* they met white men. The archaeological exploration of historic sites, such as Indian villages, missions, trading areas, and military posts, has enhanced our knowledge of the precise location, size, and construction of Indian structures and of life at the centers of frontier activity. Excavated artifacts reveal many objects previously known only through trade lists and scattered references in the written record.

Anthropologists continue to ponder the complex problems involved in estimating the aboriginal population of North America. They try to determine the effects of epidemics, warfare, and other factors on population trends during the historic period. Some tribes became extinct, others insured survival by forming intertribal alliances. New tribes formed through separation from parent ones during the historic period.

Anthropologists and historians share an interest in identifying and locating Indian villages and tribes at particular points in time. Numerous movements of tribes, even from one culture area to another, occurred before the wholesale enforced removal of many Woodland tribes to lands west of the Mississippi after 1830.

Since World War II the research interests and methods of many ethnologists and historians have been converging into a realm commonly termed ethnohistory. Traditionally ethnologists gained much of their knowledge of Indian tribes through the verbal testimony of Indian informants in the field. Historians have learned about Indians from documents in libraries and archives. There appears to be a growing recognition that both sources of information should be employed, each complementing the other, to produce richer and more insightful tribal histories. Ethnologists search archives to find significant observations concerning tribes outside the memories of Indian informants. Some historians, armed with tape recorders, have undertaken "oral history projects" on reservations.

The emphases of ethnologists and historians, however, are not identical. Most ethnologists focus on tribal cultures and the relationship of Indians to their natural and human environments. Ethnologists consider intratribal and intertribal relationships to be important factors in the history of a tribe and they tend to investigate the aspects of traditional culture that have survived an extended period of white contact. They characteristically record tribal folklore and describe religious ceremonies that have persisted long after Indians adopted the white man's technology. Such studies illumine the basic beliefs and values of the Indians which have persisted through time and thus provide important insights to understanding their character and history.

In contrast, many historians view Indian history largely in terms of Indian-white contacts. A high proportion of the articles cited in this bibliography deal with various aspects of the relations between Indians and explorers, traders, missionaries, and settlers. Many of the articles are concerned with the Indian policies of the French, English, Spanish, and American governments. The mechanisms used to implement these policies—e.g., gifts to Indians, control of trade, establishment of reservations, removals, treaties, wars, land allotments, Indian education, and health care—are examined extensively in the periodical literature. The influences of military and religious groups in the formation of Indian policies are also considered.

The study of Indian wars continues to attract many students. Articles that examine particular actions in Indian-white warfare in detail are numerous. They range from descriptions of the Jamestown Massacre of 1622 to narratives of isolated small skirmishes on western reservations, years after the Indian wars were thought to have ended. The role of the Indians in inter-colonial wars, the Civil War, and the Riel Rebellion in Canada are the subject of many citations. The character, attitudes, and performance of white leaders in the Indian wars are also studied. Custer is praised, damned, and posthumously psychoanalyzed. Other leaders in the Indian wars of the West are eulogized for their humanitarian qualities.

Even so, most white writers on the Indian wars seemingly hold peculiarly ethnocentric attitudes toward Indian warfare. To them the Indian wars were conflicts between Indians and whites which interrupted the steady expansion of white settlement. The role of intertribal warfare in regional history and its relationship to Indian-white warfare receives little attention. Noteworthy exceptions are Otterbein's "Why the Iroquois Won. An Analysis of Iroquois Military Tactics" (see abstract 1027) and Schroeder's articles (see abstracts 433 and 518) on the long-range effects of intertribal warfare upon Pueblo settlements in the Southwest.

The growing number of studies of the problems and performances of individual Indian agents is heartening. The reputation of Indian agents in general has suffered from the recorded dishonesty of a few. An examination of the experiences of a number of conscientious Indian agents certainly should reveal that the positions they held on isolated reservations were not sinecures.

Traders and missionaries were the first carriers of Western civilizations to become closely associated with Indians and to record their observations of Indian life and customs in many areas of North America. It is encouraging to observe that the records of various trading companies and of church denominations are being examined and are yielding previously unpublished information on Indian trade and missions. Furthermore, critical studies of the effects of the fur trade and mission activities upon Indian history are beginning to appear. An interest in the emergence of mixed-blood tribal leaders and communities has produced a few papers and additional studies are needed to assess their role in Canadian and United States history.

The rich possibilities for biographical studies of Indian leaders remain largely unrealized. The well-known war leaders—Pontiac, Sitting Bull, Geronimo, and Louis Riel—should continue to receive attention as little-known facts regarding their lives are found. We should also recognize that each tribe had leaders deserving of remembrance by their descendants. Too little has been written about the chiefs of smaller tribes, about Indian men and women distinguished by diplomatic abilities, their roles as religious leaders, their artistic creativity, or their written interpretations of the lives and hopes of their people for non-Indians. It is refreshing to find recent biographical accounts of the little-known chiefs Little Dog (Blackfoot) and José Maria (Anadarko), the influential 18th-century Cherokee Nancy Ward, and tributes to the late Mungo Martin, a gifted Kwakiutl wood carver.

Several papers discuss the role of the arts and the media in molding popular conceptions of the Indian and attitudes toward the Indian people. This subject probably will continue to intrigue future scholars. The Indians in Karl May's novels have impressed German youth quite as much as James Fenimore Cooper's redskins interested generations of young Americans. Pictorial images from the time of George Catlin helped create and perpetuate the popular stereotype of the American Indian as a feather-bonneted warrior. Historians should be especially appreciative of the influence that Frederick Jackson Turner and his concept of the Indian Frontier have had upon later generations of historians. Turner's seminal works have helped shape their views of the role of the Indian in American history.

Even so, many articles cited in this bibliography deal exclusively with the Indian in 20th-century America. Their inclusion reminds adherents of Turner that Indians are a lively element in American society that will continue to impose special problems—education, poverty, alcoholism, factionalism, discrimination, and the latter day problem of adjustment to urban living.

The antiquity of the Indian people, the diversity of Indian cultures, the multiplicity of Indian tribes, and their different experiences within the historic period make Indian history a rich field of inquiry for students. This bibliography of the serial literature in the field is a useful aid to students seeking information on Indian culture and history; it is a reference guide to recent accomplishments and a stepping-stone to future Indian studies.

USER'S GUIDE

The spelling of tribal and subtribal names conforms to John R. Swanton, *The Indian Tribes of North America,* Bureau of American Ethnology, Bulletin 145 (Washington, D.C.: Government Printing Office, 1952). Alternate names of tribes appear in parentheses in the textual headings.

Indians of the United States and Canada is divided chronologically, by culture area, and by tribe. The organization of each chapter will become clear with a glance at the Table of Contents. Further refinement is achieved by subdividing tribes and within each subdivision abstracts are arranged alphabetically by author.

Migrations, treaties, removal, reservation assignments, and other factors have changed and varied tribal locations. Herein, tribes are classified and indexed according to the geographic area where they resided at the time as indicated in the article. Geographic locales—cities, reservations, rivers, etc.—are indexed under the state or province in which they are located.

Abstracter credits appear at the end of each abstract. Personal names identify individual abstracters. "J" indicates the abstract was furnished by the editor of the journal; "A" indicates the author of the article provided the abstract.

INDIANS
OF THE
UNITED STATES AND CANADA

LIST OF ABBREVIATIONS

A	Author-Prepared Abstract	*IHE*	Indice Histórico Español
Acad.	Academy, Academie, Academia	*Illus.*	Illustrated, Illustration
Agric.	Agriculture, Agricultural	*Inst.*	Institute, Institut, Instituto, Institution
AIA	Abstracts in Anthropology	*Internat.*	International
Akad.	Akademie	*J*	Journal-Prepared Abstract
Am.	America, American	*J.*	Journal
Ann.	Annals, Annales, Annual	*Lib.*	Library, Libraries
Anthrop.	Anthropology, Anthropological	*Mag.*	Magazine
		Mus.	Museum, Musée, Museo
Arch.	Archives	*Natl.*	National, Nationale, Nacional, Nazionale
Archeol.	Archeology, Archeological		
Assoc.	Association, Associate	*Phil.*	Philosophy, Philosophical
Asst.	Assistant	*Photo.*	Photograph
Biblio.	Bibliography, Bibliographical	*Pol.*	Politics, Political, Politique, Político
Biog.	Biography, Biographical	*Pres.*	President
Bull.	Bulletin	*Pro.*	Proceedings
Can.	Canada, Canadian, Canadien	*Pub.*	Publication
Cent.	Century	*Q.*	Quarterly
Coll.	College	*R.*	Review, Revue, Revista, Rivista
Com.	Committee	*Res.*	Research
Comm.	Commission	*S*	Staff-Prepared Abstract
Dept.	Department	*Sci.*	Science, Scientific
Dir.	Director, Direktor	*Secy.*	Secretary
Econ.	Economy, Economic, Économique, Economico	*Soc.*	Society, Société, Sociedad, Societa
		Sociol.	Sociology, Sociological
Ed.	Editor	*Tr.*	Transactions
Educ.	Education, Educational	*Trans.*	Translator
Geneal.	Genealogy, Genealogical, Généalogique	*U.*	University, Université, Università, Universidad, Universidade, Universität
Grad.	Graduate		
Hist.	History, Historical, Histoire, Historia, Historische	*U.S.*	United States
		Y.	Yearbook

Abbreviations also apply to feminine and plural forms.
Abbreviations not noted above are based on *Webster's Third International Dictionary*
and the *United States Government Printing Office Style Manual*.

PRE-COLUMBIAN INDIAN HISTORY

General

1. Agogino, George A. THE PALEO-INDIAN RELATIVE AGE AND CULTURAL SEQUENCE. *Great Plains J. 1963 3(1): 17-24.* Points out that 35 years ago archaeologists believed no Paleo-Indian sites were more than 5,000 years old. The Folsom discovery at that time doubled the estimated time and during the past decade a number of possible pre-projectile point cultures have been investigated which may extend human occupancy of the Americas 20,000 years or more. Various point cultures are discussed and the article concludes with the prediction that in the next 35 years the sequence and evolution of point types will become firmly established.   O. H. Zabel

2. Ainsworth, Thomas H. THE STONE CARVINGS OF AN UNKNOWN PEOPLE. *Beaver [Canada] 1963 294(Winter): 44-49.* Soapstone carvings designed as bowls in zoomorphic or human form have been found along the Fraser River and on the islands of the Gulf of Georgia. An andesite example was traced to Seward Peninsula, Alaska. Discovery of further such figures will help to determine migratory routes. Illus.   L. F. S. Upton

3. Camp, Charles L. SONG OF MAN: A PROLOGUE TO HISTORY. *Am. West 1970 7(5): 18-23.* Folsom man was in the forefront of the hunters that discovered and invaded the New World some 11 thousand years ago. The first evidence of the Folsom cultural complex was discovered in New Mexico in 1926. The uniquely-fashioned spear points are the sole, conclusively identified, remaining artifacts of this early inhabitant. Their distribution, frequent location in debris underneath that of later cultures, and their association with bones of extinct animals furnish virtually the only clues from which the speculative reconstruction of Folsom culture can be made. This pre-agricultural hunter lived in migratory bands, ranging over the Canadian and American Great Plains, and perhaps as far eastward as the Atlantic coast. Successive prehistoric groups progressed up the cultural and technological ladders, maintaining a reasonable balance with

nature. The coming of the white man wrought permanent disorder to the comparatively stable prehistoric context that had evolved over several centuries. Taken from a forthcoming book; 4 illus.   D. L. Smith

4. Crahan, M. E. GOD'S FLESH AND OTHER PRECOLUMBIAN PHANTASTICA. *Masterkey 1968 42(3): 96-103*. Shows that the use of intoxicants, new mind-expanding drugs, and hallucinogens is anything but new. The author surveys the drinking habits of New World Indians as well as the use of such hallucinogens as peyote, datura, cocaine, mescal, various mushrooms, cohoba, vision-producing vines and resins, and the seeds of the morning glory. He mentions that over 40 psychomimetric drugs are known to be native to the Americas as compared to half a dozen for the rest of the world. He also briefly describes the context in which the drugs were used (usually for religious, prophetic, or divinatory purposes) and the effects of the drugs. Based on published sources by early explorers and scientists.   C. N. Warren

5. Dickinson, Dennis. A SELECTED AND ANNOTATED BIBLIOGRAPHY ON WILD RICE. *Plains Anthropologist 1968 13(40): 90-99.* "Information germane to a comprehensive anthropological study of wild rice and its use as a subsistence item is contained in the literature of several disciplines. The...annotated bibliography attempts to provide an indication of the location and nature of some of this material....This bibliography was prepared during a study of the prehistoric utilization of wild rice by the Indians in the so-called 'wild-rice district' of the northcentral United States."   J

6. Grunfeld, Frederic V. INDIAN GIVING. *Horizon 1969 11(1): 46-47.* Describes the Indian potlatch.   R. N. Alvis

7. Harrington, Mark Raymond. REMINISCENCES OF AN ARCHAEOLOGIST. *Masterkey 1962 36(4): 138-142, 1963 37(1): 22-26, (2): 66-71, (3): 114-118, 1964 38(1): 26-34, (3): 106-110, 1965 39(1): 30-35, (4): 150-153, and 1967 41(1): 34-36.* A series of reminiscences of his long career in archaeology and ethnography by Mark Raymond Harrington, who served as curator of the Southwest Museum in Los Angeles from about 1927. Based on experiences in many parts of the United States and Canada; illus.   R. S. Burke

8. Jarcho, Saul. SOME OBSERVATIONS ON DISEASE IN PREHISTORIC NORTH AMERICA. *Bull. of the Hist. of Medicine 1964 38(1): 1-19.* Discusses three of "the great infectious diseases"(malaria, yellow fever, syphilis), nutritional diseases such as scurvy and pellagra, generalized osteoporosis, symmetrical osteoporosis, and occupational diseases as revealed by the paleopathological studies of North American prehistoric man. This article comprised the Fielding H. Garrison Lecture given at the annual meeting of the American Association for the History of Medicine, in Boston, May 1963.   W. L. Fox

9. Johannessen, Carl L., Wilson, Michael R., and Davenport, William A. THE DOMESTICATION OF MAIZE: PROCESS OR EVENT? *Geographical R.*

1970 60(3): 393-413. "Domestication is considered to be a continuing process consisting of perception, selection, maintenance, and diffusion, and maize is used as an example to illustrate this process. In the papers that contain pertinent information the data most frequently found are related to selection of long ears and of large, consistently colored kernels. Information on the maintenance of varieties, once selected, is available for fewer societies. When farmers are definitely concerned about maintenance, they try to isolate each maize variety in a separate field, or they arrange with neighbors to plant similar types adjacent to each other. Few reports discuss dispersal and diffusion of seed between individuals or cultures. The hypothesis of this study provides a framework that will promote the gathering of data which will permit the analysis of the domestication process to proceed, instead of being considered impossible."   J

10. Keel, Bennie Carlton. THE CONSERVATION AND PRESERVATION OF ARCHAEOLOGICAL AND ETHNOLOGICAL SPECIMENS. *Southern Indian Studies 1963 15: 5-65.* The entire issue of this journal is devoted to archaeological methods and procedures. The author comments that few studies of this sort are available and are somewhat dated or limited in their scope. After an introduction, the author deals with the preservation of ceramics and glass. The next chapter considers artifacts made from bone, shell and antler materials as well as skeletal remains. Metals, treated in another chapter, are generally limited to historic period sites. The author also discusses techniques for preserving stone. The following three chapters deal with artifacts made of perishable materials— wood, textiles, and animal products. Since correct identification is so important for this type of work, the author covers the minimum requirements that all institutions should try to meet with regard to registration, cataloging and storage. The attacks of insects often endanger ethnological collections, so the final chapter contains a few notes on insect control. Biblio.   K. P. Davis

11. Kidd, Kenneth E. and Kidd, Martha Ann. A CLASSIFICATION SYSTEM FOR GLASS BEADS FOR THE USE OF FIELD ARCHAEOLOGISTS. *Can. Historic Sites 1970 1: 46-89.* "As a result of examination of numerous collections of glass beads in northeastern North America and elsewhere, and as a result of a study of the procedures used in their manufacture, the authors propose a classification and nomenclature which they hope will permit exact descriptions and a reference base for all beads found in archaeological excavations. New bead types may be added to the system which is expansible to accommodate all possible variations."   J

12. Minor, Nono. INDIAN CULTURE BEFORE THE WHITE MAN CAME. *Am. Hist. Illus. 1967 2(5): 4-9, 28-36.* Describes Indian customs, clothing, economic life, and religion before the arrival of Columbus. Tribes are described on a regional basis. Included is a two-page color map, "Indian Tribes and Cultures."   J. D. Filipiak

13. Ogburn, Charlton, Jr. THE FIRST DISCOVERY OF AMERICA. *Horizon 1970 12(1): 92-99.* Discusses Beringia, the land mass which connected Asia and the North American continent on several occasions during the ice ages. The

author gives evidence that men probably arrived from Asia about 28 thousand years ago. He postulates that they came in small groups, possibly only a few groups of 50 to 100. There is evidence that many of the large mammals were killed off by these comparatively small groups of human beings.   R. N. Alvis

14. Riley, Carroll L. ADOLPH BANDELIER AS ARCHAEOLOGIST. *Kiva 1963 29(1): 23-27.* "The anthropologist and historian Adolph Bandelier [1840-1914] did much of his fieldwork (especially in the Southwest) under the auspices of archaeological organizations. In reality his interests were extremely varied and he combined archaeology, ethnology, and history to reconstruct culture. In spite of inadequate methods and techniques in archaeology, Bandelier's work does foreshadow the interpretive archaeology of the present day."   J

15. Schlesier, Karl-Heinz. GESCHICHTE DER BESIEDLUNG NOR-DAMERIKAS VON DEN ANFANGEN BIS ZUM BEGINN DER CHRIST-LICHEN ZEITRECHNUNG [History of the settlement of North America from its initial stage until the beginning of the Christian Era]. *Saeculum [West Germany] 1965 16(1): 29-41.* The first settlement of North America, about 40,000 B.C., was almost certainly undertaken by Neanderthal-type tribes from northeast China. The seven subsequent population movements, culminating in the arrival of the Athabaska about 2000-1500 B.C. originated in Siberia, north China and the north Pacific areas of Asia. Three maps, biblio.   C. F. Latour

16. Wentworth, Edward N. DRIED MEAT—EARLY MAN'S TRAVEL RA-TION. *Agric. Hist. 1956 30(1): 2-10.* The preservation of meat by drying originated with primitive man. The practice was brought to North America by the Asiatic tribes that migrated across the Bering Strait and spread from the Arctic Circle to Patagonia.   W. D. Rasmussen

17. Whitaker, Kathleen. ANALYTICAL INTERPRETATIONS OF PETRO-GLYPHS. *Masterkey 1969 43(4): 132-141.* Prehistoric painted or carved pictures on rock surfaces have been found throughout the world. Who did them? When and why? Discusses the most recent theories from the men studying the western American petroglyphs, and indicates the large amount of work that remains to be done in this area. Map, 3 photos, 3 notes, biblio.   C. N. Warren

18. Willey, Gordon R. NEW WORLD ARCHAEOLOGY IN 1965. *Pro. of the Am. Phil. Soc. 1966 110(2): 140-146.* Surveys American archaeology for the period of about 10,000-1000 B.C. in terms of three major themes of culture history. Raises questions concerning how man first came to the New World, how American agriculture evolved and what effects this had on New World cultures, and under what circumstances civilization appeared. Based essentially on secondary sources; 33 notes.   W. G. Morgan

Arctic Area

19. Ackerman, Robert E. PREHISTORIC ART OF THE WESTERN ES-KIMO. *Beaver [Canada] 1967 298(Autumn): 67-71.* Alaska, the land of the Western Eskimo and Athapaskan Indian, is a vast meeting ground for Asian and American cultures, and the plentiful and varied resources of the sea and the land permitted a cultural elaboration quite unlike that of the Canadian Eskimo. Several carvings are described and their place in the culture explained. Illus.
L. F. S. Upton

20. Brown, Jerry. RADIOCARBON DATING, BARROW, ALASKA. *Arctic [Canada] 1965 18(1): 37-48.* Radiocarbon dating suggests that the present Barrow land surface is not older than 8,300 years, and the sand spit perhaps 1,100 years old; while the next inland raised beach may be considerably less than 25 thousand years old. Several wooden artifacts have been given mean dates ranging from 1,430 to 1,146 years. An extensive scientific bibliography is furnished on soils, vegetation, Eskimo prehistory, and dating studies. J. E. Caswell

21. Henoch, W. E. S. PRELIMINARY GEOMORPHOLOGICAL STUDY OF A NEWLY DISCOVERED DORSET CULTURE SITE ON MELVILLE IS-LAND: N. W. T. *Arctic [Canada] 1964 17(2): 119-125.* Reports of physical remains, as of 1962, and earlier reports of an Eskimo dwelling site. Radiocarbon dating suggests it existed ca. 1150-1740 years ago. Illus., map, 3 notes. S

22. Taylor,William E.,Jr. and Swinton, George.PREHISTORIC DORSET ART. *Beaver [Canada] 1967 298(Autumn): 32-47.* Archaeologist Taylor looks at Eskimo art as "the silent echoes of culture." Artist Swinton considers the magico-religious basis of the art form. Both have worked together studying carving and photographs of Dorset culture art, a period roughly 800 B.C. to 1400 A.D.
L. F. S. Upton

23. Taylor, William E., Jr. ARCHAEOLOGY OF THE MC CORMICK INLET SITE. MELVILLE ISLAND, N.W.T. *Arctic [Canada] 1964 17(2): 125-129.* Illus., 11 notes. S

24. Taylor, William E., Jr. THE FRAGMENTS OF ESKIMO PREHISTORY. *Beaver [Canada] 1965 295(Spring): 4-17.* Surveys the various periods of Eskimo prehistory: pre-Dorset from approximately 300 to 500 B.C.; Dorset, from 800 B.C. to 1300 A.D.; and Thule from 900 to 1750 A.D. Archaeological discoveries show that these cultures ranged from eastern Siberia to Denmark Strait between Greenland and Iceland. The Duason-Oleson theory of the origin of the Thule Eskimo is refuted. An expedition in July and August 1963 to survey prehistoric sites for the National Museum of Canada is described. Illus.
L. F. S. Upton

Subarctic Area

25. Erskine, J. S. NOVA SCOTIA PRE-HISTORY. *Dalhousie R. [Canada] 1964 44(1): 16-27.* Describes the archaeological work begun in 1957 by the Nova Scotia Museum. This work was undertaken to study the long history of the Indians of Nova Scotia before the Europeans came in contact with them. Several types of Indians are distinguished: the "Blue-whin" people (ca. 10,000 B.C.) who are considered to be the first true Nova Scotians; the Archaics (up to ca. 1500 B.C.); and the Micmacs, descendants of them all, and still in existence today. Considers particularly the most informative early site by the estuary of Bear River. Map: Indian sites in Nova Scotia, p. 27.   R. J. C. Ford

26. Gryba, Eugene M. A POSSIBLE PALEO-INDIAN AND ARCHAIC SITE IN THE SWAN VALLEY, MANITOBA. *Plains Anthropologist 1968 13(41): 218-227.* "An archaeological site uncovered in the Swan Valley of Manitoba during road construction yielded a small group of artifacts including a Paleo-Indian projectile point and side-notched Archaic points. The site is significant as it lies in a corridor which probably served as a vital migration route between the northern Plains and the diminishing lakes within the Lake Agassiz Basin."   J

27. Hall, Edwin S., Jr. SPECULATIONS ON THE LATE PREHISTORY OF THE KUTCHIN ATHAPASKANS. *Ethnohist. 1969 16(4): 317-334.* "Oral historical, archaeological, ecological, linguistic and ethnological data are drawn upon in an attempt to delineate the geographical extent of the Athapaskan-speaking Kutchin Indians of northern Alaska and northwest Canada during late prehistoric times."   J

28. Sanger, David. 7,000 YEARS: PREHISTORY IN BRITISH COLUMBIA. *Beaver [Canada] 1968 298(Spring): 34-40.* Excavations along the Fraser River Valley since 1961 have yielded some eight thousand specimens spanning over six thousand years of prehistory. Sites examined have been between Lytton and Lillooet, and at Nesikep Creek in the Lochnore-Nesikep locality. Between 7000 and 8000 B.C. the ice sheet had retreated sufficiently to allow plant life in this area, and man's appearance can be set at about 5500 B.C. From then on it is possible to trace the progressive development of man's skills.
                                                                 L. F. S. Upton

29. Webber, Alika Podolinsky. A PAINTING TOOL. *Beaver [Canada] 1968 299(Autumn): 24-26.* Shows five bone and antler tools found in Ontario in the 19th century and used in ancient times to paint clothing. Similar tools are still used by the Algonkian-speaking Naskapi Indians of the Quebec-Labrador Peninsula. Illus.   L. F. S. Upton

Northwest Coast Area

30. Jacobs, Melville. INDICATIONS OF MENTAL ILLNESS AMONG PRE-CONTACT INDIANS OF THE NORTHWEST STATES. *Pacific Northwest Q. 1964 49-54.* With fragments of information about Indians in the region, the author deduces opinions on irrational manifestations. Includes significant discussion of sources and appeals for improved methods of recreating early history.
C. C. Gorchels

Plateau Area

31. Swanson, Earl. IDAHO YESTERYEARS. *Idaho Yesterdays 1965 9(1): 17-24.* "Recent archaeological discoveries have enabled scientists to outline a thousand or fifteen hundred decades of Idaho's prehistory." Several perspectives have been employed by anthropologists to learn something of Idaho's prehistoric past. The perspectives successfully used are: the direct historical approach, the study of language, geography of the area, problem-oriented research, and time periods. The author gives an idea of both the approaches and results obtained by the methods of prehistoric archaeology. Illus.
B. B. Swift

Great Basin Area

32. Brodie, Fawn. [DISCOVERIES BY DEAN BRIMHALL]. *Am. West 1971 8.*
THE BRIMHALL SAGA: SOME REMARKABLE DISCOVERIES IN THE CLIFFS OF UTAH. PART ONE: THE MAN, (4): 4-9, 62. Octogenarian Dean R. Brimhall, retired psychologist, academician, and aviation specialist, is regarded as the foremost authority on Indian art in the canyonlands of Utah. Since 1940 he has become an intimate of the labyrinthine drainage basin of the Upper Colorado River. His findings have altered and added substantial contributions to the anthropological and archaeological understanding of the Indians of the area. A theft in 1967 of hundreds of his unique and unpublished color slides of some 200 prehistoric petroglyphs and pictographs spurred the 80-year-old Brimhall to go back and to start all over again with his collection. Today, sometimes alone, he continues on this mission into the wilderness. 5 illus.
THE BRIMHALL SAGA. PART TWO: THE DISCOVERIES, (5): 18-23, 63. Archaeological research in the Utah canyonlands near the confluence

of the Green and Colorado rivers has concentrated on nearly every aspect of the prehistoric cultures that occupied the area except for the abundant evidence of Indian art, yet therein may well be the New World's finest gallery of prehistoric pictographs. Centuries of summer flash floods have deepened the canyons, making the picture-bearing walls hard to reach. Further, in these inaccessible regions it is most difficult to get the proper photographic equipment in position and the right light for capturing the essential details. Brimhall persists in tracking down every rumor of a pictograph or petroglyph discovery. His now considerable collection of color slides covers every aspect of Indian life. Six mastodon petroglyphs may force a major revision of Indian chronology of the area or the time at which the mastodon became extinct. Other revision potentials appear in the Brimhall findings. 10 illus.   D. L. Smith

33. Husted, Wilfred M. and Mallory, Oscar L. THE FREMONT CULTURE: ITS DERIVATION AND ULTIMATE FATE. *Plains Anthropologist 1967 12(36): 222-232.* Aikens in his *Fremont-Promontory-Plains Relationships in Northern Utah* (1966), "has proposed that Fremont-Promontory culture originated on the Northwestern Plains and represents an Athabascan migration into the Utah area at *circa* A.D. 500. Their descendants, he suggests, were later forced back into the plains by the 12th century expansion of Shoshoneans from the Great Basin. He also proposes that Fremont-Promontory culture was ancestral to Dismal River culture. In this paper an alternative hypothesis is proposed, i.e., that Fremont and then Promontory cultures were sequential developments from an indigenous Utaztecan or proto-Utaztecan base and that there is no direct cultural relationship between the Utah cultures and the Dismal River aspect." Illus., biblio.   J

34. Judd, Neil M. BASKETMAKER ARTIFACTS FROM MOKI CANYON, UTAH. *Plateau 1970 43(1): 16-20.* "A bundle of 'snares' and a twined-woven bag, containing a stone-seed-shell necklace, were recovered in 1923 from caves in southeastern Utah. A description of these Basketmaker materials is published for the first time."   J

35. Manners, Robert A. HABITAT, TECHNOLOGY AND SOCIAL ORGANIZATION OF THE SOUTHERN PAIUTE. *Am. Indígena [Mexico] 1959 19(3): 179-197.* Challenges careless use of the word "tribe," showing that ecological-technological facts of precontact times will not support such a designation for the Southern Paiute Indians. Even given linguistic and cultural similarities among Indians, ecological conditions prevented their political unity. This extract from a longer study on these Indians is intended as a case history for precontact Indians in similar habitats. Based on secondary sources.   R. J. Knowlton

36. Simpson, Ruth D. MARK HARRINGTON: FATHER OF NEVADA ARCHEOLOGY. *Nevada Hist. Soc. Q. 1965 8(3/4): 5-22.* A biography and review of the work of Mark R. Harrington in the Indian ruins of prehistoric southern Nevada, 1924-63. Contains brief references to recorded Spanish visits in 1776 and radiocarbon dating as early as 2000 B.C.   W. J. Brooks

37. Tuohy, Donald R. STONE AGE MISSILES FROM A MODERN TEST SITE. *Masterkey 1965 39(2): 44-59.* Presents the results of an archaeological survey of the Nevada Test Site, which uncovered seven archaeological sites, two of which were partially excavated by the author. The artifacts recovered from the two excavated sites are probably from the Southern Paiute occupation of the area at about 1150 A.D. Based on field investigation, primary and secondary sources; 3 illus., table, biblio. C. N. Warren

California Area

38. Alliot, Hector. BURIAL METHODS OF THE SOUTHERN CALIFOR-NIA ISLANDERS. *Masterkey 1969 43(4): 125-131.* Discusses Alliot's archaeol-ogical burial finds on San Nicolas Island, a small wind- and sand-swept island in the Santa Catalina group off Southern California. Ties in his finds with other known mainland mortuary customs. An article by Alliot in the *Bulletin of the Southern California Academy of Sciences* 15(1), 1916. Photo. C. N. Warren

39. Alliot, Hector. PRE-HISTORIC USE OF BITUMEN IN SOUTHERN CALIFORNIA. *Masterkey 1970 44(3): 97-102.* Lists a myriad of ingenious uses to which the Santa Catalina Indians put the natural ocean-borne (and born) black asphaltum substance called bitumen. Bitumen, found as sticky, soft balls on the California coast, was a natural cement, glue, waterproof sealer, plastic, putty, and preserver to these people. Cites uses of bitumen by other culture groups all over the world where the substance is found. Reprinted from a 1917 article. Illus. C. N. Warren

40. Broms, R. S. D. and Moriarty, James R. THE ANTIQUITY AND INFER-RED USE OF STONE SPHEROIDS IN SOUTHWESTERN ARCHAEOL-OGY. *Masterkey 1967 41(3): 98-112.* "Stone spheroids are rare but not uncommon finds in Southwestern archaeological sites. They are consistently reported from early sites in California as ground stone objects, usually of prob-lematical use. A careful examination of the literature and an evaluation of the authors' own work in archaeological sites in Southern California tend to support the view that most stone spheres were gaming pieces. Examination of the available data shows this artifact to have been in relatively constant use in the Southwest for the last 6000 years." Based on field investigation, primary and secondary sources; 2 illus., table, biblio. J

41. Carter, George F. A CROSS CHECK ON THE DATING OF LAKE MOJAVE ARTIFACTS. *Masterkey 1967 41(1): 26-33.* Discusses the dating of Lake Mojave artifacts. Included are some suggestions for further analysis of the

artifacts currently in museum collections. Based on the author's personal experience of 30 years ago, and on primary and secondary sources; biblio.

C. N. Warren

42. Curtis, Freddie. MICRODRILLS IN THE MANUFACTURE OF SHELL BEADS IN SOUTHERN CALIFORNIA. *Masterkey 1964 38(3): 98-105.* Speculates on the possibility of shell bead industry on the Southern California coast, based upon excavations at Arroyo Sequit and Goleta, among others, which revealed microdrills in conjunction with large numbers of shell beads. Based on field investigation, primary and secondary sources; 3 illus., biblio.

C. N. Warren

43. Goodman, Ruth and Raskoff, Richard. THE BERNASCONI SITE IN SOUTHERN CALIFORNIA; AN ARCHAEOLOGICAL RECONNAISSANCE. *Masterkey 1964 38(2): 17-25.* Reports on an archaeological survey done in 1961 on a site in the northern portion of the Peninsula Plateau of Southern California. Results of test pits show an atypical technology, insofar as the stone types found indicate that a familiar range of 750 square miles must be postulated for the toolmakers, a range which is not ordinarily ascribed to the Indians of Southern California. Further study is felt to be warranted, and is planned for fall and winter of 1963-64. Based on field investigation and secondary sources; map, table, 5 illus., 2 notes.

C. N. Warren

44. Greenwood, Roberta S. A SECOND STONE SCULPTURE FROM THE BROWNE SITE. *Masterkey 1967 41(3): 84-87.* Reviews the first and describes the second stone sculpture to be recovered from the Browne site in Ventura County, California. The author assigns the second sculpture a date of approximately 5000 B.C., based on obsidian hydration analogy with other well-dated sites. Based on primary sources and personal experience; 3 illus., biblio.

C. N. Warren

45. Griffin, Dorothy W. PREHISTORY OF THE SOUTHERN SIERRA NEVADA: PARTS I AND II. *Masterkey 1963 37(2): 49-57 and (3): 105-114.* Part I. Attempts to reconstruct the culture history of the southern Sierra region of California, through use of geological, geographical, ethnographic, and linguistic data. Based on secondary sources. Part II. Discusses the archaeological data available for the Tubatulabal-Kawaissu area, with a distribution study of various artifact types such as pottery and projectile points, and the apparent conflicts between the limited archaeological and ethnographic data. Based on primary and secondary sources, as well as field investigation; 2 illus., biblio.

C. N. Warren

46. Heizer, Robert F. CALIFORNIA ARCHAEOLOGY: ITS DEVELOPMENT, PRESENT STATUS, AND FUTURE NEEDS. *Masterkey 1964 38(3): 84-90.* Discusses the history of archaeological discoveries and exploration in California during the period 1850-1964. The author evaluates current California archaeology and makes a number of suggestions, including: establishment of a

California Archaeological Society, and its publication of a journal; a uniform, statewide system of site designations, with perhaps a master file of sites; work on the types, distribution and chronology of cultures in California; a general outline of what is known of California prehistory, region by region, by which an outline of unknown or problem areas will appear.   C. N. Warren

47. Heizer, Robert F. PLANK CANOES OF SOUTH AND NORTH AMER-ICA. *Kroeber Anthrop. Soc. Papers 1966 35: 22-39.* In this revision of an article first written in 1942, the author examines the various hypotheses of origin and relationship of plank canoes in South America and the Santa Barbara, California, coast. He concludes that the South American dalca was of indigenous origin, probably in the region of the island of Chiloe in Chile, with eventual spreading as far south as the Straits of Magellan. The North American tomolo is also seen as being of indigenous origin, in the area of the Santa Barbara channel. In both cases the author finds theories of oceanic influence to be unsupportable, as well as any theory showing relationship between the dalca and the tomolo. Based on primary and secondary sources; 17 notes, biblio.   C. N. Warren

48. Heizer, Robert F. PROBLEMS IN DATING LAKE MOJAVE AR-TIFACTS. *Masterkey 1965 39(4): 125-134.* Reviews research on the dating of Lake Mojave artifacts and attempts to show alternative interpretations for the data available. Based on primary and secondary sources; 2 illus., biblio.
C. N. Warren

49. King, T. F. THREE CLAY FIGURINES FROM MARIN COUNTY. *Masterkey 1967 41(4): 138-142.* Discusses the literature relating to anthropomorphic fired clay figurines in California, and presents a discussion and description of three such figurines recovered in Marin County, California. Based on field investigation, primary and secondary sources; 3 illus., biblio.
C. N. Warren

50. Mead, George R. and Smith, Jason. MICROTOOLS FROM OWENS VAL-LEY, CALIFORNIA. *Masterkey 1968 42(4): 148-151.* Microtools are infrequently reported, no doubt from their being easily categorized as "chipping waste." In 1964 every shovelful taken from a site near Olancha in Owens Valley, California, was carefully screened and inspected. Forty-three microtools were found; all were of obsidian, which was probably obtained at Coso Hot Springs in Inyo County. The tool types were divided into three categories: spoke-shaves, burins, and end-shaves. As no cores were found at the site, the origin of manufacture remains a mystery. Illus., biblio.   C. N. Warren

51. Meighan, Clement W. A RITUAL CAVE IN TOPANGA, CALIFORNIA. *Masterkey 1969 43(3): 112-116.* In 1962 the University of California, Los Angeles, field class in archaeology excavated several small rock shelters in Topanga Canyon just north of the Los Angeles basin. Describes the finds from one of these sites, a very small cave with evidence of ritual activity. It was found that the cave was never used for habitation and that it is enigmatic in both age and function;

however, the evidence strongly suggests a ritual importarce of some kind because of the presence of four painted pebbles. These pebbles were carefully made and deliberately buried, one by one, in the clay cave floor. Biblio.

C. N. Warren

52. Meighan, Clement W. and Haynes, C. Vance. FURTHER INVESTIGA-TIONS OF BORAX LAKE. *Masterkey 1970 44(3): 112-113.* An abstract of archaeological investigations fully reported in *Science* (27 February 1970) on the Borax Lake site in California. Photo, biblio.   C. N. Warren

53. Mieghan, Clement W. and Haynes, C. Vance. NEW STUDIES ON THE AGE OF THE BORAX LAKE SITE. *Masterkey 1968 42(1): 4-9.* For 20 years the Borax Lake site in northern California has been the subject of question and controversy for west coast archaeologists and those interested in Early Man sites. The author reports the preliminary results of studies on the age of the obsidian artifacts from Borax Lake; so far these studies tend to confirm the site as indeed ancient. Based on primary and secondary sources; illus., biblio.

C. N. Warren

54. Miles, Charles. THE GUNTHER ISLAND SITES. *Masterkey 1965 39(3): 92-103.* A collection and analysis of data amassed on the two archaeological sites, Hum-62 and Hum-68, found on Gunther Island in Humboldt Bay, northwestern California. The author concludes that more research would have been desirable since the artifacts from these sites do not fit neatly into any present cultural distributions. Unfortunately, both sites have been destroyed by pothunting, tillage, and erosion. Based on primary and secondary sources; 10 illus.

C. N. Warren

55. Moriarty, James Robert. A RECONSTRUCTION OF THE DEVELOP-MENT OF PRIMITIVE RELIGION IN CALIFORNIA. *Southern California Q. 1970 52(4): 313-344.* Discusses ritual elements of prehistoric California aboriginal culture. The author divides California prehistory into four periods for which he delineates a progression from general, less specialized, and widely diffused rituals to more complex, distinct, and regional ceremonies. The chronology for the four periods is based on radiocarbon data; the author discusses the difficulty in accurately dating prehistoric periods. Concentrates on the development of religious ritual, but maintains that other aspects of California primitive culture demonstrate similar development. Based on archeological data and secondary sources; 6 maps, 4 tables, 39 notes.   W. L. Bowers

56. Pond, Gordon G. STEATITE TABLETS FROM MALAGA COVE. *Masterkey 1968 42(4): 124-131.* For many years fragments of steatite incised with geometric designs have been recovered from sites along the Southern California coast from Ventura to Seal Beach in sufficient numbers to cause speculation over their classification. The steatite was thought to have been mined at Catalina Island and brought to the coast by canoe. Three large steatite slabs were uncovered at Malaga Cove in Redondo Beach in 1953 and, until recently, were in a

Pre-Columbian Indian History 15

private collection. Upon examination by experts, these specimens solve the puzzle
concerning the identity of incised pieces found in other excavations. These tablets
are believed to have been used as part of the Gabrielino Indians' religious rites.
4 photos, biblio.   C. N. Warren

57. Smith, Gerald A. SPLIT-TWIG FIGURINES FROM SAN BERNAR-
DINO COUNTY, CALIFORNIA. *Masterkey 1963 37(3): 86-90.* Reports on
five split-twig figurines from Newberry Cave, California. A brief comparison is
made to other known split-twig figurines. Their function as items of ceremonial
hunting magic is suggested by their association with quartz crystals painted green,
pictographs, painted stones, and a sheep-dung pendant strung on sinew. At
Newberry Cave they are associated with the Amargosa Phase II artifacts. Based
on field investigation, primary and secondary sources; illus., biblio.
                                                                     C. N. Warren

58. Wallace, William J. AN ARCHAEOLOGICAL RECONNAISSANCE IN
JOSHUA TREE NATIONAL MONUMENT. *J. of the West 1964 3(1): 90-101.*
While William and Elizabeth Campbell, working under the auspices of the Southwest Museum, investigated numerous aboriginal campsites in the Joshua Tree
area in Riverside County, California, before it became a national monument, it
was not until 1957 that the National Park Service engaged the Department of
Anthropology at the University of Southern California to institute a program of
research. The purpose of the program is to record and map the previously
discovered prehistoric encampments and to supply additional information on the
manner of living of the prehistoric people who once resided within the present
limits of the national monument. Thus far the explorations have centered around
the Sheep Pass district. Artifacts reveal that the prehistoric Indians subsisted on
wild plants and upon meat from animals. Evidently the area supported neither
a large nor a permanent population. Illus., table, 13 notes.   D. N. Brown

59. Wallace, William J. ARCHAEOLOGICAL RESOURCES OF THE POSO
CREEK RESERVOIR AREA. *Masterkey 1967 41(3): 88-97.* Presents the results of an archaeological survey made in the Poso Creek Reservoir area, near
Bakersfield, California. The surveyors found two sites, one was outside the area
to be inundated by the reservoir. The site within the target area yielded only
sparse surface artifacts, none amenable to dating. Based on field investigation,
primary and secondary sources; map, 3 illus., biblio.   C. N. Warren

60. Wallace, William J. PREHISTORIC SEASONAL CAMPSITES IN
SOUTHERN CALIFORNIA. *Masterkey 1968 42(4): 134-141.* A surface survey
in Orange County recently revealed four seasonal campsites of unknown antiquity. The sparse surface finds consisted entirely of seed-grinding implements
and hammerstones and it is assumed the four camps served as temporary bases
for tiny foraging bands. Although unimpressive and meager of content, the
encampments provide useful information on the seasonal round of activities of
the region's aboriginal inhabitants. Biblio.   C. N. Warren

61. Wallace, William J. SEASONAL INDIAN CAMPSITES IN THE LAKE ISABELLA AREA, CALIFORNIA. *Masterkey 1970 44(3): 84-96.* An archaeological report done in November 1964 on three temporary foraging sites in the French Gulch Creek area of south-central California. These campsites are felt to have been used by the Tubatulabal during late-prehistoric and early-historic times. 2 illus., map, table, biblio.   C. N. Warren

Southwest Area

62. Agenbroad, Larry D. THE DISTRIBUTION OF FLUTED POINTS IN ARIZONA. *Kiva 1967 32(4): 113-120.* "A total of seventy-two fluted projectiles have been reported from seventeen localities within Arizona. The location and distribution of these points indicate that early man, using fluted projectile points, was most active in the northeast Plateau region, and the southeast Desert regions of the state."   J

63. Ayres, James E. A PREHISTORIC FARM SITE NEAR CAVE CREEK, ARIZONA. *Kiva 1967 32(3): 106-111.* "At the request of the Phoenix office of the Bureau of Land Management the Arizona State Museum surveyed an area scheduled to be used as a sanitary land fill near Cave Creek, Arizona. Two field houses and numerous field borders were discovered within the area and were mapped. One of the houses was excavated. Two additional houses were found north of the survey area." 3 illus.   J

64. Bohrer, Vorsila L., Cutler, Hugh C., and Sauer, Jonathan D. CARBONIZED PLANT REMAINS FROM TWO HOHOKAM SITES, ARIZONA BB:13:41 AND ARIZONA BB:13:50. *Kiva 1969 35(1): 1-10.* "The plant evidence from two Hohokam sites near Punta del Agua on the San Xavier Indian Reservation south of Tucson, Arizona enlarges our knowledge of plant utilization between A.D. 700-1200. The cultivated plants included maize *(Zea mays),* tepary beans *(Phaseolus acutifolius var. latifolius)* and jack beans *(Canavalia ensiformis).* The maize is similar to that from other Hohokam sites and to smaller and older kinds grown by the Papago. The uncultivated plant remains included the seeds of tansymustard *(Descurainia sp.),* pigweed *(Amararthus or Chenopodium),* and stick-leaf *(Mentzelia sp.).* The stick-leaf seed is apparently a new prehistoric record in southern Arizona. The charred buds of cholla *(Opuntia sp.)* provide direct evidence of Hohokam utilization of a food source popular with the Pima and Papago." Illus., photo.   J

65. Bohrer, Vorsila L. PALEOECOLOGY OF SNAKETOWN. *Kiva 1971 36(3): 11-19.* "The following plant communities probably existed near [the Hohokam village of] Snaketown [in Arizona]: creosote-bush, desert-saltbush, saltbush-arroweed, seepweed, mesquite thicket, and saguaro-paloverde. Agricultural

activities promoted an increase in ragweed *(Ambrosiae)* as new land was incorporated into the irrigation system in the earlier phases. Irrigation fostered the extension of many riparian plant communities. Today upriver water storage has eliminated or disrupted the riparian plant communities and altered the ecology."

J

66. Brown, Jeffrey L. AN EXPERIMENT IN PROBLEM-ORIENTED HIGHWAY SALVAGE ARCHAEOLOGY. *Kiva 1967 33(2): 60-66.* "The application of both chronological and functional objectives to a highway salvage project [in Arizona] revealed a site in which stone was quarried and tools shaped by chipping, game was hunted and vegetal material possibly gathered. These activities were spatially patterned in relation to available natural resources. The users of this site were probably small work groups or single individuals. The exploitation activities carried on at the site occurred from the San Pedro Stage of the Cochise Culture as early as 2000 B.C. to recent Papago." J

67. Burrus, Ernest J. THE BANDELIER COLLECTION IN THE VATICAN LIBRARY. *Manuscripta 1966 10(2): 67-84.* A description of Adolph F. A. Bandelier's archaeological and ethnological writings about Indians in the southwestern United States and northwestern Mexico as contained in portfolios in the Vatican Library. Bandelier's history, written before 1887, is outlined.

R. Wertz

68. Cattanach, George S., Jr. A SAN PEDRO STAGE SITE NEAR FAIRBANK, ARIZONA. *Kiva 1966 32(1): 1-24.* "Stone artifacts from a San Pedro Stage site, Arizona EE:8:7, near Fairbank, Arizona, are described and compared to artifacts from midden levels 3 to 5 at Ventana Cave. The site interpretation is confused slightly by a Salado occupation, but patination of the worked faces of many of the San Pedro tools aided separation of San Pedro and Salado artifacts. A temporal correlation of Arizona EE:8:7 with nearby Benson:5:10 (San Pedro type site) and with Ventana Cave is suggested." J

69. Clark, Geoffrey A. A PRELIMINARY ANALYSIS OF BURIAL CLUSTERS AT THE GRASSHOPPER SITE, EAST CENTRAL ARIZONA. *Kiva 1969 35(2): 57-86.* "From 1963-66 almost 200 human burials, in 7 clusters, were recovered at Grasshopper, a 14th century pueblo in east central Arizona. The burials and associated grave offerings are the data for this study. Considerable variability was observed among the clusters. Three possible causes were considered: sampling error, temporal and social factors. Sampling error was dismissed because the size of the burial population remains unknown, and the sample used was the maximum available. Temporal factors were insignificant. Grasshopper was occupied for about a century, too short a period to explain the variation as due to change through time. Two different kinds of cemeteries were defined which could accommodate all of the original burial clusters. The first were common cemeteries located in trash mounds peripheral to the site. The second was an area of high status burials associated with the plaza in the western unit of the site. Using analogies drawn from modern Western Pueblo society, a model was generated for the social structure of Grasshopper. Social units based on each of the

following were considered: kinship, territoriality, sodalities and stratification. Evidence for the first 3 categories was scanty; evidence for social stratification was abundant. It suggests that status was ascribed at birth through membership in kin groupings."   J

70. Dawson, Jerry and Judge, William J. PALEO-INDIAN SITES AND TOPOGRAPHY IN THE MIDDLE RIO GRANDE VALLEY OF NEW MEXICO. *Plains Anthropologist 1969 14(44, pt. 1): 149-163.* "The settlement patterns of Paleo-Indians are almost completely unknown. Although the use of topographic features for game drives, such as blind canyons, bluffs, and arroyo banks, is well documented both by excavated kill sites and by historical and ethnological analogy, the relationships of Paleo-Indian campsites to features of the surrounding terrain have been generally ignored, possibly because of insufficient data. Such graphic features generally chosen for campsite locations, in conjunction with portions of the terrain used for hunting activities, could provide insights into the camping needs of hunting communities, suggest reasons why some locations were chosen over others within the same locality and area, aid in the discovery of other sites, and provide an interpretive setting for viewing the occupation at any individual site...."   J

71. Euler, Robert C. THE CANYON DWELLERS. *Am. West 1967 4(2): 22-27, 67-71.* Until recently it was believed that prehistoric human occupation of the Grand Canyon of the Colorado River in Arizona was a comparatively brief experience. Starting in the 1950's archaeological reconnaissance and exploration have located some 250 ruins, thousands of artifacts, and multitudes of data that indicate the antiquity and extent of occupation. The earliest identifications made thus far date some four thousand years ago with primitive hunters and gatherers who used caves in the canyon bottom area as religious shrines. They were probably associated with the Desert Culture which was predominant over much of western North America. Their occupation probably ended long before the beginning of the Christian era. Not until the 8th century is there further evidence of human occupation. For the next three centuries the Pueblo explored and made seasonal use of the area. About 1000 A.D. a much larger influx of Pueblo developed into a major occupation of the canyon region based on a well-balanced economy of hunting, gathering, and agriculture. A smaller group, the Cohonina, appeared about the same time as the Pueblo, but located on the south rim and not within the canyon itself. By 1150 or 1200 A.D. both groups abandoned the area, probably because of climatic changes. There were later and lesser occupations by Havasupai, Walapai, and Southern Paiute. Based partly on the author's archaeological field studies; 13 illus., biblio. note.   D. L. Smith

72. Ferdon, Edwin N., Jr. THE HOHOKAM "BALL COURT": AN ALTERNATE VIEW OF ITS FUNCTION. *Kiva 1967 33(1): 1-14.* "A comparative study of Hohokam and Mesoamerican ball courts indicates a lack of shared fundamental features. It is suggested, therefore, that Hohokam courts may have served some other function. General similarities, including basic court orienta-

tions, with the Papago Vikita dance court assemblages at Santa Rosa and Quitovaca may reflect a similar use of Hohokam courts in prehistoric times."
J

73. Fish, Paul, Kitchen, Suzanne, and McWilliams, Kenneth. A SLAB-COV-ERED BURIAL FROM THE PERKINSVILLE VALLEY, ARIZONA. *Plateau 1971 43(3): 138-144.* "An extended inhumation with a sandstone slab-covering was recently excavated near Perkinsville, Yavapai County, Arizona. Ceramic associations suggest a date just prior to A.D. 1100. Although the burial is believed to be affiliated with the Prescott Branch, certain similarities with Western Pueblo, Sinagua and Salado mortuary practices are noted. A study of the skeletal material and an analysis of the associated sediments for pollen are included."
J

74. Fitting, James E. and Stone, Lyle M. DISTANCE AND UTILITY IN THE DISTRIBUTION OF RAW MATERIALS IN THE CEDAR MOUNTAINS OF NEW MEXICO. *Kiva 1969 34(4): 207-212.* "The distribution of raw materials between two quarry sites and three Mimbres village sites in the Cedar Mountains of southwestern New Mexico was not a random process. Factors of site function, differential selection of raw materials for different tool types and the knapping characteristics of these raw materials had to be studied before the finished tool weight was demonstrated to be the key selective factor. Even then an optimal distribution pattern was disrupted by known and unknown intervening opportunities." 4 tables.
J

75. Fitting, James E. and Price, Theron D. TWO LATE PALEO-INDIAN SITES IN SOUTHWESTERN NEW MEXICO. *Kiva 1968 34(1): 1-8.* "Two Late Paleo-Indian sites in southwestern New Mexico produced similar styles of projectile points, but dissimilar tool assemblages. Since these sites are in two distinct environmental zones, it is possible that they represent different stages of the yearly economic cycle. One site, located in an area of transition from semi-desert brush to open grassland today, may be a small campsite while the second site, located in an oak-pinyon upland area, can be interpreted as a workshop site where both flintworking and woodworking took place."
J

76. Forbes, Jack D. THE EARLY WESTERN APACHE, 1300-1700. *J. of the West 1966 5(3): 336-354.* An application of the ethnohistorical method to a study on the pre-Columbian habitats of the Southwestern Indian tribes, especially in Arizona. The Western Apache originated in northern Arizona and gradually migrated southward by the late 1300's. Suggests Western Apache and a portion of the Navaho formed a homogeneous group which split due to isolation, different environmental factors, and the impact of the Pueblos on the Navaho after 1600. Also deals with Spanish contact with the Apache from 1539 through 1744 and the effect this had on both Indians and whites. Based on published sources; 54 notes.
D. N. Brown

77. Gorman, Frederick. THE CLOVIS HUNTERS: AN ALTERNATE VIEW OF THEIR ENVIRONMENT AND ECOLOGY. *Kiva 1969 35(2): 91-102.* "This paper is a reevaluation of artifact assemblages associated with Clovis culture. Analytical perspective is shifted from mammoth-kill sites to the investigation of individual mammoth matrices. Patterned orientation and disarticulation of mammoth skeletons are archaeological remnants of the cultural behavior of Clovis hunters. Numbers of projectile points having culturally patterned attributes were deliberately abandoned in mammoth carcasses; these provide insight to the cultural ecology of the Clovis hunters."   J

78. Greer, John W. MICRO-ECCENTRICS FROM THE FOUR CORNERS REGION OF THE SOUTHWEST. *Kiva 1969 34(4): 251-256.* "Sixteen differing examples of a notched stone flake artifact type, termed a micro-eccentric, are described from the Southwest. The archaeological associations, and geographical and temporal distributions of the specimens are summarized. Their function and cultural relationships are considered." Illus.   J

79. Griffin, P. Bion. A HIGH STATUS BURIAL FROM GRASSHOPPER RUIN, ARIZONA. *Kiva 1967 33(2): 37-53.* "During the 1966 session of the University of Arizona Archaeological Field School an elaborate burial was excavated. The grave goods were placed in two layers. Layer 1 was approximately 90 cm. above Layer 2, which was associated with the body. Layer 1 may have been deposited some time after the grave was originally filled. Included in the two areas were 36 ceramic vessels, 128 projectile points, an incised bone wand, and many other items. The implication that Burial 140 may represent a high status burial within a socially stratified society is discussed."   J

80. Hammack, Laurens C. A PRELIMINARY REPORT OF THE EXCAVATIONS AT LAS COLINAS. *Kiva 1969 35(1): 11-28.* "Under contract with the Arizona Highway Department and the Bureau of Public Roads, the Arizona State Museum excavated Mound 8 of the Las Colinas ruin group, located in Phoenix, Arizona. This site is the last remaining mound of 12 situated northwest of the downtown section of the city. The excavation revealed the following: an artificial platform mound, rectangular, post-reinforced, adobe-walled rooms, pit houses, cremations, burials and thousands of artifacts. Occupation was during the Hohokam Classic period." Illus., photos.   J

81. Harrill, Bruce G. PREHISTORIC BURIALS NEAR YOUNG, ARIZONA. *Kiva 1967 33(2): 54-59.* "In the fall of 1965 eleven prehistoric burials were uncovered by roadgrading operations on Arizona State Route 288 near the town of Young. These burials were excavated by the Arizona State Museum in conjuction with the State Highway Salvage Archaeology Program. On the basis of ceramics the burials were found to date between A.D. 1250 and 1385."   J

82. Haury, Emil W. SNAKETOWN: 1964-1965. *Kiva 1965 31(1): 1-13.* "The 1964-1965 excavations at Snaketown [now a Registered National Historic Landmark] have verified and augmented the results obtained by Gila Pueblo in 1934-

1935. Numerous house floors, wells, pits, cremations, a crematory area, trash mounds, platform mounds and canals were located as well as an abundance of ceramic and artifactual material. There were limited excavations in adjacent Classic Period sites and canals. The analysis and description of all of these materials proceeds at the present time. It is expected that relationships with Mexican and other Southwestern groups will be clarified." J

83. Hemmings, E. Thomas. CRUCIFORM AND RELATED ARTIFACTS OF MEXICO AND THE SOUTHWESTERN UNITED STATES. *Kiva 1967 32(4): 150-169.* "Reported occurrences of cruciform artifacts and some inferences regarding them are summarized. Four types of cruciforms distinguished by metric and formal attributes are defined. These data are compared with problematical objects which may be related in form or function. Evidence is presented for the geographic and temporal distribution of ground-stone cruciform types and for a possible early tradition of chipped stone, four-pointed artifacts in North America. A hypothetical function for cruciforms is discussed." J

84. Hill, James N. A PREHISTORIC COMMUNITY IN EASTERN ARIZONA. *Southwestern J. of Anthrop. 1966 22(1): 9-30.* Presents an ethnographic description of a Pueblo Indian site in Arizona based strictly on archaeological evidence. The author holds that while his analysis should have validity of its own, the important point is the creation of a methodology, a theoretical structure which can serve as a starting point in this type of ethnographic reconstruction. Based on secondary sources; 3 maps, 6 tables, biblio.

C. N. Warren

85. Hill, T. C., Jr. and Hester, Thomas Roy. ISOLATED ARCHAIC AND LATE PREHISTORIC COMPONENTS AT THE HONEYMOON SITE (41ZV34), SOUTHERN TEXAS. *Plains Anthropologist 1971 16(51): 52-59.* "A dual component site in southern Texas is reported. One area of the site yielded Archaic lithic debris in association with a relatively intact hearth. The other recognized component is situated nearby and represents a Late Prehistoric camping area of brief duration. Artifacts in this component indicate that small dart points were coeval with presumed early styles of arrow points in the region." J

86. Honea, Kenneth. THE RIO GRANDE COMPLEX AND THE NORTHERN PLAINS. *Plains Anthropologist 1969 14(43): 57-70.* "The earliest component at the La Bolsa site in the Galisteo Basin of north-central New Mexico is an early manifestation of what is defined in this paper as the Quemado Phase of the proposed Rio Grande Complex. Relatively dated to about 7000 to 6000 years ago, this Proto-Archaic Phase is postulated to be ultimately rooted in the Agate Basin Complex of the northern Plains." J

87. Jack, Robert N. THE SOURCE OF OBSIDIAN ARTIFACTS IN NORTHERN ARIZONA. *Plateau 1971 43(3): 103-114.* "Obsidians from nine extrusions in the San Francisco volcanic field of northern Arizona have been analyzed for

20 minor and trace elements and fall into five clearly defined trace element groups; 217 artifacts (flakes and tools) from 16 sites in northern Arizona have also been analyzed by X-ray fluorescence, and the source of 186 of these has been identified. In the Flagstaff area the Government Mountain obsidian predominates as the raw material in all sites sampled. At least four different obsidian types from an unknown source have been found among samples from other sites in northern Arizona."   J

88. Johnson, Alfred E. and Wasley, William W. ARCHAEOLOGICAL EXCA-VATIONS NEAR BYLAS, ARIZONA. *Kiva 1966 31(4): 205-253.* "Under Contract No. 14-10-0333-995 with the National Park Service, the Arizona State Museum conducted excavations in two prehistoric ruins on the San Carlos Indian Reservation during April and May, 1963, as a part of the Inter-Agency Archaeological Salvage Program. A total of 88 surface rooms, 2 pit houses, and 4 cremations were excavated, and tests were made in 5 trash mounds and one sheet trash area. This project was accomplished with the aid of San Carlos Apache laborers. The two ruins, Arizona V:16:8 and 10, were nearly contemporary occupations of the area from about A.D. 1100 to 1200, on the basis of ceramic dating. Although Arizona V:16:8 was probably slightly later in time than the other village, both sites were occupied during the twelfth century and may be considered as belonging to the same cultural period, for which the designation of Bylas Phase has been suggested."   J

89. Johnston, Bernice. A NEWLY DISCOVERED TURQUOISE MINE OF PREHISTORY, MOHAVE COUNTY, ARIZONA. *Kiva 1964 29(3): 76-83.* "Current mining operations near Kingman, Arizona, have again revealed the presence of an aboriginal turquoise mine. Although the stone tools associated with the mine are reminiscent of the Hohokam culture, not enough material culture has been found at the mine or a nearby campsite to place the aboriginal workings in time or cultural context."   J

90. Kaemlein, Wilma. LARGE HUNTING NETS IN THE COLLECTIONS OF THE ARIZONA STATE MUSEUM. *Kiva 1971 36(3): 20-53.* "The Arizona State Museum has in its collections five large hunting nets in complete or fragmentary condition. These nets, from caves located in Arizona, are described and compared. One net, of human hair cordage, is compared with the net of human hair from U-Bar Cave in New Mexico. References in the literature to other large nets, both prehistoric and historic, are tabulated. The time range of known nets is ca. A.D. 350-1450. It is concluded that large nets were frequently used in the Southwest for communal hunting activities. Attached offerings or fetishes probably were placed on the nets to insure success in the hunt."   J

91. Kelly, Roger E. AN ARCHAEOLOGICAL SURVEY IN THE PAYSON BASIN, CENTRAL ARIZONA. *Plateau 1969 42(2): 46-65.* "At the request of Tonto National Forest officials, an archaeological salvage survey of terrain to be altered by proposed expansion of the Tonto Forest Seismological Observatory, headquartered near Payson, was accomplished by the Museum of Northern

Arizona. Forty-nine sites were recorded within and without an extensive array of seismometer stations. The data generated corroborates previous surveys of the region and indicates a Salado cultural occupation."   J

92. Lundquist, Karen. A VERDE VALLEY DIG. *Masterkey 1963 37(1): 18-21.* Description of archaeological excavations in 1962 at three small rock shelters in Verde Valley, Arizona, near Montezuma's Castle. Structure, storage pits, artifacts, burials, and food remains were found. It was probably a Sinagua site. 4 illus.   C. N. Warren

93. Midvale, Frank.. PREHISTORIC IRRIGATION IN THE SALT RIVER VALLEY, ARIZONA. *Kiva 1968 34(1): 28-32.* "Prehistoric irrigation in the Salt River Valley is described. Information about the re-use of prehistoric canals and their gradual obliteration since the settlement of the Phoenix area in historic times is presented. A classification for the identification of canal remains is outlined. Finally, the pre-historic canal complex in the vicinity of Mesa is discussed in detail. The map accompanying this article gives the location of more than 315 miles of prehistoric irrigation canals."   J

94. Midvale, Frank. PREHISTORIC IRRIGATION OF THE CASA GRANDE RUINS AREA. *Kiva 1965 30(3): 82-86.* "The location of 85 miles of prehistoric irrigation canal has been precisely mapped along the Gila River, near Casa Grande National Monunent. Much of this evidence is now erased by recent agricultural development and the construction of buildings and highways."   J

95. Morris, Donald H. A 9TH CENTURY SALADO (?) KIVA AT WALNUT CREEK, ARIZONA. *Plateau 1969 42(1): 1-10.* "A sub-circular kiva with some distinctive western Pueblo floor features was excavated 10 miles southeast of Young by students from Arizona State University in 1967. Associated with a pithouse horizon and paddled, non-scraped pottery, its location and occurrence in a village in which Hohokam were also living are particularly interesting."   J

96. Morris, Donald H. and El-Najjar, Mahmoud. AN UNUSUAL CLASSIC PERIOD BURIAL FROM LAS COLINAS, SALT RIVER VALLEY, CENTRAL ARIZONA. *Kiva 1971 36(4): 31-35.* "In April 1961, a contractor's excavation turned up the burial of a partially cremated male near mound 4 of the Classic period Las Colinas site in the Salt River Valley, central Arizona. Grave goods included an incised bone wand, a stone pipe, a small 3/4-grooved axe, and unworked *Glycymeris* sea shells."   J

97. Myers, Richard D. THE FOLSOM POINT FROM THE RISING SITE, SOUTHEAST ARIZONA. *Kiva 1967 32(3): 102-105.* "The occurrence of a Folsom point 31 miles east of Douglas, Arizona, moves the Folsom Culture westward into a region well known for the Clovis Culture." 2 illus.   J

98. Reilly, P. T. ISOLATED RIM SITES OF GRAND CANYON. *Masterkey 1970 44(3): 103-107.* Discusses the possible reasons early man used the temporary prehistoric campsites found along the precipitous rim of the Grand Canyon. Specifically describes one of the sites, Apache Point, located roughly 20 miles northwest of Grand Canyon Village. 3 photos.   C. N. Warren

99. Reilly, P. T. THE JUNO RUIN. *Masterkey 1966 40(1): 16-22.* Reviews the various explorations of the first three main tributaries running east from the Walhalla Plateau in the Grand Canyon, emphasizing the archaeological sites found and claimed to be found. Describes in some detail the Juno Ruin, and reviews the unsuccessful attempts to find the "lost city" in Kwagunt Canyon. Based on field investigation, primary and secondary sources; 4 illus.
C. N. Warren

100. Reilly, P. T. THE SITES AT VASEY'S PARADISE. *Masterkey 1966 40(4): 126-139.* A history of the discovery and investigation of Stanton Cave, a prehistoric site on the right bank of the Colorado River in Marble Canyon, 32 miles downstream from Lees Ferry, Arizona. This site has become well-known to investigators of the prehistoric southwest Split-Twig Figurines Complex. One of the Stanton Cave figurines has recently been radiocarbon-dated at 4095 B.C. (plus or minus 100 years). Ties in this complex with different desert cultural phases of the area. 4 photos.   C. N. Warren

101. Schreiber, John P. and Breed, William J. OBSIDIAN LOCALITIES IN THE SAN FRANCISCO VOLCANIC FIELD, ARIZONA. *Plateau 1971 43(3): 115-119.* "In an attempt to relate obsidian found in archaeological sites in northern Arizona to its source areas, nine obsidian outcrops in the San Francisco Volcanic Field were located. Although it is not possible to differentiate this obsidian megascopically, it is possible to divide the field into four chemical groups by X-ray fluorescence."   J

102. Sense, Richard. A PREHISTORIC QUARRY NEAR RAY, ARIZONA. *Kiva 1967 32(4): 170-174.* "A prehistoric chrysocolla quarry was discovered near the Kennecott open pit copper mine at Ray, Arizona. Chrysocolla, a blue copper silicate, was sought by aboriginal miners, who moved over one hundred and eighty tons of rock in the quarry to obtain the mineral. Stone tools were recovered at the site, but no pottery was found. Prehistoric ruins in the area indicate that the miners may have been Hohokam."   J

103. Smith, Calvin, Runyon, John, and Agogino, George. A PROGRESS REPORT ON A PRE-CERAMIC SITE AT RATTLESNAKE DRAW, EASTERN NEW MEXICO. *Plains Anthropologist 1966 11(34): 302-313.* "The Rattlesnake Draw Site has produced both Paleo-Indian and Archaic artifacts in a concentrated area centering about a presently dry lake basin. In addition to the artifacts discovered, investigators have found evidence of the archaic period. These wells are similar to those earlier discovered, at Blackwater Draw." Archae-

ological research with radiocarbon dates clearly established that man existed in North and South America 11 thousand to 12 thousand years ago. Illus., biblio.

K. Adelfang

104. Steen, Charlie R. EXCAVATIONS IN COMPOUND A, CASA GRANDE NATIONAL MONUMENT, 1963. *Kiva 1965 31(2): 59-82.* "Excavations were conducted with the purpose of exploring the south end of Compound A, and the compound-link enclosure which lies southeast of the Casa Grande. Besides extensive evidence of earlier archaeological and stabilization excavations, a series of house floors and associated posts, wall, and hearths were found in Compound A. Some information was obtained concerning wall construction of the Casa Grande and nearby plaza areas. The architectural remains combined with a uniform ceramic distribution leads to the conclusion that the massive-walled multi-storied building was a trait acquired from the south and not from the north as was previously thought."

J

105. Stewart, Kenneth M. EXCAVATIONS AT MESA GRANDE: A CLASSIC PERIOD HOHOKAM SITE IN ARIZONA. *Masterkey 1967 41(1): 14-25.* Reports on the results of excavations of the Mesa Grande site in Arizona. The author places the site in the Civano Phase of the Classic Period of Hohokam Indians and dates the site at approximately 1300 A.D. Based on field investigation, primary and secondary sources; 4 illus., biblio.

C. N. Warren

106. Stewart, Kenneth M. MOJAVE INDIAN AGRICULTURE. *Masterkey 1966 40(1): 5-15.* Describes in some detail the agricultural practices of the Mojave Indians, prior to contact, in the Colorado River floodlands of Southern California and Arizona. Principal crops were maize, tepary beans, melons, pumpkins, sunflowers (for the seeds), and gourds (for use as receptacles or rattles). Mojave agricultural methods were relatively simple, involving planting on the floodplain immediately following subsidence of the spring floods, and a fall harvest. Both crop rotation and artificial irrigation were superfluous, due to the richness and moisture of the silt deposited by the floods. The author also notes several agriculturally-related cultural practices. Based on primary and secondary sources; 5 illus., biblio.

C. N. Warren

107. Thompson, Raymond H. and Longacre, William A. THE UNIVERSITY OF ARIZONA ARCHAEOLOGICAL FIELD SCHOOL AT GRASSHOPPER, EAST CENTRAL ARIZONA. *Kiva 1966 31(4): 255-275.* "The University of Arizona Archaeological Field School has now completed three seasons' work at the Grasshopper Ruin, a 14th century pueblo in east-central Arizona. The teaching program stresses student participation in an ongoing research activity. Excavations thus far have uncovered 21 domestic rooms, a rectangular Great Kiva, 120 human burials and a number of masonry-lined pit ovens. Trash deposits have been tested, as has a large central plaza which was entered through a roofed corridor. Stylistic similarities in the ceramics suggest interaction with adjacent areas. Sampling problems and future research plans are discussed."

J

108. Turner, Christy G., II. CRANIAL AND DENTAL FEATURES OF A SOUTHEASTERN ARIZONA COCHISE CULTURE BURIAL. *Kiva 1969 34(4): 246-250.* "The cranial and dental features of a skull found in a Cochise Culture burial near St. David, Arizona, are described. The relationship of the skull to Brues' San Simon type is discussed. The validity of the San Simon type is questioned." Illus., photo.   J

109. Turner, Christy G., II, and Lofgren, Laurel. HOUSEHOLD SIZE OF PREHISTORIC WESTERN PUEBLO INDIANS. *Southwestern J. of Anthrop. 1966 22(2): 117-132.* Presents a system of sizing of C 2 western Pueblo Indian households, based on the ratio of sizes of serving bowls, ladles, and cooking jars from prehistoric archaeological sites in the southwestern United States. Based strictly on these ratios, the authors' resultant estimates of household and population size vary little from reliable estimates made using other techniques. Based on primary and secondary sources; 4 tables, 4 illus., biblio.   C. N. Warren

110. Ward, Albert E. A MULTICOMPONENT SITE WITH A DESERT CULTURE AFFINITY, NEAR WINDOW ROCK, ARIZONA. *Plateau 1971 43(3): 120-131.* "Surface finds at a site on the western bank of Black Creek, in northeastern Arizona, have produced projectile points usually assigned to the Pinto Basin complex of the Desert Culture. Similar artifacts contained in a Navajo medicine bundle were found to have originated at the site. Ethnographic data concerning the shaman's use of these projectile points is given. In addition, a wide range of ceramics suggests that the site consists of two components: (1) a non-ceramic occupation represented by the Pinto finds, and (2) a long Anasazi occupation represented by the ceramics."   J

111. Ward, Albert E. A NAVAJO ANTHROPOMORPHIC FIGURINE. *Plateau 1970 42(4): 146-149.* "A Navajo anthropomorphic figurine was found associated with a prehistoric Anasazi site in the Inscription House Trading Post area on the Navajo Reservation in northern Arizona. Similar finds reported from New Mexico suggest that the use of wooden anthropomorphic images among the Navajo has been borrowed from the neighboring Hopi and is of recent introduction. The description and discussion here offers new and supportive data from Arizona."   J

112. Wasley, William W. and Benham, Blake. SALVAGE EXCAVATION IN THE BUTTES DAM SITE, SOUTHERN ARIZONA. *Kiva 1968 33(4): 244-279.* "During November and December, 1966, archaeological salvage excavation was conducted in the Buttes Dam Site by the Arizona State Museum under contract with the National Park Service. Excavated were six pit houses, a Casa Grande type of ball court, four trash mounds, 21 cremations, and several cooking pits. The architecture, ceramics, and the style of some of the stone artifacts indicate that this Hohokam village site was occupied during the late Santa Cruz and early Sacaton phases. It is suggested that the occupation of the site took place between about A.D. 850 and A.D. 1000."   J

113. Weed, Carol S. TWO TWELFTH CENTURY BURIALS FROM THE HOPI RESERVATION. *Plateau 1970 43(1): 27-38.* "Early in 1969, at the request of the Hopi Tribal Council, an excavation was conducted on the Hopi Reservation. Discovered during a roadgrading operation, the site ultimately produced two burials, dating from ca. A.D. 1125, associated funeral offerings and a mealing and Massed Sherd area. The funeral offerings consist of some sixteen whole and restorable vessels, many of which prove to be variants on Tusayan White Ware and Little Colorado White Ware themes." J

114. Yarnall, Richard A. IMPLICATIONS OF DISTINCTIVE FLORA ON PUEBLO RUINS. *Am. Anthropologist 1965 67(3): 662-674.* A report of a study of the effects of Pueblo Indians of pre-Spanish times on the composition of the flora of their former habitation sites (small and large ruins, cave sites) at Bandelier National Monument, New Mexico. The author found that certain plants seldom occur in the area except on Pueblo ruins and that others are more common on ruins than elsewhere. Many of these plants (significantly so: *Solanaceae, Cleome serrulata, Lithospermum caroliniense, Salvia subincesa, Lycium pallidum, Datura*) have been extensively utilized by Pueblo Indians and semicultivated by them in some cases. Results of the study suggest to the author that the Indians introduced a number of plant species into the area, perhaps into the American Southwest. Tables of plants collected at the sites arranging plants as to degree of occurrence on and confinement to ruins, extent of relationship with Pueblo Indians archaeologically and ethnologically, and considerations of ecology and range are included in the text. Sr. B. A. Barbato

115. Zahniser, Jack L. LATE PREHISTORIC VILLAGES SOUTHEAST OF TUCSON, ARIZONA, AND THE ARCHAEOLOGY OF THE TANQUE VERDE PHASE. *Kiva 1966 31(3): 103-204.* "Nearly 20 prehistoric villages and rock shelters are known to exist in the Rincon Valley, southeast of Tucson, Arizona. With one exception, none has been excavated. The exception, Tanque Verde Ruin, was partially excavated 38 years ago. Other scattered features— bedrock mortars, petroglyphs, and pictographs—are common. Sherd collections indicate the presence of Tucson Hohokam in the Rincon Valley from late Colonial to middle Classic times. This paper reports the recent excavation of Arizona BB: 14:24, a part of the same village as Tanque Verde Ruin, at the west end of the Rincon Valley. Throughout, an attempt has been made to collect, incorporate, and evaluate the largely unpublished data from Tanque Verde Ruin. Both sites are assigned to the Tanque Verde Phase of the Tucson Basin Hohokam cultural sequence, although some things suggest that they were also occupied during the preceding Rincon and Rillito Phases. A survey in the immediate vicinity of Arizona BB:14:24 yielded evidence of widespread settlement in the Tanque Verde foothills during Tanque Verde times (approximately A.D. 1100-1300). Available information about excavated and surveyed Tanque Verde Phase sites is examined in order to provide a comprehensive statement about the Tanque Verde Phase and its cultural affinities." J

116. —. [HIGHWAY SALVAGE ARCHAEOLOGY]. *Kiva 1969 34(2/3): 53-205.*

Vivian, R. Gwinn. ARIZONA HIGHWAY SALVAGE ARCHAEOL-
OGY 1969, pp. 53-57. A general introduction to the volume combining two
numbers to cover the scope of highway salvage operations during the past 11
years in Arizona. Justifications, procedures, and benefits of the public operations
are described. Photo.

Hammack, Laurens C. HIGHWAY SALVAGE ARCHAEOLOGY IN
THE FORESTDALE VALLEY, ARIZONA, pp. 58-89. "In July 1966 under a
contract with the Arizona Highway Department and the Bureau of Public Roads
the Arizona State Museum in cooperation with the Museum of Northern Arizona
conducted salvage excavations on two sites on the Fort Apache Indian Reservation near Forestdale, Arizona. Two phases of occupation were represented at one
of the ruins investigated, the Skiddy Canyon Ruin. A kiva, pithouse and a number
of burials show cultural affiliation with the Forestdale Phase dated between A.D.
600 and 800. A series of rectangular masonry rooms, a trash area, and burials
were characteristic of the Linden Phase which has been dated provisionally
between A.D. 1100 and 1200. A second site excavated, the Gobbler Tank site,
is a small Linden Phase seasonal unit. Excavation of these sites has enabled a
preliminary description of the Linden Phase in the Forestdale region." 17 illus.,
4 tables.

Pilles, Peter J., Jr. HABITATION AND FIELD HOUSES NEAR
WINONA AND ANGELL, ARIZONA, pp. 90-102. "One habitation unit, two
field houses, and one sherd area were excavated as part of the highway archaeological salvage program for construction of Interstate 40. The habitation unit is
unusual for its time period (A.D. 1075-1100) in being a circular above-ground
masonry structure. All excavated sites date ceramically from A.D. 1070 to 1100,
although two later structures were found nearby. Observations are made regarding the surface finishing of Sunset Red pottery." 4 illus., table.

Barrera, Bill, Jr. A DESERT CULTURE SITE NEAR TWO GUNS,
NORTHERN ARIZONA, pp. 103-108. "A Desert Culture-affiliated site was
collected near Two Guns, Arizona. Projectile points, knives, cutter-scrapers,
primary decortication flakes, ground stone, and utilized flakes of chert, obsidian,
basalt, quartzite, and sandstone were recovered. A statistical treatment indicates
that chert was selected for utilized flakes and obsidian was selected for bifacial
implements." 2 illus.

Grebinger, Paul and Bradley, Bruce. EXCAVATIONS AT A PREHIS-
TORIC CAMP SITE ON THE MOGOLLON RIM, EAST CENTRAL
ARIZONA, pp. 109-123. "Archaeological excavations directed by Laurens C.
Hammack were conducted near Overgaard, Arizona, under the Statewide Highway Salvage Program. Arizona P:10:7 proved to be a prehistoric campsite with
two temporally and, to some extent, spatially separated occupations. The site was
first occupied briefly between A.D. 600 and 950. Four hearths, early Mogollon
pottery types, and an extensive lithic assemblage were associated with this occupation. After A.D. 1100 the site was occupied again, as suggested by the presence
of Snowflake Black-on-white pottery. This second use of the area was probably
a brief one, as little other cultural material and no hearths were found in association with the pottery." 7 illus., table.   J

Great Plains Area

117. Anderson, Adrian D. and Chappabitty, Franklin L. A BISON KILL FROM DOMEBO CANYON. *Great Plains J. 1968 8(1): 48-52.* A geological field party working in Domebo Canyon in Caddo County, Oklahoma, in 1963 found partial skeletal remains of a bison buried three to three and one-half feet below the surface. A small projectile point between two ribs was of the Fresno type and has been dated between 800 A.D. and about 1750 A.D. This find, coupled with type-locations for a Paleo-Indian mammoth kill and a late Pleistocene geological formation elsewhere in the canyon, "presents a unique and almost full habitational and cultural sequence of prehistoric occupation in Oklahoma and the Great Plains." Illus., biblio. O. H. Zabel

118. Anderson, Duane C. MILL CREEK CULTURE: A REVIEW. *Plains Anthropologist 1969 14(44, pt. 1): 137-143.* "The literature pertaining to the Mill Creek complex of northwestern Iowa is reviewed with particular emphasis on the taxonomic history of the assemblage, the dating of the two separate phases, their origin and spread, external relationships and ultimate disappearance. It is hoped that this survey will be useful to interested amateurs in its historical approach to the subject matter, and further, that it will serve to convey some of my thoughts to professional archaeologists working in the area." J

119. Bass, William M. A HUMAN SKELETON FROM THE GILLETTE SITE, STANLEY COUNTY, SOUTH DAKOTA. *Plains Anthropologist 1966 11(34): 290-293.* Describes a skeleton excavated from a refuse area at the Gillette Site, Stanley County, South Dakota, which proved to be that of an adult male of advanced age. Details are given in chart form of skull, teeth, and height measurements, as well as total face index. Illus., biblio. K. Adelfang

120. Bass, William M. and Grubbs, Patricia A. HUMAN SKELETAL MATERIAL FROM A KEITH FOCUS PLAINS WOODLAND SITE. *Plains Anthropologist 1966 11(32): 135-143.* Describes in detail the skeletal material from two individuals, adult male and female, found from a Keith Focus Plains Woodland site. They had lived in Kansas at about 400-800 A.D. and were members of the high headed dolichocranic populations. Illus., biblio. K. Adelfang

121. Bell, Robert E. DATING THE PREHISTORY OF OKLAHOMA. *Great Plains J. 1968 7(2): 42-52.* Discusses the reliability of radiocarbon dating and asserts that in the past 20 years a timetable, based upon some 100 radiocarbon dates, has been established for Oklahoma's prehistoric Indian populations. The oldest discovered site dates from approximately 9250 B.C. There are only a very few discovered sites dated prior to A.D. 250. Of the 49 radiocarbon dates available for Gibson aspect sites in the Arkansas drainage area, most fall in the period

from A.D. 900 to A.D. 1400. Radiocarbon dates confirm prehistoric Indian occupation of Oklahoma for the past 11 thousand years, but additional dates between 9250 B.C. and A.D. 250 are needed. Illus., biblio.   O. H. Zabel

122. Brown, Lionel A. TEMPORAL AND SPATIAL ORDER IN THE CENTRAL PLAINS. *Plains Anthropologist 1966 11(34): 294-301.* "The major archeological complexes of the Central Plains can be arranged according to the Willey and Phillips system" (the area, sub-area, region, locality, and site) "thus recognizing not only content, but time and space dimensions." Biblio.
K. Adelfang

123. Brown, Lionel A. THE GAVINS POINT SITE (39YK203): AN ANALYSIS OF SURFACE ARTIFACTS. *Plains Anthropologist 1968 13(40): 118-131.* "A descriptive analysis of surface artifacts discloses Woodland-Great Oasis elements of an earlier component and later use of the site represented by collared rims suggestive of either the Central Plains Tradition or the Initial Coalescent Horizon....Limited excavations of the site...were conducted...in 1960 and 1961."
J

124. Brown, Lionel A. THE GILLETTE SITE, OAHE RESERVOIR, SOUTH DAKOTA. *Plains Anthropologist 1966 11(34): 239-289.* "Fieldwork at the Gillette Site primarily consisted of the partial excavation of three circular houses, a cross section of a fortification ditch, and the removal of a burial." The latest occupation dates from about 1700 to 1800 A.D. The artifacts included Stanley Braced Rim Ware, Colombe Collared pottery, and trade goods such as beads and an iron knife. A single skeleton was excavated. Eleven kinds of mammals were represented. Illus., biblio.   K. Adelfang

125. Caldwell, Warren W. ARCHEOLOGICAL INVESTIGATIONS AT THE MC KENSEY VILLAGE, OAHE RESERVOIR, CENTRAL SOUTH DAKOTA. *Plains Anthropologist 1966 11(34): 4-99.* Points to heavy concentration of archaeological sites at the Oahe Reservoir in South Dakota, on the Missouri River. The McKensey Site, on the north side of the river, was composed of 17 house depressions, appearing to be arranged in regular rows or blocks. Illus., biblio.   K. Adelfang

126. Caldwell, Warren W. THE MIDDLE MISSOURI TRADITION REAPPRAISED. *Plains Anthropologist 1966 11(32): 152-157.* States that the geographic distribution of the horizons (an important integrative concept within the Willey and Phillips system), has been rephrased as a cultural stratum cutting across the tradition. Within the Middle Missouri tradition the temporal and cultural relationships are not entirely clear. Illus., biblio.   K. Adelfang

127. Clayton, Lee, Bickley, W. B., Jr., and Stone, W. J. KNIFE RIVER FLINT. *Plains Anthropologist 1970 15(50, pt. 1): 282-290.* "Twenty-four Knife River Flint quarries have been newly discovered in Dunn County, North Dakota. Five were previously known in Mercer County. The flint occurs as pebbles, cobbles,

and boulders in alluvial, slope-wash, and colluvial lag deposits of Pleistocene age. The flint in these deposits was originally derived from a silicified lignite bed in the Golden Valley Formation of Eocene age and possibly also from other lignite-bearing formations. The flint has a characteristic petrography and can be readily distinguished from all other commonly used rock types in North Dakota and adjacent areas." J

128. Coleman, John M. AN ANALYSIS OF CERAMICS FROM THE GETTYSBURG SITE, 39P0209, POTTER COUNTY, SOUTH DAKOTA. *Plains Anthropologist 1968 13(41): 228-241.* "Ceramics recovered from the Gettysburg Site during the summers of 1964, 1965, and 1966 are described and analyzed. A comparison is made with ceramic collections from 19 other sites in the Middle Missouri Valley. Concluding comments demonstrate the relationship of the Gettysburg Site to sites of the Extended Coalescent Horizon." J

129. Davis, Leslie B. AVONLEA POINT OCCURRENCE IN NORTHERN MONTANA AND CANADA. *Plains Anthropologist 1966 11(32): 100-116.* Follow-up of 1961 Keho-McCorquodale article in *Plains Anthropologist* of the Avonlea point as a horizon marker for the late prehistoric period in the northwestern Plains. Regional Montana Avonlea "culture" is discussed, compared and combined with the Canadian data about which there is some correspondence. Evidence is still lacking as to permit ready assignment of the Avonlea point to the late prehistoric period. Tables, illus., 5 notes. K. Adelfang

130. Dewdney, Selwyn. WRITINGS ON STONE ALONG THE MILK RIVER. *Beaver [Canada] 1964 295(Winter): 22-29.* Describes Indian pictographs at Writing-on-Stone Provincial Park in southern Alberta. Illus.
L. F. S. Upton

131. Dibble, David S. ON THE SIGNIFICANCE OF ADDITIONAL RADIOCARBON DATES FROM BONFIRE SHELTER, TEXAS. *Plains Anthropologist 1970 15(50, pt. 1): 251-254.* "Two hitherto unreported dates from charcoal samples associated with remains attributed to a Paleo-Indian bison kill at this site are provided. These dates further substantiate a minimal antiquity of ca. 10,000 years for the deposit and, by inference, give evidence of the use of a 'bison jump' technique of hunting at this early time period. Definitional problems, differing views on the antiquity, basic comparability of cited examples, and temporal continuity of this mode of mass killing are briefly discussed. Some suggestions are made as to the cultural implications made probable by acceptance of an early date for this practice." J

132. Eighmy, Jeff. EDWARDS II: REPORT OF AN EXCAVATION IN WESTERN OKLAHOMA. *Plains Anthropologist 1971 15(50, pt. 1): 255-281.* "Edwards II is located on the North Fork of the Red River in western Oklahoma. It is one of two sites excavated in 1968 by the University of Oklahoma Field School in Archaeology. The major excavation area consisted of 19 contiguous five foot squares. Two test pits were also dug to determine the limits of the site. Nine

features were uncovered; all were pits which exhibited a variety of shapes. Ceramic materials and projectile points are similar to Custer and Washita River foci manifestations, but the low proportion of bison bone, and the presence of a few corner notched and stemmed points suggest placement early in the time span represented by these foci."   J

133. Ford, James A. HOPEWELL CULTURE BURIAL MOUNDS NEAR HELENA, KANSAS. *Anthrop. Papers of the Am. Mus. of Natural Hist. 1963 50(1): 3-55.* Excavation of two of five conical mounds took place in the autumn of 1960. Mound C contained five long-roofed tombs in a primary mound with higher burials and a secondary mound over the earlier features. Mound B contained one large log-roofed tomb extended and bundle burials were recovered. Radiocarbon dates range from approximately 140 B.C. to 335 A.D. Burial patterns and artifacts link the Helena Crossing Site with the Hopewell culture to the south. The culture pattern appears to come ultimately from the formative period of civilization in Mesoamerica. The excavations fill in an archaeological gap 400 miles long in the central portion of the Alluvial Valley of the Mississippi River. Illus.   E. H. Swanson, Jr.

134. Frison, George. DAUGHERTY CAVE, WYOMING. *Plains Anthropologist 1968 13(42, pt. 1): 253-295.* "Daugherty Cave is a double component site in the Big Horn Basin of northern Wyoming. The earlier level is representative of a widespread Late Middle Prehistoric Period occupation. The surface material is believed to represent the Late Prehistoric Period, Crow Indian occupation of the area. The site produced considerable amounts of perishable material."   J

135. Frison, George C., Wright, Gary A., Griffin, James B., and Gordus, Adon A. NEUTRON ACTIVATION ANALYSIS OF OBSIDIAN: AN EXAMPLE OF ITS RELEVANCE TO NORTHWESTERN PLAINS ARCHAEOLOGY. *Plains Anthropologist 1968 13(4): 209-217.* "By a process of neutron activation, obsidian samples from an archaeological site may be traced to their quarry sources. The potential of this type of information remains largely unexplored and this paper is one small example of its application to Northwestern Plains Archaeology."   J

136. Frison, George C. SITE 48SH312: AN EARLY MIDDLE PERIOD BISON KILL IN THE POWDER RIVER BASIN OF WYOMING. *Plains Anthropologist 1968 13(39): 31-39.* A report of the Sheridan chapter of the Wyoming Archaeological Society's 1961 excavation of a bison kill in Powder River County, Montana. Found was a layer of bison bone and artifacts including projectile points and butchering tools. A similar bison kill was found further south in Wyoming. Radiocarbon dates are 2500 plus or minus 125 years B.C. for the first find and 650 plus or minus 200 years B.C. for the second. The evidence represents an Early Middle Period. The bison kill may have been done by four or five males or an extended family group. A good explanation of butchering and meat handling technique is still lacking. Evidence indicates that the animals were killed for immediate food needs. 5 figs., biblio.   K. Adelfang

137. Frison, George C. THE PINEY CREEK SITES, WYOMING (48 JO 311 AND 312). *U. of Wyoming Publications 1967 33(1):1-92.* Report of an archaeological excavation of a buffalo kill area along Piney Creek in Wyoming. Evidence indicates that about 120 pre-horse Indians used the village and adjacent kill area just one year (ca. 1600 A.D.) to kill about 200 bison. In addition to describing two sites, artifacts, and geographical conditions in the area, the archaeologist conjectures the process of killing and butchering buffalo. Illus., maps, tables, photos, biblio.   H. B. Powell

138. Gibson, A. M. PREHISTORY IN OKLAHOMA. *Chronicles of Oklahoma 1965 43(1): 2-8.* Archaeologists have found in Oklahoma traces of human life possibly 10 to 15 thousand years old. Situated in a great concourse of human groups, with a terrain that allowed easy access for wandering bands and a moderate climate and natural shelter, the area has revealed some of the earliest signs that have been found in North America. The first age was one of big game hunters who sought mammoths and other prehistoric creatures. These people were cave dwellers, but toward the end of their period they made homes in the valleys. From about the beginning of the Christian era to 1500 A.D. lowland village dwellings with certain refinements developed. In Oklahoma's late prehistoric period mounds were built, many over 40 feet high, sometimes as locations for villages above possible floods, others being burial places. The golden age of Oklahoma prehistory was from 900 to 1450 A.D., and the best archaeological treasure-trove dates from this period. Biblio.   I. W. Van Noppen

139. Gilbert, B. Miles. SOME ASPECTS OF DIET AND BUTCHERING TECHNIQUES AMONG PREHISTORIC INDIANS IN SOUTH DAKOTA. *Plains Anthropologist 1969 14(46): 277-294.* "Faunal remains from ten South Dakota archaeological sites, ranging temporally from ca. 600 B.C.-A.D. 1600, are identified and analyzed by the method of [Dr. Theodore E.] White (1952). This analysis shows what species were used, and in what numbers, in sites of the three major temporal divisions; Woodland, Middle Missouri and Coalescent. Bison are the preferred animals in all time periods. Group related butchering techniques are discussed." Biblio.   J

140. Gregg, John B. EAR DISEASE IN THE INDIAN SKULLS AT THE MUSEUM OF THE STATE HISTORICAL SOCIETY OF NORTH DAKOTA. *North Dakota Hist. 1965 32(4): 233-239.* A member of a team engaged in extensive research on skulls removed from Indian burials in North and South Dakota and of studies made on present-day living Indians in those states, the author attempted to discover by X ray whether middle ear disease (otitis media) and a disease of the inner ear (otosclerosis) occurred among the uncivilized Indians of this area. He found nothing that suggested the presence of cholesteatome in the middle ear nor the existence of otosclerosis in individuals represented by the bones examined. Either the latter disease did not exist in these cultures of people, or the bone formed in the otosclerotic process is less resistant to the weathering effects of the elements. Illus., biblio.

I. W. Van Noppen

141. Gregg, John B. and Steele, James P. THE PARAOCCIPITAL (PARA-CONDYLOID) PROCESS: AN ANATOMIC AND RADIOLOGICAL AP-PRAISAL. *Plains Anthropologist 1969 14(44, pt. 1): 103-106.* "A summary of the available literature relating to the subject of paraoccipital (paracondyloid) processes is presented. An anatomic description illustrated by a photograph and a radiographic analysis of an outstanding example of a paracondyloid process is submitted. In a series of 984 Indian burial specimens from South and North Dakota, anomalies in the area of the base of the skull, including occipitalization of the first cervical vertebra and paracondyloid processes, occurred in 0.3 percent. This ratio is similar to that found in other series which have been reported in the past."   J

142. Gunnerson, James H. PLAINS APACHE ARCHAEOLOGY: A RE-VIEW. *Plains Anthropologist 1968 13(4): 167-189.* "A review of the literature on the Dismal River Aspect in the light of recent additional work at Plains Apache sites has led to more specific suggestions as to probable sources of various Dismal River traits. Most of the traits that appear to have been borrowed from sedentary neighbors seem to have an Eastern Plains origin. Many trade items from the Southwest may have been secured from or through the Jicarilla Apaches. Frequency of some traits at Dismal River sites form a gradient from north to south. Many problems remain unsolved."   J

143. Heizer, Robert F. and Brooks, Richard A. LEWISVILLE—ANCIENT CAMPSITE OR WOOD RAT HOUSES? *Southwestern J. of Anthrop. 1965 21(2): 155-165.* Urges reconsideration of evidence from the archaeological site at Lewisville, Texas, holding that all published evidence could apply just as easily to wood rat houses as to human occupation. Based on secondary sources; table, biblio.   C. N. Warren

144. Hester, Thomas Roy. BURNED ROCK MIDDEN SITES ON THE SOUTHWESTERN EDGE OF THE EDWARDS PLATEAU, TEXAS. *Plains Anthropologist 1970 15(50, pt. 1): 237-250.* "Data from two groups of burned rock midden sites are presented. Occupation of the sites seems to have been heaviest during Archaic times, with some Late Prehistoric and possible Paleo-Indian components also recognized. A burial is described from one site. Problems pertaining to burned rock midden sites are briefly discussed."   J

145. Hoffman, J. J. AN UNUSUAL POTTERY OBJECT FROM SOUTH DAKOTA. *Plains Anthropologist 1968 13(39): 29-30.* A spoon or small ladle found in three fragments from the Rosa Site in Potter County, South Dakota, during the 1957 investigation of the South Dakota Archaeological Commission. It is made of local clay, heavily tempered with large grit particles, probably modeled by hand with at least one fingernail impression visible on one side. It has a volume of 15 cc. and seems too small to be utilitarian, leaving the reason for its manufacture open to question. Fig., biblio.   K. Adelfang

146. Hoffman, J. J. and Brown, Lionel A. THE BAD RIVER PHASE. *Plains Anthropologist 1967 12(37): 323-343.* "The Bad River Phase is a distinct archeological unit defined from contact period earthlodge villages in the bad-Cheyenne District of the Middle Missouri Region. The phase is outlined in terms of time, space, and salient contents. On the basis of spatial and temporal distribution, as well as comparable material culture, the Bad River Phase represents a portion of 18th century Arikara population in South Dakota." 4 figures, 2 plates, biblio.

J

147. Howard, James H. ARCHEOLOGICAL INVESTIGATIONS AT THE SPAWN MOUND, 39LK201, LAKE COUNTY, SOUTH DAKOTA. *Plains Anthropologist 1968 13(40): 132-145.* "The Spawn Mound, 39LK201, overlooking Brant Lake in eastern South Dakota, appears to be a Plains Woodland burial mound later used by historic Dakota for secondary interments. The 1966 excavations revealed two burial pits believed to be contemporaneous with the erection of the mound, which were assigned to the Plains Woodland component, and a third pit at the center of the mound which has been assigned to the historic Dakota. Each of the Woodland burial pits contained at least three individuals buried in the flexed position. The intrusive pit contained the remains of at least two individuals, apparently 'bundle' burials. These intrusive burials were accompanied by European trade items. On the basis of the limited ceramic material from the mound, including one rim sherd of the Ellis Cord Impressed type, as well as various lithic materials recovered in the mound fill, the Plains Woodland component has been tentatively assigned to the Loseke Focus. The historic burials would appear to date between A.D. 1800-1850." J

148. Jensen, Richard E. THE PETERSON SITE, AN EARTH LODGE VILLAGE IN THE BIG BEND RESERVOIR, SOUTH DAKOTA. *Plains Anthropologist 1966 11(31): 78-99.* "One circular earth lodge and an inter-house test trench were excavated at the Peterson Site by the Smithsonian Institution's Missouri Basin Project in 1958 prior to the flooding of the area by the Big Bend Reservoir. Surface features indicated the site was an unfortified village of about 40 lodges...probably occupied during the mid-18th century." Illus., plates, biblio.

J

149. Johnson, Arthur F. A BUFFALO DRIVE ON HEART RIVER. *North Dakota Hist. 1964 31(4): 231-233.* Plains Indians customarily hunted buffalo by driving them over a cliff and killing them. The site of such a "drive" is on the Heart River in Stark County, North Dakota. More than 750 arrowheads have been found in the narrow ravine into which the buffalo fell. Apparently the use of this site was abandoned with the coming of the white men, as no steel arrows have been found. Arrows were of brown flint, slate and shale, white flint, moss agate and petrified wood, chert and quartzite, obsidian, and jasper. The gully in which they were found was at one time partially filled with a packed mixture of buffalo bones and soil.   I. W. Van Noppen

150. Johnson, Elden. DECORATIVE MOTIFS ON GREAT OASIS POTTERY. *Plains Anthropologist 1969 14(46): 272-276.* "Decorative design motifs

on Great Oasis Incised rim sherds from the Great Oasis site in Minnesota are illustrated and described. The usefulness of using decorative modes in ceramic comparisons with pottery of the Over focus is suggested." Biblio.   J

151. Johnston, Richard B. AN ANALYSIS OF THE SURVEY COLLECTION FROM THE PASCAL CREEK SITE. *Plains Anthropologist 1966 11(33): 176-185.* "Descriptive analysis of a limited survey collection, including primarily ceramics, reveals the Pascal Creek Site to be an 18th century settlement resembling contemporary villages along the Missouri River in Central South Dakota affiliated with the Snake Butte Focus." It was probably an Arikara village of the late protohistoric age. Illus., biblio.   K. Adelfang

152. Johnston, Richard B. and Hoffman, J. J. AN ANALYSIS OF FOUR SURVEY COLLECTIONS FROM ARMSTRONG COUNTY, SOUTH DAKOTA. *Plains Anthropologist 1966 11(31): 41-75.* Materials collected from four sites on the Little Bend of the Missouri River, referred to as the No Heart Creek complex, are described and analyzed. Five sites were cited as similar in that all contained a thin, simple ceramic vessel, stone and base tools representing horticulture and big game hunting, lack of Euro-American material, circular housing remains, a defensive system consisting of a ditch or dry moat, and a settlement pattern of fortified enclosures with a dense cluster of lodges. Illus., plates, biblio.   K. Adelfang

153. Katz, Paul R. ARCHAEOLOGY OF THE SUTTER SITE IN NORTHEASTERN KANSAS. *Plains Anthropologist 1971 16(51): 1-19.* "The Sutter site (14JN309) is a deeply buried preceramic occupation area in northeastern Kansas. Threatened by inundation, salvage operations were conducted by the Museum of Anthropology, University of Kansas early in 1968. Surface collecting behind a grader and limited excavation resulted in the recovery of a sample of artifact categories and faunal remains. Cutting and scraping implements predominate among the former; modern bison among the latter. Geological studies indicate the site was an area of marshy conditions, and it is postulated that mired animals and wild flora were procured, processed, and consumed in the immediate vicinity of the marsh. In the absence of radiocarbon dates, attribute and assemblage comparisons were made with other preceramic complexes on the Central and Northwestern Plains. The closest similarities are with both the Frederick and McKean complexes, and the Sutter site is assigned a relative chronological position within the span from 6000 to 3000 B.C. It is thus possibly the oldest excavated site in Kansas."   J

154. Kehoe, Thomas F. THE BOARDING SCHOOL BISON DRIVE SITE. *Plains Anthropologist 1967 12(35): 1-165.* A monograph of archaeological excavations at the Boarding School Bison Site, a prehistoric bison drive and kill located five miles north of Browning, Montana, on the Blackfeet Indian Reservation. The author's approach was to obtain a broad picture of the bison drives as an important part of the Plains Indian culture, using archaeological, ethnographic, and historical data. The method of excavating 42 layers of strata is described in detail. The first two series of strata are separated from the last two

by a carbon-14 date of ca. A.D. 1590. The deepest deposits reveal remains of a single bison bull killed some time during the middle period of northwestern Plains prehistory. Remains of five bison killed about the time of Christ were also found. Between A.D. 800-1500 the site was occupied by people who made prairie side notched points. The upper deposits reveal herds of 100 and 500 bison were killed in the drives of the late prehistoric period. Historical accounts of the Blackfoot Indian were used in describing the methods of capturing and killing the bison. Most common was driving a herd to a cliff or coulee where the bison would drop off to a corral located just below. Projective points were the most numerous class of artifacts collected. Other stone artifacts were side scrapers, choppers, and knives. This site is believed to be primarily a kill and meat processing station. Comparison is made with other bison drive sites of the Northern Plains region. This study also produced information on the terrain and natural features needed for a bison drive. Illus., 5 maps, 9 tables, 26 plates, biblio.   K. Adelfang

155. Knudson, Ruth Ann. CAMBRIA VILLAGE CERAMICS. *Plains Anthropologist 1967 12(37): 247-299.* Detailed analysis of ceramic material discovered in 1913, 1916, 1938, and 1941 in order to establish a typology and description of what Cambria is. Cambria Village, a single component agricultural site, located in southern Minnesota, was occupied between A.D. 1000 and 1300. The ceramics are grit tempered jars, with smoothed and rounded bodies and well-rounded and well-defined shoulders. Cambria's strongest affiliations are with the Over Focus and Anderson phase sites in South Dakota with major influences from Cahokia, Aztalan, and some Woodland sources. The author concludes that there is a great deal of cultural integration as well as innovation. No radiocarbon dates or rigid stratigraphic controls have been established for this site. Ceramics are overwhelmingly Middle Missouri-like and appear to provide an eastern boundary for that tradition. 15 illus., 8 plates, biblio.   K. Adelfang

156. Kotch, Jonathan and Starr, Ellen L. THE FOX ISLAND SITE (39DW230), DEWEY COUNTY, SOUTH DAKOTA. *Plains Anthropologist 1968 13(42, pt. 1): 310-338.* "An examination of this site on the west bank of the Missouri River in north-central South Dakota has revealed an unfortified settlement of approximately 30 earthlodges. The settlement pattern and artifact inventory indicate that the Fox Island site is an Extended Coalescent village that appears to be a descendant of the complex defined at Molstad Village."   J

157. Logan, Wilred D. and Ingmanson, John Earl. EFFIGY MOUNDS NATIONAL MONUMENT. *Palimpsest 1969 50(5): 273-304.* Effigy Mounds National Monument is an elongate tract of land on the boundary between Allamkee and Clayton counties in northeast Iowa. The area contains ample tangible evidence of prehistoric occupation, including 87 Indian burial mounds and three rock shelters. Archaeological surveys began in 1881 in the Mississippi River Valley. In 1909 legislative attempts were made to preserve the mounds in a national park. In October 1949 President Harry S. Truman proclaimed the Effigy Mounds area a national monument because of its scenic, historic, and prehistoric features. Discusses the prehistoric mound builders, the surveys, and the efforts to make a national park. Illus.   E. M. Hade

158. Magee, Molly. THE GRASS VALLEY HORSE. *Plains Anthropologist 1966 11(33): 204-207.* "The head and part of the neck of a baked clay horse figurine from an archeological site in Lander County is described. It is suggested the presence of the Grass Valley horse in Central Nevada reaffirms the strong cultural ties between the Plateau Shoshone and the buffalo hunting, horse-nomad Shoshone of the Western Plains, ties already indicated by Shoshone pottery and other plains type artifacts indigenous to the area." Illus., biblio.   J

159. Mann, C. John. GEOLOGY OF ARCHEOLOGICAL SITE 48SH312, WYOMING. *Plains Anthropologist 1968 13(39): 40-45.* Archaeological site 48SH312 is a Paleo-ravine floor similar to the Kaycee Terrace of northeastern Wyoming. This dates the site at 3,500 to four thousand years before the present. The broad box ravine with nearly vertical walls five to 10 meters high formed a natural trap into which animals were driven by Indians. 3 figs., biblio.

K. Adelfang

160. Marshall, Richard A. A STUDY OF POTTERY IN THE RONALD ARNEY COLLECTION, JEFFERSON CITY, MISSOURI. *Plains Anthropologist 1967 12(38): 396-417.* Describes the late Woodland pottery in the Arney collections of Jefferson City, Missouri, which could be classed under Moreau Focus types. The author studied three problems: 1) the differences between the Boon Focus and the proposed Moreau Focus ceramics, 2) comparison of the Boon and Moreau ceramic with the Highland aspect as described by Marshall (1962), and 3) assessment of the validity of the Moreau Focus on the basis of ceramics. It is concluded that the Arney collection indicated an affinity between the Cole County, Moreau River material and the northern Boone County material. A clear distinction cannot be made between the Boone and Moreau Focus. A summary description of the pottery categories is included at the end indicating surface treatment, decoration, form, size and color. 5 figures, 5 tables.

K. Adelfang

161. Mayer-Oakes, William J. SOME IMPORTANT DEVELOPMENTS IN NORTHERN PLAINS PREHISTORY, 1942-1967. *Plains Anthropologist 1969 14(43): 38-45.* "The area of the Northern Plains is defined as by Wedel in his 1969 synthesis. For the period under consideration, the 'process' of archeological work is presented in terms of two main areas of growth—the River Basin Survey Program and the opening up of intensive work in Canada. Also for the period considered, the 'results' of archeological work are presented in terms of the following eight areas of both fact and theory development: 1) The Middle Missouri 'Plains Village' development; 2) Paleo-Indian diversity; 3) Meso-Indian gap filling; 4) Projectile points as diagnostics; 5) Functional interpretation; 6) Ecological perspectives; 7) Relationships outside the Plains; 8) Broad-ranging synthesis. Future developments are seen in the need and possibilities for historic work, preparation of syntheses and the deeper development of micro-analytic approaches."   J

162. McMillan, R. Bruce. FRISTOE BURIAL MOUNDS FROM THE PRAIRIE BORDER REGION OF SOUTHWESTERN MISSOURI. *Plains An-*

thropologist 1968 13(39): 46-62. Three sites—the Alberti, Amity, and Clemons mounds—are all part of the Fristoe Burial Complex, a woodland mortuary complex of the western Ozarks. Much of the archaeological research is on burial mounds since the habitation sites have been plowed over. Human bones, of which 20 percent were cremated, were found in the three areas. A large number of artifacts such as projectile points and pottery vessel fragments, both useful and ornamental, were found in all three sites. The mounds varied in content, but were sufficiently similar to be described under a single taxonomic unit—the Fristoe Burial Complex. The author discusses two views concerning the culture; a seminomadic food collecting group may have lived there, or semisedentary villagers who practiced horticulture. This identification has extended the geographic range of the Fristoe Complex to the extreme western edge of the Ozarks where it merges with the Cherokee Plains. 5 figures, 2 tables, biblio.

K. Adelfang

163. McNerney, Michael J. A DESCRIPTION OF CHIPPED STONE AR-TIFACTS FROM NORTHEASTERN SOUTH DAKOTA. *Plains Anthropologist 1970 15(50, pt. 1): 291-296.* "This article describes and illustrates a surface collection of 68 chipped stone artifacts from the shore line of Blue Dog Lake in Day County, South Dakota. The collection and site location were reported to personnel of the Smithsonian Institution, River Basin Surveys, Lincoln, Nebraska. The site was recorded and designated 39DA201."

J

164. Morse, Dan F. PRELIMINARY NOTES ON A RECENT MASTODON AND TAPIR FIND IN NORTHEASTERN ARKANSAS. *Arkansas Archaeologist 1970 11(3/4): 45-49.* "Excavation of a drainage ditch near Weona, Arkansas, in May, 1969, exposed bones of large extinct mammals. A fragment of a mandible and a chipped tooth have been identified as tapir. Some of the other bones found were a portion of the partially articulated skeleton of a mastodon. Remains of several other mastodons have been reported in northeastern Arkansas. These Pleistocene mammals may have lived as late as 6000 years ago in certain areas in America. Because Paleo and Archaic tools have been associated in several instances with fossil animal bones of the Pleistocene period, finds such as these help the anthropologist to establish a chronology for the earliest people in this area and to interpret their cultural behavior."

J

165. Muller, Jon. NOTES ON THE WHITE EARTH CREEK SITE (32MN2). *Plains Anthropologist 1968 13(39): 18-25.* The White Earth Creek Site is important for its unusual character (a fortified site of the Middle Missouri or Coalescent Tradition) and for its location. It is located outside the main valley of the Missouri and well to the north of most fortified villages in Mountrail County, North Dakota. There is no surface evidence of earth lodges, nor does the site appear to have been occupied extensively. It was partially excavated by Thaddeus C. Hecker, a self-taught pioneer of Northern Plains archaeology, in 1938. Recent work has supported many of his conclusions. He found such archaeological remains as teepee rings, fireplaces, stone drying racks, and boiling pits. The site was erected by groups from the Missouri Valley sometime before intensive Eu-

ropean contact. The author favors the possibility that it was a fortified site for women and children while the men were hunting. 3 figs., plate, biblio.

K. Adelfang

166. Mulloy, William. AN INDIAN VILLAGE NEAR POMPEY'S PILLAR CREEK, MONTANA. *Plains Anthropologist 1969 14(44, pt. 1): 95-102.* "Described is a small late prehistoric or early historic winter village in north-central Yellowstone County, Montana. It consisted of six log lodges in well protected locations among the rocks near the edge of a small cuesta. One problematical structure and a circle of stones were also present. In questionable association was a small sample of Intermountain tradition pottery and a scanty assemblage of stone artifacts."   J

167. Mulloy, William and Steege, Louis C. CONTINUED ARCHAEOLOGICAL INVESTIGATIONS ALONG THE NORTH PLATTE RIVER IN EASTERN WYOMING. *U. of Wyoming Pub. 1967 33(3): 189-233.* Report of an archaeological survey and excavation of Late Middle Period Indian sites along the North Platte River in eastern Wyoming. The collection of artifacts is one of the best for Plains Indians engaged in agrarian life during the period 1-700 A.D. Included is an extensive list and description of artifacts. Illus., maps, photos, biblio.   H. B. Powell

168. Neuman, Robert W. ADDITIONAL ANNOTATED REFERENCES: AN ARCHEOLOGICAL BIBLIOGRAPHY OF THE CENTRAL AND NORTHERN GREAT PLAINS PRIOR TO 1930. *Plains Anthropologist 1968 13(40): 100-102* "This addendum contains 23 entries dating between 1859 and 1927 relative to sites in Kansas, Nebraska, Iowa, South Dakota, North Dakota, Wyoming, and the provinces of Manitoba and Saskatchewan. The first section of this bibliography was published in Volume 7, Number 15, of *Plains Anthropologist,* 1962, and contained 302 references."   J

169. Nichols, Peter W. A COLLECTION OF HISTORIC MATERIAL FROM THE FT. COLLINS CITY MUSEUM, FT. COLLINS, COLORADO. *Plains Anthropologist 1970 15(47): 63-69.* "In the late 1930's, near Morton, Wyoming, a burial was found which included an interesting collection of artifacts. An attempt is made to answer questions regarding the date of burial, tribal origin, and sex of the individual by an analysis of the material. This material is now on exhibit at the Ft. Collins City Museum."   J

170. Pangborn, Rolland E., Ward, H. Trawick, and Wood, W. Raymond. FLYCATCHER VILLAGE: A NON-POTTERY SITE IN THE STOCKTON RESERVOIR, MISSOURI. *Plains Anthropologist 1971 16(51): 60-73.* "Excavations in an open site in the Stockton Reservoir, southwestern Missouri, yielded the remains of three lightly constructed houses, some fireplaces, and associated pits and other features. The projectile points from this non-pottery site are predominantly of forms reminiscent of the Gary type, with a few miscellaneous stemmed forms and arrowpoints. One radiocarbon date intimates it may span some part

of the period about A.D. 620 to 810. The homogeneity in the projectile point sample is especially striking, and implies the site contains but a single component, a rarity in the Ozark Highlands." J

171. Rovner, Irving and Agogino, George. AN ANALYSIS OF FLUTED AND UNFLUTED FOLSOM POINTS FROM BLACKWATER DRAW. *Masterkey 1967 41(4): 131-137.* Presents an analysis of unifluted, bifluted, and unfluted Folsom points recovered from Blackwater Draw in Texas. The authors urge, on the basis of their analysis, that these points be referred to as above, rather than through use of another designation (e.g., Midland, for unfluted Folsom). Based on field investigation, primary and secondary sources; 3 tables, biblio.

C. N. Warren

172. Sanger, David. THE HIGH RIVER MICROBLADE INDUSTRY, AL-BERTA. *Plains Anthropologist 1968 13(41): 190-208.* "A small collection of obsidian and chalcedony microblades, from a site near Calgary, Alberta, is described and compared with other microblades from the Plains and from the Plateau. Although the age and cultural affiliations of the microblades are not certain, there is some evidence to suggest that they are early in the Plains sequence. The microblades have some distinctive attributes including ridge flakes, for which a typology is suggested. A comparison of the High River microblades with a large sample from the Interior Plateau of British Columbia suggests that the stimulus for the Alberta microblades did not derive from the Plateau." J

173. Smith, Shirley and Agogino, George. A COMPARISON OF WHOLE AND FRAGMENTARY PALEO-INDIAN POINTS FROM BLACKWA-TER DRAW. *Plains Anthropologist 1966 11(33): 201-203.* "An analysis of differential breakage in a sample of Clovis, Agate Basin, and Folsom points suggests that the Clovis form is most resistant to breakage and the fluted Folsom type the most fragile." This study does not represent all of the Paleo-Indian points found by the Paleo-Indian Institute of Eastern New Mexico University at Blackwater Draw. It does include most of the projectile points from Agate Basin (7,800 B.C.), Folsom (8,300 B.C.), and Clovis (9,200 B.C.) Paleo-Indian cultures.

K. Adelfang

174. Spring, Otto F. PREHISTORIC CHERT QUARRIES IN KAY COUNTY: A REPORT. *Chronicles of Oklahoma 1966 44(1): 5-11.* The Marland Archaeological Expedition for the Oklahoma Historical Society in 1926 investigated the quarries of chert or flint near Hardy in Kay County. There are many pits dug by prehistoric man—seldom over four feet deep. Many chert chippings and broken artifacts of stone exist. The chert was suitable for rougher implements —hoes, skinscrapers, rough axes—but a "four-bladed pen knife" made of the chert from these workings was found. 5 notes. I. W. Van Noppen

175. Vis, Robert B. and Henning, Dale R. A LOCAL SEQUENCE FOR MILL CREEK SITES IN THE LITTLE SIOUX VALLEY. *Plains Anthropologist 1969 14(46): 253-271.* "Mill Creek ceramics from northwest Iowa are used to

derive a sequence of occupations for sites along the Little Sioux River and its tributaries. Previous typologies and attempts at seriation of sites are examined and tested. The methods employed in this study are evaluated, and the resulting seriation is cross-checked with stratigraphic evidence and a series of radiocarbon dates." Biblio.   J

176. Watt, Frank H. and Agogino, George A. FIRST CITIZENS OF CENTRAL TEXAS. *Texana 1967 5(4): 293-316.* The Brazos is one of many Ice Age-formed Texas rivers down which primitive man came. The question of how far these first citizens came into Texas has arisen among Texas archaeologists. Studies the Ballew site which presents the redepositing of materials by flood waters from a Paleo-American type station a short distance upstream on the Brazos. This station is fully authenticated by the nature of the inclusions and by radiocarbon datings. Illus., 3 maps.   W. A. Buckman

177. Wedel, Waldo R. A SHIELD AND SPEAR PETROGLYPH FROM CENTRAL KANSAS: SOME POSSIBLE IMPLICATIONS. *Plains Anthropologist 1969 14(44, pt. 1): 125-129.* "A petroglyph in central Kansas evidently represents a pedestrian carrying a large shield and spear. Situated near the 16th-17th century Tobias (Wichita Indian) site, and perhaps associated with it in time and origin, ethnohistoric data suggest that the figure may represent one of the non-horticultural Plains Indian groups, such as the Excanxaques, whom the Spaniards met here in the early 17th century. A review of the relevant ethnohistoric, historical, and archaeological evidence discloses no proof that the Indians of this region were using the spear at the time of their first recorded contacts with the Spanish in the 16th and early 17th centuries but that they had acquired it by the second or third decade of the 18th century."   J

178. Wedel, Waldo R. AFTER CORONADO IN QUIVIRA. *Kansas Hist. Q. 1968 34(4): 369-385.* The legendary Quivira visited by Coronado in 1541 has interested students for years. Some have argued that Quivira was located near the great bend of the Arkansas River. Since 1940 the Smithsonian Institution has been excavating Indian sites in this region. Historical and archaeological evidence suggests that the sites designated as the Little River focus, the Great Bend aspect, and the Paint Creek culture were among the Indian villages visited by Coronado. The evidence indicates that this central Kansas phase of Wichita culture was not affected by the coming of the white man. The culture, which disappeared in the 18th century before the arrival of French explorers, may have been destroyed by the Osages, the Apaches, or weather changes. The evidence shows that the inhabitants were in contact with Pueblo Indians in the Rio Grande drainage basin, and the artifacts found at the sites provide guidelines for working into both the prewhite past and ethnohistoric present. Based on articles and books; illus., 14 notes.   W. F. Zornow

179. Wedel, Waldo R. SOME OBSERVATIONS ON TWO HOUSE SITES IN THE CENTRAL PLAINS: AN EXPERIMENT IN ARCHAEOLOGY. *Nebraska Hist. 1970 51(2): 225-252.* A careful critique of a 1969 monograph exam-

ining two prehistoric Plains Village Indian House sites representing "two relatively poorly known manifestations: the Nebraska and Upper Republican complexes."   R. Lowitt

180. Wedel, Waldo R. SOME THOUGHTS ON CENTRAL PLAINS-SOUTHERN PLAINS ARCHAEOLOGICAL RELATIONSHIPS. *Great PLains J. 1968 7(2): 53-62.* The last 20 years have added a great deal of archaeological information about cultural relationships of native peoples in the Central Plains of Nebraska and northern Kansas with those of the Middle Missouri. Less attention has been devoted to southward connections of Central Plains cultures. The author surveys the findings of the 1964 Smithsonian archaeological survey of southwestern Kansas. Investigations in central Kansas in 1965-67 in the Little River focus suggest Wichita Indian occupancy of about A.D. 1500-1700. Potsherds and other items indicate considerable contact with the Southwest. The author concludes that there may have been a cultural break roughly along the watershed separating the Smoky Hill drainage from the Arkansas, but the problem is complex and requires much more work. 10 notes.   O. H. Zabel

181. Witty, Thomas A., Jr. THE WEST ISLAND SITE, A KEITH FOCUS PLAINS WOODLAND SITE IN KIRWIN RESERVOIR, PHILLIPS COUNTY, KANSAS. *Plains Anthropologist 1966 11(32): 127-137.* "Salvage excavations at a badly eroded site, now an island in the Kirwin Reservoir of west-central Kansas, produced pottery and other artifacts indicative of the Keith Focus." The Keith Focus has small occupation sites and burial places along the Republican River drainage in southwestern Nebraska and northeastern Kansas. Illus., biblio.   K. Adelfang

182. Wood, W. Raymond. THE MIDDLE MISSOURI REGION: TYPOLOGY AND CONCEPTS. *Plains Anthropologist 1969 14(44, pt. 1): 144-148.* "Three impressionistic 'stages' in the development of the present archaeological framework for the Middle Missouri region [North and South Dakota] are discussed: (1) the Period of Tribal Identification, (2) Content-ordered classification—the Midwestern Taxonomic System, and (3) Broad conceptual schemes. The problems and goals of the next period, in which cultural processes and dynamic interpretations will dominate our thinking, will reflect the data now on hand and the theoretical orientation of regional prehistorians."   J

183. Wood, W. Raymond. THE MIDDLE MISSOURI TRADITION: THE LATE STAGE. *Plains Anthropologist 1965 10(30): 250-255.* "Two prehistoric complexes in the northern part of the Middle Missouri area, the Thomas Riggs and Huff Foci, comprise the late stage of the Middle Missouri Tradition. Although transitional sites are as yet lacking, this late stage is regarded as an outgrowth of the early stages of the same tradition, localized further south along the Missouri River in South Dakota. The Huff Focus postdates the Thomas Riggs Focus and is a direct outgrowth of Thomas Riggs, both foci being assigned to the Fire Heart Aspect. This aspect is the prehistoric antecedent for the Heart River

Focus, the protohistoric expression of Historic Mandan culture. Brief comments are offered on the history, origins, distribution, characteristics, dating, and relationships of the Thomas Riggs and Huff Foci."   J

184. Wood, W. Raymond and Pangborn, Rolland E. THE EUREKA AND COMSTOCK MOUNDS, SOUTHWESTERN MISSOURI. *Plains Anthropologist 1968 13(39): 1-17.* Discussion of two separate burial mounds, called the Eureka and the Comstock, in southwestern Missouri similar to the nearby Woodland and Mississippian Mounds. Burials of the Eureka Mound contained human remains. The burial practice of this mound was unlike others of southwestern Missouri , since a Spiro engraved water bottle was found buried with an individual, indicating contact with a Caddoan population probably from northeastern Oklahoma. The author dates it sometime between A. D. 1000 and 1450. The Comstock Mound included a single primary burial in a central grave pit with trade goods. The rest of the artifacts were from earlier occupations which were accidentally included in the mound as it was being built. 3 illus., 3 figs., biblio.
K. Adelfang

185. Wood, W. Raymond, Ed. [THE HOUSE SITES IN THE CENTRAL PLAINS: AN EXPERIMENT IN ARCHAEOLOGY]. *Plains Anthropologist 1969 14(44, pt. 2): 1-112.*
INTRODUCTION, pp. 1-2.
THE MOWRY BLUFF SITE, 23FT35, pp. 3-16.
MOWRY BLUFF ARTIFACTS, pp. 17-62.
THE NUZUM SITE, 14DP10, pp. 63-68.
NUZUM SITE ARTIFACTS, pp. 69-81.
CORRELATION OF PHASES IN CENTRAL PLAINS PREHISTORY, pp. 82-96.
A CONTRASTIVE STATEMENT ON UPPER REPUBLICAN AND NEBRASKA, pp. 97-108.
CONCLUSIONS, pp. 109-112.
"New and objective basic data are offered for the Upper Republican Mowry Bluff site and the Nebraska Nuzum site and related manifestations in the Central Great Plains. Fresh interpretations are provided by new near-total recovery and analytical techniques, by a re-examination of taxonomic problems, and by inferences relating to social organization and cultural ecology. The study, focusing on a single recently excavated dwelling in each complex, was an experiment in extracting as much as possible from a limited field program. Empirical data obtained support some assumptions which were largely intuitive in the past, and challenge other assumptions. The Upper Republican and Nebraska manifestations are defined as regional variants within the Central Plains sub-areal tradition. These two regional variants are united by correspondences in social organization and in material culture which reflect processes of adaptation to a broadly similar Plains environment by the separate immediate ancestors of both complexes. The two regional variants differ primarily in subsistence and aspects of culture related to the fact that they exploited distinct physiographic provinces in their separate developmental histories. Revisions in the taxonomic systems currently in use in the Plains suggest the classification of the two sites....The techniques applied, and the approaches followed, promise to contribute to a

deeper and more meaningful understanding of the role played by these complexes in the history of the Plains Village Pattern—and the role of the Great Plains environment in the cultural ecology of its first settled peoples." Based on secondary sources; biblio.   J

186. Wyckoff, Don G. and Taylor, Lyonel. THE PUMPKIN CREEK SITE: AN EARLY ARCHAIC CAMP ON THE SOUTHERN PLAINS BORDER. *Plains Anthropologist 1971 16(51): 20-51.* "The Pumpkin Creek site is located in Love county of south-central Oklahoma. Surface investigations, indicating the site is extensively exposed by erosion, have resulted in the recovery of a rather consistent cultural assemblage. The projectile points are predominantly lanceolate in outline and relate to Plains complexes that date around 7,000 to 9,500 years ago. The site is situated on the present eastern border of the Southern Plains, and assemblage analysis suggests the station was a temporary camp at which stone working of local gravels was the primary activity."   J

Northeast Area

187. Biery, James. TRACING THE HOPEWELL. *Northwestern Report 1968 3(4): 30-32.* Describes the archaeological search for the Hopewell Indian culture which flourished in western Illinois some two thousand years ago. While little is known of the Hopewell, preliminary findings indicate that they were a highly advanced culture which practiced agriculture and which carried on an extensive trade and commerce with neighboring tribes. Undocumented; 2 illus.
                                                                    G. Kurland

188. Caine, Christy A. H. BIG-GAME HUNTING ARTIFACTS FROM MINNESOTA. *Plains Anthropologist 1968 13(40): 87-89.* "A Browns Valley type point, a Scottsbluff type point, and four Cody knives, recovered as surface finds, give evidence of the presence of the Big-Game Hunting Tradition in east-central Minnesota. These artifacts, their location, and similar finds in the Minnesota-Wisconsin area are described."   J

189. Coles, Robert R. ORIGINS OF HEMPSTEAD HARBOR. *Long Island Forum 1970 33(7): 138-142.* Hempstead Harbor was originally a part of the Appalachian mountain chain. The harbor was formed by the Wisconsin glacier which spread over the area about two million years ago and which retreated 10 to 11 thousand years ago. Hempstead Harbor was occupied by primitive food gathering Indians about 3500-1300 B.C. When the first Europeans arrived in the 17th century the area was inhabited by Indians belonging to the Matinecock chieftaincy. Captain Adriaen Block, sailing in the employ of the Dutch, is be-

lieved to be the first European to discover the harbor. An English settlement at Hempstead was established in 1643-44. Undocumented, 2 illus.

G. Kurland

190. Dustin, Fred and Fitting, James E. SAGINAW VALLEY ARCHAEOL-OGY. *Michigan Archaeologist 1968 14(1/2): 1-130.* "Between 1907 and 1957, the late Fred Dustin of Saginaw, Michigan, published many papers on the history and archaeology of the Saginaw Valley. Many of these are primary source materials on the area and are long out of print.In 1967, as part of a contemporary study of the Valley, a number of these were assembled and edited for publication as a single volume. This volume includes 2 papers on the history of archaeology in Michigan, 8 papers on archaeological sites and collections, 2 on raw materials of the region and 2 on Indian history." AIA (1:3:11)

191. Fitting, James E. THE ARCHAEOLOGY EXPLOSION IN MICHIGAN. *Michigan Hist. 1966 50(3): 219-227.* Draws attention to recent archaeological research and newer publications concerning Michigan's prehistory.

J. K. Flack

192. Fitting, James E. and Cleland, Charles E. LATE PREHISTORIC SETTLE-MENT PATTERNS IN THE UPPER GREAT LAKES. *Ethnohist. 1969 16(4): 289-302.* "Known cultural adaptations to specific ecological settings are projected back into the prehistoric period in an attempt to elucidate late prehistoric cultural patterns in the Upper Great Lakes region." J

193. Hall, Robert L. THE MISSISSIPPIAN HEARTLAND AND ITS PLAINS RELATIONSHIP. *Plains Anthropologist 1967 12(36): 175-183.* "The Cahokia site near East St. Louis, Illinois, was a gateway on the Northwestern frontier of the Mississippian heartland. Its exact relationship to other Middle Mississippi cultures and to cultures of the Plains and Upper Great Lakes area is still not fully understood. It is clear, nonetheless, that these relationships, when more completely known, will prove to be much more complicated than any suggested in current literature." Biblio. J

194. Henning, Dale R. MISSISSIPPIAN INFLUENCES ON THE EASTERN PLAINS BORDER: AN EVALUATION. *Plains Anthropologist 1967 12(36): 184-194.* "Mississippian or Mississippian-inspired elements have long been identified in sites along the Plains-Prairie border. Coupled with available Carbon-14 dates, the distribution of traits often regarded as Mississippian is suggestive of a system of interrelationships which may be important to further understanding of late Plains-Prairie prehistory." Biblio. J

195. Higgins, Robert. AN INDIAN SITE IN THE BORO OF MONTOURS-VILLE. *Now and Then 1965 14(10): 276-284.* Describes archaeology work at the juncture of the Susquehanna River and Loyalsock Creek in north-central Pennsylvania, where a number of Indian relics have been found. Recently, the author, with some professional aid, discovered a graveyard at Montoursville which con-

tained Algonkian and Iroquoian relics, some of which dated back as early as 800 A.D., and markings which indicate the probable occupation of a permanent village on the site. Illus. H. Ershkowitz

196. Kellar, James H. GLENN A. BLACK. *Indiana Mag. of Hist. 1967 63(1): 49-52.* An essay describing Glenn Black's achievements as archaeological field director for the Indiana Historical Society, stressing particularly his work with the prehistory of the Indian tribes of the Ohio Valley. J. Findlay

197. Kenyon, Walter A. THE ARMSTRONG MOUND ON RAINY RIVER, ONTARIO. *Can. Historic Sites 1970 3: 66-85.* "The Armstrong Mound, one of several mounds overlooking the Long Sault Rapids on Rainy River, Ontario, was excavated in 1966 at the request of the Historic Sites and Monuments Board of Canada. The purpose of the excavation was to inform the Board of the nature of the mounds and their relative age and cultural affiliation with relation to possible commemoration of the site. Walter Kenyon of the Royal Ontario Museum directed the work. He excavated one mound 80 feet in diameter and 8 feet high, in which he found several burials, stone and copper artifacts, and numerous fragments of pottery. The author associates the mound itself with the Late Laurel culture and dates its construction to about 1,000 years ago." J

198. Kenyon, Walter A. THE ORIGINS OF THE IROQUOIS. *Ontario Hist. [Canada] 1964 56(1): 1-4.* Attempts to show that the Iroquois are indigenous to the northeastern part of North America and were not of migratory origin. The basic elements of the Iroquois culture "were already present in southern Ontario and New York State in the pre-Iroquoian period." J. M. E. Usher

199. MacCord, Howard A., Sr. VIRGINIA INDIAN MOUNDS. *Virginia Cavalcade 1965 15(1): 29-31.* An analysis of Indian mounds in Virginia with an account of recent excavations on Lewis Creek in Augusta County. R. B. Lange

200. Mallory, Enid Swerdfeger. THE AGAWA PICTOGRAPHS. *Can. Geographical J. 1964 69(4): 127-129.* Photographs, partial description and interpretation of these pictographs. E. W. Hathaway

201. McKee, Russell. FORMATION AND HISTORY OF THE "GREATEST" LAKES. *Inland Seas 1966 22(4): 283-294.* Little is known of the preglacial conditions of the Great Lakes area beyond its submergence by the ocean. The first of the ice ages began about one million years ago. The most recent ice sheet began retiring forty thousand years ago. As the ice retreated across the Great Lakes basin, bodies of water collected in the depressions previously formed by the geology of the region and the movements of the heavy rains and the rising of land in the North Bay inlet, the lakes took their modern form. Men have inhabited the area for about eleven thousand years. About 5,000-7,000 years ago, the Old Copper Indians appeared, only to be replaced about 1100 B.C. by a new, more

sophisticated group from the south. These widely traveled mound builders were replaced, in turn, about 800 A.D. by the less advanced tribes who lasted into historical times. Illus.   K. J. Bauer

202. Nelson, Sheila. AZTALAN—1967. *Wisconsin Then and Now 1967 14(1): 1-3, 7.* Describes the ancient Indian site located at Aztalan State Park, near Lake Mills, and the archaeological excavation being carried on there under the direction of Joan Freeman, Curator of Anthropology at the State Historical Society of Wisconsin, and Jay Brandon, Associate Curator of Anthropology. Aztalan is an Indian village founded between 1100-1300 A.D. by a tribe with a highly developed culture that originated directly or indirectly in Mexico. Illus.
                                                              D. P. Peltier

203. Prahl, Earl J. and Becker, M. Joseph. PRELIMINARY ARCHAEOLOGICAL INVESTIGATIONS IN THE MAUMEE VALLEY. *Northwest Ohio Q. 1967 39(2): 40-50.* An account of a proposed investigation, scheduled for the summer of 1967, to recover and analyze prehistoric artifacts and skeletal material for meaningful cultural inferences. Three research teams will do the work; the River Survey Team will investigate areas of the Maumee Valley, the Glacial Beach Survey Team will survey and map four glacial beaches south of the Michigan State line, and the Harris Yards Site Team will examine an extensive site of a Late Woodland occupation. 2 maps.   W. F. Zornow

204. Ridley, Frank. THE ONTARIO IROQUOIAN CONTROVERSY. *Ontario Hist. [Canada] 1963 55(1): 49-59.* Sees a "stable pause in Iroquoian development" which is termed the "Lalonde culture." This had a wide geographical base but was centered in Ontario. A division of the population and the withdrawal of one southern group to the west end of Lake Ontario and the Grand River Valley formed the Neutral Nation. The northern section became the Huron nation. This is contrasted with an opposing view of the Hurons of origination in the eastern Lake Ontario area and recent arrivals in historic Huronia. Based on archaeological investigations by the author. Space and time columns appended. 21 notes.
                                                              J. M. E. Usher

205. Unsigned. AZTALAN. *Wisconsin Then and Now 1964 11(2): 1-4.* Discusses a site discovered in 1836, studied first in 1850 and excavated in 1919-21, 1932, 1949-54, and again in 1964. The people who lived at Aztalan from 1000 to 1200 A.D., first thought to have been Aztecs, are now known to have belonged to the Middle Mississippi culture, centering at Cahokia near East St. Louis, Illinois. Their houses were more or less permanently constructed. Their pyramidal mounds were probably the sites of temples. Evidence shows these people were agriculturists but also cannibals. Illus.   E. P. Stickney

206. Wright, J. V. THE APPLICATION OF THE DIRECT HISTORICAL APPROACH TO THE IROQUOIS AND THE OJIBWA. *Ethnohist. 1968 15(1): 96-111.* The direct historical approach begins with the known sites and tribes, if possible to identify, and works back. Cultural complexes of the sites are

then determined, and sequences are carried backward in time to protohistoric and prehistoric periods and cultures. An interdisciplinary approach using archaeology, ethnohistory, and ethnology is required. Such an approach reveals the culture history of the Iroquois from A.D. 900 to 1650. Although investigation of the Chippewa (Ojibwa) culture is still in its infancy, the approach does offer a general outline of cultural development at least as far back as the 10th century. Biblio.

R. S. Burns

Southeast Area

207. Baillou, Clemens de. A TEST EXCAVATION OF THE HOLLYWOOD MOUND (9 RI 1), GEORGIA. *Southern Indian Studies 1965 17: 3-11.* Test excavations were carried out at this site in Richmond County, Georgia, during the summer of 1965. A 70-foot-long trench, excavated into one side of the larger mound, revealed a thick layer of postaboriginal alluvium which covered the sides of the mound. Toward the inner part of the mound, the slopes and slump zones of two construction stages were found. Ceramics from this area were primarily of plained surfaced and Savannah Check Stamped type sherds. Two 10-foot test squares were excavated at the site of the smaller mound, which had been explored by Henry Reynolds in 1891. About five feet of modern sediments covered the aboriginal surface area. Undisturbed portions of this mound are probably still present. Further excavations at both mounds and in the nearby probable village area are recommended. Illus., map, tables, appendixes including a report of the Reynolds excavation. K. P. Davis

208. Davis, Hester A. HISTORY'S MYSTERIES IN ARKANSAS. *Arkansas Hist. Q. 1967 26(1): 3-10.* Suggestions of a few areas for archaeologists to explore in Arkansas before land use disturbs Indian artifacts and the more recent remains.

P. M. McCain

209. Dickson, Don R. EXCAVATIONS AT CALF CREEK CAVE. *Arkansas Archaeologist 1970 11(3/4): 50-82.* "Excavations at the huge Calf Creek Cave, a deeply stratified site in Searcy County, Arkansas, revealed a lengthy occupation ranging from early Archaic until late prehistoric times. The upper part of the deposits, containing Woodland and late prehistoric artifacts, was extensively disturbed by pothunters, but two undisturbed occupation zones were found beneath the altered levels. Stratum 1, the deepest, contained one unfinished fluted point and a series of dart points featuring basal notching and fine workmanship. These have been named Calf Creek points. Lanceolate specimens with slight shoulders, contracting stems, and beveled and serrated blades, Smith points, Rice points, Johnson-like specimens, and White River Archaic points were recovered from stratum 2. The lanceolate points found at the base of this stratum are called Searcy points. An atlatl hook of antler was associated with small corner-notched dart points of apparent late Archaic age. A wide variety of notched dart points

and bone tools were recovered from the disturbed upper zone along with one polished slate bead, a damaged slate gorget, and grit- and shell-tempered pottery sherds. These seem to be Woodland and late prehistoric artifacts." J

210. Gibson, Jon L. A PRELIMINARY SURVEY OF INDIAN OCCUPA-TION IN LA SALLE PARISH, LOUISIANA. *Louisiana Studies 1966 5(3): 193-238.* Surveys 45 Indian sites in the Castor Creek, Little River, and Catahoula Lake drainage system of La Salle Parish, Louisiana. James A. Ford made prelimi-nary surveys in 1936 and 1940. This report is based, for the most part, on surface surveys. However, test pits were dug at two sites, for stratigraphy, and one site was explored to ascertain feasibility of future excavation. The survey gives site locations, the physiography, and artifact types and numbers. The culture period at maximum popularity is given as the time of occupancy. Illus., tables, 18 notes and references.   G. W. McGinty

211. Gibson, Jon L. THE HOPEWELLIAN PHENOMENON IN THE LOWER MISSISSIPPI VALLEY. *Louisiana Studies 1970 9(3): 176-192.* Lists the various Hopewellian periods and their known characteristics. Discusses the complexity of Hopewellian ceramics and the difficulty of classifying them. The cultures have been scrambled in the lower Mississippi valley more, perhaps, than in any other region. This adds to the difficulty of identification. The social structure necessitates speculation in drawing conclusions. 2 illus., 2 tables, 39 notes.   G. W. McGinty

212. Gregory, Hiram Ford, Jr. PLAQUEMINE PERIOD SITES IN THE CATAHOULA BASIN, A CULTURAL MICROCOSM IN EAST CENTRAL LOUISIANA. *Louisiana Studies 1969 8(2): 111-134.* Presents a detailed study of the Catahoula Basin and justifies, by cultural and ecological data, the term "Plaquemine Period," 1200-1700 A.D. The ecology is carefully examined and the cultural developments are analyzed. Such cultural factors as ceramics, engrav-ings, dwellings, burial, and the economy are examined and compared with those of other Indian cultures to show the microcosmic makeup. Map, chart, table, 71 notes.   G. W. McGinty

213. Gregory, Hiram Ford, Jr. VESSELS FROM THE BISON SITE. *Louisiana Studies 1966 5(2): 159-161.* Pictures and a description of pottery excavated from a prehistoric Caddoan cemetery and village that will be inundated by the Toledo Bend Reservoir on the Sabine River.   G. W. McGinty

214. Haag, William G. LOUISIANA IN NORTH AMERICAN PREHIS-TORY. *Louisiana Studies 1965 4(4): 279-323.* After an overall summary of North American prehistory, the author focuses upon the prehistoric cultures that have left their mark in the present state of Louisiana. Illustrations of cultural artifacts from each period are given.   G. W. McGinty

215. Huscher, Harold A. THE STANDING BOY FLINT INDUSTRY; AN EARLY ARCHAIC MANIFESTATION ON THE CHATTAHOOCHEE

RIVER IN ALABAMA AND GEORGIA. *Southern Indian Studies 1964 16: 3-20.* This report was originally read to the 29th Annual Meeting of the Society for American Archaeology in 1964. The author suggests that a background statement ("The Archaic of the Walter F. George Reservoir Area." *Proceedings of the 19th Southeastern Archaeological Conference, 1962.* Bulletin No. 1, pp. 36-41) should be read. The Early Archaic artifact grouping from a site above Columbus, Georgia, consists of plano-convex knives, scrapers, and small triangular alternate-bevel points. Artifacts are those made of a flint. Other sites investigated (1958-63) along 100 miles of the Chattahoochee River confirm the importance of this complex as consistent Early Archaic phenomena. However, better separation is needed and may depend on sampling restricted camps at spring sites higher in the hills. Illus., maps, biblio.   K. P. Davis

216. Mason, Carol. NATCHEZ CLASS STRUCTURE. *Ethnohist. 1964 11(2): 120-133.* Reexamines and evaluates various conflicting interpretations of the sociopolitical structure of prehistoric Indian groups of the southeastern United States. Based on original French sources, the earlier translations and misunderstandings of which are discussed.   H. J. Graham

217. Michels, J. W. SETTLEMENT PATTERN AND DEMOGRAPHY AT SHEEP ROCK SHELTER: THEIR ROLE IN CULTURE CONTACT. *Southwestern J. of Anthrop. 1968 24(1): 66-82.* One of the most interesting aspects of an artifact assemblage is the nature and extent of resemblances between it and other assemblages located elsewhere. The nature of this relationship is often not made clear, even when these resemblances are used to date the components, or to define archaeological units. The author feels this relationship can best be viewed on the basis of cultural affinities and "contact networks." In this article he relates the contact networks to the settlement pattern and population density of central Pennsylvania and adjacent northeastern regions from the early Archaic (6900 B.C.) through the Proto-Historic phase (1675 A.D.) as viewed from excavation in the Raystown region, Huntingdon County, Rock Shelter. Map, chart, biblio.   C. N. Warren

218. Neitzel, Robert S. ARCHEOLOGY OF THE FATHERLAND SITE: THE GRAND VILLAGE OF THE NATCHEZ. *Anthrop. Papers of the Am. Mus. of Natural Hist. 1965 51(1): 3-108.* The Fatherland site was probably the grand village of the Natchez recorded historically between 1682 and 1729. Mounds at the site disclosed three prehistoric and one historic period of occupation, with earliest settlement possibly in the 13th century. Minor geomorphological changes support the documentary identification of the grand village. Diverse sizes and structural features recorded in early literature contradict but do not outweigh the evidence in favor of this site as the grand village of the Natchez. Illus.   E. H. Swanson, Jr.

219. Redfield, Alden and Moselage, John H. THE LACE PLACE, A DALTON PROJECT SITE IN THE WESTERN LOWLAND IN EASTERN ARKANSAS. *Arkansas Archaeologist 1970 11(2): 21-43.* "The Lace Place, a multicomponent site in Poinsett County, Arkansas, has yielded large amounts of Dalton

points and associated materials in surface collections. Three test pits, excavated in 1961 in the natural levee whereon lies the principal part of the site, indicated that midden accumulated there intermittently over thousands of years between periods of alluviation by an ancient channel of the Mississippi River, at a time when it flowed to the west of Crowley's Ridge as a braided stream. The highest levees formed in that period remained uncovered during the subsequent silting up of the stream channels, and on many of them can still be found Paleo-Indian and Archaic artifacts along with Woodland and Mississippi materials. The Dalton Project was begun in 1961 by James A. Ford after he was shown material collected by John Moselage and Charles Scheel at the Lace Place. All artifacts collected from Lace and related sites were put together for analysis. This work is being continued by Alden Redfield. Integration of the Lace Place collections into the mass of data in the Dalton Project will aid in the assessment of this site's place in prehistory and in the understanding of Paleo-Indian and Archaic cultures in Arkansas and in the eastern United States."   J

220. Reid, J. Jefferson. A COMPARATIVE STATEMENT ON CERAMICS FROM THE HOLLYWOOD AND TOWN CREEK MOUNDS. *Southern Indian Studies 1965 17: 12-25.* Compares ceramics of the Hollywood Mound in Georgia with the Town Creek Mounds of North Carolina. The author emphasizes the similarities in the appearance of the pottery and in the presence of an urn/ burial complex at both sites. Material from upper levels at the Hollywood mounds shows an amazing resemblance to the material from Town Creek. The lower levels at Hollywood possess "Southern Cult" material not seen at Town Creek. Pictures show the Hollywood Mound area and some of the excavations there. Illustrations of artifacts, pottery, and clay pipe fragments as well as a burial urn are shown. Map, biblio.   K. P. Davis

221. White, Patsy. INVESTIGATION OF THE CEMETERY AT THE GEE'S LANDING SITE, 3DR17. *Arkansas Archaeologist 1970 11(1): 1-20.* "Primary excavation at the Gee's Landing site (3DR17) was undertaken in the cemetery, in 1967-1968, by Edward and Patsy White and son Ronald. Clay-tempered sherds, stone artifacts, and projectile points found on the surface show the initial occupancy was in the late Archaic and the Woodland periods. The 34 burials excavated, with shell-tempered pottery, shell artifacts, and untyped arrow points, represent a Mississippi period occupancy. The mortuary vessels tie the site into the Glendora phase in northern Louisiana, although they may be earlier in time. This relates a late occupancy on the lower Saline River to the Caddoan sites of the lower Ouachita River valley."   J

222. —. [THE MC LEAN MOUND, CUMBERLAND COUNTY, NORTH CAROLINA]. *Southern Indian Studies 1966 18: 3-87.*
        MacCord, Howard A., Sr. THE MC LEAN MOUND, CUMBERLAND COUNTY, NORTH CAROLINA, pp. 3-66.
        Stewart, T.D. NOTES ON THE HUMAN BONES RECOVERED FROM BURIAL IN THE MC LEAN MOUND, NORTH CAROLINA, pp. 67-87. The entire issue of this journal discusses the findings of the McLean Mound on the Cape Fear River in North Carolina. MacCord discusses the mound

which he excavated between April and November of 1961. Some 1,400 square feet were excavated, uncovering over 300 burials. The physical setting, procedure, and artifacts are discussed. Thirty chipped-stone triangular projectile points, simple animal bone artifacts, shell beads, ceramics, and human bones were found. McCord concludes that the McLean Mound probably belonged to the sand-mound burial complex common to coastal regions of the southeastern United States during the Middle Woodland period—approximately 1000 A.D. Stewart discusses human bones in the McLean Mound. Illus., map, tables, biblio, 6 appendixes.   K. P. Davis

2

TRIBAL HISTORY
1492-1900

Arctic Area

General

223. Hinckley, Ted C. SHELDON JACKSON AS PRESERVER OF ALAS-KA'S NATIVE CULTURE. *Pacific Hist. R. 1964 33(4): 411-424.* Recounts the work of a Presbyterian missionary in collecting artifacts and information on Alaskan culture. Jackson (1834-1909) helped to found the Alaska Natural History and Ethnology Society and the Sheldon Jackson Museum.

J. McCutcheon

224. Hinckley, Ted C. THE INSIDE PASSAGE: A POPULAR GILDED AGE TOUR. *Pacific Northwest Q. 1965 56(2): 67-74.* Describes Alaska as a magnet of tourists, 1867-1900, including methods of traveling, attractions, the role of residents, and the names of distinguished visitors, with special attention to Sitka and Indians. Documented.

C. C. Gorchels

225. McFarland, Amanda R. LETTERS OF AMANDA R. MC FARLAND. INTRODUCTION BY CHARLES A. ANDERSON. *J. of the Presbyterian Hist. Soc. 1956 34(2): 83-102, (4): 226-244, and 1957 35(1): 33-56.* Letters written during the period 11 October 1877 to 9 January 1878 (Part I), 12 February to 11 May 1878 (Part II), and 7 June to 9 November 1878 (Part III), from Fort Wrangel, Alaska, by the first woman missionary to Alaska, sent by the Presbyterian Board of Home Missions, describing the life of the Indians at this trading post and her work with them.

W. D. Metz

226. Merbs, Charles F. ANTERIOR TOOTH LOSS IN ARCTIC POPULA-TIONS. *Southwestern J. of Anthrop. 1968 24(1): 20-32.* A reevaluation of the "ritual ablation" theory put forth by Aleš Hrdlička for the premortem loss of

anterior teeth of Arctic Mongoloid populations as compared with ritual ablations of African groups. The author presents evidence to show that the extremely high rate of tooth loss was caused by unintentional trauma occasioned by the use of the teeth as a tool and not, as had been previously supposed, by ritual removal. 2 tables, biblio.   C. N. Warren

227. Shenitz, Helen A. FATHER VENIAMINOV, THE ENLIGHTENER OF ALASKA. *Am. Slavic and East European R. 1959 18(1): 57-80.* The first biographical sketch in any Western language of Father Veniaminov (1797-1879), who rose from the obscurity of a small parish priest in Siberia to become the Metropolitan of Russia. The "Enlightener of Alaska," as he is known to historians, he developed among the natives of Alaska not only a firm belief in Christian life and Christian democracy, but also an appreciation of the value of knowledge and a desire for learning. His scholarly writings on Alaska still represent the most valuable source material on Alaska. Based on Barsukov's *Innokentii, Mitropolit Moskovskii,* Veniaminov's works, letters, manuscript diary, and various book reviews.   A

228. Smith, Lorne. ARCTIC STONEHENGE. *Beaver [Canada] 1969 299(Spring): 16-22.* The harshness of life in the Arctic meant that there was no surplus of wealth or manpower for the construction of impressive monuments. However, there are about a hundred stone monunents, some up to 7 feet tall, on Enusko Point, Foxe Peninsula, southwest Baffin Island. The author, who visited the site in 1968, speculates on the origin and purpose of these monuments, or enuskos, found only in this one place. Some may have been used as beacons, some for ceremonial purposes.   L. F. S. Upton

By Tribe

Eskimo

229. Bruemmer, Fred. MARBLE ISLAND. *Beaver [Canada] 1969 300(Autumn): 36-41.* Relates the legend of Marble Island, 25 miles from Rankin Inlet off the west coast of Hudson Bay. Eskimos visiting it for the first time crawl onto it on hands and knees; failure to do this invites catastrophe. It was here that James Knight's 1719 expedition perished. The author cites unsuccessful attempts to establish a fishery on the island and describes his recent visit there. Illus.
                                                L. F. S. Upton

230. Dunbabin, Thomas. CAPTAIN LYON IN THE ARCTIC. *Beaver [Canada] 1963 293 (Spring): 45-51.* Describes the two Arctic voyages of Captain George Francis Lyon, RN (1795-1832), from 1821 to 1823 and in 1824. Also gives an account of Eskimos met on the voyages, including the now extinct Sadlermiut people. Illus.   L. F. S. Upton

Eskimo, Alaskan

231. Bronson, William. ESKIMO: THE PEOPLE OF THE FAR AMERICAN NORTH AS THEY WERE SEEN AND RECORDED DURING THE GREAT TURN-OF-THE-CENTURY NOME GOLD RUSH. *Am. West 1970 7(4): 34-47.* A 27-photograph essay of the southern Seward Peninsula (Alaskan) Eskimo, which pictures the natives at the time of the 1898-99 gold strike and stampede in the Nome region and during the years following. Except for limited trade, the Eskimo had had little contact with the outside world. The photographs and commentary give a vivid description of Eskimo culture and the impact of the gold rush on it.   D. L. Smith

232. Montgomery, Maurice and Murray, Keith A. THE MURDER OF MISSIONARY THORNTON. *Pacific Northwest Q. 1963 54(4): 167-174.* Harrison Thornton, a missionary in Alaska, 1890-93, was murdered by Eskimos after being ineffective in Christianizing them. The article includes much about the character, habits, diseases, and superstitions of the natives, giving reasons for the murder. Murray's comments give encouragement for more research on early Alaskan history and more study of the culture of natives.   C. C. Gorchels

233. Ray, Dorothy Jean. SHELDON JACKSON AND THE REINDEER INDUSTRY OF ALASKA. *J. of Presbyterian Hist. 1965 43(2): 71-99.* Discusses the attempt of Sheldon Jackson, Presbyterian missionary and Alaska's General Agent for Education, to introduce reindeer into Alaska. Reindeer were imported from Siberia from 1892 until the Russian government stopped the trade in 1902. The author, an anthropologist, traces the general ineffectiveness of the program to Jackson's misunderstanding of the Eskimo way of life and standard of living, to personal animosities, to Jackson's mixture of humanitarian and commercial motives, and to his vacillation on the issue of Eskimo ownership of reindeer. Based on letters, manuscripts, and reports; 102 notes.

S. C. Pearson, Jr.

Eskimo, Greenland

234. Nellemann, George. HINRICH RINK AND APPLIED ANTHROPOLOGY IN GREENLAND IN THE 1860'S. *Human Organization 1969 28(2): 166-174.* Translates portions of "Om Aarsagen til Grönlaendernes og lingnende, af jagt levende, Nationers materielle Tilbagegang ved Beröring med Europaerne" [The Reason Why Greenlanders and Similar People Living by Hunting Decline Materially Through Contact with Europeans] by Hinrich Johannes Rink from *Dansk Maanedsskrift,* 1862. Presents a brief biography of Rink. The study by Rink is a concise ethnology of the Greenland Eskimos, with an analysis of the effect of European contact. Suggests some administrative changes which would correct the noted impact of European contact. 6 notes.

E. S. Johnson

Eskimo, Labrador

235. Taylor, J. G. WILLIAM TURNER'S JOURNEYS TO THE CARIBOU COUNTRY WITH THE LABRADOR ESKIMOS IN 1780. *Ethnohist. 1969 16(2): 141-164.* "In 1780 the Moravian missionary, William Turner, made two inland journeys from Nain, Labrador, one in the winter and one in the late summer. His diaries of these trips, published here for the first time, provide considerable ethnographic data concerning the Eskimos of the region, especially with respect to their subsistence activities."   J

236. Whiteley, W. H. THE RECORDS OF THE MORAVIAN MISSION IN LABRADOR. *Am. Archivist 1961 24(4): 425-430.* The Moravians established their first mission station at Nain, Labrador, in 1771. There was an early recognition of the value of record preservation, so that today an extensive archive exists. A tremendous file of correspondence of letters to and from Europe, particularly from London where the mission was supervised, has been catalogued. In addition, there are the records of each mission station in Labrador, and since the Moravians operated trading depots until 1926, many business records are available.
G. M. Gressley

237. Whiteley, William H. THE MORAVIAN MISSIONARIES AND THE LABRADOR ESKIMOS IN THE EIGHTEENTH CENTURY. *Church Hist. 1966 35(1): 76-92.* Traces the missionary efforts of Moravians among Labrador Eskimos from a first abortive effort in 1752 through the establishment of a permanent mission station in 1770 to the end of the century. Even with the support of the British government the Moravians experienced difficulties because of the fierce and lawless behavior of the Eskimos. Though the mission initially experienced success and baptism of Eskimo converts began in 1776, by 1785 increasing contacts between the Christian Eskimos and European traders and less civilized Eskimos led to considerable falling away from baptismal vows on the part of the converts. Yet by the end of the century three mission stations were in operation, and the Moravian missions continue to operate in 1966. "It is due in no small measure to the efforts of the Brethren that the Eskimos in Labrador have survived and prospered, rather than being hunted down and exterminated as were the native Beothucks of Newfoundland."   S. C. Pearson, Jr.

Tlingit

238. Hinckley, Ted C., ed. "THE CANOE ROCKS—WE DO NOT KNOW WHAT WILL BECOME OF THE US": THE COMPLETE TRANSCRIPT OF A MEETING BETWEEN GOVERNOR JOHN GREEN BRADY OF ALASKA AND A GROUP OF TLINGIT CHIEFS, JUNEAU, DECEMBER 14, 1898. *Western Hist. Q. 1970 1(3): 265-290.* The Tlingit Indians of the northern part of the Alexander Archipelago of the Alaskan panhandle were a maritime people whose sea-going canoes had been "rocked by the seas of stormy acculturation" for several decades. The Russian, British, and American cultural impact on the Tlingit was a mixed blessing. The 1898 gold rush in the Klondike was a crisis for this people. The avaricious mass crippled the Indian economy and threatened

the very future of the natives. Alaska Governor John Green Brady, a man of good intentions and enlightened actions, and who consistently fought for Indian rights, conducted a series of consultations with the Tlingit in the latter part of 1898. Presented herein are the translated and annotated transcripts of the conference held in Juneau on 14 December 1898. The principal purpose of the meetings was to record the Tlingit grievances so that they might be presented to the federal government. 49 notes.   D. L. Smith

Subarctic Area

General

239. Johnson, Patricia. MC LEOD LAKE POST. *Beaver [Canada] 1965 296(Autumn): 22-29.* This trading post, now located on the John Hart Highway north of Prince George, British Columbia, was the first permanent post erected in British territory west of the Rocky Mountains. Founded by Simon Fraser on behalf of the North West Company in 1805, it was taken over by the Hudson's Bay Company in 1821. The visits of numerous travelers are noted, including that of Governor George Simpson, who thought "McLeod Lake is the most wretched place in the Indian Country," (1828). Quotes from the McLeod Lake Journal (1845 to 1848) in the Glenbow Foundation, Calgary. Illus.
L. F. S. Upton

240. Lewis, Palmer G. BABINE LAKE. *Beaver [Canada] 1968 299(Summer): 26-35.* Babine Lake in British Columbia was first visited by white traders Daniel Harmon and James McDougall in 1812. The Hudson's Bay Company opened a post, Fort Kilmaurs, there in 1822, and this was later replaced by Fort Babine located at the northern end of the west arm of the lake. An Indian village on the site of Fort Kilmaurs, known as Old Fort, remains to this day. The lake still yields fine sockeye salmon, the mountains are well-timbered, and extensive copper deposits are now being exploited in the area. Illus.
L. F. S. Upton

241. Peake, F. A. WILLIAM WEST KIRKBY: MISSIONARY FROM ALASKA TO FLORIDA. *Hist. Mag. of the Protestant Episcopal Church 1965 34(3): 265-276.* Biographical sketch of the first Anglican missionary to reach Fort Yukon, Alaska. Kirkby (d. 1907) was recruited by the Church Mission Society in England and sailed for Ruperts' Land in 1852. Three years after his arrival in Canada, he was ordained to the priesthood. For the next 27 years he traveled and worked with the Indians and white settlers in the western preserve of the Hudson's Bay Company. His account of a journey into "Russian America" which he took in 1861 was published in the *Annual Report* of the Smithsonian Institution (1864). Documented.
E. G. Roddy

242. Reynolds, Arthur G. CHRISTMAS AMONG THE INDIANS. *Bull. of the United Church of Can. 1963 16: 34-39.* The letter reproduced here from *The Christian Guardian* of 26 January 1848 was written by Reverend Robert Brooking, Methodist missionary among the Indians at Rice Lake, Ontario. The letter gives a "complete and vivid picture" of the Methodist work among the Indians at that time. The real founder of the Rice Lake Mission was not the first missionary but Reverend William Case, whose concern for the evangelization of the Indians was his ruling passion.   E. P. Stickney

By Tribe

Athapascan

243. McKennan, Robert A. ATHAPASKAN GROUPS OF CENTRAL ALASKA AT THE TIME OF WHITE CONTACT. *Ethnohist. 1969 16(4): 335-345.* "The impact of white contact and recent linguistic data are evaluated in an effort to generalize concerning the aboriginal economies, settlement patterns, and territorial boundaries of hunting, fishing and foraging bands of Athapaskan Indians in central Alaska."   J

Cree

244. Allan, Iris, ed. A RIEL REBELLION DIARY. *Alberta Hist. R. [Canada] 1964 12(3): 15-25.* The diary of Robert K. Allan, recording his experiences while serving in the campaigns against Louis Riel and against the Indians of Chief Big Bear. Born in Ontario, Allan had been with the Winnipeg civil service prior to the outbreak of the rebellion. He died in Edmonton in 1942. Illus.   G. Emery

245. Boon, T. C. B. THE CENTENARY OF THE SYLLABIC CREE BIBLE 1862-1962. *Bull. of the United Church of Can. 1964 17: 27-33.* A Bible easily read by the Indians of the Northwest was an achievement, the climax of many years of work by Anglican and Wesleyan Methodist missionaries. The title page of the Syllabic Cree Bible bears the single name William Mason, but the records of the British and Foreign Bible Society which published it indicate it was the work of William Mason assisted by his wife Sophia Mason, Henry B. Steinhauer (a native Methodist pastor), John Sinclair, editions between 1862 and 1909 and was reset for a new edition in 1961. 28 notes.   E. P. Stickney

246. Fraser, W. B. BIG BEAR, INDIAN PATRIOT. *Alberta Hist. R. [Canada] 1966 14(2): 1-13.* Account of the career of the Cree Indian Chief, Big Bear, appraising his role in the Frog Lake Massacre, and indicating that, contrary to popular belief, this was not an attack planned in league with Louis Riel who also led uprisings in western Canada during this period.   H. M. Burns

247. Hood, Robert. SOME ACCOUNT OF THE CREE AND OTHER INDI-
ANS. *Alberta Hist. R. [Canada] 1967 15(1): 6-17.* Notes on the ethnography of
the Cree and neighboring tribes in Alberta, Canada, made by a member of an
exploring expedition in 1819.   H. M. Burns

248. Irvine, Col. A. G. A PARLEY WITH BIG BEAR. *Alberta Hist. R. [Can-
ada] 1963 11(4): 19.* Describes the incident that persuaded the Indian chief Big
Bear to stop molesting the government surveyors.   E. W. Hathaway

249. MacKay, J. A. THE JOURNAL OF THE REVEREND J. A. MACKAY,
STANLEY MISSION, 1870-72. *Saskatchewan Hist. [Canada] 1963 16(3): 95-
113.* This distinguished Anglican missionary and Cree scholar was in charge of
the Stanley mission on the Churchill River from 1864 to 1867. These extracts
from his journal, covering part of the period at the mission, give an insight into
the character of the man and his work as a pioneer missionary. Photos.
                                                                   A. H. Lawrance

250. Rogers, E. S. and Updike, Lee. MISTASSINI CREE. *Beaver [Canada] 1970
301(Summer): 22-25.* These people lived, and still live, on the east coast of James
Bay. A subsistence hunting and fishing economy was changed to one of fur
trapping by the arrival of European traders. The author describes their life by
seasons. The pressure of population has recently exceeded the resources of this
area and many of the tribe are dispersing southward. Illus.
                                                                   L. F. S. Upton

251. Shipley, Nan. PRINTING PRESS AT OONIKUP. *Beaver [Canada] 1960
291(Summer): 48-53.* Joseph Reader (d. 1928), Anglican missionary, came to
Touchwood Hills, Saskatchewan (then Northwest Territories) in 1874. He and
his family moved to The Pas, Manitoba, in 1878; he resigned from the Church
Missionary Society in 1881 and was appointed Indian agent. He built a house at
Oonikup, near The Pas, and in 1889 set up a press to print books in the Cree
syllabics invented in 1841 by James Evans. Illus.   L. F. S. Upton

Malecite

252. Christie, A. G. EXERCISE LES VOYAGEURS. *Can. Army J. 1963 17(3):
35-44.* Description of a Canadian army exercise designed to train junior officers
in independent leadership. A water and cross-country route of over 140 miles was
selected. It paralleled the 18th-century route of the Malecite Indians when they
invaded the United States. Illus.   J. H. Scrivner

Montagnais-Naskapi

253. Caron, Adrien. LA MISSION DU PERE PAUL LE JEUNE, S.J. SUR
LA CÔTE-DU-SUD, 1633-1634 [The mission of Father Paul Le Jeune, S.J., on
the south shore (of the St. Lawrence), 1633-1634]. *R. d'Hist. de l'Amérique*

Française [Canada] 1963 17(3): 371-395. The *Jesuit Relations* of 1634 described Father Le Jeune's winter with a wandering tribe of Montagnais Indians. Using this account as his guide, the author identifies places mentioned and traces the route followed. He describes the principal participants and the outstanding incidents of the voyage. No permanent mission was established in the area because there were too few Indians. Maps. L. F. S. Upton

254. Dyke, A. P. MONTAGNAIS-NASKAPI OR MONTAGNAIS AND NASCAUPI? AN EXAMINATION OF SOME TRIBAL DIFFERENCES. *Ethnohist. 1970 17(1/2): 43-48.* "The Indians of the Labrador-Ungava peninsula historically have been variously regarded as one group, the 'Montagnais-Naskapi,' and as two groups, the 'Montagnais' and 'Nascaupi.' Genetic and ethnographic data are offered to support the argument that these people represent two distinct groups, and that 'Montagnais-Naskapi' should be used solely to refer to offspring of mixed marriages between them." J

255. Rogers, E. S. and Updike, Lee. THE NASKAPI. *Beaver [Canada] 1969 300(Winter): 40-43.* The Naskapi Indians inhabited northern Quebec and Labrador, and probably never numbered more than 1,500. They lived entirely by hunting and fishing, and their mainstay was the caribou. Most Naskapi have now moved south to Schefferville, Quebec, settling near iron mines. A few still live at Davis Inlet on the Labrador coast. Illus. L. F. S. Upton

256. Williams, Glyndwr. JAMES CLOUSTON'S JOURNEY ACROSS THE LABRADOR PENINSULA IN 1820. *Beaver [Canada] 1966 297(Summer): 4-15.* Describes the first explorations of the barren lands east of Hudson Bay. Clouston's objects were to map the area and to determine trade possibilities for the Hudson's Bay Company. His journal contains much information about the life and belief of the Naskapi Indians of this region and their interdependence with the caribou. Clouston's journal has been recently published in Vol. XXIV of the *Hudson's Bay Record Society.* Illus. L. F. S. Upton

Nakotcho-kutchin (Loucheux)

257. Boon, Thomas C. B. WILLIAM WEST KIRKBY: FIRST ANGLICAN MISSIONARY TO THE LOUCHEUX. *Beaver [Canada] 1965 295(Spring): 36-43.* Kirkby (d. 1907) went to the northwest from England for the Church Missionary Society as a missionary school master. He was ordained a priest in 1856. He journeyed to Fort Yukon, at the junction of the Porcupine and Yukon rivers in what is now Alaska, in 1861 and 1862. Lengthy excerpts from the account Kirkby wrote for *The Nor'Wester* of Red River, 5 March 1862, are used to describe the trip and the customs of the Kutchin or Loucheux Indians. This people lived in the area from the Mackenzie River to Bering Strait, north of latitude 65. Illus. L. F. S. Upton

Thlingchadinne (Dog Ribs)

258. Helm, June and Thomas, Vital. TALES FROM THE DOGRIBS. *Beaver [Canada] 1966 297(Autumn): 16-20 and (Winter): 52-54.* The Thlingchadinne (Dog-Ribs) are one branch of the widespread Indian linguistic family known as the Déné or Athapascan Indians and live in the country between the Great Bear and Great Slave Lakes. Six stories are here narrated by one of the tribe, Vital Thomas: three are legends concerning the beginnings of the area; three are stories related to the first arrival of the fur traders in the late 18th century. Illus.
L. F. S. Upton

Northwest Coast Area

General

259. Beckham, Stephen Dow. LONELY OUTPOST: THE ARMY'S FORT UMPQUA. *Oregon Hist. Q. 1969 70(3): 233-257.* Originally established in 1856 to serve a military role in preventing clashes between Indians of the Oregon Pacific coast and newly-arrived white miners and settlers, Fort Umpqua had a short and unsatisfactory existence. Events in the early years of the Civil War and reduction of Indian aggressiveness brought official closure of the fort in 1862.
C. C. Gorchels

260. Deutsch, Herman J. INDIAN AND WHITE IN THE INLAND EMPIRE. *Pacific Northwest Q. 1956 47(2): 44-51.* A general account of the Indian wars in the Pacific Northwest 1880-1912. Based on government documents.
D. Houston

261. Gates, Charles M. THE INDIAN TREATY OF POINT NO POINT. *Pacific Northwest Q. 1955 46(2): 52-58.* Reproduces excerpts from the official proceedings of negotiations with various northwestern Indian tribes in 1854 over the cession of land. The treaty illustrates particularly well the problems of making such treaties and the methods used by the government in concluding them.
D. Houston

262. Geary, E. R. HISTORICAL NARRATIVE OF THE PRESBYTERY OF OREGON. *J. of the Presbyterian Hist. Soc. 1960 38(2): 103-109, (3): 166-181.* Part I. Reprint of an article first published in the *Presbyterian Home Missionary* 1885 14(7): 154-155. The author traces the history of the Presbytery of Oregon from 1846, when the Reverend Lewis Thompson, native of Kentucky and graduate of the Princeton Theological Seminary, established the first Presbyterian Church among the American settlers in Oregon. In 1851 the Presbytery was

organized at a meeting in LaFayette by Thompson, the Reverend Edward R. Geary, pastor of the church in LaFayette, and the newly-arrived Reverend Robert Robe. Deals with the years up to 1857. Part II. Covers the years 1858-76. Describes each Presbyterian church established in Oregon, and the work of each Presbyterian minister and missionary to the Indians.   W. D. Metz

263. Howell, Erle. JOHN P. RICHMOND, M.D., FIRST METHODIST MINISTER ASSIGNED TO THE PRESENT STATE OF WASHINGTON. *Methodist Hist. 1970 9(1): 26-35.* Biographical account of John P. Richmond (1811-95), who became the first Methodist minister in Washington when he was assigned to the Indian Mission at Nisqually on Puget Sound in 1840. He served there for two years. In addition to being a Methodist preacher, Richmond was a physician, politician, and superintendent of schools. 32 notes.
                                                                H. L. Calkin

264. Jessett, Thomas E. CHRISTIAN MISSIONS TO THE INDIANS OF OREGON. *Church Hist. 1959 28(2): 147-156.* Brings together the history of Indian missions in Oregon sponsored by various denominations from 1829 to the Whitman massacre in 1846, which marked the end of the first missionary phase. The missionaries' sympathy for the white settlers alienated the Indians from Christianity.   E. Oberholzer, Jr.

265. Johannessen, Carl L., Davenport, William A., Millet, Artimus, and McWilliams, Steven. THE VEGETATION OF THE WILLAMETTE VALLEY. *Ann. of the Assoc. of Am. Geographers 1971 61(2): 286-302.* "The vegetation of the Willamette Valley, Oregon, has been modified by man for centuries. The earliest white men described the vegetation as extensive prairies maintained by annual fires set by Indians. The cessation of burning in the 1850s allowed expansion of forest lands on the margins of the former prairies. Today some of these forest lands have completed a cycle of growth, logging, and regrowth. Much of the former prairie is now in large-scale grain and grass seed production and is still burned annually. The pasture lands of the Valley are still maintained as open lands with widely scattered oaks."   J

266. Kelley, Don Greame. TREES OF THE TOTEM CULTURE—THEIR ANCIENT IMPORTANCE IN THE LIFE AND ECONOMY OF THE NORTHWEST COAST INDIANS. *Am. West 1971 8(3): 18-21, 63.* The abundance of easily worked timber along the Pacific Northwest coast from Oregon to California was an important factor in the daily lives of the Indians who depended on this paradise of natural resources. Of greatest utility was the western red cedar which ranged over most of the area. Commonly known as "canoe cedar," but really an arborvitae, it was the principal material resource, after food, for the Indian culture. It provided multifamily dwellings as much as 500 feet long and 60 feet wide, totem poles, and seaworthy canoes. The bark and wood were important export trade items. The fiber was used with goat wool in the celebrated Chilkat blankets. Cedarbark also provided baskets. The Northwest Indian used

all manner of cedarwood boxes and containers, many of them exquisitely carved and painted with simple or elaborate patterns and designs. Excerpted from a forthcoming book. 7 illus.   D. L. Smith

267. Kime, Wayne R. ALFRED SETON'S JOURNAL: A SOURCE FOR IRVING'S "TONQUIN" DISASTER ACCOUNT. *Oregon Hist. Q. 1970 71(4): 309-324.* An excerpt from a recently discovered journal by Alfred Seton, a clerk in John Jacob Astor's Pacific Fur Company, is the foundation for an analysis of the accuracy of Washington Irving's account of the Indian attack on the ship *Tonquin* in 1811. Irving relied "upon the testimony of sources rather than upon what has often been claimed—the power of his imagination."

C. C. Gorchels

268. Nalty, Bernard C. and Strobridge, Truman R. THE DEFENSE OF SEATTLE, 1856: "AND DOWN CAME THE INDIANS." *Pacific Northwest Q. 1964 55(3): 105-110.* Describes the aggressiveness of Indians against the small settlement of Seattle in 1856 with details of the important role of the warship *Decatur.* Biblio.

C. C. Gorchels

269. Onstad, Preston E. THE FORT ON THE LUCKIAMUTE: A RESURVEY OF FORT HOSKINS. *Oregon Hist. Q. 1964 65(2): 173-196:* Detailed description of location and function of the U.S. Army military establishment in Oregon, said to have been constructed to protect the native Indians from the white men. A "fort" in name only, the post was generally sparsely manned throughout its history, from 1857 to 1866, and was never the scene of any warfare. The most noted army officer stationed at the post was Philip H. Sheridan. Included are contemporary letters which describe the physical features and paraphernalia of the post.

C. C. Gorchels

270. Ross, Nancy Wilson. MURDER AT THE PLACE OF RYE GRASS. *Am. Heritage 1959 10(5): 42-53, 85-91.* Describes the efforts of Marcus Whitman and his wife Narcissa to Christianize the Indians of Oregon Territory and the massacre of the Whitmans in 1847. Illus.

C. R. Allen, Jr.

271. Ruby, Robert H. A HEALING SERVICE IN THE SHAKER CHURCH. *Oregon Hist. Q. 1966 67(4): 347-355.* Report of observations by the author of vocal and energetic religious activities in the Shaker Church in the Northwest originated by John Slocum, a Puget Sound Indian who claimed that God gave him spiritual inspiration in a dream in 1882.

C. C. Gorchels

272. Taylor, Herbert C., Jr. ABORIGINAL POPULATION OF THE LOWER NORTHWEST COAST. *Pacific Northwest Q. 1963 54(4): 158-166.* Population figures and discussion of sources of information on number of aborigines living in the Puget Sound region from 1780 to 1845. Francis D. Haines, Jr., commenting on the population paper (given at the annual meeting of the Council on Regional Historical Research in Progress in Tacoma, Washington, 20 April 1963), pays

tribute to the work of anthropologists in the study of history, and comments on implications of new facts on the Indian economy of the era.

C. C. Gorchels

273. Unsigned. SEATTLE'S FIRST TASTE OF BATTLE, 1856. *Pacific Northwest Q. 1956 47(1): 1-8.* These excerpts from contemporary letters and diaries describe the Indian attack of 26 January 1856 on Seattle, Washington.

D. Houston

274. Weber, Francis J. A MISSIONARY'S PLEA FOR GOVERNMENTAL ASSISTANCE. *Records of the Am. Catholic Hist. Soc. of Philadelphia 1966 77(4): 242-249.* Reproduces a 15-page letter of Eugene Casimir Chirouse, O.M.I., to James Willis Nesmith of Oregon, 28 August 1865. Father Chirouse documented the financial position of his mission among the Indians of Puget Sound and requested government support for a school. J. M. McCarthy

By Tribe

Chinook

275. Schaeffer, Claude E. WILLIAM BROOKS, CHINOOK PUBLICIST. *Oregon Hist. Q. 1963 64(1): 41-54.* Discusses William Brooks' association with Indians in the Pacific Northwest and his efforts to publicize problems of the Indians, 1835-39. C. C. Gorchels

Cowichan

276. Brothers, Ryan. COWICHAN KNITTERS. *Beaver [Canada] 1965 296(Summer): 42-46.* Describes the cottage industry of the Cowichan Indians near Duncan, 40 miles north of Victoria, British Columbia. They learned the art of knitting from Scottish immigrants to Vancouver Island in the mid-19th century. Illus. L. F. S. Upton

Euclataw

277. Meade, E. F. A EUCLATAW CHIEF. *Beaver [Canada] 1965 296(Winter): 48-53.* The Euclataw Indians moved to their present site near Cape Mudge, British Columbia, about 1850. They were warlike, taking slaves and trading them with other tribes, and through the 1860's they terrorized the waters of Seymour Narrows. But with the arrival of the miner and logger they began to realize the need to adapt. A boy, William Assu (ca. 1867-1965), was chosen to undergo intensive training in both the ancient Indian customs and in the ways of the white man, to fit himself to become chief. Under Assu's leadership, the Euclataws took

up commercial fishing, got a government grant to rebuild their village, and preserved their morale and unity at a time when most Indian tribes were disintegrating. Illus.   L. F. S. Upton

Haida

278. Haynes, Bessie Doak. GOLD ON QUEEN CHARLOTTE'S ISLAND [SIC]. *Beaver [Canada] 1966 297(Winter): 4-11.* In August 1850 came the first news of a gold discovery at Englefield Bay, Queen Charlotte Islands. Little gold was found, and what there was had been an offshoot or "blow," a freak often found in mining areas. Nevertheless, prospectors were attracted to the islands, and there was considerable concern at the presence of Americans. Royal Navy ships were sent, and in September 1852 James Douglas, governor of Vancouver Island, was commissioned lieutenant governor of Queen Charlotte Islands in order to establish his authority to deal with the situation. There were numerous incidents between hostile Indians and gold seekers. Included are excerpts from the log of the *Georgianna* giving an account of its wreck and the capture of its passengers by Haida Indians. Illus.   L. F. S. Upton

Kake

279. McKelvie, B. A. COLONEL EBEY'S HEAD. *Beaver [Canada] 1956 (Summer): 42-45.* Describes how Kake warriors beheaded Colonel Isaac N. Ebey in 1857 and how his head was recovered three years later by Captain Charles Dodd of the *Labouchère* at the request of Governor James Douglas of Vancouver Island.   R. W. Winks

Kwakiutl

280. Piddocke, Stuart. THE POTLATCH SYSTEM OF THE SOUTHERN KWAKIUTL: A NEW PERSPECTIVE. *Southwestern J. of Anthrop. 1965 21(3): 244-264.* Challenges the orthodox view of the Kwakiutl potlatch and develops a new view. Although the Kwakiutl as a whole did have a "surplus economy," differences in wealth between groups existed. Without distribution of food from wealthier groups to poorer groups, the latter would often have died from hunger. Since the potlatch in aboriginal times was confined to various local groups of one or another tribe or winter-village group, variations in productivity were minimized, and a level of subsistence was maintained for the entire population. In this system food could be exchanged for wealth objects, and wealth objects for increased prestige. The desire for prestige and the status rivalry between chiefs directly motivated potlatching and so indirectly motivated the people to continue the system of exchange. The continuation of these practices ensured the survival of the population. Based on secondary sources; biblio.
                                                           C. N. Warren

281. Rogers, E. S. and Updike, Lee. INDIAN TRIBES OF CANADA: THE KWAKIUTL. *Beaver [Canada] 1969 299(Spring): 23-27.* First in a series of short

pictorial articles on some of the native peoples of Canada. The Kwakiutl lived on the northeast corner of Vancouver Island and along the mainland coast of British Columbia from Douglas Channel to Bute Inlet. Between 1820 and 1920 disease cut the population from almost 11 thousand to two thousand. Theirs was largely a fishing economy and much above subsistence. Woodworking was an important art, and the easily split red cedar provided material for homes, boats, cooking utensils, and ritual masks. The Kwakiutl were very conscious of social status. Illus.   L. F. S. Upton

282. Sismey, Eric D. H'KUSAM, A KWAKIUTL VILLAGE. *Beaver [Canada] 1961 292: 24-27.* Of all Indian villages, this (on Salmon Bay, Vancouver Island) is one of the best documented, photographically—from 1880 through 1918 (when it was abandoned) and up to 1953, when the last traces were becoming obliterated. A detailed account of houses and totem poles is given. Photos.
                                                                    A. P. Tracy

Lummi

283. Suttles, Wayne. POST-CONTACT CULTURE CHANGES AMONG THE LUMMI INDIANS. *British Columbia Hist. Q. [Canada] 1954 18(1/2): 29-102.* The Lummi Indians of the Puget Sound area are especially important to anthropologists and historians because they were numerous, they easily provided for their human needs, and had enough leisure to develop art and ceremony. This comprehensive article covers their contacts with white men from 1790 to 1953. Changes brought about by such institutions as the church, school, white government, and the Indian Bureau are presented in considerable detail. Based on primary and secondary sources.   C. C. Gorchels

Makah

284. Quimby, George I. JAMES SWAN AMONG THE INDIANS; THE INFLUENCE OF A PIONEER FROM NEW ENGLAND ON COASTAL INDIAN ART. *Pacific Northwest Q. 1970 61(4): 212-216.* Description of the work of James Swan, jack-of-all-trades, who became a self-trained ethnographer of merit, as he noted and recorded the rituals and cogent artwork of the Makah Indians in the Pacific Northwest, 1858-60. 7 photos.   C. C. Gorchels

285. Riley, Carroll L. THE MAKAH INDIANS: A STUDY OF POLITICAL AND ECONOMIC ORGANIZATION. *Ethnohist. 1968 15(1): 57-95.* Studies the political, economic, and social characteristics of the Makah Indians, the only people of western Washington organized on a multivillage level. They served as middlemen in coastwise trade although their orientation was primarily to the sea. The political organization was originally based on a head-chief in each autonomous village. 9 notes, biblio.   R. S. Burns

Rogue River

286. Smith, Thomas H. AN OHIOAN'S ROLE IN OREGON HISTORY. *Oregon Hist. Q. 1965 66(3): 218-232.* Letters written in primitive form by a pioneer in eastern and southern Oregon to his brother in Ohio. Details in the letters include descriptions of Rogue River Indian skirmishes, the dispositions of cross-country travelers, the cost of food and the wages received by unskilled laborers.   C. C. Gorchels

Tsimshian

287. Moeller, Beverley B. CAPTAIN JAMES COLNETT AND THE TSIM-SHIAN INDIANS, 1787. *Pacific Northwest Q. 1966 57(1): 13-17.* Documented account of conflict between the crew of an English fur-trading ship and Tsimshian Indians near the [Queen] Charlotte Islands British Columbia, based on the *Journal of the "Prince of Wales"* by sailor James Colnett.   C. C. Gorchels

Plateau Area

General

288. Beidleman, Richard G. NATHANIEL WYETH'S FORT HALL. *Oregon Hist. Q. 1957 58(3): 197-250.* An account of Wyeth's experiences in establishing and maintaining Fort Hall near the Snake River in Idaho. The author describes affairs of the Fort (mostly trade), as well as Wyeth's associates, visitors, and relations with the Indians.   C. C. Gorchels

289. Brandon, William. TWO THOUSAND MILES FROM THE COUNTING HOUSE: WILSON PRICE HUNT AND THE FOUNDING OF ASTORIA. *Am. West 1968 5(4): 24-29, 61-63.* With the Louisiana Purchase and the reports of the Lewis and Clark expedition, considerable Yankee attention focused on the Western beaver fur trade. John Jacob Astor, the leading American fur merchant, planned a chain of trading posts along the Lewis and Clark route, a monopoly of the trade with the Russians along the Pacific Northwest coast, and a vast trade cycle that would involve China, Europe, and New England. He was also aware of the political implications for the American position in the Oregon country. Two simultaneous expeditions were to set the plan in motion. The first was by sea to establish headquarters at the mouth of the Columbia River. The second was by land to win the confidence of the Indians and to determine proper locations for trading posts en route. Wilson Price Hunt commanded the overland expedition. As leader of the 1811 overland Astorians, he is credited with marking the route between the Snake River and the Columbia that later was to become

an important link in the Oregon Trail. Hunt also founded and was in command of the post at Astoria, on the Oregon side of the mouth of the Columbia. Map, biblio., note.   D. L. Smith

290. Davison, Stanley. WORKER IN GOD'S WILDERNESS. *Montana 1957 7(1): 8-17.* A study of the personality and life of the Reverend Samuel Parker, probably the earliest Christian missionary to preach in the wild territories of what is now Montana and Idaho. The author gives a detailed account of this Congregational churchman's work among the Nez Percé and Flathead (Salish) Indians.
                                                                              B. Waldstein

291. Edland, Roy E. THE "INDIAN PROBLEM": PACIFIC NORTHWEST, 1879. *Oregon Hist. Q. 1969 70(2): 101-137.* While white settlers were steadily moving into the territory of the northwest corner of the United States in the latter quarter of the 19th century, the native Indians frequently reacted violently as they resisted losing their lands. The objectives and policies at that time of the Office of Indian Affairs and the War Department (sometimes in conflict) are reviewed. Such influences as the passing of the Homestead Act and the general economic collapse in the Mississippi valley, 1837 to 1842, are considered. Compromises with the Indian tribes of the Northwest, and special consideration for Chief Moses and his followers, finally brought peace in 1879, as Chief Moses was granted his choice of a separate Indian reservation in northeastern Washington Territory.
                                                                              C. C. Gorchels

292. Garth, Thomas R. EARLY NINETEENTH CENTURY TRIBAL RELATIONS IN THE COLUMBIA PLATEAU. *Southwestern J. of Anthrop. 1964 20(1): 43-57.* A delineation of the major Indian groups and their relationships to one another, in the Dalles-Snake River region of Washington, Oregon, and Idaho, in the early 19th century. Based on field investigation, primary and secondary sources; map, biblio.   C. N. Warren

293. Garth, Thomas R. THE PLATEAU WHIPPING COMPLEX AND ITS RELATIONSHIP TO PLATEAU-SOUTHWEST CONTACTS. *Ethnohist. 1965 12(2): 141-170.* Whipping as corporal punishment in Columbia Plateau tribes is unique in American primitive societies. The diffusion of whipping and European attitudes toward it is probably the result of very early (17th century) contact with the slaveholding Spanish Southwest. 26 notes, biblio.
                                                                              R. S. Burns

294. Gossett, Gretta. STOCK GRAZING IN WASHINGTON'S NILE VALLEY: RECEDING RANGES IN THE CASCADES. *Pacific Northwest Q. 1964 55(3): 119-127.* History of changes in cattle-grazing in the mountain valley in central and western central Washington Territory and State over a span of a century, covering Indian activities, wars between cattlemen and sheepmen, and the encroachment of field agriculture. Activities in numerous valleys are described, and leading cattlemen are identified.   C. C. Gorchels

295. Green, Frank L. H. K. W. PERKINS, MISSIONARY TO THE DALLES. *Methodist Hist. 1971 9(3): 34-44.* Henry Kirk White Perkins (1814-84) served as a Methodist missionary to the Indians at The Dalles, Oregon, 1837-44. Relates the story of Perkins' personal life, his relations with others of the missionary mission, and his ministry to and experiences with the Indians. 10 notes.
H. L. Calkin

296. Howard, Helen Addison. THE STEPTOE AFFAIR. *Montana 1969 19(2): 28-36.* Summarizes events leading to and including the "Steptoe Massacre" of 1858 near Spokane. An explanation is furnished for the mysterious shortage of ammunition for the besieged soldiers: a civilian teamster forgot to bring the packs. Emphasis is placed on the assistance given the troops by Timothy, a Nez Percé chief and convert to Christianity. Illus., biblio.
S. R. Davison

297. Howell, Erle. JAMES HARVEY WILBUR, INDIAN MISSIONARY— FOUNDER OF METHODISM IN THE INLAND EMPIRE. *Methodist Hist. 1969 7(2): 17-27.* Gives a biographical account of James Harvey Wilbur, founder of Methodism in Washington and northern Idaho and one of Methodism's top-flight Indian missionaries.The author discusses his relations with the Indians and his position in the Methodist Church from 1859 to 1887. In addition there are earlier biographical data and a summary of developments on the Yakima Reservation. Based on a diary of Wilbur at Willamette University and records of the Pacific Northwest, Oregon, and Columbia River Annual Conferences of the Methodist Church; 16 notes.
H. L. Calkin

298. Knuth, Priscilla, ed. CAVALRY IN THE INDIAN COUNTRY, 1864. *Oregon Hist. Q. 1964 65(1): 5-118.* All but nine pages of this article consist of the "Private Journal" of Captain John M. Drake describing an army cavalry expedition from Fort Dalles, Oregon, into eastern Oregon Indian country. The editor states that two "editions" of Drake's journal were used, one version believed to be the original (kept in the Coe Collection at Yale University) and the second version, a typewritten copy (held at the Oregon Historical Society). The journal gives many details of the business of a small military detachment trying to locate hostile Indians. Drake's observations are candid and personal, such as (in speaking of any army officer), "He fills my mind's eye precisely of a stiff, aristocratical old fool, morbid in his sensibilities and uncivil and contemptible in his intercourse with others." There are no battles with the Indians. Strife (bloodless) is limited to the criticisms and misunderstandings among the members of the expedition and military superiors and residents of Oregon. The journal covers 20 April to 11 October 1864.
C. C. Gorchels

299. Point, Nicolas. RELIGION AND SUPERSTITION: VIGNETTES OF A WILDERNESS MISSION. *Am. West 1967 4(4): 34-43, 70-73.* Father Nicolas Point was a missionary to the Siksika (Blackfeet), Skitswish (Coeur d'Alene,and Salish (Flathead) Indians from 1840 to 1847. Later he organized his rough journals into six volumes which he titled *Recollections of the Rocky Mountains.* A painter of considerable ability, he included in the *Recollections* many of the illustrations he had executed in the field to communicate the tenets of Christianity

to the Indians and to record his day-to-day life in the mission. Point's journals were translated and edited by Joseph P. Donnelly and published in 1967 as *Wilderness Kingdom—Indian Life in the Rocky Mountains: 1840-1847* (New York: Holt, Rinehart and Winston). Anecdotal selections from the journal, with 14 illustrations, are presented here bearing out Father Point's conviction that Indian "medicine" was the principal obstacle in the way of their conversion and civilization.   D. L. Smith

300. Walker, Deward E., Jr. NEW LIGHT ON THE PROPHET DANCE CONTROVERSY. *Ethnohist. 1969 16(3): 245-256.* "A re-examination of ethnographic and documentary materials combined with a look at recent archaeological data suggest that the Prophet Dance among Indians of the Plateau and Northwest Coast was inspired by indirect, protohistoric influences stemming from Euroamericans. This is contrary to the view that the Prophet Dance was a purely 'aboriginal' innovation."   J

301. Wood, C. E. S. PRIVATE JOURNAL, 1878-79. *Oregon Hist. Q. 1969 70(1): 5-38, (2): 138-170.* Part I. Observations and comments of a young lieutenant in the U.S. Army as recorded in his personal journal while in Oregon and the territories of Washington and Idaho in 1878. A wide range of experiences is covered, including association with many people (actresses, soldiers, pioneer settlers, Indians, and boatmen). Part II. Tells of his experiences in going from Vancouver to Walla Walla and vicinity for important meetings with Indians (1879). The journal reflects a wide range of experiences—from the "monotony and melancholy" of February days in Goldendale (covered with 27 inches of snow) to life-and-death Indian problems. Included are reports of negotiations between J. H. Wilbur, Indian Agent at the Yakima reservation, Indian Chief Moses, and Lieutenant Wood which led to the U.S. Government's decision to create for Chief Moses a new Indian reservation.   C. C. Gorchels

By Tribe

Cayuse

302. Thompson, Erwin N. NARCISSA WHITMAN. *Montana 1963 13(4): 15-27.* As the recent bride of Dr. Marcus Whitman, missionary and physician, Narcissa Prentiss Whitman was one of the first two white women to cross the plains and mountains to the Oregon country. She lived at the Waiilatpu Mission to the Cayuse Indians from 1836 to 1847, gradually losing both health and hope as mission efforts showed little result in improving the natives. The tragedy culminated in a general massacre of whites at the mission in 1847. Undocumented.   S. R. Davison

Klamath

303. Stern, Theodore. THE KLAMATH INDIANS AND THE TREATY OF 1864. *Oregon Hist. Q. 1956 57(3): 229-273.* A historical sketch of the Klamath Indians up to 1864, when they signed a land treaty with the government of the United States. Includes information on the relations of the Klamaths with other Indians of the area, their relations with whites, and the tribal characteristics which influenced their development.   C. C. Gorchels

Kutenai

304. Dempsey, Hugh A., ed. THOMPSON'S JOURNEY TO THE RED DEER RIVER. *Alberta Hist R. [Canada] 1965 13(1): 1-8, (2): 7-15.* The portion of David Thompson's journals covering his trip to the Red Deer River in October 1800. At this time, the Hudson's Bay Company and the North West Company had both established their first posts in the Rocky Mountains. Thompson, representing the latter company, made this trip to intercept the Kutenai Indians before they reached the Hudson's Bay post with their furs. The second part covers Thompson's trip of November 1800, his second trip of the year. Traveling with Duncan McGillivray, he went south to the Bow River country from Rocky Mountain House to learn the country and to look for mountain passes. Illus.
                                                   G. Emery

305. Schaeffer, Claude E. EARLY CHRISTIAN MISSION OF THE KUTENAI INDIANS. *Oregon Hist. Q. 1970 71(4): 325-348.* Probes the background of Christian forms of worship among Indians of the Columbia plateau, with special reference to Kutenai Indians among the Flathead region in Montana. Treats the period 1824-39. Describes the school life of the Indians as directed by Anglican missionaries. Depicts disappointing results of attempts by white missionaries to train Indian neophytes to assume a missionary role.
                                                   C. C. Gorchels

306. Schaeffer, Claude E. THE KUTENAI FEMALE BERDACHE: COURIER, GUIDE, PROPHETESS, AND WARRIOR. *Ethnohist. 1965 12(3): 193-236.* Describes the assumption of male role and status by a woman of the Kutenai in the early 19th century. Her social and sexual deviancy was infrequent; more often, the homosexuality or intersexuality involved a shift from male to female role. 22 notes, biblio.   R. S. Burns

Nez Percé

307. Alcorn, Rowena L. and Alcorn, Gordon D. AGED NEZ PERCE RECALLS THE 1877 TRAGEDY. *Montana 1965 15(4): 54-67.* Josiah Redwolf, now 93, recalls incidents of the Nez Percé War, which he witnessed as a boy of five. His comments confirm that the Indian retreat was led by others than Chief Joseph, who is traditionally credited.   S. R. Davison

308. Alcorn, Rowena L. and Alcorn, Gordon D. OLD NEZ PERCE RECALLS TRAGIC RETREAT OF 1877. *Montana 1963 13(1): 66-74.* Suhm-Keen, an Indian lad of 10, witnessed most of the action in the Nez Percé War, including the battles at Clearwater, the Big Hole, and Canyon Creek, before the surrender at Bear Paw. He escaped into Canada with his parents, where Sitting Bull and other Sioux refugees befriended them. Now 95 years old, and known as Sam Tilden, this Nez Percé recounted these episodes for the authors in 1962, surely one of the last interviews with survivors of this war. L. G. Nelson

309. Barsness, John and Dickinson, William. MINUTE MEN OF MONTANA. *Montana 1960 10(2): 2-9.* Montana's somewhat irregular militia was first called to arms by Acting Governor Thomas F. Meagher during premature Indian scares in 1867. In the Nez Percé campaign 10 years later, informally organized volunteers took part in several engagements and suffered some casualties. A claim is made here for their recognition as soldiers of the militia. Based on the standard published accounts of the Indian wars. S. R. Davison

310. Brown, Mark H. YELLOWSTONE TOURISTS AND THE NEZ PERCE. *Montana 1966 16(3): 30-43.* Summarizes the encounters between fleeing Nez Percé Indians and several groups of tourists and prospectors in Yellowstone National Park in 1877. Varied treatment of the whites reflected Nez Percé uncertainty after the Big Hole battle, where settlers joined troops in attacking the unwary fugitives. Illus. S. R. Davison

311. Brown, Mark K. CHESSMEN OF WAR. *Idaho Yesterdays 1966 10(4): 22-29.* "An analysis of the strategy of troop movements in the Nez Percé War of 1877." The author compares the game of chess with the war, where the positions of U.S. troops dictated the final outcome of the conflict. General Oliver Otis Howard (1830-1909) requested reinforcements from all three geographic divisions of the Continental Army to contain the movements of the Nez Percé under the leadership of Chief Joseph (1840-1904). Included are the engagements from the Battle of White Bird Canyon to the final confrontation by Colonel Nelson Appleton Miles in northeast Montana. 6 illus. D. H. Swift

312. Dozier, Jack. 1885: A NEZ PERCE HOMECOMING. *Idaho Yesterdays 1963 7(3): 22-25.* Describes the return in 1885 of the remnants of Chief Joseph's band of Nez Percé Indians to the region from which they had been driven during the Nez Percé War of 1877, with particular attention to the organized efforts of local citizens (Lewiston, Idaho) to prevent their return. M. Small

313. Haines, Francis. PIONEER PORTRAIT: ROBERT NEWELL. *Idaho Yesterdays 1965 9(1): 2-9.* "A mountain man who became one of the very first Idaho pioneers, Robert Newell was a friend of the Nez Percé Indians in the years of the fur trade and the gold rush." The author gives a brief biography of Newell's life and describes his adventures with other mountain men, his political activities, his success with various Indian tribes, and his several marriages. 2 photos. B. B. Swift

314. Harlan, Gilbert Drake, ed. FARMING IN THE BITTERROOT AND THE FIASCO AT "FORT FIZZLE." *J. of the West 1964 3(4): 501-516.* Wilson Barber Harlan settled in the Bitterroot Valley of Montana as a farmer. In 1875 he married Mary Horn who had been teaching at Corvallis. To this union were born three children; one daughter still survives. In 1877 apprehension spread throughout the valley because the Nez Percé Indians under Chief Joseph were reported headed for the Bitterroot. Harlan joined a group of settlers who, in conjunction with the Army, built a fort in a canyon on the Lodo trail. Although the situation was tense, the Indians did not attack and after consultation left the valley. Illus.   D. N. Brown

315. Josephy, Alvin M., Jr. THE NAMING OF THE NEZ PERCES. *Montana 1955 5(4): 1-18.* Historical highlights of the association of white men with the Nez Percé Indians, centering on the question of whether or not these Indians were properly named. Evidence presented includes scholars' and writers' research as well as quoted observations of David Thompson, Meriwether Lewis and William Clark, and other explorers.   C. C. Gorchels

316. Morrill, Allen and Morrill, Eleanor. TALMAKS. *Idaho Yesterdays 1964 8(3): 2-15.* Tells how the Talmaks camp (Christian camp-meeting of the Nez Percé Indians) grew out of the wild Indian celebration of the Fourth of July in northern Idaho.   M. Small

317. Morrill, Allen C. and Morrill, Eleanor D. THE MEASURING WOMAN AND THE COOK. *Idaho Yesterdays 1963 7(3): 2-15.* Tells of the work of anthropologist Alice Cunningham Fletcher and her companion Jane Gay among the Nez Percé of north Idaho from May 1889 to September 1892. Sent by the U.S. government to measure and allocate land to the Indians under the provisions of the Dawes Act of 1887, the two women worked to overcome the hostility of the remnants of Chief Joseph's band. The authors depend largely on the letters of Jane Gay in the Women's Archives at Radcliffe College and on the published works of missionary Kate McBeth.   M. Small

318. Peterson, Ernst. REV. SAMUEL PARKER AND THE SOUTHERN NEZ PERCE TRAIL. *Montana 1966 16(4): 12-27.* The Protestant missionary Samuel Parker, passed through the southwestern tip of present Montana in 1835, en route to the homeland of the Nez Percé Indians, who were his escort on this occasion. The author attempts to identify the trail they followed. Based on Parker's published account, supported by the author's field reconnaissance and illustrated with his recent photos.   S. R. Davison

319. Ruby, Robert H. RETURN OF THE NEZ PERCE. *Idaho Yesterdays 1968 12(1): 12-15.* The Nez Percé, exiled in Oklahoma since 1877, were given but little time to dispose of their stock and visit the graves of loved ones after the decision to move the band came in 1885. The people were permitted to select either the Colville or Lapwai reservations; Chief Joseph chose Colville because of white antipathy in Idaho. The Indians, with Dr. W. H. Faulkner in charge, made the

trip to the Pacific Northwest by wagon and train, arriving at Wallula Junction, Washington Territory, 27 May 1885. Faulkner remained with the ill and personally delivered them to the post surgeon at Fort Spokane. 24 notes.

G. Barrett

320. Wells, Merle W. THE NEZ PERCE AND THEIR WAR. *Pacific Northwest Q. 1964 55(1): 35-37.* Indians were in no sense engaged in warfare when U.S. troops pursued fleeing Nez Percé 1,500 miles to the Canadian border in 1877. Individualism and relationship of warriors to chiefs are expounded.

C. C. Gorchels

321. Young Joseph. AN INDIAN'S VIEW OF INDIAN AFFAIRS. *North Am. R. 1969 6(1): 56-64.* A Nez Percé chief speaks on behalf of his people in a reprint from an 1879 issue of *The North American Review.* He describes the series of events which led to the deprivation of the Indians' land and liberty. He mentions the friendship of such white men as Lewis and Clark, but describes how Indians later encountered less friendly white men as the government increased pressure to force them from their home. The Indian concept that land is not owned by man and therefore cannot be bought or sold was always in conflict with the materialism of the white men who eventually squeezed the Indian out of his rich land and imprisoned him on tiny reservations—by white law, of course. The author is a peace-loving man who, above all, did not want the blood of white men on his people's hands, but finally felt he was left with no alternative in the face of innumerable broken promises and threats. He ends with a heavy heart, a witness of the Indians' transition from peaceful, friendly men to sick, resentful men.

S. L. McNeel

Salish (Flathead)

322. Harrison, Michael. CHIEF CHARLOT'S BATTLE WITH BUREAU-CRACY. *Montana 1960 10(4): 27-33.* Reviews Chief Charlot's refusal to acknowledge the contract which moved the Salish (Flathead) Indians from the Bitterroot Valley to a reservation in the Jocko Valley, stressing that the conflict between the government and the Indians arose over Chief Charlot's mark being on one copy and not being on a second copy.

L. G. Nelson

323. Holmes, Oliver W., ed. PEREGRINATIONS OF A POLITICIAN. *Montana 1956 6(4): 34-45.* One provision in the Stevens Treaty with the Salish (Flatheads) in 1855 was construed to allow the President at his discretion to remove the Indians from their ancestral home in the Bitterroot Valley. In 1872 President Grant so ordered, to clear the valley for white settlement. He sent Congressman James Garfield to arrange with the Indians for their removal to the Jocko Reservation. Garfield's diary, quoted extensively, shows his reactions to life and travel in the West. Footnotes supply substantial excerpts from his official report, detailing his difficulties and limited success in accomplishing his mission.

S. R. Davison

324. Howard, Helen Addison. INDIANS AND AN INDIAN AGENT: CHIEF CHARLOT AND THE FORGED DOCUMENT. *J. of the West 1966 5(3): 379-397.* Charlot was a peaceful chief of the Salish (Flathead) Indians who offered passive resistance to the federal government for a period of 20 years. In 1872 the Secretary of the Interior appointed James A. Garfield as special commissioner to persuade the Flatheads to comply with an order of President Grant that they move to a reservation. Garfield entered into negotiations with Charlot and other chiefs, but the former refused to sign that he would accept the government's offer of houses and supplies if he would move his people to a reservation. Garfield then allegedly forged the chief's mark to the published agreement which was sent to the Senate for ratification. This forgery was later discovered. The action embittered Charlot and made him distrustful of the government. In 1891, however, after long negotiations Charlot capitulated and led his people to the Jocko Reservation. Based on government reports and other published sources; illus., 36 notes.   D. N. Brown

325. Seiber, Richard A. DAVID E. BLAIN: THE METHODIST CHURCH IN WASHINGTON, 1853-1861. *Methodist Hist. 1963 1(3): 1-17.* David E. Blain was the founder of Methodism in Seattle, Territory of Washington, in 1853. Discusses the organizing of the Methodist Episcopal Church by Blain, his subsequent pastorates in Washington and Oregon until 1861, the difficulties of travel in a frontier area, society during territorial days, and his relationships with the Salish (Flathead) Indians. Some details of his earlier and later activities are included. Based on unpublished letters and letters printed in the *Christian Advocate* of that period.   H. L. Calkin

326. Wells, Oliver N. RETURN OF THE SALISH LOOM. *Beaver [Canada] 1966 297(Spring): 40-45.* Blankets were one of the principal trade items of the Salish and an index of wealth before the Hudson's Bay Company introduced fur and salmon trading with the opening of the Fort Langley post in 1827. Gold seekers and missionaries ended the blanket economy. The recent revival of blanket weaving and one of the looms now in use are described. Illus.
                                                                L. F. S. Upton

Shuswap

327. Rogers, E. S. and Updike, Lee. THE SHUSWAP. *Beaver [Canada] 1970 300(Spring): 56-59.* The Shuswap live in east-central British Columbia on a plateau at an elevation of 2,500-6,000 feet. They were first met by Europeans in the late 1700's. The Shuswap lived by hunting and fishing. Relying on dried foods in the winter, they left their winter homes in April, digging for roots until the trout fishing began. Salmon were caught in late summer, and the fall was spent hunting deer, caribou, bear, and smaller animals. The author describes their artifacts and pastimes. Today, the Shuswap live by ranching, farming, and lumbering. Illus.   L. F. S. Upton

328. Sanger, David. INDIAN GRAVES PROVIDE CLUES TO THE PAST. *Beaver [Canada] 1966 296(Spring): 22-27.* Bulldozers discovered the Chase burial

site of the Shuswap Indians in 1960 on the north bank of the South Thompson River, three miles west of Chase, British Columbia. The burials were in a sandy ridge about 200 feet long. Much damage was done by curiosity seekers before professional archaeologists arrived. The artifacts are among the most spectacular ever found from a prehistoric site on the Canadian Plateau. Suggests that the burial site was used between 1400 and 1750 A.D. Notes early descriptions of the Shuswap about 1800. Illus.   L. F. S. Upton

Yakima

329. Reese, J. W. OMV'S FORT HENRIETTA: ON WINTER DUTY, 1855-56. *Oregon Hist. Q. 1965 66(2): 133-160.* History of the construction of a military fort on the Umatilla River in Oregon and its use by the Oregon Mounted Volunteers during the Yakima Indian War of 1855-56. Incidents at the fort and nearby territory show harrassing actions of Indians.   C. C. Gorchels

Great Basin Area

General

330. Athearn, Robert G. WAR PAINT AGAINST BRASS. *Montana 1956 6(3): 11-22.* A study of the policies and problems of the U.S. Army in the late 1860's and 1870's in coping with gold-seeking white and warlike Indians in the Bozeman Trail area of the United States.   C. C. Gorchels

331. Baker, Galen R. EXCAVATING FORT MASSACHUSETTS. *Colorado Mag. 1965 42(1): 1-16.* Excavation of the first permanent American military post in Colorado has been valuable chiefly in revealing the design for the fort and the materials used in construction, plus a few Indian artifacts.
I. W. Van Noppen

332. Bigler, David L. THE CRISIS AT FORT LIMHI, 1858. *Utah Hist. Q. 1967 35(2): 121-136.* Describes how units of the Nauvoo Legion, the volunteer militia of Utah Territory, under the command of Lieutenant Colonel Benjamin Franklin Cummings moved northward from the Utah Valley to rescue a Mormon missionary and colonizing group in Oregon Territory from Indian attack. This article is a chapter from a study *Massacre at Fort Limhi, Early Mormons in Oregon Territory, 1855-58.*   S. L. Jones

333. Chandler, W. B., ed. SOME PIONEER EXPERIENCES OF GEORGE CHANDLER. *Oregon Hist. Q. 1965 66(3): 197-207.* Autobiographical reminis-

cences of George Chandler, edited by his son. Includes his experiences in traveling from Missouri to Baker, Oregon, in 1862 and descriptions of early Indian violence in Baker until 1878.   C. C. Gorchels

334. Egan, Ferol. WARREN WASSON, MODEL INDIAN AGENT. *Nevada Hist. Soc. Q. 1969 12(3): 3-26.* Warren Wasson, a native New Yorker raised in Illinois, emigrated to the Far West in 1849. In 1851 he went back to the East but returned the following year. Wasson became friendly with the Washo and Paiute Indian tribes and, by 1858, had become an intermediary between the appointed Indian agent and his Indian charges. In September 1860, Wasson was made acting Indian agent for Nevada. Although he was appointed U.S. marshal for the territory of Nevada in March 1862, he continued settling disputes between various Indian tribes. Wasson was a rarity in Indian-white relations and was respected by both ethnic groups. Based mostly on primary sources, government reports, memoirs, and letters; illus., photos, 20 notes.   E. P. Costello

335. Faulkner, Mont E. EMIGRANT-INDIAN CONFRONTATION IN SOUTHEASTERN IDAHO, 1841-1863. *Rendezvous 1968 2(2): 43-58.* Seeks to explain the causes of violence between the Shoshoni and Bannock tribes with the white emigration to and through southeastern Idaho from 1841 to 1863. The author cites as causes: first, the nature of tribal political organization was toward an extreme individualism as opposed to a national loyalty, so that decisions by chief spokesmen were not binding upon the whole; second, the settlers and emigrants pastured the best grass land (bottomland), thereby destroying the basis of Indian wealth and power in raising horses; third, the lack of central authority in the emigrant trains west of Fort Laramie caused them to break up into small groups averaging 2.5 wagons per group.   H. F. Malyon

336. Hafen, LeRoy R. FORT VASQUEZ. *Colorado Mag. 1964 41(3): 198-212.* During the 1830's fur men of the West turned from the beaver-skin business to trade in buffalo robes. Four adobe forts were established in competition with each other on the South Platte River in Colorado for trade with the Cheyennes and Arapahoes. One of these, Fort Vasquez, was established in 1835 by Louis Vasquez and Andrew Sublette, both experienced fur traders, who shipped buffalo robes and tongues to St. Louis. In 1840 the fort was sold and when the new purchasers soon became bankrupt the place was abandoned. During the 1930's the WPA reconstructed the fort, mixing the old adobe remains with new materials. Based on letters, earlier accounts by the author, newspaper accounts, and memoirs.
I. W. Van Noppen

337. Haines, Francis, Sr. GOLDILOCKS ON THE OREGON TRAIL. *Idaho Yesterdays 1965 9(4): 26-30.* An account of various attempts by Indians to trade horses for blond children of the pioneers traveling on the Oregon Trail. Indian relations with the pioneers are detailed in three exacting tales of warfare and travel after reaching Oregon.   D. H. Swift

338. Hart, Newell. RESCUE OF A FRONTIER BOY. *Utah Hist. Q. 1965 33(1): 51-54.* Tells how Shoshoni and Bannock Indians in Utah carried off a 10-year-old boy, Reuban Van Orman, after killing his parents and of how his uncle Zachias, with the help of federal troops, recovered him two years later. Based on records of Zachias Van Orman in the Oregon State Historical Society and the *Official Records.*   S. L. Jones

339. Madsen, Brigham D. SHOSHONI-BANNOCK MARAUDERS ON THE OREGON TRAIL, 1859-1863. *Utah Hist. Q. 1967 35(1): 3-30.* Shows how the Shoshoni and Bannock Indians in their traditional territories north and west of Utah were disturbed by the overland migration to Washington, Oregon, and California and recites the stories of various hostile encounters between these Indians, the overland migrants, and U.S. military forces sent into the area to protect white settlers. Mormon leaders are described as favoring a pacific policy of feeding and clothing the Indians rather than fighting them, but the narrative reveals that Mormon settlers were not always prepared to follow such a policy. Based in part on Records of the Bureau of Indian Affairs in the National Archives, contemporary newspaper accounts, and *The War of the Rebellion.*
                                                                        S. L. Jones

340. Metschan, Phil. CANYON CITY "FORT-UP," 1878. *Oregon Hist. Q. 1969 70(1): 56-59.* A letter describing violent troubles in Grant County, Oregon, in 1878, with Indians who left the Malheur Agency and pillaged and killed white men in the region.   C. C. Gorchels

341. Nash, John D. SALMON RIVER MISSION OF 1855: A REAPPRAISAL. *Idaho Yesterdays 1967 11(1): 22-31.* "The Pacific Northwest's earliest Mormon colony brought several hundred missionaries to central Idaho between 1855 and 1858." Explains the reasons for establishing a Mormon mission among the Bannock and Shoshoni Indians on the Salmon River. The mission was built and manned as a fort in an isolated valley. Outlines the relationships between the Mormons and the mountaineers and illustrates the collision of three frontier cultures, which resulted in an Indian raid that closed the mission in 1858. 2 illus., 52 notes.   D. H. Swift

342. Povlovich, Charles A., Jr., ed. WILL DEWEY IN UTAH. *Utah Hist. Q. 1965 33(2): 134-140.* Provides editorial comment on and the text of five letters written by Will Dewey to his brother after a sudden, unannounced departure from his home in Missouri. His destination was Utah. The letters contain a lively account of his adventures with white settlers and with the Indians.
                                                                        S. L. Jones

343. Richards, Kent D. WASHOE TERRITORY: RUDIMENTARY GOVERNMENT IN NEVADA. *Arizona and the West 1969 11(3): 213-232.* Although American mountain men were traversing Washoe (the early name for Nevada) as early as 1827, permanent settlement was not established until 1851 when the Mormons located a way station en route to the California gold fields.

In the absence of any governmental authority, some 50 Mormons and Gentile prospectors and cattle ranchers drew up a Washoe code concerned with land claims. In time, its coverage was enlarged. Mormon-Gentile relations deteriorated and letters and petitions were soon reaching Washington. Gentiles even asked to be annexed to California. Utah Territory countered this by incorporating the area as a county. When federal troops were sent to Utah in 1857, the Mormons left Washoe. The Gentiles took over and launched a move for separate territorial status. The end of an Indian war in 1860, new problems occasioned by the mining boom of 1859 and the national North-South cleavage, and the failure of a newly formed provisional territorial government led to the creation of Nevada Territory by Congress in 1861. The pragmatic attempts to establish workable frontier institutions had failed and the paternalistic territorial system was welcomed. According to the author, Nevada's experience was similar to the evolution of government struggle on many other western frontiers. 4 illus., 4 maps, 40 notes.   D. L. Smith

344. Spence, Clark C. A CELTIC NIMROD IN THE OLD WEST. *Montana 1959 9(2): 56-67.* A detailed account of the fabulous hunting expedition undertaken by Sir St. George Gore, an Irish baronet, in the wilds of Montana, Wyoming and Colorado from 1854 to 1857. The author describes Gore's relations with the various Indians he encountered, as well as with the official Indian agents, who resented the killing of so much game simply in the name of sport. Based on contemporary articles, letters and documents.   B. Waldstein

345. Sunder, John E. UP THE MISSOURI TO THE MONTANA MINES: JOHN O'FALLON DELANY'S "POCKET DIARY FOR 1862". *Missouri Hist. Soc. Bull. 1962/63 19(1): 3-22.* A biographical sketch, followed by a portion of the diary. Member of a wealthy St. Louis family, Delany in 1862, at the age of 20, accompanied a famous missionary to the Indians, Father Pierre-Jean De Smet, on a trip up the Missouri River and then overland to Montana and the Rockies. This portion of the diary consists of brief sketches of steamboat life and of the country traversed through 7 July 1862. Additional information is provided about Indian problems and the Montana gold strikes. Notes.   R. J. Hanks

346. Taylor, Morris. ACTION AT FORT MASSACHUSETTS: THE INDIAN CAMPAIGN OF 1855. *Colorado Mag. 1965 42(4): 292-310.* A reinterpretation of the Indian campaigns of 1855 throughout southern Colorado, using heretofore overlooked primary sources—the personal letters of DeWitt Peters (assistant surgeon attached to the campaigns) and observations of Rafael Chacon (a participant in the campaigns). They were successfully directed against the Moache Utes and Jicarilla Apaches, leading to the cessation of hostilities by these two tribes against the white people.   R. Sexauer

347. Taylor, Morris F. SOME ASPECTS OF HISTORICAL INDIAN OCCUPATION OF SOUTHEASTERN COLORADO. *Great Plains J. 1964 4(1): 17-28.* In 1706 Juan de Ulibarri's expedition found Apaches in the area, but soon thereafter apparently the Comanches, followed by the Kiowas, Arapahoes and Cheyennes, replaced them. In the mid-19th century the Apaches and their allies,

the Utes, were again hunting in the area. Conflicts between them and the plains Indians continued there into the seventies. Based on newspapers and secondary sources; map, 67 notes. O. H. Zabel

348. Vandembushe, Duane. LIFE AT A FRONTIER POST: FORT GARLAND. *Colorado Mag. 1966 43(2): 132-148.* This fort, constructed in 1858, replaced Fort Massachusetts which had been established in 1852 to protect the "cradle of Colorado history" settlements in northern New Mexico, recently acquired from Mexico. Fort Garland, one of the most important of the frontier posts, protected settlers from the Ute, Apache, and other Indian tribes. Kit Carson was commandant, 1866-67, from which time the Indians were relatively peaceful until 1879, when the Meeker Massacre caused the strengthening of the garrison to 1,500 men. After 1881 the troops were reduced to a skeleton force and in 1883 the fort was abandoned. I. W. Van Noppen

349. Wilmot, Luther Perry. A PLEASANT WINTER FOR LEW WILMOT. *Colorado Mag. 1970 47(1): 1-25.* A personal account of the winter of 1860-61 which the author spent away from the diggings in Georgia Gulch, working in southeastern Colorado. Describes his trip to Bent's Fort to get a freight wagon from Majors' and Russell's camp, his brush with the Indians, his service as a hunter for Zan Hicklan's Ranch (where he met Kit Carson), and his observation of recruiting activities by both the Confederacy and the Union. Wilmot was especially proud of his success in target shooting, at which he won 740 dollars. Except for the Indian scare, "it was a pleasant winter for Lew Wilmot." Illus., 24 notes. O. H. Zabel

By Tribe

Bannock

350. Brimlow, George F., ed. TWO CAVALRYMEN'S DIARIES OF THE BANNOCK WAR, 1878. *Oregon Hist. Q. 1967 68(3): 221-258.* Biographical sketches and diaries of a second lieutenant and a private who participated in a military campaign against Indians in Oregon and Nevada in 1878. Details include descriptions of the countryside, experiences on marches, and reports of minor conflicts. C. C. Gorchels

351. Watson, Chandler B. RECOLLECTIONS OF THE BANNOCK WAR. *Oregon Hist. Q. 1967 68(4): 317-329.* Personal experiences of the author during a period of friction, 1877-79, with Indians in southern Oregon. Raids on cattle and depredation of settlements made living hazardous for the white man in the midst of unfriendly Indians, but actual violence was limited. C. C. Gorchels

Paiute, Northern (Snake)

352. Kenny, Judith Keyes. THE FOUNDING OF CAMP WATSON. *Oregon Hist. Q. 1957 58(1): 5-16.* Camp Watson was established in eastern Oregon to prevent depredations of the Snake (Northern Paiute) Indians in the 1860's. Details here include a report of the battle which cost the life of Stephen Watson.
C. C. Gorchels

353. Onstad, Preston E. CAMP HENDERSON, 1864. *Oregon Hist. Q. 1964 65(3): 297-302.* Description of a brief military expedition of the First Oregon Volunteer Cavalry against the Snake (Northern Paiute) Indians in rugged countryside of eastern Oregon, 1864.
C. C. Gorchels

354. Speth, Lembi Kongas. POSSIBLE FISHING CLIQUES AMONG THE NORTHERN PAIUTES OF THE WALKER RIVER RESERVATION, NEVADA. *Ethnohist. 1969 16(3): 225-244.* "Oral historical, ethnographic, and documentary data are used to provide the delineation of heretofore undescribed and now-defunct cooperative economic and social units, 'fishing cliques,' among male Northern Paiute Indians."
J

Sheepeater

355. Dominick, David. THE SHEEPEATERS. *Ann. of Wyoming 1964 36(2): 131-168.* Attempts to establish the identity of the "Sheepeaters," or primitive Indians living in Wyoming and Idaho from prehistoric times until the 1870's. Suggests that they shared all the intellectual and social customs of the Basin-Plateau Shoshoni, and discusses their archaeological remains and cultural development. Based on personal field work among the Fort Hall Shoshoni, and published anthropological material; illus., map, 144 notes, biblio.
R. L. Nichols

356. Shearer, George M. THE BATTLE OF VINEGAR HILL. *Idaho Yesterdays 1968 12(1): 17-21.* The author's eyewitness account of the defeat of the mounted infantry high on a ridge removed from water. Held down by the Sheepeater Indians, the soldiers had only vinegar to drink, but they escaped in the night after a 14-hour siege. This defeat of the Army in Idaho led to a general court-martial for the commanding officer. Shearer considered him a "coward," and "totally unfit to take command of any body of troops."
G. Barrett

Shoshoni

357. Chandler, M. G. SIDELIGHTS ON SACAJAWEA. *Masterkey 1969 43(2): 58-66.* With the vast amount of territory obtained by the Louisiana Purchase, it became necessary to explore and occupy this new land. The author describes the advance preparations made by the explorers chosen by President Jefferson to lead the first expedition into the Far West—Meriwether Lewis and William Clark. After outfitting the group in St. Louis, they made their way up the Missouri to

a Minitaree village where they took on Toussaint Charbonneau and his pregnant 14-year-old Shoshoni slave girl, named Sacajawea (Bird Woman) by the Minitaree. As the Shoshoni were a hostile tribe, Sacajawea was not only a godsend as a guide, but also insured the expedition's safe conduct through Shoshoni territory. In later life Sacajawea left Charbonneau and married a Comanche warrior. The son she bore while on the expedition, Jean Baptiste, and a nephew she adopted while in Shoshoni country, Bazil, were educated in Europe at Clark's expense. Both boys returned to the Wind River Shoshoni Reservation to be joined later by the widowed Sacajawea, who died on 9 April 1884 in her mid-90's. Based primarily on discussions with C. A. Eastman, noted Sioux Indian authority.

C. N. Warren

358. Fowler, Don D., ed. NOTES ON THE EARLY LIFE OF CHIEF WASHAKIE TAKEN DOWN BY CAPTAIN RAY. *Ann. of Wyoming 1964 36(1): 34-42.* Discusses the importance of such documents for the anthropologist and historian. "Notes" were taken by Captain Patrick Henry Ray during the 1890's and are in the form of a reminiscence. Describes a Shoshoni Council with American Peace Commissioners in 1851 and the Indians' rejection of peace with their enemies, the Cheyennes and Blackfeet. The "Notes" show the chief's attitudes toward raiding and warfare and his participation in such events. The document is located with other Shoshoni materials at the Bancroft Library.

R. L. Nichols

359. James, Rhett S., ed. BRIGHAM YOUNG-CHIEF WASHAKIE INDIAN FARM NEGOTIATIONS, 1854-1857. *Ann. of Wyoming 1967 39(2): 245-256.* Presents a series of six letters from Brigham Young to Shoshoni Chief Washakie during the years 1854 to 1857. These demonstrate Brigham Young's desire to live peacefully with the Indians, as well as his realization that the Indians had to become farmers if they were to survive. Based on the Brigham Young Papers, Church Historian's Office, Salt Lake City, Office of Indian Affairs material in the National Archives, and published material; 39 notes.

R. L. Nichols

360. Stewart, Omer C. SHOSHONI HISTORY AND SOCIAL ORGANIZATION. *Idaho Yesterdays 1965 9(3): 2-5.* "A reinterpretation of Shoshoni culture since the coming of the horse." The author explains the three social groups of the Shoshoni: 1) those who rode horses and hunted for their living; 2) those who made their living by fishing; and 3) those who lived on roots and plants. Described is the geographical location of the tribe from the Wind River Range in Wyoming, southwest to Death Valley, California, between 1700 and 1870. The movements and composition of various tribes are analyzed through prominent chiefs and the economic activities of the people are discussed. 2 illus., 29 notes.

D. H. Swift

Ute

361. Benjamin, Peggy H. THE LAST OF CAPTAIN JACK. *Montana 1960 10(2): 22-31.* The Ute uprising in 1879, culminating in the murder of Agent Nathan C. Meeker and 11 others, was led by "Captain Jack," a sub-chief of the

White River band, and not to be confused with the Modoc Captain Jack. Less well known is Jack's part in the ambush massacre of Major Thomas T. Thornburgh's command just before the Meeker episode. Jack took refuge with the Arapahoe Indians near Lander, Wyoming. The next year he was killed by troops who surprised him in camp with a local cattleman's crew. This rancher, "Cap" Haskell, then age 20, recorded the event in his journal, the source of this account.

S. R. Davison

362. Johnson, Jerome W. MURDER ON THE UNCOMPAHGRE. *Colorado Mag. 1966 43(3): 209-224.* A discussion of a seemingly insignificant pair of murders which took place in Colorado in 1880 and had statewide repercussions. Before the murderers were brought to trial there was widespread fear of the possibility of an Indian war, agitated by the Utes in retaliation for the murder of the chief's son; the event had become an issue in the state election of 1880, and both the state and the federal government had become involved in a jurisdictional dispute which threatened to precipitate a clash between state militia and the U.S. Army. Illustrates the additional conflicts between the Indian and white man of the 1870's and 1880's, leading to lynch law justice, the exploitation of the Indian problem by politicians, and the constant encroachment on the Indian lands by the whites. Based mainly on newspapers published at the time, especially the *Denver Daily News;* illus., map, 53 notes.   R. Sexauer

363. Stewart, Omer C. UTE INDIANS: BEFORE AND AFTER WHITE CONTACT. *Utah Hist. Q. 1966 34(1): 38-61.* Reviews anthropological controversy regarding the origins, movements, and culture of the Ute Indians who lived in the Great Basin area of Colorado and Utah and then traces the developments among the Utes after white penetration of their tribal grounds beginning with Spanish contacts which were first reported in 1623. Based principally on the author's anthropological investigations and published studies of other anthropologists. Illus., map.   S. L. Jones

364. Walker, Don D., ed. COWBOYS, INDIANS & CAVALRY: A CATTLEMAN'S ACCOUNT OF THE FIGHTS OF 1884. *Utah Hist. Q. 1966 34(3): 255-262.* Contains an explanatory introduction and the text of a letter written by Harold Carlisle and published in the *Denver Republican* on 29 July 1884 describing a fight between several cattlemen and a group of Ute Indians near Durango, Colorado.   S. L. Jones

Ute, Moache

365. Taylor, Morris F. KA-NI-ACHE. *Colorado Mag. 1966 43(4): 275-302, 44(2): 139-161.* Part I. Surveys the origins of a skirmish between the Moache Utes under Ka-ni-ache and the U.S. Cavalry under Colonel A. J. Anderson at Trinidad on 3 October 1866. The author presents a history of the Moache tribe and a biographical sketch of Ka-ni-ache. He suggests that the chief cause of this skirmish was the raids the Moache, compelled by hunger, had been making. Illus., 19 notes. Part II. Traces the activities of Ka-ni-ache, the leading chief of the Moache Utes from 1866 until his death in 1880. Pressures for the removal of the

Utes to reservations were mounting, and, while a treaty for such a purpose was negotiated in 1868, the government did not have its way until 1877. Such questions as the size and location of the reservation and the terms of the treaty were constantly disputed. In 1874 a new treaty was made and the chiefs agreed to a reduction of their former claims. 7 illus., 141 notes.   I. W. Van Noppen

California Area

General

366. Bekeart, Philip Kendall. CALIFORNIA GUNSMITHS FOR THREE GENERATIONS. *Pacific Historian 1966 10(2): 4-14.* Frank Bekeart, of Flemish descent, migrated from London and was apprenticed to an American gunsmith, fought in the Mexican War, was wounded, came to gold rush California, panned gold, sold and repaired guns, and traded with the Indians in Coloma and San Francisco. By 1849 his son, Philip Bekeart, worked for E. T. Allen, first repairing then selling guns in the Santa Clara Valley. The third generation of gunsmiths is represented by the author who kept the family company going from 1913 through 1965. Illus., photos.   T. R. Cripps

367. Bowman, J. N. THE BIRTHDAYS OF THE CALIFORNIA MISSIONS. *The Americas 1964 20(3): 289-308.* "A critical and analytical study of the founding dates" of the 21 Franciscan Indian missions in California. In discussing the discrepancies that have arisen and the definition of "founding," the article offers a review of the normal procedures (military-political as well as ecclesiastical) followed in the establishment of the missions. From archival and other sources.   D. Bushnell

368. Burrus, Ernest J. KINO EN ROUTE TO SONORA: THE CONICARI LETTER. *Western Explorer 1964 3(2): 37-42.* The first published English translation of a letter (preserved in the Huntington Library, San Marino, California) sent from Conicari, Sonora, by Father Eusebio Francisco Kino, well-known Spanish missionary, to the Portuguese Duchess of Aveiro, wife of the Spanish Duke of Arcos and resident in Madrid. This was the last letter of Kino's extant correspondence with the duchess, who intervened repeatedly with the highest Spanish authorities to keep alive missionary activities among the Indian tribes of northwestern Mexico and Upper and Lower California. Introduction, 10 notes.   W. L. Bowers

369. Carranco, Lynwood. BRET HARTE IN UNION (1857-1860). *California Hist. Soc. Q. 1966 45(2): 99-112.* The three years (1857-60) Bret Harte spent in the town of Union (now Arcata, California) have been referred to as his lost years. He never cared to discuss these years in which he learned so much about writing

and of frontier life because of the tragic massacre of 26 February 1860 when a large number of peaceful Indians were brutally slain by a few whites who were never brought to trial. Harte, temporarily in charge of the local newspaper, bitterly attacked the perpetrators of the massacre, though not by name. Apparently the tide of opinion against Harte, as the author of the editorial, was strong enough to force him to leave Union. He profited by his experience there. 29 notes.

E. P. Stickney

370. Caughey, John Walton. CALIFORNIA IN THIRD DIMENSION. *Pacific Hist. R. 1959 28(2): 111-129.* Surveys California literature or "creative writing" from the Indians, as found by the Spaniards, to the present. The author shows how this literature adds a new dimension or insight into an understanding of California history by supplementing the work of more formal historians. In studying California "the addict of verse, the essay, and the novel would do well to read such history as is available, and the student of history neglects at his peril the works of literature."

R. Lowitt

371. Duckett, Margaret. BRET HARTE AND THE INDIANS OF NORTHERN CALIFORNIA. *Huntington Lib. Q. 1954 18(1): 59-83.* Francis Brett Harte's writings about the Indians reflect genuine knowledge and a courageous and thoughtful approach to the problem of relations between whites and Indians.

H. D. Jordan

372. Evans, William Edward. THE GARRA UPRISING: CONFLICT BETWEEN SAN DIEGO INDIANS AND SETTLERS IN 1851. *California Hist. Soc. Q. 1966 45(4): 339-349.* Sees the Garra uprising near San Diego in 1851 as an example of a fight for survival by the Indians in a primitive, highly competitive environment. The Anglo-American migration into California after 1849 was interpreted by the Indian as a threat to his culture. He responded accordingly. Antonio Garra chose to lead an uprising rather than pay a property tax to which all Southern California was opposed. This decision was unwise because there was a movement on foot to obtain the franchise for Christianized Indians. Had Garra acted otherwise "he might have prevented many deaths, and perhaps led the way to Indian suffrage in California." Based on material in the National Archives and newspapers; 33 notes.

E. P. Stickney

373. Fireman, Janet R. and Servín, Manuel P. MIGUEL COSTANSO: CALIFORNIA'S FORGOTTEN FOUNDER. *California Hist. Soc. Q. 1970 49(1): 3-19.* Costansó (1741-1814) was a military engineer who accompanied Junípero Serra and Gaspar de Portolá on the expedition to colonize Alta California in 1769. Costansó rendered service as a cartographer, and he was the first man to compose a map of San Francisco Bay. In later years, Costansó, an intelligent and enlightened servant of the Crown, offered plans and advice for the settlement of Alta California. These plans included integration of the Spanish and Indian societies, the importation of settlers under favorable inducements, and the training of the Indians by artisans. These suggestions, and Costansó's condemnation of Church ownership of large areas of land, drew opposition from the Franciscan clergy. Costansó also served his monarch through his work in designing fortifica-

tion, churches, and monuments; as an engineer he assisted in the project to supply water to Mexico City. In spite of his enormous contributions, Costansó has been almost entirely neglected by historians who have preferred perpetuating the Portolá-Serra viewpoints in the settlement of Alta California. Based on archival material, memoirs, contemporary documents, and secondary works; illus., photo, 57 notes.   A. Hoffman

374. Foreman, Louise. COME WITH ME TO THE CALIFORNIA HALL. *Masterkey 1969 43(4): 152-155.* Examines the California Hall of the Southwest Museum in Highland Park, California. The hall, at the north end of the lower floor of the museum, contains exhibits from many of California's 100 or more tribes, although the majority of the exhibits are from the Canaliño culture of Southern California. Photo.   C. N. Warren

375. Franklin, William E. THE RELIGIOUS ARDOR OF PETER H. BURNETT, CALIFORNIA'S FIRST AMERICAN GOVERNOR. *California Hist. Soc. Q. 1966 45(2): 125-131.* Traces the religious development of Peter Hardeman Burnett from his youth when he was a deist, through his 30's when he joined the Disciples of Christ Church, to the time he became a Catholic convert. After the massacre of 14 inhabitants of the Waiilatpu Mission in 1847, he defended his faith in answer to a scathing denunciation from the pulpit accusing certain Catholics of having incited the Indians to the barbarous massacre. 27 notes.
E. P. Stickney

376. Geiger, Maynard, O.F.M., ed. REPLY OF MISSION SAN GABRIEL TO THE QUESTIONNAIRE OF THE SPANISH GOVERNMENT IN 1812 CONCERNING THE NATIVE CULTURE OF THE CALIFORNIA MISSION INDIANS. *The Americas 1955 12(1): 77-84.* A report dated 28 June 1814 by the senior missionary of San Gabriel Mission dealing with the social and cultural habits and the religious and economic condition of the native Indian population, and describing the mission's evangelical efforts among the Indians of Southern California.   R. Mueller

377. Gould, Richard A. SEAGOING CANOES AMONG THE INDIANS OF NORTHWESTERN CALIFORNIA. *Ethnohist. 1968 15(1): 11-42.* Proves the existence of and describes in detail the redwood dugout seagoing canoe, its construction, role in the tribe, and general uses. Refers to the Yurok, Tolowa, Tututni, and Wiyot tribes. 7 notes, biblio.   R. S. Burns

378. Guest, Florian F. THE INDIAN POLICY UNDER FERMIN FRANCISCO DE LASUEN, CALIFORNIA'S SECOND FATHER PRESIDENT. *California Hist. Soc. Q. 1966 45(3): 195-219.* That the policy of the Spanish government was one of peace toward the California Indians is clear from the correspondence of the viceroys of New Spain and the governors of New Spain. These peaceful intentions are also illustrated in the matter of legal punishments for Indian delinquents and criminals. Unfortunately, Junípero Serra, Fermín Francisco de Lasuén and their successors followed the cruel practices of punish-

ment which were common in Europe and in New Spain for over two centuries but which the Enlightenment at home was at the time decrying. A crisis at San Francisco in 1796 showed that the Indians were overworked and underfed. Lasuén made two visits to investigate. He exonerated two missionaries (Danti and Landaeta) of crimes of which they had been accused but recommended more moderate punishment, lighter work, and cooked rations. Based chiefly on the Archive of California, Bancroft Library; the Archivo General de la Nación, Mexico; and Lasuén's writings; 88 notes.   E. P. Stickney

379. Halpin, Joseph. MUSICAL ACTIVITIES AND CEREMONIES AT MISSION SANTA CLARA DE ASIS. *California Hist. Q. 1971 50(1): 35-42.* One of the more prosperous missions in the California system, Santa Clara featured an Indian choir and orchestra. The Indians learned music from Father Magín Catalá and Father José Viader. They learned two-part and four-part singing and participated in the singing at Masses, religious festivals, and special services. Musical instruments included violins, small drums, triangles, and flutes. Following secularization, Mission Santa Clara de Asís declined rapidly; the Indians scattered, and most of the musical instruments were lost or stolen. Based on secondary sources; photo, 20 notes.   A. Hoffman

380. Heizer, R. F. HOW ACCURATE WERE CALIFORNIA INDIANS WITH THE BOW AND ARROW? *Masterkey 1970 44(3): 108-111.* Various investigators have searched early explorers' records, experimented with modern and ancient bows and arrows, and checked out surviving natives' prowess with their indigenous weapons to ascertain just how accurate the Indians were with the bow and arrow. Presents the findings of these investigators and answers the question. Chart, 2 notes.   C. N. Warren

381. Heizer, Robert F. ONE OF THE OLDEST KNOWN CALIFORNIA INDIAN BASKETS. *Masterkey 1968 42(2): 70-74.* Describes an oval coiled basket decorated with encircling rows of shell beads and red feathers which the author found in the Jos. Dombey collection housed in the Musée de l'Homme, Paris, in 1960. It is suggested that the basket came from the area between San Francisco and Bodega Bay, that it may have been made by a Pomo Indian or by any one of four other tribes, and that it was made earlier than 1785. Photo, 7 notes.   C. N. Warren

382. Hoopes, Chad L. REDICK MC KEE AND THE HUMBOLDT BAY REGION, 1851-1852. *California Hist. Soc. Q. 1970 49(3): 195-219.* McKee was one of the three Indian agents authorized to negotiate treaties with the California Indians. A niggardly Congress, white settlers, and ambiguous authorizations and instructions plagued McKee and his associates. McKee assumed the responsibility of negotiating with Indian tribes in northern California. He traveled to Humboldt Bay and sought to establish a reservation for the Eel River Indians, to protect the Indians from the settlers' demands. McKee found himself jammed between the needs of the Indians and the claims of the white settlers. A series of 18 treaties concluded by the three agents in 1851 established reservations. The U.S. Senate rejected these treaties on the grounds that the agents had granted

immense areas, including choice lands, to the Indians. Meanwhile, California launched a policy of extermination against the Indians. Finally a system of military posts in conjunction with Indian reservations was adopted. McKee's humanitarian efforts contrast with the attitudes of Governor John Bigler and several California legislators. Based on congressional and state documents and published sources; 62 notes. A. Hoffman

383. Hutchinson, C. Alan. THE MEXICAN GOVERNMENT AND THE MISSION INDIANS OF UPPER CALIFORNIA, 1821-1835. *The Americas 1964 21(4): 335-362.* Efforts to promote the development of California inevitably involved the status of the Indian missions, which had been adversely affected by the Mexican War of Independence but whose Indian charges provided the main labor force. Measures for gradual secularization, with a view to converting the Indians into independent farmers, were followed in 1833 by a law for full, immediate secularization. But the latter left unsettled the disposition of the mission lands, which became a subject of considerable confusion and debate. Based on a wide variety of primary and secondary sources; 126 notes. D. Bushnell

384. Jensen, Joan M. THE INDIAN LEGENDS OF MARIA ALTO. *Western Explorer 1965 3(3): 25-28.* Legends performed the function for the Indian that history performs for more civilized peoples. Thus, they give valuable insight into the world view of the Indian. Mary Elizabeth Johnson published 12 legends of the San Diego Indians in her book, *Indian Legends of the Wyomaca Mountains* (San Diego: Frye and Smith, 1914). The legends were told to her by Mary Alto, a member of that declining tribe. To Mary Johnson, these stories were "a revelation of the poetic instinct, the dramatic impulse, and the nobility of character hidden beneath the social mask of our primitive people," and they allowed a glimpse of the "inner shrine of their lives." Reproduces one of the legends, "The Old Woman's Whip" which explains how the birds and beasts received their major distinguishable physical characteristics. W. L. Bowers

385. Kibby, Leo P. CALIFORNIA, THE CIVIL WAR, AND THE INDIAN PROBLEM: AN ACCOUNT OF CALIFORNIA'S PARTICIPATION IN THE GREAT CONFLICT. *J. of the West 1965 4 (3): 377-410.* During the Civil War, when federal troops were withdrawn from western territories, President Lincoln authorized volunteers to be recruited to protect the vacated region. The California volunteers proceeded to Arizona and New Mexico where they performed valuable service. Units of the volunteers also were assigned to protect the overland route to California and others to protect supply lines from Indian uprisings and depredations. Three of every four volunteers spent the full period of enlistment in the struggle with the Indians. Peace was finally restored in late 1864 when a treaty was concluded. By October 1866 all California soldiers had been returned to civilian life. Based on official records and other published material. 205 notes, biblio. D. N. Brown

386. Kibby, Leo P. SOME ASPECTS OF CALIFORNIA'S MILITARY PROBLEMS DURING THE CIVIL WAR. *Civil War Hist. 1959 5(3): 251-262.* Examines the unique military problems of the state of California during the Civil

War. Though the state was not assigned a quota, there were numerous volunteers for the Union cause. California soldiers did not participate in any of the major battles of the war, but were concerned with a variety of assignments, all in the West. These assignments included 1) guarding overland mail routes against Indian attacks; 2) suppressing minority elements which supported directly or indirectly the Confederate cause; 3) preventing Confederate forces from gaining a foothold in the western territories and in California; and 4) relieving Union regular troops stationed at western outposts so that they might be reassigned to active duty in the main theaters of the war.   B. Waldstein

387. Kornweibel, Theodore, Jr. THE OCCUPATION OF SANTA CATALINA ISLAND DURING THE CIVIL WAR. *California Hist. Soc. Q. 1967 46(4): 345-357.* On 1 January 1864 federal troops occupied Santa Catalina Island, off the coast of Southern California, for the purpose of securing the island for use as an Indian reservation. The purpose was never announced; local opinion concluded that the action was taken to forestall a Confederate attempt to seize the island for a privateer base, and this unfounded idea continued to be repeated in history books. The author disproves the Confederate base theory and shows the series of circumstances that prevented the use of the island for an Indian reservation for tribes from the north. The War Department was cool toward the plan; accordingly the Department of the Interior, after sounding out the Bureau of Indian Affairs, which was negative, defeated the proposal. When it was certain that the island would not be used for a reservation, it was evacuated on 14 September 1864. By removing most of the population of miners from the island, the occupation "served only to prolong its isolation." Based largely on Army records; 45 notes.   E. P. Stickney

388. Marrant, Doris E. VARIATIONS ON A THEME: SOME NORTHERN CALIFORNIA INDIAN HORROR STORIES. *Western Folklore 1970 29(4): 257-267.* Discusses some of the means of expressing traditional beliefs and the problem encountered as story elements change from place to place and generation to generation. Studies Indians from all parts of Northern California. Within this framework, believes some conclusions may be drawn about the stability of belief systems. Uses common horror tales as the vehicle of study. Examines in detail six categories of horror tales. Notes the relationships between similar stories among different tribes. Concludes that the research tends to support the idea that the mythmaking process is one of a continual sorting of generally familiar materials. Based on secondary sources; 27 notes.   R. A. Trennert

389. Nunis, Doyce B., Jr. A CALIFORNIA GOLD RUSH LETTER FROM THE "HARTFORD COURANT." *Southern California Q. 1964 46(3): 265-279.* An anonymous letter dated 22 February 1850, printed in the 18 May 1850 issue of the *Hartford Courant.* It is an account of the writer's experiences in crossing the Colorado River, dealing with the Yuman Indians, crossing the "great American Desert" to Los Angeles, and journeying up the San Joaquin Valley to Stockton and San Francisco.   J. Jensen

390. Ziegler, Alan C. QUASI-AGRICULTURE IN NORTH-CENTRAL CALIFORNIA AND ITS EFFECT ON ABORIGINAL SOCIAL STRUCTURE. *Kroeber Anthrop. Soc. Papers 1968 38: 52-67.* In terms of the general welfare, quasi-agricultural acorn-salmon economies of north-central California seem to have been reasonably equivalent to proto- or semi-agricultural societies elsewhere. Manifestations of leisure time and resultant diversity of labor allowed by this type of existence are evident not only in the presence of highly specialized "non-vital" occupations but also in the apparent overelaboration of assignments in even the "vital" professions. Recognized competence in at least certain occupations placed the professional on a recognized but not sharply delineated higher social plane than unskilled workers, thus forming an incipient "middle class." Map, biblio.   C. N. Warren

By Tribe

Canaliño

391. Barthol, Johannes. A WESTERN EXPLORER'S GUIDE TO SAN MIGUEL ISLAND. *Western Explorer 1965 3(3): 3-24.* An encyclopedic discussion of a tiny windswept island, westernmost of the Santa Barbara Channel Islands which lie scattered off the coast of Southern California. Approximately 37 square miles of desolate beauty, San Miguel Island was discovered in 1542 by Juan Rodriguez Cabrillo, a Portuguese in the employ of Spain. The Canaliño Indians were the only inhabitants until the early 1800's when they moved to the mainland. For nearly 50 years the island was uninhabited, but in 1848 the United States acquired it from Mexico and between 1850 and 1946 leased it to cattle and sheep raisers. Since 1946 the U.S. Navy has owned the island. The author was an employee of one of the last lessees of the island and lived and worked there for some time. He describes in detail the history, physical features, and wildlife of the island.   W. L. Bowers

Chumash

392. Geiger, Maynard. FRAY ANTONIO RIPOLL'S DESCRIPTION OF THE CHUMASH REVOLT AT SANTA BARBARA IN 1824. *Southern California Q. 1970 52(4): 345-364.* A translation and edition of Franciscan missionary Antonio Ripoll's report (5 May 1824) to Vincente Francisco Sarría, acting president of the missions, concerning the Chumash Indian uprising at Santa Barbara Mission in late February 1824. The Indians, mistreated by the soldiers at the presidio, revolted against them rather than the missionaries. Ripoll's report reveals that he was a compassionate advocate of the Indians and was angry with the military authorities for creating the occasion for the uprising. Part of the document has been translated in Zephyrin Engelhardt's *Santa Barbara Mission,* but the second half, in which Ripoll gave his reactions to the uprising, was previously untranslated. Based on a copy of Ripoll's report in the Santa Barbara Mission Archive Library; 97 notes.   W. L. Bowers

393. McElrath, Clifford. THE LAST TOMOLO. *Noticias 1966 12(4): 1-4.* Tomolos were canoes made by Santa Barbara Channel Indians. The only canoes made by California Indians, their design was possibly influenced by the Aleuts. Planks were sewed together by thongs and then coated with tar. Traders along the channel coast and around Catalina and Santa Cruz Islands used these vessels. The author tells of an Indian who lived on Santa Cruz Island in the 1870's and used a tomolo, probably the last ever made, though he makes "no claim as to the historical correctness" of this story which he heard from older residents. Photo.

T. M. Condon

Gabrielino

394. Robinson, W. W. LOS ALAMITOS: THE INDIAN AND RANCHO PHASES. *California Hist. Soc. Q. 1966 45(1): 21-30.* Discusses the Indian and rancho phases of Los Alamitos, a seven and one half acre parcel within the city limits of Long Beach. It includes a charming house and garden dating from Spanish days and was the site of an important Indian village, a community sometimes called Pubu, of Shoshonean-speaking Gabrielino Indians who were fishermen. Father Geronimo Boascana, who served as missionary there from 1814 to 1826, wrote down their beliefs and traditions. In 1784 Manuel Perez Nieto of Sinaloa, Mexico, secured from Governor Pedro Fages a large land concession which included Los Alamitos. By 1790, Perez Nieto had settled in fertile land near Whittier, where he had large cattle operations. In a sense, the rancho period continued until 1952. Illus., 20 notes.   E. P. Stickney

Maidu

395. Gruber, Abraham. THE PATRICK RANCHERIA. *Masterkey 1963 37(1): 30-34.* Describes the Patrick Rancheria in Butte County, California, and its historically recorded use as a center for the Ghost Dance by the Maidu tribe. Based on a visit to the site and secondary historical records; 2 illus., biblio.

C. N. Warren

396. Riddle, Francis A. ETHNOGEOGRAPHY OF TWO MAIDU GROUPS. *Masterkey 1968.*
    I: THE SILOM MA'A MAIDU, 42(2): 44-52.
    II: THE TASAIDUM MAIDU, 42(3): 85-93.
    For one interested in the ethnology of a group, a basic familiarity with the ethnogeography is a primary requisite. To know their village, camp, cemetery, and physiography place-names and locations allows the investigator a base line to which all his other data are ultimately referrable. This also applies to the archaeologist who eagerly utilizes information of houses, period of occupation, and like information. Such data are useful in his probe into the full prehistoric period of the group. The author shows in these two articles just how useful charting the ethnogeography of an area can be. Data were obtained from native informants. 2 maps, 8 photos.   C. N. Warren

Miwok

397. Colley, Charles C. THE MISSIONIZATION OF THE COAST MIWOK INDIANS OF CALIFORNIA. *California Hist. Soc. Q. 1970 49(2): 143-162.* An account of the impact of Spanish civilization upon the Miwok Indians. First contacted by the Cermenño expedition in 1595, the Coast Miwok were among the most accessible of the California Indians to missionary work. The Mission San Francisco de Asís, established in 1776, served as an important base for Christianizing northern California Indians. The experiences of the Coast Miwok with mission life were mostly negative. Their language, culture, and freedom were ignored by the padres, who sought to impose an inhibiting, rigid code of Christian society upon them. Lashing was a frequent method of punishment. Mortality among the Coast Miwok ran high and many Indians became "fugitives" from the missions. Venereal disease was also spread. By the end of the mission period the Coast Miwok, the northern California tribe most exposed to the practices of the mission system, was decimated. Based on anthropological and historical writings; illus., map, 70 notes.   A. Hoffman

Tolowa

398. Gould, Richard A. INDIAN AND WHITE VERSIONS OF "THE BURNT RANCH MASSACRE": A STUDY IN COMPARATIVE ETHNOHISTORY. *J. of the Folklore Inst. 1966 3(1): 30-42.* A comparison of a white account of an Indian massacre in northwestern California with several accounts gathered from Tolowa Indians who had heard of the "massacre" when very young reveals little "objective" history but is evidence that historians select "the happenings and impressions which had meaning in the light of the values and attitudes of their respective cultures." 11 notes.   J. C. Crowe

399. Gould, Richard A. THE WEALTH QUEST AMONG THE TOLOWA INDIANS OF NORTHWESTERN CALIFORNIA. *Pro. of the Am. Phil. Soc. 1966 110(1): 67-89.* Analyzes the quest for wealth exhibited by the Tolowa Indians of northwestern California. Noting that these efforts revolved primarily around the acquisition and disposal of women, the author treats: Tolowa subsistence, division of labor, the household, "treasures" as capital, trade, fines, inheritance, gambling, and prestige. The operations of this seeking for wealth were significantly different from those suggested by earlier commentators. Essentially, Tolowa "treasures" were all-purpose money, with female labor providing the link between the subsistence and prestige areas of the economy. Drawn largely from secondary works and personal interviews; 56 notes, appendix, and biblio.
                                                                    W. G. Morgan

Southwest Area

General

400. Avillo, Philip J., Jr. FORT MOJAVE: OUTPOST ON THE UPPER COLORADO. *J. of Arizona Hist. 1970 11(2): 77-100.* The Mexican War and the discovery of gold in California inspired a heavy migration from the eastern United States to the Southwest and the Pacific Coast. This necessitated protection of the emigrants from the hostile Indians and intensified the need for adequate roads. Numerous army posts were soon established throughout the Southwest to guard the routes of travel. One of these, Fort Mojave, Arizona, was founded in 1859 along a wagon route from Fort Defiance, New Mexico, at a crossing of the Colorado River from Arizona into California to the north of Needles. By 1865, with the Indians generally pacified and with the road to California well established, Fort Mojave had virtually fulfilled its purpose. Life at the post became very uneventful and settlers lived unmolested in the vicinity. The army abandoned the fort in 1890. 3 illus., map, 67 notes.   D. L. Smith

401. Ayres, J. E. AN EARLY HISTORIC BURIAL FROM THE VILLAGE OF BAC. *Kiva 1970 36(2): 44-48.* "In February, 1970 a burial was found in the village of Bac on the San Xavier Indian Reservation. Of special interest was the discovery of a Hopi polychrome bowl included as part of the burial goods. The bowl dates about A.D. 1700. The presence of this bowl indicates some type of trading relations between the Indians of northern and southern Arizona at that time."   J

402. Brand, Donald D. THE EARLY HISTORY OF THE RANGE CATTLE INDUSTRY IN NORTHERN MEXICO. *Agric. Hist. 1961 35(3): 132-139.* The range cattle industry in northern Mexico began with the settlement of the region by Spanish ranchers moving out of the central Mexican region after the middle of the 16th century. Great herds of Spanish cattle were established by ranchers and missions as far north as California, New Mexico and Texas. Revolutions and Indian raids caused temporary setbacks, but herds of tens of thousands of cattle were often found from the 16th to the 20th century. New ranching methods have been introduced into the northern Mexican states in the 20th century.   W. D. Rasmussen

403. Brinckerhoff, Sidney B. "STEADFAST" GREGG IN ARIZONA. *Arizoniana 1964 5(2): 31-37.* Following service with General Winfield Scott during the Mexican War and with a cavalry brigade in the Army of the Potomac, Colonel J. Irvin Gregg came to Arizona Territory as commander of the 8th Cavalry. Here he became measurably involved in Indian affairs and campaigns in the Fort Whipple area and, subsequently, at Churchill Barracks, Nevada.   W. Unrau

404. Chapman, Hank and Chapman, Toni. MIDAS OF NEW MEXICO. *Am. West 1971 8(1): 4-9, 62-63.* After a Jesuit education as a boy, an informal apprenticeship in his grandfather's fur and pelt shop in St. Louis, and two years with the American Fur Company, Lucien Bonaparte Maxwell (ca. 1818-75) went to Taos, New Mexico, in 1841 as a trapper. He signed on with three Charles Frémont expeditions as a hunter and married into the local Beaubien family. The Miranda and Beaubien families had received a vaguely described land grant in northeastern New Mexico from the Mexican governor. Maxwell's father-in-law stocked a ranch and gave him permission to use it as the base for a trading post and settlement. His trading post attracted Indians, served travelers on the Santa Fe Trail, and supplied provisions to American troops. He bought the Miranda share of the grant and, when his father-in-law died, bought out the other Beaubien heirs. Now named "Cimarron," the baronial Maxwell colony flourished and became the scene of a considerable gold rush. Selling the grant in 1870, Maxwell turned to banking for a few years and then went back to ranching until his death in 1875. The Maxwell Land Grant contained 1,714,764 acres, the largest individually owned tract in the continent. 7 illus., map, biblio. note.

D. L. Smith

405. Chavez, Fr. Angelico. THE HOLY MAN OF ZIA. *New Mexico Hist. R. 1965 40(4): 309-318.* Biographical sketch of Fray Bernardo de Marta, for some years minister of Zia Pueblo, an Indian reservation. A Catalan by birth, he and his brother Juan joined the Franciscan Providence of Santiago in 1597, were ordained, and decided to go to the Indies. They arrived in the New World in 1606, where Fray Juan was allowed to proceed to the Far East. Fray Bernardo, however, was ordered to remain in America where he was in charge, successively, of Santo Domingo (a reservation), Galisteo, and finally of Zia. 16 notes.

D. F. Henderson

406. Clark, Laverne Harrell. EARLY HORSE TRAPPINGS OF THE NAVAJO AND APACHE INDIANS. *Arizona and the West 1963 5(3): 233-248.* Navajo and Apache Indians were proud horsemen. From the early 17th century, when they began to acquire their horses in raids from Spaniards, Mexicans, Anglo-Americans, and other Indians, they began to work with their own resources to provide trappings for the horses by blending imitation and ingenuity. Ropes were made of rawhide, buckskin, horsehair, wool, or yucca leaves. Bridles were fashioned from animal skins. Metal bits came later. Silversmithing developed as an ancillary skill for decorative purposes. The saddles were closely patterned after the popular Spanish and Mexican ones in use in the Southwest. Saddle blankets were either woven by Navajo women or serapes acquired in Mexico were used. Saddlebags were made from skins and were frequently decorated with beadwork. Boots were fashioned from hides to protect the hoofs. Not until late in the prereservation period did the Indians learn to work metal to copy the horseshoes used by whites. Even today a splendid set of trappings is a prestige factor for a Navajo or Apache. Based on monographic studies and published source material; illus., 60 notes.

D. L. Smith

407. Conrad, David E. THE WHIPPLE EXPEDITION IN ARIZONA, 1853-1854. *Arizona and the West 1969 11(2): 147-178.* From mid-July 1853 to late March 1854, Lieutenant Amiel Weeks Whipple conducted an exploring and survey expedition from Fort Smith, Arkansas, to Los Angeles, California, along the 35th parallel. A feasible transcontinental rail route was the principal object of the expedition, although a substantial amount of ethnological and scientific data was an important by-product. The party moved across present Arizona during the months of December, January, and February, which proved to be a challenging and trying experience. U.S. Highway 66 and the Santa Fe Railroad have approximated the Whipple route across the Southwest, especially in Arizona. Scientists on the expedition named scores of new plant and animal species and geological formations. The report made on the Indian tribes that were encountered was long considered as a standard reference. 5 illus., map, 58 notes.

D. L. Smith

408. Dobyns, Henry F. INDIAN EXTINCTION IN THE MIDDLE SANTA CRUZ RIVER VALLEY, ARIZONA. *New Mexico Hist. R. 1963 38(2): 163-181.* Attempts to explain the disappearance of the native Indian population in the middle Santa Cruz River Valley between 1700 and 1850. Whereas there were dozens of villages in the first quarter of the 18th century, there was only one at the end of the century. Two causes were pre-eminent: Apache raids and disease.

D. F. Henderson

409. Faulk, Odie B. and Brinckerhoff, Sidney B. SOLDIERING AT THE END OF THE WORLD. *Am. West 1966 3(3): 28-37.* The mission, the major agency of frontier colonization in the Spanish push northward from Mexico City into the American Southwest, had failed to civilize, Hispanicize, and Christianize the Indians. The Royal Regulation of Presidios in 1772 inaugurated a new program intended to bring about pacification of the natives by force of arms here in the region often referred to as *el fin del mundo* the end of the world. The equipment, living conditions, discipline, morale, and fighting techniques of the less than a thousand soldiers stationed in 15 to 20 presidios scattered throughout the northern tier of provinces of New Spain designated as the Interior Provinces, an area larger than most of Europe, are described and discussed. All the necessary ingredients were present for a successful military pacification of the Indians, but Spanish officials failed to make proper use of them. This policy was replaced by another in 1786. Illus., biblio., note.   D. L. Smith

410. Fraser, James H. INDIAN MISSION PRINTING IN NEW MEXICO: A BIBLIOGRAPHY. *New Mexico Hist. R. 1968 43(4): 311-318.* Although the first missionary activity in New Mexico can be dated from approximately 1539, not until 1877 was mission printing produced. John Menaul, a Presbyterian missionary, "must be given credit for being the first missionary-linguist-printer" in New Mexico. The bibliography, containing 17 entries, is divided into three language groups. 13 notes.   D. F. Henderson

411. Gilles, Albert S., Sr. THE SOUTHWESTERN INDIAN AND HIS DRUGS. *Southwest R. 1970 55(2): 196-203.* Traces the use of stimulants and

sedatives among American Indians, including various liquors, tobacco, mescal, peyote, jimsonweed, locoweed, and the narcotic mushroom *teonanácatl*. Although various tribes are mentioned, emphasis is placed on the Comanche.

D. F. Henderson

412. Green, Fletcher M. JAMES S. CALHOUN: PIONEER GEORGIA LEADER AND FIRST GOVERNOR OF NEW MEXICO. *Georgia Hist. Q. 1955 39(4): 309-347.* Reviews the career of the Georgia legislator (1802-52), who was appointed Indian agent and first territorial governor of New Mexico.

C. F. Latour

413. Hagemann, E. R., ed. "THOU ART THE MAN": AN ADDRESS ON THE INDIAN QUESTION IN 1892 BY COLONEL GEORGE BLISS SANFORD. *J. of Arizona Hist. 1968 9(1): 33-38.* After a distinguished career with the Sixth Cavalry, serving both in the Civil War and on the western frontier, Colonel Sanford retired and gave this address to the Litchfield Scientific Association in the winter of 1892. In this speech, Colonel Sanford described the customs and life patterns of the Pima and Apache Indians. He felt strongly that the Indians, especially the Pima who had long been allies of the Americans, had become the innocent victims of white aggression. He added that it was not only the government, but also the people of the United States who, in a very real sense, broke treaties and displaced the Indians. He closed his address by appealing for justice for the Indian and "an equal share" in this country. Based on a privately owned manuscript; 7 notes.

R. J. Roske

414. Haines, Francis. HOW THE INDIAN GOT THE HORSE. *Am. Heritage 1964 15(2): 16-21, 78-81.* Legend has it that the Indian acquired the horse by capturing strays from De Soto or Coronado or both. The author shows why this cannot be true and then proposes that the Indians acquired them from the Spaniards by various means later, in the 17th century. Illus.

C. R. Allen, Jr.

415. Heaston, Michael D. THE GOVERNOR AND THE INDIAN AGENT: 1855-1857. *New Mexico Hist. R. 1970 45(2): 137-146.* Analyzes the conflict between territorial governor David Meriwether and one of three Indian agents for the territory, Abraham G. Mayers. Strife developed over expenses, territorial politics, and supplies for the Indians. Mayers eventually took his complaints to Washington, D.C., without success. Based primarily on letters received by the Office of Indian Affairs, 1849-80, in the National Archives; 34 notes.

D. F. Henderson

416. Hogan, William F. JOSEPH SEXTON HOPLEY, DISPENSER OF JUSTICE. *Arizoniana 1963 4(3): 41-45.* Hopley "traversed Arizona terrain during its territorial years as a United States cavalryman, rancher, and lawman." A 15-year veteran of Indian warfare, he was discharged at Tucson in 1885. He began a business life as a dairyman and worked at cattle raising 30 miles east of Tucson.

For eight years he carried the mails operating a mail stage and express line. As marshal of Tucson for four terms, he effectively enforced antigambling legislation and new antiliquor laws. Documented; illus.   E. P. Stickney

417. Horgan, Paul. CHURCHMAN OF THE DESERT. *Am. Heritage 1957 8(6): 30-35, 99-101*. Describes the career of Archbishop John Baptist Lamy (originally Jean Baptist l'Amy), 1814-88, of Santa Fe, as he contended with "Indians, ignorance, and a recalcitrant clergy" in the vast territory which now forms part of Nevada, about one fourth of Colorado, and most of Arizona and New Mexico. Illus.   C. R. Allen, Jr.

418. Huscher, Harold A. SALT TRADERS OF CIBOLA. *Great Plains J. 1966 5(2): 73-83*. Discusses the identification of the Indian tribes in the Puebloan area of the American Southwest at the opening of the historic period. The generic names for salt, buffalo, trade, and trader are key words for identifying old trade routes, commodities traded, and contacts between peoples. Biblio.
                                                                            O. H. Zabel

419. Karnes, Thomas L. GILPIN'S VOLUNTEERS ON THE SANTA FE TRAIL. *Kansas Hist. Q. 1964 30(1): 1-14*. The Mexican War caused a break-down of defense on the Santa Fe Trail, but Major William Gilpin organized a "Separate Battalion of Missouri Volunteers" to restore peace along the trail. Gilpin was successful in keeping the northern tribes from cooperation with the southern, but he was unable to do more than postpone the Indian struggles for a short time. The entire operation in 1847-48 was characterized by dishonest and humorous events. Many of Gilpin's subordinates proved thoroughly unreliable; there were accusations of murder, horse stealing and indiscipline. One man even enrolled his mistress as a "private." Based on material in the National Archives.
                                                                            W. F. Zornow

420. Kent, H. R., ed. BISHOP LAY'S PROPOSED MISSIONARY JOURNEY TO NEW MEXICO. *Hist. Mag. of the Protestant Episcopal Church 1966 35(1): 99-103*. Bishop Henry Champlin Lay (1823-85) was consecrated missionary bishop of the Southwest in 1859. His territory included Arkansas, Indian Terri-tory, and "parts adjacent." Keenly interested in the New Mexican portion of his vast district, Lay sought the assistance of fellow Episcopal clergymen in planning an 1861 exploration of New Mexico and Arizona. The Civil War put an end to his proposed journey.   E. G. Roddy

421. Kessell, John L. DOCUMENTS OF ARIZONA HISTORY: A PER-SONAL NOTE FROM TUMACACORI, 1825. *J. of Arizona Hist. 1965 6(3): 147-151*. Tumacacori, now a national monument, was one of eight pioneer mis-sions in the Pimeria Alta established by the Franciscan order. Quoted here is a letter from Fray Ramon Liberos, then serving as resident missionary, to an unknown friend, dated 20 November 1825. The letter comments on church and

Indian affairs and is believed to be the last letter from the last Franciscan at the mission. Introduction and 20 notes, many from Spanish and Mexican archives.

J. D. Filipiak

422. Kessell, John L. SAN JOSE DE TUMACACORI—1773: A FRANCISCAN REPORTS FROM ARIZONA. *Arizona and the West 1964 6(4): 303-312.* Franciscan Father Bartholomé Ximeno was sent as a missionary to the Pima Indians in Pimería Alta on the far northwestern frontier of New Spain and stationed at Tumacacori in present southern Arizona. His tenure there was for a little over a year. In 1773 he made a report of conditions at Tumacacori. It is also a commentary on the Apache-harrassed frontier of northwestern New Spain. Based on microfilm copy, University of Arizona Library, facsimile Library, and reproduction of a 1772 Ximeno burial record; map, 23 notes.

D. L. Smith

423. Knowlton, Clark S. CHANGING SPANISH-AMERICAN VILLAGES OF NORTHERN NEW MEXICO. *Sociol. and Social Res. 1969 53(4): 455-474.* "The Spanish Americans of northern New Mexico and southern Colorado living in isolation from other European groups for almost three hundred years developed a unique rural farm village culture based upon subsistence agriculture, pastoral activities, barter, handicrafts, and trade with the Indians."

J

424. McConnell, Virginia. CAPTAIN BAKER AND THE SAN JUAN HUMBUG. *Colorado Mag. 1971 48(1): 59-75.* Describes the operations of Captain Charles Baker as he promoted expeditions into the San Juan, Colorado, region with reports of gold and good agricultural lands. Various parties entered the wilderness of the San Juan in the fall and winter of 1860-61, only to be disappointed. Feelings rose against Baker. In the fall of 1861 he joined the Confederate Army. After the war, in 1867, Baker reportedly was killed by Indians (or perhaps by a member of one of his former expeditions) along the Colorado River. In the 1870's rich ores were found in the San Juan region. Baker, however, had not discovered them, "he was merely a promoter." 4 photos, map, 70 notes.

O. H. Zabel

425. McNitt, Frank. FORT SUMNER: A STUDY IN ORIGINS. *New Mexico Hist. R. 1970 45(2): 101-117.* Discusses the reasons a military post was established at Bosque Redondo (on the Pecos river), and the reasons that post was made the center of a reservation for Navaho and Apache Indians. Various military surveys are analyzed, including those by Brevet Colonel John Munroe in 1850 and Brevet Major James H. Carleton in 1852 and 1854. A post was finally established at the Bosque in November 1862. In 1863, Carleton, now a general and commander of the Military Department of New Mexico, converted the post into a reservation for 400 Apache, which accommodated over 40 thousand Navaho the following year. Based on various U.S. Army Records in the National Archives; 29 notes.

D. F. Henderson

426. Meyer, Roy W. THE WESTERN FICTION OF MAYNE REID. *Western Am. Literature 1968 3(2): 115-132.* With references to over a dozen of Thomas Mayne Reid's (1818-83) nearly 60 novels, the author describes the Irishman's writings about the American Southwest as less than literary. His adventure stories all had similar plot structure. His three major character types were mountain men, Indians, and Mexicans, usually in Southwestern American or Mexican settings. He was obviously influenced by James Fenimore Cooper and many similarities are found to the works of Josiah Gregg. Even though Reid's wife insists in a biography of her husband that he was personally familiar with the areas about which he wrote, it is suggested that Reid at least borrowed from many others to supplement his own accounts, which sometimes lacked in geographic factuality. His three virtues lie in a vivid narration of action, lucid and direct language, and a fairly good view of the Southwest. Though not a literary giant, Reid did show a genuine enthusiasm for the Southwest in his writings. 32 notes.

S. L. McNeel

427. Moorman, Donald R. HOLM O. BURSUM, SHERIFF 1894. *New Mexico Hist. R. 1964 39(4): 333-344.* Evidently a chapter from the author's doctoral dissertation, "A Political Biography of Holm O. Bursum, 1899-1924," relates in detail the three principal problems of a New Mexican territorial sheriff: law enforcement, finances, and politics. The most taxing was law enforcement. The sheriff not only had to deal with ordinary criminals, but also with Indian depredations. Financially the sheriff had difficulty collecting rewards, obtaining just claims from the territorial legislature for mileage, and extracting money from the federal government for prisoners kept in the county's jail. The sheriff was also an important political figure; Bursum used the position as a stepping stone into the U.S. Senate.

D. F. Henderson

428. Moseley, M. Edward. THE DISCOVERY AND DEFINITION OF BAS-KETMAKER: 1890-1914. *Masterkey 1966 40(4): 140-154.* Gives the history of the early exploration and exploitation of the Four Corners region of the Southwest by turn-of-the-century antiquarians and commercial relic-hunters. Cites the earliest records available, which, in their own time, led to the differentiation between Pueblo and Basketmaker cultures by both the explorer-collectors themselves and later by trained professional investigators. 3 notes, biblio.

C. N. Warren

429. Murphy, Lawrence R. RECONSTRUCTION IN NEW MEXICO. *New Mexico Hist. R. 1968 43(2): 99-115.* Analyzes and evaluates Reconstruction activities in New Mexico "as they affected the abolition of Indian slavery and debt peonage." Although various attempts were made to end slavery—the Civil Rights Bill of 1866, the 13th amendment, and special acts concerning New Mexico—they encountered determined and effective opposition. After Reconstruction, "with economic and social change, involuntary servitude in New Mexico disappeared." Based chiefly on newspapers and Territorial Papers of the U.S. Senate, New Mexico, NA-RG 46; 63 notes.

D. F. Henderson

430. Rasch, Philip J. THE TULAROSA DITCH WAR. *New Mexico Hist. R. 1968 43(3): 229-235.* Bordering the eastern marches of the White Sands, the small village of Tularosa (first settled in 1858) had only one problem—water. The only water supply was the Tularosa River, and attempts to dam the stream and use the water for irrigation were constant sources of irritation. Several minor clashes between the villages and neighboring Indians and ranchers occurred in the 1870's. The final clash occurred in 1881 when several employees from the James West ranch annihilated a posse attempting to arrest them. The ranchhands were eventually arrested, indicted, but never convicted. 19 notes.   D. F. Henderson

431. Robinson, William J. EXCAVATIONS AT SAN XAVIER DEL BAC, 1958. *Kiva 1963 29(2): 35-57.* "Excavations at the historic Franciscan Mission of San Xavier [Arizona] revealed an architectural complex which represented workshops related to the construction of the present mission building. The paucity of artifacts and fragility of construction indicate a temporary structure which may have been intentionally destroyed at the completion of the mission church ca. AD 1796."   J

432. Rusho, W. L. LIVING HISTORY AT LEE'S FERRY. *J. of the West 1968 7(1): 64-75.* A glimpse at the history of the West through the people (missionary, cowboy, Indian, outlaw, lawman, trader, settler, and government scientist) who have used Lee's Ferry, Arizona, to cross the Colorado River. Based on narratives of western expeditions and secondary sources; illus., map, 33 notes.   E. A. Erickson

433. Schroeder, Albert H. SHIFTING FOR SURVIVAL IN THE SPANISH SOUTHWEST. *New Mexico Hist. R. 1968 43(4): 291-310.* Discusses Indian population shifts in New Mexico from the 17th to the 19th centuries and concludes that the Indian territories and pueblos shifted, contracted, or expanded not because of the Spanish intrusion but because of hostilities "(many probably originating in prehistoric times) between Indian groups." 5 maps, 53 notes.   D. F. Henderson

434. Smith, R. A. INDIANS IN AMERICAN-MEXICAN RELATIONS BEFORE THE WAR OF 1846. *Hispanic Am. Hist. R. 1963 43(1): 34-64.* Detailed accounts of Apache, Navaho, Ute, Comanche, and Kiowa Indian raids into northern Mexico in the 1830's and 1840's. The author carefully traces the plunder trails used by the Indian tribes, and discusses the Indian strategy of capturing horses, other animals, and women and children. As treaties signed with the Indians were not honored, it is shown that the Mexican federal and state governments could evolve no more effective solution to the problem than to resort to the Spanish colonial practice of providing payment for Indian scalps. The raids increased in severity in the early 1840's as the Indians in general, and the Comanches in particular, took advantage of worsening relations between Mexico and the United States. No solution had been found when war came in 1846.   B. B. Solnick

435. Smith, Ralph A. THE SCALP HUNTER IN THE BORDERLANDS, 1835-1850. *Arizona and the West 1964 6(1): 5-22.* From the late 18th century Apache and Comanche Indians crossed the present U.S.-Mexico boundary to terrorize much of northern Mexico. Destruction of life and property was probably greater in the 1840's than in any other decade. Over 10 major plunder trails the marauders raided and carried the stolen livestock and other loot. The Mexican states of Sonora, Chihuahua, Coahuila, and Durango launched extensive scalp bounty systems to eliminate the raiders or to cow them into a cessation of their activities. The scalp industry boomed, especially as some unemployed Americans during the Panic of 1837 seized this opportunity for quick riches. James "Don Santiago" Kirker was the most famous of these entrepreneurs, making a systematic business out of it, even working at times for the Indians against the Mexicans. There was a reward of several thousands of dollars posted a number of times for Kirker's scalp. Ironically, during the Mexican War when Mexican authorities were unable to pursue the bounty system because of involvements with American armies, the Yankee enemy gave the Mexican countryside more security from the Indians than it had had for many years. When not battling Mexicans the Americans found sport in fighting the Indian marauders. Although Mexico continued to have troubles with these Indians until the 1880's, the scalp bounty industry phase ended almost completely in the spring of 1850. The source of supply had been seriously decimated and "unethical" practices were making it unhealthy for American bounty hunters. Illus., map, 41 notes.   D. L. Smith

436. Tanner, Clara Lee. PAPAGO BURDEN BASKETS IN THE ARIZONA STATE MUSEUM. *Kiva 1965 30(3): 57-76.* "Keehos (kiahas) are burden baskets formerly made and used by Papago and Pima Indians of southern Arizona. All-over and generally four-part designs were produced in the lace-like coil-without-foundation weave; these patterns were emphasized by rubbing red and blue coloring over them. Desert plants supplied materials for this all-purpose carrying basket."   J

437. Taylor, Morris F. CAMPAIGNS AGAINST THE JICARILLA APACHE, 1855. *New Mexico Hist. R. 1970 45(2): 119-136.* Describes the spring 1855 campaign against the Moache Ute and the Jicarilla Apache Indians. Colonel Thomas T. Fauntleroy, First Dragoons (U.S. Army), was given command of the campaign and was assisted by both regular army troops and a battalion of New Mexican Volunteers under the command of Lieutenant Colonel Ceran St. Vrain. St. Vrain's volunteers never inflicted a defeat on the Jicarilla of sufficient certitude to end their depredations. Colonel Fauntleroy and his mixed force, however, dealt the Moache Ute heavy blows so that they quickly became peaceful. Treaties were eventually signed with both Indian groups, but were not ratified by the U.S. Senate. 59 notes.   D. F. Henderson

438. Thrapp, Dan L. DAN O'LEARY, ARIZONA SCOUT: A VIGNETTE. *Arizona and the West 1965 7(4): 287-298.* Dan O'Leary's youth and last days are shrouded in mystery and obscurity. During his prime, however, he was an outstanding figure of the Southwest. Arriving in Arizona sometime in the 1850's or 1860's, he acquired guide and scout experience, probably for the Army. He

scouted for the Army against hostile Indians, was a guide to a railroad survey across northern Arizona, freighted for the Army and local merchants, piloted wagon trains through dangerous areas, tracked Indian thieves, became a friend and confidante of unfortunate Indians, probably named Tombstone, and traveled over much of the Southwest. Many of these items can be authenticated, although some of the stories about O'Leary are probably legend. 38 notes.

D. L. Smith

439. Thrapp, Dan L. THE "MARRIAGE" OF AL SIEBER. *J. of Arizona Hist. 1970 11(3): 175-178.* In his biography of Al Sieber, a famous Indian scout of Arizona, the author asserted that Sieber succeeded so well with the Indians because "he left their women alone." In the 1960's, progeny of Al Sieber by Apache women began to cast doubt on the author's assertion. To his satisfaction, however, he has now established that the Sieber children were offspring of a Yavapai Al Sieber. The Indian was probably an orphan raised by the famous bachelor scout, and probably took the scout's name as his own. 6 notes.

D. L. Smith

440. Utley, Robert M., ed. CAPTAIN JOHN POPE'S PLAN OF 1853 FOR THE FRONTIER DEFENSE OF NEW MEXICO. *Arizona and the West 1963 5(2): 149-163.* Brevet Captain John Pope of the Corps of Topographical Engineers worked on mapping missions, surveying boundaries, and making railroad surveys on the western military scene during the 1850's. After more than two years in New Mexico he was so concerned with the Indian problems that plagued the territory that he formulated an unsolicited plan to solve them. His observations were "acute" and his solutions were "well-reasoned." Pope's recommendations concerning communications, defense, deployment of troops, relations with the Indians, and other details were never adopted. Map, 26 notes.

D. L. Smith

441. Vigness, David M. INDIAN RAIDS ON THE LOWER RIO GRANDE, 1836-1837. *Southwestern Hist. Q. 1955 59(1): 14-23.* Describes Indian raids in southern Texas and northern Mexico during the early days of the Republic of Texas and traces efforts to defend against them.

J. A. Hudson

442. Vivian, R. Gwinn. AN ARCHAEOLOGICAL SURVEY OF THE LOWER GILA RIVER, ARIZONA. *Kiva 1965 30(4): 95-146.* "During January and February 1964, an archaeological survey of the Lower Gila River was undertaken by the Arizona State Museum to locate sites endangered by future Gila River channel alterations. The 85 sites located in the survey reflected occupation in the river valley by several culturally distinct groups. Anglo American, modern Papago, historic Western Yavapai, historic and prehistoric Yuman, and prehistoric Hohokam sites were represented."

J

443. Weber, Francis J. ARIZONA CATHOLICISM IN 1878: A REPORT BY JOHN BAPTISTE SALPOINTE. *J. of Arizona Hist. 1968 9(3): 119-139.* Salpointe was a French-born missionary who came to the West eight years after his

ordination as a priest. He was sent in September 1868 to the newly established Vicariate Apostolic of Arizona (which then included a small portion of southern New Mexico and west Texas). After 10 years of service, Salpointe, then a titular bishop, prepared a report on the state of Arizona Catholicism. In his survey of the Church in Arizona, Salpointe reported that missionary activity by the Jesuits had begun in the latter years of the 17th century. This promising beginning was swept away by a great Indian rebellion which occurred in the mid-18th century. Before the Jesuit missionaries could rebuild their missions, as was done in other Spanish colonies at that time, they were banished by order of the crown. Their successors, the Franciscans, made a great deal of progress until the 1820's. At that time, when Mexico won its independence from Spain, the missionaries had to take an oath of allegiance to the new state or leave. All the missionaries in Arizona elected to go. As a result, they could not be replaced and the missions decayed. When the United States took possession of Arizona, there was a period when Church activities were greatly neglected. By 1864 only San Xavier del Bac remained open for religious services. Consequently, Pope Pius IX created the Vicariate Apostolic of Arizona. There then followed a period of rapid growth in both Catholic population and church construction. Based largely on Salpointe's report in the archives of the Archdiocese of Los Angeles; 51 notes.

R. J. Roske

444. Whilden, Charles E. LETTERS FROM A SANTA FE ARMY CLERK, 1855-1856. *New Mexico Hist. R. 1965 40(2): 141-164.* Seven letters from Charles E. Whilden, clerk in the Commissary Department, Third Infantry, to his brother and sister-in-law, William G. and Ellen Whilden of Charleston, South Carolina. The letters "describe the exciting experiences Charles Whilden had with the wagon train on the way west—inquisitive Indian chiefs, stampeding cattle, and prairie fire—and paints a clear picture of a relatively quiet but interesting existence in the city of Santa Fe."

D. F. Henderson

By Tribe
Apache [1]

445. Brinckerhoff, Sidney B. THE LAST YEARS OF SPANISH ARIZONA, 1786-1821. *Arizona and the West 1967 9(1): 5-20.* The efforts of the Spanish to terminate the expanding war with the Apache in Arizona and northern Sonora were discouraging. Not infrequently the undermanned Spanish garrisons along the northern frontier were forced on the defensive. A new policy was inaugurated in 1786 designed to break the Apache will to resist and to make them dependent on the Spanish. Strong, coordinated, and continued military pressure with peace rewarded with gifts, food, and supplies, it was hoped, would induce the Indians to settle on reservations near the presidios. Agricultural pursuits, liquor, and antiquated firearms should corrupt them and keep them under control. If the Indians did not subscribe to this program they were to be hunted down and killed.

1. See also Apache, Cuartelejo (abstract 712); Jicarilla Apache (abstracts 484-87); Lipan Apache (abstract 489).

In these twilight years of Spanish control the Apache menace was sharply reduced by large-scale military expeditions, the missionaries stepped up their Christianization, and mining, ranching, and farming foundations in Arizona were laid. Peace continued after the end of the Spanish period for another decade, until the restless Apache once again went on the warpath. The Mexican government accepted the Spanish system but financial stringency and problems of stabilizing the new government left much of the control in the hands of the local presidial officers. And, by their very nature, the Apache were not to be content very long in a sedentary and agricultural situation. 4 illus., map, 35 notes.   D. L. Smith

446. Byars, Charles, ed. GATEWOOD REPORTS TO HIS WIFE FROM GERONIMO'S CAMP. *J. of Arizona Hist. 1966 7(2): 76-81.* A letter from First Lieutenant Charles B. Gatewood in Arizona to his wife, written 26 August 1886, describing Geronimo's agreement to surrender to the military forces. Gatewood had been selected by General Nelson Miles to follow Geronimo into Mexico to try to obtain his surrender. The editor supplies a biographical sketch of Gatewood and 8 notes.   J. D. Filipiak

447. Christiansen, Paige W. THE APACHE BARRIER. *Rocky Mountain Social Sci. J. 1966 3(2): 93-108.* An outline of the role played by the Apache as a barrier to Spanish, and later Anglo-American, occupation of the Southwest. The Apache entered the Southwest by 1100 A.D., secured territory, and underwent a change from hunters to predators. The author dwells upon Apache-Spanish conflicts, correcting what he considers the omissions of earlier historians. 37 notes.   R. F. Allen

448. Ellis, Richard N. COPPER-SKINNED SOLDIERS: THE APACHE SCOUTS. *Great Plains J. 1966 5(2): 51-67.* A detailed description of the use of Apache scouts by the U.S. Army between 1871 and 1886. General George Cook inaugurated the practice. He and his successors, even the skeptical General Nelson Miles, found them essential in dealing effectively with hostile Apaches. In spite of their exceptional loyalty, the loyal Indians were removed to Florida with the hostiles and not until 1913 were the survivors allowed to return to New Mexico. Biblio.   O. H. Zabel

449. Forrest, Earle. THE FABULOUS SIERRA BONITA. *J. of Arizona Hist. 1965 6(3): 132-146.* The Sierra Bonita, founded in 1872 by Henry Clay Hooker and made famous in literature and drama, is still in the possession of the same family—the fifth generation—and is still the largest ranch in southern Arizona. Covers the ranch's history, with emphasis on its close association with nearby Camp (later Fort) Grant, and the founder's many friends, who included military leaders as well as Cochise, famous Apache Indian. 20 notes.   J. D. Filipiak

450. Gordon, Dudley, ed. LUMMIS AS WAR CORRESPONDENT IN ARIZONA. *Am. West 1965 2(3): 4-12.* Charles F. Lummis was sent by the Los Angeles *Times* to cover the army campaign under General George Crook against the Apaches under Geronimo. For months in 1886 this assignment took him

through Arizona, New Mexico, Sonora, and Chihuahua. Printed here is the Lummis field report about the pursuit and surrender of Geronimo on 17 March 1886, written at Fort Bowie, Arizona Territory. Also included are a short notice from the *Times* of Lummis' assignment and editorial comments on Lummis, Geronimo, and Crook. The holographic field report is in the Southwest Museum. Illus.   D. L. Smith

451. Hagemann, E. R. SCOUT OUT FROM CAMP MC DOWELL. *Arizoniana 1964 5(3): 29-47.* Captain George B. Sanford, with four officers and 91 men, left Camp McDowell 27 September 1866 in pursuit of Apaches. His report 10 days later was highly commended by General McDowell. By the end of November *The Arizona Miner* was fulsome in its praise of Sanford for having killed 15 men and taken many prisoners. The Third Legislative Assembly passed a resolution, "Thanking the Arizona Volunteers." Sanford "had committed the Army to a war with the Apaches that the federal government could not henceforth disavow and which would last for more than twenty years." Sanford led many more scouts until the regiment was transferred in 1873. Illus., map, 48 notes.
E. P. Stickney

452. Hall, Martin Hardwick. PLANTER VS. FRONTIERSMAN: CONFLICT IN CONFEDERATE INDIAN POLICY. *Essays on the Am. Civil War (Austin: U. of Texas Press, 1968), pp. 45-72.* Describes the controversy over Colonel John Paul Baylor's "Indian Order" in 1862-63. Baylor, an old Indian fighter, was in command of Confederate troops in West Texas-Arizona, an area which had been badly victimized by Apache Indians. Under the mistaken impression that the Confederate government had authorized a policy of Indian extermination, Baylor issued an order that all adult Apaches be killed and the children enslaved. When Jefferson Davis learned of the order, he demanded an explanation from Baylor, who replied that all those familiar with Apache atrocities against whites would heartily approve his order. Unconvinced, Davis revoked Baylor's commission. The author holds that Baylor's "Indian Order" was representative of frontier thinking and that his dispute with Richmond reflected a breakdown in communications between those who had battled Apache Indians all their lives and those who had never seen an Indian. Based on primary sources, newspapers, and the *Official Records.*   E. C. Murdock

453. Kessell, John L. ANZA, INDIAN FIGHTER, THE SPRING CAM-PAIGN OF 1766. *J. of Arizona Hist. 1968 9(3): 155-163.* Discusses Juan Bautista de Anza's ability as an Indian fighter by describing in detail his spring campaign of 1766. Born in 1735 in a frontier outpost as the son of an Indian-fighting captain, Anza seemed predestined to be a soldier. Enlisting in the Spanish Army at 16, he became a lieutenant at 19 and obtained his own command as a captain at 24. In 1766, after six years' experience as a captain, he led an expedition against the hostile Apache Indians in the mountains south of the Gila River. Anza succeeded, by hard marching and various stratagems, in killing or capturing 40 Apache. However, he was able to recover few of the horses previously stolen by

the Apache. This affair proved significant only as a training exercise for Anza and his men. Based largely on Anza's report in the Biblioteca Nacional; illus., map, 22 notes.   R. J. Roske

454. Kessell, John L. CAMPAIGNING ON THE UPPER GILA, 1756. *New Mexico Hist. R. 1971 46(2): 133-160.* Provides a background to the campaign of 1756, and an account by Chaplain Bartolomé Sáenz, S.J., of the campaign against the Gila Apache in 1756. Over 300 fighting men (60 under Captain Bernardo Antonio de Bustamante y Tagle, from Chihuahua, the remainder under Captain Gabriel Antonio de Vildósola from Sonora) made their base camp at Todos Santos, near present-day Cliff, New Mexico. The campaigners killed some Apache warriors and captured Apache women and children, but failed to deter future Apache raiding. 78 notes.   D. F. Henderson

455. Kessell, John L. THE PUZZLING PRESIDIO SAN PHELIPE DE GUEVAVI, ALIAS TERRENATE. *New Mexico Hist. R. 1966 41(1): 21-46.* Traces in minute detail the history of the presidio from its establishment in 1742 until its demise in 1775. Located on a spot known locally as San Mateo de Terrenate, in Sonora, Mexico it was designated by at least six different names during its first 10 years, thus creating a puzzle about its true location. It was an outpost of defense against Apache raids, especially for the Guevavi Mission in what is now Arizona. Based on printed and archival materials.
                                                                    D. F. Henderson

456. King, James T. GEORGE CROOK: INDIAN FIGHTER AND HUMAN-ITARIAN. *Arizona and the West 1967 9(4): 333-348.* General George Crook enjoyed a well-earned reputation as a vigorous fighter who campaigned tirelessly through most of the major Indian wars of the trans-Mississippi West. He is probably best remembered as "conqueror of the Apaches." Often overlooked is that the olive branch, as well as implements of war, was carried in the talons of the American eagle. This is epitomized in General Crook who conceived and executed one of the most enlightened Indian policies in American frontier history. Much of his humanitarian program rested upon his experiences in Arizona Territory, especially during his second tour of duty, 1882-86. Possessed with a remarkable ability to replace war's ruthlessness with humanity in peace, Crook was willing to treat the Indian with decency and fairness. On his first assignment to Arizona in 1871, he found that American cruelty and viciousness had attained "exquisite perfection" aimed toward literal extermination. He felt that in such circumstances the Indian would have to be conquered before he could be pacified. A further innovation was to enlist friendly natives as scouts, not only for the intelligence value they could offer but also as a demoralizing factor against the hostiles. Implementation was delayed until his second Arizona tour because less satisfactory programs were imposed from the federal government. Meanwhile his voice was heard increasingly as a champion of justice for the Indian. Granted unusual freedom of action upon his return to the Southwest in 1882, Crook was determined to give the Apache the opportunity to adjust himself to a civilized sedentary culture and to treat him as an equal. A steady barrage of letters, articles, and speeches supplemented his military actions. Unfortunate policy differences

with superiors led to Crook's resignation from the Arizona command before fulfillment of his dreams. He remained, nevertheless, an active champion of Indian rights. Illus., 34 notes.   D. L. Smith

457. Lyon, Juana Frazer. ARCHIE MC INTOSH, THE SCOTTISH INDIAN SCOUT. *J. of Arizona Hist. 1966 7(3): 103-122.* A biographical sketch of an Indian scout who was the son of a Hudson's Bay Company employee and a Chippewa woman. In part educated in Scotland, he served as a valuable scout for General George Crook in the campaigns against the Apache Indians in Arizona.
                                                                              J. D. Filipiak

458. Moseley, Edward H. INDIANS FROM THE EASTERN UNITED STATES AND THE DEFENSE OF NORTHEASTERN MEXICO: 1855-1864. *Southwestern Social Sci. Q. 1965 46(3): 273-280.* Through use of strong military outposts, the Spanish were able to contain the Indians of northeastern Mexico until the 18th century when Mescalero and Lipan Apaches from the United States were pushed into the region. The outposts did little to halt their depredations. The war for Mexican independence, the Texas revolt, and the Mexican War left the situation unaltered. From 1855 to 1864 the governor of Coahuila, Santiago Vidaurii, used so-called civilized Indians from the United States, Seminoles and Kickapoos, to help suppress the Apaches.   D. F. Henderson

459. Myers, Lee. FORT WEBSTER ON THE MIMBRES RIVER. *New Mexico Hist. R. 1966 41(1): 47-57.* First located at Copper Mines, now Santa Rita, and later moved to the Mimbres River, Fort Webster was the first post established to combat the Apache menace in southwestern New Mexico. The location of the second site has remained in doubt. After a careful analysis of several reports and a comparison of mileage, Myers believes that the Horace Bounds ranch site was the location of old Fort Webster. Based on printed sources and materials in the National Archives; 20 notes.   D. F. Henderson

460. Myers, Lee. THE ENIGMA OF MANGAS COLORADAS' DEATH. *New Mexico Hist. R. 1966 41(4): 287-304.* Leader of the Copper Mine band of Apache Indians, Mangas Coloradas was killed while under guard of soldiers at abandoned Fort McLane, sometime during the night of 18 January 1863. Four versions— all supposedly by eyewitnesses—are presented. Documented; 26 notes.
                                                                              D. F. Henderson

461. Nalty, Bernard C. and Strobridge, Truman R. CAPTAIN EMMET CRAW-FORD, COMMANDER OF APACHE SCOUTS, 1882-1886. *Arizona and the West 1964 6(1): 30-40.* Civil War veteran Emmet Crawford was assigned to cavalry duty against the Indians in the West in late 1870. In 1882, as military commandant of the San Carlos Reservation in Arizona Territory, he enlisted Apache and trained them for service as scouts. In his efforts to work with civilian authorities to maintain peace and to make the Indians self-sustaining, and in his leadership of the scouts on campaigns with General George Crook throughout northern Mexico, Arizona, and New Mexico, Crawford earned the respect of

soldiers and Indians alike. In pursuit of a Geronimo-led renegade band in northern Mexico in January 1886, Crawford was asked for a truce. Mexican irregulars came upon the scouts, and, in the confusion as to their identity, Crawford was mortally wounded by a Mexican bullet in a brief skirmish. Geronimo, who was prepared to surrender, was further pursued for several months before he finally capitulated. 2 illus., 40 notes. D. L. Smith

462. Nalty,. Bernard C. and Strobridge, Truman R. EMMET CRAWFORD, PENNSYLVANIA VOLUNTEER TURNED INDIAN FIGHTER. *Pennsylvania Hist. 1966 33(2): 204-214.* Crawford entered the Union Army as a private and frequently saw action, particularly during the Peninsular Campaign and at Antietam. After the war, he was commissioned a second lieutenant in the Regular Army. With the Third Cavalry, he helped to round up the Apache in 1871, chased Cheyenne at the Kansas-Nebraska border in 1875, and saw action in the Sioux War of 1876. Promoted to captain in 1879, he became provost marshal at the San Carlos Apache Reservation in 1882, where he became known as a friend of the Indian. On 10 January 1886, he had succeeded in routing Geronimo's renegades and had received a peace feeler from the famed Apache leader. That night Mexican scalp-hunters attacked Crawford's scouts, and the captain was killed signaling to the Mexicans that his Apache were scouts. Had Crawford lived, the authors argue, Geronimo would have surrendered with little delay. Based largely on primary sources; 43 notes. D. C. Swift

463. Ryan, Pat M. JOHN P. CLUM, "BOSS-WITH-THE-WHITE-FORE-HEAD." *Arizoniana 1964 5(3): 48-60.* The 22-year-old Clum was appointed agent on the San Carlos Apache Reservation of Arizona, arriving 8 August 1874. He had an embattled three-year career, being at odds with the U.S. Army. In 1877 he refused to "submit to inspection by the army." His colorful career included being a lawyer, newspaper editor, postmaster, and city auditor at Tombstone; 20 years with the Office of Post Office Inspectors, traveling extensively; a spectacular part in the Klondike Gold Rush of 1898; and lecturer on the West to promote tourism for the Southern Pacific Railway. Illus., biblio. E. P. Stickney

464. Sacks, Ben. THE ORIGINS OF FORT BUCHANAN: MYTH AND FACT. *Arizona and the West 1965 7(3): 207-226.* The Gadsden Purchase from Mexico added land south of the Gila River to the territory of New Mexico, which area is primarily within the present-day state of Arizona. The principal threat to the peace and security of settlers and travelers in the 1853 purchase were the wild Apache Indians. Not until 1856 were troops dispatched to the troubled region. In June of 1857 they established Fort Buchanan south of the Gila at the head of the Sonoita Creek Valley. The fort continued in existence until it was evacuated and destroyed in July 1861. The author untangles the confusion, misinformation, conflicting accounts, and mistaken conclusions drawn concerning the evacuation of the Mexican military from the Gadsden Purchase, the arrival and establishment of American military authority, and the antecedents and early history of Fort Buchanan. 72 notes. D. L. Smith

465. Salzman, M., Jr., ed. GERONIMO, THE NAPOL፤ON OF INDIANS. *J. of Arizona Hist. 1967 8(4): 215-247.* Originally published at the time of Geronimo's death in March 1909, in a long-defunct publication *The Border.* It is essentially a collection of source materials thinly held together by a narrative which traces Geronimo's life and career as an Indian leader. The article is generally accurate, except for a reliance on incorrect traditions for the Indian scout meeting at Cibecue Creek in 1881. Editorial notes correct the account. Based on personal interviews, printed documents, and records in the National Archives; illus., 29 notes.   R. J. Roske

466. Stevens, Robert C. THE APACHE MENACE IN SONORA, 1831-1849. *Arizona and the West 1964 6(3): 211-222.* Civil strife weakened Sonora, Mexico, economically and militarily to such an extent that the state was unable to organize an effective defense against Arizona and New Mexico-based Apache raiders in the 20 years following Mexican independence. The Apache swept down on Sonora from their north-of-the-border mountain retreats, raiding and pillaging almost at will. No relief was forthcoming from Mexico City. The devastation of the marauders was so appalling and furious that the line of settlement in the state receded southward while other parts of the nation were gaining rapidly in settlement. Attacks continued almost unchecked until the 1850's when Apache enmity shifted to westward advancing Anglo-Americans. 33 notes.   D. L. Smith

467. Tweedie, M. Jean. NOTES ON THE HISTORY AND ADAPTATION OF THE APACHE TRIBES. *Am. Anthropologist 1968 70(6): 1132-1142.* Gathers together the widely scattered information about the prehistoric movements, economy, and general style of adaptation to the southwest of the Athapaskan-speaking tribes known as the Apache. Traces the movements and development of the Apache as they migrated sometime between A.D. 1100 and 1600 from northwestern North America to settle in the southwestern United States. Uses the mythology of these Indians, early 17th-century accounts of the Spanish, and archaeological evidence as well as later accounts. Discusses folklore, linguistic characteristics, and glottochronology. Geographical location, the economy suitable for it, and the pressures from other groups had considerable influence on the social structure and distribution of the Apache. Studies the Jicarilla, Lipan, Chiricahua, Mescalero, Western, and Kiowa Apache, and the Navaho. Table, charts.   Sr. B. A. Barbato

468. Tyler, Barbara Ann. COCHISE: APACHE WAR LEADER, 1858-1861. *J. of Arizona Hist. 1965 6(1): 1-10.* The frequently explored "Bascom affair"— an incident named after Lieutenant George N. Bascom which resulted in a number of dead, both soldiers and Indians—is presented as an event which brought Cochise to the front rank of Apache leadership. Relying on recent reexaminations by other historians, the writer emphasizes that "the Bascom affair merely gave Cochise a motive for revenge." It did not transform him into a hostile, for he had raided American settlements prior to February 1861, when the altercation with Lieutenant Bascom occurred. Based on published and government (National Archives) sources; notes.   J. D. Filipiak

469. Unsigned. ALL ABOUT COURTESY: IN A VERBAL WAR JOHN P. CLUM HAS A PARTING SHOT. *Arizoniana 1963 4(2): 11-18.* In 1877 the Indian agent Clum was ordered by the Commissioner of Indian Affairs to take Indian police, request military aid if needed, arrest marauding Indians at the Southern Apache Agency, remove them to the San Carlos Reservation and confine them there. During the carrying out of this order misunderstandings developed with General August Valentine Kautz, commanding the Department of Arizona, who complained to his divisional commander about the agent's discourtesy. M. Petrie

470. Utley, Robert M. ARIZONA VANQUISHED: IMPRESSIONS AND RE-FLECTIONS CONCERNING THE QUALITY OF LIFE ON A MILITARY FRONTIER. *Am. West 1969 6(6): 16-21.* Before the arrival of the railroad in the 1880's, Arizona was regarded as the most odious assignment that a soldier could receive. As much as one-fifth of the entire U.S. Army was stationed there at times. A mass of reminiscent and contemporary literature produced by military officers and their wives record impressions and feelings about their residence in Arizona. In general, it was regarded as an intolerable place in which to live. The scorched and malarial valleys of the Gila River and its tributaries were the basis of the Army's impression of Arizona. The Indians, chiefly the Apache, were respected for their skill and prowess; the Mexicans received no more than passing notice from these observers; and the white civilian Arizonans were viewed as parasites on the Army. Nostalgia, nevertheless, does pervade the reminiscences of most of the Arizona veterans; some of it is characteristic of the things for which Arizona is noted today. 12 illus. D. L. Smith

471. Utley, Robert M. THE PAST AND FUTURE OF OLD FORT BOWIE. *Arizoniana 1964 5(4): 55-60.* The legislation creating Fort Bowie National Historic Site is the successful culmination of a campaign that goes back a quarter of a century. In 1963 Senator Barry M. Goldwater and Representative Morris K. Udall introduced identical bills in Congress which resulted in Public Law 88-15 (signed into law on 30 August 1964). Fort Bowie commanded the eastern entrance to Apache Pass. "From 1858 until the outbreak of the Civil War the famed Butterfield Company ran its stagecoaches over the rocky slopes of the Pass." In 1861 the pass was the scene of Lieutenant George N. Bascom's attempt to arrest Cochise. Fort Bowie was established in July 1862. Illus. E. P. Stickney

472. Utley, Robert M. THE SURRENDER OF GERONIMO. *Arizoniana 1963 4(1): 1-9.* In 1876, after the federal government moved the Apache Indians from the Chiricahua Mountains to San Carlos, a group of so-called "renegades" under Geronimo began a reign of terror that lasted three years. The successful attack upon them in 1886 was led by Brigadier General Nelson A. Miles in a difficult campaign demanding the utmost in endurance and perseverance from the men under his command because of the climate, terrain, and nature of the enemy. The details are based largely on Miles' *Personal Recollections* (1897) which included Captain Leonard Wood's narrative. Illus. E. P. Stickney

473. Wallace, Andrew. GENERAL AUGUST V. KAUTZ IN ARIZONA, 1874-1878. *Arizoniana 1963 4(4): 54-65.* August Valentine Kautz "represents in the American Southwest the highest kind of self-sacrificing character which the Army occasionally sent to the frontier." He was a steadying influence and the instrument of orderly progress and law. His troubles with the Apaches, the Indian Office, and politicians are surveyed. Based on a preliminary study for a doctoral dissertation at the University of Arizona; illus.   E. P. Stickney

474. Wharfield, H. B. APACHE KID AND THE RECORD. *J. of Arizona Hist. 1965 6(1): 37-46.* Includes an extract of the court-martial of the former sergeant of Apache Indian scouts, Apache Kid, in this biographical sketch. After that conviction in 1887, Apache Kid was retried and found guilty by an Arizona Territorial Court in 1889, but escaped. It is not known when he died, but he may have lived in Mexico to as late as 1924.   J. D. Filipiak

Apache, Chiricahua

475. Ball, Eve. THE APACHE SCOUTS: A CHIRICAHUA APPRAISAL. *Arizona and the West 1965 7(4): 315-328.* An intra-Apache power struggle led to an 1883 Mexican-based raid into New Mexico resulting in the massacre of a white couple and the taking of their child into captivity. This status assertion incident provoked General George Crook to swiftly organize an expedition against the offenders. He enlisted a band of Apache scouts to guide his troops. Subsequently other Apache enlisted and the scouts were used in various capacities for Crook, even against the Apache themselves. The author interviewed some of the scouts and their descendants and found, contrary to the generally accepted notion, that the Chiricahua hold nothing but contempt for those who served as scouts. Based extensively on personal interviews; 5 illus., 62 notes.   D. L. Smith

Apache, Mescalero

476. Basehart, Harry W. THE RESOURCE HOLDING CORPORATION AMONG THE MESCALERO APACHE. *Southwestern J. of Anthrop. 1967 23(3): 277-291.* The Mescalero Indians of the southwestern United States were characterized during the 1850's as a very loosely-knit "tribe" composed of numerous autonomous bands. The tribe itself is a nebulous concept and especially so for the Mescalero. The bands held all the power, yet all of the bands existed in a transhumance situation, moving over a broad range of territory. While each band might have its own favorite area, there was totally free access to all of the resources used by all of the bands by any other Mescalero band. Outsiders were delineated and repulsed. Thus it seems that, despite the lack of a leader and the absence of power, the Mescalero did possess some sort of tribal organization, here termed a resource holding corporation as a reflection of its function. Based on field investigation, primary and secondary sources; map, biblio.   C. N. Warren

477. MacLachlan, Bruce B. ON "INDIAN JUSTICE." *Plains Anthropologist 1963 8(22): 257-261.* "In 1908 a Mescalero Apache who had killed a white man was tracked down and killed by an all-Mescalero posse. The crime of the fugitive and the behavior of his pursuers do not reflect some cross-culturally inexplicable, specifically 'Indian justice', as various published comments have suggested. The Indian justice involved has to do with the precautions taken by the Indian leaders to discourage the development of an intra-community feud on the basis of the execution."   J

478. Mehren, Lawrence L., ed. SCOUTING FOR MESCALEROS: THE PRICE CAMPAIGN OF 1873. *Arizona and the West 1968 10(2): 171-190.* The restive Mescalero Apache, neither happy with a new reservation created for them in southeastern New Mexico in mid-1873 nor with the regular rations allotted to them, continued to steal large quantities of horses, mules, and cattle from ranchers in the vicinity. Apparently, in addition to other reasons, the Mescalero believed that the whites owed them tribute in the form of horses and mules. Major William Redwood Price, experienced in recovering stolen stock from other Apache, was assigned to recover the considerable loot accumulated by the Mescalero and to see that they settled peacefully on the reservation. In four reports, herein edited, Price and his principal officers detail the fall campaign of 1873, in which the Mescalero were pursued in the mountains of southeastern New Mexico and into Texas. He succeeded in driving them from New Mexico but failed both to keep them on the reservation and to recover the stolen stock. 2 illus., map, 66 notes.   D. L. Smith

Apache, Tonto

479. Hagemann, E. R., ed. SURGEON SMART AND THE INDIANS: AN 1866 APACHE WORD-LIST. *J. of Arizona Hist. 1970 11(2): 126-140.* Assistant surgeon Lieutenant (later Brigadier General) Charles Smart (1841-1905) was stationed at Camp McDowell, Arizona Territory. In midsummer 1866, while peace negotiations were going on with the Tonto Apache, Smart made detailed notes and observations on them. He compiled a word-list with 173 entries and prepared a short article, "Notes on the 'Tonto' Apaches." The article later appeared in a government document, but the vocabulary was never published. Both appear herein. Although Smart was neither a linguist, philologist, nor anthropologist, his is one of the earliest reports of its kind and is of considerable value to scholars. 2 illus., 14 notes.   D. L. Smith

Apache, White Mountain

480. Measer, Forrest W., Jr. NA'ILDE': THE GHOST DANCE OF THE WHITE MOUNTAIN APACHE. *Kiva 1967 33(1): 15-24.* "Revitalizing movements are defined according to the theories of Anthony F. C. Wallace. With this in mind, a revitalizing movement which occurred among the White Mountain Apache in 1881 is described and ultimately related to the 1870 Paiute Ghost Dance. A three plane analysis is then made of this Apache movement using Wallace's classification."   J

Chemehuevi

481. Stewart, Kenneth M. A BRIEF HISTORY OF THE CHEMEHUEVI INDIANS. *Kiva 1968 34(1): 9-27.* "The Chemehuevi were originally a branch of the Southern Paiute who, prior to the middle of the nineteenth century, ranged over the Mohave Desert hunting and gathering. At the invitation or upon the sufferance of the Mohave they began to filter over to the Colorado River to take up floodwater farming in the Colorado Valley and Chemehuevi Valley. Here they underwent a degree of acculturation as a result of Yuma contacts. The Mohave also brought some Chemehuevi to Cottonwood Island. War broke out with the Mohave in 1865, and the Chemehuevi fled back into the desert. After peace had been restored in 1867, many Chemehuevi returned to the river to live on the Colorado River Reservation or in the Chemehuevi Valley."   J

Halchidhoma

482. Dobyns, Henry F., Ezell, Paul H., and Ezell, Greta S. DEATH OF A SOCIETY: THE HALCHIDHOMAS. *Ethnohist. 1963 10(2): 105-161.* Traces the decimation by slave raiding, slave trading, intertribal warfare, and pestilence, of the Halchidhomas, a Yuman-speaking, lower Colorado River tribe, vanquished by their hereditary enemies, the Yuma and Mohave, 1827-29. The remnants amalgamated with neighboring Gila River societies, the present day Maricopa. Multitribal alliances, aggression, and warfare between "inimical" societies proved fatal. Modern parallels are noted.   H. J. Graham

Havasupai

483. Casanova, Frank E., ed. GENERAL CROOK VISITS THE SUPAIS: AS REPORTED BY JOHN G. BOURKE. *Arizona and the West 1968 10(3): 253-276.* In November 1884 General George Crook, commanding officer at Whipple Barracks, Arizona, led a party to visit the Havasupai Indians who lived in Cataract Canyon, a tributary of the Grand Canyon. Captain John Gregory Bourke, then Acting Inspector General of the Department of Arizona, detailed the journey in his diaries. His meticulous and perceptive observations, herein edited, describe the terrain, the perilous trails, inscriptions on the walls, vegetation, and matters of ethnology such as food, dress, shelter, weapons, crops, and trade. 4 illus., map, 74 notes.   D. L. Smith

Jicarilla Apache

484. Gordon, B. L. HEROES AND ETHOS OF THE JICARILLA APACHE. *Masterkey 1970 44(2): 54-62.* Retells the Jicarilla Apache story of their two rival legendary heroes. Relates these heroes, "Knowing-Glance" and "Strikes-the-Enemy," to the Apache ethos of conflicting aspirations and ways of life: plains versus mountains, war versus peace, east versus west, and stability versus adventure. Recounts the story of the Apache-Comanche truce negotiations of 1897.   C. N. Warren

485. Lecompte, Janet. THE MANCO CURRO PASS MASSACRE. *New Mexico Hist. R. 1966 41(4): 305-318.* In Manco Curro Pass Jicarilla Apache attacked a party of 14 men and two children on 19 June 1848 killing four men and capturing the children. The annotated account of one of the survivors is reproduced. Based on manuscripts and newspapers, 33 notes.
D. F. Henderson

486. Skinner, S. Alan. TWO HISTORIC PERIOD SITES IN THE EL RITO VALLEY, NEW MEXICO. *Plains Anthropologist 1968 13(39): 63-70.* Two sites were found on the sides of a stream which drains into the El Rito from the east. A constant supply of water may have been the reason for their location. The architectural features are scanty. Three isolated finds of pottery dating in the 19th century (1853-81) and the location on Jicarilla Territory suggest the presence of Jicarilla Apaches during the second half of the 19th century. 3 figs., biblio.
K. Adelfang

487. Taylor, Morris F. CAMPAIGNS AGAINST THE JICARILLA APACHE, 1854. *New Mexico Hist R. 1969 44(4): 269-291.* Examines the Jicarilla Apache raids in 1854—their background and the reactions to them. The trouble began in February with a raid on cattle belonging to Samuel B. Watrous, and ended with a massacre of the inhabitants of a small fur traders' post, Fort Pueblo, on Christmas Day. Military units from Fort Union pursued the Indians and fought several engagements without decisive results during 1854. Based on documents in the National Archives; 70 notes.
D. F. Henderson

Karankawan

488. Wolff, Thomas. THE KARANKAWA INDIANS: THEIR CONFLICT WITH THE WHITE MAN IN TEXAS. *Ethnohist. 1969 16(1): 1-32.* "The Karankawa Indians, whose aboriginal homeland was on the east coast of Texas, were first encountered by non-Indians when Alvar Nuñez Cabeza de Vaca and his men came upon them soon after A.D. 1528. From then until the demise of the Karankawa in 1858 the relationship between these Indians and Spaniards, Frenchmen, Englishmen, Mexicans and Anglo-Americans passed through various phases, all of which are outlined here."
J

Lipan Apache

489. Brant, Charles S. JOE BLACKBEAR'S STORY OF THE ORIGIN OF THE PEYOTE RELIGION. *Plains Anthropologist 1963 8(21): 180-181.* The story of the origin of the peyote religion. "Long ago," when the Indians were still fighting each other, a group of Lipan Apache was camped on the other side of New Mexico when they were attacked by other bands of Indians. The tribe was scattered, leaving behind a woman and her son. The boy went out early in the morning to look for the tribe. As he walked around, a voice spoke to him from above, telling him of the peyote and that he should eat some. He ate some with his mother and they were soon full. The mother prayed to the providing spirit

for rain and it rained. That night she dreamed of finding the tribe on a mountain to the east. The next morning they set out toward the mountain and found the tribe. He introduced peyote to the tribe and since then it has been used on special occasions such as Thanksgiving and Easter.   C. B. Schroeder

Mohave (Mojave)

490. Kroeber, Clifton B. THE MOHAVE AS NATIONALIST, 1859-1874. *Pro. of the Am. Phil. Soc. 1965 109(3): 173-180.* Traces the story of tribal leadership of the Mohave of the Colorado River as it relates to contacts with the white men and to other Indians in the period after submission to the U.S. Army in 1859. The policy of a southern group under the leadership of Yara tav is contrasted with that of a more northern group of Mohave. The southern group reflecting a traditionally strong sense of autonomy that lay at the "religious core of national feeling among the Mohave" actively promoted peaceful relations among other Indian tribes and between Indians and whites. As settlement proceeded, the opportunity for Mohave leadership was reduced, and the policy failed. Documented.   R. G. Comegys

491. Sherer, Lorraine M. THE NAME MOJAVE, MOHAVE: A HISTORY OF ITS ORIGIN AND MEANING. *Southern California Q. 1967 49(1): 1-36.* Mojave (or Mohave) Indians of today insist that their tribal name has always been *Aha macave,* meaning "along or beside the water." For centuries they inhabited the land near the Colorado River. The author discovered that over the span of time from the first white contacts with these Indians in 1704, 71 different spellings of the name with five different meanings have been used. The chief explanation for the variations is the difficulty in translating the oral name into Spanish and English, the languages of the whites who were most involved with these Indians. The name Mojave, or Mohave, originated during the 1820's when the Southwest was controlled by Mexico and it was perpetuated by Americans when they acquired the area. Of the five meanings for the tribal name, the best-known, although erroneous according to the author, is "three mountains." It was assumed to have reference to either three mountains or three mountain ranges surrounding the valley in which the Mohave lived. The author states that both the vowels and the word order of the Mohave words for "three mountains" differ from the words for the true tribal name. Based on interviews with Mohave Indians, government documents, and various secondary sources; illus., map, 80 notes.   W. L. Bowers

492. Sherer, Lorraine M. THE NAME MOJAVE, MOHAVE: AN ADDENDUM. *Southern California Q. 1967 49(4): 455-458.* Shows parts of three maps made between 1854 and 1858 which show that one of the erroneous names for the Mojave (or Mohave) Indians, *Hamok avi,* was used to designate both the tribe and a mountain range. However, the maps make clear that the name did not refer to a group of mountains known as the Needles as is commonly believed. *Hamok avi,* which means "three mountain" or mountains, was used on the maps to designate a mountain range other than the one of which the Needles were a part. Based on the maps.   W. L. Bowers

493. Stewart, Kenneth M. A BRIEF HISTORY OF THE MOHAVE INDIANS SINCE 1850. *Kiva 1969 34(4): 219-236.* "Descriptions of Mohave culture in the middle of the nineteenth century are contained in such writings as [R. B.] Stratton's account of the captivity of the Oatman girls *[The Captivity of the Oatman Girls,* 1857], the reports of railroad surveyors ([Lorenzo] Sitgreaves and [Amiel Weeks] Whipple), and accounts of the steamboat captains ([Joseph C.] Ives). The long period of intertribal warfare was ending, but the apprehensive Mohave fought the white intruders on several occasions before they were finally subdued. Reservations were established, but the Mohave had to undergo many hardships before making a better adjustment to changing times."   J

494. Stewart, Kenneth M. MOHAVE INDIAN GATHERING OF WILD PLANTS. *Kiva 1964 31(1): 46-53.* "Aboriginally the Mohave Indians of the lower Colorado River gathered about half of their food supply. Besides fishing and hunting activities, a large variety of plant foods was collected. Most important of these were the pods of mesquite and screwbean trees. Others included numerous wild seeds, nuts, greens, roots, and berries. Some of these were used for medicinal purposes."   J

495. Stewart, Kenneth M. THE ABORIGINAL TERRITORY OF THE MOHAVE INDIANS. *Ethnohist. 1969 16(3): 257-276.* "Archaeological, documentary, and ethnographic sources pertaining to the Mohave Indians of Arizona and California are reviewed in an effort to establish their areas of aboriginal use and occupancy."   J

496. Stewart, Kenneth M. THE MOHAVE INDIANS IN HISPANIC TIMES. *Kiva 1966 32(1): 25-38.* "The Mohave Indians, who were visited only at great intervals by the Spaniards, maintained their independence without hindrance throughout Hispanic times. The first Spaniard who is known with certainty to have contacted the Mohave was [Juan de] Oñate, in 1604. Garcés, in 1776, was the first Spaniard to travel through the Mohave Valley. The rather scanty ethnographic accounts left by the Spanish chroniclers suggest a way of life quite similar to that reported for the Mohave by modern ethnographers."   J

497. Walker, Henry Pickering. TEACHER TO THE MOJAVES: THE EXPERIENCES OF GEORGE W. NOCK, 1887-1889. *Arizona and the West 1967 9(2): 143-166, (3): 259-280.* Part I. Nock and his family lived on the Colorado River Indian Reservation from 1887 to 1890. The 300,800-acre reserve was located on the Colorado River between Yuma, Arizona, and Needles, California, largely within the present state of Arizona. Nock served as superintendent and principal teacher at the Colorado Indian Agency school on the reservation and his wife as matron and teacher. A seamstress, a cook, and a laundress completed the personnel roster of the school. Enrollment during the Nock period varied from 55 to 70, about 60 percent of the eligible Mojave children on the reservation. The fundamentals of reading, writing, arithmetic, and the vocational arts were the concerns of the school. Within a year or so after the Nocks left the reservation he prepared his recollections of the experience among the Mojave as part of a book-length manuscript which he probably hoped to publish. Edited and an-

notated here are five chapters which describe their stay of several weeks in Yuma and the steamboat trip up the river en route to the reservation; the climate and the country, the agency, and the routine of the school. 4 illus., map, 60 notes. Part II. Contains nine chapters of the Nock manuscript concerning his experiences. They are, essentially, an ethnohistorical account of Mojave life and culture—dress, homes, customs, religion. Included is an eyewitness account of the death rites of the second-in-authority among the local Mojave. The narrative closes with the return of the Nocks to Yuma, en route back to their home in Virginia. 4 illus., 29 notes.   D. L. Smith

Navaho (Navajo)

498. Brugge, David M. NAVAJO USE OF AGAVE. *Kiva 1965 31(2): 88-98.* "The use of plants of the genus *Agave* by the Navajos was of limited importance economically because of the restricted distribution of these plants within the Navajo range, but the Navajo agave complex shows some time depth and includes some traits not reported for other tribes. In spite of being a well defined set of traits, there are significant differences between the usual practices of the western Navajos and those in the southeast."   J

499. Brugge, David M., ed. VIZCARRA'S NAVAJO CAMPAIGN OF 1823. *Arizona and the West 1964 6(3): 223-244.* José Antonio Vizcarra, Mexican governor of New Mexico (1822-25), negotiated a treaty with the Navajo in February 1823. This was an attempt to bring peace between the Navajo and New Mexicans whose expanding economies were based on livestock. In mid-June Vizcarra's 1,500-man army set out on a campaign to enforce the terms of the treaty. The elusive Navajo constantly retreated, scattered, and vanished into their hideouts. Translated and edited here are Vizcarra's journal with entries from 18 June through 31 August, and a diary report of an officer who led a detachment separate from the army with entries for 3-18 August. These documents detail the expedition on its march through west-central New Mexico, across northeast Arizona, into southern Utah, and return. Map, 89 notes.   D. L. Smith

500. Firestone, Melvin and Rodriquez, Antonio. NOTES ON THE DERIVATION OF THE NAJA. *Plateau 1970 42(4): 139-145.* "(1) Evidence for the presence of the crescent amulet in Spain and Mexico is sparse; writers maintaining its derivation [to the Navaho] via those areas supply no documentation for its existence there. (2) Despite what certain writers have maintained, the crescent amulet is neither specifically Phoenician in derivation nor does it come from the Moorish Hand of Fatima. (3) The term *naja* is similar to an unrelated, widely-spread term for the evil eye in the area of the Old World from which the naja is felt to have derived."   J

501. Hopkins, Richard C. KIT CARSON AND THE NAVAJO EXPEDITION. *Montana 1968 18(2): 52-61.* An account of Kit Carson's campaign against the Navajo in the Canyon de Chelly region in 1864. With Captain Albert H. Pfeiffer,

Carson broke the Navajo power by a series of raids against their villages and fields, leading to their early surrender. Based on military correspondence among officers concerned.   S. R. Davison

502. Jones, Oakah L., Jr. THE ORIGINS OF THE NAVAJO INDIAN PO-LICE, 1872-1873. *Arizona and the West 1966 8(3): 225-238.* The warlike Navaho (Navajo) who returned from military imprisonment in New Mexico in 1868 to a northeastern Arizona reservation were finding it difficult to change suddenly to a peaceful agrarian way of life. Recurrent drought and poor crops, unsatisfactory reservation boundaries, and irregular distribution of government rations served only to intensify their predicament. Soon mounted Navajo bands were raiding settlements in New Mexico and stealing livestock from the ranches. Both civilian and military observers believed that the Navajo could be guided into useful citizenship if a Navajo regulatory body replaced the present military guardianship. The lean winter of 1871-72 and imminent starvation provoked the Indians to increasingly uncontrollable raids on horse, sheep, and cattle herds. At an August Navajo-Apache peace conference the Navajo warchief Manuelito himself openly proposed the establishment of a native police force. Manuelito became the captain of the Navajo Indian Police, a force of 100 men. They provided their own horses, but were uniformed and equipped by the army. The Navajo Police were so efficient and effective in returning stolen property and discouraging further incidents that they were dissolved in late 1873. There is evidence, however, that a similar arrangement was continued for some time on an informal basis by the Indian agent to maintain law and order. This experiment was an important forerunner of a later general governmental policy for administering Indian reservations through native police forces. Based in part on Bureau of Indian Affairs records in the National Archives; 2 illus., 27 notes.
                                                              D. L. Smith

503. Kelly, Lawrence C. WHERE WAS FORT CANBY? *New Mexico Hist. R. 1967 42(2): 49-62.* From June 1863 until October 1864 New Mexican volunteers used Fort Canby as a headquarters camp in their campaign against the Navaho Indians. Previous historians placed the site of Fort Canby at Pueblo, Colorado, but the author, by a careful reading of military correspondence, locates the correct site at Fort Defiance. Based on records in the National Archives, Record Group 98; 19 notes.   D. F. Henderson

504. Kurtz, Ronald J. HEADMEN AND WAR CHANTERS: ROLE THE-ORY AND THE EARLY CANYONCITO NAVAJO. *Ethnohist. 1969 16(1): 83-111.* "Ethnohistorical studies of early contacts between separate cultures and of subsequent stability and change can profit from the use of role theory. As a demonstration of this fact, role concepts are employed to enlighten the history of the Canyoncito Navajo Indians of New Mexico in terms of their relationships with other Navajo, Hispanos, and Anglo-Americans."   J

505. McNitt, Frank. NAVAJO CAMPAIGNS AND THE OCCUPATION OF NEW MEXICO, 1847-1848. *New Mexico Hist. R. 1968 43(3): 173-194.* A narrative of two expeditions against the Navajo following the American occupation of

New Mexico. The expedition of 1847, led by Major Robert Walker, nearly ended in a disaster, and failed completely to force the Navajo to cease their raids on New Mexican livestock. The expedition of 1848, under Colonel Edward W. B. Newby, resulted in the "second American treaty with the tribe which...was never ratified and was not much worse or better than the treaties that preceded it." Based on Record Group 94, National Archives, and various newspapers; 26 notes.

D. F. Henderson

506. Reeve, Frank D., Adams, Eleanor B., ed., and Kessell, John L., ed. NAVAHO FOREIGN AFFAIRS, 1795-1846. *New Mexico Hist. R. 1971 46(2): 101-132, (3): 223-251.* Part I. Details the efforts by Spanish authorities to negotiate successful treaties with the Navaho Indians. The period of relative peace from 1720 to 1770 was ended by violence in the 1770's and early 1780's. A treaty in 1786 preserved calm until 1796. The new trouble stemmed partly from New Mexico's rising population and the need for more land. A compromise effected in 1808 by Governor Real Alencaster permitted the Navaho to remain at peace with the New Mexicans for the next several years. Based on records at the Archivo General de la Nacion, the Spanish Archives of New Mexico, and the Mexican Archives of New Mexico; 67 notes. Part II. After two years of trouble, a new governor, don Facundo Melgares, undertook a major military campaign against the Navaho in October 1818. The 49-day campaign failed to produce significant results. The following year, Melgares launched a more successful campaign that brought about a formal treaty, signed at Santa Fe on 21 August 1819. The resulting peace lasted but two years, and by 1821 the Navaho again were raiding. During 1822 several individuals exercised civil or military authority, or both. The confusion prevented effective action against the Indians. Finally in 1823 Bartolomé Baca became the political chief; Colonel José Antonio Vizcarra became the military chief. Vizcarra took to the field for ten weeks, from 18 June to 31 August, with considerable success. On 20 January 1824, 14 articles of peace were signed at Jémez. Based on various manuscript collections; 56 notes.

D. F. Henderson

507. Warner, Michael J. PROTESTANT MISSIONARY ACTIVITY AMONG THE NAVAJO, 1890-1912. *New Mexico Hist. R. 1970 45(3): 209-232.* Commencing with the so-called Quaker Peace Policy formulated by President Ulysses S. Grant, the increase in missionary activities was dramatic. The Peace Policy was terminated in 1882. Although the government continued to allot reservation lands to those missionary societies which expressed a desire to begin or expand their efforts with the Indians, activity declined. The author discusses general missionary activity during the years 1890-1901 and 1901-12, and Presbyterian activity during the years 1901-12. 60 notes.

D. F. Henderson

Papago

508. Clark, Geoffrey A. A CACHE OF PAPAGO MINIATURE POTTERY FROM KITT PEAK, SOUTH-CENTRAL ARIZONA. *Kiva 1967 32(4): 128-142.* "The Kitt Peak cache is composed of a number of miniature pottery vessels, found in a rock crevice near the summit of Kitt Peak in southern Arizona. Such

caches are widespread phenomena in the southwestern United States. Practically anything may be included in them, from projectile points to village fetishes. The cache may have been a personal offering to Ee-e-toy (Nature personified). Such gifts were given by the individual in order to replace objects taken from the natural environment. This idea of reciprocation is widespread among the Papago. The cache was probably deposited during the period A.D. 1725 to 1860." J

509. Hoy, Wilton E. A QUEST FOR THE MEANING OF QUITOBAQUITO. *Kiva 1969 34(4): 213-218.* "The desert oasis of Quitobaquito is a shallow pond, one half acre in size, fed by springs from the granitic Quitobaquito Hills in the southwestern corner of Organ Pipe Cactus National Monument. Because of its role as a dependable water source on the formidable *Camino del Diablo* between Sonoyta and Yuma, travelers have long stopped at the pond, while Sand Papago Indians, Mexicans and Anglo-Americans have occasionally made it their home. The first recorded European visitor to the springs was the Jesuit Padre Eusebio Kino in 1698. The Papago name for the pond has been variously retained, replaced, misinterpreted, and corrupted by both Spanish and English speaking peoples. This compilation explores some of the names and meanings that have been used in historical times." J

Pima

510. Anderson, Charles A. DAY BOOK OF REV. CHARLES H. COOK. *J. of the Presbyterian Hist. Soc. 1959 37(2): 104-121.* The day-by-day record of a journey from Chicago to the Pima Indian Agency in Arizona Territory between 1 September 1870 and 24 February 1871. Travel was by train as far as the railroads extended in east Colorado, then by stagecoach to a point on the Santa Fe trail, and finally with traders' caravans drawn by bullocks. Cook had been born in Germany, came to the United States as a young man, served in the Civil War, studied for the ministry, and served in Halsted Street Methodist Episcopal Church in Chicago before deciding to become a missionary among the Pima Indians. His account therefore contains observations on religious conditions and activities as well as travel conditions. W. D. Metz

Pueblo

511. Brugge, David M. PUEBLO FACTIONALISM AND EXTERNAL RELATIONS. *Ethnohist. 1969 16(2): 191-200.* "Contrary to popular opinion, at various times throughout history the Pueblo Indians of the American Southwest were allied with Apache and Navajo Indians against non-Indians and in fights among themselves. Several documented instances of such alliances from 1583 to the 1860's are cited. It is suggested that intratribal factionalism, as well as diverse economic, religious and kin interests have to be taken into account in order to understand these changing political alignments." J

512. Chavez, Angelico. POHE-YEMO'S REPRESENTATIVE AND THE PUEBLO REVOLT OF 1680. *New Mexico Hist. R. 1967 42(2): 85-126.* The

Pueblo Revolt of 1680 put to an end for a time the Spanish colony and the Franciscan missions in New Mexico. The causes were several, but the main rallying cry was the "ancient ones" of the pueblos versus the God and the saints of the Spaniards. In previous histories, the tactical genius of the revolt was thought to be El Popé of San Juan, but Governor Otermín and his captains felt at the time that El Popé could not have done it all alone. The interrogation of prisoners revealed that an "Indian representative of Pohé yemo" had ordered them to rebel. This Indian was reported to be very tall and black with very large yellow eyes. In Pueblo mythology Pohé-yemo made the sun shine upon the people when they first came out upon the dark and dreary earth's surface. The tall black man with yellow eyes who was called the representative of Pohé-yemo was probably two people—Domingo Naranjo, the representative of Pohé-yemo in Taos, and Pedro Naranjo, carrying out his orders at San Felipe. Based on various records in the Biblioteca Nacional and the Archivo General de la Nación, Mexico, and the Spanish Archives of New Mexico; 80 notes.

D. F. Henderson

513. Lange, Charles H. ADOLPH F. BANDELIER AS A PUEBLO ETH-NOLOGIST. *Kiva 1963 29(1): 28-34.* "The activities of Adolph Bandelier in the Southwest during the late 19th century have long been of interest to scholars with a variety of interests. This paper is limited to a consideration, or evaluation, of his ethnological investigations among the Puebloan tribes. In terms of the present day, his work reveals the shortcomings typical of the efforts of most scholarly pioneers; nonetheless, Bandelier's findings have great value in the study of Puebloan peoples."

J

514. Reno, Philip. REBELLION IN NEW MEXICO—1837. *New Mexico Hist. R. 1965 40(3): 197-214.* For a short time during August and September 1837, a successful revolt by northern New Mexico's village poor, aided by Pueblo Indians, vested New Mexico governmental authority first in a revolutionary canton, then in a *Junta Popular,* or "People's Assembly," with José Gonzales of Taos named governor. The revolt was smashed and the rule of law reestablished in September 1837. While the rebels, except in matters of taxation, hoped to carry on under the same government and laws as before, they did make two modifications in the focus of political power: first, governmental power was to reside in the village leaders, second, the Pueblo Indians were to be included in councils on government policy. 33 notes.

D. F. Henderson

515. Simmons, Marc. NEW MEXICO'S SMALLPOX EPIDEMIC OF 1780-1781. *New Mexico Hist. R. 1966 41(4): 319-326.* Brief assessment of the effects and causes of the epidemic of 1780-81 which was estimated to have claimed the lives of 5,025 Pueblo Indians alone. The disease came to New Mexico either from the south through various Indian tribes, or from the interior of Mexico which suffered a major epidemic in 1779. Based on records in the Spanish Archives of New Mexico, State Records Center and Archives; 31 notes.

D. F. Henderson

Pueblo, Hopi

516. Adams, Eleanor B. FRAY SILVESTRE AND THE OBSTINATE HOPI. *New Mexico 1963 38(2): 97-138.* The fame of Fray Silvestre Velez de Escalente, who lived in New Mexico from 1774 to 1800, rests chiefly on his exploration into Utah in 1776 in search of a land route to Monterey, California. The author concentrates on his unsuccessful attempt to convert the Hopi in 1775. Fray Silvestre was shocked and disappointed by the actions and attitudes of the apostate Hopi. He recommended a show of force as the only means of setting them on the right track. A translation of the journal he kept during his stay with the Indians occupies the last 20 pages of the article.   D. F. Henderson

517. Harrison, Michael. FIRST MENTION IN PRINT OF THE HOPI SNAKE DANCE. *Masterkey 1964 38(4): 150-155.* Presents the first printed reference to the Hopi Snake Dance, taken from the weekly newspaper *The Long-Islander,* of Huntington, Long Island, issue of 10 October 1879. The story was based on information supplied by William Ross Mateer, "Agent of the Moqui Pueblos of Arizona." Unfortunately, Mateer's account seems to be second-hand, and the story itself is open to question. Based on primary and secondary sources; illus.
C. N. Warren

Pueblo, Salineros

518. Schroeder, Albert H. THE LANGUAGE OF THE SALINE PUEBLOS: PIRO OR TIWA? *New Mexico Hist. R. 1964 39(3): 235-249.* By the middle 1670's the Saline (Salineros) Pueblos, beset by droughts that began in the 1660's and by Apache raids, abandoned their homes and joined "other pueblos on the Rio Grande." All statements labeling Indians of the Saline Pueblos as Tiwa-speaking were made after the abandonment of those pueblos in the 1670's. Reports made prior to 1670, where reference is made to language, indicate that it was not Tiwa, but either Piro or Tompiro. An array of sources was used to substantiate the thesis. A map of "Pueblo Groups of Central New Mexico" is included.   D. F. Henderson

Pueblo, Taos

519. Jenkins, Myra Ellen. TAOS PUEBLO AND ITS NEIGHBORS, 1540-1847. *New Mexico Hist. R. 1966 41(2): 85-114.* A summary of the encroachments on lands claimed by the Taos Indians from the visit of Hernando de Alvarado in 1540 to the transfer of the lands to the United States in 1847. Based on printed sources and the Spanish Archives of New Mexico, Series I, Bureau of Land Management; 80 notes.   D. F. Henderson

Pueblo, Zuñi

520. Buchanan, William J. LEGEND OF THE BLACK CONQUISTADOR. *Mankind 1968 1(5): 21-25, 93.* In 1539 Estevancio de Dorantes, the Negro slave of a Spanish master, wandered through the lands of Nueva España. The folklore of the Zuñi Indians contains a legend pertaining to his last journey: One of the survivors of the ill-fated Narvaez expedition of 1528, he wandered across Texas and New Mexico with Cabeza de Vaca. During the eight-year period of wandering, Estevan learned to speak at least six Indian languages. In the spring of 1539, Estevan was sent to the North to discover the "Cities of Gold." He soon began to assert himself at the expense of the friar with whom he was traveling. Now adorned with brightly colored plumes and practicing the weird ritual of a medicine man, he began to tell the Indians he met that he was a god, and he attracted a group of followers. From each group of new Indians which he met, he demanded and received women and gifts. Success clouded his judgment, and his arrogance with the Indians of Zuñi led to his death in 1539. Illus.

P. D. Thomas

521. Proper, David R. THE ZUÑI VISITATION TO SALEM. *Essex Inst. Hist. Collections 1968 104(1): 80-85.* Over the years many visitors to Salem have evinced special interest in witchcraft. In 1882, Salem was visited by five Zuñi Indians from New Mexico, representatives of a tribe whose religious practices recognized and exorcised witchcraft. To the town's surprise, they commended Salem for its work in 1692 in "using up its bad spirits" and one advised a startled audience to put witches or wizards immediately to death should any reappear.

J. M. Bumsted

522. Rinaldo, John B. NOTES ON THE ORIGINS OF HISTORIC ZUÑI CULTURE. *Kiva 1964 29(4): 86-98.* "Surveys and excavations in the Zuñi area have indicated that the culture of the earlier periods in that district was broadly Puerco-Chacoan in character, and that it was strongly influenced during the later periods by a Mogollon culture that probably stemmed directly from the 'budding off' of late Mogollon pueblos of the northern branches. Evidence for this relationship is noted in the continuum between these areas not only of styles of ceramic design and complexes of pottery types, but also in certain architectural traits such as types of masonry construction, settlement patterns, and types of stone artifacts of a ceremonial nature. This relationship is outlined as having developed in three stages beginning with trade in pottery and axes of a Puerco-Chacoan character to the Mogollon villages and culminating in a period when the Zuñi were making black-on-white and black-on-red polychrome pottery in the Tularosa style and building a characteristic type of rectangular kiva."   J

523. Vroman, Adam Clark. ZUÑI. *Am. West 1966 3(3): 42-55.* Adam Clark Vroman, a photographer, went on several expeditions to the Indian pueblos of New Mexico and Arizona in the late 1880's and through the early 1900's. The portraits and photographs of Zuñi homes, dances, and occupations reproduced here were selected from the collection of hundreds of original Vroman glass plate

negatives in the Los Angeles County (California) Museum. Vroman's descriptive essay, "The Pueblo of Zuñi," is reprinted from *Photo Era,* August 1901.

D. L. Smith

Sobaipuri

524. Ellinwood, Sybil. CALABASAS. *Arizoniana 1964 5(4): 27-41.* The Sobaipuri Indians (who later merged with the Papago) farmed on this beautiful spot before the 17th century. Here Father Eusebio Kino established a ranch to support his mission at nearby Guebabi. "Calabasas became successively a fortified hacienda in Mexican times, a U.S. military encampment after the Gadsden Purchase, and finally a bustling town, envisioned as a hub of the cattle and mining industries." The action of the Court of Private Land Claims in 1894 voiding all Spanish land grants along the border decided against the Boston investors in Calabasas. Since the buildings burned in 1927 only a few bricks and adobes mark the site. Illus., biblio.

E. P. Stickney

Yuma

525. Ives, Ronald L., ed. RETRACING THE ROUTE OF THE FAGES EXPEDITION OF 1781. *Arizona and the West 1966 8(1): 49-70, (2): 157-170.* Part I. As early as 1540 the Yuma crossing on the Colorado River was known. Its economic and strategic importance increased as it developed as a gateway on the trail from Sonora, Mexico, through Arizona to Alta California. Two mission-presidio settlements were established at the crossing in 1780, but the Yuma Indians soon became disgruntled and massacred all but the women and children in July 1781. Don Pedro Fages, a veteran infantry officer with extensive service in California and Sonora, was sent from Sonora to Yuma to rescue the captives, execute the leaders of the rebellion, and restore peace with the other Indians. Highly literate and competent, Fages kept a diary of his 106-day, 980-mile expedition over the difficult terrain of the desolate Sonoran frontier. The Fages diary places the Yuma relief expedition of 1781 in a much clearer historical perspective. Although its existence has been known by historians for some time, the itinerary of the expedition has remained elusive and vague because few of the sites mentioned by Fages appear on modern maps. The editor has resolved the mystery to a large extent by personal field investigations. 2 maps, 60 notes. Part II. The expedition led by Don Pedro Fages in the late summer of 1781 from Pitic near present Hermosillo, Sonora, Mexico, to Yuma, Arizona, was to rescue captives, punish the participants of the massacre of the Yuma mission-presidio-settlements, and restore peace. It is traced from the rest retreat at Sonoyta back to Yuma to search for the Franciscan martyrs, and the subsequent return back to Pitic. The manuscript is in the Bancroft Library. 2 maps, 20 notes.

D. L. Smith

526. Kessell, John L. THE MAKING OF A MARTYR: THE YOUNG FRANCISCO GARCES. *New Mexico Hist. R. 1970 45(3): 181-196.* A brief biographical sketch of Father Francisco Garcés, killed by the Yuma Indians at Yuma Crossing, New Mexico, on 17 July 1781. Born in 1738 in Aragon, Spain, he was

educated at the convent of San Crístobal de Alpartir. Inspired by two friars from a missionary college in Mexico, he left Spain in 1763, survived a shipwreck, and arrived in Mexico late in 1763. After five years at the college, he volunteered to serve in Sonora. 44 notes.   D. F. Henderson

Great Plains Area

General

527. Adams, Donald K., ed. THE JOURNAL OF ADA A. VOGDES, 1868-1871. *Montana 1963 13(3): 2-17.* A young army wife relates the experiences and sensations encountered during residence at Fort Laramie and Fort Fetterman, deep in the country of hostile Indians. The observations of this sensitive white woman on such matters as Indian dress and behavior, and primitive social life at these remote posts, are stressed in these selections from the original diary which is held in the Henry E. Huntington Library.   L. G. Nelson

528. Anderson, Harry H., ed. A FORTIFIED EARTHLODGE VILLAGE NEAR FORT THOMPSON, SOUTH DAKOTA AS IT APPEARED IN 1866. *Plains Anthropologist 1968 13(39): 26-28.* The letters of Noah M. Glatfelter, an army surgeon stationed at Fort Thompson, South Dakota, in 1866, describe a fortified earthlodge village about 500 yards from the fort extending over four or five acres. There was a zigzag type of fortification around the town. Fragments of pottery made of clay, but not glazed, with some attempts at ornamentation were strewn over the grounds. Pieces of hard stone and fragments of shell were found. Source material such as letters and documents could result in discovery of material pertaining to other locations. Biblio.   K. Adelfang

529. Anderson, Harry H., ed. STAND AT THE ARIKAREE. *Colorado Mag. 1964 41(4): 337-342.* A letter from Major S. Brisbane of the Second U.S. Cavalry describing the battle of Beecher Island, 17-25 September 1868, one of the most spectacular of a long series of conflicts with Plains Indians. Major George A. Forsyth with a company of 50 enlisted scouts was attacked by a much larger number of Cheyennes and Dakota (Sioux). Five of Forsyth's company were killed and 16 wounded. Indian losses were greater.   I. W. Van Noppen

530. Andrews, Ralph W. THE 'VANISHING RACE' OF EDWARD S. CURTIS. *Beaver [Canada] 1963 294(Autumn): 46-49.* Edward S. Curtis (1863-1952) spent 40 years amassing data on some 80 Indian tribes and bands west of the Red, Assiniboine and Missouri Rivers. He made a photographic record of their vanishing civilization, and through the friendship of Theodore Roosevelt was able to publish the *North American Indian* (20 vols., 1907-20).   L. F. S. Upton

531. Andrews, Thomas F. FREEDMEN IN INDIAN TERRITORY: A POST
CIVIL WAR DILEMMA. *J. of the West 1965 4(3): 367-376.* In 1866 the Five
Civilized Tribes and the United States concluded new treaties. During the Civil
War factions of all these tribes had aided the Confederacy, and the United States
forced the tribes to cede land for the use of other Indians and freedmen. Initially
the Choctaw and Chickasaw asked that the ex-slaves be removed from their
district and settled on ceded land. This was in accordance with the wishes of the
freedmen, but in 1869 they held a meeting and expressed a desire to stay in the
district. This was agreeable to the Choctaw and Chickasaw, but at a later date
the Indian leaders sought to have the Negroes removed. In 1881 a Freedmen's
Oklahoma Association was formed for the purpose of promoting colonization of
surplus Indian land by freedmen. Little came of this, but in the 1880's the
Choctaw adopted their freedmen as citizens with full tribal rights. The Chickasaw
did not. The author maintains that the dilemma of the freedmen attracted the
nation's attention to the unoccupied lands of Oklahoma and led to their settlement by whites. Based on congressional documents and published sources; 56
notes.   D. N. Brown

532. Anson, Bert. VARIATIONS OF THE INDIAN CONFLICT: THE EF-
FECTS OF THE EMIGRANT INDIAN REMOVAL POLICY, 1830-1854.
Missouri Hist. R. 1964 59(1): 64-89. The removal policy of the United States
forced numerous tribes that had become partially civilized by years of contact
with white men into a region populated by tribes that were still primitive. The
rate of destruction of acculturation among the emigrant Indians varied from tribe
to tribe, but the evidence suggests that most of the Indians kept the skills and tools
they brought from the East. The influence of the eastern Indians on the tribes of
the Plains was one of deterioration. The Plains Indians often fell heirs to the most
degrading influences of the eastern tribes. It was a repetition of the case where
two groups adopt each other's least desirable characteristic when brought in
contact. Based largely on Bureau of Indian Affairs Papers.   W. F. Zornow

533. Antrei, Albert. FATHER PIERRE DE SMET. *Montana 1963 13(2): 24-43.*
A summarized biography of the first Jesuit missionary in the northern Rocky
Mountains. De Smet, born in Belgium in 1801, spent 10 years among Indians of
the lower Missouri Valley before his establishment of a mission for the Salish of
western Montana in 1841. His vigor and ability led to further assignments in
founding missions to other tribes, including a temporarily unsuccessful attempt
among the Blackfeet. Particular emphasis is placed on De Smet's later service in
winning Indian support of projected treaties, especially the noted Fort Rice
Treaty of 1868.   S. R. Davison

534. Ashcroft, Allan C. CONFEDERATE INDIAN TERRITORY CONDI-
TIONS IN 1865. *Chronicles of Oklahoma 1965 42(4): 421-428.* For four years
the Indian Territory experienced the horrors of the Civil War. Military conditions
in 1865 are delienated in inspector general reports on the state of affairs in Indian
Territory. 12 notes.   I. W. Van Noppen

535. Ashcroft, Allan C. CONFEDERATE INDIAN TROOP CONDITIONS IN 1864. *Chronicles of Oklahoma 1964 41(4): 442-449.* Captain B. W. Marston was sent to inspect the regiments and companies of General Douglas H. Cooper's Indian Division. Discipline was lax. Arms and equipment were poor. The Indians had to disperse to their homes because there were no houses or food for them. Many white men were in the Indian regiments to get out of service. Marston urged the removal of the causes of disorganization. He stated that General Cooper had no command over the men. Cooper asked permission to separate the white soldiers from the Indian troops. By 1865 Captain Marston was in command of a separate battalion in the Indian Division. The division was lacking in basic military attributes. Leadership and command were weak, yet the individual soldiers had an interest in "the cause." 11 notes.   I. W. Van Noppen

536. Ashcroft, Allan C. CONFEDERATE INDIAN DEPARTMENT CONDITIONS IN AUGUST, 1864. *Chronicles of Oklahoma 1963 41(3): 270-285.* Confederate relations with the Indians have seldom been given sufficient consideration. With the coming of secession the Confederate States Government made strong attempts to win the support of the Indians residing within its borders. Eventually a dozen Indian regiments fought for the Confederacy. But the care of the nonmilitary tribal member caused a serious problem. The basis of this article is a report in August 1864, by R. W. Lee, Assistant Superintendent of Indian Affairs, CSA, delineating the problems in supervising the various tribes. He had continued difficulty in obtaining food and supplies for the Cherokee, Creek, Osage, Seminole, Chickasaw, Choctaw, and "Reserve Indians." There was also the problem of maintaining amicable relations among the tribes. Supply depots were established. Looms, spinning wheels, wagon shops, and blacksmith shops were provided for the subsistence of the Indians. The number of the Indians of each tribe needing subsistence were listed and the need for schools was emphasized. The Indians were exempted from taxation. 12 notes.

I. W. Van Noppen

537. Ashcroft, Allan C., ed. A CIVIL WAR LETTER OF GENERAL STEELE, CSA. *Arkansas Hist. Q. 1963 22(3): 278-281.* The general in command of Fort Smith, Arkansas, and of Confederate Indian Territory, wrote to Acting Brigadier General S. P. Bankhead, recently named commander of the Northern Sub-District of Texas. The letter, dated 11 July 1863, discussed overall conditions of Steele's command, offered some information concerning the Union's strength and probable future plans, and dealt with common problems of western Arkansas, southeastern Indian Territory, and northern Texas.   E. P. Stickney

538. Asplin, Ray. A HISTORY OF COUNCIL GROVE IN OKLAHOMA. *Chronicles of Oklahoma 1968 45(4): 433-450.* Now a part of the Oklahoma City complex, Council Grove was the site of councils of Plains Indians. In 1858, Jesse Chisholm recognized the importance of the location and established a trading post there. Chisholm was a scout, trader, and interpreter of considerable renown. The contruction of a nearby ranch house about 1873 may have marked the arrival of Oklahoma's first permanent settlers. Later Council Grove's timber was set

aside by the government for fuel, lumber, and fence posts for nearby Fort Reno. It was opened for general settlement in 1889. 2 illus., map, 76 notes.

D. L. Smith

539. Banks, Dean. CIVIL WAR REFUGEES FROM INDIANA TERRI-TORY, IN THE NORTH, 1861-1864. *Chronicles of Oklahoma 1963 41(3): 286-298.* Describes the plight of the Upper Creek and Seminole who fled from the Indian Territory into Kansas because they were loyal to the Union. They were attacked, pursued, and arrived in Kansas naked and without supplies. They froze, starved, suffered, and many died. Food, clothing, and medical care supplied by the federal government were inadequate in quality and quantity. Many braves, however, enlisted in and fought for the Union Army. In 1864, these loyal Indians were able to return to their homes. 41 notes.

I. W. Van Noppen

540. Barnes, Lela, ed. LETTERS OF ALLEN T. WARD, 1842-1851, FROM THE SHAWNEE AND KAW (METHODIST) MISSIONS. *Kansas Hist. Q. 1967 33(3): 321-376.* Eighteen letters written by Ward to his parents, brother, and sister between 25 June 1842 and 23 February 1851. They are now in the posses-sion of his descendants in Topeka, Kansas, and Urbana, Illinois. The most important letters are the dozen that Ward wrote while teaching at the mission's Indian manual labor school. The letters provide information about the many problems associated with missionary activities on the frontier and the day-by-day operation of a school dedicated to providing Indian children with instruction in English, manual arts, and agriculture. Illus., 26 notes.

W. F. Zornow

541. Barrett, Francis A. THE GREATEST RIDE IN WYOMING HISTORY. *Ann. of Wyoming 1966 38(2): 223-228.* Describes briefly the Fetterman massacre and the weakness of the remaining garrison at Fort Philip Kearny in December 1866. In this situation, John "Portugee" Philips, a civilian employee, agreed to ride to Fort Laramie 236 miles away asking for aid. This he did in four days, traveling through snow and below zero cold, hiding from hostile Indians, and eating only a few biscuits. Based on published secondary material, illus., 30 notes.

R. L. Nichols

542. Barry, Louise. THE RANCH AT WALNUT CREEK CROSSING. *Kansas Hist. Q. 1971 37(2): 121-147.* In 1855 a trading post was constructed at Walnut Creek Crossing on the Santa Fe Trail on the great bend of the Arkansas River, in Kansas. Until it was finally burned down by marauding Cheyenne and Arapaho in 1868, this ranch played an important role in supplying goods to traders moving along the trail and to military expeditions against the Indians. In 1969 the Kansas State Historical Society and Kansas Anthropological Associa-tion conducted excavations on the site of the old ranch. Illus., 101 notes.

W. F. Zornow

543. Barry, Louise, compiler. KANSAS BEFORE 1854: A REVISED AN-NALS. *Kansas Hist. Q. 1963 29(1): 41-81, (2): 143-189, (3): 324-359, (4): 429-486, 1964 30(1); 62-91, (2): 209-244, (3): 339-412, (4): 492-559, 1965 31(2):*

138-199, (3): 256-339, 1966 32(1): 33-112, (2): 210-282, (4): 426-503, 1967 33(1): 13-64, (2): 172-213. Part 9, 1836-37, Part 10, 1838-39, and Part 11, 1840-41: summary of some of the key events which took place in the Kansas area, by two-year periods. Major attention is given to events concerning military affairs, Indian relations, missionary activities, the movement of settlers through the area, land surveys, federal laws pertaining to the area, and vital statistics. Parts 12-15, 1842-46: summary of the key events which took place in the Kansas region during 1842-46. Major attention is given to events concerning military affairs, Indian relations, missionary activities, floods, vital statistics, trade caravans, the movement of settlers and traders over the Santa Fe and Oregon Trails, land surveys, federal laws pertaining to the area, and operations against the Pawnee. The years 1844-45 were marked by the expeditions of Colonel Stephen W. Kearney to the Rockies, and John C. Frémont to California. Part 16, 1847, Part 17, 1848: summary of the key events which took place in the Kansas region during these years. The major topics include the construction of Fort Mann, an investigation of irregularities at the agency of the Mississippi Sauk and Fox and the arrest of Frémont, the discovery of gold in California, traffic on the trails to Oregon and Santa Fe, the return march of the soldiers from Mexico, and the fourth exploration trip led by Frémont. Part 18, 1849, Part 19, 1850: the California gold rush is the major topic. Many Forty-niners traveling along the Oregon-California trail kept extensive diaries. There were also many military expeditions moving across Kansas toward Santa Fe, Oregon and California. The traffic along the western trade routes was unusually heavy. Part 20, 1851: steamboats on the Missouri, the movement of immigrants and goods along the trails to Santa Fe, California, and Oregon, the activities of the U.S. Army, the government's dealings with the Indians, and a cholera epidemic were topics of particular interest during the year. Part 21, 1852, Part 22, 1853, Part 23, 1854: concludes a chronological summary of the key events which took place in the Kansas region, 1540 to 1854. Steamboats on the Missouri, the movement of immigrants and merchandise along the trails to Santa Fe, California, and Oregon, the activities of the U.S. Army, the government's dealings with the Indians, birth notices, and obituaries are the topics of particular interest. Based largely on newspapers, government publications, and microfilms of papers in the National Archives; illus., map of Indian landholdings in 1853, 6 tables of Indian traders, livestock shipments, distances, ship arrivals and departures.   W. F. Zornow

544. Barry, Louise, ed. CHARLES ROBINSON—YANKEE '49ER. HIS JOURNEY TO CALIFORNIA. *Kansas Hist. Q. 1968 34(2): 179-188.* A journal covering some of the experiences that physician Charles Robinson and his 50 associates of the Congress and the California Mutual Protective Association had in Kansas during their trip from Boston to the California gold fields in 1849. Robinson's journal-narrative is drawn from a pamphlet *Nebraska and Kansas. Report of the Committee of the Massachusetts Emigrant Aid Co.* published in Boston in 1854; a letter he published in the *Worcester Spy* (Massachusetts, 1854); *The Kansas Conflict,* which he published in 1892. The journal-narrative contains much information about Kansas geography, Indians, missions, and Kansas City. 10 notes.   W. F. Zornow

545. Bass, Althea. THE CHEYENNE TRANSPORTER. *Chronicles of Oklahoma 1968 46(2): 127-140.* The newspaper *Cheyenne Transporter* was started in December 1879 in Darlington, Indian Territory. Its initial purpose was educational, but its coverage soon broadened to serve the interests of cattlemen and the military. It was a champion of the Indian point of view and a reflector of the society of this frontier outpost; its files, now in the archives of the Oklahoma Historical Society, furnish a valuable body of source material. Publication ceased in 1886. 3 illus.   D. L. Smith

546. Bate, Walter N. EYEWITNESS REPORTS OF THE WAGON BOX FIGHT. *Ann. of Wyoming 1969 41(2): 192-202.* Disputes the small number of Indian casualties in the Wagon Box Fight at Fort Phil Kearny on 2 August 1867. Using the published reports and memoirs of both white and Indian participants, the author tries to determine actual Indian losses. Estimates vary from five to 1,500, but none of the participants give a figure below 180. By comparing the various white and Indian reports of the battle, and using a ratio of two wounded to one dead, the author concludes that Chief Red Cloud's report of between 1,100 and 1,300 Indian casualties is accurate. Based on archival material, published reminiscences, and secondary sources; illus., photos, 13 notes.
                                                                    R. L. Nichols

547. Bearss, Edwin C. GENERAL COOPER'S CSA INDIANS THREATEN FORT SMITH. *Arkansas Hist. Q. 1967 26(3): 256-284.* An account of an attack by Confederate forces on 31 July 1864 against Fort Smith. Both federal and Confederate forces were handicapped by shortages of supplies and difficulties in communications. Based on Official Records; 2 maps, 66 notes.
                                                                    B. A. Drummond

548. Bearss, Edwin C. IN QUEST OF PEACE ON THE INDIAN BORDER: THE ESTABLISHMENT OF FORT SMITH. *Arkansas Hist. Q. 1964 23(2): 123-153.* Land was acquired from the Osages along the Arkansas under Jefferson in 1808-09, in order to enable the Cherokees at their request to leave the Appalachians. The constant friction of the Cherokees and the Osages, and the Indians' dissatisfaction with the encroachments of the whites were soon apparent to the national government. In 1817, despite the dissatisfaction of the Cherokees of the Old Nation with the new Treaty of Hiwassee, the treaty was approved by the Senate, and the construction of Fort Smith began near Belle Point. By 1819, four thousand more Cherokees had, with government assistance, moved to the Arkansas. The eastern Cherokees helped their western brothers in a savage attack on the almost defenseless village of the Osages. This massacre is known as the "Battle of Claremore's Mound." The new fort was intended to prevent future attacks on the Osages by the Cherokees, "prevent the whites from trespassing on Indian lands, and secure the frontier settlements of the Arkansas against raids by the Indians." Illus., 63 notes.   E. P. Stickney

549. Bearss, Edwin C. THE ARKANSAS WHISKEY WAR: A FORT SMITH CASE STUDY. *J. of the West 1968 7(2): 143-172.* Covers the history of Fort Smith, Arkansas, from 1830 to 1834 when it was ordered vacated in favor of a

site some 10 miles distant to be named Fort Coffee. During this period a number of Indian tribes including Choctaw and Chickasaw were moved into the territory from east of the Mississippi. The "whiskey war" refers to the efforts of the army to halt the sale of whiskey to the Indians by the Arkansans.   R. N. Alvis

550. Boles, David C. EDITORIAL OPINION IN OKLAHOMA AND IN- DIAN TERRITORIES ON THE CUBAN INSURRECTION, 1895-1898. *Chronicles of Oklahoma 1969 47(3): 258-267.* Between 1895 and 1898 the eastern part of the present state of Oklahoma was called Indian Territory, while the western area was called Oklahoma Territory. Newspapers in both sections criti- cized the Spanish Government's actions in Cuba, as well as the inaction by the U.S. Government. *The Daily Oklahoman* and the *Tecumseh Herald* are the most often cited sources in this article, though the Muskogee *Phoenix, The Cherokee Advocate,* and other papers are also mentioned. By 1897 many editorials in- cluded statistical reports on noncollected taxes, unemployment, and army prob- lems in Cuba. Neither the Dupuy de Lôme letter nor the sinking of the *Maine* brought comment from Oklahoma editors, but soon thereafter they began to demand war with Spain and favored annexation of Cuba. 45 notes.
                                                        K. P. Davis

551. Boller, Henry A. JOURNAL OF A TRIP TO, AND RESIDENCE IN, THE INDIAN COUNTRY. *North Dakota Hist. 1966 33(3): 261-315.* From 1 September until 31 December 1858 Henry Boller, Upper Missouri fur trader, reported daily his preparation for his first trading expedition, the Assiniboin camp, his stock in trade, traveling experiences, Indian customs, descriptions of the country, the building of Fort Atkinson (a trading post) and life there, and the coming and going of the Indians to the fort. Boller and a rival trader, accom- panied by assistants with ox-drawn wagons, went with the Atsina (Gros Ventres) as they moved on 30 October to their winter quarters where both traders had houses built for their stock. During November several trips were made back to Fort Atkinson for additional goods. Most of December was spent keeping store and hunting. Illus., 10 notes.   I. W. Van Noppen

552. Bonney, David. THE INDIAN AND THE HORSE. *Am. Hist. Illus. 1966 1(5): 44-54.* The emergence of the horse on the American Continent, his crossing into Asia, and reintroduction by Spaniards are traced. Emphasis is on the impact of the horse on the Plains tribes and the methods of catching, training, and equipping him. 4 illus., 3 photos.   E. Brown

553. Bray, Martha. PIERRE BOTTINEAU: PROFESSIONAL GUIDE. *North Dakota Q. 1964 32(2): 29-37.* Covers the career of a French-Indian guide in North Dakota during the 19th century. Bottineau, though occasionally a farmer or businessman, served primarily as guide to governmental, business and railroad parties crossing the northern Plains. His career spanned development of the area from individual exploration to the railroad. Documented.   J. F. Mahoney

554. Brooks, George R., ed. GEORGE C. SIBLEY'S JOURNAL OF A TRIP TO THE SALINES IN 1811. *Bull. of the Missouri Hist. Soc. 1965 21(3): 167-207.* Presents, with editorial introduction and notes, the journal of a man who, at the time, was chief factor in the new Indian trading post of Fort Osage up the Missouri River. Based on a letter to his father, Sibley's journal describes at considerable length the territory and Indian tribes in the area west and south of Fort Osage. He visited and described the Osage, Konsee, and Pawnee tribes and found further information about the earlier Zebulon Pike expedition. 40 notes.

R. J. Hanks

555. Brown, Alice E. THE FUR TRADE POSTS OF THE SOURIS-MOUTH AREA. *Hist. and Sci. Soc. of Manitoba Papers, 1961-62 [Canada] 1964 series 3(18): 78-91.* Two kinds of evidence are examined: the physical evidence of the sites themselves and the written evidence from letters and journals of fur traders, 1793-1821. One journal not previously studied, that of William Yorstone, the man in charge of Brandon House from 1810 to 1821, provides important materials. Archaeological investigation should be fruitful, for the whole area was an important point-of-pause in the Indians' yearly migrations and was certainly one of the original centers of fur trade activity in the plains area of Manitoba. 2 maps, 16 notes.

E. P. Stickney

556. Brown, D. Alexander. THE MILLION DOLLAR WAGON TRAIN RAID. *Civil War Times Illus. 1968 7(6): 12-20.* Tells of a Confederate raid on a rich Union supply train of 205 wagons in Indian Territory on 18 September 1864. The 29th and 30th Texas regiments, plus an Indian brigade, numbered about two thousand men. The force was commanded by Brigadier General Stand Watie, a three-quarter-blood Cherokee Indian, Acting Brigadier General Richard M. Gano, and Colonel Charles DeMorse. The wagon train, under Major Henry Hopkins, had about 800 men. Meeting at Cabin Creek Stockade, the Union soldiers were driven off and the Confederates captured the wagon train. Casualties were light on both sides. The Texans were to have made a raid into Kansas to draw off Union forces from Sterling Price who was launching an invasion of Missouri. Had they done so, the Confederates "might have gained a great deal more than the spoils of a rich wagon train."

R. N. Alvis

557. Brown, George A. THE SETTLEMENT OF CHEROKEE COUNTY. *Ann. of Iowa 1963 36(7): 539-556.* Several families set out from Milford, Massachusetts during the winter of 1855-56. They were to settle in Cherokee County, Iowa. Although troubled by Indians, prairie fires, wind storms, and long harsh winters, these families managed to build a settlement including a school and the services of a Methodist minister.

W. F. Peterson

558. Brown, Mark H. and Felton, W. R. L. A. HUFFMAN, BRADY OF THE WEST. *Montana 1956 6(1): 29-37.* Laton A. Huffman came to Montana in 1878 as post photographer at Fort Keough. There and at nearby Miles City, over a period of some 50 years, he photographed the people and sights on this colorful frontier. Using the crude equipment and awkward methods then current, Huffman made an unmatched record of the closing scenes of the Indian Wars, the

extermination of the bison, the open-range phase of the cattle business, and the establishment of routine civilization. This documentary photography causes him to be likened to Matthew Brady, famed for similar work in the Civil War. Huffman was also noted as a guide for hunting parties.   S. R. Davison

559. Brugge, David M. SOME PLAINS INDIANS IN THE CHURCH RECORDS OF NEW MEXICO. *Plains Anthropologist 1965 10(29): 181-189.* "The information found relating to four Plains tribes, Aa (Ae), Shuman (Jumano), Kiowa and Pawnee, in the baptismal and burial records of the Catholic Church in New Mexico for the period from 1694 to 1875 is summarized in tabular form. A brief description is given of the circumstances resulting in these records and their possible significance to Plains history."   J

560. Caldwell, Dorothy J. THE BIG NECK AFFAIR. TRAGEDY AND FARCE ON THE MISSOURI FRONTIER. *Missouri Hist. R. 1970 64(4): 391-412.* Within five years after the Iowa, Sauk, and Fox Indians relinquished some land claims in Missouri, a group of whites moved into the area and formed a settlement known as "The Cabins" on the Chariton River. The author describes a minor confrontation between Big Neck's band of Indians and these settlers, producing widespread fear that the entire frontier was threatened by hordes of Indians. Troops were needlessly rushed in to defend the frontier. After they were captured, Big Neck and some of his lieutenants were brought to trial. There was no great protest when they were acquitted. The commander of the militia was also acquitted by a court-martial. What had looked like a major crisis suddenly turned into a situation in which both sides appeared innocent of any real intent to plunge the frontier into a bloodbath. Based on books, articles, newspapers, county histories, and manuscripts in the Kansas State Historical Society and the State Historical Society of Missouri; illus., 76 notes.   W. F. Zornow

561. Caldwell, Warren W. FORTIFIED VILLAGES IN THE NORTHERN PLAINS. *Plains Anthropologist 1964 9(23): 1-7.* "The varied defensive systems of [Indian] villages in the northern Plains are used as the basis for an inference of change in the patterns of warfare."   J

562. Chapman, Berlin B. THE BARNES FAMILY OF BARNESTON. *Nebraska Hist. 1966 47(1): 57-83.* Examines the Barnes family and their role in the history of the Oto and Missouri tribe, particularly with regard to the tribal lands in Nebraska and western Iowa that were ceded to the United States. Francis M. Barnes (1832-1916) acted as an advisor to the tribe on business matters while tribal property accrued to his family through his half-breed wife, Mary Jane Drips Benoist Barnes (1829-1920).   R. Lowitt

563. Chilcott, Winona Hunter. SYLVESTER WITT MARSTON. *Chronicles of Oklahoma 1967 45(1): 68-72.* Briefly describes Dr. Marston and his tenure as Indian agent of the Union Mission in Muscogee, Indian Territory. Born in Maine, he received his D.D. degree in 1852 and later became president of Burlington University in Iowa. After some additional religious work, Dr. Marston accepted

the Indian agency appointment from President Grant. He stayed at the agency until it was closed in 1878. The author believes Marston could have accomplished more in some other capacity, for he was a talented man. Appendix describing the agency's physical assets and an invoice of property. K. P. Davis

564. Coffman, Edward M., ed. BEN MC CULLOCH LETTERS. *Southwestern Hist. Q. 1956/57 60(1): 118-122.* Reprints three letters from Ben McCulloch to General Albert Pike in 1861 concerning efforts of the Confederacy to obtain an alliance with the Indians. J. A. Hudson

565. Corwin, Hugh D. PROTESTANT MISSIONARY WORK AMONG THE COMANCHES AND KIOWAS. *Chronicles of Oklahoma 1968 46(1): 41-57.* Protestant missionary work among the Comanche and Kiowa of southwestern Oklahoma began as early as 1869 with Quakers appointed by the government to serve as agents. Subsequent efforts have been conducted under the aegis of the Baptist, Mennonite, Methodist, Presbyterian, and Reformed denominations. 25 notes. D. L. Smith

566. Currin, Jean McCulley. WHY INDIAN TERRITORY JOINED THE CONFEDERACY. *Lincoln Herald 1967 69(2): 83-91.* Presents evidence that the pro-Southern and proslavery proclivities of the Five Civilized Tribes coupled with the withdrawal of federal troops and general misunderstanding of Indian attitudes in the territory by the Union government at the beginning of the war enabled Confederate agents to draw the Indians into an alliance in 1861. S. L. Jones

567. Daniell, Forrest. TEXAS PIONEER SURVEYORS AND INDIANS. *Southwestern Hist. Q. 1956/57 60(4): 501-506.* Relates several incidents of Indian raids against surveying crews in Texas in the 1830's and 1840's. J. A. Hudson

568. Danziger, Edmund J., Jr. CIVIL WAR PROBLEMS IN THE CENTRAL AND DAKOTA SUPERINTENDENCIES: A CASE STUDY. *Nebraska Hist. 1970 51(4): 411-424.* Examines the work of the Office of Indian Affairs during the Civil War in protecting and caring for the friendly Indians of Kansas, Nebraska, and Dakota, and in pacifying the hostiles while pioneers pushed up the Kansas, Platte, and Missouri rivers, trespassing on Indian lands and destroying game. R. Lowitt

569. Danziger, Edmund J.,Jr. THE OFFICE OF INDIAN AFFAIRS AND THE PROBLEM OF CIVIL WAR INDIAN REFUGEES IN KANSAS. *Kansas Hist. Q. 1969 35(3): 257-275.* The poor care provided by the Office of Indian Affairs for its charges became even poorer during the Civil War. Thousands of Indians driven into Kansas from Indian Territory during the war faced a grim future. No one wanted them in Kansas, but no one could guarantee their safety in Indian Territory. For more than three years they were allowed to wander or were herded back and forth across the border. The Office of Indian Affairs was

hampered by corruption, jurisdictional quarrels, low morale, administrative weaknesses, inordinate demands imposed by the war, and the inability to antici- pate how many Indians would become refugees because of the war. Based on books, articles, annual reports of the Commissioner of Indian Affairs, records of the Department of the Interior, of the War Department, and of the Southern Superintendency, and material in the National Archives; illus., map, photos, 71 notes.   W. F. Zornow

570. Davison, Stanley. HAZARD AND THE CENTENNIAL SUMMER. *Montana 1955 5(4): 24-33.* Describes the work of Governor Isaac I. Stevens of Montana in negotiating with the various Indian tribes of the region prior to the treaty council of 1855. The author recounts the significant ride of the governor's 13-year-old son, Hazard, who acted as messenger to the savage Atsina (Gros Ventre) tribe just before the council.   B. Waldstein

571. Day, Daniel S. FORT SEDGWICK. *Colorado Mag. 1965 42(1): 16-35.* From 1864 to 1871 Fort Sedgwick, at first named Camp Rankin, served as a protector of travelers, settlers, and stage lines from depredations of hostile Indi- ans. Comments on the life of the camp and activities of the troops.
I. W. Van Noppen

572. Debo, Angie. THE LOCATION OF THE BATTLE OF ROUND MOUN- TAINS. *Chronicles of Oklahoma 1963 41(1): 70-104.* Between a command of Creeks, Seminoles, Choctaws, and Chickasaws, and a detachment of Texas cav- alry on one side, and a group of Creeks loyal to the Union led by Opothle Yahola on the other, 19 November-26 December 1861, three battles were fought, but the locations of the battles are indefinite. The Unionists were attacked and finally fled to Kansas leaving behind 60 to 100 dead plus 17 wagons loaded with supplies and countless other objects. The author examines the legends that have grown and the newspaper accounts that have appeared, and contests most of the supposed sites of the battles and the routes of Yahola's retreat except those of Indian survivors. She concludes that white investigators have failed to relate Indian testimony to known facts and that "the time has come now for a definite identifi- cation of the place."   I. W. Van Noppen

573. Dempsey, Hugh A. SWEETGRASS HILLS MASSACRE. *Montana 1957 7(2): 12-18.* Less well known than the Cypress Hills Massacre in 1873, the Sweetgrass Hills affair a year earlier and on the Montana side of the international boundary was an equally important and colorful incident. These fights led to much debate and some court action to determine whether white wolf-hunters who killed Indians on each occasion were acting in self-defense or aggressively against harmless natives. Based on contemporary newspapers.   S. R. Davison

574. Dippie, Brian W. JACK CRABB AND THE SOLE SURVIVORS OF CUSTER'S LAST STAND. *Western Am. Literature 1969 4(3): 189-202.* Gives "Jack Crabb," the main character in Thomas Berger's 1964 *Little Big Man* (New York: Dial Press), consideration among the historical and fictional "sole survi-

vor" claimants of the Battle of the Little Big Horn (1876). A knowledge of Berger's sources would help illuminate the text, since the novel is thoroughly based on research. "Crabb's" literary antecedent is "John Clayton," and his historical antecedent is perhaps Jack Cleybourne. Berger's realization of the equal importance of myth and historical fact is crucial, enabling him to produce "a myth within a myth" that is based on history. S. L. McNeel

575. Dunn, Adrian R. A HISTORY OF OLD [FORT] BERTHOLD. *North Dakota Hist. 1963 30(4): 157-240.* Traces events from the migration of the three tribes, Mandans, Hidatsa, and Arikara to the Upper Missouri: the coming of fur traders, devastation of the three tribes by smallpox brought in with a steamboat cargo in 1837, building of Fort Berthold and establishment of a highly competitive fur trade there, the strife of the 1860's, the end of the Berthold trade in the 1870's, and efforts to educate the Indians and teach them useful trades. By 1880 the three tribes had lost half their reservation to the Northern Pacific Railroad and in 1884 individual allotments of land were made to heads of families for farms. The tribal culture was to be replaced with that of the white man. The balance of the tribal reservation was allotted to homesteaders. Illus., biblio. I. W. Van Noppen

576. Ellis, Richard N. AFTER BULL RUN: THE LATER CAREER OF GENERAL JOHN POPE. *Montana 1969 19(4): 46-57.* Following an undistinguished campaign in Virginia in 1862, General John Pope was transferred to a post in Minnesota with orders to chastise the Indians responsible for recent massacres in that area. Success during the next two years restored Pope's military reputation, and most of his remaining career consisted of important assignments on the frontier. His observation of Indian problems led him to advocate new policies toward hostile tribes. His enlightened program failed largely because of incompetent subordinates and because of political pressures to retain the old methods of treaties and annuities. Illus., 28 notes. S. R. Davison

577. Ellis, Richard N. GENERAL JOHN POPE AND THE SOUTHERN PLAINS INDIANS, 1875-1883. *Southwestern Hist. Q. 1968 72(2): 152-169.* As commander of the Department of the Missouri, Major General John Pope had put down the hostilities of the Kiowa, Comanche, and Southern Cheyenne. With the conclusion of hostilities in 1875, Pope entered into a protracted struggle with the Bureau of Indian Affairs to maintain the peace and to treat the Southern Plains Indians with humanity. He believed that ultimate assimilation was the proper goal but that the process of conversion must be one of sympathetic firmness and instruction in white ways. He insisted that they could not be permitted to starve. Pope's continuous battle with the bureau over the treatment of the Indians brought little improvement before he was transferred to another command in 1883. 47 notes. D. L. Smith

578. Ellis, Richard N. VOLUNTEER SOLDIERS IN THE WEST, 1865. *Military Affairs 1970 34(2): 53-55.* One of the major reasons for the failure of the 1865

campaign against the Dakota (Sioux) and the Cheyenne was the insubordination of many of the troops who were volunteers awaiting demobilization following the Civil War. 11 notes.   K. J. Bauer

579. Ellis, Richard N., ed. BENT, CARSON AND THE INDIANS, 1865. *Colorado Mag. 1969 46(1): 55-68.* An introduction gives the setting for the report (27 October 1865) of William Bent and Kit Carson to General John Pope, commander of the Department of the Missouri. The report is reproduced. It recommends that Indians be controlled by the War Department and placed on reservations. Furthermore, it suggests that posts be garrisoned by regular troops and officers of "known discretion and judgment," that both white and Indian offenders be punished by law, and that strict regulations be enforced over trade with the Indians. Illus., 25 notes.   O. H. Zabel

580. Enochs, James C. CLASH OF AMBITION: TAPPAN-CHIVINGTON FEUD. *Montana 1965 15(3): 58-67.* Indian fighting on the Plains during the Civil War was complicated by a feud between John M. Chivington and Samuel F. Tappan, commanders of the troops in eastern Colorado. Based on correspondence of the two men, and on newspapers and other printed sources; photos.
                                                                                    S. R. Davison

581. Ewers, John C. "CHIEFS FROM THE MISSOURI AND MISSISSIPPI" AND PEALE'S SILHOUETTES OF 1806. *Smithsonian J. of Hist. 1966 1(1): 1-26.* In response to an invitation to visit the United States issued by President Thomas Jefferson in 1803 with the intention of cementing relations with the Indians of the territory of the Louisiana Purchase, numerous tribes sent delegates eastward in the years immediately following. The second large contingent visited Washington and other centers in the winter of 1805-06. While in Philadelphia, the profiles of many of the members of the party were drawn by the renowned artist Charles Wilson Peale. Ten of these silhouettes survive in the collections of the Smithsonian Institution and the author here identifies some of them while telling the story of their journey and of Peale's work. Among the more prominent of the men identified are Sagessaga, or the Wind, head chief of the Little Osage, and two interpreters, Paul Chouteau and Joseph Barron. Based on contemporary manuscript sources and newspaper accounts as well as on the 10 surviving profiles which form a part of the 15 illustrations. 89 notes.   J. J. McCusker

582. Ewers, John C. DEADLIER THAN THE MALE. *Am. Heritage 1965 16(4): 10-13.* Among the Indians the female could also be deadly. Related are the following stories of Indian women: 1) Elk Hollering in the Water, a Blackfoot, who often accompanied Blackfeet war and horse-stealing parties; 2) The Other Magpie, a Crow, who went with the Crow scouts that assisted General George Crook against the Dakota (Sioux) in 1876, and who returned with one of the 11 scalps taken from the Dakota by the Crow at the Battle of the Rosebud 17 June 1876; 3) Woman Chief, an Atsina (Gros Ventre) who grew up with the Crow and who even became a member of their council of chiefs; and, perhaps, the most noted of all, 4) Running Eagle, a Blackfoot woman warrior who led many raids on enemy tribes.   J. D. Filipiak

583. Ewers, John C. PLAINS INDIAN PAINTING: THE HISTORY AND DEVELOPMENT OF AN AMERICAN ART FORM. *Am. West 1968 5(2): 4-15, 74-76.* Some primitive art of the Plains Indians survives in the form of pictures incised on vertical rock surfaces or painted on cave walls from Alberta, Canada, to Texas. Although precise dating is difficult at best, there is general agreement among archaeologists that pictograph paintings in a Montana cave date from the late prehistoric period, 500-1800 A.D. Crudely painted representations of men and animals on less durable surfaces may well have been created for thousands of years before the contact period of Indian history. The author traces the influence of the techniques of artists who accompanied explorers and soldiers, the adoption of paper and paint and water colors which the whites used, the encouragement of Indian agents and others, the formal training and schooling offered to budding Indian artists, the collection and competitive exhibitions of their art, and the awakening awareness of the world to Plains Indian painting. Although the themes, styles, and functions have changed over the years, the tradition of this art form persists and is very active today. Derived from a forthcoming book, 14 illus.   D. L. Smith

584. Ewers, John C. PLAINS INDIAN REACTIONS TO THE LEWIS AND CLARK EXPEDITION. *Montana 1966 16(1): 2-12.* Although the Northwest Plains Indians had earlier met white men, their contact with Lewis and Clark was decisive in establishing a hostile attitude, especially toward Americans. Diplomacy apparently was the least successful aspect of the expedition. Published sources.   S. R. Davison

585. Ewers, John C. THOMAS M. EASTERLY'S PIONEER DAGUERREOTYPES OF PLAINS INDIANS. *Bull. of the Missouri Hist. Soc. 1968 24(4, pt. 1): 329-339.* Easterly, a professional daguerreotypist, was probably the first to make photographs of the Plains Indians. It is also probable that he took these daguerreotypes while he worked as an itinerant in the vicinity of Liberty, Missouri, not too far from a Sauk and Fox reservation. 8 illus., 27 notes.
D. L. Smith

586. Ewers, John C. WAS THERE A NORTHWESTERN PLAINS SUB-CULTURE? AN ETHNOGRAPHICAL APPRAISAL. *Plains Anthropologist 1967 12(36): 167-183.* After briefly examining the economy, political organization, intertribal warfare, and the importance of the horse, the author concludes that there is no distinct division of a Northwestern Plains culture within the Plains Indian culture area. Almost all of the tribes resident in this area had not lived in it prior to 1800 and therefore were immigrants. To answer the cultural problems of these tribes one must look to the east for the origins of the older traits in their cultures. Biblio.   K. Adelfang

587. Faulk, Odie B. RANCHING IN SPANISH TEXAS. *Hispanic Am. Hist. R. 1965 45(2): 257-266.* An examination of the growth of the cattle industry in Spanish Texas. Included are details of attempts to regulate and tax cattle ranching, protests by ranchers and clergy, and problems with the Indians of the area. By the late 18th century cattle had proved to be a source of revenue for the

government and for the ranchers as they were exported eastward to Louisiana—illegally after Louisiana became part of the United States. Based on materials in the Béxar Archives of the University of Texas. Documented, 33 notes.

B. B. Solnick

588. Filipiak, Jack D. THE BATTLE OF SUMMIT SPRINGS. *Colorado Mag. 1964 41(4): 343-354.* Tall Bull led a band of Cheyennes and Dakota (Sioux) in a last stand against encroachments of white men and railroads. From 1 May to 2 June 1869, they raided in the Saline and Solomon River Valleys. Appeals of settlers for protection led to the Republican River Expedition of eight under-manned companies of the Fifth Cavalry commanded by Brevet Major General Eugene A. Carr and a battalion of Pawnee Indian scouts led by Major Frank J. North, with "Buffalo Bill" Cody as the chief scout. This was the last conflict with Plains Indians in Colorado Territory. It was reenacted as the climax to Cody's Wild West Show for years.

I. W. Van Noppen

589. Fisher, A. D. CULTURAL CONFLICTS ON THE PRAIRIES, INDIAN AND WHITE. *Alberta Hist. R. [Canada] 1968 16(3): 22-29.* Describes the unique features of the prairie culture of Indians and the impact of European culture upon this established form. There is a discussion of geographic consider-ations in the evolution of Indian culture and the development of tribal life.

H. M. Burns

590. Fisher, John R. THE ROYALL AND DUNCAN PURSUITS: AFTER-MATH OF THE BATTLE OF SUMMIT SPRINGS, 1869. *Nebraska Hist. 1969 50(3): 293-308.* An account of the futile searches by the Fifth Cavalry under Major William Bedford Royall for refugee bands of Cheyenne and Dakota (Sioux) Indians in the Republican River valley of southern Nebraska in 1869 following the Battle of Summit Springs. After reaching Fort McPherson, Thomas Duncan replaced Royall as commander of the Republican Valley Expedition. The Battle of Summit Springs "had been a major defeat of hostile Indians of the central plains," and the expeditions of Royall and Duncan "made it plain to the Indians that it was not a chance encounter....The military intended to keep the Indians and the plains in a semblance of order." 42 notes.

R. Lowitt

591. Fletcher, Robert H. THE DAY OF THE CATTLEMAN DAWNED EARLY—IN MONTANA. *Montana 1961 11(4): 22-28.* Traces the origin of Montana's cattle industry, starting with the oxen of travelers on the emigrant trails. These animals, often foot-sore and trail-weary, were bought cheaply or acquired by trade and driven into Montana's western valleys as foundations of beef herds. Some were marketed in the Oregon country, while others were sold to the missions, whose herds helped to feed the Indians as the buffalo became scarce. This meat supply was a welcome resource when the area's gold rush began shortly in the 1860's.

S. R. Davison

592. Forbis, Richard G. THE DIRECT HISTORICAL APPROACH IN THE PRAIRIE PROVINCES OF CANADA. *Great Plains J. 1963 3(1): 9-16.* Points

out that the "Great Plains" extends into Canada in a vast wedge called the "Palliser Triangle." The article discusses three methods utilized in attempts to identify historic Indian tribes with prehistoric remains in the Palliser triangle: the direct historical approach, the direct ethnological approach, and the inferential historical approach. While all three have weaknesses, when several lines of evidence converge toward a single conclusion, their cumulative testimony cannot be lightly dismissed.   O. H. Zabel

593. Gage, Duane. OKLAHOMA: A RESETTLEMENT AREA FOR INDIANS. *Chronicles of Oklahoma 1969 47(3): 282-297.* Discusses the reasons Oklahoma became the principal resettlement area for Indians of the United States. Because of its inaccessibility during colonial times, reported barrenness, and Indian barrier, few whites moved to Oklahoma before the 19th century. The government was pressured to move eastern tribes beyond the Mississippi River. Then Arkansas and Texas became states and the Kansas-Nebraska bill was passed. The Indians were therefore gradually squeezed into the area of present-day Oklahoma. 58 notes.   K. P. Tavis

594. Gephart, Ronald M. POLITICIANS, SOLDIERS AND STRIKES: THE REORGANIZATION OF THE NEBRASKA MILITIA AND THE OMAHA STRIKE OF 1882. *Nebraska Hist. 1965 46(2): 89-120.* Examines the transition of the Nebraska militia system, 1879-82, from a frontier outfit fighting Indians to a more "eastern" organization designed to curb industrial violence. The differences between the eastern militia and that of Nebraska and the use of the Nebraska organization in the Omaha strike of 1882 are examined.   R. Lowitt

595. Gibson, A. M. CONFEDERATES ON THE PLAINS: THE PIKE MISSION TO WICHITA AGENCY. *Great Plains J. 1964 4(1): 7-16.* Describes the Confederacy's interest in Indian Territory and General Albert Pike's mission there in August 1861. He was successful in treating with both the civilized tribes in the east and the Comanches in the west. He was unable to meet with the Kiowas, the most hostile toward neighboring Texas. About one-half of the article is composed of two long quotations from Pike's report to the Confederate Government. Published government records and some unpublished letters provide the main additional sources. 13 notes.   O. H. Zabel

596. Gilles, Albert S., Sr. UNCLE SIM'S TRADING STORE. *Southwest R. 1964 49(4): 342-351.* Folksy reminiscences of six years spent by Albert S. Gilles, Sr. in his father's trading store at Faxon, Oklahoma, serving settlers and Indians alike. Relates type of products sold, problems of bill collection, and freighting.   D. F. Henderson

597. Gilstrap, Harry B., Jr., ed. COLONEL SAMUEL LEE PATRICK. *Chronicles of Oklahoma 1968 46(1): 58-63.* Samuel Lee Patrick served as an Indian agent to the Sauk and Fox near Stroud, Oklahoma, from 1889 to 1895. His "Notes" contain miscellaneous information including comments on some of the leaders. 2 illus.   D. L. Smith

598. Gray, John S. WILL COMSTOCK, SCOUT: THE NATTY BUMPO OF KANSAS. *Montana 1970 20(3): 2-15.* Identifies frontier scout William Averill Comstock (1842-68) as the child of a prominent Michigan family and as a grandnephew of James Fenimore Cooper. Orphaned early, Will Comstock became an Indian trader in Nebraska before he was 18 years old. In the Indian troubles of the 1860's he served as an army scout, including some service under George A. Custer in Kansas. He died while on a peace mission to the Cheyenne Indians in 1868. Derived from published material and U.S. Census records; illus., 23 notes.   S. R. Davison

599. Hagan, William T. KIOWAS, COMANCHES, AND CATTLEMEN, 1867-1906: A CASE STUDY OF THE FAILURE OF U.S. RESERVATION POLICY. *Pacific Hist. R. 1971 40(3): 333-355.* The treaty which these two tribes signed with the United States in 1867 provided a reservation of 3 million acres closed to all white men. Relates the gradual encroachment of whites onto this land. First came the cattlemen, whose payment for the leasing of the lands was gradually welcomed by most of the Indians. Then potential settlers began to put pressure on the government for open land. In 1901 legislation opened a portion of the land to them, and brought to an end the cattleman's era. It was also the final blow to the principle of isolation inherent in the treaty. History might have been different had the government subsidized the experiment properly. 91 notes.
E. C. Hyslop

600. Haines, Francis. HORSES FOR WESTERN INDIANS. *Am. West 1966 3(2): 4-15, 92.* That the Plains Indians had been horsemen from time immemorial is historically inaccurate. The advent of horses to the western United States is comparatively recent. The hypothesis that bands of stray horses from the expeditions of Hernando De Soto (1539-42) and Francisco Coronado (1540-42) furnished the parent stock is untenable. With only minor adaptations, the Indians borrowed the entire horse-culture complex from the Spanish New Mexican colony between 1650 and 1700. The manner in which this was accomplished and the spread of the horse frontier into the Great Plains grassland areas and into the Pacific Northwest are explained. Map, illus., biblio. note.   D. L. Smith

601. Hall, Peter Nelson. MINIRARA, MINNEAPOLIS' INTERNATIONALLY HISTORIC FALLS. *Historic Preservation 1971 23(3): 36-44.* A sketch of the history of Minirara Falls (the Falls of St. Anthony) in Minneapolis. The first white man to see the falls was Father Louis Hennepin in 1680. An Indian legend tells of a distraught young woman who paddled her canoe over the falls, but who lived in the spray over Spirit Island below the falls. The island was removed by the Corps of Engineers in 1950. American soldiers built a grist mill on the falls in 1823, and the village of St. Anthony grew from this beginning. In 1852 a settlement on the west bank of the Mississippi became Minneapolis. Because of the water power potential a number of flour mills were established there. The most famous of these mills was the Pillsbury A Mill, which in 1881 was the world's largest. This mill is still in operation. Describes efforts to preserve the falls area. In 1971 the St. Anthony Historic District was created. Illus.
J. M. Hawes

602. Hampton, H. D. POWDER RIVER INDIAN EXPEDITION OF 1865. *Montana 1964 14(4): 2-15.* In response to popular demand, General Patrick E. Connor was given responsibility for clearing hostile Indians from the Oregon Trail in Wyoming. Connor accompanied one of three columns marching against the Dakota (Sioux), Cheyenne, and Arapahoe. Hampered by unseasonable cold, "incompetent guides and vague maps," and with forces largely made up of recruits and unwilling Civil War veterans, the campaign accomplished little. Indicated sources are congressional documents and standard published accounts.

S. R. Davison

603. Harris, Frank H. NEOSHA AGENCY 1838-1871. *Chronicles of Oklahoma 1965 43(1): 35-57.* These annals of an Indian agency reveal the ineptitude with which the government dealt with the situation after the removal of the tribes to Indian Territory. Promises made in the treaties, such as provision for schools, were not kept, and, although agents were appointed, quarters were not provided for them. Under these conditions agents seldom remained long, and those who accepted the positions were sometimes unqualified for the work. The tribes included in the Neosha Agency were Senecas from Sandusky, Ohio, Quapaws from Arkansas, Seneca and Shawnees from Lewistown, Ohio, and later the so-called "New York Indians," parts of the Seneca, Tuscarora, Oneida, St. Regis, Onondaga, and Cayuga tribes. When the Civil War began, some of them served with the Confederacy while others were loyal to the Union. In 1875 the Neosha Agency ceased to exist, being replaced by the Quapaw Agency, which was much more efficient. 38 notes.

I. W. Van Noppen

604. Heath. Gary N. THE FIRST FEDERAL INVASION OF INDIAN TERRITORY. *Chronicles of Oklahoma 1967 44(4): 409-419.* The Battle of Pea Ridge, Arkansas, 6-8 March 1862 was the turning point of the war for Indian Territory. The Confederates were defeated, the Union forces were in the ascendancy, and Union commanders decided to invade Indian Territory, with victorious results. The defeated men spread fear and panic and caused the disintegration of Confederate alliances with the Indians. Many sought refuge within federal lines. 33 notes.

I. W. Van Noppen

605. Hiatt, Burritt M. JAMES M. HAWORTH, QUAKER INDIAN AGENT. *Bull. of Friends Hist. Assoc. 1958 47(2): 80-93.* Haworth (1832-85) was appointed agent to the Kiowa and Comanche Indian tribes in the region near Fort Sill (Oklahoma) in 1873. His appointment was the result of President Grant's peace policy after the failure of attempts at military repression of the Indians. Haworth had to deal with hostile military men and whites who abused, or wished to deal harshly with the Indians. He managed to gain the confidence of the Indians, thus helping to ease some of the tensions between them and the soldiers.

N. Kurland

606. Hiemstra, William L. PRESBYTERIAN MISSIONS AMONG CHOCTAW AND CHICKASAW INDIANS, 1860-1861. *J. of the Presbyterian Hist. Soc. 1959 37(1): 51-59.* Describes the disruptive effect of the sectional controversy and secession upon missionary work in the Indian Territory, and relates how the

Choctaw and Chickasaw Indians were induced in July 1861 to enter into treaties of amity and alliance with the Confederacy. Although a Choctaw regiment was organized for service in the Confederate Army, the Indians were not zealous in their support of the Confederacy. By 1863 at least four hundred Choctaws and Chickasaws had fled to federal territory in Kansas.   W. D. Metz

607. Hill, Burton S. THE GREAT INDIAN TREATY COUNCIL OF 1851. *Nebraska Hist. 1966 47(1): 85-110.* Discusses the great gathering of over 10 thousand Indians from numerous tribes near Fort Laramie, Wyoming where they assembled to confer with white officials, numbering, with troops, less than 300 men, on problems emanating from loss of forage and game owing to heavy traffic on the Oregon Trail. The treaty that emerged from the council was amended by the Senate and did not insure the harmonious relations the negotiating commissioners hoped would follow.   R. Lowitt

608. Hlady, Walter M. INDIAN MIGRATIONS IN MANITOBA AND THE WEST. *Hist. and Sci. Soc. of Manitoba Papers, 1960-61 [Canada] 1964 Series 3(17): 24-53.* Considers in detail the chief Indian tribes that have lived in Manitoba: Cree, Assiniboin, Ojibwa, Chipewyan, Dakota (Sioux), Blackfeet, Sarcees, and the Hidatsa and Atsina. Notes.   E. P. Stickney

609. Hollon, W. Eugene. RUSHING FOR LAND: OKLAHOMA 1889. *Am. West 1966 3(4): 4-15, 69-71.* Much of Oklahoma was assigned to various Indian tribes. A part of the Seminole and Creek reservations, a two-million-acre tract in the center of Oklahoma, was never occupied. Popularly called "the District" it soon tempted land-hungry whites. Congress had legalized the opening of the District to homesteaders. Based on photographic collections and other manuscript sources sources in the University of Oklahoma Library, contemporary articles in various national periodicals, and secondary histories; 19 illus., map, biblio. note.   D. L. Smith

610. Hood, Fred. TWILIGHT OF THE CONFEDERACY IN INDIAN TERRITORY. *Chronicles of Oklahoma 1964 41(4): 425-441.* A description of the Battle of Honey Springs and the capture of Fort Gibson and Fort Smith. The Confederates were badly armed, clothed, fed, and were defeated and scattered. Stand Watie raided near Fort Gibson and up the Neosha Valley but was defeated. These Confederate defeats impaired relations with their Indian allies. General Kirby Smith assured Watie that the Confederate position would be strengthened. There was friction between Generals Cooper and Steele. General Maxey was sent to take command and he found the army demoralized. He sought to make full use of the Indians. Stand Watie captured a steam ferryboat and a wagon train of 300 wagons with over one million dollars worth of federal supplies. In November 1864 Indian troops had still not been armed. Few federal troops were left. Cooper was finally placed in command of the Indian Territory just a month before Lee surrendered. 49 notes.   I. W. Van Noppen

611. House, R. Morton. "THE ONLY WAY" CHURCH AND THE SAC AND FOX INDIANS. *Chronicles of Oklahoma 1966 43(4): 443-446.* This is the story of the Sauk and Foxes, joined as the Sac and Fox Tribe. The author begins with "The Only Way" Church which he first saw as a lad in 1889. The treaties of 1842, 1860, 1867, and 1890 are discussed. The dates span most of the life of Moses Keokuk, who signed the tribal documents. There are descriptions of the pleasant life on the reservation, of the mission school, and of Sunday school and church services in "The Only Way" Church. 5 illus., 13 notes.

                                                              I. W. Van Noppen

612. Hughes, Willis B. THE FIRST DRAGOONS ON THE WESTERN FRONTIER, 1834-1846. *Arizona and the West 1970 12(2): 115-138.* The mounted volunteers who were pressed into service for the Black Hawk War (1832) were unsatisfactory and the mounted rangers who succeeded them were merely a stopgap measure to reckon with the fast-moving horse Indians. Congress created the elite First Dragoon Regiment which patrolled the thousand-mile frontier between the Red Rivers of Minnesota and Texas, with Colonel Henry Dodge (1782-1867) as its commander from 1834 to 1836, and General Stephen Watts Kearny (1794-1848) as his successor from 1836 to 1846. With nine major expeditions over much of the Great Plains and as many treaties to its credit, the regiment fulfilled its mission with great success. Escort duty down the Santa Fe trail, assistance in settling removal-emigrant Indians, and contacting and overawing Plains tribes were the principal activities. The dragoons maintained this peace on the western frontier for 12 years without a single battle with the Indians, an amazing feat in itself. The experiences of the period also schooled the army in campaigning on the Great Plains, lessons that were to serve it well in later years. 4 illus., 2 maps, 57 notes.   D. L. Smith

613. Johnson, Dorothy M. THE HANGING OF THE CHIEFS. *Montana 1970 20(3): 60-69.* Attempts to identify those responsible for the hanging of two or more Indians charged with kidnapping and other crimes, in the Fort Laramie area in 1865. The author concludes that all accounts are questionable, even as to the number of Indians executed and the details of charges against them. Based on published sources, including official documents; 16 notes.

                                                              S. R. Davison

614. Jones, Dorothy V. A PREFACE TO THE SETTLEMENT OF KANSAS. *Kansas Hist. Q. 1963 29(2): 122-136.* Before Kansas was opened for white settlement, it had already become a haven for many Indian tribes of the eastern states. During 1832, while Chief Black Hawk led some Sauk and Fox in a war against the United States and a cholera epidemic swept through the tribes of the Middle West, Colonel James B. Gardiner was assigned the job of moving several groups of Indians in Ohio to Kansas. This article, which is based largely on the five-volume collection of correspondence on the subject of Indian emigration compiled by the Twenty-third Congress, recounts the grim journey from Ohio to Kansas. The Shawnees and Ottawa found much to admire in the white man's culture. There was not total harmony between both races, but they were closer

in Kansas than in many other states. The author regards this incident as the first step toward the settlement of Kansas and mutual tolerance between the races.

W. F. Zornow

615. Josselyn, Daniel W. INDIAN CAVALRY. *Great Plains J. 1963 2(2): 77-79.* Based on Theodore R. Davis' account of his personal experiences following Custer in Kansas as an artist for *Harper's New Monthly Magazine.*   S

616. Karklins, Karlis. THE FIRE CLOUD SITE (39BF237), BUFFALO COUNTY, SOUTH DAKOTA. *Plains Anthropologist 1970 15(48): 135-142.* "A bottle-necked cache pit was excavated near Old Fort Thompson, Buffalo County, South Dakota in June of 1955 by a University of Kansas field party as part of a non-reservoir salvage project. The site is interesting due to the presence of three variants of Talking Crow Straight Rim pottery apparently unreported up to this time. These consist of a square orifice vessel, a vessel incorporating what most closely resembles Stanley Tool Impressed incised lip decoration, and a vessel bearing three bands of differing design motifs on the lip and upper rim exterior. This site is tentatively assigned to the Fort Thompson focus of the Pahuk aspect. It probably dates to the first half of the 18th century."   J

617. Kay, Marvin. TWO HISTORIC INDIAN BURIALS FROM AN OPEN SITE, 23AD95, ADAIR COUNTY, MISSOURI. *Plains Anthropologist 1968 13(40): 103-115.* "Two historic Indian burials from Adair County, Missouri are discussed. A summary of the site and description of the find are given; ethnohistoric inferences are made on the basis of the available data....The most probable range for the interments at 23AD95 is from 1785 to 1809."   J

618. Kearns, Kevin C. THE ACQUISITION OF ST. LOUIS' FOREST PARK. *Missouri Hist. R. 1968 62(2): 95-106.* An account of how the land that became the site of the Louisiana Purchase Exposition of 1904 was first taken over by St. Louis between 1870 and 1875 for a city park. The bills that were introduced in the state legislature for this purpose are described briefly and some attention is given to court cases growing out of the affair. Supporters of the plan argued that when property is acquired for a park eminent domain is simply redemption by the people of their own property. Indian sites excavated while the site was being prepared for the exposition produced hot debates among experts unable to agree on whether they were ancient or quite recent. Based on newspapers, court records, and local histories; illus., 23 notes.   W. F. Zornow

619. Kehoe, Alice B. ABORIGINAL POTTERY FROM SITE FHNA-3, THE FRANÇOIS LE BLANC TRADING POST. *Plains Anthropologist 1964 9(23): 18-21.* "Aboriginal pottery excavated at a peddlar's post, dated 1768-1774, is described and named the François Variety of the fabric-impressed type of Wascana Ware. The diagnostic feature of François sherds is the use of European cloth for impressing the vessel surfaces. It is suggested that the François Variety can be a horizon marker for the early historic period in Saskatchewan."   J

620. Kehoe, Alice B. THE FUNCTION OF CEREMONIAL SEXUAL IN-
TERCOURSE AMONG THE NORTHERN PLAINS INDIANS. *Plains Anthropologist 1970 15(48): 99-103.* "Sexual intimacy as a means of transferring
spiritual power appears to have been a Mandan-Hidatsa ceremonial trait borrowed by three Algonkian Plains tribes as part of the graded men's societies
complex. The Algonkian tribes modified the rite, which in the village tribes
emphasized the role of father's clan. The Arapaho emphasized the cosmic symbolism of the rite, the Atsina made it a test of self-discipline, and the Blackfoot
[Siksika] stressed the dangerous power commanded by those who performed it.
These modifications parallel the differences in kinship structure between village
and nomadic Plains tribes discussed by [Fred] Eggan."   J

621. Kelsey, Harry. BACKGROUND TO SAND CREEK. *Colorado Mag. 1968
45(4): 279-300.* Asserts that politics offers a fertile field for research on the
background of the Sand Creek Massacre (1864). Discussed are the activities of
three "totally unqualified political appointees" who served as Indian agents in
Colorado Territory prior to the massacre. The inept Samuel G. Colley, cousin of
the newly named Commissioner of Indian Affairs William P. Dole, was appointed
to the Upper Arkansas Indian Agency in 1861. There is some evidence that his
son, Indian trader Dexter Colley, traded and sold Indian "annuity" goods. John
W. Wright, crony of John P. Usher, secretary of the interior, received a lucrative
contract to survey lands on the Upper Arkansas reservation and also to serve as
special agent to the Caddo Indians. After completing a useless survey opposed
by Governor John Evans, Wright attacked Evans by linking him with the causes
of the Indian wars. The third agent was Simeon Whiteley, friend of Simon
Cameron and Senator James R. Dolittle, who was appointed agent to the Middle
Park Indian Agency apparently with the main function of organizing support for
the Lincoln administration in the West. Largely to blame for the "scandalous
state of affairs in the Indian service" in the 1860's was Commissioner William
P. Dole who accommodated "political cronies, greedy relatives, well-meaning
amateurs and conniving rascals" in the Indian service. Illus., 89 notes.
                                                              O. H. Zabel

622. Kennedy, Michael S. PAUL DYCK PORTFOLIO: INDIANS OF THE
OVERLAND TRAIL. *Montana 1962 12(3): 56-66.* Praises Dyck's 15 Indian
portraits. These are presented with his captions. The artist plans to complete a
series depicting all the Plains tribes of 1840-50.   L. G. Nelson

623. Kidder, John. MONTANA MIRACLE: IT SAVED THE BUFFALO.
Montana 1965 15(2): 52-67. During the years 1885-90 the American bison escaped extinction largely because two Montana stockmen, Michel Pablo and
Charles P. Allard, bought a tiny herd from Samuel Walking Coyote and built it
up to 300 head. This account traces the origin of this herd and its dispersal to
provide stock for most of the bison preserves now in existence, including Yellowstone Park.   S. R. Davison

624. King, James T. FORGOTTEN PAGEANT—THE INDIAN WARS IN
WESTERN NEBRASKA. *Nebraska Hist. 1965 46(3): 177-192.* An interpreta-

tive survey of the military frontier in Nebraska emphasizing the period (1854-90) when the Indian-fighting army was most closely associated with the people of western Nebraska.   R. Lowitt

625. Kroeker, Marvin. COLONEL W. B. HAZEN IN THE INDIAN TERRI-TORY. *Chronicles of Oklahoma 1964 42(1): 53-73.* Deals with Hazen's career as a special military agent at Fort Cobb, 1868-69. Following the Congressional Act of 1867 Hazen sought to bring the peaceable Southern Indians—Kiowa Comanche, Kiowa Apache, Wichita, Cheyenne, and Arapaho—in to restricted reservations and to teach them an agricultural mode of life. Treaties had been made with these Indians at Medicine Lodge in 1867. Congress failed to appropri-ate sufficient funds. The Indians were destitute and resentful. Generals Sheridan and Sherman were in command of the military. Hazen had the task of separating the friendly from the hostile Indians. He refused to deal with the Cheyenne and Arapaho tribes who were considered hostile by Sherman and Sheridan, and he urged these tribes to make peace. His funds were inadequate to provide for eight thousand Indians, some of whom raided in Texas. Too few troops were available to restrain these malcontents. Strenuous efforts were made to introduce farming. Hazen's services as special agent were concluded in 1869. He had only partially succeeded in establishing a reservation system but he had prepared the way to lead the Indian on the white man's road. 90 notes.   I. W. Van Noppen

626. Lass, William E. THE "MOSCOW EXPEDITION." *Minnesota Hist. 1965 39(6): 227-240.* An account of the Moscow Expedition of 1863. Following the Sioux uprising of the previous year and the removal of most of the Indians to the Dakota Territory, it became necessary to provide them with food, clothing, and other supplies. Two businessmen named James B. Hubbell and Clark W. Thomp-son contracted to transport the supplies overland, through 292 miles of wilder-ness, with the help of a troop of soldiers who almost proved to be more hindrance than help. The whole affair turned into a farce with political overtones and is another sordid chapter in the story of the poor treatment of the Indians by the white man. Based on letters and newspapers in the Minnesota Historical Society.
                                                                        P. L. Simon

627. Lass, William E. THE REMOVAL FROM MINNESOTA OF THE SIOUX AND WINNEBAGO INDIANS. *Minnesota Hist. 1963 38(8): 353-364.* Following the great Dakota (Sioux) uprising of 1862, the U.S. Government bowed to local pressure and took steps to remove all Indians from southern Minnesota—the relatively peaceful Winnebago as well as the Sioux. They were to be removed beyond the limits of the state to an area along the upper Missouri. Steamboats were chosen to transport them since it was felt this would be cheaper for the government and easier on the Indians than an overland trek. The trip was difficult and uncomfortable. There was considerable over-crowding and insuffi-cient food and water. The white missionaries who accompanied their charges were so appalled by the treatment of the Indians that one wrote to his Bishop, "...if I were an Ind[ian] I would never lay down the war club while I lived." Based largely on Indian Office *Reports* and newspaper accounts.   P. L. Simon

628. Lecompte, Janet. GANTT'S FORT AND BENT'S PICKET POST. *Colorado Mag. 1964 41(2): 111-125.* Locates and identifies three forts on the Arkansas River for trading with the Arapahoe, Cheyenne, Kiowa, and other Indians, two of which were known as Fort Cass and Fort William. Later all were supplanted by a great adobe trading post, Bent's Fort. I. W. Van Noppen

629. Lehman, Leola. A DEPUTY U.S. MARSHAL IN THE TERRITORIES. *Chronicles of Oklahoma 1965 43(3): 289-296.* Deals chiefly with the career of William Bartley Murrill as a deputy U.S. Marshal in Oklahoma, but in doing so depicts the problems of law and order in a territory where no U.S. courts existed. The Indians had their own courts and law enforcement officers, but those had no jurisdiction over white men. Consequently Oklahoma was the hideout of many gangs of outlaws, including some women. 13 notes. I. W. Van Noppen

630. Lehmer, Donald J. THE PLAINS BISON HUNT—PREHISTORIC AND HISTORIC. *Plains Anthropologist 1963 8(22): 211-217.* "Nicholas Perrot, one of the giants of the fur trade, was active in the west for nearly three decades of the latter half of the 17th century. Among his writings he has left a detailed description of the buffalo hunting techniques of the northern Prairie tribes. The individual elements of Perrot's description show a close trait for trait similarity with the hunting complex of the historic Omaha. Those similarities, plus certain elements of the Omaha hunt ritual which may be survivals from the pre-horse period, provide a good indication that the historic hunting complex derived from one which was in existence during pre-contact times." J

631. Lemley, Harry J. LETTERS OF HENRY M. RECTOR AND J. R. KANNADAY TO JOHN ROSS OF THE CHEROKEE NATION. *Chronicles of Oklahoma 1964 42(3): 320-329.* Henry M. Rector, governor of Arkansas, wrote to John Ross, principal chief of the Cherokee Nation, urging the Cherokee to side with the Confederacy. J. R. Kannaday, commander of Fort Smith, wrote Ross asking the intentions of the Cherokee in the war. Ross answered that their treaties were with the U.S. government but that he would advise the Cherokee to be neutral. There follow sketches of the lives of Rector and Ross. After the Confederate victories at the first Battle of Manassas (Bull Run) and the Battle of Wilson Creek, Ross and the Cherokee signed a treaty uniting the Cherokee Nation with the Confederate States. After the Confederate defeat at Locust Grove, Chief Ross went north and favored the Union. 4 notes. I. W. Van Noppen

632. Leutenegger, Benedict, ed. and trans. NEW DOCUMENTS ON FATHER JOSÉ MARIANO REYES. *Southwestern Hist. Q. 1968 71(4): 583-602.* Franciscan Father José Mariano Reyes, apparently well-loved by the Indians with whom he worked, was a poor manager of mission affairs and conducted business and correspondence with ecclesiastical and political superiors directly rather than through prescribed channels. He was transferred from mission to mission in Texas. Charges were brought against him repeatedly and some of his actions were reversed. The four translated and edited letters, two from Reyes himself, are

concerned with some of these matters. They reveal the character of Reyes and give a view of some of the internal problems of the mission system. 52 notes.
D. L. Smith

633. Lewitt, Robert T. INDIAN MISSIONS AND ANTISLAVERY SENTIMENT: A CONFLICT OF EVANGELICAL AND HUMANITARIAN IDEALS. *Mississippi Valley Hist. R. 1963 50(1): 39-55.* In 1816, the American Board of Foreign Missions sent Cyrus Kingsbury to establish a mission among the Cherokees and Choctaws. As laborers on the missions Kingsbury used slaves freely. This policy conflicted with the abolitionist sentiment on the American Board. Kingsbury elected to retain the slaves and thereby lost the abolitionist support to the North.
G. M. Gressley

634. Liberty, Margot P. PRIEST AND SHAMAN ON THE PLAINS: A FALSE DICHOTOMY? *Plains Anthropologist 1970 15(48): 73-79.* "For a number of years, anthropologists have tended to classify religious leaders of more or less primitive peoples into shamans on the one hand, and priests on the other. Such terms are analytically useful, but like many polarities of their kind, they tend to break down when applied to 'real world' situations. The Crow and Northern Cheyenne Indians of Montana provide interesting contrasts in this area, where two powerful religious themes—the tribal Sun Dance and the individual Vision Quest—interact in various societies to produce a wide range of ceremonial expression. The literature on these two societies combines with modern field observation to suggest that in one case, shamans prevail entirely—while in the other, a real stage of separation between priest and shaman has developed, with one man serving in both capacities at various times."
J

635. Littlefield, Daniel F., Jr. and Underhill, Lonnie E. NEGRO MARSHALS IN THE INDIAN TERRITORY. *J. of Negro Hist. 1971 56(2): 77-87.* It is little known that several of the lawmen in Indian Territory (now Oklahoma) during the late 19th century were Negroes. Their duties pertained to the regions occupied by the Five Civilized Tribes—the Cherokee, Choctaw, Creek, Chickasaw, and Seminole—and were used by the Indian police and the U.S. marshal's office. The Indians preferred the black law officers, who unlike the white officials had lived all or most of their lives among the Indians and Indian freedmen. A fee system and the lack of available courts also made the Indians distrust white officers. Based mostly on Indian newspapers of the region, and on secondary sources; 45 notes.
R. S. Melamed

636. Loomis, Augustus W. SCENES IN THE INDIAN TERRITORY: KOWETAH MISSION. *Chronicles of Oklahoma 1968 46(1): 64-72.* In 1851, Augustus W. (Gustavus) Loomis published *Scenes in the Indian Territory* from his observations as an army commander in the area in the 1840's. Reprinted here is the portion dealing with a visit he made to the Kowetah Mission, near present Coweta, Oklahoma. Education, Negro interpreters, recreation, and a history of the mission are briefly described. 8 notes.
D. L. Smith

637. MacLeod, Margaret Arnett. DICKSON THE LIBERATOR. *Beaver [Canada] 1956(Summer): 4-7.* A brief account of the only filibustering expedition that ever entered Minnesota. In 1837 James Dickson, self-styled "Liberator of the Indian Nations," attempted to organize an army of liberation to march from Red River to Santa Fe to free the Indians and found a kingdom in California.
R. W. Winks

638. Mallory, Enid Swerdfeger. LUXTON MUSEUM AT BANFF. *Can. Geographical J. 1965 71(2): 64-67.* This museum, based on the collection of Norman Luxton, presents "Old West" Canadiana. Its chief exhibits relate to the Indians of the Banff area, i.e., the Assiniboin (Stonies) and the Blackfoot Confederacy. Photos.
A. H. Lawrance

639. Mardock, Robert W. THE PLAINS FRONTIER AND THE INDIAN POLICY, 1865-1880. *Nebraska Hist. 1968 49(2): 187-201.* Surveys the gradual shift in public opinion on the Plains, evident by the late 1870's, from favoring a policy of exterminating the Indians to one of educating and civilizing them by breaking up tribal relations and making them self-sustaining. Federal policies with regard to the Indians are examined within this context.
R. Lowitt

640. Martin, Charles W., ed. A ROUND TRIP TO THE MONTANA MINES: THE 1866 TRAVEL JOURNAL OF GURDON P. LESTER. *Nebraska Hist. 1965 46(4): 273-313.* Following an overland stage coach route from Iowa to Montana and a water route on the Missouri River back to Iowa, Gurdon Lester gives a description of his travels in the year 1866. Traveling along the Platte River following severe Indian attacks and down the Missouri River at the height of the passenger traffic period, his diary conveys information about the trials and tribulations confronting travelers.
R. Lowitt

641. Mattison, R. H., ed. HENRY A. BOLLER, UPPER MISSOURI RIVER FUR TRADER. *North Dakota Hist. 1966 33(2): 106-219.* Born in 1836 in Philadelphia, Boller early fell in love with the West, reading tales of Indian life during his youth. In the spring of 1858 he fulfilled his dreams and became a clerk for Frost, Todd and Company, an "opposition" company to the American Fur Company, which usually dominated the Upper Missouri trade. Most of his correspondence, which later enabled him to write *Among the Indians,* was penned during the years 1858 to 1860. The letters, printed here for the first time, are invaluable as a guide to the important events of the fading years of the western fur trade. In addition, he was an avid observer of Indian customs and life during what was to be the last years of Indian freedom. Illus., 64 notes.
R. Sexauer

642. McCann, Frank D., Jr. GHOST DANCE: LAST HOPE OF WESTERN TRIBES. *Montana 1966 16(1): 25-34.* In the late 1880's the Ghost Dance religion arose among the Paiutes and spread to other western tribes. Based on the teachings of Wavoka the Prophet, with elements derived from earlier mystic cults and from several Christian denominations, the religion later added a variety of Indian

innovations. The Dakota (Sioux) version contributed to the disorders which ended in the Wounded Knee episode, after which the movement soon faded away. Based on publications of the U.S. Bureau of Ethnology and other professional papers.   S. R. Davison

643. McDermott, John D. FORT LARAMIE'S SILENT SOLDIER—LEODE-GAR SCHNYDER. *Ann. of Wyoming 1964 36(1): 4-18.* Discusses the army career of Ordinance Sergeant Schnyder at Fort Laramie from 1848 until 1886 when he was ordered to New Bedford, Massachusetts. The article traces events such as the gold rush to the Black Hills and Indian attacks on the post, through Schnyder's career. Shows how Schnyder solved financial difficulties by becoming fort postmaster while continuing as ordinance sergeant. Based on records at Fort Laramie, published government documents, and state histories.

R. L. Nichols

644. McFarland, Carl. ABRAHAM LINCOLN AND MONTANA TERRI-TORY. *Montana 1955 5(4): 42-47.* Describes the far-seeing achievements of Abraham Lincoln for the state of Montana, his concern for the development of mineral resources, his commendation of land grants to railroads, his interest in the territory as a settlement area, and the laws he signed for surveying the territory and for the care of the Indian tribes. The author recalls how the slavery question almost prevented the organization of the Territory of Montana. The Supreme Court finally ruled that Congress could not prohibit slavery in the territories, but that Negroes could not be citizens. After much controversy the Senate decided to adopt, by reference, the identical provisions of the Idaho territorial statue, a maneuver which obviated the necessity of including a "Negro clause," since there were no Negroes in Montana.   B. Waldstein

645. McNeil, Kenneth. CONFEDERATE TREATIES WITH THE TRIBES OF INDIAN TERRITORY. *Chronicles of Oklahoma 1965 42(4): 408-420.* Early in the war the Confederate Congress established a Bureau of Indian Affairs and appointed a commissioner to negotiate alliances with the tribes of the Indian Territory. Many Indians resented their removal in the 1830's, others wished to remain neutral. Treaties were concluded with the Choctaw, Seminole, Chickasaw, with one faction of the Creek, with a number of small tribes, and with the Plains Indians. After the Confederate victory at Wilson's Creek on 10 August 1861, the Cherokee joined the Confederate alliance on 7 October. The Confederacy was to be the protector of each tribe and it assumed the payment of all money Washington owed the tribes. The Indians promised to furnish troops to protect the Indian Territory. There was proposed, and rejected, a provision for ultimate statehood. The treaties gave official recognition to slavery. The Confederate government was unable to meet its obligations to the tribes but they remained loyal. 44 notes.

I. W. Van Noppen

646. Millbrook, Minnie Dubbs. THE WEST BREAKS IN GENERAL CUS-TER. *Kansas Hist. Q. 1970 36(2): 113-148.* George Armstrong Custer's first year on the Great Plains was not a success. His actions did not bear out his superiors' impressions that he was a born leader and fighter. During a lengthy campaign

against the Indians from March to September 1867, Custer complained about the food and weather, showed little interest in fighting, cracked down with unnecessary severity on deserters, and at one point even left his command in the field to rush back to his family and civilization. This final offense brought Custer before a court-martial that found him guilty and suspended him from service for a year. When he returned to his regiment, Custer responded with vigor to every opportunity to show that he was a good soldier and became a skilled member of the Indian fighting army. Based on books, articles, government publications, newspapers, and manuscripts in the National Archives and Kansas State Historical Society; illus., 129 notes.   W. F. Zornow

647. Mitchell, Michael Dan. ACCULTURATION PROBLEMS AMONG THE PLAINS TRIBES OF THE GOVERNMENTAL AGENCIES IN WESTERN INDIAN TERRITORY. *Chronicles of Oklahoma 1966 44(3): 281-289.* The Friends sought a more humane Indian policy and after 1869 President Grant gave the management of certain reservations to them. Numerous Quakers established homes among the Indians. There were too few doctors and drugs and little knowledge of sanitation. The white border element brought smallpox and whiskey to the reservations. Schools were needed. In 1870 Congress passed the first appropriation act specifically for Indian education. The first school was established among the Kiowa-Comanche in 1870, another in 1872. By 1874 there were 60 scholars. In 1871 a school was begun for the Cheyenne and the Arapahoes. The Indian school at Carlisle had 70 Cheyennes. A compulsory education law helped. By 1877 Indians began to wear clothing and by 1878 a number lived in houses. By 1876 they evidenced a desire for law and order. 37 notes.
                                                                    I. W. Van Noppen

648. Monahan, Forrest D., Jr. THE KIOWA-COMANCHE RESERVATION IN THE 1890'S. *Chronicles of Oklahoma 1968 45(4): 451-463.* The Kiowa-Comanche Indian Reservation in southwestern Oklahoma Territory became an island in a sea of white settlement in the late 19th century. The three million acres of rich grasslands and timber were coveted by the whites. Encroaching settlers generated considerable friction. With the passage of the Dawes Act (1887) ending the reservation system, a commission was appointed to handle the allotment of lands in the Kiowa-Comanche Reservation. By coercion, the commission forced an agreement on the Indians and obtained their signatures. Such negative notoriety attended the contract, however, that Congress waited until 1901 to ratify it and open the reservation for settlement. 78 notes.   D. L. Smith

649. Moodie, D. W. and Kaye, Barry. THE NORTHERN LIMIT OF INDIAN AGRICULTURE IN NORTH AMERICA. *Geographical R. 1969 59(4): 513-529.* "At the time of European contact the northern limit of Indian agriculture on the Great Plains was in the Upper Missouri region. Then in 1805 a gift of seed corn to some immigrant Ottawas at Netley Creek, at the southern end of Lake Winnipeg, led to the establishment of Indian gardens there. From Netley Creek, and later from Plantation Island in Lake of the Woods (to which the Netley Creek Ottawas migrated in 1812), agriculture spread among the Saulteaux Indians of the Manitoba plains and of the adjacent woodlands of Ontario and Minnesota.

Indian corn reached its northern limit in the Mossy River area. All evidence suggests that short-season Mandan flint corn from the Upper Missouri was the source of the original seed. The traditional corn-bean-squash-pumpkin complex of the North American Indians was found as far north as Plantation Island, beyond which it could not survive as a complete complex. Except for potatoes, few crops of European origin were grown."   J

650. Moore, Waddy W. SOME ASPECTS OF CRIME AND PUNISHMENT ON THE ARKANSAS FRONTIER. *Arkansas Hist. Q. 1964 23(1): 50-64.* There were two types of crimes committed on the Arkansas frontier: unprofessional (dueling, crimes of drunkenness, selling whiskey to the Indians, cutting trees on federal land) and professional (horse stealing, highway robbery, counterfeiting). The causes of crime were the abundant opportunities to rob pioneer families of their material possessions and the difficulties of detecting, arresting, holding, and convicting wrongdoers. Punishment for a convicted criminal, however, was severe. Arkansas Territory was lawless because of frontier conditions and because of the lawless heritage of the frontiersmen.   G. B. Dodds

651. Morris, Wayne. TRADERS AND FACTORIES ON THE ARKANSAS FRONTIER, 1805-1822. *Arkansas Hist. Q. 1969 28(1): 28-48.* The U.S. factory system was comprised of "trading houses" which "attempted to make the Indians dependent on government goods" by underselling (and thereby protecting them from) private traders. The author gives a concise account of the three Arkansas factories and of their chief private competitors. Many of the factories' difficulties are attributed to inadequate cooperation of Indian agents, federal regulations, and persistent Indian warfare. 105 notes.   B. A. Drummond

652. Mortensen, A. R. MORMONS, NEBRASKA AND THE WAY WEST. *Nebraska Hist. 1965 46(4): 259-271.* Survey of early Mormon history, stressing the significance of the sojourn on Indian lands in Nebraska in 1847-48.
                                                                      R. Lowitt

653. Morton, W. L. A CENTURY OF PLAIN AND PARKLAND. *Alberta Hist. R. [Canada] 1969 17(2): 1-10.* Discusses the role of the plains in the life of the Indian, the fur trader, and the early farmer, considering the impact of the East upon the settlement of the West and of the significant differences that existed.
                                                                      H. M. Burns

654. Munkres, Robert L. THE PLAINS INDIAN THREAT ON THE OREGON TRAIL BEFORE 1860. *Ann. of Wyoming 1968 40(2): 193-221.* Examines 66 diaries of travelers using the Oregon Trail between 1834 and 1860 to determine the actual danger from Indian attack on that route. The vast majority of diarists studied encountered no overt threat of attack in either Nebraska or Wyoming. Indian harassment of travelers was mainly through begging, demanding tolls, and theft of livestock. These acts occurred more often than did physical attack.

Carelessness of the travelers induced some Indian harassment. Based on printed and manuscript diaries kept by travelers on the Oregon Trail; 87 notes.

R. L. Nichols

655. Murray, Robert A. THE WAGON BOX FIGHT: A CENTENNIAL APPRAISAL. *Ann. of Wyoming 1967 39(1): 104-108.* Discusses past research on the Wagon Box Fight in August 1867 near Fort Philip Kearny. The author examines the Wagon Box Fight from the usually neglected manuscript reports of that engagement submitted by Captain James Powell and by Major Benjamin F. Smith, both participants. Major Smith's unit frightened the Indian attackers and rescued the surrounded troops under Captain Powell. As a result of this attack, the troops received more organized target practice and gained confidence in their units and firepower. Based on correspondence in Record Group 98, National Archives, and secondary material; 11 notes.   R. L. Nichols

656. Nielsen, George R., ed. BEN MILAM AND UNITED STATES AND MEXICAN RELATIONS. *Southwestern Hist. Q. 1970 73(3): 393-395.* A letter written in 1825 from Benjamin Rush Milam, an early Anglo-American in Texas, to Joel Poinsett, U.S. Minister to Mexico, regarding the drawbacks of the land market in Texas. Milam also described the frontier problems resulting from Indian raids and a growing number of refugee slaves and outlaws, suggesting the possibility of a reciprocal arrangement between Mexico and the United States for their return. No further communication between the two has been found to date.

R. W. Delaney

657. Parry, Henry C. OBSERVATIONS ON THE PRAIRIES: 1867. *Montana 1959 9(4): 22-35.* In 1867 the author was assigned as medical officer to General Grenville M. Dodge's Union Pacific Commission charged with planning the westward route of the new transcontinental railroad and the protection of crews against hostile Indians. In the 10 letters reproduced in this article, written to his father during this period, the young doctor provides a concise documentary summary of the geographical conditions in the raw frontier region, the rough population, the exigencies of soldiering, facts about homesteading, ranching and commerce, as well as significant commentary on the Indians, of whose character, habits and customs he had a very low opinion.   B. Waldstein

658. Parsons, John E. STEAMBOATS IN THE "IDAHO" GOLD RUSH. *Montana 1960 10(1): 51-61.* Describes the fortunes and vicissitudes of the steamboats of the 1860's, as they brought gold-seekers, Indian fighters, and prospective solid citizens to the vast three-state territory still known as "Idaho," encompassing the present states of Idaho, Montana, and Wyoming. The author gives biographical notes on some of the well-known passengers, including the missionary Jesuit priest, Pierre-Jean de Smet, renowned for his work among the hostile Dakota (Sioux).   B. Waldstein

659. Petersen, Karen Daniels. ON HAYDEN'S LIST OF CHEYENNE MILITARY SOCIETIES. *Am. Anthropologist 1965 67(2): 469-472.* Comments on

Hayden's annotated listing of Cheyenne and Dakota dances and their manner of performance. The listing is concerned with the five extant military societies of the Cheyenne and Dakota tribes which intermarried, one society that early became extinct, and the (questionable) Elk society. This earliest known publication (Philadelphia: C. Sherman and Son, 1862) was drawn up by Ferdinand V. Heyden, geologist, who at the age of 30 spent the winter 1859-60 with the U.S. Exploring Party under Captain William F. Reynolds. The group encamped 100 miles north of Fort Laramie on the North Platte where Hayden obtained his information from Cheyenne hunters who worked with the Indian agent there. Documented.

Sr. B. A. Barbato

660. Peterson, Clell T. CHARLES KING: SOLDIER AND NOVELIST. *Am. Book Collector 1965 16(4): 8-12.* Charles King wrote fiction about army life and Indian warfare on the Plains in the years 1870-80. It was based on his experiences as a second lieutenant in the army. Although his novels were subliterary, they were very popular and have been used as background material for numerous westerns. Documented; illus.   D. Brockway

661. Peterson, Walter F., ed. CHRISTMAS ON THE PLAINS: ELIZABETH BACON CUSTER'S NOSTALGIC MEMORIES OF HOLIDAY SEASONS ON THE FRONTIER. *Am. West 1964 1(4): 53-57.* Elizabeth Bacon Custer traveled with and personally attended General Custer, her husband, during his western campaigns against the Indians in Texas, Kansas, and Dakota Territory. These recollections do not relate specifically to Christmas at any particular army post but range over the whole of her western yuletide experiences. Unpublished manuscript from Milwaukee-Downer College archives. Illus.   D. L. Smith

662. Peterson, William J., ed. INDIANS OF IOWA. *Palimpsest 1969 50(4): 209-272.* Discusses the tribes of Iowa, including the prehistoric Indians, the Iowa, Omaha, Oto, Missouri, Sauk, Fox, Dakota (Sioux), Winnebago, and Potawatomi. Mentions the dispossession of the tribes, Indian home life, amusements, wars, and religion. Illus., biblio.   E. M. Hade

663. Pfaller, Louis. THE FORGING OF AN INDIAN AGENT. *North Dakota Hist. 1967 34(1): 62-76.* Beginning his service at the Indian Agency of Devil's Lake (near Fort Totten) in Dakota Territory as a blacksmith in 1871, James McLaughlin won the respect of Major Forbes, the agent, and of the soldiers at Fort Totten, the Indians, and his fellow employees. Forbes paid McLaughlin a tribute and won for him an increase in salary. When Forbes died in 1875, McLaughlin applied to the vicariate apostolic of northern Minnesota for the position of agent. The Indian agencies had been assigned to the denominations as a means of civilizing the natives. Although all who knew McLaughlin supported his application, Paul Beckwith was appointed by the commissioner of Indian affairs at the suggestion of Father J. B. A. Brouillet, head of the Commission of Catholic Indian Missions. Beckwith was soon jealous of McLaughlin's prestige with the Indians and soldiers. A lack of harmony led Beckwith to dismiss

McLaughlin, but Beckwith was inexperienced and unsuccessful. He resigned 1 July 1877, and McLaughlin was then appointed to the post, serving until his death in 1923. Illus., 33 notes.   I. W. Van Noppen

664. Pope, Polly. TRADE IN THE PLAINS: AFFLUENCE AND ITS EF-FECTS. *Kroeber Anthrop. Soc. Papers 1966 34: 53-61.* Points to a relationship between Euro-American trade with the Plains Indians and changes in Plains Indian culture. The author includes specific examples of trading and their cultural effects among such Plains Indians as the Blackfoot, Kiowa, Omaha, Sioux, and Mandan. Based on secondary sources; 2 notes, biblio.   C. N. Warren

665. Porter, Kenneth W. NEGROES AND INDIANS ON THE TEXAS FRONTIER, 1831-1876. *J. of Negro Hist. 1956 41(3): 185-214, (4): 285-310.* An examination of the relations between Negroes and Indians on the Texas frontier, revealing a "general pattern of mutual hostility similar to that which existed between Indians and white frontiersmen." Nevertheless, examples are "sufficiently numerous to demonstrate that the pattern of relations between Negro and Indian was not absolutely identical with that between white and Indian."
W. E. Wight

666. Presley, James. SANTA ANNA'S INVASION OF TEXAS: A LESSON IN COMMAND. *Arizona and the West 1968 10(3): 241-252.* In February 1836 General Antonio López de Santa Anna marched northward to put down the rebellion in the Mexican state of Texas. He relied on traditional methods to organize and equip his army: forcing loans and mortgages; recruiting whomever and wherever he could, including convicts and non-Spanish-speaking Indians; and permitting an equal number of non-soldier camp followers to come along. His army, ill-equipped and accustomed to a tropical climate, moved into the Texas winter, suffering from a multitude of troubles—shortage of food and supplies, inadequate transportation, wretched medical facilities, weakened morale from lack of chaplains to administer last rites to those dying, harassment by hostile Indians, insufficient feed for draft animals and beef cattle, lack of adequate water supplies, and desertions. Despite these difficulties, Santa Anna marched toward San Antonio, hoping to prove that his generalship was invincible. Although he won the Battle of the Alamo, it was a near-Pyrrhic victory. It was, nevertheless, a new war and he moved on to other victories and toward ultimate success. Suddenly, ingloriously, and unexpectedly, however, Santa Anna was defeated at San Jacinto in 1836 and was captured by the Texans. The 1836 campaign demonstrated that Santa Anna's army, more effective at stamping out political revolts in the interior, was not adequate to cope with logistic, supply, and strategy problems on the northern frontier. 2 illus., map, 25 notes.   D. L. Smith

667. Reid, Russell. SAKAKAWEA. *North Dakota Hist. 1963 30(2/3): 101-113.* North Dakota claimed that Sacagawea (Sakakawea), the bird woman, young Indian wife of Charbonneau and member of the Lewis and Clark expedition, was the Snake squaw who died in 1811 at the age of 25 in South Dakota. This claim is based on the journal of John Luttig, a clerk of Manuel Lisa's Missouri Fur Company. Wyoming accepts the claim of Dr. Grace Raymond Hebard in her

1933 book, *Sacajawea* (Glendale, Calif.: A. H. Clark, 1967) (the accepted spelling in Wyoming), that the Indian woman was a Shoshoni who lived to the age of 100 years and died in Wyoming in 1884. Illus., map.   I. W. Van Noppen

668. Richardson, Ernest M. THE FORGOTTEN HAYCUTTERS AT FORT C. F. SMITH. *Montana 1959 9(3): 22-33.* Outlines some of the main incidents in Montana during the Indian wars, including the forgotten defensive stand of 19 white soldiers and haycutters against more than one thousand Sioux, Cheyenne and Arapaho Indian warriors some two miles north of Fort C. F. Smith on 1 August 1867.   B. Waldstein

669. Riley, Paul D. DR. DAVID FRANKLIN POWELL AND FORT MC PHERSON. *Nebraska Hist. 1970 51(2): 153-170.* A brief account of Powell's interesting frontier experiences in 1873 in the vicinity of Fort McPherson, Nebraska, one of the most noted military posts on the Great Plains. Powell was a contract surgeon at Fort McPherson and extensive quotes are included from the diary and letters written by him about travels and Indian warfare.
                                                                    R. Lowitt

670. Rodee, Howard D. THE STYLISTIC DEVELOPMENT OF PLAINS INDIAN PAINTING AND ITS RELATIONSHIP TO LEDGER DRAWINGS. *Plains Anthropologist 1965 10(30): 218-232.* "This paper attempts to trace the stylistic development of Plains Indian figurative hide painting. Beginning with its possible origins in the petrographs and bark drawings of the pre and early historic Northeast and Southwest it ends with the ledger drawings of the late 19th century. The early (pre-1860) hides are shown to have indicated events through a form of visual shorthand in contrast to the detailed refinement of the illustrated scenes on later hides. The ledger drawings include both traditional warfare themes and scenes from reservation life, ending with views of the white world drawn in the white man's manner. One drawing by Bears Heart, a Cheyenne prisoner in Florida, is examined in some detail and in relationship to the historical, biographical and cultural world in which it was created."   J

671. Rolston, Alan. THE YELLOWSTONE EXPEDITION OF 1873. *Montana 1970 20(2): 20-29.* Describes the effort to locate a route for the Northern Pacific Railroad between Bismarck (North Dakota) and Bozeman (Montana). In the early 1870's the company sent out surveying parties and the army furnished military escorts. Progress was hampered by weather and rough terrain, as well as by Indian resistance. The survey in 1873 particularly brought out the rivalry between the army and the Department of the Interior concerning the scientific aspects of such an exploration, as well as conflicts over Indian policy. Based on contemporary reports and correspondence; illus., 14 notes.
                                                                    S. R. Davison

672. Sanderson, James F. INDIAN TALES OF THE CANADIAN PRAIRIES. *Alberta Hist. R. [Canada] 1965 13(3): 7-21.* Series of stories relating feats of the Blackfoot, Cree, and Gros Ventres Indians in western Canada.
H. M. Burns

673. Schock, Jack M. and Bass, William M., III. SOME ADDITIONAL AR-TIFACTS FROM THE FANNING SITE. *Plains Anthropologist 1966 11(33): 208-219.* A report of the contents of 11 cache pits found at the Fanning site, situated in the extreme northeastern corner of Kansas, occupied between 1650 and 1750. Some important artifacts reported are a blond French gunspall, first evidence of the presence of firearms and European trade goods. Illus., biblio.
K. Adelfang

674. Schusky, Ernest L. THE UPPER MISSOURI INDIAN AGENCY, 1819-1868. *Missouri Hist. R. 1971 65(3): 249-269.* Agency is often used as a synonym for reservation, but actually is a much more restricted enterprise dealing with trade. The Upper Missouri Agency developed during this half-century from essentially a paper organization that supplied many tribes with yearly presents to preserve peace and assist the fur trade, into a number of reservations where the Indians were confined and made dependent on the federal government. Only the Sioux to the west remained strong; the tribes along the Missouri were reduced to living under agents who had great power over them and often little interest in their problems. Based on articles, books, and manuscripts in the National Archives; illus., 46 notes.
W. F. Zornow

675. Shirk, George H. CONFEDERATE POSTAL SYSTEM IN THE INDIAN TERRITORY. *Chronicles of Oklahoma 1963 41(2): 160-218.* Assumption of jurisdiction of the postal service by the Confederate States disrupted mail service in Indian Territory, in operation since 1824, although Albert Pike, Confederate commissioner to the Indian tribes, negotiated nine Indian treaties, and a postal system existed on paper. The postmaster general advertised for bids on the different mail routes and contracts were let, but military operations and money shortages interfered. The author concludes: "It is heartening to know that the Confederate States of America attempted to...bring the benefits of civil government to what is now Oklahoma." Contains the correspondence between the agent of the Post Office Department, James H. Starr, and the various postmasters.
I. W. Van Noppen

676. Sinclair, F. H. WHITE MAN'S MEDICINE FIGHT. *Montana 1956 6(3): 1-10.* Report of a battle between Indians and a small detachment of U.S. troops in 1867 near Fort Phil Kearney, Wyoming, in which 28 whites successfully repulsed Indians, killing 1,137.
C. C. Gorchels

677. Smith, Cornelius C., Jr. CROOK AND CRAZY HORSE. *Montana 1966 16(2): 14-26.* Two indecisive battles, fought in the same year and in the same vicinity as Custer's famous fight, contributed to that disaster. A victory by troops

under General George Crook at either the Powder River or Rosebud battles in the spring and summer, respectively, of 1876, would have prevented the Custer affair.

                                                                S. R. Davison

678. Steckmesser, Kent L. CUSTER IN FICTION. *Am. West 1964 1(4): 47-52, 63-64.* An analysis of the novels concerned with George Armstrong Custer confirms that literary interpretation changes when historical interpretation changes. Frederick Whittaker's 1876 eulogistic biography and his 1882 Beadle's "dime biography" established the initial pattern. Juvenile and adult literature portrayed Custer with profound indifference to historical facts, as a truly romantic, heroic and legendary figure. This tradition came to an abrupt end with Frederick F. Van de Water's 1934 biography portraying Custer as an "impetuous and irresponsible egotist." This and Helen Hunt Jackson's 1881 plea for the Indians has changed the literary approach to a debunking effort. An "admirable" Custer has now been replaced by a "petulant and self-seeking neurotic" in Custerana. Illus.

                                                                D. L. Smith

679. Steffen, Randy. WAR DRESS AND WEAPONS OF THE PLAINS INDIANS, 1874. *Military Collector and Historian 1965 17(1): 16-18.* Describes the war dress and weapons of Dakota (Sioux) and Cheyenne braves in 1874. Two types of saddles which the Plains Indians used are described and illustrated.

                                                                C. L. Boyd

680. Stevens, Harry R. A COMPANY OF HANDS AND TRADERS: ORIGINS OF THE GLENN-FOWLER EXPEDITION OF 1821-1822. *New Mexico Hist. R. 1971 46(3): 181-221.* On 5 August 1821, Hugh Glenn received a license from Major William Bradford to trade with Indians in the country beyond Fort Smith, Arkansas. Of the 18 men named in the license, only nine made the trip; 12 others joined them later. Several accounts of the expedition survive, including the extensive *Journal of Jacob Fowler.* By delving into the background of eight of the men, in particular Hugh Glenn and Jacob Fowler, the author attempts to determine the origins of the expedition. 81 notes.

                                                                D. F. Henderson

681. Stevens, O. A. PLANTS USED BY INDIANS IN THE MISSOURI RIVER AREA. *North Dakota Hist. 1965 32(2): 101-106.* Discusses various plants found in the Missouri River area that are known to have been used by American Indians for food and medicinal purposes. The author notes some of the observations of several 19th-century travelers in the area. Knowledge of plants used for medicine was probably learned through a long process of trial and error. Smoking and chewing gum were also supplied by various plants. 3 illus., 2 notes, biblio.

                                                                M. J. McBaine

682. Taylor, Morris F. THE MAIL STATION AND THE MILITARY AT CAMP ON PAWNEE FORK, 1859-1860. *Kansas Hist. Q. 1970 36(1): 27-39.* An account of the military forces that provided protection for the U.S. mails moving along a 150-mile stretch of the Santa Fe Trail during the Kiowa and

Comanche uprising during 1859-60. This protective measure is shown to have been largely ineffective because of bad weather conditions, an insufficient number of troops along the portion of the trail being protected, a lack of escort from Pawnee Fork eastward to Council Grove, and the uncertainty of making connections with patrols coming northward from Fort Union in New Mexico Territory. Based on books, articles, local newspapers, and records of the Office of Indian Affairs, Office of the Adjutant General and U.S. Army Command, and Department of Missouri records in the National Archives; 57 notes.

W. F. Zornow

683. Thane, James L., Jr. THE MONTANA "INDIAN WAR" OF 1867. *Arizona and the West 1968 10(2): 153-170.* In the spring of 1867, a rumor started with the army at Fort C. F. Smith in Montana Territory that an all-out uprising of 11 thousand Sioux Indians was being planned. Territorial officials barraged Washington with letters and telegrams demanding that the regular army take the field. Meanwhile steps were taken to raise a local volunteer force to protect the threatened settlements until the army should arrive. The confusion and breakdown in communications between territorial and federal officials resulted in a so-called "Indian War." Only a few minor raids occurred in the summer of 1867. Four Indians were killed. Montana Territory expended over a million dollars in its efforts. The federal government eventually reimbursed Montana for about half of the amount. 7 illus., 42 notes.

D. L. Smith

684. Unrah, William F. INDIAN AGENT VS. THE ARMY: BACKGROUND NOTES ON THE KIOWA-COMANCHE TREATY OF 1865. *Kansas Hist. Q. 1964 30(2): 129-152.* It is too easy to see the Indian problem of 1865 as a simple one to be solved either by military force or treaties and civilian control. The debate over whether the War or Interior Department should control Indian affairs was complicated by such factors as the difficulty and cost of conducting military operations in an era when men were tired of war and anxious to economize, an era of corruption, illicit livestock trade, land claims, town rivalries, and railroad speculation. The army was not anxious to fight, and other interests demanded peace. Jesse Leavenworth (1807-85) negotiated the treaty. The army criticized him, but actually his treaty gave military men time to build up their forces for a later war and, in the meantime, saved the country much added expense. Based on records from the National Archives.

W. F. Zornow

685. Unrau, William E. INVESTIGATION OR PROBITY? INVESTIGATIONS INTO THE AFFAIRS OF THE KIOWA-COMANCHE INDIAN AGENCY, 1867. *Chronicles of Oklahoma 1964 42(3): 300-319.* It was charged in *Harper's New Monthly Magazine* and throughout the nation that there was an "Indian Ring" of Congressmen, commissioners, and Indian agents, formed especially to defraud the Indians. Indian agents were given jobs for party work and on 1,500 dollars a year could retire with fortunes in four years. The worst charges were directed against the son of General Henry Leavenworth, Kiowa-Comanche agent Jesse Henry Leavenworth, who had been dishonorably discharged from the army in 1863. In 1867 Leavenworth was charged with illegal

sale of arms to the Indians. He protested that the Indians would starve unless they had guns for hunting. Corrupt traders and correspondents made false charges. Indicates that Leavenworth was not guilty. 34 notes.   I. W. Van Noppen

686. Unsigned. A BRITISH JOURNALIST REPORTS THE MEDICINE LODGE PEACE COUNCIL OF 1867. *Kansas Hist. Q. 1967 33(3): 249-320.* Henry Morton Stanley (who later found David Livingston in Africa) was a special correspondent for the St. Louis *Daily Missouri Democrat* during the 1867 campaign against the Plains Indians. His reports were published in the *Democrat* between 19 October and 2 November 1867. Some of them were later republished in greatly edited form in the first volume of his *My Early Travels and Adventures in America and Asia* (London: 1895). Given here are the articles pertaining to the peace negotiations as they appeared in the *Democrat.* Obvious errors have been corrected. Illus., 47 notes.   W. F. Zornow

687. Unsigned. BATTLE OF THE ARICKAREE (OR BEECHER ISLAND), SEPTEMBER 17-25, 1868. *Kansas Hist. Q. 1968 34(1): Frontispiece.* Four pages describe the battle between Brevet Colonel George A. Forsyth's 50 civilian scouts from Kansas and hundreds of Cheyenne and Dakota (Sioux) warriors on the Arickaree branch of the Republican River in what is now Yuma County, Colorado. It provides background material for the cover illustration "The Battle of the Arickaree (or Beecher Island)" by Robert Lindneux, a painting now owned by the State Historical Society of Colorado. Forsyth's six-page dispatch on 19 September is reproduced. 3 photos.   W. F. Zornow

688. Unsigned. [CORRESPONDENCE OF WILLIAM HAMILTON 1811-91]. *J. of the Presbyterian Hist. Soc.*
   LETTERS OF WILLIAM HAMILTON, 1811-1891. 1957 35(3): 157-170. From 1837 to 1853, Hamilton served among the Iowa, Sauk, and Fox Indians under the Presbyterian Board of Foreign Missions, and for 13 years thereafter among the Omaha Indians of Nebraska. The eight letters, dated from 7 July 1846 to 8 January 1847, and directed to Walter Lowrie, secretary of the Board of Foreign Missions, recount the difficulties and expense of travel from Jersey Shore, Pennsylvania, to the mission station by way of Pittsburgh, Cincinnati, St. Louis, and St. Joseph, Missouri, and describe the problems faced in educating the Indians.
   MORE LETTERS OF WILLIAM HAMILTON, 1811-1891. 1958 36(1): 53-65. In eight letters, dated between 28 January and 2 September 1847, Reverend William Hamilton, one of the pioneer missionaries to the American Indians on the western Plains, to Walter Lowrie, secretary of the Presbyterian Board of Foreign Missions, the difficulties encountered in his efforts to educate the Indian children at the Ioway and Sac Mission. The language barrier, illness, irregularity of attendance, lack of support from the parents, and the limited resources of the mission made progress slow and uncertain.   W. D. Metz

689. Unsigned. MINUTES OF THE NEBRASKA PRESBYTERY: 1849-51, AND MINUTES OF THE PRESBYTERY OF HIGHLAND, 1857-1858. *J. of the Presbyterian Hist. Soc. 1957 35(2): 120-139.* Records of the establishment and

early work of presbyteries of the Presbyterian Church in the United States among the Indian missions and white settlements in the Nebraska country west of Missouri and Iowa. The Highland Presbytery was in Kansas Territory.

W. D. Metz

690. Utley, Robert M. CUSTER: HERO OR BUTCHER? *Am. Hist. Illus. 1971 5(10): 4-9, 43-48.* Summarizes the image of Major General George Armstrong Custer with a focus on his career as an Indian fighter from 1867 to June 1876. Historians have had as much difficulty in judging Custer as his contemporaries did. There are still those who are either Custerphobes or Custerphiles, although the current emphasis on red history and the Vietnam War is not likely to improve the image of an Indian-fighting cavalryman. Other field commanders deserved equal or greater recognition but they lacked the distinctive personal style that captures popular fancy—and an autobiography, and wife-biographer. Yet Custer's attitudes that Indians should be civilized under army guidance, combined with his admiration for many Indian customs as well as their physical proficiencies, were contradictions shared by most frontier commanders. Based on primary and secondary sources; 11 illus.

D. B. Dodd

691. Utley, Robert M. KIT CARSON AND THE ADOBE WALLS CAMPAIGN. *Am. West 1965 2(1): 4-11, 73-75.* The Santa Fe Trail was the only supply and communication line to the federal troops stationed in Santa Fe during the Civil War. They were guarding against the possibility of another Confederate threat to New Mexico similar to the one in 1862. The long, richly-laden supply trains along the trail were a temptation to the southern Plains Indians. Kiowa and Comanche raiding accelerated throughout the summer of 1864. With approaching winter, when the Indians preferred peace so that they could spend the time gathering food, the American offensive was prepared. Colonel Christopher Carson led New Mexico and California volunteer troops and friendly Ute Indian auxiliaries on a campaign highlighted 25 November 1864 by the Battle of Adobe Walls on the South Canadian River in the Texas Panhandle. Carson's victory lessened the hostile forays along the Santa Fe Trail the following summer, but also proved to be the opening of a decade of intermittent warfare that ended with the Red River War of 1874-75. Illus., map, note, biblio.

D. L. Smith

692. Utley, Robert M. "PECOS BILL" ON THE TEXAS FRONTIER. *Am. West 1969 6(1): 4-13, 61-62.* William R. Shafter had risen to the brevet rank of brigadier general in the Michigan Volunteers in the Civil War. Under the 1869 reorganization of the army he was commissioned a lieutenant colonel of infantry. His assignment was to one of four Negro regiments garrisoning the little frontier forts of the West and fighting hostile Indians over the next three decades. Except for a brief period in Dakota, Pecos Bill Shafter's role in the opening of the West was played out largely on the sterile frontiers of Texas and Mexico. Ironically, one minority (black troops) was being used to subjugate another minority (Indians). This was compounded by the increasing employment of Indian scouts by the army against the Indians. The use of black troops was "a calculated humiliation" against conquered Texans but it was turned to discrimination against the blacks who for nearly two decades were left to police the most disagreeable sectors

of the American frontier. Tough, aggressive, and persevering, Shafter enjoyed the respect, if rarely the affection, of his troops and fellow officers. Although his racism was barely concealed, he still proved an effective commander of Negro troops. Shafter was one of the frontier army's more effective leaders. Heretofore this has been larely unknown and his chief claim to fame has been that of a caricatured figure in the Spanish-American War. 7 illus., map, biblio. note.

D. L. Smith

693. Vincent, John R. MIDWEST INDIANS AND FRONTIER PHOTOGRA-PHY. *Ann. of Iowa 1965 38(1): 26-35.* Discusses eight photographs of Iowa area Indians taken before 1880. Short accounts are given of the wars and migrations of the Sauk, Fox, Iowa, Potawatomi, Oto, Missouri, Omaha, and Dakota Indians. Despite the diverse original locations of the tribes discussed, it is emphasized that a common prairie style of dress existed. Illus.

D. C. Swift

694. Warner, Sister Mildred. [INDIANS AND THE NEBRASKA TERRITO-RIAL GOVERNMENT]. *Great Plains J. 1970 9(2): 53-66.*

INDIANS CHALLENGE THE NEBRASKA TERRITORIAL GOV-ERNMENT: I, pp. 53-58. Reviews the problems between the Indians and the Nebraska Territory between 1854 and 1859. Early governors not only asked the federal government for assistance when the Indians failed to stay in designated areas or attacked emigrants along the Oregon Trail, but several times sent territo-rial militia into the field. The policy of peaceful coexistence of whites and Indians slowly strangled the Indians. The reservation system and the destitution of the Indians disrupted coexistence. Hostilities along the western border increased as the 1850's ended. 9 notes.

THE ATTITUDE OF THE NEBRASKA TERRITORIAL GOVERN-MENT TOWARDS THE INDIANS: II, pp. 59-66. In the latter part of Nebras-ka's territorial period the clash of Indians and whites was precipitated by the Colorado gold rush and the Civil War. By the Treaty of Fort Wise (1861) the Cheyenne and Arapaho ceded most of their lands between the Platte and the Arkansas rivers. With the 1862 Dakota (Sioux) uprising in Minnesota, the Second Nebraska Cavalry was organized as Nebraskans demanded severe measures against the Indians. Indians took the warpath in the summer of 1864 and attacks were made in the valley of the Little Blue in eastern Nebraska. Late in the fall of 1864 the Chivington Massacre occurred at Sand Creek in Colorado. Three widely-held frontier concepts help explain it: the Indians could be controlled by severe measures, the Confederates were inciting the Indians, and the Indians should be exterminated. In 1865 peace was made with the Cheyenne and Ara-pahoe, but a Sioux war began. In 1867 Congress appointed a peace commission to study the Indian problem. In the 1870's most Indians were removed from Nebraska. 30 notes.

O. H. Zabel

695. Weddle, Robert S. THE SAN SABA MISSION: APPRAOCH TO THE GREAT PLAINS. *Great Plains J. 1965 4(2): 29-38.* Deals primarily with failure of the Spanish attempt to maintain a northern military and religious outpost at the San Sabá Mission (now Menard, Texas) from 1757 to 1770. The failure

resulted from vacillating Spanish policies and the power of the Plains Indians—especially the Comanches. It marked the turning point for the Spanish Empire in Texas. Based on both primary and secondary sources.   O. H. Zabel

696. Weinstein, Robert A. and Belous, Russell E. INDIAN PORTRAITS: FORT SILL, 1869. *Am. West 1966 3(1): 50-63.* Solely for his personal satisfaction, William S. Soule left home in Boston in 1869 to photograph the Indians of the western Plains. With few photographic or daguerreotype records of Plains Indians made before Soule, he must be regarded as a pioneer in this form of documentation. The 14 photographs in this picture essay were made from the wet-plate collodion negatives taken at Fort Sill, Oklahoma Territory, in 1869, now in the collection of the Los Angeles County Museum.   D. L. Smith

697. West, G. Derek. THE BATTLE OF SAPPA CREEK (1875). *Kansas Hist. Q. 1968 34(2): 150-178.* A detailed account of a small engagement in Kansas on 23 April 1875 between some Cheyenne warriors and a small detachment of U.S. regulars and civilians. Drawing upon the accounts written by four participants in the engagement, the author tries to show that the facts concerning the location of the battle, the size of the Indian encampment, the identity of the Indians involved, the number of Indian casualties, and the identity of the civilian participants have been incorrectly given by modern writers on western lore who have relied on hearsay for their versions of the battle. Based on articles, books, and official records; illus., 71 notes.   W. F. Zornow

698. West, Larry L. DOUGLAS H. COOPER, CONFEDERATE GENERAL. *Lincoln Herald 1969 71(2): 69-76.* Outlines developments in Indian Territory during the Civil War. Emphasis is placed on Cooper's role and his emergence in 1865 as military commander of Indian Territory, which had been designated as a separate department.   S. L. Jones

699. White, Lonnie J. INDIAN BATTLES IN THE TEXAS PANHANDLE, 1874. *J. of the West 1967 6(2): 278-309.* In May and June of 1874 there began what was to be the last major Indian uprising on the southern Plains. This Red River Indian War resulted from the dissatisfaction of the Kiowas, Comanches, and Cheyennes with the policies of the government and their concern over the continued slaughter of the buffalo by hidehunters. The most spectacular of the battles were fought in the Texas Panhandle. They included the Battle of Adobe Wells which was fought between hunters and representatives of five tribes in late June and early July; the first Battle of Palo Duro Canyon fought in late August; the Battle of Lyman's Wagon Train in early September; the Battles of Buffalo Wallow and Price's Fight in September; and the second Battle of Palo Duro Canyon which occurred late in that month. The author details all of these fights and some other minor skirmishes. The defeats suffered by the Indians ended their last stand in this area. Based on published sources; illus., 61 notes.
D. N. Brown

700. White, Lonnie J. THE BATTLE OF BEECHER'S ISLAND: THE SCOUTS HOLD FAST ON THE ARICKAREE. *J. of the West 1966 5(1): 1-24.* Indian depredations in Kansas and Colorado resulted in Major General Philip Sheridan's directing Major George A. Forsyth to employ 50 frontiersmen to be used as scouts against the hostiles. Securing his men, Forsyth, with Lieutenant Frederick Beecher as second-in-command, left Fort Wallace, Kansas, on 10 September 1868, in an attempt to locate the Indians. On 16 September the scouts camped on the Arickaree Fork of the Republican River in present Colorado. At daybreak on 17 September the scouts were attacked by several hundred Cheyenne, Arapaho, and Dakota (Sioux). Retreating to a small island in the Arickaree, the scouts repulsed several charges by the Indians. Two scouts slipped through the Indian lines to seek assistance. On 21 September the main body of Indians withdrew, but the scouts remained on the island, subsequently named for Beecher who was killed in the fight, until a relief column reached them on 25 September. Because of its sensational nature, this battle became one of the best known Indian fights of all time. Based on material in the Kansas State Archives, illus., maps, 56 notes.   D. N. Brown

701. White, Lonnie J. THE HANCOCK AND CUSTER EXPEDITIONS OF 1867. *J. of the West 1966 5(3): 355-378.* Depredations of scattered bands of Cheyenne, Dakota (Sioux), and Kiowa committed in 1865 and 1866 caused many frontiersmen and local military commanders to believe that the Indians would eventually embark on a full-scale war on the southern Plains. Major General Winfield S. Hancock, commander of the Department of the Missouri, concluded the Indians meant to take the warpath in the spring of 1867. To forestall this, Hancock led an expedition to convince the Indians that further hostile acts would be punished. Part of his command included four companies of the Seventh Cavalry under Lieutenant Colonel George Custer. The author gives a detailed account of the movement of this expedition. He concludes that neither Hancock's nor a subsequent expedition led by Custer succeeded in accomplishing its objectives. Hancock's unduly harsh attitude and rash actions provoked an Indian uprising rather than preventing one. Nor was Custer successful in punishing the Cheyenne and Dakota (Sioux) or in relieving pressure on the overland road. Based on published sources, illus., 37 notes.   D. N. Brown

702. White, Lonnie J. WARPATHS ON THE SOUTHERN PLAINS: THE BATTLES OF SALINE RIVER AND PRAIRIE DOG CREEK. *J. of the West 1965 4(4): 485-503.* In 1867 Kansas was feeling the effect of raids conducted by bands of Dakota (Sioux), Cheyenne, and Kiowa. Efforts were made by the U.S. Army to bring the hostiles under control. In August 1867 cavalry units were attacked and defeated by the Indians in battles on the Saline River and Prairie Dog Creek in northwestern Kansas. The author concludes that the failure to punish the hostiles in 1867 made necessary Major General Philip H. Sheridan's winter campaign of 1868-69. Based principally on records in the War Department and National Archives; illus., map, 33 notes.   D. N. Brown

703. White, Lonnie J. WHITE WOMEN CAPTIVES OF THE SOUTHERN PLAINS INDIANS, 1866-1875. *J. of the West 1969 8(3): 327-354.* Tells of the

experiences of several women captured by the Indians during raids in Kansas. The stories are related in detail and transcripts and newspaper stories are included. All of the experiences are similar. Men in the party were killed immediately and the younger women were carried off. If the Indian camp was attacked, the prisoners were killed. When the women were returned, they told of cruel treatment and were often pregnant. R. N. Alvis

704. White, Lonnie J. WINTER CAMPAIGNING WITH SHERIDAN AND CUSTER: THE EXPEDITION OF THE NINETEENTH KANSAS VOLUNTEER CAVALRY. *J. of the West 1967 6(1): 68-98.* As a result of Indian forays in Kansas during the summer of 1868, General Philip Sheridan decided to conduct a winter campaign to punish the hostiles. Governor Samuel Crawford of Kansas offered to organize a regiment of volunteers which would augment the regular Army and, when the offer was accepted, resigned as governor to accept appointment as the regiment's colonel. Early in November the regiment, numbering slightly over twelve hundred men, was ordered to join the forces under Colonel George Custer at Camp Supply in Indian Territory. Due to the ineptitude of the guides, a raging storm, and the weak condition of the regiment's mounts, it arrived too late to participate in Custer's attack on Black Kettle's camp on the Washita. Later, however, the regiment marched with Sheridan and Custer through the western and southern part of the Indian Territory. The author concludes that, while the volunteers did not engage the Indians in combat, the additional strength they gave to Custer's expedition caused the hostiles to abandon any thought of resistance. Based largely on published sources, illus., 62 notes. D. N. Brown

705. Willey, William J. THE SECOND FEDERAL INVASION OF INDIAN TERRITORY. *Chronicles of Oklahoma 1967 44(4): 420-430.* Following the first invasion of Indian Territory, Union commanders organized a second invasion under Brigadier General James E. Blunt. Union forces conquered northwest Arkansas. On 17 October 1862 General Blunt defeated Brigadier General Douglas H. Cooper at Old Fort Wayne, a disaster for the Confederacy. Union forces seized Fort Gibson on 18 April 1863 in the Creek Nation. Using this as a base, U.S. commanders seized control of the whole Indian Territory. The largest battle of the war in the Indian Territory took place at Elk Creek, near Honey Springs, on 17 July. General Cooper and his force of six thousand men were defeated. These federal successes were due chiefly to superior arms. The deciding factor was ammunition. Many Confederate units were useless because of wet gunpowder. On 22 August General Blunt advanced, defeated the Confederates at Perryville, and captured Fort Smith. The Battle of Honey Springs was decisive in the contest for the Indian Territory. The Confederates were badly armed, the Indian troops were undisciplined, and there was intense rivalry between Generals Cooper and William Steele. 30 notes. I. W. Van Noppen

706. Wilson, Wesley C. DOCTOR WALTER A. BURLEIGH: DAKOTA TERRITORIAL DELEGATE TO 39TH AND 40TH CONGRESS: POLITICIAN EXTRAORDINARY. *North Dakota Hist. 1966 33(2): 93-103.* One of the early pioneers of North Dakota, Walter A. Burleigh served the territory as an Indian

agent and as a Republican delegate to the U.S. Congress. While agent, he employed the Dakota (Sioux) as adjuncts for the U.S. Army and also began encouraging them to adopt an agrarian way of life. Congressman from 1864-69, Burleigh was a strong force in politics and engaged in enterprises connected with the Dakota Territory and the Missouri River areas. Documented from contemporary newspapers and related works; illus., 33 notes.　　　　　　　R. Sexauer

707. Zimmerman, Jean L. COLONEL RANALD S. MACKENZIE AT FORT SILL. *Chronicles of Oklahoma 1966 44(1): 12-21.* Colonel Mackenzie, Indian fighter, was placed in command of Fort Sill to oversee the Kiowa-Comanche Agency. He believed moral restraint was superior to brute force. He faced three problems: Indians off the reservation, poor administration of Indian affairs, and white thieves in Indian Territory. Mackenzie handled affairs with firmness, sympathy, and justice. 42 notes.　　　　　　　I. W. Van Noppen

708. —. [THE FISK EXPEDITION OF 1864]. *North Dakota Hist. 1969 36(3): 208-278.*
　　　Mattison, Ray H., ed. THE FISK EXPEDITION OF 1864: THE DIARY OF WILLIAM L. LARNED, pp. 208-274. In 1864 James W. Fisk led a wagon train from Minnesota through the western Dakota Territory, trying to open a new and shorter route to Bannack and Virginia City, Montana Territory. The Fisk train was the only one of eight trains of the 1860's that had serious Indian trouble along the route to the gold fields. William L. Larned and his family were members of the expedition. Larned kept a diary of the trip starting on 29 June 1864 and concluding 31 January 1866. The Indian trouble is recorded by Larned beginning with the entry of 2 September 1864. The diary is taken from a typed copy owned by the Minnesota Historical Society; the original has been lost. Illus., photos, 37 notes.
　　　Paulson, Norman, ed. A LETTER FROM HORATIO H. LARNED TO KATE LARNED ALEXANDER, pp. 275-278. Horatio H. Larned was the son of William L. Larned and accompanied his father on the 1864 Fisk Expedition from Minnesota to Montana Territory. The part of the Horatio Larned letter that is published in this article provides additional details on the expedition. This letter is dated 1 July 1910. Illus., photos.　　　　　　　E. P. Costello

709. —. THE INDIAN FRONTIER. *Military Affairs 1959 23(2): 85-96.*
　　　Hardin, Edward E. AN ARMY LIEUTENANT IN MONTANA, 1874-76, pp. 85-91. A narrative of garrison duty in Montana with the 7th Infantry. Based on the original in the files of the Order of Indian Wars.
　　　Rickey, Don, Jr. THE ENLISTED MEN OF THE INDIAN WARS, pp. 91-96. Describes the life and services of the army enlisted men during the Indian wars of 1865-90.　　　　　　　K. J. Bauer

710. Olson, James C. THE "LASTING PEACE" OF FORT LARAMIE. *Am. West 1965 2(1): 46-53.* Despite the inconclusive army campaign of 1865 in its attempt to clear the Sioux and Cheyenne from the Powder River road to the Montana gold fields, army and Indian Bureau officials were hopeful of getting the Indians to quit the warpath and to agree to "a lasting peace." A June 1866

peace conference at Fort Laramie appeared to be making progress until the arrival of an army colonel in advance of a contingent of troops. This apparently upset Red Cloud, Dakota (Sioux) chief, who withdrew from the council with his band. The treaty that was negotiated in 1868 was assented to by Indians who really had no stake in the Powder River area. Those concerned with the Powder River road stepped up their attacks on the army, culminating in the December 1866 Fetterman massacre, the worst defeat the army had yet suffered in warfare with the Indians. Derived from a forthcoming book; illus., note, biblio.

D. L. Smith

By Tribe

Anadarko

711. Neighbors, Kenneth F. JOSE MARIA: ANADARKO CHIEF. *Chronicles of Oklahoma 1966 44(3): 254-274.* José Maria, an Anadarko, was reportedly born on the Sabine River in 1806. He was a Master Mason and, on one occasion, freed some surveyors that a chief wanted to kill because one was a Mason. José defeated 48 men under Benjamin Bryant on the Brazos River. When a lad suffered from malaria, José took him to winter camp and cured him. In 1843 U.S. commissioners worked out a peace treaty between the Texas Indians and the whites. At Bird's Fort, near the present Fort Worth, José Maria and the chiefs of the agrarian tribes and Texas agreed to a treaty, and in 1844 he signed a treaty with Sam Houston and the nomadic tribes. In 1845 the members of José Maria's tribe had 150 acres of fine corn, melons, beans, and peas. When the republic of Texas became a state, José signed peace treaties with the United States and visited President Polk in Washington. The Indians settled on reservations and made rapid progress in the arts of civilization. In the Civil War he fought with the Confederacy. He was a brave warrior who always sought peace. 3 illus., 43 notes.

I. W. Van Noppen

Apache, Cuartelejo

712. Gunnerson, James H. A HUMAN SKELETON FROM AN APACHE BAKING PIT. *Plains Anthropologist 1969 14(43): 46-56.* "A human skeleton found in an Apache baking pit in Scott County, Kansas, is that of a 22 or 23 year old male, about 5 feet 7 inches tall. It is probable that he was a Cuartelejo Apache of ca. 1700."

J

Arapaho

713. Murphy, James C. THE PLACE OF THE NORTHERN ARAPAHOES IN THE RELATIONS BETWEEN THE UNITED STATES AND THE INDIANS OF THE PLAINS, 1851-1879. *Ann. of Wyoming 1969 41(1): 33-61, (2): 203-259.* Part I. Claims that, unlike their warlike neighbors the Northern Cheyenne and the Sioux, the Arapaho considered themselves peaceful people.

There is an ethnological discussion of the tribe. The Fort Laramie Treaty of 1851 is depicted as the basis for peace between the northern Plains Indians and the United States. Based on newspapers, government documents, and other published sources; illus. Part II. A narrative of white-Indian relations supports the author's contention that, despite American provocations, the Arapaho usually maintained peace with the United States. He notes that federal Indian policy—locating army garrisons in Indian country, continuing public hostility toward all Indians—and the determination of the Arapaho to retain their culture combined to prevent assimilation. Based on newspapers, government documents, and other published sources; 257 notes, biblio.   R. L. Nichols

Arikara

714. Gray, John S. ARIKARA SCOUTS WITH CUSTER. *North Dakota Hist. 1968 35(2): 442-478.* The Fort Berthold Reservation in North Dakota supplied some of the most effective Indian scouts the army could obtain in the Indian wars in the West. In a book published in 1912 as *The Arikara Narrative* (State Historical Society of North Dakota Collections, VI), O. G. Libby records data he collected from nine survivors of the Sioux campaign of 1876 in which George A. Custer was defeated at the Little Big Horn. The National Archives has microfilmed the "Register of Enlistments of Indian Scouts, 1866-1914." Two tables of names and data on the scouts are compiled from these two sources and biographical information is gleaned from other sources. 15 illus., 30 notes.
                                                                                    D. L. Smith

715. Hurt, Wesley R. SEASONAL ECONOMIC AND SETTLEMENT PATTERNS OF THE ARIKARA. *Plains Anthropologist 1969 14(43): 32-37.* "That the Arikara were characterized by seasonal economic activities accompanied by varying settlement patterns during the Late Prehistoric and Early-Contact Periods is amply documented in the archaeological records and journals of the first explorers of the Missouri Valley. In spite of the abundant data, however, several aspects of the seasonal changes of economic and settlement patterns still remain subjects of speculation. Since there seems to have been so much regional and time variation in these patterns the observations presented in this report should be considered tentative...."   J

716. McRill, Leslie A. FERDINANDINA: FIRST WHITE SETTLEMENT IN OKLAHOMA. *Chronicles of Oklahoma 1963 41(2): 126-159.* The history of Ferdinandina, the first white settlement in Oklahoma. Part I deals with discoveries and settlements by Claude du Tisné and Bénard de la Harpe at the Arikara (Pani) village on the Deer Creek site, on the Arkansas River south of the northern boundary of Oklahoma in 1719. Here du Tisné established a forest trading post. Bénard de la Harpe reported conditions here and near the present Haskell, Oklahoma. Part II deals with the discoveries made on the sites of these villages by Joseph B. Thoburn in 1926. His manuscripts on the Oklahoma Historical Society shelves include photographs of Indian and French artifacts found in the

Deer Creek and Buffalo Cliff sites. These artifacts are evidence of French-Indian occupancy after 1719. 9 illus., 45 notes, summary, appendix.

I. W. Van Noppen

717. Morgan, Lewis H. THE STONE AND BONE IMPLEMENTS OF THE ARIKAREES. *North Dakota Hist. 1963 30(2/3): 115-135.* The Mandans were practically exterminated by smallpox in 1838 and their village was taken over by the Arikara, a Pawnee tribe then still virtually shut out from intercourse with the white race and thus still practicing their primitive arts. Implements left by the Mandans and used by the Arikara were abandoned by the latter in 1861 when nearby Fort Clark, established in 1829 by the American Fur Company, was destroyed by fire depriving them of protection against Dakota (Sioux). The author, an ethnologist and archaeologist, in 1862 obtained from the village a series of stone and bone implements which he described in this article. The Arikara also used wooden implements including the corn mortar, the ladder, and willow matting, and they made pottery. Their village of circular houses five feet high surrounded by a 10 or 12 foot stockade, was left intact just as they had lived in it. It served as an illustration of the aboriginal period of the American Indian of higher culture. Illus.

I. W. Van Noppen

718. Stephenson, Robert L. BLUE BLANKET ISLAND (39WW9) AN HISTORIC CONTACT SITE IN THE OAHE RESERVOIR NEAR MOBRIDGE, SOUTH DAKOTA. *Plains Anthropologist 1969 14(43): 1-31.* "The Blue Blanket Island site (39WW9), a small, fortified, proto-historic Indian village on an island in the Missouri River, in Walworth County, South Dakota, was partially excavated by a River Basin Surveys crew in August 1961. One centrally located earthlodge, sections of the fortification, storage pits, and middens were excavated. Artifacts were scanty but architectural details were informative. The lodge was 18 sided with a short entryway to the south (river side) and leaner posts of split cedar. The palisade was of split posts and the ditch was wide and shallow. The site appears to have been an Arikara village of short duration probably occupied during the 1780's and 1790's. The abandoned remains of this village were noted by Lewis and Clark in 1804."

J

Assiniboin (Stoney)

719. Andersen, Raoul R. ALBERTA STONEY (ASSINIBOIN) ORIGINS AND ADAPTATIONS: A CASE FOR REAPPRAISAL. *Ethnohist. 1970 (1/2): 48-61.* "Historical and ethnographic data are reviewed in an attempt to discern the origins of the Siouan-speaking Stoney (Assiniboin) Indians of modern Alberta, Canada. The histories of various bands and of their particular cultural adaptations are outlined."

J

Blackfoot (Siksika)

720. Cutright, Paul Russell. LEWIS ON THE MARIAS 1806. *Montana 1968 18(3): 30-43.* Recounts the adventures of Meriwether Lewis in his reconnaissance of the Marias River as a side trip on the return journey in 1806. A skirmish with the Blackfeet Indians was the most prominent single incident. The author, a biologist, points out Lewis' interest in collecting plant specimens even while fleeing the country after this dangerous encounter. Based on the Lewis and Clark journals, and on guided visits to the area; illus.   S. R. Davison

721. Doty, James. A VISIT TO THE BLACKFOOT CAMP. *Alberta Hist. R. [Canada] 1966 14(3): 17-23.* Report of a journey from Fort Benton, Montana north into Alberta by U.S. Representative Doty to secure attendance of the tribes and bands of the Blackfoot Nation at a treaty conference arranged by the American government to be held on the upper Missouri River. Reproduced from a manuscript copy in the U.S. National Archives.   H. M. Burns

722. Ewers, John C. THE LAST OF THE BUFFALO INDIANS. *Am. West 1965 2(2): 26-31.* A portrait picture essay of a half dozen of the last of the Blackfeet (Siksika) Indians who survived the winter of 1883-84 when the last of the great northern buffalo herd was destroyed on the grasslands of Montana. Photographs by Donald Schmidt.   D. L. Smith

723. Halliburton, R., Jr. JOHN COLTER'S RUN FOR LIFE. *Great Plains J. 1963 3(1): 32-34.* Gives a brief biography of John Colter, the first "mountain man" and describes his narrow escape from the Blackfoot Indians in the upper Missouri area in 1808.   O. H. Zabel

724. Harrod, Howard L. EARLY PROTESTANT MISSIONS AMONG THE BLACKFEET INDIANS: 1850-1900. *Methodist Hist. 1967 5(4): 15-24.* During the period from 1850 to 1900 Protestant missions to the Blackfeet Indians evolved from abortive efforts of the Presbyterians to a well established Methodist ministry. An institutional foundation was firmly established, but the missionaries were not well trained and often supported government policies which involved coercion of the Blackfeet. The author discusses the early Presbyterian attempts, Methodist evangelism in the 1870's and 1880's, the permanent Methodist mission, and the reasons for failures and successes. 33 notes.   H. L. Calkin

725. Rowand, John. A LETTER FROM FORT EDMONTON. *Alberta Hist. R. [Canada] 1963 11(1): 1-6.* The New Year's letter of 10 January 1840 from John Rowand, chief factor at Fort Edmonton to Governor George Simpson and the chief factors and traders in the Northern Department of the Hudson's Bay Company. Gives news and gossip about his district, freely attacks his superiors, and is candid about problems in trading with the Blackfeet. Photos.   R. J. C. Ford

726. Schoenberg, Wilfred P., S.J. HISTORIC ST. PETER'S MISSION. *Montana 1961 11(1): 68-85.* The first Jesuit missions for the Blackfeet proved temporary; in 1862 a new site midway between present Great Falls and Helena, became the permanent St. Peter's Mission. Here the "Black Robers" and Ursulines struggled against poverty and hardship until a government policy of indifference brought its final destruction in 1918. Based on published writings of the missionary priests and on manuscripts in church archives.   L. G. Nelson

727. Schultz, James Willard. RETURN TO THE BELOVED MOUNTAINS. *Montana 1957 7(3): 26-33.* The author lived as a member of the Blackfoot tribe for more than 20 years until his Indian wife died in 1903. In this extract from his book, *Blackfeet Tales of Glacier National Park* (Boston, 1916), he describes his return to the Glacier region in 1915 to visit his Indian relatives, and recalls some of his early exploratory trips in northwestern Montana.
                                                                            D. I. Blanchard

728. Sharp, Paul F. BLACKFEET OF THE BORDER: ONE PEOPLE DI-VIDED. *Montana 1970 20(1): 2-15.* In addition to the problems facing all Indians in the 19th century, the Blackfeet suffered because they straddled the invisible boundary between the United States and Canada. Uncertainty as to jurisdiction and responsibility led to neglect and harrassment on both sides of the line. The intrusion of stockmen into their dwindling reservation in 1875, and rivalry between the military and the Department of the Interior over control of the Indians, brought a crisis. In 1882, after fruitless negotiations with Canada, the United States unilaterally forced across the border those deemed to be Canadian subjects. Since that time the United States has assumed responsibility for those remaining. Reprinted from the book *Whoop-up Country: the Canadian-American West, 1865-1885* (Minneapolis: U. of Minnesota Press, 1955). Based primarily on correspondence, official reports, and published accounts; 39 notes.
                                                                            S. R. Davison

729. Tims, John W. ANGLICAN BEGINNINGS IN SOUTHERN AL-BERTA. *Alberta Hist. R. [Canada] 1967 15(2): 1-11.* An account of the early history of the Anglican church in Alberta. Work with various Blood and Blackfoot Indian tribes is described.   H. M. Burns

730. Weber, Francis J., ed. GRANT'S PEACE POLICY: A CATHOLIC DIS-SENTER. *Montana 1969 19(1): 56-63.* A letter from missionary John Baptist Camillus Imoda, S.J., to his superior Father J. B. A. Brouillet concerning the replacement of Catholic clergy by Methodist agents on the Blackfeet Reservation early in the 1870's. The letter is dated 30 January 1874. His complaint is based on the arbitrary breaking of the long Catholic contact with the Indians, and the relatively little previous Protestant activity. The editor provides background facts and a sketch of Father Imoda's life. Illus.   S. R. Davison

731. West, Helen B. BLACKFOOT COUNTRY. *Mor.tana 1960 10(4): 34-44.* "An original map and a carefully researched guide to the rich historical treasures of the land once ruled by the mighty Blackfeet Nation." L. G. Nelson

732. West, Helen B. ROBARE: ELUSIVE POST IN BLACKFEET COUNTRY. *Montana 1965 15(3): 44-57.* Montana's floods of 1964 washed away the last traces of early trading towns along the Blackfeet reservation's southern border. Robare, a center of whisky trade and other illicit business from 1874 to 1900, witnessed its share of fights, murders, and lynchings. Derived from letters and reports in archives of the Blackfeet Agency; illus. S. R. Davison

733. West, Helen B. STARVATION WINTER OF THE BLACKFEET. *Montana 1959 9(1): 2-19.* Describes the "starvation winter" (1883-84) during which one-quarter of the Blackfeet Indian tribe—some 600 in all—died due to disappearance of the buffalo and the shortage of rations provided by the Indian Agency. New evidence exonerates to some degree Major John W. Young, the much maligned agent who was blamed for the tragedy and resigned his post in April 1884. B. Waldstein

734. —. BELOVED STORYMAKER OF THE BLACKFEET—JAMES WILLARD SCHULTZ. *Montana 1960 10(4): 2-18, 22-26.*
    Schultz, Jessie Donaldson. ADVENTURESOME, AMAZING APIKUNI, pp. 2-18.
    Dusenberry, Verne. AN APPRECIATION OF JAMES WILLARD SCHULTZ, pp. 22-23.
    James, Harry C. APIKUNI'S AGELESS AUDIENCE, pp. 24-26.
    Three authors have prepared a reflection on the life of James Willard Schultz, emphasizing his years spent with the Indians and his stories written about these people. L. G. Nelson

Blackfoot, Blood

735. Gladstone, James. INDIAN SCHOOL DAYS. *Alberta Hist. R. [Canada] 1967 15(1): 18-24.* Recollections of school days spent at St. Paul's Mission schools on the Blood Reservation and at Calgary Industrial School. H. M. Burns

Blackfoot, Piegan

736. Hopwood, V. G. NEW LIGHT ON DAVID THOMPSON. *Beaver [Canada] 1957(Summer): 26-31.* The author has unearthed the missing 30 pages from Thompson's (1770-1857) *Narrative* which the original editor, J. B. Tyrell, was forced to omit. These pages tell of Thompson's first trip to the West, his first meeting with the Piegan war chief Kootenae Appee, and how Thompson lost the sight of his right eye. R. W. Winks

737. Wilson, Wesley C. THE U.S. ARMY AND THE PIEGANS—THE BAKER MASSACRE OF 1870. *North Dakota Hist. 1965 32(1): 40-58.* The massacre of 173 men, women, and children in their camp on a bitterly cold morning, by U.S. soldiers under Colonel Eugene M. Baker, was in retaliation for the murder of two white men by Piegan Indians. Baker was praised by his superior officers, but when public opinion in the East denounced the heartless affair a demand arose for a modified Indian policy, already put into planning by an Indian Commission appointed by President Grant. Because of the influence of humanitarians, several changes were made. Army officers were excluded from being Indian agents. Efforts were made to civilize the Indians, teach them skills, and prepare them for living in accordance with the standards of the white community. Treaties with tribes were discontinued and Indians were treated as individual members of society. The Piegan Massacre contributed impetus to the reform. 3 illus., 40 notes. I. W. Van Noppen

Cherokee

738. Chapman, Berlin B. THE ENID "RAILROAD WAR": AN ARCHIVAL STUDY. *Chronicles of Oklahoma 1965 43(2): 126-197.* An account of a town and railroad contest. When the Chicago, Rock Island and Pacific Railway and its subsidiary the Chicago, Kansas and Nebraska Railway built a road through the Indian Territory a controversy ensued over the locations of townsites and county seats. Sites were chosen, and the railroad company "induced some Cherokee Indians to take their allotments at these stations and bought them out in the same deal." White speculators resented this fact. Secretary of the Interior Hoke Smith had the sites changed to less desirable locations with bogs and quicksands. Violence erupted in the "railroad war." Appendix and 96 notes.
I. W. Van Noppen

739. Foreman, Carolyn Thomas, ed. AN OPEN LETTER FROM TOO-QUA-STEE TO CONGRESSMAN CHARLES CURTIS, 1898. *Chronicles of Oklahoma 1969 47(3): 298-311.* Presents a letter written by DeWitt Clinton Duncan to protest the Curtis Act before Congress which would have ended the tribal governments in Indian Territory and would have allotted the lands to the individual Indians. Duncan was a powerful writer of the Cherokee, who was born in Dahlonega in the eastern Cherokee nation and moved west along the Trail of Tears. He graduated from Dartmouth College in 1861, taught school in Indian Territory, served as a lawyer, and wrote poetry under his Cherokee name— "Too-qua-stee." Additional material provides biographical information on Duncan and a booklet he wrote entitled *Story of the Cherokees.* 2 notes.
K. P. Davis

740. Hermann, Robert K. THE CHEROKEE TOBACCO CASE. *Chronicles of Oklahoma 1963 41(3): 299-322.* Following the Civil War Cherokees and Choctaws set up tobacco factories near the Arkansas line in Oklahoma. They believed their product was exempt from the U.S. excise tax. This contention was denied by the U.S. Supreme Court in 1871. The case was brought because E. C. Boudinot and Stand Watie believed that, according to the Cherokee Treaty of 1866 as a

separate "nation," they were exempt from U.S. taxation. The 1871 Supreme Court decision erased any idea that an American "nation" could be preserved within U.S. borders. Illus., 21 notes.   I. W. Van Noppen

741. Johnson, N. B. THE CHEROKEE ORPHAN ASYLUM. *Chronicles of Oklahoma 1966 44(3): 275-280.* Prior to Oklahoma's statehood the Cherokee Nation was governed under a constitution similar to that of the United States. It maintained public schools and two institutions of higher learning. It housed the insane and gave aid to orphans. Because of the Civil War, there were many orphans whose support was a problem. After the New Echota Treaty of 1835 the Cherokees set aside 50 thousand dollars for orphans. By 1875 the Cherokees had built an orphanage at Salina at a cost of 28 thousand dollars to house 150 children. There were 340 acres of land. Prior to that time orphans had been cared for in private homes. The orphanage was administered by the Board of Education and its academic course was similar to that in modern schools. After school hours the children worked in the kitchen, laundry, sewing room, dining room, and black-smith's shop, as well as at stock raising and farming. Farm and dairy products aided the support of the home. The Cherokees supported the asylum from their tribal funds for one-third of a century.   I. W. Van Noppen

742. Kilpatrick, Jack F. and Kilpatrick, Anna G. A CHEROKEE CONJURA-TION TO CURE A HORSE. *Southern Folklore Q. 1964 28(3): 216-219.* That the Cherokee Indians had an enormous repertoire of conjurations for human ills has been well known; the authors point out, however, that they also had conjura-tions for the ills of animals. They proceed to translate two versions of such a conjuration to doctor a horse suffering from the blind staggers; they place the document in Oklahoma and date it "from the late 19th century."
                                                              H. Aptheker

743. Kilpatrick, Jack F. and Kilpatrick, Anna G. LETTERS FROM AN AR-KANSAS CHEROKEE CHIEF (1828-29). *Great Plains J. 1965 5(1): 26-34.* The text of three letters published in the *Cherokee Phoenix* in 1828 and 1829, written by the Cherokee chieftan, The Glass, to fellow tribesmen in the east. The Glass had moved west, and in his letters he describes life in Arkansas, Texas, and Oklahoma. 40 notes.   O. H. Zabel

744. Neet, J. Frederick, Jr. STAND WATIE: CONFEDERATE GENERAL IN THE CHEROKEE NATION. *Great Plains J. 1966 6(1): 36-51.* A discussion of Cherokee support for the Confederacy during the Civil War. The main leader of the Indians throughout the war was Brigadier General Stand Watie, CSA. Watie campaigned with considerable success in Indian Territory, Arkansas, and Mis-souri against federal forts, troops, and supply trains. When General Watie surren-dered on 23 June 1865 he was probably the last Confederate general to do so. Photo, 28 notes.   O. H. Zabel

745. Oates, Stephen B. CONFEDERATE CAVALRYMEN OF THE TRANS-MISSISSIPPI. *Civil War Hist. 1961 7(1): 13-19.* Western Confederate horsemen

were mostly cowboys and farmers who cared little for military tactics. They were organized in 115 regiments and 39 battalions which lived largely by depredations upon Yankees. They had no notable leaders comparable to Jeb Stuart or Philip Sheridan, but they were energetic and courageous and performed well. A Cherokee, Stand Watie, in the Choctaw country, was still opposing surrender to federal troops until June 1865, when his group finally laid down arms.   L. Filler

746. Warren, Hanna R. RECONSTRUCTION IN THE CHEROKEE NATION. *Chronicles of Oklahoma 1967 45(2): 180-189.* The Ridge faction of the Cherokee Nation in Oklahoma joined the Confederacy in the Civil War. After 1863, the Ross faction repudiated their Southern commitments, freed their slaves, and supported the Union. When the Ross faction confiscated the Ridge faction's property during the war, the long-standing bitterness between the two groups increased. This hampered federal treatymaking efforts and caused considerable hardship to the Indians in the winter of 1865-66. The Northern group signed the Reconstruction Treaty of 1866 and the Southern element accepted the terms without signing. It was a year later before harmony was restored and 1870 before all the legal technicalities were resolved. The status of their former Negro slaves remained a touchy question. 40 notes.   D. L. Smith

Cheyenne

747. Berthrong, Donald J. CATTLEMEN ON THE CHEYENNE-ARAPAHO RESERVATION, 1883-1885. *Arizona and the West 1971 13(1): 5-32.* In 1883 seven cattle companies got approval from the Arapaho and Southern Cheyenne Indians to run stock on some three million acres of rented land on the reservation in western Oklahoma. The arrangements had the sanction of the Indian agent. The impact of this and other white incursions disturbed the Indians, especially a hard core of the Cheyenne. The Cheyenne Dog Soldiers, as they were called, led the opposition and were able to enforce their will on the agent, mixed-bloods, and the Indians who were succumbing to white institutions. A presidential order forced the cattlemen to leave the reservation. Cattlemen who hoped to get the order withdrawn spread rumors that the fierce Southern Cheyenne planned to raid southwestern Kansas in retaliation. In the summer of 1885, thousands of settlers fled to nearby towns in terror, abandoning their homes, livestock, and crops. The dissident Cheyenne had protected their reservation land by exercising traditional forms of control over their people. 10 illus., map, 50 notes.   D. L. Smith

748. Collings, Ellsworth. ROMAN NOSE: CHIEF OF THE SOUTHERN CHEYENNE. *Chronicles of Oklahoma 1965 42(4): 429-457.* The Cheyennes were a proud and fearless people. Formerly agricultural, they gave up settled abodes to follow the buffalo herds. In 1867, after numerous battles with whites, Medicine Lodge Treaty was signed allotting the Southern Cheyenne and the Arapaho a reservation together. Schools, teachers, clothing, and money were to be provided. Bunton Darlington, who became agent, taught the women to bake and sew. Roman Nose, a Cheyenne, was born in 1856 and became chief in 1897, seeking peace and education. For 18 years he assisted the Indians and the Com-

missioner of Indian Affairs to improve living conditions. In 1906 he organized the Roman Nose Gypsum Company. He died June 12, 1917. Appendix includes Roman Nose genealogy and a description of Roman Nose State Park.

I. W. Van Noppen

749. Dusenberry, Verne. HORN IN THE ICE. *Montana 1956 6(4): 26-33.* The Cheyenne, long considered typical Indians of the western Plains, are now shown to have been recent migrants from the woodlands of the north and east. Apparently the migration occurred slowly during the 18th century. Archaeological excavations and reexamination of linguistic and other ethnological evidence support the revised opinion. Based on the published works of explorers and of authorities on the Cheyenne, and on interviews with elderly members of the tribe.

S. R. Davison

750. Gage, Duane. BLACK KETTLE: A NOBLE SAVAGE? *Chronicles of Oklahoma 1967 45(3): 244-251.* An examination of the conflicting opinions concerning the character and performance of the Cheyenne Indian chief Black Kettle, and the circumstances under which he was compelled to act, leads to the conclusion that he was a victim of the times in which he lived. Black Kettle was a powerful and controversial figure in the post-Civil War Indian wars on the Great Plains. Illus., 22 notes.

D. L. Smith

751. Garrard, Lewis H. IN THE LODGE OF VI-PO-NA: A VISIT TO THE CHEYENNE. *Am. West 1968 5(4): 32-36.* Narrates his travels and observations of his 1846 trip over the Santa Fe Trail and the Southwest, first published in 1850 as *Wah-to-Yah and the Taos Trail.* The present narrative is excerpted from a 1968 facsimile reproduction of the 1936 edition. It describes Garrard's visit to a Cheyenne village on the Purgatoire River where he was hospitably received by Chief Vi-Po-Na. Recorded are numerous ethnographic details. Illus.

D. L. Smith

752. Grange, Roger T. TREATING THE WOUNDED AT FORT ROBINSON. *Nebraska Hist. 1964 45(3): 273-294.* Presents the surgeons' reports prepared after treating the wounded, both white and Indian, after the Cheyenne outbreak at Fort Robinson in 1879 and analyzes medical practice and knowledge of the time.

R. Lowitt

753. Hill, Burton S. FRONTIER POWDER RIVER MISSION. *Ann. of Wyoming 1966 38(2): 214-222.* Discusses the efforts of the German Evangelical Lutheran Synod of Iowa to establish an Indian mission on the Powder River in 1859-60. The missionaries spoke only German, had little knowledge of Indian culture, and lacked adequate economic support, and their first efforts failed. Still, they did establish a headquarters at Deer Creek, and from there they worked among several tribes. They enjoyed a degree of success among the Cheyenne tribes, but apparently were not able to maintain their work because of Indian wars and U.S. Indian policy which moved the tribes to other areas. Illus.

R. L. Nichols

754. Kircus, Peggy D. FORT DAVID A. RUSSELL: A STUDY OF ITS HIS-TORY FROM 1867 TO 1890. *Ann. of Wyoming 1968 40(2): 161-192, 1969 41(1): 83-111.* Part I. Discusses the building and operations of Fort David A. Russell in Wyoming at present-day Cheyenne. Built to protect construction crews of the Union Pacific Railroad, it remained in use as a supply depot. Described are the post facilities, health and diet problems, and relations between the garrison and the nearby Cheyenne Indians. Based on published journals, government records, and secondary accounts; illus., 32 notes. Part II. Discusses health and dietary problems at the post. Unsanitary conditions and poorly constructed living quarters caused high rates of sickness and lowered efficiency and morale. The author then examines the role of troops from the fort in the Indian wars on the northern Plains against the Sioux, Cheyenne, and Ute tribes, as well as their participation in the battle at Wounded Knee (1890). Briefly traced are the activities at the post since the close of the Indian wars. During the ensuing decades the army used the post to house units during peacetime, as a regional processing center during war, and most recently as a missile base. Based on published journals, government records, and secondary accounts; 94 notes.				R. L. Nichols

755. Liberty, Margot. "I WILL PLAY WITH THE SOLDIERS." *Montana 1964 14(4): 16-26.* During the Ghost Dance excitement of 1890, two young Cheyennes deliberately murdered a white youth and prearranged their own deaths by announcing the time and place of their attack against U.S. troops at Lame Deer, on Northern Cheyenne Reservation. In view of almost the entire Cheyenne tribe, assembled for distribution of rations, the two charged down a hillside, firing at the waiting soldiers, and were killed by volleys of rifle fire. Their exploit has become a tribal legend, and primitive stone markers have been placed to indicate the site. Derived from recent testimony of elderly Indians who witnessed the event, and early published accounts.				S. R. Davison

756. Ottaway, Harold N. A POSSIBLE ORIGIN FOR THE CHEYENNE SACRED ARROW COMPLEX. *Plains Anthropologist 1970 15(48): 94-98.* "This paper examines known origin myths and describes how the four Sacred Arrows were utilized by the Cheyenne in time of hunger and battle. By combining the existing folklore with an examination of Cheyenne prehistory, a more precise time and geographical point of origin of the whole Cheyenne Sacred Arrow 'complex' is developed."				J

757. Parsons, John E., ed. THE NORTHERN CHEYENNE AT FORT FET-TERMAN. COLONEL WOODWARD DESCRIBES SOME EXPERIENCES OF 1871. *Montana 1959 9(2): 16-27.* An account by Colonel George A. Woodward, commander of Fort Fetterman, Wyoming, of his experiences during the year 1871 with the Cheyenne Indians.				B. Waldstein

758. Petersen, Karen Daniels. CHEYENNE SOLDIER SOCIETIES. *Plains Anthropologist 1964 9(25): 146-172.* "There has been considerable ambiguity as to the identity of the Cheyenne soldier societies. This paper examines all known

original sources and on the basis of internal evidence, comparatively analyzed, established the identity and characteristics of the Cheyenne military societies."
                                                                                          J

759. Peterson, Karen Daniels. THE WRITINGS OF HENRY ROMAN NOSE. *Chronicles of Oklahoma 1965 42(4): 458-478.* Roman Nose, 19, was one of three Cheyennes imprisoned in St. Augustine, Florida, to insure pacification of the tribe. They were given much freedom and some schooling. Roman Nose's writings reveal Indian life, his prison years, and life at Hampton Institute and Carlisle Institute. He praised the kindness of Captain R. H. Pratt and the people of St. Augustine. After three years Roman Nose and 21 other Indian boys were given three years of education in the East. Roman Nose took the name of his benefactors and called himself Henry Caruthers Roman Nose—the Henry for Captain Pratt and the Caruthers for Mr. and Mrs. Horace Caruthers who had raised the money for the education of the Indian boys. Roman Nose wanted to stay at Hampton three years and then educate his people. As evidenced by his writings, Roman Nose became an evangelist for the white man's way of life, which he continued after he became a chief. 54 notes.   I. W. Van Noppen

760. Powell, Peter J. OX'ZEM: BOX ELDER AND HIS SACRED WHEEL LANCE. *Montana 1970 20(2): 30-41.* "For the Cheyenne people, two disasters assumed such spiritual proportions that they cast their shadow across all subsequent tribal history. To this day, older Cheyennes speak of these twin misfortunes: the capture of the Sacred Arrows by the Skidi Pawnees, and the mutilation of the Sacred Buffalo Hat by the Keeper's own wife." These events, in 1830 and 1874 respectively, are shown to have been forerunners of catastrophe for the tribe, in the form of white invasion and suppression. The author describes the two sacred objects and the related ceremonials and beliefs. The title refers to a lance likewise held in veneration for its power to shield the people from harm. Based on letters from and interviews with Cheyenne leaders; illus., 23 notes.
                                                                                          S. R. Davison

761. White, Lonnie J. FROM BLOODLESS TO BLOODY: THE THIRD COLORADO CAVALRY AND THE SAND CREEK MASSACRE. *J. of the West 1967 6(4): 535-581.* Details the relations between Indians and whites in Colorado during the two years preceding the battle between the Third Colorado Cavalry and the Cheyennes on Sand Creek in November 1864 and concludes that the commander of the Third, Colonel John M. Chivington, may have been motivated by the hope that a decisive victory would advance his political fortunes. The author details the battle and the controversy which resulted from it, suggesting that the massacre might not have been so controversial had it not been for the political and personal animosities prevalent in Colorado at that time and had the Third not attacked a village that had seemingly been granted temporary immunity. He maintains that other politicians and military men, as well as all the white inhabitants of Colorado, must share the blame with Chivington if Sand Creek is to be condemned. He does not believe that the subsequent investigations of the affairs were thorough or objective. Based on newspaper and government reports as well as secondary sources; map, illus., 86 notes.   D. N. Brown

762. Wright, Kathryn. INDIAN TRADERS' CACHE. *Montana 1957 7(1): 2-7.*
The history of the monument erected by W. P. Moncure, an Indian trader, to the
memory of Two Moons, the Cheyenne Indian chief who led his men against
General Custer in the battle of the Little Big Horn on 25 June 1876. The rock-
built monument contains a vault in which many objects of historical interest have
been hidden. Among these is an envelope, "not to be opened until 1986," containing legends and tribal secrets of the Cheyennes and, allegedly, instructions covering sources of buried treasure within the confines of the Northern Cheyenne
Indian Reservation in southeastern Montana. The author appeals for a legal
opening of the monument's vault before 1986 and the transfer of the contents to
an appropriate museum.   B. Waldstein

763. Wright, Peter M. THE PURSUIT OF DULL KNIFE FROM FORT
RENO IN 1878-1879. *Chronicles of Oklahoma 1968 46(2): 141-154.* After the
Battle of the Little Big Horn in 1876, American troops pursued and separated
the Dakota (Sioux) and Cheyenne Indians into smaller groups. In the peace
settlement that followed it was decided that the Northern Cheyenne should rejoin
their southern kinsmen in Indian Territory. About half of the band, a faction led
by Dull Knife, were restive and wanted to return to Dakota (Sioux) territory in
the northern Plains. When they defied orders and fled in late 1878 they were
pursued by Fort Reno-based troops. A network of troops, made possible by
telegraph and rail communications, joined in efforts to stop the fleeing Indians.
The Fort Reno troops were in pursuit into Nebraska. 53 notes.
                                                                  D. L. Smith

764. —. [SAND CREEK.] *Colorado Mag. 1964 41(4): 277-335.*
    Unsigned. A CENTURY OF CONTROVERSY, pp. 277-278. Introduces
the authors of these anniversary articles, a century after the Sand Creek massacre
or battle.
    Carey, Raymond G. THE PUZZLE OF SAND CREEK, pp. 279-298. On
29 November 1864 Colonel John Chivington and the Third Regiment of Colorado Volunteer Cavalry, "hundred-daysters," attacked an encampment of one
hundred Cheyenne lodges at Sand Creek. Figures vary as to the number killed.
The "massacre" evoked nationwide disapproval and was studied by two congressional commissions and a military commission. Certain facts of the battle remain
a mystery; how many were killed, whether the Indians were hostile, and whether
the killed included a large number of women and children.
    Unrau, William E. A PRELUDE TO WAR, pp. 299-313. The period
1860-63 in Colorado Territory was confused. Two successive territorial governors, two Indian agents serving concurrently, and a novice Indian commissioner
in Washington tried to make satisfactory treaties with Cheyennes and Arapahoes,
but they were unsuccessful, and war soon followed.
    Lecompte, Janet. SAND CREEK, pp. 314-335. The Indian War in Colo-
rado in 1864 was provoked by the political aspirations of Territorial Governor
John Evans. The massacre cannot be justified. Evidence of the guilt of Evans and
Chivington was suppressed in Colorado for one hundred years, while people there
have continued to debate the propriety of the attack.   I. W. Van Noppen

Chickasaw

765. James, Parthena Louise. THE WHITE THREAT IN THE CHICKASAW NATION. *Chronicles of Oklahoma 1968 46(1): 73-85.* After 1871, the influx of whites into the Chickasaw Nation in Oklahoma posed a threat. Civil War veterans leased land from the Chickasaw or hired themselves out to the Indians as laborers. As with the emancipated Negroes in their midst, the whites as citizens were not subject to the jurisdiction of the Indians. The Chickasaw were fearful of the time when they might be outnumbered. Their one hope, they believed, was allotment of their lands to individuals. Legal technicalities prevented this in the 1870's. 70 notes.   D. L. Smith

766. Sparger, Julia K. YOUNG ARDMORE. *Chronicles of Oklahoma 1965 43(4): 394-415.* From 1855 the Ardmore area was held communally by the Chickasaw Nation. From 1865 to 1900 a white person could settle there by marrying a Chickasaw or by buying land from Chickasaw citizens. In 1880 Alva Roth, who had married a Chickasaw, built the 700 Ranch on the site of Ardmore. After 1897 the Indians held land in severalty instead of communally. This caused a problem for those who had leased land. In 1898 telephones and electric lights were installed, in 1902 water mains were laid. Hargrove College was established in 1895. Oil was found in 1913 and the county filled up overnight. Biblio.
                                                            I. W. Van Noppen

767. James, Parthena Louise. RECONSTRUCTION IN THE CHICKASAW NATION: THE FREEDMAN PROBLEM. *Chronicles of Oklahoma 1967 45(1): 44-57.* The Dawes Commission destroyed the Chickasaw Nation in 1894 by appropriating the land to individual tribal members. It was at this time that the problem of Chickasaw freedmen was solved. From the Civil War to 1894 much confusion existed with regard to the status of the freedmen. This made law and order in the Chickasaw Nation difficult. This confusion could have been avoided if the United States had acted to remove the freed slaves as the Chickasaw elected to have done under the treaty of 1866. But after the freedmen settled and built in the Nation they no longer wanted to move. The Chickasaw, however, were equally determined to move the black men for fear of losing control of their Nation. Fortunately for the Chickasaw, other Reconstruction problems were not so difficult. 50 notes.   K. P. Davis

Choctaw

768. Baird, W. David. SPENCER ACADEMY, CHOCTAW NATION, 1842-1900. *Chronicles of Oklahoma 1967 45(1): 25-43.* Spencer Academy stood as an important educational institution among the Choctaw. It educated many of the principal chiefs, leaders, and military officers from the tribe who served in the Civil War. The school was administered at various times by the Northern and Southern Presbyterians and by the tribe itself. Subject matter included geography, history, algebra, and music, as well as classical Greek and Latin at times. Based

on the criteria of ability to teach English, the school was a failure, yet many felt it was the equal of New England schools. Illus., map, 43 notes.

K. P. Davis

769. Bryant, Keith L., Jr. THE CHOCTAW NATION IN 1843: A MISSIONARY'S VIEW. *Chronicles of Oklahoma 1966 44(3): 319-321.* On 9 February 1843 the Reverend Jared Olmstead wrote a letter to his brother which reveals his concern for conditions in the Choctaw Nation and his hope for improvement. He tells that the General Council of the Nation had appropriated 18 thousand dollars for nine schools, which were to be given to the Methodist and Presbyterian Societies provided they put up one-fifth as much money. Sanction by Congress was necessary. 10 notes.

I. W. Van Noppen

770. Edwards, John. AN ACCOUNT OF MY ESCAPE FROM THE SOUTH IN 1861. *Chronicles of Oklahoma 1965 43(1): 58-89.* Never before published, this narrative by a Presbyterian missionary begins on 11 May 1861 when a vigilance committee visited the Choctaw Reservation to check the allegiance of the missionaries and to warn those who were not willing to fight for the Confederacy to leave the Indian Territory. They believed that John Edwards was an abolitionist and threatened to hang him, but he convinced them that he had no objection to slavery so they merely commanded him to leave the territory. Later, word came to him that the vigilance committee of Texans was coming to hang him. Most of the narrative relates the events of his escape as he and his family traveled first on horseback, then by wagon, boat, and train, eventually reaching Bath, New York. After the war he returned to minister to the Choctaw.

I. W. Van Noppen

771. Spalding, Arminta Scott. FROM THE NATCHEZ TRACE TO OKLAHOMA: DEVELOPMENT OF CHRISTIAN CIVILIZATION AMONG THE CHOCTAWS, 1800-1860. *Chronicles of Oklahoma 1967 45(1): 2-24.* Legend among the Choctaw people tells of their ancient migration into the Mississippi area from a land far to the west. Relying on corn for food, the Choctaw lived a stoical existence, believing their creator had given them rules to live by and left them. Not until contact with Christian missionaries did the Indians conceive of worshipping a god. The first mission school was established in 1818 and became a major influencing factor in the history of the Choctaw civilization. This school, though disrupted, moved with the tribe when they migrated to present-day Oklahoma in 1831. The American Board for Foreign Missions continued to underwrite the tribal educational system with funds and missionaries. By 1860 the Indians were able to undertake the administering of the school system themselves. Maps, 81 notes.

K. P. Davis

772. Unsigned. LETTER OF CYRUS KINGSBURY TO MISSION HEADQUARTERS. *J. of the Presbyterian Hist. Soc. 1959 37(1): 50.* Writing from Pine Ridge, Indian Territory, on 16 January 1861, Kingsbury described conditions among the Choctaw Indians and the progress of his missionary work among them.

W. D. Metz

Comanche

773. Day, James M. TWO QUANAH PARKER LETTERS. *Chronicles of Oklahoma 1966 44(3): 313-318.* Quanah Parker was the son of a chief of the Nocone and Cynthia Ann Parker, a white girl captured in the massacre of Parker's Fort in 1836. He was born in 1852, died in 1911. Up to 1875 he fought frontiersmen. After that he surrendered himself and his people and became a "reservation" Indian. He became a shrewd businessman and a just judge in cases involving the Comanches. On a visit to Washington he became friendly with President Theodore Roosevelt. His mother was buried in Henderson County, Texas. He wanted her body moved to Oklahoma so he could be buried beside her. In 1909 Congress appropriated money for this purpose. Included are two of his letters to the governor of Texas in which he expressed concern for his tribesmen over hunting regulations, and about the removal of his mother's body. Illus., 15 notes.   I. W. Van Noppen

774. Duffield, Lathel F. THE TAOVAYAS VILLAGE OF 1759: IN TEXAS OR OKLAHOMA? *Great Plains J. 1965 4(2): 39-48.* Reviews the background and the events of Colonel Don Diego Ortiz Parilla's campaign of 1759 against the Comanches in northern Texas. Using Parilla's descriptions, present geographical conditions, and archaeological evidence, the author concludes that the Indian village of Taovayas, where the climax of the campaign occurred, was on the north bank of the Red River in present Oklahoma rather than in Texas as is generally believed. Maps. Based on both primary and secondary sources listed at the end.   O. H. Zabel

775. Faulk, Odie B. SPANISH-COMANCHE RELATIONS AND THE TREATY OF 1785. *Texana 1964 2(1): 44-53.* The Spanish government had little trouble with the eastern and northern Indian tribes of Texas. The Lipan Apache gave trouble when the Spanish forces were occupied elsewhere than with them. The Comanches were the greatest Indian adversaries to the Spanish. The Spanish learned that neither Hispanicizing in missions nor coercion worked with the Comanches. The Spanish turned to treatying with them. Reproduces a report from Pedro de Nava, Commandant-General of the Interior Provinces, to Viceroy Miguel Joseph de Azanza, dated 23 July 1799. This document gives the terms of the Treaty of 1785 and illustrates the continuing menace of the Comanches and a desire by some Spanish officials to return to the policy of coercion. 18 notes.   W. A. Buckman

776. Faulk, Odie B. THE COMANCHE INVASION OF TEXAS, 1743-1836. *Great Plains J. 1969 9(1): 10-50.* Traces the background of the Spanish conflicts with the Indians on their northern frontier prior to 1743. After that date the major concern was with the Comanche Indians who were expanding into Texas. The author traces in some detail the gradual withdrawal of the Spanish until, by 1821, the population of Texas, "exclusive of Indians, was 3,500, or half of what it was reported to have been fifteen years earlier." One of the reasons Anglo-Americans petitioned the Mexican government to make Texas a separate province in 1833 was the failure of Coahuila to provide aid against the Comanche.

By the end of the Spanish and Mexican era in 1836, the Comanche were still in control of the Plains and were raiding San Antonio and areas below the Rio Grande. Only years later did "an advancing technology and increasing numbers of settlers...bring defeat to this tribe and confine it within a reservation, bringing permanent peace." 119 notes.   O. H. Zabel

777. Fleming, Elvis Eugene. CAPTAIN NICHOLAS NOLAN: LOST ON THE STAKED PLAINS. *Texana 1966 4(1): 1-13.* Captain Nicholas Nolan, in search of marauding Comanches, led a detachment of Negro cavalrymen and a group of buffalo hunters into the Staked Plains of northwest Texas and eastern New Mexico in the summer of 1877. Although the expedition became lost and suffered from lack of water, it indirectly removed the last major Indian impediment to settlement of the area.   W. Elkins

778. Gilles, Albert S., Sr. CA-VO-YO, GIVER OF NAMES. *Southwest R. 1968 53(1): 56-62.* During a lifetime, a Comanche male might have a number of names, all given to him by respected name givers, such as Ca-Vo-Yo. The attributes of a name-giver included a keen ear and an extensive knowledge of the vocabulary and "he must have a successful reputation as a warrior-hunter and a willingness to share his medicine."   D. F. Henderson

779. Gilles, Albert S., Sr. POLYGAMY IN COMANCHE COUNTRY. *Southwest R. 1966 51(3): 286-297.* In defense of the Comanche practice of having several wives, the author contends that the loss of men in war, the numerous tasks necessary to keep a camp functioning properly, and the necessity for a woman to become a wife once she left her father's house, forced the Comanches to adopt the practice of polygamy which proved, at least for most, to be successful.
                                                                      D. F. Henderson

780. Gilles, Albert S., Sr. THE LOST ONES: COMANCHES ON THE SCHOOL TRAIL. *Southwest R. 1965 51(1): 63-74.* Reflections on the ineffectiveness of the training at the Indian school at Carlisle, Pennsylvania. The teachers drilled into the children's minds what terrible people their parents were. After returning home, the children refused to speak English.   D. F. Henderson

781. Gilles, Albert S., Sr. WER-QUE-YAH, JESUS-MAN COMANCHE. *Southwest R. 1968 53(3): 277-291.* Captured and taken to Fort Sill in 1874 or 1875, Wer-que-yah became one of the Gilles' first customers at their trading store at Old Faxon, Oklahoma Territory. Reflections on the problem of Indian credit, conflict with the government trader, and an explanation of the "grass payment" are included.   D. F. Henderson

782. Harrison, Jeanne V. MATTHEW, CONFEDERATE AGENT AT THE WICHITA AGENCY INDIAN TERRITORY. *Chronicles of Oklahoma 1969 47(3): 242-257.* Matthew Leeper served as both the U.S. government agent and the Confederate agent to the Comanche Indians. A native of North Carolina, Leeper was educated at Chapel Hill. He and his family moved often, living in

Georgia, Tennessee, Mississippi, and Arkansas where he served as receiver of the public moneys. President Buchanan offered Leeper the position of Consul to Smyrna (in the Mediterranean) or Cuba, but Leeper did not want to leave the United States, so he was given the job of Indian agent. When the Civil War began, Leeper was reappointed to the same job by the Confederate government. In the massacre which occurred at the Wichita Agency in Indian Territory on 23 October 1862, Leeper was feared slain. He escaped, however, and was aided by some friendly Comanche. This account is based on the memory of the author, Leeper's daughter; illus., 12 notes.   K. P. Davis

783. Harrison, Lowell H. INDIANS VS. BUFFALO HUNTERS AT ADOBE WALLS. *Am. Hist. Illus.* *1967 2(1): 18-27.* The Texas Panhandle was the locale of a fight between Comanche Indians and a small settlement housing nearly 30 people. The author provides the background of the battle, including the development of a new tanning process which encouraged the buffalo hunters to venture into territory claimed by the Indians. The major battle took place 27 June 1874, and there were brief exchanges for a few days afterward before the Indians departed to make other attacks to the south. Retaliation came with a military campaign in 1874-75 under Generals Nelson A. Miles and Ranald S. Mackenzie.
J. D. Filipiak

784. Jones, William K. THREE KWAHARI COMANCHE WEAPONS. *Great Plains J. 1968 8(1): 31-47.* A discussion of the source and the acquisition by the Smithsonian Institution of two Comanche shields and their covers and of an Osage orange bow. A detailed description of the designs on the shields and covers is provided and the author concludes, "These Comanche weapons were uniquely well documented. They should serve in the future as significant keys to the better documentation of similar objects whose origin and history are less well known."
Illus., 23 notes.   O. H. Zabel

785. Neighbours, Kenneth F. THE GERMAN-COMANCHE TREATY OF 1847. *Texana 1964 2(4): 311-322.* Account of the arrangement of a treaty between the Comanche Indians and a German land company. The land company, headed by J. O. Meusebach, needed to survey certain areas in the Comanche hunting grounds. Meusebach and his party, joined by Indian agent Major Robert S. Neighbors, met the Indians at their camp in February 1847 to make preliminary arrangements. A description of the encampment and the council was taken down by Doctor Ferdinand von Roemer, who accompanied Neighbors. The Comanche agreed to the survey on their lands for one thousand dollars. The treaty was signed on 9 May 1847 in the German town of Fredericksburg by the land company officers, the Indian agent, and the Comanche chiefs Santa Anna, Buffalo Hump, Old Owl, and Ketumse. 24 notes.   W. A. Buckman

786. Oates, Stephen B. THEY DID RIGHT BECAUSE IT WAS RIGHT. *Southwest R. 1963 48(4): 387-395.* Brief narrative of the experiences of John S. Ford's company of Texas Rangers from 23 August 1849, when they were sworn into the service of the United States, to 23 September 1851, when they were

mustered out. The mission of the Rangers was the protection of residents between the Nueces and Rio Grande Rivers from renegade Comanches and Mexican outlaws who had terrorized the area.   D. F. Henderson

787. Tyler, Ronnie. QUANAH PARKER'S NARROW ESCAPE. *Chronicles of Oklahoma 1968 46(2): 182-188.* Comanche chiefs Quanah Parker and Yellow Bear went to Fort Worth, Texas, 19 December 1885, on business. Yellow Bear died from coal gas fumes in his hotel room and Parker nearly died. Although Comanche terror had been subdued, there was apprehension that their fellow tribesmen would not understand the circumstances of Yellow Bear's death and might cause trouble. Fortunately, this did not develop. 22 notes.
                                                        D. L. Smith

Cree, Plains

788. Rogers, E. S. and Updike, Lee. PLAINS CREE. *Beaver [Canada] 1969 300(Autumn): 56-59.* In the early years of the 18th century the Cree moved west from the Subarctic to the Great Plains, along the North and South Saskatchewan rivers. The buffalo became their staple of life. The focal point of their year was the Sun Dance held in late June or early July. The author describes their artifacts. The disappearance of the buffalo ruined the Cree way of life. Illus.
                                                        L. F. S. Upton

Creek

789. Barnett, Leona G. ESTE CATE EMUNKV: RED MAN ALWAYS. *Chronicles of Oklahoma 1968 46(1): 20-40.* Alexander Posey, half-Creek and of literary talent, served in the tribal legislature and in administrative capacities in tribal schools. As an interpreter, poet, journalist, and employee of the Dawes Commission, he served his people well in the transition from collective to individual ownership and rights. 4 illus., 33 notes.   D. L. Smith

790. Dale, Edward Everett, ed. THE JOURNAL OF ALEXANDER LAWRENCE POSEY, JANUARY 1 TO SEPTEMBER 4, 1897. *Chronicles of Oklahoma 1968 45(4): 393-432.* Alexander Lawrence Posey, half-Creek, was superintendent of a Creek orphanage near Okmulgee, Oklahoma. His journal for 1897 reveals his personality, his love of nature, and the everyday details of running an orphanage and school. 6 illus., 35 notes.   D. L. Smith

791. Debo, Angie. THE LOCATION OF THE BATTLE OF ROUND MOUNTAINS. *Chronicles of Oklahoma 1963 41(1): 70-104.* Marshals and evaluates the evidence, oral and written, concerning the site of the Battle of Round Mountains. The Creek Indians with Union sympathies were seeking to emigrate to Kansas with all their household belongings. They were persued by Confederate troops and caught near the Round Mountains at the mouth of the Cimarron and above

Tulsa. There is much controversial evidence concerning the location. From fragments of dishes, cooking pots, and a buggy step, the author presents conclusions concerning the location of the battle.   I. W. Van Noppen

792. Hodges, Bert. NOTES ON THE HISTORY OF THE CREEK NATION AND SOME OF ITS LEADERS. *Chronicles of Oklahoma 1965 43(1): 9-18.* Traces the migration of the Creeks from their homelands on the Chattahoochie River and the surrounding country to what later became Oklahoma, and the self-government practiced by the tribe after its removal. The McIntosh family has always played a leading role among the Lower Creeks (so-called because they originally resided along the lower creeks in Georgia) and among the survivors of the Five Civilized Tribes, in their effort to become a separate state. The movement for separate statehood was brought to a standstill with the passage of the Dawes General Allotment Act which provided for making up rolls of the five Indian nations and alloting them lands in severalty. Oklahoma became a state in 1907. The McIntosh family has been well known during the entire history of Oklahoma. Descendants of Captain William McIntosh, a Scot, and his Creek Indian wife, have served in the War of 1812 and the Confederate Army in the Civil War. They have been well-educated and are ardent members of the Baptist Church. W. E. "Dode" McIntosh is the present chief of the Creek people. 10 notes.
                                                                          I. W. Van Noppen

793. King, Jerlene. JACKSON LEWIS OF THE CONFEDERATE CREEK REGIMENT. *Chronicles of Oklahoma 1963 41(1): 66-69.* A full-blooded Creek Indian, Jackson Lewis was six years old when his tribe was removed from Alabama and Georgia to Oklahoma. Earning the respect of his people as he grew up, he became an excellent doctor, a Baptist deacon, a Mason, and a member of the House of Warriors. He served as a doctor in the army of the Confederate States in Company K of the Second Regiment Creek Indian Volunteers. He died in 1910.   I. W. Van Noppen

794. Pickens, Donald K. A NOTE IN OKLAHOMA HISTORY: HENRY C. BROKMEYER AMONG THE CREEK INDIANS. *Chronicles of Oklahoma 1967 45(1): 73-76.* Henry C. Brokmeyer (1828-1906) was a German who migrated to the United States and worked his way to Saint Louis. After attending Georgetown University (Kentucky) and Brown University, he began to seriously study German literature and philosophy. His first interest was the work of Hegel. After the Civil War, Brokmeyer served as lieutenant governor of Missouri and continued his philosophic activities. He developed an interest in the Creek Indians while acting as lawyer for a railroad in Oklahoma. His activities among the Creeks are little known. "The detailed story of this missionary of Hegelian speculation among the Creeks must remain a curio of Oklahoma history." 6 notes.   K. P. Davis

795. Posey, Alexander Lawrence. JOURNAL OF CREEK ENROLLMENT FIELD PARTY 1905. *Chronicles of Oklahoma 1968 46(1): 2-17.* The "Creek Enrollment Field Party of the Commission to the Five Civilized Tribes" was charged with collecting further evidence for applications of Creek Indians who

wished to participate in the distribution of tribal property; locating "lost Creeks," whose names appeared on tribal rolls but whose identity still had to be determined; and conciliating the "Snakes," renegade Creek who were opposed to relinquishment of tribal authority. Alexander Posey and another man composed the field party. Posey's journal, with entries for 18 August 1905-30 March 1906, concerns its work. Illus., 24 notes.   D. L. Smith

Crow

796. Humphreys, A. Glen. THE CROW INDIAN TREATIES OF 1868: AN EXAMPLE OF POWER STRUGGLE AND CONFUSION IN UNITED STATES INDIAN POLICY. *Ann. of Wyoming 1971 43(1): 73-89*. As a result of northern Plains tribes' violent resistance to white encroachment upon Indian lands during the 1860's, Congress appointed an eminent commission in 1867 to arrange permanent reservations for the affected tribes. In contrast to the previous practice of conquest and destruction, the treaties proffered by the Indian Peace Commission represented a humanitarian approach to Indian policy. Several tribes accepted commission treaties, and the Mountain Crow signed after the commissioners promised to close army forts on the Bozeman Trail and to protect the Crow from their traditional enemies, the Sioux. Although the Senate ultimately ratified this treaty, the government displayed its usual inefficiency in dealing with Indians when a House-Senate dispute over control of Indian policy, and Congress' preoccupation with Reconstruction, prevented ratification of a similar treaty which a special agent had negotiated with the Prairie Crow. Based primarily on newspapers and government documents; 53 notes, biblio.
                                                                    G. R. Adams

797. Krieg, Frederick C. CHIEF PLENTY COUPS: THE FINAL DIGNITY. *Montana 1966 16(4): 28-39*. Biographical sketch of the Crow chieftain who led his people to accept rather than to resist white ways. His homestead cabin, bequeathed by him as a memorial park for public use, is now being developed as part of the Montana State Park System. Based on newspaper accounts and the author's personal knowledge.   S. R. Davison

798. Wiltsey, Norman B. PLENTY COUPS: CROW CHIEF. *Montana 1963 13(4): 28-39*. From early childhood, Plenty Coups showed the intelligence and adaptability that characterized his leadership of the Crow tribe in the years 1875-1932. Almost alone among Indian leaders, he chose a path of collaboration, appeasement, and surrender, rather than one of resistance to the whites. This policy spared the Crows the wars and defeats that destroyed so many other tribes, and enabled his people to retain their traditional land as a reservation.
                                                                    S. R. Davison

Dakota (Sioux)

799. Anderson, Harry H. INDIAN PEACE TALKERS AND THE CONCLU-
SION OF THE SIOUX WAR OF 1876. *Nebraska Hist. 1963 44(4): 233-254.*
Examines the role of influential leaders among the agency Sioux, notably Spotted
Tail (Sinte Galeski), who traveled in the winter of 1876-77 to the hostile Indian
camps and after extensive talks with the fighting chiefs, persuaded them to come
in and surrender to the military authorities.   R. Lowitt

800. Anderson, Harry H. THE BENTEEN BASEBALL CLUB: SPORTS EN-
THUSIASTS OF THE SEVENTH CAVALRY. *Montana 1970 20(3): 82-87.*
Losses suffered at Custer's fight on the Little Big Horn in June 1876 are often
described, but rarely mentioned is the damage to the baseball team fielded by
Captain Frederick W. Benteen's "H" Company. Four men in the starting lineup
were killed or wounded in the battle. Yankton newspapers preserved details of
the team and its members' style of play during the season or two before the
disastrous engagement in Montana.   S. R. Davison

801. Andrist, Ralph K. MASSACRE! *Am. Heritage 1962 13(3); 8-17, 108-111.*
Recounts the Dakota (Sioux) uprising of August 1862 in southwestern Minnesota. Illustrated in color by a panorama painted by John Stevens from contemporary accounts and accompanied by the original commentary.
                                                              C. R. Allen, Jr.

802. Babcock, Willoughby M. MINNESOTA'S FRONTIER, A NEGLECTED
SECTOR OF THE CIVIL WAR. *Minnesota Hist. 1963 38(6): 274-286.* In the
late summer of 1862 while the Civil War was raging in the East, the citizens of
Minnesota were faced with an uprising of the Dakota (Sioux). Under the general
command of General John Pope, federal troops plus Wisconsin volunteers
managed to defeat the Indians and establish military posts for the protection of
the settlers by 1864. The account is based largely on War Department Records
and other papers, both published and unpublished, in the Minnesota Historical
Society.   P. L. Simon

803. Baker, Miriam Hawthorn. INKPADUTA'S CAMP AT SMITHLAND.
Ann. of Iowa 1967 39(2): 81-104. Discusses the background of the Spirit Lake
Massacre of 1857. A band of Wahpetuke Dakota (Sioux) led by Chief Inkpaduta
had spent several winters with the settlers of Smithland, Iowa. Relations with the
settlers were peaceful until the winter of 1856-57, when unusually severe weather
made food gathering difficult for both whites and Indians. A series of incidents
provoked an armed band of settlers to disarm the Dakota and demand their
withdrawal. Humiliated, Inkpaduta and his followers left a trail of destruction
in the Little Sioux River valley and climaxed their depredations with the massacre
at Spirit Lake. Smithland was untouched since the Indians feared the local militia.
Based largely on secondary sources; illus., 14 notes.   D. C. Swift

804. Barnds, William Joseph. THE MINISTRY OF THE REVEREND SAMUEL DUTTON HINMAN, AMONG THE SIOUX. *Hist. Mag. of the Protestant Episcopal Church 1969 38(4): 393-401.* Reverend Hinman served as a missionary to the Sioux Indians in the Dakota and Nebraska Territories and Minnesota for almost three decades after the beginning of the Civil War. Most of this time was spent in Dakota, and his success owed much to his willingness to live among the Indians and speak and minister in their language. He organized schools, ordained native ministers, and taught them practical skills in a "trade school." After his wife died, he became involved in a nasty dispute with Bishop William Hobart Hare over some supposed improprieties. Nevertheless, the author declares him to be the "Godfather" of Episcopal work among the Sioux. Based primarily on research in Episcopal periodicals; 23 notes.　　　J. B. Boles

805. Barsness, John and Dickinson, William. THE SULLY EXPEDITION OF 1864. *Montana 1966 16(3): 23-29.* General Alfred Sully's campaign against the Dakota (Sioux) in Dakota and Montana demonstrated the effectiveness of a large force and adequate arms, including cannon, in making war against the Plains tribes. His column not only routed a concentration of warriors but safely escorted a wagon train en route from Minnesota to Montana's newly opened gold mines. Illus., map.　　　S. R. Davison

806. Bean, Geraldine. GENERAL ALFRED SULLY AND THE NORTHWEST INDIAN EXPEDITION. *North Dakota Hist. 1966 33(3): 240-259.* Reviews the almost unnoticed Battle of White Stone Hill near present Ellendale, North Dakota, on 3 September 1863 when General Sully and troops of the Northwest Indian Expedition decisively defeated some 1,500 Dakota (Sioux) warriors. Fears of the settlers were somewhat calmed and some who had abandoned their farms returned. Land companies had enticed settlers since 1861 when Dakota Territory was created. Gold discoveries in Montana had boosted activities in the Upper Missouri country. Major General John Pope, who had been placed in charge of military operations on the northwest frontier after his defeat at Bull Run in 1862, had devised a pincers movement, one column commanded by Colonel Henry H. Sibley and the other by Sully. While Pope fumed at Sully's slow progress, he was pleased with the outcome of the battle. Other officials disagreed as to its effectiveness, as the Dakota Territory was not freed of the Indian menace. Illus., 51 notes, biblio.　　　I. W. Van Noppen

807. Bell, Gordon L. and Bell, Beth L. GENERAL CUSTER IN NORTH DAKOTA. *North Dakota Hist. 1964 31(2): 101-113.* Discusses the campaign of the Seventh Cavalry led by General George Armstrong Custer against Chief Sitting Bull and his tribes. The expedition left Fort Abraham Lincoln on 17 May 1876 with 1,200 men and 150 wagons. A day-by-day account is given of the progress of the march until 3 June 1876, just 22 days before the Battle of the Little Big Horn. Attention is given to the events leading up to this confrontation, particularly the settler expansion into the sacred Indian grounds of the Black Hills. The author discusses some of the more important diaries and personal accounts of Custer's years in North Dakota. Based on primary and secondary sources; photo, map.　　　M. J. McBaine

808. Brown, D. Alexander. THE GHOST DANCE AND BATTLE OF WOUNDED KNEE. *Am. Hist. Illus. 1966 1(8): 4-16.* Summarizes the Ghost Dance movement among the American Plains Indians that climaxed with the battle known as Wounded Knee, between Chief Big Foot's band of Dakota (Sioux) and the 7th U.S. Cavalry. The immediate events leading to the battle on 29 December 1890 are given in detail. Illus.   J. D. Filipiak

809. Coburn, Wallace David. THE BATTLE OF THE LITTLE BIG HORN. *Montana 1956 6(3): 28-41.* Gives details of General Custer's "last stand" against the Indians in Montana in 1876 (as told to the author by Major Will A. Logan).   C. C. Gorchels

810. Collins, Dabney Otis. THE FIGHT FOR SITTING BULL'S BONES. *Am. West 1966 3(1): 72-78.* Sitting Bull, Dakota (Sioux) Indian chief, was killed by Sioux Indian police on 15 December 1890, on the Standing Rock Indian Reservation in South Dakota. Soldiers removed his body for burial to Fort Yates, across the line into North Dakota. For 63 years a nephew tried to get the remains brought back to Sitting Bull's home, an effort which involved local, state, and federal officials. He succeeded in 1953. Illus., map, biblio. note.   D. L. Smith

811. Cullens, J. CUSTER'S LAST STAND. *Army Q. and Defence J. [Great Britain] 1965 90(1): 104-109.* Describes the Battle of Little Big Horn and the subsequent skirmishes with the Indians. No other single event in American history has captured public imagination more completely. It is rather like the charge of the Light Brigade at Balaclava in that both were exercises in military futility which led to disaster and a place in history. Maps.   K. James

812. Dippie, Brian W. BARDS OF THE LITTLE BIG HORN. *Western Am. Literature 1966 1(3): 175-195.* Traces the persistence of versified accounts and tributes to the Little Big Horn battle. Using a variety of poetic quotations, the author reconstructs the progress of the battle. The habitually positive attitude toward Custer and the typical sentimental treatment of the event are described. The essay includes a discussion of the ballad and poetic treatment of the "Comanche" legend. The poets (all minor) created and sustained a myth about the man and the event. 63 notes, all published, but many from obscure sources.   R. N. Hudspeth

813. Ege, Robert J. ISAIAH DORMAN: NEGRO CASUALTY WITH RENO. *Montana 1966 16(1): 35-40.* The Indians who overran Major Reno's original position in the Little Big Horn Battle were surprised to find the body of a Negro civilian. Sitting Bull identified him as Azimpa, a runaway slave who had married a Dakota (Sioux) woman and lived at times among her people. Later he worked around frontier army posts, where he was known as Isaiah Dorman. Apparently he had accompanied General Terry's command as a guide and interpreter, in the hope of meeting old friends among the Sioux.   S. R. Davison

814. Ege, Robert J. LEGEND WAS A MAN NAMED KEOGH. *Montana 1966 16(2): 27-39.* Fictionized and undocumented biographical sketch of Myles Walter Keogh, stressing his dramatic death with Custer in 1876. S. R. Davison

815. Eggleston, Edward. GEORGE W. NORTHRUP: THE KIT CARSON OF THE NORTHWEST. *North Dakota Hist. 1966 33(1): 5-21.* Called by the Dakota Indians "The-Man-That-Draws-the-Handcart," George W. Northrup by the age of 18 had mastered the Dakota tongue and customs. After having served as a trader's clerk in the Yankton country for three years he outfitted himself with a handcart of supplies and attempted to go from St. Cloud, Minnesota, to Fort Benton and on to the Pacific Coast alone, traveling 36 days before Dakota (Sioux) attackers forced him to seek a trading post. During the next few years as he guided several parties in the upper Great Plains and narrowly escaped death from Yankton and Teton Dakota Indians, he became a skilled naturalist. During the Civil War he served in the Union Army first as a scout in the Army of the Cumberland and later in Brackett's Battalion in suppressing the Dakota on the frontier in 1864. In the Battle of Killdeer Mountain, 28 July 1864, he was killed at the age of 27 years. Illus., 29 notes. I. W. Van Noppen

816. Ewers, John C. THE GUN OF SITTING BULL. *Beaver [Canada] 1956 (Winter): 20-23.* The author discusses the authenticity of an 1875 Winchester rifle that is reputed to be the gun surrendered by Sitting Bull to Major David A. Brotherton, commander of Fort Buford, on 20 July 1881.
H. J. Silverman

817. Feraca, Stephen E. and Howard, James H. THE IDENTITY AND DEMOGRAPHY OF THE DAKOTA OR SIOUX TRIBE. *Plains Anthropologist 1963 8(20): 80-84.* The authors discuss the cultural, linguistic, and historical situation of the Dakota or "Sioux" Indian tribe (first mentioned by white explorers ca. 1640), who lived in a region just west of the Great Lakes. By 1750, the westernmost groups had begun to cross the Missouri River and filter into the Black Hills region. Until after the War of 1812, the Dakota were allies of the British. In 1862, the eastern or Santee bands rose against the whites in what is called the Minnesota uprising. Defeated by government forces, many of the Santee sought refuge in Manitoba and Saskatchewan, Canada. Those remaining in the United States were placed on reservations further west, though some were allowed to stay, or filtered back, into Minnesota. "The dialect of the Eastern or Santee division is *Dakota,* that of the Middle or *Wiciyela* division *Nakota,* and that of the Teton division *Lakota.*" 5 notes, biblio. D. D. Cameron

818. Fife, Austin. BALLADS OF THE LITTLE BIG HORN. *Am. West 1967 4(1): 46-49, 86-89.* An important legacy of those who wrestled with nature and the Indians to win the West is a folklore which preserves the past as it seemed to be in their hearts and minds, but not necessarily the way it was in reality. This lore is preserved in ballads and songs, anecdotes and stories, legends and tall stories, rhymes and riddles, place names and proverbs. The defeat of George Armstrong Custer at the Battle of Little Big Horn 25 June 1876 inspired several multiversed ballads. The music and lyrics of six and the ballads of two more are

reproduced along with related commentaries. "Custer's Last Fierce Charge," "The Dying Scout," and "Custer's Last Stand" are typical titles. Biblio. note.

D. L. Smith

819. Gray, John S. CUSTER THROWS A BOOMERANG. *Montana 1961 11(2): 2-12.* Several years before the Custer "Massacre" of 1876, the general took a leading part in the feud between the army and the Interior Department over Indian policy for the tribes along the upper Missouri River. It is contended here that Custer, then in charge at Fort Abraham Lincoln (Bismarck, North Dakota), in an effort to discredit the Indian Agent Edmund Palmer, trespassed upon the latter's jurisdiction and arrested the influential Dakota chief Rain-in-the-Face for an alleged murder. In an exchange of complaints to Washington, Palmer seems to have had the better of the argument. Custer soon met a greater retribution, when the chief escaped and helped to organize the Indian forces which overwhelmed the general in the Battle of the Little Big Horn. Based principally on correspondence of Custer and Palmer to their respective superiors, and related official records.   S. R. Davison

820. Gray, John S. THE NORTHERN OVERLAND PONY EXPRESS. *Montana 1966 16(4): 58-73.* The need for rapid mail service to the gold rush area of Montana led to an experimental horseback mail between Fort Abercrombie, North Dakota, and Diamond City, near Helena, Montana. The line operated in the latter half of 1867 but was withdrawn the next year because of the distance involved, the severe climate, and resistance by the Dakota (Sioux) Indians. Based on newspaper accounts and other contemporary sources.   S. R. Davison

821. Hill, Burton S. THOMAS S. TWISS, INDIAN AGENT. *Great Plains J. 1967 6(2): 85-96.* Twiss (1803-71), a graduate of the U.S. Military Academy at West Point (1826), taught at South Carolina College (1829-47), worked for industry (1847-55), and became a U.S. Indian agent of the Upper Platte District in 1855 first at Fort Laramie and then at Deer Creek. He took an Oglala Dakota wife, worked well with the Indians and supported more western military posts and the introduction of agriculture and Christianity to the Indians. He was charged with misusing government property and had difficulty cooperating with the military. In 1861, after Lincoln's election, he resigned but continued, for a time, to live at Deer Creek. His last years were spent at Nebraska City and Rulo, Nebraska. His wife and six children survived him. Two sons were scouts for General Crook in 1876 and one was among the first recruits for Carlisle Indian School in 1879. The name "Twiss" is still common among the Sioux. Illus.

O. H. Zabel

822. Hutchins, James S. POISON IN THE PEMMICAN. *Montana 1958 8(3): 8-25.* The Yellowstone Valley, a part of the Crow Indian Reservation, was entered in 1874 by an expedition of about 150 heavily-armed men from Bozeman. The ostensible errand was to mark out a wagon road; the real one was to investigate rumors of gold in the area south of the river. On the Rosebud River the party suffered three attacks by Dakota (Sioux) Indians. The whites defended

themselves, but had to retreat to Bozeman without accomplishing either of their objectives. Based on newspaper accounts and reports by the participants.

S. R. Davison

823. Johnson, Dorothy M. GHOST DANCE: LAST HOPE OF THE SIOUX. *Montana 1956 6(3): 42-50.* Tells the story of the despairing Dakota (Sioux) Indians on a reservation in Dakota Territory who embraced a "religion" which led to a final tragic massacre by white soldiers in 1890. Other Indian religions of the time are mentioned.

C. C. Gorchels

824. Johnson, Emeroy. WHAT AN OLD MINNESOTA CHURCH REGISTER REVEALS. *Swedish Pioneer Hist. Q. 1967 18(3): 157-168.* Analyzes entries in the register of the First Swedish Lutheran Church of Scandean Grove, Minnesota, located near the village of Norseland, Minnesota. The register contains significant reflections of member's names, the Indian outbreak of 1862, births, deaths, mortality rates from disease, occupations, Civil War service of members, emigration certificates issued by parish pastors in Sweden, and other details of life in a small pioneer parish. The document of organization, dated 30 May 1858, is quoted verbatim and includes the names of the signatories. Based on the original church register; 10 notes.

E. P. Costello

825. Jones, Robert Huhn. THE NORTHWESTERN FRONTIER AND THE IMPACT OF THE SIOUX WAR, 1862. *Mid-Am. 1959 41(3): 131-153.* In the summer of 1862 the Dakota (Sioux) struck in Minnesota and threatened the entire northwestern frontier from Dakota to Kansas. Checked at first by the Minnesota volunteers under Colonel Henry Hastings Sibley, the frontier was soon militarily organized under the federal command of Major General John Pope. "The entire northwestern frontier was vitally concerned, and the disturbance was serious enough to trouble the federal government for years to come." Based almost entirely on official records of the United States and of the states along the northwestern frontier.

R. J. Marion

826. Jordan, Weymouth T., Jr. LIEUTENANT C. D. COWLES AT NORTH PLATTE STATION, 1876. *Nebraska Hist. 1971 52(1): 89-91.* An 1876 letter from Lieutenant Calvin Duvall Cowles (1849-1937) to his father, written at the height of the Sioux campaign. Cowles mentioned his personal affairs and the "indian news."

R. Lowitt

827. Keenan, Jerry. EXPLORING THE BLACK HILLS: AN ACCOUNT OF THE CUSTER EXPEDITION. *J. of the West 1967 6(2): 248-261.* Despite the Laramie Treaty of 1868, which guaranteed the Dakota (Sioux) that their sacred Black Hills would not be violated by the white man, General Philip Sheridan received permission to send a scouting expedition into the area. On 2 July 1874 a large force led by Lieutenant Colonel George Custer left Fort Abraham Lincoln. Accompanying the expedition were two geologists, a zoologist, a botanist, a photographer, a mapmaker, and two veteran miners. The expedition was to learn as much of the region as possible. The information gathered triggered a

massive rush of miners into the area. This invasion of the Black Hills angered the Indians and was an important factor in the Sioux War of 1876. Based on published sources; illus., 4 notes, biblio.   D. N. Brown

828. King, James T. NEEDED: A RE-EVALUATION OF GENERAL GEORGE CROOK. *Nebraska Hist. 1964 45(3): 223-235.* Calls for a new biography of General Crook and examines the 1876 campaign against the Dakota (Sioux). The author contends that Crook was not always a consummate military commander and was overtly concerned with his public "image." He failed not only in his objective of defeating the Indians but even of meeting them.
                                                                                            R. Lowitt

829. Kutzleb, Charles R. EDUCATING THE DAKOTA SIOUX, 1876-1890. *North Dakota Hist. 1965 32(4): 197-215.* Although Indian policy after 1870 provided for education of children, results were disappointing. During the 1870's each reservation was assigned to a religious denomination and money was appropriated for sectarian schools, but by 1891 all schools receiving congressional appropriation were placed under the supervision of the Bureau of Indian Affairs. Four types of schools were used: day schools, reservation boarding schools, training schools, and others including public schools. Few opportunities for educated Indians existed, and the tendency was for the younger Indians to forget what they had been taught and return to the customs of their people. Authorities disagreed as to curricula, standards, aims, and practicability of educating Indians. Based chiefly on government documents and other primary sources; 6 illus., 31 notes.   I. W. Van Noppen

830. Nye, E. L. CAVALRY HORSE. *Montana 1957 7(2): 40-45.* When in his 80's, Charles Varnum, a lieutenant in Custer's cavalry at the Little Big Horn Battle in 1876, related this episode about a balky horse which refused to jump even the slightest barrier until confronted with a deep ravine during flight from the counter-attacking Indians. The previously stubborn animal soared across the ditch, carrying her grateful master to safety among the number who survived with Reno.   S. R. Davison

831. Ourada, Patricia K., ed. THE HAT SITTING BULL WEARS. *Ann. of Wyoming 1969 41(2): 272-274.* Andrew Fox, a son-in-law of Sitting Bull, relates how William F. Cody (Buffalo Bill) gave the Dakota (Sioux) chief a hat when he traveled with the Wild West show in 1885. Based on manuscripts, government documents, and published secondary material; 15 notes.   R. L. Nichols

832. Pfaller, Louis. SULLY'S EXPEDITION OF 1864 FEATURING THE KILLDEER MOUNTAIN AND BADLANDS BATTLES. *North Dakota Hist. 1964 31(1): 25-77.* The author admits that this account of the battles is a bit "white-flavored" since it was based on the diaries of white men who participated. After General Alfred Sully's indecisive campaign against the Dakota (Sioux) in 1863, he was determined to bring the tribes under control in 1864, and

at the campaign's close he expressed satisfaction. Small Indian bands of raiders continued to harass white settlers, but as a unit they were no longer a threat. 16 illus., 4 maps, 150 notes. I. W. Van Noppen

833. Pfaller, Louis L., ed. THE GALPIN JOURNAL: DRAMATIC RECORD OF AN ODYSSEY OF PEACE. *Montana 1968 18(2): 2-23.* In 1868 Father Pierre-Jean DeSmet traveled from Fort Rice, North Dakota, to the camp of hostile Dakota (Sioux) in southeastern Montana, to induce tribal leaders to attend a peace conference. Charles Galpin, a Fort Rice trader, served as guide and interpreter. To supplement his own notes, DeSmet asked Galpin to keep a record of the journey; this diary, discovered in Europe in 1924, provides the body of this article. In addition to extensive verbatim reports of speeches by Sitting Bull and other prominent Dakota, the document also supplies information on the land as it then appeared, circumstances of travel, habits of the Indians, and the personality of the missionary priest. Illus., map. S. R. Davison

834. Radabaugh, J. S. CUSTER EXPLORES THE BLACK HILLS 1874. *Military Affairs 1962/63 26(4): 162-170.* The Treaty of 1868 guaranteed Dakota (Sioux) ownership of the Black Hills. The treaty, however, granted to the government the right to explore the area. In July and August 1874, a force of one thousand men under Brevet Brigadier General George A. Custer explored the area. The expedition confirmed rumors of gold which filled the Black Hills with miners, convinced the hostile Indians that resistance was the only course open to them, and led to Custer's death on the Little Big Horn. Based on primary sources. K. J. Bauer

835. Rawlings, Gerald S. CUSTER'S LAST STAND. *Hist. Today [Great Britain] 1962 12(1): 57-66.* An analysis of the conflicting versions of the annihilation of Lieutenant Colonel George Armstrong Custer and his command in 1876 by Sioux Chief Sitting Bull during the last great battle of the American Indian wars. L. D. Kasparian

836. Rector, William G. THE RENO-BENTEEN DEFENSE PERIMETER. *Montana 1966 16(2): 65-72.* Modern research shows that some soldiers in Major Marcus A. Reno's command at the Little Big Horn were deployed in a position allowing only a limited field of fire. Casualty figures suggest that the Indians took advantage of this situation to sneak in close enough for effective shots at troops on the opposite side of the defense circle. Based on examination of the site, with some reference to standard printed sources. S. R. Davison

837. Rickey, Don, Jr. THE BATTLE OF WOLF MOUNTAIN. *Montana 1963 13(2): 44-54.* Relates the tactical details of a minor skirmish, important only because it marked the end of Dakota (Sioux) and Cheyenne resistance which had continued since the Custer Battle the previous summer. On 8 January 1877, Colonel Nelson A. Miles led a small infantry force against the winter camp of Chiefs Crazy Horse and Big Crow on the Tongue River near present Birney, Montana. Casualties amounted to two or three dead on each side and a few

wounded. Routing of the Indians from their camp and loss of their supplies, coupled with the demoralizing effect of Big Crow's death, led to the band's surrender within the next few weeks. Principal source is official reports, augmented by unpublished first-hand accounts.   S. R. Davison

838. Rosenberg, Marvin and Rosenberg, Dorothy. "THERE ARE NO INDIANS LEFT NOW BUT ME." *Am. Heritage 1964 15(4): 19-23, 106-111.* Sitting Bull tried to preserve the integrity and possessions of the Dakota (Sioux) by combat, treaty, and flight; all failed. In 1890 he and other Dakota, badgered by land agents and living on short rations, adopted a frenzied religion that promised immunity from the white man's guns. A ghost dance was the religion's chief ritual. The new faith regenerated the spirit of the Dakota, but it was finally crushed by the death of Sitting Bull at the hands of arresting authorities. Illus.
                                                                        H. F. Bedford

839. Rowen, Richard D., ed. THE SECOND NEBRASKA'S CAMPAIGN AGAINST THE SIOUX. *Nebraska Hist. 1963 44(1): 3-53.* A journal, a diary, and a series of drawings, all previously unpublished, by the colonel in command, a corporal, and a private, respectively, illuminate the activities of the Second Nebraska Volunteer Infantry in 1863 in Dakota Territory in the campaign to crush the Dakota (Sioux) uprising.   R. Lowitt

840. Schoenberger, Dale T. CUSTER'S SCOUTS. *Montana 1966 16(2): 40-49.* Accounts for the action of each of the 39 scouts who went into the Little Big Horn battle with Custer in 1876. In general, their conduct was praiseworthy.
                                                                        S. R. Davison

841. Stewart, Edgar I. THE LITTLE BIG HORN: 90 YEARS LATER. *Montana 1966 16(2): 2-13.* Factual and interpretive summary of events culminating in the Battle of the Little Big Horn on 25 June 1876. Lt. Colonel George A. Custer and five companies of his 7th Cavalry were annihilated, while a secondary command under Major Marcus A. Reno and Captain Frederick W. Benteen suffered heavy losses in a separate engagement a few miles away. Almost at once, controversy developed over several aspects of the affair, and none of the questions seemed near settlement as the 90th anniversary approached. Illus.; photos.
                                                                        S. R. Davison

842. Stewart, Edgar I. WHICH INDIAN KILLED CUSTER? *Montana 1958 8(3): 26-32.* Examines the most recently published theories and evidence on this phase of the Custer controversy, and concludes that the details of his death will remain a mystery. There is little chance that conclusive proof will ever appear on these questions that have been disputed since the event in 1876.
                                                                        S. R. Davison

843. Stewart, Edgar I. and Luce, Edward S. THE RENO SCOUT. *Montana 1960 10(3): 23-28.* At the outset of General Alfred H. Terry's campaign against the Sioux in June 1876, he sent Major Marcus A. Reno with six companies of the

7th Cavalry on a scouting sweep in the valleys of the Powder and Tongue rivers. Reno exceeded his orders by going as far west as Rosebud Creek. In view of the Custer disaster, occurring in his area two weeks later, students of the affair attach importance to Reno's failure both to obey instructions and to find the Indians. The recent (1958) publication of Dr. James M. DeWolf's diary of this expedition has provided the only first-hand account of the scout and has stimulated fresh interest in the whole Custer controversy. Although based on the DeWolf diary, this account is largely an analysis of the Reno scout.   S. R. Davison

844. Stewart, William J. SETTLER, POLITICIAN, AND SPECULATOR IN THE SALE OF THE SIOUX RESERVE. *Minnesota Hist. 1964 39(3): 85-92.* Following the vicious Dakota (Sioux) uprisings that swept the Minnesota frontier in 1862, the Indians were forced to migrate beyond the line of white settlement, and their lands (totaling more than one half million acres) were sold. Speculators rather than small farmers grabbed up most of the choice land, with the help of powerful Minnesota politicians. Based largely on abstracts of public land sales.
P. L. Simon

845. Unsigned. GEORGE W. NORTHRUP: YOUNG MAN OF THE NORTHWEST FRONTIER. *Gopher Historian 1968 22(3): 18-22.* George W. Northrup, wilderness scout, frontiersman, and soldier, left New York in 1853 at the age of 15 for Minnesota Territory. There he found work as a buffalo hunter and fur trader. His exploits among the Indians and on buffalo hunts made him something of a folk hero, and accounts of his adventures appeared in newspapers across the Nation. In 1863, he joined the Union Army as a scout in service against the Rebels and the Indians. In 1864 he died in battle fighting the Dakota (Sioux) on the frontier. Edward Eggleston wrote "Thus lived and died, at the too early age of 27, George W. Northrup. No braver, purer, kindlier, or more modest young man ever lived." Based on a small collection of letters from George W. Northrup to his mother and sister, now in the Minnesota Historical Society.
G. T. Sharrer

846. Unsigned. SITTING BULL'S VERSION OF LITTLE BIG HORN. *Am. Hist. Illus. 1966 1(5): 27-31.* An interview of Sitting Bull with a correspondent of the *New York Herald* a year after the battle took place. Sitting Bull was in the village when Custer's force attacked, but took no part in the final destruction. What he knew was told him by other Indians. Two photos, two-page color painting of "Custer's Last Fight" by Gayle P. Hoskins.   E. Brown

847. Wertenberger, Mildred. FORT TOTTEN, DAKOTA TERRITORY, 1867. *North Dakota Hist. 1967 34(2): 125-146.* A discussion of the history of Fort Totten, the most perfectly preserved military post on the Indian frontier. Founded in 1867 as a part of the military posts built for the protection of the overland route from southern Minnesota into western Montana, the fort went the way of many frontier posts when, after its abandonment in 1890, it became part of the Fort Totten Military Reservation for the Dakota Indians within the area. Today the fort is preserved as a historical site under the auspices of the North

Dakota Historical Society. Included are photographs of individuals connected with the fort and of the fort as it stands today. Maps, photos, 45 notes.

R. Sexauer

848. —. [MAJOR GENERAL GEORGE ARMSTRONG CUSTER]. *Montana 1971 21.*

Hofling, Charles K., M.D. GEORGE ARMSTRONG CUSTER: A PSY-CHOANALYTIC APPROACH, (2): 32-43. Analyzes Custer's character and personality for clues to his performance in the disastrous campaign against the Sioux and Cheyenne in 1876. Traces his career in terms of frequent reverses mingled with occasional brilliant successes, all with indications of instability and a desire to attract attention. Custer had reasons to feel both guilt and resentment, leading to an urge to accomplish spectacular feats. Inner conflict may have dulled his judgment and led him to the fatal errors that insured the annihilation of his command. Based mainly on secondary sources; illus., 9 notes.

Stewart, Edgar I. A PSYCHOANALYTICAL APPROACH TO CUS-TER: SOME REFLECTIONS, (3): 74-77. The author, a historian, takes exception to the psychiatrist's findings that early childhood influences determined Custer's performance in the Sioux War of 1876. Discusses factual matters involved in the attack by Custer's men and the ensuing Battle of the Little Big Horn in which the whole command was killed.

S. R. Davison

849. —. [SIOUX WAR OF 1876]. *Montana.*

Brown, Mark H. A NEW FOCUS ON THE SIOUX WAR, 1961 11(4): 76-85. A revisionist essay on the causes of the Sioux War of 1876, focusing blame on the Indians and on the government's mild policy toward them. Based on War Department Reports and the published accounts of witnesses and participants.

Anderson, Harry H. A CHALLENGE TO BROWN'S SIOUX INDIAN WARS THESIS, 1962 12(1): 40-49. Anderson blames white intrusion on Indian land, and eagerness of the army high command for a campaign against the Sioux. Based on press dispatches and official records.

S. R. Davison

Dakota, Brulé

850. Clough, Wilson O. MINI-AKU, DAUGHTER OF SPOTTED TAIL. *Ann. of Wyoming 1967 39(2): 187-216.* Examines the sources from which the story of the death and burial of Spotted Tail's daughter Mini-Aku at Fort Laramie, Wyoming, in 1866 has developed. The author discusses the original accounts of the incident, traces the additions, and shows the sources for later secondary descriptions. He concludes that Mini-Aku was one of Spotted Tail's elder daughters, that she was about 18 when she died and was buried at Fort Laramie, and that she probably helped persuade her father to remain at peace. Based on Indian Office records, military reminiscences, and secondary material; illus., 30 notes, biblio.

R. L. Nichols

851. Worcester, Donald E. SPOTTED TAIL: WARRIOR, DIPLOMAT. *Am. West 1964 1(4): 38-46, 87.* Sinte Galeski or Spotted Tail was a chief of the numerous and powerful horse and buffalo culture, Brulé Sioux of the High Plains.

In 1854 he led a party that killed or fatally wounded all the 30 soldiers sent from Fort Laramie to arrest a Sioux who violated a treaty agreement which guaranteed emigrant safe passage across Sioux territory. Incarcerated at Fort Leavenworth, he concluded it was futile for the Sioux to continue resisting the whites. Pardoned in 1856, he returned to his people and urged them to live in peace with the whites. The Sioux seemed justified in their hostility, and it was with considerable difficulty that Spotted Tail kept his friendly Brulés intact through the trying aggravations caused by Chivington and others. He resisted government efforts to convert his people to agriculture; and with several trips to Washington and other means, he gained concessions and slowed the process. He guided the Sioux through the difficult adjustment to reservation life and avoided open warfare that would have been disastrous. His death in 1881 at the hands of a rival did not end his policies and program. Illus., biblio. D. L. Smith

Dakota, Oglala

852. Grange, Roger T., Jr. THE GARNIER OGLALA WINTER COUNT. *Plains Anthropologist 1963 8(20): 74-79.* "This article makes available the text of a previously unpublished Dakota winter count which covers the period 1759 to 1908. The calendrical record is written in a journal volume which belonged to John B. Garnier, a son of Baptiste 'Little Bat' Garnier." J

853. Herman, Jake. THE SACRED POLE. *Masterkey 1963 37(1): 35-38.* Describes a method of acquiring a sacred pole for the Sun Dance and the symbolism associated with it among the Oglala Sioux of South Dakota. The account is taken from the history explained in the Oglala Sioux language and translated into English by Chief Red Cloud. C. N. Warren

854. Ripich, Carol A. JOSEPH W. WHAM AND THE RED CLOUD AGENCY, 1871. *Arizona and the West 1970 12(4): 325-338.* The Dakota (Sioux), among the most warlike of the Plains Indians, roamed the vast expanse between the Platte and Yellowstone rivers, the Upper Missouri, and the Rockies. This area was astride the path of westward American expansion and emigrant roads, stage and freight lines, and a transcontinental railroad. In addition, the Dakota and Montana gold fields were in the area. By an 1868 treaty the western half of present South Dakota was to be a Sioux reservation, the Bozeman Trail and military posts were to be abandoned, agencies were to feed and clothe the Indians, and the government promised to educate the Sioux and train them to become self-supporting farmers. In March 1871 Joseph Washington Wham was sent as a government agent to the Oglala band of Sioux to implement the treaty as it pertained to them. Charismatic Red Cloud, principal chief of the Oglala, was more than Agent Wham could handle. Problems of locating the agency, the presence of whiskey traders, the matter of rations to the Indians, the temptation to raid the herds of Wyoming ranchers, gold in the Black Hills, and other thorny problems plagued Wham's efforts. A November scandal at the agency exposed Wham's inefficiency and contributed to his dismissal in mid-January 1872. Al-

though he had been unequal to the situation, he had managed somehow to maintain peaceful relations with the Oglala Sioux. Illus., map, 36 notes.

D. L. Smith

Dakota, Santee

855. Guenther, Richard L. THE SANTEE NORMAL TRAINING SCHOOL. *Nebraska Hist. 1970 51(3): 359-378.* Discusses the education of the Santee Dakota (Sioux) Indians at the training school at the reservation established along the Niobrara River in Nebraska. The school was founded in 1870, but economic exigencies forced it to close in 1936. R. Lowitt

856. Meyer, Roy W. THE ESTABLISHMENT OF THE SANTEE RESERVA-TION, 1866-1869. *Nebraska Hist. 1964 45(1): 59-97.* Traces the history of the Santee Sioux, chiefly by examining government policies and actions, from their exile from Minnesota in 1863, as a result of the Sioux uprising in 1862. The focus is on their disheartening experiences in Nebraska where they were brought in 1866 to the Niobrara River. Concludes that by 1869 the Santee Sioux "were on their way back from the nadir of their history." R. Lowitt

857. Stirling, Everett W. BISHOP HENRY B. WHIPPLE: INDIAN AGENT EXTRAORDINARY. *Hist. Mag. of the Protestant Episcopal Church 1957 26(3): 239-247.* Describes the activity of the first bishop of Minnesota in his capacity as U.S. agent (1858-69) for the distribution of goods to two bands of Santee Dakota (Sioux) Indians. This was an experiment in the nonpartisan appointment of Indian agents. E. Oberholzer, Jr.

Dakota, Teton

858. Smith, J. L. A CEREMONY FOR THE PREPARATION OF THE OF-FERING CLOTHS FOR PRESENTATION TO THE SACRED CALF PIPE OF THE TETON SIOUX. *Plains Anthropologist 1964 9(25): 190-196.* "The following ceremony, according to my informants, must be performed each and every time an offering is made to the Sacred Calf Pipe of the Teton Sioux. When it is completed the Sacred Pipe Bundle can then be opened and prayed over."

J

Dakota, Yanktonai

859. Pfaller, Louis. THE BRAVE BEAR MURDER CASE. *North Dakota Hist. 1969 36(2): 120-139.* Brave Bear was a member of the Cut Head band of Yanktonai Dakota Indians who turned renegade and led a small gang of Indians in an eight-year reign of terror against Indian and white. Robbery and murder were the gang specialities and brutality was the usual trademark. Brave Bear was captured and escaped twice. The third time he was captured he was convicted for murder at a trial on 5 January 1882. Appeals were made as far as the president of the United States who refused clemency. On 16 November 1882 Brave Bear was hung

at Yankton, North Dakota. Article presented originally on 11 February 1969 in a series of lectures on Western history by the author at Assumption Abbey, Richardton. Based on primary source materials; illus., photos, 30 notes.

E. P. Costello

Fox

860. Stucki, Larry R. ANTHROPOLOGISTS AND INDIANS: A NEW LOOK AT THE FOX PROJECT. *Plains Anthropologist 1967 12(37): 300-317.* The "'Fox Project' is re-examined through the use of the primary documents contained within the report *Documentary History of the Fox Project: A Program of Action Anthropology* (Gearing, et al., 1960)." The Fox Indians, originally residents along the St. Lawrence, were pushed westward by the federal government and finally settled near Tama, Iowa. The role of the "action anthropologist"—the man who seeks theoretical knowledge and also strives to assist in local improvement—is examined. The pitfalls of the case study method are illustrated and "the need for independent evaluative studies of action projects is pointed out." Biblio.

K. Adelfang

Hidatsa

861. Matthews, Washington. ETHNOGRAPHY AND PHILOLOGY OF THE HIDATSA INDIANS. *Plains Anthropologist 1969 14(45): 1-72.* Deals with the history of the Hidatsa, or Minnetaree, or Grosventre Indians, one of the three tribes which inhabited the permanent village at Fort Berthold, Dakota Territory, and who hunted on the waters of the Upper Missouri and Yellowstone Rivers in northwestern Dakota and eastern Montana. Among the topics discussed are the location of the village, dwellings, caches, burial customs, places of worship, fortifications, farming, population, arts, food, inter-tribal trade, and intercourse with whites. In a second part, the author deals with the three names of the tribe, its history, character, appearance, ceremonies, mythology and superstitions, marriage customs, names, hunting, warfare, stories, and divisions of time. 69 notes.

D. D. Cameron

Iroquois

862. Ewers, John C. IROQUOIS INDIANS IN THE FAR WEST. *Montana 1963 13(2): 2-10.* Presents evidence that members of the Iroquois tribe migrated to the Canadian prairies and the Rocky Mountains as early as 1789. Iroquois in considerable numbers were found among the Salish and associated tribes during the territorial period of the northern mountain states, and individuals frequently took leading roles which have been credited to endemic Indians. Research is suggested in eastern Canadian archives to ascertain the importance of this migration to the remaining Iroquois community. Largely derived from published works on western fur trade and missionary activities.

S. R. Davison

Kansa

863. Hoffhaus, Charles E. FORT DE CAVAGNIAL: IMPERIAL FRANCE IN KANSAS, 1744-1764. *Kansas Hist. Q. 1964 30(4): 425-454.* This small base marked the western end of a series of French forts stretching westward from Fort Duquesne to Kansas. It was built mainly to foster trade among the Kansa Indians. The article centers around the commanders and their small detachments of men at this outpost, and the role played by this fort in French imperial history is traced. Later explorers passing through this region commented on the remnants of the fort that were still standing. In a sense, the fort was the "first city" of Kansas. Based on French archival material, unpublished theses, and western historical literature.   W. F. Zornow

Kickapoo

864. Wallace, Ernest and Anderson, Adrian S. R. S. MACKENZIE AND THE KICKAPOOS: THE RAID INTO MEXICO IN 1873. *Arizona and the West 1965 7(2): 105-126.* Indian hostilities increased steadily on the undefended Texas frontier after the Civil War. In response to mounting pleas that the distress be removed, the army established a line of posts across west Texas. This did not include what was called the Upper Rio Grande Border Region, an area from Laredo to Del Rio on the Rio Grande extending about 100 miles into Texas— a sparsely settled but well-stocked region. Forays made by Mexico-based Kickapoo Indians, with the connivance of Mexican officials, thoroughly terrorized the ranchers. In 1873 Cavalry Colonel Ranald S. Mackenzie was ordered to attack the Kickapoo villages some 35 miles across the border in the Mexican state of Coahuila. Although a jingoist Texas Congressman urged annexation of parts of northern Mexico and newspapers reported military plans of some magnitude on both sides of the border, the purpose of Mackenzie's expedition was to restore peace and order by removing the Kickapoo menace. The May 1873 raid destroyed the Kickapoo villages, forced them to remove to a reservation in the United States, and led to a revision of Mexican border policies. Based on government documents, Department of State files (microfilm), and newspaper accounts; illus., map, 65 notes.   D. L. Smith

Kiowa

865. Metcalf, George. SOME NOTES ON AN OLD KIOWA SHIELD AND ITS HISTORY. *Great Plains J. 1968 8(1): 16-30.* In 1947 a collection of Indian materials acquired between 1889 and 1897 by the late Brigadier General James D. Glennan was presented to the United States National Museum. Included was an old shield Glennan had purchased from the Kiowa, Big Bow. Four accounts of the exploits of the man who made the shield, Kowalty, are available. The author presents the version Glennan received in interviews with Tahbone, an Indian soldier at Fort Sill. Extracts from the interview are provided describing the rites of the shield and its use. Illus., 19 notes, biblio.   O. H. Zabel

866. Monahan, Forrest D., Jr. THE KIOWAS AND NEW MEXICO, 1800-1845. *J. of the West 1969 8(1): 67-75.* The Kiowa moved into the southern Plains country in the late 18th century. Their hunter economy depended heavily on trade with the Spanish New Mexicans and later the Anglo-American traders. For three quarters of a century government gifts and private trade brought changes in Kiowa culture. 67 notes.   D. L. Smith

Kiowa Apache

867. Brant, Charles S. WHITE CONTACT AND CULTURAL DISINTEGRATION AMONG THE KIOWA APACHE. *Plains Anthropologist 1964 9(23): 8-13.* "By means of documentary sources and field data, the history and white contacts of the Kiowa Apache are traced from 1837 to about 1910. A reconstruction is presented, in broad outlines, of the impact of removal, diminished sources of subsistence, disease and land allotment, upon Kiowa Apache society and culture. Nativistic movements, towards the close of the period, are briefly mentioned as responses to cultural disintegration."   J

Mandan

868. Jackson, Donald, ed. JOURNEY TO THE MANDANS, 1809; THE LOST NARRATIVE OF DR. THOMAS. *Bull. of the Missouri Hist. Soc. 1964 20(3): 179-192.* Thomas, an obscure physician, still unidentified except for his last name, accompanied the 1809 expedition to the upper Missouri River sponsored by the St. Louis Missouri Fur Company. Apart from commercial purposes, one of the principal objectives of the expedition was to return safely to his village the Mandan chief, Sheheke (Shahaka), who had returned with the Lewis and Clark expedition and had been honored in Washington and the East. The account, from contemporary newspapers, consists primarily of descriptions of geography and of the Indians.   R. J. Hanks

Nez Percé

869. Nieberding, Velma. THE NEZ PERCE IN THE QUAPAW AGENCY. *Chronicles of Oklahoma 1966 44(1): 22-30.* After the famous two thousand mile retreat of Chief Joseph and the Nez Percé warriors, they surrendered in 1877 and were brought to the Quapaw Agency in 1878, staying there for a year. Chief Joseph and his people wanted to return to their tribal lands in Idaho or Oregon but General William T. Sherman was vengeful and they were sent to die in a malarial camp at Fort Leavenworth. Agent Hiram Jones was severe with the Nez Percé because Chief Joseph appealed directly to Washington. The Nez Percé relinquished all claims to their lands and were transported to their new home in the Ponca Agency. Chief Joseph was a symbol of the heroism of his people who wanted only peace and a place where they could live as they had always lived. 24 notes.   I. W. Van Noppen

Omaha

870. Green, Norma Kidd. FOUR SISTERS: DAUGHTERS OF JOSEPH LA FLESCHE. *Nebraska Hist. 1964 45(2): 165-176.* Briefly relates through the life stories of four daughters of Joseph La Flesche, the last recognized chief of the Omaha tribe, how they made their place in a new culture and became competent and accepted citizens in the white man's society.   R. Lowitt

871. Green, Norma Kidd. THE PRESBYTERIAN MISSION TO THE OMAHA INDIAN TRIBE. *Nebraska Hist. 1967 48(3): 267-288.* Discusses the work of various Presbyterian missionaries to the Omaha tribe from 1856 to the 1930's, when the last mission church succumbed to the Depression.

R. Lowitt

872. Unsigned. MISSION WORK AMONG OMAHA INDIANS. *J. of the Presbyterian Hist. Soc. 1960 38(3): 182-190.* A lengthy letter, dated 1 February 1868, from the Reverend William Hamilton, missionary to the Omaha Indians by appointment of the Board of Foreign Missions of the Presbyterian Church in the United States, to the Reverend J. C. Lowrie, one of the corresponding secretaries of the Board of Foreign Missions. The mission was located one hundred miles to the northwest of Omaha City, Nebraska, and had been founded in 1846. Hamilton served there from 1853 until his death in 1891. In the letter he describes the educational and religious activity of the mission, discusses the staff and physical plant of the mission, and analyzes the mission's impact on the Indians.   W. D. Metz

Osage

873. Baird, Donald. SOME EIGHTEENTH CENTURY GUN BARRELS FROM OSAGE VILLAGE SITES. *Great Plains J. 1965 4(2): 49-62.* Asserts that a reliable historical picture of Indian trade guns of the 18th century may emerge from collecting and analyzing trade gun parts found at Indian sites. In the process of analyzing frontier gun barrels from Osage Indian sites in Missouri, the author provides information on cleaning and preserving the relics, manufacturing methods, markings, national origins, and dating. Based on examination of the gun barrels and on secondary printed sources, illus., tables.   O. H. Zabel

874. Myer, Mrs. Max W. and Chapman, Carl H., eds. JOURNEY TO THE LAND OF THE OSAGES, 1835-1836: BY LOUIS CORTAMBERT. *Bull. of the Missouri Hist. Soc. 1963 19(3): 199-229.* A biographical sketch accompanies this account by an educated young French immigrant, Louis Cortambert, of his travels to and in the Osage Indian country just west of Missouri and the Arkansas Territory. The account gives some description of the area and its inhabitants, but the informative material is subordinated to the author's provocative personal reactions and reflections on the frontier, Indian life, religion, French society,

American society, philosophy and history. Also included are short comments on some major American cities and on other Indian tribes to which he paid a brief visit—chiefly the Creeks and Cherokees.   R. J. Hanks

Ottawa

875. Holmes, Norman G. THE OTTAWA INDIANS OF OKLAHOMA AND CHIEF PONTIAC. *Chronicles of Oklahoma 1967 45(2): 190-206.* Combining tribal oral history and information contained in published accounts, biographical data of the Ottawa chief Pontiac are established. Genealogical information reveals patrilineal descendants among the Oklahoma Ottawa, knowledge heretofore not well established. 5 illus., 2 appendixes, 20 notes.   D. L. Smith

Pawnee

876. Troike, Rudolph C. A PAWNEE VISIT TO SAN ANTONIO IN 1795. *Ethnohist. 1964 11(4): 380-393.* Edits and interprets relevant portions of a document in the Archivo General, Mexico, recording a visit to the seat of government for the Spanish province of Texas of a group of Pawnee and other plains tribes in February 1795. Spanish-U.S. border rivalries and tribal disruption and pressures resulting from the westward movement are linked with the incident; tribes and chieftains are identified.   H. J. Graham

Pawnee, Skidi

877. Jones, Dorothy V. JOHN DOUGHERTY AND THE PAWNEE RITE OF HUMAN SACRIFICE: APRIL, 1827. *Missouri Hist. R. 1969 63(3): 291-316.* The Skidi Pawnee had been pressured into giving up their custom of making human sacrifices to the Morning Star, but in 1827 hunger or personal rivalry may have prodded them into capturing a Cheyenne squaw for sacrifice. This is an account of the sacrificial ritual as a religious custom of the Skidi Pawnee and the efforts of John Dougherty, the acting Indian agent for the Upper Missouri Agency, to arrange her ransom. Although the tribe hacked her to pieces as she was being led to safety, Dougherty consoled himself with the thought that she had been spared the torture that accompanied the sacrificial ritual. The incident demonstrated the width of the gulf that lay between Indian and white cultures on the frontier in 1827. Based on books, articles, newspapers, the Dougherty Papers in the State Historical Society of Missouri, and the William Clark Papers in the Kansas State Historical Society; illus., 32 notes.   W. F. Zornow

878. Thurman, Melvin D. THE SKIDI PAWNEE MORNING STAR SACRIFICE OF 1827. *Nebraska Hist. 1970 51(3): 269-280.* Discussion and analysis of the 1827 Skidi Pawnee effort to sacrifice a captive woman to the Morning Star. The Skidi believed such a ritual ceremony would insure good crops, a plentiful buffalo supply, and a secure military position in the face of enemies.
                                                                      R. Lowitt

Ponca

879. Howard, James H. KNOWN VILLAGE SITES OF THE PONCA. *Plains Anthropologist 1970 15(48): 109-134.* "This study contains a listing and description of the traditional village sites of the Ponca Indians. Five principal sources of information have been utilized: standard published historical references; archival materials; the J. O. Dorsey 'Omaha Map;' oral testimony gathered from Ponca informants in connection with the Omaha land claims case in 1912 and 1914; and information secured by the author from Ponca informants, including a listing and description of all sites known to him prepared by Peter Le Claire, the Ponca historian. Throughout the study an attempt is made to synthesize all available ethnographic, historical, and archaeological data. Thirty-one separate villages or camps are noted in the study, 21 of which are named in either Ðégiha (the Indian language) or English. Archaeological work has been done at five of the sites. At two of the sites this work has yielded materials of the Redbird focus, estimated to date between A.D. 1600 and 1700, and materials at two others are not inconsistent with a Redbird focus identification. The fact that two Redbird focus sites have been independently identified as long standing villages of the Ponca tribe, with associated native names, together with other data on Ponca village locations and dates, tends to confirm the identification of the Redbird focus as the archaeological remains of the Ponca Indians."   J

880. King, James T. "A BETTER WAY": GENERAL GEORGE CROOK AND THE PONCA INDIANS. *Nebraska Hist. 1969 50(3): 239-256.* Discusses the background of the 1879 case *United States ex rel. Standing Bear vs. Crook* wherein, through the efforts of General Crook and others, Standing Bear and his Ponca tribesmen were allowed to remain on their Nebraska lands and were not forced to return to lands set aside for them in the Indian Territory. For the Ponca, the affair showed that justice was not impossible within the white man's law.

R. Lowitt

Potawatomi (Fire Nation)

881. Clifton, James A. SOCIOCULTURAL DYNAMICS OF THE PRAIRIE POTAWATOMI DRUM CULT. *Plains Anthropologist 1969 14(44, pt. 1): 85-93.* "The Drum Cult, a revitalization movement founded by the Santee Dakota prophetess Wananikwe in 1872, was diffused to the Prairie Potawatomi in Kansas in the early 1880's. This paper discusses contemporary social, cultural and ritual aspects of the Potawatomi Drum Cult in terms of both internal and external processes of change, examines and attempts to account for a major re-direction of the Cult's manifest goals, and discusses the functions of its ritual activities in the contemporary reservation community."   J

882. Jacobs, Hubert, S.J. THE POTAWATOMI MISSION 1854. *Mid-Am. 1954 36(4): 220-236.* An introduction to an accompanying letter (pp. 227-236) from Maurice Gailland, a Swiss Jesuit missionary assigned to the Mission of St. Mary, Kansas, to his former spiritual director in Rome, Franz Xavier Huber. The introduction describes the background of Jesuit missionary activity in the United

States and relates how Father Gailland came to be assigned to this mission established for the Potawatomi Indians in Kansas. Discusses Gailland's missionary activities there and indicates where some of his letters have been published. The letter contains a brief account of the life and culture of the Potawatomi Indians. It mentions the controversy concerning slavery in the territories and makes specific reference to the pending Kansas-Nebraska Bill.

R. F. Campbell

Shawnee

883. Nieberding, Velma. SHAWNEE INDIAN FESTIVAL: THE BREAD DANCE. *Chronicles of Oklahoma 1964 42(3): 253-261.* The "Loyal Shawnees" are those of Shawnee blood who by the agreement of 1869 became incorporated with the Cherokee Nation and who were loyal to the Union during the Civil War. A booklet privately printed for the use of tribal members contains accounts of the origin of the Shawnees and of the Ceremonial Bread Dance. There are spring and fall bread dances and a green corn dance. This booklet lists the ceremonies and the rituals for the bread dances. It gives also the prayer of the speaker who blesses the crops and the animals.

I. W. Van Noppen

Wyandot (Huron)

884. Socolofsky, Homer E. WYANDOT FLOATS. *Kansas Hist. Q. 1970 36(3): 241-304.* By treaty in 1842 the Wyandots ceded land in Ohio and Michigan for 148 thousand acres west of the Mississippi. Article 14 granted, by patent in fee simple, a section of land to each of 35 named persons. These were "floating" grants, not tied to a particular piece of land; their location on unclaimed land provided an almost unlimited region from which the choice could be made. A new treaty in 1855 made the floats easily assignable. The author shows that, by the time the last float was filed in 1858, all 35 had become important factors in the land history of Kansas. While some floats provided important sites for such towns as Lecompton, Topeka, Lawrence, Manhattan, Emporia, Burlington, Kansas City, and Doniphan, others covered valuable farm and business sites in the Blue and Neosho river valleys, and in Atchison, Johnson, Douglas, and Shawnee counties. Based on books, articles, government publications, and manuscripts in the Kansas State Historical Society, National Archives, and Bureau of Land Management in Washington; illus., maps, 173 notes.

W. F. Zornow

Northeast Area

General

885. Adams, Elizabeth S. THE STATE LINE HISTORICAL SITE. *Michigan Hist. 1964 48(4): 373-375.* Remarks at the 23 July 1964 dedication of the State Line Historical Site at Brule Lake on the Michigan-Wisconsin border. It was here that treaties were negotiated with Indian tribes of the upper Great Lakes to permit a survey of the boundary in 1840-41.   J. K. Flack

886. Adams, O. Burton. THE VIRGINIA REACTION TO THE GLORIOUS REVOLUTION, 1688-1692. *West Virginia Hist. 1967 29(1): 6-12.* The autocratic rule of King James II in dealing with Virginia alienated many members of that colony. Despite this, however, an uprising was barely averted when news was received of the accession to the throne of William and Mary. There were rumors that Catholics and certain Indian tribes intended to destroy all Protestants, and armed men prepared for combat. The Colonial Council prevented bloodshed. In May 1689, William and Mary were solemnly proclaimed as the monarchs of Virginia. The change in English sovereigns did not bring any immediate relief to the Virginians in such crucial matters as tobacco prices and Indian raids. When Lieutenant Governor Francis Nicholson took office in 1690 matters improved. During the two years he was in office significant accomplishments were made. The most significant outcome of the Glorious Revolution in Virginia was that the members of the House of Burgesses used the occasion to enhance their power and prestige. Based on published sources; 34 notes.   D. N. Brown

887. Adams, Thomas B. OF PLIMOUTH PLANTATION. *Pro. of the Massachusetts Hist. Soc. 1963 75: 3-9.* Discusses briefly and informally the leaders of the Plymouth colony, including John Robinson, the divine who never came to New England, William Brester, Edward Winslow, William Bradford, and the Indian Squanto. Based primarily on Bradford's *Of Plimouth Plantation* (1630-51, 1912) and Winslow's *Good Newes From New-England* (1624).
                          J. B. Duff

888. Adney, John R. WHO WAS FATHER MAZZUCHELLI? *Ann. of Iowa 1969 39(7): 552-560.* Discusses the accomplishments of Father Samuel Charles Mazzuchelli (1806-64), a missionary, architect, scientist, author, and educator. Born in Milan, Italy, Father Mazzuchelli, a member of the Dominican Order, came to the United States in 1828 after learning of the need for priests and teachers. From Cincinnati he was sent to the Mackinac Island region and then to the Green Bay-Fort Winnebago area where he was responsible for numerous Indian conversions. During the 1830's, he was largely responsible for the founding of churches in Dubuque, Bellevue, Maquoketa, and Davenport, Iowa, and Galena, Illinois. Father Mazzuchelli designed the Galena court house and some authorities believe he was the architect of the Old Capitol at Iowa City. In 1843

he unsuccessfully attempted to convert Joseph Smith from Mormonism to Catholicism. Based on Mazzuchelli's memoirs and several secondary sources; 2 illus.

W. R. Griffin

889. Alexander, Edward P. AN INDIAN VOCABULARY FROM FORT CHRISTANNA, 1716. *Virginia Mag. of Hist. and Biog. 1971 79(3): 303-313.* Transcribes a portion of an unpublished 1840 copy of the manuscript journal of John Fontaine (1693-1767), written between 1710 and 1719, giving an Indian vocabulary of 46 words, phrases, or sentences recorded in 1716. Indicates tribal identification of 77 individual words. Provides a facsimile of three journal pages. 31 notes.

C. A. Newton

890. Badger, Margaret. FACTS AND FANCIES OF TAUGHANNOCK. *New York Folklore Q. 1963 19(3): 202-210.* Indian legends about the origins and naming of Taughannock Falls at Trumansburg, New York, the highest falls in the northeastern United States. Also some legends of early settlers, and an account of the Taughannock Giant hoax of 1879. 2 illus.

M. A. Booth

891. Baillargeon, Noël. QUELQUES ADVIS POUR SERVIR DE REGLE AUX MISSIONNAIRES DONNEZ AUX MOIS DE JUILLET 1699 [Some advice to serve as guide to the missionaries given in the month of July 1699]. *R. de l'U. Laval [Canada] 1963 17(5): 396-403.* Text taken from a work in preparation treating the foundation of the first missions of the Séminaire de Québec on the Mississippi. The rules, found in the archives of the Séminaire de Québec, were not intended by Bishop Laval and the directors of the Séminaire to be "a complete treatise of missionology" but were simply concerned with advising missionaries, isolated in the midst of barbarians, to avoid too great relaxation in carrying out their devotions. At the same time there was a warning against too great abstinence and austerity.

G. H. Kelsey

892. Bandel, Betty. DANIEL CLARKE SANDERS AND THE INDIANS: A BELATED FOOTNOTE TO A CONTROVERSIAL BOOK. *Vermont Hist. 1968 36(2): 91-93.* Sander's book *A History of the Indian Wars with the First Settlers of the United States, Particularly in New England,* published in 1812, was not "fabricated" as was charged. The story was first told by Jean Baptiste Trudeau (Truteau) in his journal kept during his explorations of 1794-95. This journal was translated and published in the 1809 *Medical Repository.*

T. D. S. Bassett

893. Barbour, Philip L. [CAPTAIN NEWPORT]. *Virginia Cavalcade.*
THE FIRST RECONNAISSANCE OF THE JAMES, 1967 17(2): 35-41. Discusses the initial exploration of the James River by Captain Christopher Newport (1565-1617) and 24 others beginning 21 May 1607, one week after the first English settlers arrived at Jamestown. Their encounters with various Indian tribes, such as the Weanoc and Arrohattoc, and their arrival at Powhatan village are described. Illus.

CAPTAIN NEWPORT MEETS OPECHANCANOUGH. 1968 17(3): 42-47. Describes the meetings of Captain Newport with Powhatan's son Parahunt and half-brother Opechancanough during the first English exploration of Virginia, in May 1607. Based on the eyewitness accounts of George Percy, Gabriel Archer and John Smith; illus.   N. L. Peterson

894. Barbour, Philip L. THE EARLIEST RECONNAISSANCE OF THE CHESAPEAKE BAY AREA: CAPTAIN JOHN SMITH'S MAP AND INDIAN VOCABULARY. *Virginia Mag. of Hist. and Biog. 1971 79(3): 280-302, 1972 80(1): 21-51.* Part I. Lists and where possible locates Indian place-names recorded by Captain John Smith in his writings and on his map. Discusses problems of the sources and handwriting and lists titles of sources used. Part II. A glossary of 137 Chesapeake Bay area Indian words, drawn from writings by John Smith and William Strachey, with references to other but lesser recorders of local Indian language. Describes and analyzes the primary sources and some other early transcriptions of Indian words. Includes a linguistic bibliography.
C. A. Newton

895. Bertin, Eugene P. FRONTIER FORTS ON THE SUSQUEHANNA. *Now and Then 1965 14(12): 376-393.* Describes the forts which were used by the settlers on the west branch of the Susquehanna River during the darkest days of the Revolutionary War in this region from 1777 to 1779. Most were erected by private individuals and are compared to a modern bomb shelter. During periods of Indian attack, local citizens would take shelter there. The largest of these forts were built by the colony and were staffed with militia. Despite these precautions, an Indian and Tory attack depopulated the region during the summer of 1779. Illus., maps.   H. Ershkowitz

896. Binford, Lewis R. AN ETHNOHISTORY OF THE NOTTOWAY, MEHERRIN AND WEANOCK INDIANS OF SOUTHEASTERN VIRGINIA. *Ethnohist. 1967 14(3/4): 103-218.* Studies the Nottoway, Meherrin, and Powhatan (Weanoc) Indian tribes of southeastern Virginia in the 17th and 18th centuries, assesses available historical resources, and describes contextual phenomena deemed meaningful to the material covered, such as clarification of the term "Mangoake" as a generic Algonquin term for Iroquois speakers, and a more accurate tracing of Edward Bland's southern explorations in 1650. Discusses the physicobiological and superorganic environments of the cited events. The rationale behind such an approach stems from the conviction that culture is most profitably viewed as man's extrasomatic means of adaptation. Using 1650 as an initial point for a baseline of the form of the systems and the structure of their ecological articulations, documents the relationship between geography, ecology, and social organizations. 38 notes, biblio.   R. S. Burns

897. Blackburn, George M. FOREDOOMED TO FAILURE: THE MANISTEE INDIAN STATION. *Michigan Hist. 1969 53(1): 37-50.* Lucius Garey, government farmer and agent in charge of the Manistee Indian Station during its brief and troubled existence (1837-39), viewed the insuperable difficulties of establishing and maintaining the seven thousand-acre reservation in northern

Michigan. Garey's vivid reports are part of the Records of the Michigan Superintendency of Indian Affairs (1814-51) in the National Archives. Microfilmed portions are in the Clarke Historical Library, Central Michigan University. 4 illus., 53 notes. J. K. Flack

898. Blackburn, George M. GEORGE JOHNSTON AND THE SIOUX-CHIPPEWA BOUNDARY SURVEY. *Michigan Hist. 1967 51(4): 313-322.* Uses both primary and secondary sources to describe the futile efforts to end difficulties between Indian tribes in the northern reaches of the Michigan Territory.
J. K. Flack

899. Blackmon, Joab L., Jr. JUDGE SAMUEL SEWALL'S EFFORTS IN BEHALF OF THE FIRST AMERICANS. *Ethnohist. 1969 16(2): 165-176.* "Samuel Sewall, who was presiding judge at the Salem, Massachusetts, witchcraft trials of 1692, is more widely-remembered in this connection than any other. He had a considerable involvement with Indians in the Massachusetts area, however, which has been largely overlooked by historians. His relationships with these Indians are examined here." J

900. Bogert, Frederick W. MARAUDERS IN THE MINNISINK. *New Jersey Hist. Soc. Pro. 1964 82(4): 271-282.* An area from the Delaware Water Gap to a point just west of Kingston, New York, is called the Minnisink, which includes parts of New Jersey, Pennsylvania, and New York. During the Revolution this was the scene of devastating raids by British and Indians. 40 notes.
E. P. Stickney

901. Bolt, Robert. REVEREND LEONARD SLATER IN THE GRAND RIVER VALLEY. *Michigan Hist. 1967 51(3): 241-251.* An account of the Thomas Indian Mission administered by the Reverend Leonard Slater, a Baptist, between 1827 and 1836, where Grand Rapids now stands. Following a brief period of success this effort was abandoned because of the disharmonious relationship of Slater and his superior, competition from Catholic missionaries, the negative influence of whiskey traders, and the federal government's unsympathetic attitude toward Indians. J. K. Flack

902. Brand, Irene B. ALBERT GALLATIN IN WEST VIRGINIA. *West Virginia Hist. 1964 26(1): 35-46.* Details experiences of Gallatin as a land speculator in western Virginia. He and his partner, Jean Savary, obtained property in the Monongahela River region. Questions arose as to the validity of their title to the land, but most of their claims were upheld. Gallatin traveled throughout the area making surveys, but plans to dispose of the land went awry because of Indian difficulties. Documented from published sources. D. N. Brown

903. Bronner, Edwin B. INDIAN DEED FOR PETTY'S ISLAND, 1678. *Pennsylvania Mag. of Hist. and Biog. 1965 89(1): 111-114.* Publishes the 1678 deed, signed by four Indians, which turned over to Elizabeth Kinsey the island in the Delaware River opposite Kensington, Maryland. D. P. Gallagher

904. Brown, Elizabeth G., ed. JUDGE JAMES DOTY'S NOTES OF TRIALS AND OPINIONS: 1823-1832. *Am. J. of Legal Hist. 1965 9(1): 17-40.* Edited documents of Judge James Duane Doty of the U.S. Circuit Court for Brown County, Michigan Territory. The case notes concern several trials involving Indians and reveal a high level of judicial expertise.   N. C. Brockman

905. Bruemmer, Fred. THE CAUGHNAWAGAS. *Beaver [Canada] 1965 296(Winter): 4-11.* Caughnawaga, Quebec, was originally a Jesuit missionary settlement for Christianized Indians. In 1672 there were more than 400 Indians, principally from the Mohawk, Onondaga, and Huron tribes. They proved to be staunch allies of the French in war and good traders with the English in peace. After the British conquest of Canada, the Caughnawagas enrolled as canoe-men with the fur brigades, and steered log booms on the Ottawa River. Their career as high steel workers began in 1886 with the construction of the CPR bridge across the St. Lawrence at Lachine. Today more than 75 percent of Caughnawaga's men work on high steel. Illus.   L. F. S. Upton

906. Burghardt, Andrew F. THE ORIGIN AND DEVELOPMENT OF THE ROAD NETWORK OF THE NIAGARA PENINSULA, ONTARIO, 1770-1851. *Ann. of the Assoc. of Am. Geographers 1969 59(3): 417-440.* "During the American Revolution, white settlers entered the Niagara Peninsula by way of the four entry points previously established by the Indians. The aboriginal trails served as the avenues of penetration, but with fuller settlement these trails were improved, abandoned, or extended according to the needs of the settlers. The river road became the most prevalent type of route because of the felt need for a juxtaposition of land and water transport. New roads were cut across the inherited network to tie remote areas to the administrative centers. With full settlement of the land the survey roads came to dominate. The analysis leads to the conclusions that the Indian trails did not predetermine the road alignments, that towns create roads rather than vice versa, that the true urban centers were the foci for six or more through routes, and that the sequence of development has been strongly at variance with the model suggested by Taaffe, Morrill, and Gould."   J

907. Coad, Oral S. JERSEY GOTHIC. *Pro. of the New Jersey Hist. Soc. 1966 84(2): 89-112.* Describes a large number of stories of the strange and horrifying that have a New Jersey setting. Some are related to landscape, others to Indian legends, to historical figures, episodes, and deepwater pirates, or to New Jersey superstitions of witches, devils, and ghosts. 23 notes.   E. P. Stickney

908. Coles, Robert R. INDIAN AND OTHER PLACE-NAMES. *Long Island Forum 1971 34(5): 94-97.* Explains the Indian origins of various place-names on Long Island. Based largely on William Wallace Tooker's *The Indian Place-Names on Long Island* (1911); illus.   G. Kurland

909. Cummings, Hubertis M. THE PAXTON KILLINGS. *J. of Presbyterian Hist. 1966 44(4): 219-243.* Traces the frontier conditions in Pennsylvania during

the French and Indian Wars, the conflict between the Scotch-Irish settlers of Paxton, Derry, and Hanover townships in Lancaster County and Quaker assemblymen, and the organization of the settlers to protect themselves. A militia was recruited and effectively used in 1755-56, but the area suffered from Indian attacks in 1757. The "Paxton Boys," an expedition lacking approval of the government or of the local pastor who had previously commanded two companies of men, destroyed a compound of government-protected Indians at Conestoga Village and another in Lancaster in late 1763. When the government demanded arrest and trial of the group, 500 settlers went to the Philadelphia area and presented a list of grievances to the commissioners. Through these events the Pennsylvania government was effectively aroused to frontier sentiment. Based primarily on published sources; 17 notes.   S. C. Pearson, Jr.

910. Day, Gordon M. THE INDIAN OCCUPATION OF VERMONT. *Vermont Hist. 1965 33(3): 365-374.* Historians have treated Vermont as virtually unoccupied, but Missisquoi, Coos, and Memphramagog villages are well known and artifacts are numerous and widespread. Iroquois and colonial wars kept northern New England Indians moving; but their annual economy also required migration between home village cornfields, summer fishing grounds and family hunting tracts. Swanton Falls was probably reoccupied in 1732 by Abnaki who had been there a generation or more earlier. The Mahican refugees of 1676 who settled at Schaghticoke, New York, probably hunted north to Lake Bomoseen. The Squakeags or Sokwakis centering on Northfield, Massachusetts, probably hunted in the whole of upper Connecticut and are the same Indians as the Sokokis of the French sources, hitherto erroneously located on the Saco River.
                                                                T. D. S. Bassett

911. Deardorff, Merle H., ed. and Snyderman, George S., ed. A NINETEENTH-CENTURY JOURNAL OF A VISIT TO THE INDIANS OF NEW YORK. *Pro. of the Am. Phil. Soc. 1956 100(6): 582-612.* John Philips (1753-1846) kept a journal of a trip by a committee of Quakers to the Seneca Indian Reservation in the Allegany region of New York in 1806. The journal records economic, political, religious and social data on an Indian people in the process of change. Philips describes the plight of dispossessed refugee Munsee Delaware Indians in some detail, and also notes the rapidly contracting reservations, conflict between the youths and elders, encroaching whites, and rising alcoholism. The full annotated text of the journal is preceded by a history of the Quaker work with the Senecas, with particular attention to the role of Cornplanter and Handsome Lake, the Seneca leaders most influenced by the Quakers.   N. Kurland

912. Dever, Harry. THE NICOLET MYTH. *Michigan Hist. 1966 50(4): 318-322.* Seeks to correct the theory that Jean Nicolet, in 1634, discovered Lake Michigan, Green Bay, and Wisconsin, and calls for a "reinterpretation of the tribal wars, fur trade, and exploration of that period."   J. K. Flack

913. Douville, Raymond. JACQUES LARGILLIER DIT "LE CASTOR", COUREUR DES BOIS ET "FRERE DONNE" [Jacques Largillier, called "Le Castor": trapper and lay brother]. *Cahiers des Dix [Canada] 1964 29: 47-69.* The

first account of the life of Jacques Largillier (1644-1708), who arrived in New France about 1664. He accompanied Louis Jolliet on his explorations to the Mississippi and Père Marquette on his expeditions. In 1675 Largillier turned his worldly possessions over to the Society of Jesus and was listed in 1681 as a servant at their mission to the Ottawas. By contrast to the normally licentious fur traders, Largillier was a living proof of the virtues taught by the missionaries. He ended his days at Kaskaskia, working with the Illinois tribes. A hitherto unpublished letter of 25 February 1715, from Father Mermet at Kaskaskia to Father Germain, Superior of the Jesuit missions in Canada, describes the death of Largillier and Father Marest. 41 notes.   L. F. S. Upton

914. Dreyer, Fred. THREE YEARS IN THE TORONTO GARRISON. *Ontario Hist. [Canada] 1965 57(1): 29-38.* The experiences of Gilbert Elliot, a younger son of the Earl of Minto, as a subaltern doing garrison duty in Toronto. Included are Gilbert's impressions of Toronto society, of Canadian weather, of Indians, and of desertion in the army. Also mentioned is Gilbert's engagement, broken by his parents because his Toronto fiancée was too colonial and without dowry. Based on Gilbert's letters to his family.   G. Emery

915. Faben, Walter W. LISTEN FOR THE THUNDERERS. *Northwest Ohio Q. (Part I) 1963 35(4): 164-171, (Part II) 1964 36(2): 99-112.* Part I. A description of the sights and events a typical *voyageur* might behold as he paddled his canoe southward from Detroit to the Maumee. The forests, wildlife, and local Indians receive brief attention. At Manhattan the Indians gathered to council, dance and play games, of which lacrosse was the most popular. Pontiac's village on the Maumee was most important for it was here that the chief was to be found. Part II. This part is divided into four sections. The first and the longest is an account of Roche de Bout, a huge stone rising from the Maumee River near Waterville, Ohio. A young Ottawa warrior killed his wife and cast her body over the cliff, when he discovered that she had slain their child on the rocks. He was slain by members of her family; this sparked a violent massacre, which was finally stopped by an old Indian who offered to adopt the man who had slain his grandson. The second and third sections are brief descriptions of some of the history and legends of the Algonquins, Iroquois, Potawatomi and Ottawa tribes. The final section is a summary of tribal beliefs in Gitchi Manitou, the Great Spirit, and Animoki, the Thunderer, who ruled over the upper air.   W. F. Zornow

916. Feest, Christian F. THE VIRGINIA INDIAN IN PICTURES, 1612-1624. *Smithsonian J. of Hist. 1967 2(1): 1-30.* The image of the American Indian from Virginia during the 17th century was determined not so much in America as in Europe where busy engravers compiled, multiplied, and altered a small number of original pictures. The author indicates that the drawings made by John White during the Roanoke voyages form the basis for all later pictures of the Virginia Indians. Théodore de Bry, the engraver, publicized White's Indian pictures. 19 illus., 90 notes.   W. L. Willigan

917. Franklin, W. Neil. ACT FOR THE BETTER REGULATION OF THE INDIAN TRADE, VIRGINIA, 1714. *Virginia Mag. of Hist. and Biog. 1964 72(2): 141-151.* Reprints the act with an introduction.   K. J. Bauer

918. Gerwing, Anselm J. THE CHICAGO INDIAN TREATY OF 1833. *J. of the Illinois State Hist. Soc. 1964 57(2): 117-142.* The Chicago Treaty of 1833 was the last removal treaty involving a large tract of land east of the Mississippi and north of the Ohio. Three Algonquin tribes—Chippewa, Ottawa, Potawotomi—surrendered their title to a five million-acre isosceles triangle shaped area. Its base was in Illinois north of Chicago, and it pointed into Wisconsin, extending somewhat above Milwaukee. Also, the Wood Potawatomi ceded three small tracts in southwestern Michigan Territory which totaled some 152 sections. The land thus released and the unprecedented sums of money involved in the transaction attracted traders, creditors, and others desiring to benefit from the occasion. Charges of foul play and fraud delayed ratification of the treaty, which brought disillusionment to the Indians and caused difficulties with their removal itself. Illus., map, 55 notes.   D. L. Smith

919. Guy, Camil. L'ART DECORATIF DES INDIENS DE L'EST [The decorative art of the Indians of the East]. *Culture Vivante [Canada] 1969 14: 9-18.* By diffusion from a Laurentian center, the Algonquin and Iroquois of the Great Lakes and Saint Lawrence Valley developed a distinctive geometric style very early, which featured the double curve and bilateral symmetry. Materials included birchbark, quill, skins, and hair. The Naskapi, with plenty of game to provide materials for their art, could preserve their style from white influence until this century. Ochre and roe provided reds and yellows. The tools for applying the dye were of bone, horn, and wood. From the 17th century, their art form was influenced by French floral patterns, glass beads, and textiles. Beadwork became the leading Indian art form, as the woodland tribes were stimulated to develop new botanical and imaginative motifs. 12 illus.
                                                        T. D. S. Bassett

920. Hagan, William T. GENERAL HENRY ATKINSON AND THE MILITIA. *Military Affairs 1959 23(4): 194-197.* Describes Atkinson's difficulties with the militia during the Black Hawk War, 1832.   K. J. Bauer

921. Hamilton, Kenneth G. THE MORAVIAN ARCHIVES AT BETHLEHEM, PENNSYLVANIA. *Am. Archivist 1961 24(4): 415-423.* The Moravian archives contain 500,000 manuscript items, plus music, painting and library collections of a significant size. A unique historical record is the Bethlehem Diary, 1742-1871, which was a daily record (33,352 pages) compiled by individual congregations and sent to the main church office. The personal papers of individual leaders, and the files of missionaries among both the Indians and the German immigrants, enrich the Moravian archives.   G. M. Gressley

922. Hoffman, Bernard G. ACCOUNT OF A VOYAGE CONDUCTED IN 1529 TO THE NEW WORLD, AFRICA, MADAGASCAR, AND SUMA-

TRA, TRANSLATED FROM THE ITALIAN, WITH NOTES AND COMMENTS. *Ethnohist. 1963 10(1): 1-79.* Translates, edits and reproduces in facsimile, along with related maps and complementary materials, "one of the earliest, most interesting" descriptions of the coasts and natives of North America (vicinity of Newfoundland, 1529). The expedition is identified as that of Jean and Raoul Parmentier, the former being the balladist, courtier and "great French sea captain from Dieppe" whose account, first published by the French cosmographer Pierre Crignon (in 1531), was reproduced anonymously in the third volume of Ramusio's *Navigationi e Viaggi Raccolta* (Venice, 1556). Rasmusio's version is the one translated and facsimiled here in toto.   H. J. Graham

923. Hoffman, Bernard G. AN UNUSUAL EXAMPLE OF VIRGINIA INDIAN TOPONYMICS. *Ethnohist. 1964 11(2): 174-182.* Observes "that the name *Mattaponi* attached to the northern main branch of the York River was formed by the simple combination of the names of its principal tributaries—the *Mat, Ta, Po,* and *Ni* Rivers—and that the names of these tributaries also combined in pairs" to form the Matta River and the Poni River. 5 maps.
                                                                H. J. Graham

924. Hoffman, Bernard G. ANCIENT TRIBES REVISITED: A SUMMARY OF INDIAN DISTRIBUTION AND MOVEMENT IN THE NORTHEASTERN UNITED STATES FROM 1534 TO 1779. PARTS I-III. *Ethnohist. 1967 14(1/2): 1-46.* Outlines basic features of tribal distribution in the colonial period. Based on contemporary primary sources; maps, tables, 8 notes, biblio.
                                                                R. S. Burns

925. Hoffman, Bernard G. JOHN CLAYTON'S 1687 ACCOUNT OF THE MEDICINAL PRACTICES OF THE VIRGINIA INDIANS. *Ethnohist. 1964 11(1): 1-40.* Reprints and annotates a letter (British Museum Add. Ms. 4437), heretofore published only in part, written to Dr. Nehemiah Grew by John Clayton, a minister at Jamestown, 1684-87, afterwards dean of Kildare, Ireland. The focus is comparative and on materia medica and therapeutics. Facsimile.
                                                                H. J. Graham

926. Horsman, Reginald. AMERICAN INDIAN POLICY IN THE OLD NORTHWEST, 1783-1812. *William and Mary Q. 1961 18(1): 35-53.* The consistent aim throughout this period was to acquire Indian land from the Ohio to the Mississippi. The view of Washington and Philip Schuyler, that land seizures were justified by the Indians' aid to the British, prevailed until 1787, at which time Henry Knox's policy of peace and absorption was substituted. Jefferson sought to encourage Indian agriculture and manufacturing, to release hunting land for settlers, transmuting acquisitiveness into "lofty moral purpose." The acquisition policy succeeded, but peace was not achieved, for "wholesale land acquisition and friendship with the Indians were incompatible."   E. Oberholzer, Jr.

927. Horsman, Reginald. THE BRITISH INDIAN DEPARTMENT AND THE ABORTIVE TREATY OF LOWER SANDUSKY, 1793. *Ohio Hist. Q.*

1961 70(3): 189-213. Relates the attempts of the Indian nations of the Old Northwest and agents of the U.S. government to negotiate a treaty in the summer of 1793 for the purpose of establishing a definitive boundary between the Indian nations and the United States in the Ohio region. The Indians, divided among themselves, were unable to agree upon a boundary line. The British watched developments closely, hoping that the negotiations would lead to the establishment of an Indian buffer state between Canada and the United States. When it became apparent to the American agents that no basis for discussion existed, they abandoned their attempts to open formal negotiations.   S. L. Jones

928. Horsman, Reginald. THE BRITISH INDIAN DEPARTMENT AND THE RESISTANCE TO GENERAL ANTHONY WAYNE, 1793-1795. *Mississippi Valley Hist. R. 1962/63 49(2): 269-290.* The British Indian Department at Detroit strove, at first with some success, to thwart the American advance in the Old Northwest. However, the Indian Department was seriously hampered by the lack of substantial military support from the British. After Anthony Wayne's victories in 1794, the Indians became less tractable. Only the constant pressure of American expansion made the Indians temporary allies of the British after 1807.   G. M. Gressley

929. Horsman, Reginald. WISCONSIN AND THE WAR OF 1812. *Wisconsin Mag. of Hist. 1962/63 46(1): 3-15.* The joint action of the English and the Indian tribes of the Dakota (Sioux), Chippewa, Menominee, and Winnebago against the Americans during the War of 1812 is discussed, as well as various commentaries by British commanders of the time as to the actual worth of the Indian assistance. Highly successful, the British were in control of most of the Wisconsin area by the time the Treaty of Ghent ended the conflict. The treaty, however, gave control of this entire area to the Americans and the British were forced to leave. Thus the Indian tribes, who might have kept to the old ways of life had the British remained, became victims of westward movements of Americans to the area.   W. F. Peterson

930. Jackson, Donald. OLD FORT MADISON—1808-1813. *Palimpsest 1966 47(3): 1-64.* Fort Madison was built in 1808 to help pacify the frontier and to provide a refuge for traders on the long and lonely trip up the Mississippi from St. Louis to Prairie du Chien. In 1813, during the War of 1812, the fort was abandoned and burnt as it was subject to repeated Indian attacks and its commander believed he would be unable to maintain his position. The location of the fort is now the parking lot for the Sheaffer Pen Company in downtown Fort Madison. Illus.   D. W. Curl

931. Jackson, Donald. WILLIAM EWING, AGRICULTURAL AGENT TO THE INDIANS. *Agric. Hist. 1957 31(2): 3-7.* Thomas Jefferson and the men about him believed that the problems of persuading the American Indian to live at peace with white men could be solved by teaching agriculture to him, because the Indian could thus sustain himself on a much smaller area of land. With this objective, William Ewing was sent as an agricultural agent to the Sauk and Fox nations along the upper Mississippi in 1805. His efforts were, however, unsuccess-

ful. The Indians were already adept at raising corn, squash, pumpkins and other crops, and were not willing to give up hunting for livestock husbandry.

J. (W. D. Rasmussen)

932. Jackson, Harry F. BISHOP MADISON'S SPECULATIONS ON THE INDIAN MOUNDS. *West Virginia Hist. 1963 24(4): 363-369.* Bishop James Madison gave the first good report on the Indian mounds in the Kanawha and Guyandot river valleys of western Virginia. His speculations, published in the *Transactions of the American Philosophical Society* in 1804, are in the background of all that has been done since his time to piece together the Adena culture. Madison erred in assuming the Kanawha mounds were the same as that of the Rivanna described by Jefferson, but most of the rest of his work is sound and contributed to the work of later observers.   E. P. Stickney

933. Jennings, Francis P. A VANISHING INDIAN: FRANCIS PARKMAN VERSUS HIS SOURCES. *Pennsylvania Mag. of Hist. and Biog. 1963 87(3): 306-323.* Considers the way in which Parkman handled the many-sided negotiations in 1758 by which peace was reestablished between British and Indian inhabitants after the hostilities of Pennsylvania's first Indian conflict and finds from a comparison of Parkman's text with his cited sources that his account is substantially erroneous. Parkman rejected the idea that Indian initiative was involved in negotiating the peace. "The diplomacy of the Indians themselves, epitomized in the Easton treaty which they organized and managed from first to last, was the crucial factor in bringing peace to the Ohio," not, as Parkman would have us believe, the influence of the Moravian missionary Christian Frederick Post. Based on *Colonial Records* (Harrisburg, 1838-53); *Pennsylvania Archives, First Series* (Philadelphia, 1852-60); and two journals of Christian Frederick Post (London, 1759); 46 notes.   E. P. Stickney

934. Jennings, Francis P. THE INDIAN TRADE OF THE SUSQUEHANNA VALLEY. *Pro. of the Am. Phil. Soc. 1966 110(6): 406-424.* Examines the Indian trade with whites in Pennsylvania's Susquehanna Valley during the period 1675 to 1740. This trade led to a significant alteration in the economic outlook and activities of the Indians, causing them to neglect agricultural endeavors to concentrate on trapping and hunting furs. The drive for furs led in turn to destructive exploitation of available game which further led to clashes among the tribes for the reduced hunting areas. There was also a considerable struggle between the French and British traders for control of the lucrative traffic. James Logan, William Penn's secretary, was at once merchant, land speculator, and colonial official; his efforts were instrumental in determining the development of the Indian trade and of the advancing frontier. Conditions during the formative period in the Susquehanna Valley differed substantially from those postulated in the customary frontier theory: both the Indians and the whites were dependent on Logan—for the fur trade and for land titles, respectively—thus causing an authoritarian rather than a democratic milieu to exist on the Pennsylvania frontier. Based on primary sources; 89 notes.   W. G. Morgan

935. Jennings, Francis P. THE SCANDALOUS INDIAN POLICY OF WIL-
LIAM PENN'S SONS: DEEDS AND DOCUMENTS OF THE WALKING
PURCHASE. *Pennsylvania Hist. 1970 37(1): 19-39.* Examines the famed Walk-
ing Purchase and the dispute over ownership of lands in the Lehigh Valley. The
Penns desperately hoped to reduce their debts by selling lands in the Lehigh
Valley. For some time they recognized the obligation of clearing Indian title to
these lands by purchase. When they realized how expensive this would be, they
tried to prove that their father had already paid for lands at the fork of the
Delaware and Lehigh Rivers in 1686. The boundaries of this purchase were
determined by a man's walking for a day and a half from a given point. They
produced a copy of the supposed deed which the author concludes was at best
"an unconsummated *draft.* " Although the copy had several blank spaces, it also
contained signatures and seals. In 1737 the Indians were pressured and tricked
into confirming the 1686 document. Thomas Penn misled the Indians by implying
he was discussing lands at the fork of the Delaware River and Tohickon Creek
rather than at the fork of the Delaware and Lehigh. Provincial adversaries of the
Penns never saw the minutes of the meeting and they cannot be found in the
records of the Provincial Council. A copy of the minutes is in the report of Sir
William Johnson to the Board of Trade in 1762. 50 notes.   D. C. Swift

936. Johnson, Robert C., ed. A POEM ON THE LATE MASSACRE IN VIR-
GINIA. *Virginia Mag. of Hist. and Biog. 1964 72(3): 259-292.* Reproduces in
facsimile the only known copy of Christopher Brooke's poem published in London in 1622. The editor discusses the Indian massacre of 1622 and Brooke's
interest in Virginia.   K. J. Bauer

937. Johnson, Robert C., ed. THE INDIAN MASSACRE OF 1622: SOME
CORRESPONDENCE OF THE REVEREND JOSEPH MEAD. *Virginia Mag.
of Hist. and Biog. 1963 71 (4):408-410.*   S

938. Kawashima, Yasu. JURISDICTION OF THE COLONIAL COURTS
OVER THE INDIANS IN MASSACHUSETTS, 1689-1763. *New England Q.
1969 42(4): 532-550.* Massachusetts followed a general policy of assimilating
Indians into the dominant white society. In conformity with this policy, courts
tended to assert a jurisdiction over Indians within their borders, looking toward
a breakdown of tribal structures. An attempt in the 17th century to establish
Indian magistrates and Indian County Courts with jurisdiction over plantation
Indians was not successful and white commissioners were appointed by 1694 to
exercise the authority of justices of the peace over Indians. Otherwise, extension
of colonial jurisdiction over Indians was taken for granted. Based mainly on court
records and colonial laws; 52 notes.   K. B. West

939. Kawashima, Yasu. LEGAL ORIGINS OF THE INDIAN RESERVA-
TION IN COLONIAL MASSACHUSETTS. *Am. J. of Legal Hist. 1969 13(1):
45-56.* The Massachusetts Indian reservations developed in the 17th and 18th
centuries into political, economic, and cultural centers. The probable original
purpose of the reservations was to provide a means to assimilate the Indians into

white society. By 1786, when the state reservation system was replaced by federal reservation policy, the system "had virtually come to an end...." Based on government documents; 47 notes.   L. A. Knafla

940. King, David R. MISSIONARY VESTRYMAN. *Hist. Mag. of the Protestant Episcopal Church 1965 34(4): 361-368.* Biographical sketch of Elias Neau (1662-1722), Huguenot veteran of Louis XIV's galleys, convert to Episcopalianism and, by 1703, "one of the most prominent merchants" in New York City. In this year he offered his services to the Society for the Propagation of the Gospel as lay missionary to the thousand-odd Negro and Indian slaves of the city. For most of the remainder of his life he ministered to the spiritual and material needs of several hundred of these unfortunates. Despite their ignorance and the opposition of many of their masters to baptism, the missionary vestryman won the respect and confidence of his spiritual wards and the admiration of influential clergymen and colonial officials. Documented.   E. G. Roddy

941. Klein, Milton M. POLITICS AND PERSONALITIES IN COLONIAL NEW YORK. *New York Hist. 1966 47(1): 3-16.* In the 18th century, New York parties represented broad alliances of different interest groups on Indian policy, the independence of the council, and the administration of local government. 31 notes.   B. T. Quinten

942. Lecompte, Janet. TWO OLD BATTLES FOUGHT BY BARONET VASQUEZ. *Bull. of the Missouri Hist. Soc. 1971 27(4, pt. 1): 243-247.* Antoine ("Baronet") Vasquez was an interpreter for the explorer Zebulon Pike in 1806 and later pursued a career in the U.S. Army. His military service included a stint with the force that William Henry Harrison massed to crush an Indian uprising led by Tecumseh. Contains the texts of two letters written by Vasquez in Harrison's Indian campaign and later on duty at Fort Madison (now in Iowa) when Winnebago Indians attacked the fort. Based on manuscript materials at the Missouri Historical Society; note.   H. T. Lovin

943. Lobdell, Jared C. SOME INDIAN PLACE NAMES IN THE BERGEN-PASSAIC AREA. *Pro. of the New Jersey Hist. Soc. 1966 84(4): 265-270.* Gives tentative conclusions as to derivations of such Indian place-names in New Jersey as Hackensack, Passaic, Preakness, and many others, to serve as a point of departure for further research. 34 notes.   E. P. Stickney

944. Lydecker, Leigh K. HISTORY OF NEW NETHERLAND REVIEWED. *Halve Maen 1964 39(3): 5-6, 16.* Sketches Dutch colonial activities in America, from Hudson's voyage until the English take-over in 1664. The emphasis is on Dutch troubles with the English and the Indians. This essay was first delivered orally to the Holland Society of New York.   B. T. Quinten

945. MacCord, Howard A., Sr. A VIRGINIA INDIAN FAMILY IN 1680. *Virginia Cavalcade 1967 17(1): 39-42.* A report on the archaeological discoveries made at a small site on the Camden farm along the Rappahannock River in

Caroline County, Virginia. The size of the excavation measured only 30 feet by 40 feet, but in it were found potsherds (Indian and European), tobacco pipes, tools, articles of personal adornment, and two coins (a 1662 Spanish silver *real* and a 1672 English copper farthing). A find of special significance was a coin silver medal, two and one-half inches long and one and one-half inches wide, inscribed "The King of Machotick," similar to a medal found on the same site in 1832, inscribed "The King of Patomeck." Illus. N. L. Peterson

946. MacCulloch, Susan L. A TRIPARTITE POLITICAL SYSTEM AMONG CHRISTIAN INDIANS OF EARLY MASSACHUSETTS. *Kroeber Anthrop. Soc. Papers 1966 34: 63-73.* Traces the political growth of the 20 Indian Praying Towns of 17th- and 18th-century Massachusetts, based on three political systems: English colonial, traditional tribal, and biblical (Exodus 18: 20-22). The rulers in these towns are studied, and the author finds that in spite of the inauguration of an elective system, the rulers continued to be those who would also have ruled in the native system. Finally, a comparison is made between the Sagamore-ruler and the modern African chief, indicating that the Sagamore-ruler faced a more cheerful prospect at reconciling two cultures than does his modern African counterpart. An epilogue follows the towns' steady deterioration during the period of 1675 to 1760 due to war, persecution, and disease. Based on primary and secondary sources; 2 tables, 4 notes, biblio. C. N. Warren

947. Malchelosse, Gérard. PEUPLES SAUVAGES DE LA NOUVELLE-FRANCE (1600-1670) [The Indians of New France, 1600-70]. *Cahiers des Dix [Canada] 1963 28: 63-92.* Locates the principal groups of Indians in New France. Algonquin territory was in a vast circle from the Delaware to the Ottawa to the Wisconsin rivers. There were nomadic hunters without government or sophistication. About 40 of these tribes are identified. The Huron-Iroquois group lay north and south of Lakes Ontario and Erie and were sedentary, hard-working cultivators with a more complex social and political organization. Gives a chronology of French-Indian contacts. L. F. S. Upton

948. Manders, Eric and Snook, George A. NEW ENGLAND INDEPENDENT COMPANIES, 1675-1676. *Military Collector and Historian 1964 16(2): 50-51.* Describes the weapons and clothing of friendly New England Indians and settlers during King Philip's War. "The bow and arrow was seldom used as the Indian had been accustomed to using the musket for many years and had lost the knack." Illus. C. L. Boyd

949. Marshall, Peter. SIR WILLIAM JOHNSON AND THE TREATY OF FORT STANWIX, 1768. *J. of Am. Studies [Great Britain] 1967 1(2): 149-179.* Reinterprets the career of Sir William Johnson, New York land-speculator and superintendent of Indian affairs for the northern department. Johnson's effort at the Treaty of Fort Stanwix has been treated too simplistically and negatively by historians. A variety of political and material interests influenced his conduct. Moreover, he concluded a treaty which must be considered a success and "which incorporated those policies and assumptions reflected over the years in his official correspondence: the maintenance of imperial regulation of Indian affairs, the

according of special position to the Iroquois, and the satisfaction of speculators' demands for additional land." The relationship between Johnson, royal officials in England, and other English and colonial figures—Thomas Penn, for example —are also discussed. Based on such published primary sources as *Documents Relative to the Colonial History of the State of New York* (Albany, 1853-58) and *The Papers of Sir William Johnson* (Albany, 1921-62).   D. J. Abramoske

950. Massay, G. F. FORT HENRY IN THE AMERICAN REVOLUTION. *West Virginia Hist. 1962/63 24(3): 248-257.* Once the American Revolution materialized the West began to play a major role. The English and the Americans recognized the importance of the Indians in the West and each sought to gain their support. Fort Henry, located in what is now Wheeling, was a ready target for the Indians. Describes several efforts made by the Indians to take the fort.   M. Kanin

951. Massie, Dennis. JACOB SMITH IN THE SAGINAW VALLEY. *Michigan Hist. 1967 51(2): 117-129.* Using a variety of published works the author synthesizes a biographical sketch of Jacob Smith, an early 19th-century fur trader and successful land treaty negotiator with the Indians.   J. K. Flack

952. McNew, George L. THE PARADISE WORLD OF THE RED MAN IN WESTCHESTER COUNTY. *Yonkers Hist. Bull. 1968 15(1): 9-15.* The people of the Wappinger Council, including the Siwanoy to the east, the Weckquaeskeck to the north, their cousins to the nearby east at Aquehung in Tuckahoe hills, and the Manhattan Indians to the south, had a loose but effective confederation. They were organized to protect themselves from the warlike Iroquois nation to the north, especially from the fierce Mohawk and the Delaware Indians west of the Hudson River. These tribes were part of the Algonquin people who had moved eastward as the Mohican (or Mohegan) tribes until they encountered the great river which they had named the Mohicanituck. They settled in the estuaries along the Mohicanituck at the Nepperhan, Dobbs Ferry, Croton River, and the Harlem River. These "pre-Dutch" Indians lived in an assortment of environments depending on the underlying soil and moisture content of the land. They produced fairly substantial acreages of corn, sieva beans, tobacco, and pumpkin. These people preferred to build the so-called longhouses in their permanent villages. It is significant that the Indian never multiplied to the extent that he overran the natural resources of the area.   J. K. Huhta

953. Medlicott, Alexander, Jr. RETURN TO THIS LAND OF LIGHT: A PLEA TO AN UNREDEEMED CAPTIVE. *New England Q. 1965 38(2): 202-216.* An account of the life of Eunice Williams, who was captured at the age of seven when Deerfield, Massachusetts, was destroyed by the Indians, remained with her captors at Caughnawaga in Canada near Montreal, married an Indian, reared children, paid visits to her brother Stephen at Longmeadow, Massachusetts, and lived to the age of 88. The account is based on printed sources, manuscript letters, and the manuscript diary kept by Stephen Williams now at the First Church of Christ Congregational, Longmeadow.   A. Turner

954. Meyers, Arthur N. "COXEY" BIVENS—DELAWARE VALLEY CAVE DWELLER. *New York Folklore Q. 1963 19(3): 197-202.* Joseph "Coxey" Bivens, Jr., was a fishing guide on the Delaware River. For the last two years of his life, 1910-12, he chose to live in a cave—or actually under a rock overhang—on the Pennsylvania shore of the Delaware River, across from Narrowsburg, New York. Archaeological expeditions have since proved that the cave was once used by Iroquois and Algonkin Indians, and local legend is that Tom Quick, the Indian slayer, also used it. Newspaper obituary reprinted. 2 illus.   M. A. Booth

955. Miles, William. JOHN TANNER—MAN WITHOUT A RACE. *Am. Book Collector 1970 20(6): 12-15.* When he was nine years old, John Tanner was captured by Indians. In 1817 he returned to his white family. The homecoming was less than successful. In 1830 he published an account of his capture by the Ottawa and Chippewa Indians, *[A Narrative of the Captivity and Adventures of John Tanner].* He then lived 16 years at Sault Sainte Marie in Michigan where his attempts to gain status as a white man failed. When James Schoolscraft was murdered on 4 July 1846 he was accused of the crime and disappeared, not to be heard from again. Illus.   D. Brockway

956. Mochon, Marion Johnson. STOCKBRIDGE-MUNSEE CULTURAL ADAPTATIONS: "ASSIMILATED INDIANS." *Pro. of the Am. Phil. Soc. 1968 112(3): 182-219.* An analysis "of an adaptive response to the surrounding dominant Euro-American society by a community with a self-perception as 'assimilated Indians,'" specifically the Stockbridge-Munsees, who now live in Wisconsin. This sociological study traces the group's cultural-political-economic development from the early 17th century to the present, and describes the current nature of their society. The fur traffic and other trade provided contact with the Europeans in America, and in the 18th century substantial efforts were made to convert these Indians to Christianity. During the early years of the 19th century, they considered themselves as brokers between whites and Indians; in 1822 the first group of Stockbridge and Munsees moved west to Wisconsin. After removal west, the community split into a Citizen's Party and an Indian Party; this factional strife continued until 1910. Conclusions about the adaptation process are presented, along with areas for subsequent research. Based on printed sources, government reports, and secondary materials; 144 notes, biblio.
                                                                                    W. G. Morgan

957. Mohl, Raymond A. EDUCATION AS SOCIAL CONTROL IN NEW YORK CITY, 1784-1825. *New York Hist. 1970 51(3): 219-237.* In the half-century after the American Revolution, numerous primary schools were established in New York City. Most were church supported, and religion constituted a major portion of the curriculum. Founded for the education of the poor, Negroes, and Indians, they provided a basic education but stressed the inculcation of middle-class values and attitudes. The schools also found employment for their students as domestics or as apprentices in the trades. It was hoped that the schools could cure New York's poverty and social ills by training lower-class students to

fit into a middle-class society. Social control and the prevention of social radicalism were the primary functions of the New York school system. Based on primary and secondary sources; 5 illus., 29 notes.   G. Kurland

958. Nelsen, Anne K. KING PHILIP'S WAR AND THE HUBBARD-MATHER RIVALRY. *William and Mary Q. 1970 27(4): 615-629.* Places the histories of the war by William Hubbard and Increase Mather in the context of a rivalry between the two men. Hubbard blamed King Philip's War (1675-76) on over-confidence, lack of understanding of the Indian problem, and greed. Mather took a more theological stance, bewailing the loss of Puritan mission. A case is also made for Hubbard's recognition of the need for dissent. Of the two histories, Hubbard created a drama of flesh and blood "actors," while Mather believed that King Philip's War was a scourge of the people. Included are brief comments on the careers of the two men. 52 notes.   H. M. Ward

959. Nicholas, Roger L. THE FOUNDING OF FORT ATKINSON. *Ann. of Iowa 1965 37(8): 589-597.* Construction of this fort began in 1840 under the direction of General Henry Atkinson. Located on the Turtle River in northeastern Iowa, the post was designed to protect the Winnebago from their Sac-Fox neighbors. The former refused to migrate from Wisconsin without this assurance of protection. Within nine years, the tribe was relocated in Minnesota and the rather costly fort was abandoned. Since 1958, the state of Iowa has restored the stockade walls and parts of the fort. Illus.   D. C. Swift

960. Nichols, Roger L. THE BLACK HAWK WAR: ANOTHER VIEW. *Ann. of Iowa 1963 36(7): 525-533.* While some Sauk and Fox Indians followed Black Hawk into Illinois in 1832 to fight the Sioux, many others stayed peaceably at home in Iowa, cooperating with the whites. The U.S. government was called in to keep the peace between the tribes as provided in an 1825 treaty. The minutes of one of the meetings between General Henry Atkinson and the tribal chieftains give an insight into the situation. The document used is from the Mrs. Mason Barret Collection in the Tulane University Library.   W. F. Peterson

961. Nuschke, Marie Kathern. THE LITTLE PORTAGE TRAIL. *Pennsylvania Hist. 1964 31(4): 397-405.* A summary of the Little Portage Trail, which ran from Costello to Canoe Place and the Allegheny River. Describes information from pioneers about the Little Portage and the manner in which Indians and settlers used it. Illus., 7 notes.   D. H. Swift

962. O'Donnell, Thomas F. MORE APOLOGIES: THE INDIAN IN NEW YORK FICTION. *New York Folklore Q. 1967 23(4): 243-252.* Gives plot sketches of early novels to show that the New York Indians have long been represented in fiction as either fierce warriors or noble savages. Although much factual material has been available, writers have relied on these two prototypes in their romanticized versions of New York history. James Fenimore Cooper's

early novels reflected a clearer image of the Indians, but he too fell into the use of the easy formula and created his famous character "Chingachgook," who appeared in three of his more successful novels. 5 notes. W. S. Rinaldo

963. Oedel, Howard T. SLAVERY IN COLONIAL PORTSMOUTH. *Hist. New Hampshire 1966 21(3): 3-11.* After the failure of Indian slavery and indentured servitude in the 17th century, Negro slaves, usually children, were brought from the West Indies for domestic service with the well-to-do. Based on family MSS., reminiscences, newspapers, and state documents.
T. D. S. Bassett

964. Painter, Levinus K. QUAKER SETTLEMENTS IN ERIE COUNTY, NEW YORK. *Quaker Hist. 1966 55(1): 24-37.* Post-revolutionary Quaker travelers passed through Erie County from Philadelphia, but the first settlers came from Vermont, eastern New York, and Pennsylvania, 1804-12, taking up residence near the Indian reservations.
T. D. S. Bassett

965. Patterson, Gerard A. "...THE ENEMY CAME IN LIKE A FLOOD UPON US." *Am. Hist. Illus. 1966 1(7): 14-19.* The Deerfield settlement, located on the Connecticut River in Massachusetts, was the northernmost settlement in the colony and thus had long been exposed to Indian and French raids from Canada. On 28 February 1704, a force of 250 French and Indians attacked the settlement, killing 49 and taking 111 prisoners. The expedition was ordered by the governor of Canada who was pressured from two sources: from Indians who wanted retaliation for previous English raids and from a Jesuit priest who wanted to reclaim a church bell that had been pirated away and was hanging in the Deerfield meeting house. Many of the captives were sold or bartered while others remained captives of the Indians. Several prisoners were exchanged in 1706. Based partly on a diary left by John Williams, the Protestant pastor of Deerfield; 5 illus.
M. J. McBaine

966. Patton, Glenn. THE COLLEGE OF WILLIAM AND MARY, WILLIAMSBURG AND THE ENLIGHTENMENT. *J. of the Soc. of Architectural Historians 1970 29(1): 24-32.* By relating the growth of William and Mary College to the development of the town of Williamsburg, suggests that the whole can be viewed as an illustration of the unity and order of the Anglo-American Enlightenment of the late 17th and early 18th centuries. The new concept of empire associated with John Locke and the Board of Trade, and growing need for trained men, led to the founding of a multipurpose college in 1693. The college was to combine a common school for Indian and white children, a grammar school, a liberal arts college, and a theological college. 7 illus., 18 notes.
D. McIntyre

967. Provost, Honorius. UN JESUITE AMBASSADEUR [A Jesuit ambassador]. *Soc. Can. d'Hist. de l'Eglise Catholique. Rapport 1965: 101-112.* Father Gabriel Druillettes made three voyages overland into the country of the Abnakis and to New England to further a defensive alliance between the English colonies

and New France against the Mohawk Indians, who were threatening both the French colony and the Abnaki Indians, the latter under the territorial jurisdiction of New England. 32 notes.   C. Thibault

968. Saunders, Robert. WHEN NEWFOUNDLAND HELPED SAVE CANADA. *Newfoundland Q. [Canada] 1963 62(3): 15-17, 20-23.* A description of the last days of the British at Fort McKay in Prairie du Chien in May 1815, taken from data by the Northwest historian Thwaites, which include a report by Capt. Bulger, an officer of the Royal Newfoundland Regiment. His father had assembled a large force of Indians at the fort to carry on the war. News of the Peace of Ghent was not received by him until five months later and he then had difficulty and had to use great discretion to persuade the Indians to accept the terms of the peace.   M. Petrie

969. Schulte Nordholt, J. W. NEDERLANDERS IN NIEUW NEDERLAND [The Dutch in New Netherland]. *Bijdragen en Mededelingen van het Historisch Genootschap [Netherlands] 1966 80: 38-94.* Deals with the war of 1643-45 between the Dutch and the Indians. At that time Willem Kieft was the governor of New Netherland. Discusses the events that led to the outbreak of hostilities beginning with the imposition of taxation in 1639. One of the consequences of this war was the replacement of Kieft by Peter Stuyvesant.   G. van Roon

970. Séguin, Robert-Lionel. LES TECHNIQUES AGRICOLES EN NOUVELLE-FRANCE [Agricultural techniques in New France]. *Cahiers des Dix [Canada] 1963 28: 255-288.* Opens with a description of Indian agriculture in the early 17th century but concentrates on the French Canadian settler: his methods of plowing, pasturage, drainage, sowing, harvesting, threshing; the height of his haystacks; the cultivation of peas, tobacco, and corn. The colonist generally lacked experience in, and taste for, farming. The result was poor use of land which became quickly exhausted because of not being fertilized. Draws much evidence from contemporary wills and leases.   L. F. S. Upton

971. Sifton, Paul G. THE WALKER-WASHINGTON MAP. *Lib. of Congress Q. J. 1967 24(2): 90-96.* The Library of Congress has received a map copied by George Washington from a map made by Thomas Walker in 1769 to accompany a memorandum from Walker to the Virginia House of Burgesses concerning the boundary between the western settlements and the Indians. It is believed that Washington added information to the map copied from Lewis Evans' map of 1755 and from his own personal knowledge. The Walker map has disappeared. The map was probably used by Washington on his mission to survey the lands between the Little and Great Kanawha Rivers in 1770. Illus., 2 maps, 26 notes.
                                                              H. E. Cox

972. Sisser, Fred, III. LIFE AND TIMES OF JACOB JANSEN STOL. *Halve Maen 1967 42(1): 11-12, 14, (2): 11-12, 15, (3): 21-22, 1968 42(2): 13-14, 17.* Part I. Relates the early life of a drunken, brawling, profane ferryman (ca. 1618-59) who resided near Fort Orange, New Netherland. Based on published, translated

records of New Netherland; 32 notes. Part II. Stol moved to the Esopus (later Ulster County, New York) in 1657 and soon became a leading citizen, his heretofore concealed better side apparently brought out by the Indian menace. Trouble with the natives in 1658 brought Director-General Petrus (Peter) Stuyvesant (1592-1672) to the area with troops; he built the fortified settlement of Wiltwyck (later Kingston) for the endangered pioneers. To contain further unrest, much of it focused about Indian depredations on Stol's property, Stuyvesant garrisoned 50 men at Wiltwyck in the fall of 1658. 26 notes. Part III. Tension between settlers and Indians mounted at Wiltwyck during 1659. A nighttime clash in September saw Stol wounded and an Indian killed, precipitating war. His house burned, Stol endeavored to send for help from Stuyvesant, but was captured just outside the fort with 11 others. After hideous torture he was burnt at the stake. 12 notes. Part IV. By the time Stuyvesant arrived with a contingent in October, the Indians had returned to their villages. Stol's wife, Geertruyd Andriesen van Doesburgh Stol (ca. 1619-80), married Aert Martensen Doorn in 1661. The Indians burned most of Wiltwyck in 1663. Jan Jacobsen Stol, her only son, became a substantial farmer in Ulster County. 44 notes.   G. L. Owen and S

973. Snook, George A. NOTES CONCERNING THE INDEPENDENT COMPANIES IN KING PHILIP'S WAR, 1675-1676. *Military Collector and Historian 1964 16(3): 74-76.* Describes the use made of friendly Indians who were encouraged to enlist on the same basis as Englishmen in independent companies. The independent companies were military units enlisted by such individuals as Captain Benjamin Church, Captain Samuel Mosley, and Captain Daniel Hinchman who were granted commissions by their respective colonies. Detailed plans for the hit-and-run tactics of Church are given in a letter to the governor of Massachusetts Bay. Secondary sources, 12 notes.   C. L. Boyd

974. Sosin, Jack M. THE BRITISH INDIAN DEPARTMENT AND DUNMORE'S WAR. *Virginia Mag. of Hist. and Biog. 1966 74(1): 34-50.* In 1774 many of the western Indian tribes were unhappy over the land cessions of the Treaties of Hard Labor (1770), Lochaber (1770), and Fort Stanwix (1768). Their animosities were chiefly directed against the Virginians who used some retaliatory Indian raids as a pretext to drive the tribes from western lands claimed by the colony. The ensuing Lord Dunmore's War forced the Indians to remain north of the Ohio River. Only intensive diplomacy by the British Indian Department kept other tribes from coming to the aid of the Shawnee and Delaware and attacking portions of the Virginia frontier denuded of protection by the campaign. Based on the Gage Papers in the William L. Clements Library, Ann Arbor, Michigan, and other contemporary sources, published and manuscript.
                                                              K. J. Bauer

975. Stealey, John E., III. GEORGE CLENDINEN AND THE GREAT KANAWHA VALLEY FRONTIER: A CASE STUDY OF THE FRONTIER DEVELOPMENT OF VIRGINIA. *West Virginia Hist. 1966 37(4): 278-296.* As was so often the case with land speculators, it was the expectation of profits, not the actual existence of them, that led George Clendinen to promote the settlement of western lands. After participating in Lord Dunmore's campaign of

1774 against the Ohio Indians, he served in the Virginia militia on the frontier during the Revolution. Elected from Greenbrier County to the Virginia Assembly in 1781, he served until 1789. In this office he promoted the interests of the West by championing internal improvements. He was a typical frontiersman who used his political position to promote his personal interests. Based on published primary and secondary sources.   D. N. Brown

976. Suelflow, Roy A. LUTHERAN MISSIONS IN THE SAGINAW VALLEY. *Michigan Hist. 1967 51(3): 226-240.* Studies the general failure of the Missouri Synod's Indian missions in Michigan between 1845 and 1868. Curiously, this was a period in which German Lutheran communities flourished throughout the Saginaw Valley and the lack of success of missionary work has never been satisfactorily explained. Drawing evidence from publications and manuscript sources of the Concordia Historical Institute, St. Louis, Missouri, unpublished dissertations, and German documents, the author maintains that too few Lutherans understood Indian culture.   J. K. Flack

977. Talley, William M. SALT LICK CREEK AND ITS SALT WORKS. *Register of the Kentucky Hist. Soc. 1966 64(2): 85-109.* In Lewis County, Kentucky, where the Salt Lick Creek enters the Ohio River, there was a salt lick which was a popular spot for Indians to hunt game. The early settlers in the area, the founding of the town of Vanceburg, and the difficulties encountered in building a salt-making industry are described. Documented.   J. F. Cook

978. Tanis, Norman Earl. EDUCATION IN JOHN ELIOT'S UTOPIAS, 1645-1675. *Hist. of Educ. Q. 1970 10(3): 308-323.* John Eliot (1604-90), "the apostle to the Indians," taught in 14 Indian villages he founded from 1646 to 1675. His efforts were an organized attempt at adult education, based on a literal and nonspeculative reading of the Bible. Eliot drew support from the Society for the Propagation of the Gospel in New England, which he had helped found. The venture ended during King Philip's War in 1675, when the General Court ordered the Indians removed to Deer Island. Only four Indian villages remained after the war. 32 notes.   J. Herbst

979. Thurston, Helen M. A SURVEY OF PUBLICATIONS ON THE HISTORY AND ARCHAEOLOGY OF OHIO, 1969-70. *Ohio Hist. 1969 78(4): 288-296.* Lists books, articles, and other materials under the headings of Archaeology, Arts and Crafts, Bibliography, Biography, Business and Industry, Education and Culture, Genealogy, Indians and the Wars, Literature, Local History, Miscellaneous, Ohio in the Wars, Politics and Government, Religion, Slavery, Civil War, Reconstruction, Urban History, and Theses and Dissertations on Ohio Subjects in Ohio Colleges and Universities.   S. L. Jones

980. Tremblay, Victor. LE MARTYRE BLANC DES MISSIONNAIRES EN SAGUENAY [The white martyrdom of the missionaries of Saguenay]. *Soc. Can. d'Hist. de l'Eglise Catholique. Rapport 1964 31: 45-53.* Supplements an earlier paper (1946) on the evangelization of Saquenay, Quebec, by the Jesuits. The

author emphasizes a generally ignored aspect of their work, the particular conditions which rendered so hard and laborious the life and work of these missionaries —a true martyrdom without the shedding of blood. Experiences close to suffocation in the Indian huts are recorded, as well as long and perilous trips by canoe or snowshoe in the attempt to meet the needs of the people of this country isolated by the Laurentian Mountains. Twenty-one missionaries participated in the task. Quotations from the *Jesuit Relations.*   E. P. Stickney

981. Trigger, Bruce G. THE MOHAWK-MAHICAN WAR (1624-28): THE ESTABLISHMENT OF A PATTERN. *Can. Hist. R. 1971 52(3): 276-286.* Examines the relationships between the Indian tribes of eastern Canada and upper New York who were allied with the French and Dutch between 1610 and 1635. Emphasizes the Mohawk-Mahican War of 1624-28 and readjustments in intertribal relations after the return of the French to the St. Lawrence in 1632. Offers a new explanation for the murder of Etienne Brûlé. Concludes that even at this early period north-south relations were as important as east-west ones and that it is impossible to understand Dutch-Indian relations in New York independently of French-Indian ones in Canada. Based on published documents.   A

982. Trudel, Marcel. LA NOUVELLE-FRANCE, 1604-1627 [New France, 1604-27]. *R. d'Hist. de l'Amérique Française [Canada] 1965 19(2): 203-228.* Population comparison show that the Dutch and English outnumbered the French in North America in this period by 27 to one. Although the French were not successful in colonization, they did show progress in adapting to the climate, resisting disease, learning new transportation methods, and solving the language barrier with the Indians, which led to the successful exploitation of the fur trade.
                          G. Sylvester

983. Trudel, Marcel. LA RENCONTRE DES CULTURES [The confrontation of cultures]. *R. d'Hist. de l'Amérique Française [Canada] 1965 18(4): 477-516.* The period 1604-27 produced the first generation of French Americans in the New World. The French learned new transportation techniques and how to survive the Laurentian winters; they solved the language barrier with the Indians. The breaking down of language bars made it possible for both sides to profit from cultural exchange.   J. M. Bumsted

984. Unsigned. A PRECISE JOURNAL OF GENERAL WAYNE'S LAST CAMPAIGN IN THE YEAR 1794 AGAINST THE WESTERN INDIANS TAKEN DOWN IN THE COURSE OF THE CAMPAIGN WITH AN ACCOUNT OF AN ATTACK MADE ON FORT RECOVERY BY THE INDIANS ON THE 30th JUNE PRECEDING. *Pro. of the Am. Antiquarian Soc. 1954 64(2): 273-302.* Printed by John Gruber in Hagerstown, Maryland, in 1795, and known only by the single copy at the American Antiquarian Society, this journal covers 28 June to 2 November 1794. It is especially valuable for march routine, soldiers' activities, the Battle of Fallen Timbers, and evidences of white-Indian contacts and British activity in the Northwest Territory. The editor con-

cludes that: 1) author "Randolph" was not an officer and was not interested in strategy and tactics, and 2) the journal was extensively edited after the campaign. Other journals of the campaign are listed.   P. Johnson

985. Unsigned. CAPITAL PUNISHMENT IN MICHIGAN, 1683: DULUTH AT MICHILIMACKINAC. *Michigan Hist. 1966 50(4): 349-360.* Letter from Daniel Greysolon Duluth (or Dulhut), commandant at Michilimackinac (now Mackinac) to Joseph-Antoine Le Febvre de La Barre, governor general of New France, 12 April 1684, justifying the execution of two Indians in retribution for the robbery and murder of two French traders.   J. K. Flack

986. Unsigned. NEW JERSEY: THE FIRST HUNDRED YEARS. *New Jersey Hist. Soc. Pro. 1964 82(1): 1-28.* Presents excerpts from the *New Jersey Archives* taken roughly at 10-year intervals, from the Patent of Charles II to the eve of the Revolutionary War. In 1744 Governor Morris' speeches to the Assembly at Burlington emphasized the importance of the militia and the need for legislation providing for its payment; the Assembly's reply, a refusal on grounds of expense, is given. The 1754 selection comments on the failure of the legislature to provide resources for the common defense against the French. In 1764 attacks by the Indians are feared. The selections include the notes supplied by the original editors. Illus.   E. P. Stickney

987. Unsigned. RELATIVES OF PAYNE COUNTY MEN CONTRIBUTED ROMANCE TO EARLY AMERICAN HISTORY. *Concordia Hist. Inst. Q. 1966 39(3): 120-129.* Focuses on the romantic adventures of Regina and Barbara Leininger, who were living in western Pennsylvania in 1755 when they were taken captives by an Indian raiding party. One of the girls eventually escaped to find refuge at Pittsburgh. The other was freed in 1764. Reprinted from the Stillwater, Oklahoma, *Daily Press,* 9 June 1932.   D. J. Abramoske

988. Vachon, André. VALEUR DE LA SOURCE HURONNE [Worth of the Huron source]. *R. de l'U. Laval [Canada] 1964 18(6): 495-515.* In the face of disagreement among the French accounts of the engagement between the Iroquois and the French under Daulac, reinforced by 40 Wyandot (Huron) warriors at the Long Sault in 1660, how much credence can be placed in the accounts given by Hurons who deserted to the Iroquois during the siege? Chaumont, Marie de l'Incarnation, and the Jesuit *Relation* for 1660 all derived their information from Huron deserters but it is suggested that the *Relation* was slanted in favor of the religious aspects of the engagement, and the conclusion is reached that the Huron source is "of incontestable value for the historian."   G. H. Kelsey

989. Van Every, Dale. PRESIDENT WASHINGTON'S CALCULATED RISK. *Am. Heritage 1958 9(4): 56-61, 109-111.* Describes the efforts of President George Washington to secure the "old Northwest" from the Indians, a strategy which climaxed in the Battle of Fallen Timbers with the defeat of the Indians by General Anthony Wayne (1794) and the ultimate Indian session in the Treaty of Greenville (1795). Illus.   C. R. Allen, Jr.

990. Vaughan, Alden T. A TEST OF PURITAN JUSTICE. *New England Q. 1965 38(3): 331-339.* The New England Puritans are recorded as normally severe in their dealings with the Indians. In the 1830's the colonists in Massachusetts and Rhode Island suffered heavily at the hands of the Pequot and the Narragansett. Chief Sequin of the Wongunk tribe sold land to the settlers at Wethersfield, Connecticut, with the understanding that he might live in the area and be protected against the Pequot. The settlers did not live up to their bargain and drove him away. With help from the Pequot, he killed nine people and numerous cows. The colonists carried out a war of retaliation, but afterward, in reestablishing relations with the Indians, they considered Chief Sequin's revenge justified, since he had been wronged without redress. The Connecticut General Court accepted the decision 5 April 1638. 21 notes.   A. Turner

991. Vogel, Virgil J. THE MISSIONARY AS ACCULTURATION AGENT: PETER DOUGHERTY AND THE INDIANS OF GRAND TRAVERSE. *Michigan Hist. 1967 51(3): 185-201.* Traces the 33-year ministry of the Reverend Peter Dougherty among the Ottawa and Chippewa (Ojibwa) Indians in the northwest part of Michigan's Lower Peninsula. Dougherty, whose manuscript diary is in the Michigan Historical Collections at the University of Michigan, served as a Presbyterian missionary between 1838 and 1871, during which time he played a singular role in adapting the Indians to white ways of life.
                                        J. K. Flack

992. Waitz, Lawrence T. THE INDIANS OF EASTERN LONG ISLAND. *Long Island Forum 1970 33(9): 182-186.* The Indians of eastern Long Island did not form distinct tribes. They were basically of Algonkian stock and included Delaware, Niantick, and Mohegan Indians. By the time the first whites arrived on Long Island around 1640, the island's Indians were paying tribute to the Pequot and Narragansett of New England. Having no conception of private property, they felt that the white settlers were paying them tribute when they purchased their ancestral lands. Economically, the Indians of eastern Long Island were food gatherers and fishermen living primarily on clams, scallops, and oysters. Agriculture was practiced by the squaws who cultivated corn, squash, and beans. Their lodgings were constructed of thatch over a framework of bent saplings. A serious plague from 1615 to 1620 seriously weakened their ability to resist white encroachment. 2 illus., biblio.   G. Kurland

993. Walton, Frank L. THE WADING PLACE. *Yonkers Hist. Bull. 1968 15(2): 3-7.* Few people realize that it is possible to walk from the Bronx mainland to Manhattan Island without crossing a bridge or getting one's feet wet. Today, boats come up the Harlem River and through the ship canal to the Hudson River without knowing they have travelled through a portion of Manhattan Island instead of around its tip. To explain this, the author first considers the early history of the Indian inhabitants of the present Bronx and the Dutch on Manhattan Island. Originally, the narrow waterway at the tip of the island was shallow and became known as the "wading place." Attention is then directed to the

building of King's Bridge which served as a valuable water crossing for both American and British forces in the American Revolution. In 1895 the water route around the top of the island was filled. Map.   J. K. Huhta

994. Watrall, Charles R. VIRGINIA DEER AND THE BUFFER ZONE IN THE LATE PREHISTORIC-EARLY PROTOHISTORIC PERIODS IN MINNESOTA. *Plains Anthropologist 1968 13(40): 81-86.* "Hickerson has proposed the existence of an unoccupied buffer zone in Minnesota and Wisconsin, between the Chippewa and the Dakota, in the period 1780 to 1850. He suggests that the shape and character of the unoccupied region relates to the distribution and density of Virginia Deer populations which became a contested resource. This paper attempts to statistically test the possibility that an unoccupied buffer zone did exist in Minnesota during the Late Prehistoric and Protohistoric periods from about A.D. 1200 to A.D. 1800, and that site distributions for this period seem to substantiate the existence of such a zone."   J

995. Wentzler, J. Donald. ANCIENT ART OF MEDICINE IN LYCOMING COUNTY. *Now and Then 1964 14(8): 211-219.* Discusses the practice of medicine in early Pennsylvania. Early doctors, who were largely unschooled despite a three to seven year apprenticeship, relied upon home and Indian remedies to treat their patients. Concludes that death was frequently caused by the treatment and by a lack of proper sanitary conditions. Illus.   H. Ershkowitz

996. Weslager, C. A. WHO SURVIVED THE INDIAN MASSACRE AT SWAANENDAEL? *Halve Maen 1965 40(3): 9-10, 15.* In the spring of 1631 a colony was founded at Swaanendael on Delaware Bay. However, about a year later, Indians attacked the settlement, burned the fort, and killed the colonists. Descendants of one Swaanendael colonist later contended that two boys escaped the slaughter but were carried away by the Indians. This account was accepted by the historian Jerome Wiltse and spread widely, but this article rejects Wiltse's claim and presents contradictory contemporary documentation.
                                                              B. T. Quinten

997. Wolfe, George D. THE BIG RUNAWAY OF 1778. *Pro. and Collections of the Wyoming Hist. and Geological Soc. 1970 23: 3-19.* In 1778 the "Big Runaway" occurred along the west branch of the Susquehanna River. With the coming of independence the "Fair Play" settlers of that region faced potential terror from Great Britain and the Indians. Describes the situation confronting these settlers and the events that led to a massacre. When news of the Wyoming Massacre (3 July 1778) reached the area, panic reigned as people emptied the valley north of Sunbury, Pennsylvania. Many of the men remained at Fort Augusta (Sunbury) to help secure the frontier against any further encroachment to the south. 56 notes.   H. B. Powell

998. Zimmerman, John J. CHARLES THOMSON, "THE SAM ADAMS OF PHILADELPHIA." *Mississippi Valley Hist. R. 1958 45(3): 464-480.* A study of the emergence of Thomson as the leader of the Philadelphia radicals in the decade

prior to 1774. A brief biographical sketch of Thomson's early activities as a teacher, secretary at several Indian conferences, and merchant is included. During the Stamp Act crisis Thomson stood out as the only Quaker party supporter who actively opposed the act. A significant result of the crisis was the entente formed between Thomson and Benjamin Franklin, then Pennsylvania's colonial agent in London. The cooperation between the two during the Townshend crisis (1767-70) led to Thomson's leadership of the radicals when the First Continental Congress met.

999. Zoltvany, Yves F. NEW FRANCE AND THE WEST, 1701-1713. *Can. Hist. R. 1965 46(4): 301-322.* Examines the effects on New France's western policy of the edict of May 1696, which abolished the 25 *congés* and ordered the garrisons withdrawn from the western posts, and of the foundation of Detroit in June 1701 by Antoine de La Mothe Cadillac. The basic thesis is that both of these measures were diplomatically ill-advised, for they gravely weakened New France's alliance with the western Indians. They were also basic causes of the outbreak of the Fox War in 1712 which obliged Governor Philippe de Rigaud, Marquis de Vaudreuil, to proceed with a reoccupation of strategic points in the Great Lakes and Mississippi Valley regions that same year. Based principally on the *Archives des colonies,* on deposit at the *archives nationales* in Paris.   A

By Tribe

Algonquin

1000. Chaput, Donald. PRONUNCIATION OF ALGONQUIAN PLACE NAMES. *Inland Seas 1965 21(4): 322-324.* Demonstrates "the elusive character of Indian place-name origins in the Great Lakes region," particularly the *ac* ending.   K. J. Bauer

Beothuk

1001. Whitby, Barbara. THE BEOTHUCKS: A PORTRAYAL OF THEIR BACKGROUND FROM TRADITIONAL SOURCES. *Newfoundland Q. [Canada] 1963 62(2): 3-6, 24-25, 34-35.* Outlines the life of the Indians as found in traditional sources, written and oral. The Beothuk were a people of surprising contrasts. They were able to cooperate in large-scale hunting operations yet were intolerant of strong central leadership in their everyday life. They ignored the special characteristics of some neighboring tribes while adapting selected ideas from other tribes. The author leaves us with questions concerning the origins and predecessors of the Beothuk.   L. Beckom

Chippewa (Ojibwa)

1002. Cumming, John. A PURITAN AMONG THE CHIPPEWAS. *Michigan Hist. 1967 51(3): 213-225.* Analyzes the personal character and historical significance of Abel Bingham, who operated a Baptist school and church for Indians at Sault Saint Marie, Michigan, between 1827 and 1855. Using extensively the Bingham Papers at Central Michigan University and those contained in the Michigan Historical Collections, University of Michigan, the author concludes that his subject, a New Englander by birth whose formative years were spent in western New York, was permanently influenced by intense emotional revivalism and remained so humorlessly pietistic that he brought the Chippewa a God too stern to accept.   J. K. Flack

1003. Donnelly, Joseph P., S.J. FATHER JACQUES MARQUETTE AND THE INDIANS OF UPPER MICHIGAN. *Records of the Am. Catholic Hist. Soc. of Philadelphia 1969 80(1): 39-52.* Presents a brief account of the life of missionary and explorer Jacques Marquette, S.J., and summarizes the history and habits of the Chippewa (Ojibwa). Based mostly on primary sources; 29 notes.
                                                        J. M. McCarthy

1004. Emmert, Darlene Gay. THE INDIANS OF SHIAWASSEE COUNTY. *Michigan Hist. 1963 47(2): 127-155, (3): 243-272.* Part I. Seeks to present a credible picture of an Indian society during the first half of the 19th century. Focusing on the Saginaw Valley Chippewa (Ojibwa), the author describes aspects of social and political life. She also discusses language and the origin of place-names, as well as locating village sites within the particular county. Part II. Deals principally with Indian-white relations, the cession of territory, and land treaties which preceded the Indians' removal to Kansas. Shiawassee County Indians participated in wars and uprisings against whites although the county itself was never a battleground.   J. K. Flack

1005. Hickerson, Harold. WILLIAM T. BOUTWELL OF THE AMERICAN BOARD AND THE PILLAGER CHIPPEWA: THE HISTORY OF A FAILURE. *Ethnohist. 1965 12(1): 1-29.* A Dartmouth alumnus and Presbyterian missionary to the Pillager Chippewas of the Lake Superior region, William T. Boutwell, labored five years (1832-37) "to encourage the Pillagers to move in the direction of private production and private ownership. His failure to accomplish this and his failure on other grounds to establish rapport with the chiefs and warriors forms the subject matter for this paper." Based on personal journals and fur company and American Board of Missions archives.   H. J. Graham

1006. Howard, James H. THE HENRY DAVIS DRUM RITE: AN UNUSUAL DRUM RELIGION VARIANT OF THE MINNESOTA OJIBWA. *Plains Anthropologist 1966 11(32): 117-126.* Description of the drum religion or dream dance as a variant of the "old-time" ceremonial grass dances of the Prairie-Plains region. Many Christian elements are incorporated into it, such as the idea of brotherhood and goodwill between the Indian and the white man, visions and messages from the Virgin Mary, and ceremonies on Easter Sunday. The author relates a visit to a ceremony at Mille Lacs, Minnesota, and describes the proceeding in detail. Illus., biblio. K. Adelfang

1007. Lambert, Bernard. MISSION PRIORITIES: INDIANS OR MINERS? *Michigan Hist. 1967 51(4): 323-334.* Discusses the work of Catholic and Protestant missionaries in Michigan's Keweenaw Peninsula during the 1840's. Primary and secondary sources are cited to show that the copper miners as well as the Chippewa stood in need of salvation. J. K. Flack

1008. Schoenfuhs, Walter P. "O TEBENINGEION"—"O DEAREST JESUS." *Concordia Hist. Inst. Q. 1964 37(3): 95-114.* An account of Lutheran missionary activity among the Chippewa (Ojibwa) Indians of Michigan. The author concludes that the Lutheran Indian Mission failed "because the church could not comprehend and adjust to the swiftly moving events of the day and because the church was either unable or unwilling to make those sacrifices which a determined Indian mission program demanded!" Based on primary and secondary sources; illus. D. J. Abramoske

Delaware

1009. Brown, D. Alexander. BLACK BEAVER. *Am. Hist. Illus. 1967 2(2): 32-41.* "Sikitomaker," or Black Beaver, the anglicized name he chose, was a Delaware Indian and a famous scout for military and scientific explorers in the West. In the 1830's he had been a trapper for the American Fur Company, and in the late 1840's he served in the Mexican War. Respected by both white men and Indians, Black Beaver was the last chief of the Delaware. J. D. Filipiak

1010. Jennings, Francis P. THE DELAWARE INTERREGNUM. *Pennsylvania Mag. of Hist. and Biog. 1965 89(2): 174-198.* Argues that the Delaware Indians "were not so much passive as suppressed," and that "their eruption in 1755 was not a sudden thing, though its dramatic qualities made it seem so...." The details of the deceitful manner in which Pennsylvania officials acquired Indian lands are presented, and it is shown how these transactions incurred the lasting enmity of the natives. Based on the Penn Papers and the Logan Papers in the Historical Society of Pennsylvania, other primary materials, and secondary sources. 71 notes. D. P. Gallagher

1011. Wurster, L. E. THE EARLY HISTORY OF THE LOYALSOCK. *Now and Then 1964 14(9): 239-249.* A general survey of the Loyalsock Valley in Lycoming County, Pennsylvania, beginning with the period of occupation by the Delaware Indians. The earliest white settlers consisting of immigrants from Scotland, Ireland, and Germany built an economic base for the region during the early 19th century on the leather and lumber industries. H. Ershkowitz

Iroquois (Five Nations, Six Nations)

1012. Chafe, Wallace L. LINGUISTIC EVIDENCE FOR THE RELATIVE AGE OF IROQUOIS RELIGIOUS PRACTICES. *Southwestern J. of Anthrop. 1964 20(3): 278-285.* An attempt to apply linguistic analysis to the Iroquois language in order to determine the relative age of Iroquois religious practices. Based on secondary sources; biblio.   C. N. Warren

1013. Day, Gordon M. IROQUOIS: AN ETYMOLOGY. *Ethnohist. 1968 15(4): 389-402.* Offers a new theory of the source of the word "Iroquois" as coming from a Montagnais pronunciation of an Iroquois name. 7 notes, biblio. on local Indian languages.   R. S. Burns

1014. Desrosiers, Leo-Paul. FRONTENAC ET LA PAIX, (1672-1682) [Frontenac and the Peace (1672-1682)]. *R. d'Hist. de l'Amérique Française [Canada] 1963 17(2): 159-184.* Appreciating the vulnerability of New France, Governor Frontenac pursued a peaceful defensive policy with regard to the Iroquois in his first term of office. He tried to "Frenchify" and neutralize the Iroquois and to prevent them from falling into the arms of the English. He kept his Indian allies on the defensive but at the same time promised to help them if they were attacked; he occupied the island of Montreal to protect the settlements. By keeping a dialogue open with the Iroquois and using his *coureurs des bois* to stiffen his Indian allies, Frontenac pursued a careful and subtle policy. He had no intention of letting matters reach the point of war, and he succeeded.

L. F. S. Upton

1015. Desrosiers, Léo-Paul. FRONTENAC L'ARTISAN DE LA VICTOIRE [Frontenac, architect of victory]. *Cahiers des Dix [Canada] 1963 28: 93-145.* The policy of friendship with the Iroquois pursued by the Marquis de Tracy, Sieur de Courcelle, Talon, and Frontenac was thrown away by La Barre with disastrous results. Marquis de Denonville understood the situation but failed to follow a peaceful policy. English influence with the Iroquois grew in the 1680's, but its use was temporarily halted by the friendship of the kings of England and France. With Frontenac's return as governor in 1689 the French reopened negotiations with the Iroquois, the fur trade resumed, and an attempt was made to break the Anglo-Iroquois alliance. Describes these maneuvers and the reactions in Albany, New York.   L. F. S. Upton

1016. Desrosiers, Léo-Paul. LE PAIX DE 1667 [The Peace of 1667]. *Cahiers des Dix [Canada] 1964 29: 25-45.* Peace treaties with the Iroquois in 1645 and 1653 had not protected New France. In the early 1660's the Iroquois stepped up their guerrilla warfare. French campaigns into Indian country under de Salières and de Tracy proved indecisive: the enemy simply disappeared and his fighting power remained intact. Yet the English, who had recently taken over at Albany, wanted their Indian allies to be at peace and were unwilling to aid them. In these circumstances de Tracy determined on a policy of friendship with the Iroquois.

The development of this policy and of its acceptance at Versailles is traced. Friendship remained the basis of French and Iroquois policy until the governorship of Joseph de La Barre. L. F. S. Upton

1017. Fenton, William N., ed. THE JOURNAL OF JAMES EMLEN KEPT ON A TRIP TO CANANDAIGUA, NEW YORK. *Ethnohist. 1965 12(4): 279-334.* A transcription of Emlen's journal which supplements William Savery's account of the 1794 treaty between the United States and the Six Nations. 32 notes. R. S. Burns

1018. Garratt, John G. THE FOUR INDIAN KINGS. *Hist. Today [Great Britain] 1968 18(2): 93-101.* Queen Anne invited four Indian chiefs of the sachems from the Confederacy of the Five Nations to London in 1710. They were lavishly entertained in order that they might be so impressed with Britain that they would encourage Indians in the Northeast to ally with Britain. As did many other British schemes, this one came to nothing. Illus. L. A. Knafla

1019. Hamilton, Milton W. SIR WILLIAM JOHNSON: INTERPRETER OF THE IROQUOIS. *Ethnohist. 1963 10(3): 270-286.* Johnson's success and fame as a trader, linguist, militia commander, and superintendent of Indian affairs for the northern colonies have obscured his importance as an authoritative interpreter of Iroquois life and culture. Peter Kalm's *Travels,* James Adair's *History of the American Indians,* the Royal Society *Transactions,* and 13 published volumes of the Sir William Johnson *Papers* all testify to significant contributions that Johnson made to ethnology and materia medica. H. J. Graham

1020. Hassler, William W. THE REAL HIAWATHA. *Am. Hist. Illus. 1966 1(2): 35-38, 53.* A biographical account of Hiawatha, an Onondaga medicine man who in many ways was even greater than Longfellow's epic hero. Hiawatha is believed to have lived during the 16th century. He and Deganawidah, another "spiritual statesman," formed the League of Five Nations which drew together the five segments of the Iroquois tribe. "The paramount objectives of the League were peace and unification." For over two centuries this league was a powerful force among Indians and colonists along the east coast. 2 illus. M. J. McBaine

1021. Jezierski, John V., ed. and trans. A 1751 JOURNAL OF ABBE FRANÇOIS PICQUET. *New York Hist. Soc. Q. 1970 54(4): 360-381.* Discusses and presents the first complete translation in English of the journal of the Jesuit, François Picquet (1708-81). The journal concerns his journey in the Great Lakes area in 1751. Abbé Picquet tried to gain recruits for his mission (located on the St. Lawrence River in northern New York) and to ascertain the situation in the area, in particular French relations with the Iroquois. Based on primary sources; 7 illus., 45 notes. C. L. Grant

1022. Lesage, Germain, O.M.I. L'ARIVEE DU REGIMENT DE CARIGNAN [The arrival of the Carignan Regiment]. *R. de l'U. d'Ottawa [Canada] 1965 35(1):*

11-34. Describes the expedition under the Marquis de Tracy sent to New France in 1665 to protect the colony from the Iroquois. The troops, about one thousand in number, departed from La Rochelle in three separate groups in April and May, and the last detachment reached Quebec in September. Emphasis is given to biographical data about the officers of the expedition, details of the voyages from France, and the initial reception of the force in Quebec. Based primarily on correspondence from the Archives Publiques du Canada and early ecclesiastical records; 180 notes.   J. H. Smart

1023. Lewin, Howard. A FRONTIER DIPLOMAT: ANDREW MONTOUR. *Pennsylvania Hist. 1966 33(2): 153-186.* Centers on Montour's services as diplomat and interpreter from 1742 to 1768. Excluding some success during Pontiac's Rebellion, Montour's activities as a soldier left something to be desired. Part Indian, he was trusted by Indians and was made a counselor by the Six Nations. As a diplomat, he served Virginia, Pennsylvania, and Indian Superintendent Sir William Johnson. Montour's relations with George Washington, Conrad Weiser, and George Croghan are described in detail. Montour received large tracts of land for his services, but he lost most of these rewards and was frequently in debt. He was noted for his attachment to whiskey, but he managed to remain sober when his services were most needed. Based on a variety of primary sources; 128 notes.
                                                              D. C. Swift

1024. McAdams, Donald R. THE SULLIVAN EXPEDITION—SUCCESS OR FAILURE. *New York Hist. Soc. Q. 1970 54(1): 53-81.* In the late summer of 1779 Major General John Sullivan led an expedition against the Iroquois. The expedition was considered a success and has been so regarded by subsequent historians. Although more careful study raises several questions which need further research, one conclusion seems valid. In view of the Indian activities in the years following the expedition, the expedition did not break the power of the Iroquois. Thus, the expedition did not succeed in its major objective. Based on primary sources; 5 illus., 48 notes.   C. L. Grant

1025. Naroll, Raoul. THE CAUSES OF THE FOURTH IROQUOIS WAR. *Ethnohist. 1969 16(1): 51-82.* "Historians and others have generally cited economic causes, most especially those involving the fur trade, for the various wars in which the Iroquois and French were involved during the 17th century. A detailed study of the Fourth Iroquois War (1657-1667) suggests that other factors, and lack of cross-cultural understanding between the French and Iroquois, are more important in understanding the conflict."   J

1026. Nash, Gary B. THE QUEST FOR THE SUSQUEHANNA VALLEY: NEW YORK, PENNSYLVANIA, AND THE SEVENTEENTH-CENTURY FUR TRADE. *New York Hist. 1967 48(1): 3-27.* William Penn realized that the Susquehanna River system held the key to the Iroquois fur trade as well as watered a vast region of fertile land. In 1683, he purchased the Susquehanna Valley from the local Indian tribes but, since they were vassals of the Iroquois, he had to clear the sale with the Iroquois Confederation. Governor Thomas Dongan of New York, fearing that Penn's acquisition of the Susquehanna would destroy New York's dominance of the fur trade, sought to block the transfer to Penn. In return for arms and the promise of English support against the French, the Iroquois transferred the title of the Susquehanna to Dongan, who in turn agreed to yield the title to Penn as soon as Indian relations had been stabilized and the French threat removed. He reneged on his pledge, however, desiring to safeguard New York's fur trade. It was not until 1697, when Dongan was in desperate financial straits, that he finally yielded the Susquehanna to Penn for 100 pounds. Based on primary and secondary sources; map, 78 notes.

G. Kurland

1027. Otterbein, Keith F. WHY THE IROQUOIS WON: AN ANALYSIS OF IROQUOIS MILITARY TACTICS. *Ethnohist. 1964 11(1): 56-63.* Attributes Iroquois military success and the subjugation of adjoining tribes to superior tactics and weapons—specifically, to better defensive armor and guerrilla action in the 1630's; to arquebusses in the 1640's; and, in the period beginning 1660, to better-fed warriors, each a master of sniper tactics armed with his own musket (as members of poorer, nonagricultural adjacent tribes often were not).

H. J. Graham

1028. Rogers, E. S. and Updike, Lee. THE IROQUOIS. *Beaver [Canada] 1971 301(1): 46-49.* In 1600, some 16 thousand Iroquois lived between the Hudson Valley and Lake Erie, grouped in a confederacy of five tribes. Their natural environment was diversified, with much wildlife, but they were primarily horticulturalists living in permanent villages. Describes their religious observations: the Maple ceremony, Green Corn ceremony, Mid-Winter ceremony. Spring was a time for fishing and sowing, summer for leisure and warfare, autumn for storing and hunting, and winter for leisure. Illus.

L. F. S. Upton

1029. Stanley, G. F. G. THE SIGNIFICANCE OF THE SIX NATIONS' PARTICIPATION IN THE WAR OF 1812. *Ontario Hist. [Canada] 1963 55(4): 215-231.* The support of the British by some Indians in the Seven Years War "revealed a break in the unity of the Iroquois League. The American Revolution witnessed its complete disruption." In spite of an early policy of neutrality by American and Canadian Iroquois, the Indians were involved in fighting in 1812 and 1813. Significance is attached to the Battle of Beaver Dam where "Iroquois were pitted against Iroquois," to the timely action of the Canadian Indians at Queenston Heights, and to the importance of their numbers when few British troops were available.

J. M. E. Usher

1030. Stanley, George F. G. THE SIX NATIONS AND THE AMERICAN REVOLUTION. *Ontario Hist. [Canada] 1964 56(4): 217-232.* Having long occupied a buffer zone between competing colonial powers, the Iroquois were at last driven from their lands during the American Revolution when their old allies, the British and the American colonies, had divided in civil war. Though their neutrality was early encouraged by both sides, first the British and then the Americans forced them to adopt a belligerent role. Because the main threat to their lands was the advancing American settlement, most fought with the British and gained by doing so. The Iroquois, already losing to American settlement, received new lands from Britain in reward for their military aid.		G. Emery

1031. Tooker, Elisabeth. THE IROQUOIS WHITE DOG SACRIFICE IN THE LATTER PART OF THE EIGHTEENTH CENTURY. *Ethnohist. 1965 12(2): 129-140.* The account of the Iroquois Midwinter, or New Year's festival—in which a white dog was ritually strangled, painted with red spots, decorated, hung from a pole, and later burned as an offering to the Great Creator—is not by Samuel Kirkland, as was formerly believed. 7 notes, biblio.		R. S. Burns

1032. Trigger, Bruce G. CRITERIA FOR IDENTIFYING THE LOCATIONS OF HISTORIC INDIAN SITES: A CASE STUDY FROM MONTREAL. *Ethnohist. 1969 16(4): 303-316.* "Criteria which should be universally helpful in the identification of locations of historic Indian sites are tested in the case of a site in downtown Montreal, Quebec, long believed by many to be the Iroquoian village of Hochelaga, visited by Jacques Cartier in 1535. Results suggest the site is not that of Hochelaga."		J

1033. Voget, Fred. A SIX NATIONS' DIARY, 1891-1894. *Ethnohist. 1969 16(4): 345-360.* "A ledger-type diary kept by an Iroquois Indian farmer on the Six Nations Reserve in Ontario, Canada, during the late 19th century is examined for the information it contains concerning the seasonal cycle, income, labor exchange, and other aspects of Iroquois life of the period."		J

1034. Wessel, Thomas R. AGRICULTURE AND IROQUOIS HEGEMONY IN NEW YORK, 1610-1779. *Maryland Historian 1970 1(2): 93-104.* Suggests that Iroquois power was derived from the sophisticated societal nexus surrounding agriculture. Discounts previous theories, which variously attribute Iroquois hegemony to their early use of firearms, to a desire to control the fur trade, or to their political organization. Each hypothesis ignores the basic fact about the Iroquois: they were sedentary agriculturalists and their opponents were not. This relative freedom from want allowed the development of the Iroquois Confederation and permitted the Iroquois to develop and maintain hegemony over interior New York for over 150 years. Based on Smithsonian Institution and secondary sources; 22 notes.		G. O. Gagnon

Iroquois, Mohawk

1035. Hamilton, Milton W. JOSEPH BRANT—THE MOST PAINTED INDIAN. *New York Hist. 1958 39(2): 119-132.* Traces briefly the events in the life of this 18th-century Mohawk leader which led to portraits by Gilbert Stuart, George Romney, Charles Willson Peale, Benjamin West and Ezra Ames. The author concludes from the portraits and from current comment that the contemporary image of Brant was a far less cruel one than that popularized by 19th-century historians.		A. B. Rollins

1036. Johnston, C. M. WILLIAM CLAUS AND JOHN NORTON: A STRUG-
GLE FOR POWER IN OLD ONTARIO. *Ontario Hist. [Canada] 1965 57(2):
101-108.* A Scot, John Norton, was an adopted Mohawk chief on the strength
of his influence with the Six Nations Indians and his military leadership of them
during the War of 1812. When the British government gave Norton the power
to distribute British gifts to worthy Six Nations warriors, William Claus of the
Indian Affairs Department, jealous of Norton's influence with the Indians and
fearful that Norton might abuse his patronage power, criticized Norton and
impeded him whenever possible. Norton responded with criticism of Claus for
his petty obstructionism.   G. Emery

1037. Johnston, Charles M. JOSEPH BRANT, THE GRAND RIVER LANDS
AND THE NORTHWEST CRISIS. *Ontario Hist. [Canada] 1963 55(4): 267-
282.* Joseph Brant claimed the Indians were a separate nation and were able to
sell their Grand River lands without reference to the Crown. He faced the
determined opposition of Lieut. Governor Simcoe. After Simcoe's withdrawal
Brant was able to take advantage of a frontier crisis in 1797, the prospect of
Franco-Spanish aggression in the Mississippi region and rumors of an Indian
uprising in Ontario to extort from Peter Russell a confirmation of the land sales.
The honesty of Brant's own financial dealings was often doubted, as the Six
Nations appeared to gain little from the sale of the land. Based on the Powell
Papers and various papers relating to the Six Nation Indians in the possession
of the New York Historical Society. 59 notes.   J. M. E. Usher

1038. Johnston, Jean. MOLLY BRANT: MOHAWK MATRON. *Ontario Hist.
[Canada] 1964 56(2): 105-124.* In 1759 an upper-class Mohawk, Molly Brant,
became housekeeper for Sir William Johnson, beloved British Indian agent living
with the Iroquois. Molly managed Johnson's large household establishment well,
and she bore Johnson nine children. When Johnson died in 1774, Molly and her
brother Joseph inherited his influence with the Six Nations Indians. Molly proved
influential in keeping the confederacy largely on the British side during the
American Revolution. In 1796 Molly died with doubts that her people, who had
lost their ancestral lands in the war, could rest secure in their cultural identity
among the European civilizations.   G. Emery

1039. Kelsay, Isabel T. JOSEPH BRANT: THE LEGEND AND THE MAN.
New York Hist. 1959 40(4): 368-379. Discusses the difficulties of research on this
prominent Mohawk Iroquois leader, particularly the problem of separating legend from fact in the Revolutionary period. The author describes some of Brant's
personal characteristics and certain facets of American Indian culture illustrated
by his career.   A. B. Rollins

1040. Klinck, Carl F. NEW LIGHT ON JOHN NORTON. *Tr. of the Royal Soc.
of Can. 1966 4(Section 2): 167-177.* John Norton (ca. 1760- 1825) was the son
of a man who lived with the Cherokees and of a Scotswoman and was adopted
into the Mohawks as Teyoninhokarawen. The adopted nephew and deputy of
Joseph Brant, whom he succeeded as chief, he has unjustly been written off as
a failure. A fair copy of a 1,000-page manuscript written by him describing his

life and travels among the Indians has been recently brought to light in the library of the Duke of Northumberland at Alnwick Castle and will shortly be published by the Champlain Society. This paper is a literary biography, a study of the man in relation to his manuscript. 37 notes.   L. F. S. Upton

1041. Lingard, Bill. LACROSSE—THE FASTEST GAME ON TWO FEET. *Beaver [Canada] 1969 300(Autumn): 12-16.* The first French explorers of the St. Lawrence River in 1535 found the Indians playing a game with a netted stick that looked like a crozier—hence the name, lacrosse. Sometimes opposing tribes, one thousand strong, would play a very violent form of the game, lasting several days and ending in pitched battles. The author describes the manufacture of lacrosse sticks at the present day: 97 percent of the world's supply comes from a factory on an island in the St. Lawrence 60 miles upstream from Montreal, and the craftsmen are all Mohawk Indians. Illus.   L. F. S. Upton

1042. Torok, C. H. THE TYENDINAGA MOHAWKS. *Ontario Hist. [Canada] 1965 57(2): 69-77.* Studies the Iroquois confederacy during the period of the American Revolution to show that the Iroquois tribes grew by groups splitting off from parent bodies to form fairly autonomous new villages. The example of the Tyendinaga Mohawks is used to support the thesis that the local village autonomy had been in uneasy balance with the centralized league authority ever since the league's creation. As the league grew old, the village autonomy reasserted itself and marginal factions broke away to form new tribes based on the village.   G. Emery

Iroquois, Oneida

1043. Ricciardelli, Alex F. THE ADOPTION OF WHITE AGRICULTURE BY THE ONEIDA INDIANS. *Ethnohist. 1963 10(4): 309-328.* Reexamines Oneida society and culture through three stages, in three environments (New York, Wisconsin, Ontario), stressing five factors that made farming the prevailing mode of life by 1860: necessity, tribal ideals, a strong horticultural tradition among women, precept and example of helpful Indian and white neighbors, relocation.   H. J. Graham

Iroquois, Seneca

1044. Berkhoffer, Robert F., Jr. FAITH AND FACTIONALISM AMONG THE SENECAS: THEORY AND ETHNOHISTORY. *Ethnohist. 1965 12(2): 99-112.* Tests Neil Smelser's modal concept of collective behavior against the Handsome Lake religion and its opposing missionary movement in the 1790's to 1820's. A continuing factionalism in the Senecas is unaccounted for by the modal. 7 notes, biblio.   R. S. Burns

1045. Congdon, Charles E. THE GOOD NEWS OF HANDSOME LAKE. *New York Folklore Q. 1967 23(4): 290-297.* Quotes from a 1799 diary of Henry Simmons, Jr., a school teacher who spoke to Handsome Lake (ca. 1735-1815) at the time the Seneca had his first visions. Gai-wee-yo of Gan-i-o-dai-yo (the good news of Handsome Lake) has been repeated word-for-word traditionally in Seneca religious ceremonies for 140 years.　　　　　　W. S. Rinaldo

1046. Fenton, William N. ANSWERS TO GOVERNOR CASS'S QUESTIONS BY JACOB JAMESON, A SENECA [CA. 1821-25]. *Ethnohist. 1969 16(2): 113-140.* "Sometime in the 1820's, Governor Lewis Cass, compiling data on the tribes of the Northwest Territory, used a questionnaire in asking questions of Jacob Jameson, a literate Seneca Indian. The schedule of replies survived, and a copy made by Vernon Kinietz many years later is presented here with an introduction and notes by the editor."　　　　　　J

1047. Fenton, William N. TOWARD THE GRADUAL CIVILIZATION OF THE INDIAN NATIVES: THE MISSIONARY AND LINGUISTIC WORK OF ASHER WRIGHT (1803-1875) AMONG THE SENECAS OF WESTERN NEW YORK. *Pro. of the Am. Phil. Soc. 1956 100(6): 567-581.* Describes changes in Seneca culture after Sullivan's raid in 1779 in terms of modern disaster-theory. The author discusses the cosmology, demography, and social and political organization of the Seneca, using the notes written in 1859 by Asher Wright, a Dartmouth graduate who learned the Seneca language and developed a written language for teaching. Fundamental in Seneca culture were the principles of unanimity in all tribal decisions, and land as common property. The author describes the disintegrating effect of the violation of these principles by the whites, and then gives an account of the reconstruction promoted by Wright and other Christian missionaries. One of their major efforts was the establishment in 1855 of the Thomas Indian School on the Cattaraugus Reservation. Illus.
　　　　　　N. Kurland

1048. Painter, Levinus K. JACOB TAYLOR: QUAKER MISSIONARY STATESMAN. *Bull. of Friends Hist. Assoc. 1959 48(2): 116-127.* Discusses the settlement of Jacob Taylor in what is now Collins, New York, and the work of the Quakers among the Seneca Indians on the Cattaraugus Reservation. In 1808 the Quakers purchased a tract of 700 acres on the site of the present town of Collins, just east of the Cattaraugus Reservation. Here Taylor labored from 1808 to 1821 to teach the Indians the ways of civilized life, but with limited success. He was, however, able to prevent land speculators from dislodging the Indians. Although work among the Senecas languished after Taylor's retirement, a Quaker community grew up at Collins. Based on the records of the Indian Committee of Philadelphia Yearly Meeting in the Department of Records, Philadelphia.
　　　　　　T. L. Moir

1049. Snyderman, George S. THE MANUSCRIPT COLLECTIONS OF THE PHILADELPHIA YEARLY MEETING OF FRIENDS PERTAINING TO THE AMERICAN INDIAN. *Pro. of the Am. Phil. Soc. 1958 102(6): 613-620.* Summary and evaluation of documentary sources primarily on the Seneca Indians, indicating kinds of questions which can be answered from documents and giving details of some of the more important subjects covered in the manuscripts.
　　　　　　N. Kurland

1050. Snyderman, George S., ed. HALLIDAY JACKSON'S JOURNAL OF A VISIT PAID TO THE INDIANS OF NEW YORK (1806). *Pro. of the Am. Phil. Soc. 1957 101(6): 565-588.* Presents the annotated text of this journal, with an introduction by the editor relating the background of the mission sent by the Quakers to the Seneca Indians in 1806 and giving an account of the condition of the Indians at the time and Jackson's relations with them. As a member of the mission Jackson noted the progress and problems of Indians arising from the Quaker work with them. This journal provides another view of the same visit described in the journal of John Philips. Documented.   N. Kurland

1051. Wayman, Dorothy G. [QUAKER PIONEERS: THE CLENDENONS]. *Quaker Hist.*

QUAKER PIONEERS IN MC KEAN COUNTY, PENNSYLVANIA, 1962 51(1): 20-31. Editorial introduction with annotated journal, accounts and letters of Robert Clendenon, 1812-13. Friends settled with the Senecas on Tunesassa Creek (Cattaraugus County, N.Y.) in 1798. Clendenon moved from Lancaster County to Ceres in 1812.

FRIENDS ON THE FRONTIER: THE CLENDENON FAMILY, 1965 54(1): 3-23. Contains two letters from a Seneca, an account of an 1826 journey up the Susquehanna River from Maryland to Pennsylvania, and family history and documents.   T. D. S. Bassett

Massachusetts

1052. Adams, Thomas Boylston. BAD NEWS FROM VIRGINIA. *Virginia Mag. of Hist. and Biog. 1966 74(2): 131-140.* Argues that the March 1623 surprise attack by the Plymouth settlers on the Massachusetts Indians resulted from knowledge of the March 1622 massacre in Virginia and reports of a similar conspiracy among the Massachusetts Bay tribes. "From this time forth the Indians dwelt in terror of the whites, and the whites of the Indians."

K. J. Bauer

Menominee

1053. Cope, Alfred and Haygood, William C., ed. A MISSION TO THE MENOMINEE: ALFRED COPE'S GREEN BAY DIARY. *Wisconsin Mag. of Hist. 1966 49(4): 302-323, 50(1): 18-42, (2): 120-146, 1967 50(3): 211-241.* Part I. The federal government on 18 October 1848 forced the Menominee Indians to relinquish their Wisconsin lands in return for 300 thousand acres in Minnesota and 350 thousand dollars. The tribe stipulated that 40 thousand dollars would go to people of mixed Menominee blood who had aided the tribe in the past. Thomas Wistar (1789-1876), chosen to handle the disbursement, selected his fellow Quaker and Philadelphian Cope (1806-75) to accompany him to Green Bay to attend a tribal council. 2 illus., map, 6 photos, 43 notes. Part II. Relates the arrival of the chiefs, including Oshkosh (a Menominee), and describes the council. 8 illus., 25 notes. Part III. Wistar left by stagecoach and steamer for New York to pick up 40 thousand dollars in gold, the only kind of payment the Indians would take for their land. Cope stayed on in Wisconsin, recording his impression of the country around Green Bay—trees, animals, insects, and Indian "farms." He noted many customs of the Menominee and Oneida, including the Oneida version of lacrosse and their 4th of July celebrations. Mentions Oneida chiefs Daniel Bread, or Tega-wia-tiron (1800-73), and Elijah Skenadore, or Shónesés. 8 illus., 3 photos, 20 notes. Part IV. Details the payment of the money to the Indians. Pictures the minutiae of the report by Cope and Wistar to President Zachary Taylor and the Secretary of the Interior. Cope left a "vivid and valuable picture of Indian-white relations in Wisconsin's first year of statehood and the contemporary social scene." 10 photos, 82 notes. H. A. Negaard

Miami

1054. Anson, Bert. CHIEF FRANCIS LAFONTAINE AND THE MIAMI EMIGRATION FROM INDIANA. *Indiana Mag. of Hist. 1964 60(3): 241-268.* Discusses the activities of whites and Indian leaders involved in the evacuation of the Miami tribe from Indiana to lands farther west in the 1840's. Emphasizes the significance of Lafontaine, chief of the Miamis at the time, in leading and shaping the response of this tribe to the pressures of whites for removal, a factor in the negotiations previously underplayed or overlooked. Based principally on records of the Bureau of Indian Affairs, in the National Archives.
J. Findlay

1055. Blain, Harry S. LITTLE TURTLE'S WATCH. *Northwest Ohio Q. 1965 37(1): 17-32.* Chief Little Turtle or Michikinikwa (1752-1812) of the Miami tribe urged his people to make peace with the United States shortly before the Battle of Fallen Timbers in 1794. The British made an unsuccessful attempt to win his allegiance shortly before the War of 1812 by giving him a valuable gold watch. The article describes this relic in detail. W. F. Zornow

1056. Faben, Walter W. INDIANS OF THE TRI-STATE AREA. THE MIA-MIS, 1654-1752. *Northwest Ohio Q. 1969 41(4): 157-162.* A few random and unrelated comments on the Miami Indians, from their first contact with white hunters near their villages northwest of Green Bay to the eve of the outbreak of the French and Indian War. The author touches briefly on such topics as: 1) the long migration of the Miamis from their original home near Hudson Bay to the headwaters of the Miami; 2) the Miamis at war with their Indian neighbors; 3) Miami dealings with the British and French traders; and 4) the Miamis and the missionaries. Based on secondary sources; 21 notes. W. F. Zornow

Micmac

1057. Hutton, Elizabeth A. INDIAN AFFAIRS IN NOVA SCOTIA, 1760-1834. *Nova Scotia Hist. Soc. Collections [Canada] 1963 34: 33-54.* Explains how contact between the primitive Micmac Indians and the Europeans resulted in a clash of cultures, which eventually caused a breakdown of the more primitive way of life and a dependence upon white men. Reasons for this dependency, and a consequent acceptance of land on a reservation, are given as the encroachment upon the Micmacs' habitual hunting areas and the decline in their fur-trading operations.   R. J. C. Ford

Ottawa

1058. Bauman, Robert F. THE OTTAWA TRADING SYSTEM. *Northwest Ohio Q. 1964 Part I, 36(2): 60-78, Part II, (3): 146-167.* Michilimackinac, Manitoulin Island, Saulte Saint Marie and several islands of Lake Huron were areas rich in furs, fish and game. They also provided the Indian tribes with convenient assembly points and were easy to defend against any hostile operation. The Ottawas built a formidable trading empire in this region. Most of their furs flowed into French Canada. After learning that the British and Dutch paid more for furs than the French, they tried to establish trade relations with these two nations via the Iroquois. They were aware of the commercial advantage offered by the British, but they feared the Iroquois too much to be drawn into their orbit. By 1700 the Ottawa still controlled the fur trade of this region. During the closing decades of the 17th century the Ottawa expanded their trading system southward from Michilimackinac into the Lake Erie-Lake Ontario region. Furs that once flowed to Canada along a northern route now flowed there along the shorter Erie-Ontario-St. Lawrence route. England claimed that this land was conquered by the Iroquois, but since the Ottawa shipped a steady stream of furs to Canada, the only possible conclusion is that the Iroquois really exerted limited control in an area allegedly "conquered" by them. Based on *Jesuit Relations* and other documentary material.   W. F. Zornow

1059. Kurtz, Henry. THE RELIEF OF FORT PITT, AUGUST 1763. *Hist. Today [Great Britain] 1963 13(11): 784-794.* The British defeat of the Pontiac Conspiracy stymied the Indian attempt to oust the British from their western frontier and, perhaps, to wrest all of North America from the white man.
L. A. Knafla

1060. Orians, George H. PONTIAC IN LITERATURE. *Northwest Ohio Q. 1963 35(4): 144-163, 1964 36(1): 31-53.* Part I. Although he apparently alluded to Pontiac in his journals of 1760, Major Robert Rogers did not specifically identify him before his *Concise Account of North America* in 1765. Rogers also wrote a play about Pontiac in 1766, and Alexander Macomb used him as the central figure in a play written in 1835. *Wacousta,* by the Canadian John Richardson in 1832, was the first important novel to use Pontiac as a theme. Francis Parkman's *History of the Conspiracy of Pontiac* (1851) provided a classic account of his career. Historical material turned up since Parkman's day has corrected or supplemented his narrative without taking any luster off his penetrating study. Pontiac passed out of literature for several years, but at the turn of the century he returned as a theme in *A Spectre of Power* (1903) by Charles Egbert Craddock (Mary Noailles Murfree), *A Sword on the Old Frontier* (1903) by Randall Parrish, and *The Heroine of the Strait* (1902), by Mary Crowley. Based on secondary sources; illus., 15 notes. Part II. Although historical fiction revived him in 1925 after 20 years of submergence, Pontiac did not reappear as a significant literary figure until 1937. The author describes the post-1938 fiction in which Pontiac played a role, concentrating on those novels centering around affairs in Detroit and those based on events at Fort Pitt.   W. F. Zornow

Pawtuxet

1061. Adolf, Leonard A. SQUANTO'S ROLE IN PILGRIM DIPLOMACY. *Ethnohist. 1964 11(3): 247-261.* Collates materials and reexamines standard accounts relating to the Pawtuxet Indian, who befriended the Pilgrims, from December 1620 until his death in September 1622. It is suggested that Squanto's services as guide-pilot, negotiator, and diplomat—especially his friendliness and his knowledge of English acquired during a series of visits and residences in England, Spain, and Virginia 1614? - 1620—were "equally [as] important to the survival and prosperity of the early Plymouth colony" as his better known teaching of the colonists to fish, trap, and plant corn.   H. J. Graham

Pequot

1062. Vaughan, Alden T. PEQUOTS AND PURITANS: THE CAUSES OF THE WAR OF 1637. *William and Mary Q. 1964 21(2): 256-269.* Observes that the accepted theory that the Pequots were chronically unable to get along with any neighbors, although partly valid, "is not the whole story." The harshness of the Puritans and "the assumption of the right to discipline neighboring Indians" caused the war, the aim of which was not land, per se, but jurisdiction over the region.   E. Oberholzer Jr.

Potawatomi *(Fire Nation)*

1063. Clifton, James A. CHICAGO WAS THEIRS. *Chicago Hist. 1970 1(1): 4-17.* Traces the history of the Potawatomi Indians. Their origins are obscure but, by 1500 at the latest, they were moving westward along the northern shores of Lakes Huron and Superior. They first came to the attention of the French explorer Samuel de Champlain in 1616. By the opening decades of the 18th century they were no longer small, scattered bands of hunters. As they pushed southward into prairie and woodland belts around Lake Michigan during the late-18th century, their mastery of agriculture and other pursuits promoted the growth of semisedentary bands. Their villages of Fort Saint Joseph, Fort Detroit, and Chicago had become quite large. Allied with the British, they took up arms against the United States during the Revolution. In 1833 the Federal Government expelled the Potawatomi from their lands in Wisconsin, Illinois, Michigan, and Indiana. After their removal west of the Mississippi River, they continued to resist change and assimilation, as they do to this day. Based on the author's forthcoming book, *The Prairie People;* illus.   D. J. Abramoske

1064. Faben, Walter W. INDIANS OF THE TRI-STATE AREA, THE POTOWATOMIS, THE REMOVAL. *Northwest Ohio Q. 1968 40(2): 68-84.* A historical summary of the Indian Removal Act of 1830 and an account of the

250   *Indians of the United States & Canada*

removal of some Potawatomi bands from Indiana, Ohio, and Michigan. Records concerning removals from Ohio are scant, and so the author focuses on minor operations in Fulton and Williams counties. More attention is given to removals from Indiana and Michigan. The story of removals from Indiana is centered around the case of Chief Mi-no-mi-nee, whose stubborn, but unsuccessful, fight to remain in the land of his fathers finally prompted the U.S. government to raise a monument to him and his 859 followers. The story of Potawatomi removals from Michigan is more depressing and dishonorable, since U.S. troops were used to herd the Indians from their homes. Based on government publications on Indian removals, articles, and books; illus., 43 notes.   W. F. Zornow

1065. Wakefield, Francis. THE ELUSIVE MASCOUTENS. *Michigan Hist. 1966 50(3): 228-234.* Discusses the many attempts to identify the Potawatomi (Mascouten), or "Fire Nation," a polygenetic Algonquian group whose exact location has been a matter of great confusion ever since they were first described by 17th-century French explorers.   J. K. Flack

Sauk

1066. Aumann, F. R., Briggs, J. E., and Peterson, William J. KEOKUK. *Palimpsest 1965 46(5): 225-272.* A biography of the Sauk chief and warrior. While a warrior and a masterful politician, Keokuk was in the tradition of the great Indian orators. His desire for peace with the white man led him into a bitter rivalry with the belligerent and better known Black Hawk, and his oratory ultimately won the day for peace. Illus.   D. W. Curl

Sokoki

1067. Day, Gordon M. THE IDENTITY OF THE SOKOKIS. *Ethnohist. 1965 12(3): 237-249.* The Sokoki tribe is not the group of Indians that lived on the Saco River in the early 17th century. Actually, the Sokokis, or Soquackicks (Spuakheags) as the English knew them, lived on the Connecticut River north of the Pacomtucks. 9 notes, biblio.   R. S. Burns

St. Francis

1068. Potter, Gail M. THE CAPTIVITY OF JEMIMA HOWE. *New-England Galaxy 1966 8(1): 10-15.* Jemima Howe (1723-1805) was captured by the St. Francis Indians at Vernon, Vermont, in 1755. She remained a captive of the Indians and the French until 1760 when she returned to Vermont.   T. J. Farnham

Susquehanna

1069. Jennings, Francis. GLORY, DEATH, AND TRANSFIGURATION: THE SUSQUEHANNOCK INDIANS IN THE SEVENTEENTH CENTURY. *Pro. of the Am. Phil. Soc. 1968 112(1): 15-53.* Studies the Susquehanna

(Susquehannock) Indians in America during the 17th century. Knowledge of Susquehannock history is essential to the proper understanding of the colonial period, for these Indians were dispersed from their homeland as the result of Lord Baltimore's unsuccessful attempts to seize and claim the Delaware Bay for Maryland. Fearsome reprisals came from his attack on the Susquehannock, and these weakened his political control. His sorties against Delaware Bay alienated those colonies which could have helped protect him. The self-imposed isolation diluted his claims in the boundary dispute which developed along with the chartering of Pennsylvania. The varying relations of power and dependency among specific Indian peoples and specific European colonies are traced. Although relying on printed sources and secondary works, the author has attempted to compare previously unrelated groups of data and to extract fresh interpretations from them; this often involves considerable hypothesizing in order to fill in the substantial information gaps. Appendix, 4 maps, 160 notes. W. G. Morgan

Tulpehocken

1070. Jennings, Francis P. INCIDENT AT TULPEHOCKEN. *Pennsylvania Hist. 1968 35(4): 335-355.* Focuses upon a neglected aspect of Pennsylvania history—James Logan's loss of power in 1732. When Thomas Penn came to the colony in that year, he was aware that Logan had abused his power as agent for the proprietary family and its creditors to enrich himself. In addition to manipulation of Indian lands on the Brandywine and Penn lands on the Susquehanna, Logan had cheated the Tulpehocken, unlawfully attempted to sell land belonging to them, and had endeavored to diminish Penn family claims in the same area. Thomas Penn quietly stripped Logan of his position as land agent and secretary of the colony but permitted him to continue as chief justice and council member. The proprietor still employed Logan's knowledge, but he never again exercised the power he formerly enjoyed. The Tulpehocken were particularly hostile when war came to the province in 1755. Based on a variety of primary sources; 45 notes.
D. C. Swift

Wappinger

1071. Handlin, Oscar and Mark, Irving, eds. CHIEF DANIEL NIMHAM VS. ROGER MORRIS, BEVERLY ROBINSON, AND PHILIP PHILIPSE—AN INDIAN LAND CASE IN COLONIAL NEW YORK, 1765-1767. *Ethnohist. 1964 11(3): 193-246.* Reprints and edits British Museum Lansdowne MSS, 707, fol. 24 ff., "A geographic, historical Narrative or Summary," which documents the editors' article, "Land Cases in Colonial New York, 1765-1767," in the *New York Law Quarterly Review* 1942 19: 165-194. This deals with conflicts which resulted when "poor tenant farmers, settlers from New England, and civilized Wappinger Indians fought for their lands, in the courts and on the fields, against the great patentees who were striving to build up estates in Dutchess and Westchester Counties." The anonymous author, still unknown, was a Connecticut lawyer friendly to the Indian title and claimants. A sketch map shows the Beekman, Philipse, and Cortland Manor lands involved. H. J. Graham

Wyandot (Huron)

1072. Borkowski, Joseph A. SANDUSKY—INDIAN OR POLISH ORIGIN? *Polish Am. Studies 1968 25(1): 6-9.* Discusses whether the city is named for Sadowski, a Polish pioneer, or for Sandesti, the Indian phrase meaning "at the cold water." Cites sources for both sides, but decides on the Wyandot Indians.
S. R. Pliska

1073. Jury, Elsie McLeod. INDIAN VILLAGE AND MISSION SITES OF HURONIA. *Can. Geographical J. 1963 67(3): 94-103.* Tells of Indian settlements and Jesuit mission sites in the region south of Georgian Bay in Ontario. Recent archaeological work has added significantly to our knowledge of "a once-great nation." Maps, photos.
A. H. Lawrance

1074. Leitch, Adelaide. LAND OF THE WENDATS. *Beaver [Canada] 1963 294(Autumn): 14-19.* The earliest farmers and traders of Ontario, the Wyandot (Huron) called themselves "Wendats." Their descendants now live in Quebec, practicing some of the old crafts, particularly snowshoe making. The history of Huronia is being learned through archaeology. The Jesuit headquarters at Fort Ste. Marie has been located, as have some 400 Huron sites. The largest Huron center, Cahiagué, has been tentatively identified near Orillia. Illus.
L. F. S. Upton

1075. Trigger, Bruce G. THE FRENCH PRESENCE IN HURONIA: THE STRUCTURE OF FRANCO-HURON RELATIONS IN THE FIRST HALF OF THE SEVENTEENTH CENTURY. *Can. Hist. R. 1968 49(2): 107-141.* This reexamination of published sources in the light of anthropological information probes various aspects of the French-Wyandot (Huron) trading alliance between 1615 and 1650 in the region around Lake Simcoe in Ontario. Evidence is presented concerning the development of factions among the Huron representing different reactions to the activities of the Jesuit missionaries that the French-Huron alliance permitted to work in Huronia.
A

1076. Trigger, Bruce G. THE JESUITS AND THE FUR TRADE. *Ethnohist. 1965 12(1): 30-53.* Reexamines the "tripartite relationship between priests, fur traders and Indians which constituted the foundation for the Huron missions" and which ended ultimately in the destruction of Huron and Jesuit power during the wars with the Iroquois in the 17th century. Discounts both the "historical teleology" of Francis Parkman's classic *The Jesuits in North America in the Seventeenth Century* (1867) and the "economic determinism" of G. T. Hunt's *Wars of the Iroquois* (Madison: U. of Wisconsin Press, 1940). Undertakes a brief narrative-synthesis in which individual, tribal, national, pagan, and Christian aspirations and rivalries are given scope along with geographic, economic, climatic, and ethnographic influences.
H. J. Graham

Southeast Area

General

1077. Alderson, William T. A PLEA FOR THE MEN OF THE PAST. *Tennessee Hist. Q. 1964 23(3): 237-245.* Reprints the full text of an editorial by William Wales in the *South-Western Monthly, A Journal Devoted to Literature and Science, Education, the Mechanic Arts and Agriculture* (1852). Wales was a strong believer in the value of the study of history, and he notes that "no State...presents a more glorious train of events for contemplation...to stir the hearts of future generations as their history is recited, than Tennessee." After tracing the history of selected areas and people of the State, he concentrated on the newly formed Tennessee Historical Society. At the time, the society was requesting information and materials on 15 points of history, from facts about early forts or stockades, to histories of Tennessee Indians and information about the previous name for Tennessee, Frankland. In his introduction, Alderson states there is still a need to preserve historical documents.   M. W. Machan

1078. Anderson, Robert L. THE END OF AN IDYLL. *Florida Hist. Q. 1963 42(1): 35-47.* For 131 years, Negro slaves from the English colonies and, later, the United States, fled to Florida and found a comfortable refuge among the Indians. They sometimes cooperated with Indian warriors in raiding Georgia plantations, until American forces occupied Florida.   G. L. Lycan

1079. Bittle, George C. THE FLORIDA MILITIA'S ROLE IN THE BATTLE OF WITHLACOOCHEE. *Florida Hist. Q. 1966 4(4): 303-311.* Evidence indicates that the Florida militia under Brigadier General Richard Keith Call did about as much as it could to aid the regular army troops under Brigadier General Duncan Lamont Clinch in the Battle of Withlacoochee, December 1835. Contends that subsequent slurs arising out of the controversy over the battle against Call and his men are not well founded. Based on private and state papers, secondary works, and newspapers.   G. L. Lycan

1080. Bonner, James C. CHATTAHOOCHEE OLD TOWN: A FOOTNOTE IN HISTORIOGRAPHY. *Georgia Hist. Q. 1967 51(4): 443-448.* Demonstrates the value of linguistics in historical research. The exact location of the old Indian village of Chattahoochee has been a matter of dispute. The traditional explanation places the town according to the assumed derivation of the Indian word Chattahoochee: chat-to, a stone, and ho-che, meaning marked or flowered. Thus the village has been located at a point in Heard County, Georgia, where distinctively marked stones have been found. The author contends, however, that "flower" really should be transcribed as "flour." If this interpretation is correct, Chattahoochee was a place where Indians ground and pounded corn into meal and was located some 15 miles from the traditionally accepted site. 12 notes.   R. A. Mohl

1081. Bonner, James C., ed. JOURNAL OF A MISSION TO GEORGIA IN 1827. *Georgia Hist. Q. 1960 44(1): 74-85.* Selections from the journal of Lieutenant John R. Vinton, who was chosen by Secretary of War James Barbour to deliver a message to the governor of Georgia, George M. Troup. The message concerned the controversy over Indian affairs between Georgia and the United States. The journal presents an insight into the character of the people of Milledgeville, the frontier capital of Georgia, where Vinton spent most of his time while in the state.   R. Lowitt

1082. Carmony, Donald F., ed. MESSAGE OF PENNSYLVANIA AND NEW JERSEY QUAKERS TO INDIANS OF THE OLD NORTHWEST. *Indiana Mag. of Hist. 1963 59(1): 51-58.* In this document Quakers in the Philadelphia area are shown seeking to reconcile Indian-white antagonisms in the Old Northwest in the 1780's. The document is important since Anthony Wayne used it in 1795 to buttress his arguments in negotiations with the Indians following the Battle of Fallen Timbers. The editor also includes correspondence between Wayne and some of the Philadelphia Quakers in order to place the latter's message to the Indians in a proper historical context.   J. Findlay

1083. Coulter, E. Merton. THE OKEFENOKEE SWAMP, ITS HISTORY AND LEGENDS. *Georgia Hist. Q. 1964 48(2): 166-192, and (3): 291-312.* Part I. Discusses the natural history, the descriptions of early visitors, the tall tales, and the explorations and surveys of Okefenokee Swamp, particularly in the 1800-60 period. Also included is an account of early settlers, chiefly Indians, and the Seminole War as it affected "the swamp" area. Part II. Describes the abortive and largely speculative 19th-century efforts first to construct a canal through the swamp in order to join the Atlantic seaboard with the Gulf of Mexico and then, by the 1880's, also to drain the area. By the end of the 19th century successful lumber operations were developed. After World War I the Okefenokee Swamp was secured by the U.S. government which set up the Okefenokee National Wildlife Refuge and, after World War II, created the Okefenokee Swamp Park so that in the modern era commercial exploitation ended and scientific, recreational and cultural uses now prevail.   R. Lowitt

1084. Coulter, E. Merton. WAS GEORGIA SETTLED BY DEBTORS? *Georgia Hist. Q. 1969 53(4): 442-454.* Reviews the historical controversy about the accuracy of colonial Georgia's image as a haven for British debtors. In a 1943 study of Georgia history, Albert B. Saye argued that not more than a dozen imprisoned debtors ever came to the colony. He claimed that more important among the colony's objectives were the following: to serve as a buffer against Spaniards in Florida; to promote British trade and prosperity; to Christianize Indians; and to provide a refuge for persecuted Protestants in Europe. Gradually, the author contends, the results of Saye's research are beginning to find their way into textbooks and standard accounts of Georgia history. 50 notes.
                                                                        R. A. Mohl

1085. Covington, James W. TRADE RELATIONS BETWEEN SOUTHWESTERN FLORIDA AND CUBA—1600-1840. *Florida Hist. Q. 1959 38(2): 114-*

128. Enumerates the items of trade and describes the nature of commercial relations between the Indians (and later the white men) of Florida and the Spanish colonials of Cuba during the period 1600-1840. Based on U.S. state papers and on autobiographies, travel accounts, secondary works, and newspapers. G. L. Lycan

1086. Craig, Alan K. and Peebles, Christopher S. CAPTAIN YOUNG'S SKETCH MAP, 1818. *Florida Hist. Q. 1969 48(2): 176-179.* An unpublished map, "Sketch of the Indian and Negro Towns on the Suwaney River," discovered in the records of the Office of the Chief of Engineers in the National Archives and Records Service, Washington, is believed to be the work of Captain Hugh Young, an assistant topographical engineer in the Corps of Topographical Engineers. As General Andrew Jackson's adjutant-general, Young prepared a special report in 1818 entitled "A Topographical Memoir on East and West Florida with Itineraries," which has been published in three parts (in 1934 and 1935) in *The Florida Historical Quarterly.* Careful consideration of the evidence, including the mention by Young of a map accompanying his report, seems to indicate that it was Captain Young who drafted the sketch map. Although the map was filed with other 1839 maps connected with the Second Seminole War, it is believed that it actually belongs with the 1818 report. Illus., 9 notes. R. V. Calvert

1087. Defina, Frank P. "EL SENDERO DE LAS LAGRIMAS": LA EXPULSION DE LOS INDIOS DE LUISIANA Y FLORIDA A CONSECUENCIA DEL TRATADO DE SAN LORENZO ["The trail of tears": The expulsion of the Indians from Louisiana and Florida in consequence of the Treaty of San Lorenzo]. *R. de Indias [Spain] 1967 27(109/110): 415-425.* Analyzes the situation of the five great tribes, inhabitants of the final stretch of the Mississippi, and the consequences for them of the treaty of 1795 which placed them under North American sovereignty. The final result was their transference in the 1830's from Georgia to the West. Based on part of the unpublished doctoral dissertation of the author, submitted in 1962, mostly documented from the Archivo Histórico Nacional in Madrid. V. C. (IHE 70878)

1088. Defina, Frank P. REALIDADES Y CONTACTOS ENTRE ESPAÑA, NORTEAMERICA Y LAS NACIONES INDIAS CHACTAS, CHICASAS, CHEROKIS Y CRIKS EN LA SEGUNDA MITAD DEL SIGLO XVII [Rivalries and contacts between Spain, North America and the Indian tribes of the Choctaws, Chickasaws, Cherokees, and Creeks in the second half of the 18th century]. *R. de la U. de Madrid [Spain] 1963 12(48): 808-809.* Summary of doctoral dissertation submitted during the 1962-63 academic year to the faculty of the University of Madrid. S. E. Roberts

1089. Delaney, Caldwell. A NEWLY-FOUND FRENCH JOURNAL, 1720. *Alabama R. 1966 19(2): 146-153.* Edited excerpts from the journal of Jean François de la Clüe, member of a detachment of French soldiers on the frigate *Comte de Toulouse* which sailed into Mobile Bay in June 1720. Describes the entry into the bay, a brief excursion ashore, and the Indians living near Mobile Bay. D. F. Henderson

1090. DeVorsey, Louis, Jr. INDIAN BOUNDARIES IN COLONIAL GEORGIA. *Georgia Hist. Q. 1970 54(1): 63-78.* Describes the changing boundary dividing Indian territory from that settled by whites, and postulates the dual nature of the frontier (a frontier of whites advancing westward and a retreating Indian frontier). Four maps delineate Indian boundaries established by treaty-making process with the tribes, especially with the Creek and Cherokee Indians. Although the Indians lost territory at each stage, most of Georgia was still controlled by the tribes at the outbreak of the American Revolution. 25 notes.
R. A. Mohl

1091. Evans, Oliver. MELTING POT IN THE BAYOUS. *Am. Heritage 1963 15(1): 30-51, 106-107.* A survey of the various influences which made New Orleans the first melting pot in the United States. The author feels that the mixing of French, Spanish, Indian, Negro and American cultures and blood before the Civil War produced a culture which was unique. The text is supplemented by sketches by A. R. Waud done in 1866. Undocumented.
C. R. Allen, Jr.

1092. Fike, Claude E. THE ADMINISTRATION OF WALTER LEAKE (1822-1825). *J. of Mississippi Hist. 1970 32(2): 103-115.* Describes the 1822-25 administration of Walter Leake (1762-1825), the third governor and first two-term governor of Mississippi. Leake's administration dealt with such matters as revision of the legal code, movement of the state capitol to Jackson, Indian affairs, education, finance, internal improvements, county boundaries, petitions for clemency, many private manumission bills, and abolition of imprisonment for debt. A distinguished governor, Leake achieved an impressive legislative record and was a "prudent, sound and capable" administrator. Based chiefly on various published and unpublished primary sources; 31 notes.
J. W. Hillje

1093. Gaines, George S. NOTES ON THE EARLY DAYS OF SOUTH ALABAMA. *Alabama Hist. Q. 1964 26(3/4): 133-229.* Reprint of a series of articles published in the Mobile *Register* in 1872. The series was composed of the reminiscences of Colonel Gaines while he was Indian agent for the United States in the Mississippi Territory and later in Alabama. Contains names of many of the early settlers of south Alabama as well as some description of their contributions. Emphasis is on Gaines' activities among the Indians with details of their life and their treatment by the government. The tribes Gaines was most concerned with were the Choctaw and the Chickasaw. The War of 1812 in Alabama, and the part Gaines had in getting General Jackson to lead an army into that section of the country during the war, are discussed.
E. E. Eminhizer

1094. Gannon, Michael F. ALTAR AND HEARTH: THE COMING OF CHRISTIANITY. *Florida Hist. Q. 1965 44(1/2): 17-44.* The Spanish government, dedicated officials, and Catholic priests persisted in their efforts to Christianize the Indians of Florida; and they succeeded at last, in 1565, in establishing a permanent foothold for the Church at St. Augustine. Based on church records, state papers, personal papers and secondary works.
G. L. Lycan

1095. Gannon, Michael V. SEBASTIAN MONTERO, PIONEER AMERICAN MISSIONARY, 1566-1572. *Catholic Hist. R. 1965 51(3): 335-353.* An interrogatory and a royal *cédula,* both dated 1572, preserved in the Archivo General de Indias in Seville disclose the name and deeds of the Spanish secular priest who accompanied Captain Juan Pardo on his 1566 expedition to the interior of Orista, present-day South Carolina, then a part of Spanish *La Florida.* The priest, Sebastian Montero, remained behind to work among the Siouan Indians at Guatari, probably located in today's Anderson County. During six years (1566-72) Father Montero taught Christian doctrine and duties, also reading and writing—one of the first authenticated missionary successes with the American Indians.   A

1096. Garvin, Russell. THE FREE NEGRO IN FLORIDA BEFORE THE CIVIL WAR. *Florida Hist. Q. 1967 46(1): 1-17.* After the Spanish in 1704 opened Florida to fugitive slaves from British plantations, Carolina and, later, Georgia were plagued with the problem of runaways. In 1740 British colonists destroyed the Negro fort three miles north of Saint Augustine. After the Revolution, several unsuccessful expeditions were made to capture runaway slaves living with or near the Creek and Seminole. Negroes joined the Indians in resistance against white penetration into Florida. 93 notes.   R. V. Calvert

1097. Gold, Robert L. CONFLICT IN SAN CARLOS: INDIAN IMMIGRANTS IN EIGHTEENTH-CENTURY NEW SPAIN. *Ethnohist. 1970 17(1-2): 1-10.* "From April, 1763, to February, 1764, immediately following the British takeover of Florida, eighty-nine Christianized Yamasee and five Apalachee Indians voluntarily migrated to New Spain to the vicinity of modern Veracruz, Mexico. Details of their migration and of the beginnings of their new village, San Carlos de Chachalacas, are presented. This colony of Indian migrants remained extant at least until 1774."   J

1098. Gold, Robert L. THE DEPARTURE OF SPANISH CATHOLICISM FROM FLORIDA, 1763-1765. *The Americas 1966 22(4): 377-388.* Following the loss of Florida in the Seven Years' War, the Spanish inhabitants (including the clergy) and certain Christianized Indians were evacuated to Cuba and Mexico. Based chiefly on photostated documents from Seville archives and other primary sources; 30 notes.   D. Bushnell

1099. Gold, Robert L. THE EAST FLORIDA INDIANS UNDER SPANISH AND ENGLISH CONTROL: 1763-1765. *Florida Hist. Q. 1965 44(1/2): 105-120.* One hundred and fifty Indians followed the Spaniards out of Florida when it was lost to the British in 1763. The English continued giving presents to the Indians in Florida to keep peace, but conditions were quite uneasy when the American Revolution began. Based on state papers, private papers, secondary works, and periodical material.   G. L. Lycan

1100. Gold, Robert L. THE SETTLEMENT OF THE PENSACOLA INDIANS IN NEW SPAIN, 1763-1770. *Hispanic Am. Hist. R. 1965 45(4): 567-576.*

The transfer of Florida to Great Britain by the Treaty of Paris of 1763 saw the Spanish population of Florida leave the colony. Among the exiles were Christianized Indians. A group of Indians from Pensacola was resettled in a village called San Carlos, outside of Vera Cruz, New Spain (Mexico). Traces the history of this Indian group from their departure from Florida through the evolution of a functioning settlement by 1770. 37 notes.   B. B. Solnick

1101. Goodall, Elizabeth J. THE RADIOCARBON DATING OF THE WOODEN IMAGE ON DISPLAY IN THE STATE MUSEUM. *West Virginia Hist. 1964 26(1): 47-52.* In 1895 a statue on a pedestal was discovered in a cave near Lewiston, West Virginia. Of undetermined origin, it remained on display for years in a museum at Charleston. In 1964 a radiocarbon dating of the statue was made which indicated that it was from 250 to 450 years old. This has led to the conclusion that the Kanawha Valley was created by farming Indians who inhabited the area between 1400 and 1600 A.D. It is a significant artifact in that it is the first evidence that Indians east of the Mississippi did woodcarving. Documented, illus.   D. N. Brown

1102. Green, E. R. R. QUEENSBOROUGH TOWNSHIP: SCOTCH-IRISH EMIGRATION AND THE EXPANSION OF GEORGIA, 1763-1776. *William and Mary Q. 1960 17(2): 183-199.* Traces the unsuccessful effort to attract Scotch-Irish emigrants to a settlement on the Ogeechee River. Although Queensborough received but few settlers because of Indian raids and did not survive the Revolution, the effort is significant because of the attempt to settle the back country directly from Europe, and because it indicates the desire for territorial expansion.   E. Oberholzer, Jr.

1103. Hatfield, Joseph T. GOVERNOR WILLIAM CLAIBORNE, INDIANS, AND OUTLAWS IN FRONTIER MISSISSIPPI, 1801-1803. *J. of Mississippi Hist. 1965 27(4): 323-350.* Describes the "sound record" of William Claiborne (1775-1817), a lawyer and former Democratic-Republican Congressman from Tennessee (1797-1801), as governor and superintendent of Indian affairs in the Mississippi Territory from 1801 through 1803. Although he favored acquiring some land from the Choctaw and Chicasaw, Claiborne was generally "sympathetic and conciliatory" toward Indians. He "worked long and patiently to iron out differences that arose, and to improve the material well-being of the Indians." Based on published and archival material.   J. W. Hillje

1104. Hawes, Lilla Mills, ed. THE FRONTIERS OF GEORGIA IN THE LATE EIGHTEENTH CENTURY: JONAS FAUCHE TO JOSEPH VALLANCE BEVAN. *Georgia Hist. Q. 1963 47(1): 84-95.* Recollections written in 1823 by Fauche, a former adjutant general of Georgia (1796-1806) with regard to Indian affairs and the settlement of some portions of the frontiers of Georgia from 1785 to 1795.   R. Lowitt

1105. Haynes, Robert V. THE SOUTHWEST AND THE WAR OF 1812. *Louisiana Hist. 1964 5(1): 41-51.* Reassesses the causal factors which influenced the people of the Orleans and Mississippi territories in their strong support of the entry into war with Great Britain in 1812. By 1810 belief in the policy of economic coercion was waning in the Southwest, while desire for unrestricted trade as well as for vindication of national honor was rising, intermingled with desire for Spanish Florida. Problems of land claims, Indians, internal improvements, and statehood issues continued, however, to excite more local interest than the coming of war. Most saw no conflict between war issues and local interests; in fact, some foresaw war as a way of resolving certain local problems. Based largely on pertinent manuscript collections, particularly those in the Mississippi Department of Archives and History. D. C. James

1106. Herndon, G. Melvin. INDIAN AGRICULTURE IN THE SOUTHERN COLONIES. *North Carolina Hist. R. 1967 44(3): 283-297.* Southeastern Indians were not only hunters but sedentary farmers as well, and they contributed much to the survival of the early colonists and to American agriculture. Their cleared fields enabled whites to survive in the early years, for example. Indians did not sow broadcast as Europeans did, but planted in rows and hoed out the weeds; they practiced field rather than crop rotation, and had well developed techniques for growing such indigenous American plants as corn. All of these practices were adopted by the settlers, as were most of their crops, not only corn, but melons, tobacco, and squash. 58 notes. J. M. Bumsted

1107. Holmes, Jack D. L. NOTES OF THE SPANISH FORT SAN ESTEBAN DE TOMBECBE. *Alabama R. 1965 18(4): 281-290.* Contends that Fort San Esteban, or St. Stephens, on the Tombigbee, was not to protect Spanish West Florida against the Americans, but rather American settlers against Indian hostilities. A brief résumé of the economic and religious activities of the settlers, and the hardships encountered by the troops stationed at the post is included. Documented, including numerous references from the Spanish archives; 42 notes. D. F. Henderson

1108. Holmes, Jack D. L. SPANISH TREATIES WITH WEST FLORIDA INDIANS, 1784-1802. *Florida Hist. Q. 1969 48(2): 140-154.* Treaties between Spain and American Indians from 1784 to 1802 included both defensive alliances for mutual protection and agreements ceding land on which Spanish fortifications and trading goods warehouses were erected. A defensive alliance against American frontiersmen was arranged with Sewanee and Talapuche chieftains in Pensacola in 1784. The Indian promise to defend Spanish territory was exchanged for the Spanish guarantee of Creek tribal lands south of 32 degrees and 28 minutes latitude against encroachment from Georgia. Alliances were also concluded with the Alibamon, Chickasaw, and Choctaw (in Mobile) in 1784. The most significant accomplishment was the Treaty of Nogales, containing provision for an offensive and defensive alliance among the Chickasaw, Creek, Talapuche, Alibamon, Cherokee, and Choctaw Indians. The sites for Fort Nogales, Fort Confederation, and Fort San Fernando de las Barrancas were all ceded by treaties. Both the land cession treaties and the Indian alliances were vital to Spanish defenses and indicated a sound southern Indian policy. Based partly on unpublished Spanish documents; 54 notes. R. V. Calvert

1109. Howard, R. Palmer. A HISTORIOGRAPHY OF THE FIVE CIVI-
LIZED TRIBES: A CHRONOLOGICAL APPROACH. *Chronicles of Oklahoma 1969 47(3): 312-331.* Summarizes the most important authors and works
written about the Five Civilized Tribes. James Adair, a trader, wrote first in 1775,
followed by missionaries, George Catlin, Washington Irving, and various military
men. Thomas L. McKenney of the Bureau of Indian Affairs traveled and wrote
extensively among the Indians and is known, as are Henry Rowe Schoolcraft and
Helen Hunt Jackson, for his sympathy for the red man. James Mooney, Frederick
Webb Hodge, and John Reed Swanton are known for their work with the Bureau
of American Ethnology around the turn of the century. More recent scholars
include Annie Heloise Abel, James Henry Malone, Grant Foreman, Edward
Everett Dale, Marion L. Starkey, Grace Steele Woodward and Angie Debo. 12
notes, biblio.   K. P. Davis

1110. Jones, George F. JOHN MARTIN BLOZIUS REPORTS ON
GEORGIA. *Georgia Hist. Q. 1963 47(2): 216-219.* A letter written in the 1730's
commenting upon the religions found among the various peoples, including Indians, living in Georgia.   R. Lowitt

1111. Jones, George F. VON RECK'S SECOND REPORT FROM GEORGIA.
William and Mary Q. 1965 22(2): 319-333. This is an account of the second
Georgia journey of Phillip Georg Friedrich von Reck in 1735-36. Von Reck was
engaged in transporting Salzburg exiles to Georgia. He gives an entertaining
description of the Spaniards, Indians, and wildlife. The document is reproduced.
                                                                 H. M. Ward

1112. Krebs, A. L'EXPLORATION DU DELTA DU MISSISSIPPI PAR LE
MOYNE D'IBERVILLE [Le Moyne d'Iberville's exploration of the Mississippi
delta]. *R. Maritime [France] 1963 (202): 1022-1030.* In 1698 Pierre Lemoyne,
Sieur d'Iberville obtained the approval of Louis Phélypeaux, Seigneur de Pontchartrain, Minister of the French Navy, for the settlement of Louisiana. His
squadron sailed past Pensacola, Mobile, and Biloxi. Leaving the ships, Iberville,
with 50 men in two boats and two canoes, followed the coast and investigated
every indentation. The muddy, fresh water of a great river, with an accumulation
of debris on each bank, enabled Iberville, after two days of progress upstream,
to identify the Mississippi. Peaceful relations were established with the Bayagou-
las and the Mugulasha. The French continued as far as Baton Rouge; there the
Oumas conducted them several leagues inland to their village. Before returning
to the ships in Bay St. Louis by a short cut (Iberville River-Maurepas Lake-Lake
Pontchartrain), Iberville obtained a letter from a Bayagoula chief written by
Henry Tonty to René-Robert Cavelier, Sieur de La Salle, conclusive proof that
La Salle had found the mouth of the Mississippi. The letter is quoted in part. Illus.
                                                                 J. S. Gassner

1113. Latimer, Margaret Kinard. SOUTH CAROLINA—A PROTAGONIST
OF THE WAR OF 1812. *Am. Hist. R. 1956 61(4): 914-929.* A reassessment of
the work of the "War Hawks" of 1812, particularly that of the South Carolina
congressmen John C. Calhoun, William Lowndes, and Langdon Cheves. The

author modifies the thesis of Julius Pratt *(Expansionists of 1812,* New York, 1925) who saw South Carolina war sentiment as the result of a desire for the settlement of the Indian problem which it held in common with the frontier states of the Southwest. South Carolina Republicanism was a conservative Federal-Republicanism, and its congressmen were motivated by a desire to protect the socioeconomic organization of their state. By 1812 the whole state was committed to cotton and was totally dependent on unrestricted foreign trade, and therefore desired war to protect this interest. "Paradoxical as it may seem, the desire of South Carolina to preserve and extend the status quo produced a determination not to be undone by the caprices of warring European powers. Going to Congress with the conviction that the older Republican measures would not solve the problems of 1812, South Carolina's young congressmen...spoke for the protection of America's foreign commerce and...for the well-being of South Carolina's trade in cotton."   D. Houston

1114. Mahon, John K. BRITISH STRATEGY AND SOUTHERN INDIANS: WAR OF 1812. *Florida Hist. Q. 1966 44(4): 285-302.* Discusses the failure of a complex British scheme by officers operating in the Gulf of Mexico during the War of 1812 to conquer the southwestern part of the United States by means of an alliance with the Indians, escaped Negro slaves, Spaniards, and others. Based on British and American state papers, private papers, and secondary works.
                                                                              G. L. Lycan

1115. Mahon, John K. MILITARY RELATIONS BETWEEN GEORGIA AND THE UNITED STATES, 1789-1794. *Georgia Hist. Q. 1959 43(2): 138-155.* Examines the hostility between Georgia and the federal government over the Indian menace on the frontier. Georgia desired additional federal forces and funds to protect frontier dwellers from the Creek Indians, but Secretary of War Henry Knox needed his limited forces in the Northwest and was unable to aid Georgia effectively. Friction between the state and the nation mounted, until in May, 1794 militiamen and regulars almost clashed. Thereafter, with the defeat of the Northwest Indians at the Battle of Fallen Timbers, tension eased and Georgia was able to obtain further protection from the federal government, although a squabble over funds continued until 1828.   R. Lowitt

1116. Mahon, John K. and. THE TREATY OF MOULTRIE CREEK, 1823. *Florida Hist. Q. 1962 40(4): 350-372.* In this treaty, the diverse bands of Indians ceded to the United States their claim to all of Florida in return for a reservation of four million acres east and northeast of Tampa Bay. Based on American and Florida state papers, and on secondary works.   G. L. Lycan

1117. Mattfield, Mary S. JOURNEY TO THE WILDERNESS: TWO TRAV-ELERS IN FLORIDA, 1696-1774. *Florida Hist. Q. 1967 45(4): 327-351.* Jona-than Dickinson's *Journal* (published 1699) and William Bartram's *Travels through North and South Carolina, Georgia, East and West Florida* (published 1791) have literary merit beyond that of good travel narratives. Analysis of the two would perhaps aid in understanding the development of American literature, since each reflects a dominant viewpoint of the century in which it was written.

Dickinson's account of his struggle in the northeastern Florida wilderness, while he and his shipwrecked family and companions were half-starved captives of Indians, is that of a devout 17th-century traveler interpreting his experience in the light of the working of Divine Providence. Originally regarding both the pagan Indians and primitive nature as decivilizing influences, Dickinson gradually recognized nature as his chief enemy. On the other hand, traveler-naturalist Bartram, traveling in the vicinity almost a century later, viewed nature as a challenge to his curiosity, seeking to study nature for the purpose of both admiring the Almighty Creator's work and finding unknown natural specimens of use to society. Bartram's romanticism, then, was modified with practicality so that nature, the Indian, and civilization were all composites of both good and evil. 33 notes.   R. V. Calvert

1118. McWilliams, Richebourg Gaillard. IBERVILLE AND THE SOUTHERN INDIANS. *Alabama R. 1967 20(4): 243-262.* Analyzes the material on Indians pertaining to "food quest, religion, social life, including sex, and 'cultural spying'" contained in the journals of Pierre Lemoyne d'Iberville, discoverer of the mouth of the Mississippi. 63 notes.   D. F. Henderson

1119. Murdoch, Richard K. INDIAN PRESENTS: TO GIVE OR NOT TO GIVE. GOVERNOR WHITE'S QUANDARY. *Florida Hist. Q. 1956/57 35(4): 326-346.* A description of the Spanish policy of keeping peace with the Indians by giving presents to chiefs. Based on annotated excerpts from official Spanish colonial records.   J. L. Lycan

1120. Olson, Gary D. THOMAS BROWN, LOYALIST PARTISAN, AND THE REVOLUTIONARY WAR IN GEORGIA, 1777-1782. *Georgia Hist. Q. 1970 54(1): 1-19, and 54(2): 183-208.* Part I. Details British efforts to defeat the rebellious colonies in the South. To this end the British governor of East Florida, Patrick Tonyn, directed the activities of a small provincial garrison, friendly Indians, and Loyalist refugees from Georgia and the Carolinas. Planter Thomas Brown became a leader of Tory exiles, worked closely with Tonyn, led "Brown's rangers" on border raids into Georgia, and made several efforts to organize backcountry Loyalists as a fighting force. He also gathered military intelligence for the British. These efforts generally had few positive results, for overall British military strategy failed in the South and reports of Loyalist sympathies of the backcountry residents were mistaken. 44 notes. Part II. "Brown's Raiders" was composed of Loyalists and Creek and Cherokee Indians. After the surrender of Charlestown to the British, Brown was sent into Cumberland to stem the flow of western volunteers to the rebels. Returning, he assumed the defense of Savannah. Later, going to East Florida, he aided in the British evacuation and cession to Spain. An extreme Loyalist, Brown migrated to the Bahamas where he became a planter and was active in politics until his death in 1825. Documented from military correspondence and area histories; 67 notes.   R. A. Mohl

1121. Posey, Walter B. PRESBYTERIAN CHURCH INFLUENCE IN LOWER MISSISSIPPI VALLEY. *J. of the Presbyterian Hist. Soc. 1955 33(1): 35-50.* Examines the activities and attitudes of the Presbyterian church in the

lower Mississippi Valley in the beginning of the 19th century. The church contributed to the establishment of law and order, took a lead in establishing educational facilities and supported the antislavery movement. It also engaged in missionary activities among the Indians but did not protest against the Indians' removal from their own land. Based on church records and published sources.
S

1122. Purser, Joyce. THE ADMINISTRATION OF INDIAN AFFAIRS IN LOUISIANA, 1803-1820. *Louisiana Hist. 1964 5(4): 401-419.* Analyzes the problems of the Natchitoches Indian agency in the Orleans Territory, 1803-12, and in Louisiana, 1812-20. The three agents of those years were John Sibley, 1803-14, Thomas Gales, 1814-15, and John Jamison, 1816-19. The agency's main purposes were to keep the Indians at peace and to keep them from succumbing to Spanish subversion. Therein the agency achieved "reasonable success" despite illegal trade, intruders, undermanned garrisons, complex land claims, and other problems typical of U.S.-Indian relations elsewhere as well.   D. C. James

1123. Rainwater, Percy L. CONQUISTADORS, MISSIONARIES, AND MISSIONS. *J. of Mississippi Hist. 1965 27(2): 123-147.* Beginning with De Soto's expedition in 1540, traces the slow progress of missionary activity in the territory which became the state of Mississippi in 1817. French missionaries labored for one hundred fifty years but accomplished nothing. In 1773 Samuel Swayze, a Congregational minister, established the first Protestant church in the area. During their rule from 1779 to 1798 the Spanish prohibited Protestant worship. Many Baptists entered Mississippi from 1800 to 1810; several Methodist itinerants and missionaries served the area from 1799 to 1813; and four Presbyterian ministers settled in the territory between 1804 and 1817. Based largely on secondary sources.   J. W. Hillje

1124. Rea, Robert R. A NEW LETTER FROM MOBILE, 1763. *Alabama R. 1969 22(3): 230-237.* Presents a copy of a letter from James Campbell, Captain Lieutenant of the 34th Regiment of Foot, to John Campbell, the 4th Earl of Loudoun, from Mobile on 15 December 1763. The letter contains information about a meeting between several Indian tribes and the French governor of New Orleans, comments on the weather, and relates the exodus of French inhabitants from the region. Based on the letter located in the William L. Clements Library, University of Michigan; 12 notes.   D. F. Henderson

1125. Rea, Robert R. REDCOATS AND REDSKINS ON THE LOWER MISSISSIPPI, 1763-1776: THE CAREER OF LT. JOHN THOMAS. *Louisiana Hist. 1970 11(1): 5-35.* British acquisition of West Florida increased British activity on the lower Mississippi, but at the same time exposed them to "the danger of redskinned highwaymen." To meet this threat, they established Fort Bute and Panmure and stationed Indian agents at the "critical juncture" of the Mississippi and Iberville Rivers. The most notable of these agents was Lieutenant John Thomas, "whose long association with Fort Bute and the lower Mississippi vividly illustrates the problems and conditions of Britain's southwestern frontier." The author traces Thomas' career there, with his frequent and unfortunate conflicts with the Spaniards and with his superiors. Based on manuscript sources from archives in the United States, Canada, and England; 40 notes.

R. L. Woodward

1126. Smith, Hale G., Doherty, Herbert J., Jr., and Tebeau, Charlton W. FLORIDA BIBLIOGRAPHY AND HISTORIOGRAPHY. *Florida Hist. Q. 1958 37(2): 156-177.* A selective annotated bibliography of works on Florida Indians and general historical writings on Florida for the periods 1821-60 and 1900-57.

G. L. Lycan

1127. Spellman, Charles W. THE "GOLDEN AGE" OF THE FLORIDA MISSIONS, 1632-1674. *Catholic Hist. R. 1965 51(3): 354-372.* Following pioneer secular priests and Jesuit missionaries, Franciscan friars came to Spanish Florida in 1573 to work among the Guale, Timucua, and Apalache Indians. The years 1632-74 mark the height of the expansion of the Franciscan missions, or *doctrinas,* in Florida. One chain of missions stretched north from St. Augustine along the coast as far as St. Catherines Island; another went west across the peninsula to the Apalachicola River. In 1674-75 visiting Bishop Gabriel Díaz Vara Calderón of Cuba found 36 missions and about 30 thousand Christian Indians under Franciscan care. The mission chains were destroyed by English Carolinians in 1702-04.

A

1128. Tanner, Helen Hornbeck. ZESPEDES AND THE SOUTHERN CONSPIRACIES. *Florida Hist. Q. 1959 38(1): 15-28.* Vicente Manuel de Zéspedes, Spanish governor of East Florida, 1784 to 1790, steered warily through a morass of conspiracies involving nationals of the United States, Britain, and Spain whose objectives were the acquisition of private lands in the Floridas, control of the fur trade with the Indians, free navigation of the Mississippi, or even a revolution against Spain aimed at creating a new republic on the Gulf of Mexico or annexation of the territory to the United States. Based on Spanish colonial records and secondary works.

G. L. Lycan

1129. Wallace, Katherine T. ELK COUNTY, ALABAMA. *Alabama R. 1966 19(3): 227-233.* Although short-lived, the creation of Elk County is an example of "how squatters moved into unsettled areas and forced the national and territorial government to act on their behalf in quieting Indian claims, establishing titles to land and creating county governments." 17 notes.

D. F. Henderson

1130. Wheeler, E. Milton. DEVELOPMENT AND ORGANIZATION OF THE NORTH CAROLINA MILITIA. *North Carolina Hist. R. 1964 41(3): 307-323.* Reviews development of the militia system from the Carolina Charter of 1663 through the American Revolution. The institution developed in trial and error response to various exigencies of the 18th century, notably Indian attacks and the wars with France and Great Britain. Details particularly the militia acts of 1715, 1756, and the revolutionary period. Based on published colonial and state records.

L. R. Harlan

1131. Willis, William S. DIVIDE AND RULE: RED, WHITE, AND BLACK IN THE SOUTHEAST. *J. of Negro Hist. 1963 48(3): 157-176.* Poses the thesis that hostility between Negroes and Indians in the southeastern states during the colonial period was directly the result of white policy of divide and rule. Whites tried to prevent the mingling of Negroes and Indians. Indians were used to catch fugitive slaves and to put down slave rebellions; Negroes were used in military operations against the Indians. All these devices contributed to the mutual hostility which divided the two groups and prevented their combining in insurrection against the white man's rule. Most of the examples used relate to South Carolina. Documented.   L. Gara

1132. Willis, William S., Jr. PATRILINEAL INSTITUTIONS IN SOUTH-EASTERN NORTH AMERICA. *Ethnohist. 1963 10(3): 250-269.* Reviews evidence of strong patrilineal institutions among the large tribes (Cherokee, Choctaw, Chickasaw, and Creeks) of the southeast interior during the 18th century. "Heretofore matriliny has been stressed in studies of this area for this century...possibly the entire subject has to be revaluated."   H. J. Graham

1133. Young, Mary. INDIAN REMOVAL AND LAND ALLOTMENT: THE CIVILIZED TRIBES AND JACKSONIAN JUSTICE. *Am. Hist. R. 1958 64(1): 31-45.* Land allotment policies were applied to the southeastern Indian tribes in the 1830's with a twofold purpose: to cause the Indians to emigrate or to force them to take up a stable agricultural pursuit which would limit the amount of acreage they occupied. The motives were to make more land available for white settlement without giving the appearance of having violated the principle of voluntarism. The effects of the policy were to leave the Indians landless and to deliver the lands into the hands of speculators.   R. C. Raack

By Tribe

Apalachee

1134. Stout, Wilbur W. LAMAHATTY'S ROAD MAP. *Southern Q. 1964 2(3): 247-254.* An effort to reconstruct the travels of Lamahatty, an Apalachee Indian of a tribe friendly to the French, who was captured near Mobile by a band of Creeks and Carolinians in the spring of 1707. He was taken north and east to the foot of the Appalachians where he was sold to a band of migratory Shawnees who took him much further north. He escaped and drifted into northern Virginia, where Robert Beverly interviewed him and made a crude map from Lamahatty's account. A facsimile of the map and a glossary of rivers accompanies the article.
D. A. Stokes

Atakapa

1135. Burch, Marvin C. THE INDIGENOUS INDIANS OF THE LOWER TRINITY AREA OF TEXAS. *Southwestern Hist. Q. 1956/57 60(1): 36-52.* Discusses the customs, practices, and language of the Attacapan (Atakapa) and related Indian tribes of southeastern Texas and southwestern Louisiana.

J. A. Hudson

1136. Butler, Joseph T., Jr. THE ATAKAPA INDIANS: CANNIBALS OF LOUISIANA. *Louisiana Hist. 1970 11(2): 167-176.* The Atakapa Indians of southwest Louisiana were known for their cannibalism, which seems to have been ceremonial only. The first European to come in contact with the Atakapa was the Spanish explorer Cabeza de Vaca in 1528, and he reported that the Atakapa did not practice cannibalism at that time and that they were vehemently opposed to the practice. In 1703, however, Frenchmen reported a case of Atakapa cannibalism. Similar reports followed and their reputation for eating human flesh spread, although there is little evidence that they ever did so for the satisfaction of hunger. Based on published sources; 23 notes.   R. L. Woodward

1137. Post, Lauren C. SOME NOTES ON THE ATTAKAPAS INDIANS OF SOUTHWEST LOUISIANA. *Louisiana Hist. 1962 3(3): 221-242.* Presents most of the meager information known about the Attakapas (Atakapa), who lived mainly along the banks of the Vermilion, Mermentau, Calcasieu, Sabine, and Neches rivers of southwestern Louisiana and eastern Texas. Considerable attention is given to their registration and disposal of cattle brands as well as to their land ownership and claims. The tribe numbered 3,500 in 1698, though by 1805 only 175 were left in Louisiana, due to "diseases, use of liquor, starvation, wars, maladjustment, and all of the difficulties that befell other Indians." Based largely on *American State Papers—Public Lands* and John R. Swanton, *Indians of the Southeastern United States* (Washington, 1929).   D. C. James

Caddo

1138. McGinty, G. W. VALUATING THE CADDO LAND CESSION OF 1835. *Louisiana Studies 1963 2(2): 59-73.* Ways to determine the value of the land the Caddo Indians ceded to the United States by treaty, 1 July 1835, are considered. The value established was 2,068,419 dollars, whereas the Caddoes sold it for 80,000 dollars in cash and goods to be delivered over a four-year period.

A

1139. McRill, Leslie A. FERDINANDINA: FIRST WHITE SETTLEMENT IN OKLAHOMA (1719). *Chronicles of Oklahoma 1963 41(2): 126-159.* Established more than 200 years ago by Lieutenant Claude du Tisné, under auspices of Sieur de Bienville of New Orleans among the Caddoan Indians along the middle Arkansas River, above the mouth of the Canadian River, this settlement was a fur trading establishment. The study has two parts: 1) discoveries made by Claude du Tisné and Bérnard de la Harpe; 2) discoveries of the sites made by residents of more recent times. Lengthy quotations are made from an unpublished manuscript by Dr. Joseph B. Thoburn, describing the culture of the Caddoan tribes as revealed by the sites of their villages. Illustrations include artifacts, photographs of panoramic views, and a map showing the location of Ferdinandina. An appendix relates the founding of the settlement to the history of Europe at the time. Based on translations of contemporary French accounts and the Thoburn manuscript, 1930.   I. W. Van Noppen

Cherokee

1140. Allen, Ben and Lawson, Dennis T. THE WATAUGANS AND THE "DANGEROUS EXAMPLE." *Tennessee Hist. Q. 1967 26(2): 137-147.* An account of the first trans-Appalachian settlements. After the conferences of Fort Stanwix and Hard Labor, immigrants began to settle by mistake on Cherokee lands along the Watauga River in Tennessee and North Carolina. Defying orders of the British to leave, they formed the Watauga Association to lease the land from the Indians. The royal governors of North Carolina and Virginia vetoed the purchase of the land from the Cherokees by the Transylvania Company. With the beginning of hostilities in 1776 the Wataugans threw their support with the rebels and fought. They were included as the delegates from Washington County in the North Carolina Constitutional Convention. The pioneers provided a "dangerous example" of defiance of royal power, helped hold the West against the Indians, and maintained American interests in the Ohio Valley against British and Spanish claims. Based on secondary sources; 20 notes.   C. F. Ogilvie

1141. Ballenger, T. L. SPRING FROG. *Chronicles of Oklahoma 1966 44(1): 2-4.* Spring Frog, Cherokee leader and a contemporary of Sequoyah, was born near Lookout Mountain, Tennessee, in 1754. The log cabin stands. He was noted for skill in trapping, hunting, and fighting wars; he fought under Andrew Jackson against the Creeks. He was with the Cherokees who went to the Indian Territory in 1828, where he settled on a farm near Briartown. He died in 1859. 2 illus., 5 notes.   I. W. Van Noppen

1142. Coulter, E. Merton. DAVID MERIWETHER OF VIRGINIA AND GEORGIA. *Georgia Hist. Q. 1970 54(3): 320-338.* A brief biographical sketch of Meriwether (1755-1822). He was born in Virginia, served in the revolutionary war, and became a friend of Washington and Jefferson. Moving to Georgia after the war, Meriwether served as state legislator, congressman, and as an Indian commissioner, in which function he was instrumental in removing the Cherokee from Georgia. Among his other accomplishments, Meriwether helped found the University of Georgia. A brief account of Meriwether's immediate family is also included. Based largely on state, local, and genealogical records; 80 notes.   R. A. Mohl

1143. Coulter, E. Merton. JOHN HOWARD PAYNE'S VISIT TO GEORGIA. *Georgia Hist. Q. 1962 46(4): 333-376.* Recounts Payne's 1835 visit to Georgia, wherein he spent most of his time among the Cherokees, and the later legends that have appeared about this visit.   R. Lowitt

1144. Cross, Jasper W., ed. JOHN MILLER'S MISSIONARY JOURNAL—1816-1817: RELIGIOUS CONDITIONS IN THE SOUTH AND MIDWEST. *J. of Presbyterian Hist. 1969 47(3): 226-261.* John E. Miller (1792-1847), a Presbyterian minister in the temporary employ of the New York Northern Missionary Society, maintained for the society a journal of his missionary tour of the South and West from 1 November 1816 to 14 May 1817. The manuscript journal, fully reproduced here, is in the possession of the Miller family. Miller traveled through Maryland, Washington, D.C., Virginia, the Carolinas, Georgia, Tennessee, Kentucky, and Ohio before returning to Pennsylvania. Miller noted the population, climate, and religious and social conditions of the communities which he visited. Many of his observations coincided with those of other early 19th-century visitors to the South and West. The moral, religious, and educational level of the South dismayed Miller. He was compassionate toward slaves and provided documentation for very early hostility of Southern slaveholders toward religious instruction for the slaves. Less compassionate toward the Cherokee Indians, he termed them "an indolent, filthy, worthless set." 58 notes.

S. C. Pearson, Jr.

1145. De Baillou, Clemens. JAMES VANN, A CHEROKEE CHIEF. *Georgia R. 1963 17(3): 271-283.* A descriptive account of life in the Cherokee country in the early years of the 19th century. It shows the great revolution that took place in the Cherokee civilization at this time.

H. G. Earnhart

1146. De Baillou, Clemens. THE DIARIES OF THE MORAVIAN BROTHERHOOD AT THE CHEROKEE MISSION IN SPRING PLACE, GEORGIA FOR THE YEARS 1800-1804. *Georgia Hist. Q. 1970 54(4): 571-576.* Describes the diaries of the Moravian missionaries among the Cherokee in north Georgia, revealing much of their Pietist spirit. Most efforts to Christianize the Indians were unsuccessful, but after several years missionaries and Cherokee began to understand each other. A school was begun and friendly relations prevailed until both Cherokee and Moravians were driven out of the area by the state of Georgia in 1832. Based on diaries in the Moravian Archives (Winston-Salem, North Carolina); 4 notes.

R. A. Mohl

1147. Ganyard, Robert L. THREAT FROM THE WEST: NORTH CAROLINA AND THE CHEROKEE, 1776-1778. *North Carolina Hist. R. 1968 45(1): 47-66.* In 1766 North Carolina faced two threats: a British invasion supported by local Tories, and an uprising of the Cherokee Indians, which was beginning just as the British were defeated. The Cherokee were stirred by westward expansion of the white man and their own young hotheads. There is no proof that either the Tories or the British encouraged them, and much evidence that attempts were made on the British side to dissuade the Indians from indiscriminate violence. North Carolina, with the assistance of militia from Virginia and South Carolina, dispersed the Indians and destroyed many villages and crops in the late summer of 1776. A peace treaty was made in 1777 which kept the Cherokee quiet until late in 1780. 53 notes.

J. M. Bumsted

1148. Goff, John H. THE PATH TO OAKFUSKEE: UPPER TRADING ROUTE IN GEORGIA TO THE CREEK INDIANS. *Georgia Hist. Q. 1955 39(1): 1-36, (2): 152-171.* A geographical and historical discussion of an important Indian trading route in eastern Georgia during the 18th and early 19th centuries.   C. F. Latour

1149. Goldsmith, Adolph O. THE ROARING LYON OF VERMONT. *Journalism Q. 1962 39(2): 179-186.* Matthew Lyon (1750-1822), first person convicted under the Sedition Act of 1798, also cast the vote which made Thomas Jefferson president instead of Aaron Burr in 1801. He served with the Green Mountain Boys in the American Revolution, but later in the war was cashiered. Elected to Congress from Vermont in 1796, he spat in the face of a Connecticut member who spoke against him and twice escaped expulsion by lack of a two-thirds majority. He started an anti-Federalist newspaper and was "railroaded" to jail for four months, being released just in time to go to Washington to help break the tie between Jefferson and Burr. He had been reelected while in jail. Later that year he moved to Kentucky, established the first printing office in that state, and was elected congressman from Kentucky in 1803. He later served as factor of the United States to the Cherokee nation and was elected territorial delegate to Congress from Arkansas, but did not live to serve.   S. E. Humphreys

1150. Kilpatrick, Jack Frederick. AN ADVENTURE STORY OF THE ARKANSAS CHEROKEES, 1829. *Arkansas Hist. Q. 1967 26(1): 40-47.* An account published in the 9 March 1829 issue of the *Cherokee Phoenix.* Thirty Cherokee warriors set out from Arkansas on an exploration of rivers toward the Rocky Mountains. The group refused to accompany a similar party of Creeks. Further on the Cherokees killed two friendly Indians and were later attacked themselves. The author uses this account to illustrate the impartiality of Elias Boudinot, the editor of the *Phoenix.*   P. M. McCain

1151. Kilpatrick, Jack Frederick. DOCUMENTS FROM ECHOTA METHODIST MISSION. *Southern Indian Studies 1962 14: 29-31.* The documents reproduced are in the Inoli Letters of the Bureau of American Ethnology. Inoli, who lived in the 19th century, was a Cherokee Methodist minister at the Echota Methodist Mission in North Carolina. The file contains church registers, committee lists, minutes of Sunday School singing classes, four lists of new church members (21 names altogether) and two memos written in 1868 and 1869. A final, undated work is entitled "How The Apostles Who Lived Over There In Ancient Times Died." Based on secondary sources; 3 notes, biblio.   K. P. Davis

1152. Kilpatrick, Jack Frederick. FOLK FORMULAS OF THE OKLAHOMA CHEROKEES. *J. of the Folklore Inst. 1965 1(3): 214-219.* A list of common formulas recited by the laity, especially children "to protect and encourage and bestow small advantages in minor contingencies." 18 notes.   J. C. Crowe

1153. Kilpatrick, Jack Frederick. VERBS ARE KINGS AT PANTHER PLACE: THE CHEROKEE TONGUE VERSUS "ENGLISH." *Southwest R.*

1965 50(4): 372-376. Discusses the differences between two languages—the Cherokee, where each verb has upward of 100 thousand distinct forms, and English, which tends to "group highly diverse actions under the label of a single verb."

D. F. Henderson

1154. Kilpatrick, Jack Frederick and Kilpatrick, Anna Gritts. RECORD OF A NORTH CAROLINA CHEROKEE TOWNSHIP TRIAL (1862). *Southern Indian Studies 1964 16: 21-23.* When most of the Cherokee were moved west in 1838, those left in North Carolina reverted to something like their old township organizations. This record of a trial before the Council of Wolftown in 1862 tells of a man accused of stealing a hoe. The account, written in Cherokee, is muddled but instructive; humorous and, at the same time, pathetic for it reveals the abject poverty of the Indian people. Based on a document in the Inoli Letters in the Smithsonian Institution.

K. P. Davis

1155. Knapp, David, Jr. THE CHICKAMAUGAS. *Georgia Hist. Q. 1967 51(2): 194-196.* A résumé of the history of the Chickamauga, a small segment of the Cherokee tribe that seceded from the parent group in 1777 under the leadership of Chief Chincobacina (Dragging Canoe). The Cherokee had previously allied with the British in colonial conflicts but remained neutral during the American Revolution. The Chickamauga, however, retained their British connections and launched a series of attacks on American settlements between 1777 and 1792. The death of Chincobacina in 1792 was followed by the reintegration of the Chickamauga into the Cherokee tribe. Documented; 2 notes.

R. A. Mohl

1156. Kutsche, Paul. THE TSALI LEGEND: CULTURE HEROES AND HISTORIOGRAPHY. *Ethnohist. 1963 10(4): 329-357.* A comparative analysis stressing the "creative forgetting" and cultural biases evident in four versions of the incident which allowed the eastern (Qualla Reservation, North Carolina) band of Cherokees to escape forced removal by the Army in 1838. The original military reports, the Whig newspaper versions of the 1840's, a humanitarian-ethnologist's use of reminiscence (1890), and modern tribal tradition, are all assayed.

H. J. Graham

1157. Longaker, Richard P. ANDREW JACKSON AND THE JUDICIARY. *Pol. Sci. Q. 1956 71(3): 341-364.* Jackson's attitude toward the judiciary was more complex than has commonly been held. More important than his distaste for John Marshall was his attitude on enforceability in the controversy with Georgia over the Cherokee Territory and his belief, as reflected in the Bank veto, that the president had a right to judge the constitutionality of legislation. On the other hand, he showed respect for the Supreme Court in the Nullification Controversy.

G. Stourzh

1158. Peacok, Mary Thomas. METHODIST MISSION WORK AMONG THE CHEROKEE INDIANS BEFORE THE REMOVAL. *Methodist Hist. 1965 3(3): 20-39.* The earliest mission work among the Cherokee Indian tribe was by a Jesuit in 1736. The Moravians started extensive missionary work in 1752-53, followed by the Presbyterians, Baptists, and Congregationalists. Methodist missions among the Cherokees began in 1821 and continued until the removal of the Indians across the Mississippi in 1839. Information is provided on the organization of the mission work, the leaders, the camp meetings, and the success of the movement.   H. L. Calkin

1159. Robinson, W. Stitt. VIRGINIA AND THE CHEROKEES: INDIAN POLICY FROM SPOTSWOOD TO DINWIDDIE. *The Old Dominion: Essays for Thomas Perkins Abernethy (Charlottesville: The U. Press of Virginia, 1964), pp. 21-40.* Attempts to combine the usual study by historians of the effects of the Indians upon the oncoming white civilization and the ethnological approach to Indian culture. At the beginning of the century the Cherokees were organized by towns; not until 1730 was a structure created for tribal government, the "Tribal Half-Government by Warriors" which led to the election of a Cherokee "emperor." Contact with the white man's civilization was directly responsible for this development. The value of Cherokee trade and the need for Indian allies in the international struggle for North America were positive factors in developing Virginia's policy toward the Cherokees. 64 notes.   E. P. Stickney

1160. Tucker, Norma. NANCY WARD, GHIGHAU OF THE CHEROKEES. *Georgia Hist. Q. 1969 53(2): 192-200.* A biography of a woman leader of the Cherokee during the revolutionary and national periods who received the honored title of Ghighau, meaning "beloved woman." When her Cherokee husband died in a 1755 battle with the Creek, Nancy Ward joined the fight with his weapon. She later married a British Indian trader named Brian Ward. She helped promote peaceful relations with Americans during the Revolution and after, encouraged agricultural improvements among her people, and fought against Indian removal.   R. A. Mohl

1161. Wright, Muriel H. NOTES ON COLONEL ELIAS C. BOUDINOT. *Chronicles of Oklahoma 1964 41(4): 382-407.* Elias C. Boudinot was a Cherokee leader, soldier, statesman, and Confederate Congressman. Boudinot believed that the Indians should be U.S. citizens, that they should own their lands individually with deeds to their property, and that the Indian Territory should be an organized territory of the United States. He established a tobacco factory because the Treaty of 1866 "provided for no regular taxation of any property or enterprise in the Cherokee Nation." His factory was seized by U.S. revenue collectors for his nonpayment of excise taxes. He took his case to the courts, but the Supreme Court decided against him in 1871. He continued to practice law and to operate his farm. He opened a new townsite on the M.K. and T. Railway, and furthered the sale of the Cherokee Outlet by his nation. He died 27 September 1890. This article contains 20 pages of tributes to Boudinot by distinguished fellow citizens.
                                                    I. W. Van Noppen

Chiaha (Chehaw)

1162. Coulter, E. Merton. THE CHEHAW AFFAIR. *Georgia Hist. Q. 1965 49(4): 369-395.* A detailed and comprehensive discussion of the Chiaha (Chehaw) affair when, in 1818, a large Indian town, home of the Chehaws, was burned and some of its residents massacred by Georgia troops while Andrew Jackson was subduing hostile Seminole Indians in Florida. Controversy immediately raged over the questions of whether the Chehaws were hostile or friendly to the Americans and of how many Chehaws were killed.   R. Lowitt

Chickasaw

1163. Phelps, Dawson A. COLBERT FERRY AND SELECTED DOCU- MENTS. *Alabama Hist. Q. 1963 25(3/4): 203-226.* In the treaty of 1801 the United States secured from the Chickasaw Indians the right to open a road south of the Tennessee River, the necessary ferries to be the property of the Chickasaw nation. George Colbert, half-Scot and half-Indian, the negotiator for the Indians, had risen to become the leader of his people "and remained so until the mid-1820's." He played a decisive role in the negotiations by which the Indians surrendered larger parts of their domain in 1805, 1816, and 1818. He operated the ferry until 1817. "By his example he encouraged his people to abandon the traditional primitive village life and to settle on individuals farms." 33 notes, illus.
E. P. Stickney

1164. Rainwater, Percy L. INDIAN MISSIONS AND MISSIONARIES. *J. of Mississippi Hist. 1965 28(1): 15-39.* Describes the mission of the Reverend Joseph Bullen, a Presbyterian minister, at the Chickasaw Towns, 1799-1802; the development of the federal policy of encouraging agriculture and domestic manufacturing among Indians, which culminated in the enactment of "the so-called Civilization Law" of 1819; and the Presbyterian mission which the Reverend Thomas C. Stuart established in the Chickasaw nation in 1821. Bullen closed his mission because his assistants displeased the Chickasaw. By 1834 Stuart's mission converted more than a hundred Indians, Negroes, and whites and established schools which taught several hundred children. Based on secondary works and published diaries, letters, and federal papers.   J. W. Hillje

1165. Bullen, Robert W. JOSEPH BULLEN, SOME BIOGRAPHICAL NOTES. *J. of Mississippi Hist. 1965 27(3): 265-267.* Sketches the New England background of a Congregationalist minister who resided in Mississippi from 1800 and did missionary work among the Chickasaw Indians. Based on published material.   J. W. Hillje

1166. Williams, Schafer. PRESIDENT WASHINGTON'S MESSAGE TO THE CHICKASAW NATION. *Jahrbuch für Amerikastudien [West Germany] 1964 9: 145-148.* A reprint of four documents relating to Washington's policy toward the Chickasaw Indians with explanations concerning the history of these and related documents.   G. Bassler

Choctaw

1167. Baird, W. David. ARKANSAS'S CHOCTAW BOUNDARY: A STUDY OF JUSTICE DELAYED. *Arkansas Hist. Q. 1969 28(3): 203-222.* A study of the western boundary of the territory and state of Arkansas as set by treaties between the United States and the Choctaw Nation. Accepts the traditional argument that the official line of 1825 was drawn irregularly for the benefit of white settlers. Not until 1888, by a decision of the U.S. Supreme Court, was the Choctaw Nation's claim adjudicated by the award of nearly three million dollars. The Choctaw actually received only half of this amount, the remainder going to the lawyers and the heirs of the Choctaw delegates who instituted the cases. Photos, map, 66 notes.   B. A. Drummond

1168. Bearss, Edwin C. FORT SMITH AS THE AGENCY FOR THE WESTERN CHOCTAWS. *Arkansas Hist. Q. 1968 27(1): 40-58.* An account of the difficulties in removing white settlers and Choctaw from lands on either side of the boundary established in 1825 by treaty between the Choctaw Nation and the United States. William McClellan as Indian agent for the Choctaw west of the Mississippi established his agency at Fort Smith to effect the removals. Based on official records; illus., maps, 36 notes.   B. A. Drummond

1169. De Rosier, Arthur H., Jr. ANDREW JACKSON AND NEGOTIATIONS FOR THE REMOVAL OF THE CHOCTAW INDIANS. *Historian 1967 29(3): 343-362.* Discusses the developments leading to and immediately emanating from the Treaty of Dancing Rabbit Creek 27 September 1830 arranged on the part of the United States by Secretary of War John Eaton and General John Coffee, both close personal friends of President Jackson, and the Choctaw Nation, whose principal negotiator was Chief David Folsom. The militancy shown by Jacksonian officials in the handling of Indian affairs "represented the completion of an evolving Indian policy from Thomas Jefferson's desire to move all Eastern Indians across the Mississippi River, through John C. Calhoun's implementation of this desire by educating the Indians to realize the need for removal, to Andrew Jackson's forcing removal as the only alternative to war or subjection by state legislation." Based on material in the Mississippi Department of Archives and History (Jackson), on manuscripts in the Bureau of Indian Affairs and of the War Department in the National Archives, on Margaret L. O'Neill Eaton's "Autobiography," and the Andrew Jackson manuscripts in the Library of Congress, as well as on published sources; 65 notes.
Sr. M. McAuley

1170. DeRosier, Arthur H., Jr. THE CHOCTAW REMOVAL OF 1831: A CIVILIAN EFFORT. *J. of the West 1967 6(2): 237-247.* In the Treaty of Dancing Rabbit Creek, ratified by the Senate in February 1831, the Choctaw of Mississippi agreed to surrender all of their eastern land and move westward. The United States pledged to use its resources to make the movement as orderly and comfortable as possible. To oversee the removal the government appointed George Gaines of Alabama, a white civilian highly respected by the Indians. The author traces the efforts of Gaines and the many problems which arose but concludes that the frequently repeated charge that removal agents cared little about the well-being of the Indians is false. That the removal did not proceed smoothly was due to faulty preparations, bad weather, political trickery, and pure inefficiency rather than to any lack of concern on the part of Gaines. Based largely on records in the Bureau of Indian Affairs, National Archives; 56 notes.

D. N. Brown

1171. DeRosier, Arthur H., Jr. THOMAS JEFFERSON AND THE RE-MOVAL OF THE CHOCTAW INDIANS. *Southern Q. 1962 1(1): 52-62.* Although Jefferson considered making private land-owning farmers and mechanics of the Indians, as president his policy was simply that of acquiring land from them. From 1801 to 1803 negotiators signed three separate treaties with the Choctaw nation in the Mississippi Territory which netted some three million acres. The whites of the southwest were not satisfied, however, so federal policy grew devious in an effort to hold white loyalties against various separatist intrigues. The Indians were encouraged to purchase more goods than they could pay for and then were called to account. In 1805 the Choctaw agreed to exchange 4,142,720 acres for 50 thousand dollars cash, nearly all of which was needed to settle debts the Indians had incurred with a single trading firm. Jefferson was not proud of his agents' handiwork and he withheld the treaty from the Senate until trouble with Spain became acute in 1807. The Senate ratified the treaty early in 1808.

D. A. Stokes

1172. Holmes, Jack D. L. THE CHOCTAWS IN 1795. *Alabama Hist. Q. 1968 30(1): 33-49.* Consists of the names and ranks of outstanding men of the Choctaw as indicated by a 1795 Spanish census. Biblio.

E. E. Eminhizer

Creek

1173. Bryan, Mary Givens. PASSPORTS ISSUED BY GOVERNORS OF GEORGIA 1810-1820. *Natl. Geneal. Soc. Q. 1963 51(2), Supplement: 59-74; and 51(3), Supplement: 75-90.* Records the names of all persons who were issued passports by governors of Georgia "to travel through the Creek Nation of Indians."

D. D. Cameron

1174. Foreman, Carolyn Thomas. LEE COMPERE AND THE CREEK INDIANS. *Chronicles of Oklahoma 1964 42(3): 291-299.* The Reverend Lee Compere, missionary to the Creek, was abused and vilified by the white commissioners of Georgia because of his attitude when, in 1824, the Creek agreed not to cede any more land. William McIntosh and a few other chiefs did sign an agreement at Indian Springs that enabled the whites to take a vast part of the Creek land. Then the Creek signers were shot by avenging Creek led by Menawa or Big Warrior. Compere and his family lived among the Creek for six years and he was held in high esteem as a missionary and teacher. He gave the Indian Bureau a complete vocabulary of the Creek language. Later, when Georgia commissioners, meeting with a few chiefs at their council, became prejudiced against Compere as a troublemaker, the Comperes moved to Alabama where he became minister of the Rehoboth Baptist Church in Montgomery County in 1829. 17 notes.

I. W. Van Noppen

1175. Hatfield, Dorothy B. and Current-Garcia, Eugene. WILLIAM ORRIE TUGGLE AND THE CREEK INDIAN FOLK TALES. *Southern Folklore Q. 1961 25(4): 238-255.* The life and activities of Tuggle, a Georgia Civil War soldier, member of the Georgia Constitutional Convention (1877), attorney, tax authority, and agent for the Creek Indians. In the late 1870's and early 1880's in particular, he spent much time among the Creek Indians in Georgia and made very careful notes on customs, myths, folktales, etc. The valuable collection had been considered lost—though fragments had been known to and used by Joel Chandler Harris and other writers—but has now been located and is described in detail here.

H. Aptheker

1176. Holland, James W. ANDREW JACKSON AND THE CREEK WAR: VICTORY AT THE HORSESHOE BEND. *Alabama R. 1968 21(4): 243-275.* Detailed account of the Creek War (1813-14), described as "a war to punish the Indians, a civil war among the Indians, and a war within the War of 1812." The war resulted in the addition of some 20 million acres to the public domain; and along with his victory at New Orleans, it propelled Andrew Jackson into national prominence. Based on manuscript collections and newspapers; 136 notes.

D. F. Henderson

1177. Hryniewicki, Richard J. THE CREEK TREATY OF WASHINGTON, 1826. *Georgia Hist. Q. 1964 48(4): 425-441.* Carefully examines the events in 1825 and 1826 leading to the Treaty of Washington, by which Georgia acquired virtually all of the Creek lands remaining in the state. Besides differences among the Creeks, federal-state relations as they affected Indian policy were involved in tensions arising over this treaty.

R. Lowitt

1178. Hryniewicki, Richard J. THE CREEK TREATY OF NOVEMBER 15, 1827. *Georgia Hist. Q. 1968 52(1): 1-15.* In 1825 federal Indian commissioners succeeded in convincing General William McIntosh, chief of the Lower Creek towns, to sign a treaty ceding remaining Creek tribal lands in Georgia. McIntosh, however, did not represent the Upper Creek tribes, who protested the treaty. At the urging of President John Quincy Adams, a second agreement (Treaty of Washington, 1826) abrogated the 1825 negotiation, satisfied the Upper Creeks, and secured the desired cession. The discovery of a surveying error left a small portion of Georgia land in Creek hands; further complicating the issue, Georgia refused to recognize the abrogation of the 1825 treaty. This article, based on research in published and unpublished Indian Office records, details the circumstances surrounding the Creek Treaty of 15 November 1827 which terminated Creek title to the disputed land. The final agreement represented the result of successful intrigue by Indian Agents Thomas McKenney and John Crowell. In return for 47,429 dollars in cash and goods, the Creeks surrendered about 192,000 acres, thus ending Georgia's long struggle with that southern tribe. Map, 40 notes.

R. A. Mohl

1179. Mauelshagen, Carl and Davis, Gerald H. THE MORAVIANS' PLAN FOR A MISSION AMONG THE CREEK INDIANS, 1803-1804. *Georgia Hist. Q. 1967 51(3): 358-364.* Two documents elaborate plans of the Moravian Brotherhood to reestablish missions among the Creek which had been disrupted in 1740 during the War of Jenkins' Ear (1739-42). The first document is a preliminary report by three Moravian mission directors announcing the benevolent intentions of the "assembled brethren." The second document is a more detailed report describing desirable locations in the Creek country for mission stations, with additional interesting comments on Indian society. Despite the original optimism, the mission was never established.   R. A. Mohl

1180. Murdoch, Richard K. MISSION TO THE CREEK NATION IN 1794. *Florida Hist. Q. 1956 34(3): 266-284.* After the American Revolutionary War the Indians along the Georgia (U.S.)-Florida (Spanish) border were an uncommitted force in the international rivalry. In 1793 the Spanish governor of East Florida dispatched a special agent, John Hambly, to the Creek Indians to report on their political outlook. Hambly kept a diary which is reproduced in English, with annotations. The original is in the Archivo General de Indias, Seville.   C. W. Arnade

1181. O'Donnell, J. H. ALEXANDER MC GILLIVRAY: TRAINING FOR LEADERSHIP, 1777-1783. *Georgia Hist. Q. 1965 49(2): 172-186.* Traces the emergence of McGillivray as "Head Warrior" of the Creek Nation following the slaying of Euristisigus in 1782. It is concluded, however, that it is problematical whether McGillivray would have been elevated to that position had it not been for the experience and influence he gained through his service in the British Indian Department during the American Revolution.   R. Lowitt

1182. Owsley, Frank L.,Jr. BENJAMIN HAWKINS, THE FIRST MODERN INDIAN AGENT. *Alabama Hist. Q. 1968 30(2): 7-13.* Discusses Benjamin Hawkins' success as Indian agent among the Creek in advancing them toward white civilization. His success is attributed to his increasing the power of the chiefs and using them to administer justice and enforce the laws. He also controlled the white traders who were a source of trouble. In addition, he took an interest in the women who did the farming, giving them new seeds and teaching them new methods, thereby helping to create a better food supply. He also taught them to weave cloth. Indians near to him did not take part in the Creek War of 1813.   E. E. Eminhizer

1183. Owsley, Frank L., Jr. BRITISH AND INDIAN ACTIVITIES IN SPANISH WEST FLORIDA DURING THE WAR OF 1812. *Florida Hist. Q. 1967 46(2): 111-123.* Prior to 1813, the Spanish had followed a policy of supporting the Creek and Seminole Indians in the gulf coast area as a barrier to expansion by the United States. When the Indians were aroused to war with the United States, the Spanish provided munitions for the Creek. Earl Bathurst, British secretary of state for war, was urged to arm the Indians and send British officers to lead them as part of the gulf coast campaign. Serious British blunders precluded success. Based on unpublished Spanish, English, and U.S. documents and letters; 47 notes.   R. V. Calvert

1184. Owsley, Frank L., Jr. FRANCIS SCOTT KEY'S MISSION TO ALABAMA IN 1833. *Alabama R. 1970 23(3): 181-192.* In an effort to resolve a conflict between the state of Alabama and the United States over enforcement of the Treaty of Cusseta (1832) negotiated with the Creek Indians, President Jackson sent Francis Scott Key to Alabama late in 1833. Key successfully carried out his mission, but the "disputation produced personal divisions which were never repaired." Based primarily on Creek Agency Records in the National Archives; 34 notes.   D. F. Henderson

1185. Owsley, Frank L., Jr. THE FORT MIMS MASSACRE. *Alabama R. 1971 24(3): 192-204.* Following a successful attack on a white expedition at the Battle of Burnt Corn, the Red Sticks, a hostile faction of the Creeks, determined to attack and destroy Fort Mims in the Mississippi Territory. Absolves Brigadier General Ferdinand L. Claiborne, commander of the Mississippi militia, of blame for the massacre, but accuses Major Daniel Beasley of gross negligence. Poor scouting, an attack at noon when most of the garrison was eating, seizure of the port holes by the Indians, and inability to close the main gates were all elements in the defeat (30 August 1813). "Of the 275 to 300 whites and half-breeds in Fort Mims at the time of the attack, between 20 and 40 escaped; therefore, around 247-260 whites, half-breeds and friendly Indians were killed in the battle." Creek losses were at least 100 killed. The massacre had significant short- and long-range implications. Immediately, the fall of the fort started a major Indian war in the South that resulted in a "substantial build-up" of U.S. forces in the area, which probably prevented the British from occupying an undefended Gulf Coast in 1814. More important, the relationships between Americans and the southern Indians drastically changed. The Creeks, who had been living peacefully and in close contact with the settlers of the Mississippi Territory, lost more than half their land, and within 20 years had to move west of the Mississippi. 30 notes.   D. F. Henderson

1186. Roberts, Frances C. POLITICS AND PUBLIC LAND DISPOSAL IN ALABAMA'S FORMATIVE PERIOD. *Alabama R. 1969 22(3): 163-174.* The key events in the area which would shortly become the state of Alabama included the defeat of the Creek Indians at Horseshoe Bend in 1814, the Treaty of Ghent, and an act of 17 February 1815 which established the boundaries of the Creek cession, created a survey district within it, and provided for the appointment of land officials for a land office. The strong political influence of the Georgia faction in Congress, headed by Secretary of the Treasury William H. Crawford, was early evident, and most of the land officials were handpicked by Crawford. Lands were opened for sale in 1817. Based on various printed sources, the Records of the General Land Office, and the Ledgers of the Register and Receiver of the Land Office at several Alabama locations; 46 notes.   D. F. Henderson

1187. Smith, Daniel M. JAMES SEAGROVE AND THE MISSION TO TUCK-AUBATCHEE, 1793. *Georgia Hist. Q. 1960 44(1): 41-55.* Presents background of the relations between the Creek Indians and the United States. The author reveals how James Seagrove succeeded in his mission, despite heavy odds—federal weakness, Spanish intrigue, Georgia interference—in preventing a major war between the powerful Creeks and the United States.   R. Lowitt

1188. Thomason, Hugh M. GOVERNOR PETER EARLY AND THE CREEK INDIAN FRONTIER, 1813-1815. *Georgia Hist. Q. 1961 45(3): 223-237.* Examines Indian affairs in Georgia and along its frontiers during the administration of Governor Peter Early, which took place while the War of 1812 was raging.   R. Lowitt

1189. Wright, J. Leitch, Jr. CREEK-AMERICAN TREATY OF 1790: ALEXANDER MC GILLIVRAY AND THE DIPLOMACY OF THE OLD SOUTHWEST. *Georgia Hist. Q. 1967 51(4): 379-400.* Traces the background of the Creek-American Treaty of New York City of 1790 and explains the reasons for its ineffectiveness. The treaty, signed by the supposed leader of the Creek Indians Alexander McGillivray, provided for permanent peace between the U.S. government and the Southern Indians, stipulated the cession of Indian lands to the Americans, and placed the Creeks under the protection of the national government rather than the state of Georgia or some foreign power. Secret clauses granted McGillivray a monopoly of the Indian trade and a duty-free port for the importation of trading goods. But the treaty was ineffective. McGillivray did not represent all of the southern Indians; the state of Georgia claimed sovereignty over the Indians and the land of the southern territory; and both Great Britain and Spain had important interests in the area. The failure of the U.S. negotiators, especially Secretary of War Henry Knox, to take account of their interests caused these four parties to work actively for the demise of the agreement. Thus the British stirred up the anti-McGillivray Indians, the Spanish weaned McGillivray from his bargain with the United States, and the terms of the treaty were never executed. Based on research in published and unpublished diplomatic manuscripts; 49 notes.   R. A. Mohl

Natchez

1190. Tooker, Elisabeth. NATCHEZ SOCIAL ORGANIZATION: FACT OR ANTHROPOLOGICAL FOLKLORE? *Ethnohist. 1963 10(4): 358-372.* Questions the now accepted yet inherently incongruous view of Natchez society as one which combined caste and exogamy; shows from analysis that John Reed Swanton possibly misread once-scanty documentary evidence relating to this extinct tribe.   H. J. Graham

Seminole

1191. Adams, George R. THE CALOOSAHATCHEE MASSACRE: ITS SIG-
NIFICANCE IN THE SECOND SEMINOLE WAR. *Florida Hist. Q. 1970
48(4): 368-380.* The significance of the Caloosahatchee River attack was its
influence in prolonging the Second Seminole War. Occurring during a brief
period in 1839 when it seemed that tempers had cooled and peace might prevail
between whites and Seminoles in Florida, the Caloosahatchee River Indian attack
on a poorly protected white trading post served to inflame white Floridians who
became more insistent about Seminole removal. Neither public opinion nor the
lack of Seminole unity had been considered in anticipating a peaceful settlement
of white-Indian hostilities in Florida. Seminole Indians who had not been represented at the peace agreement at Fort King in May 1839 were not eager to accede
to what amounted to merely a temporary postponement of their removal from
Florida. Following the Caloosahatchee attack and massacre during the truce
period (23 July 1839), new hostilities erupted all over the territory, with both civil
and military authorities criticized for policies considered ineffectual. Disagreement between the federal and territorial officials resulted in the replacement of
Florida's territorial governor. Not until 1842 was the war successfully closed,
after several changes of military command. The additional two and one-half years
of the war were necessitated because the truce was broken by the Caloosahatchee
massacre. Based on published material; map, 40 notes.   R. V. Calvert

1192. Bittle, George C. FIRST CAMPAIGN OF THE SECOND SEMINOLE
WAR. *Florida Hist. Q. 1967 46(1): 39-45.* Differing opinions abound on the cause
of the Second Seminole War. Apparently it was merely part of the border warfare
characteristic of all American frontier areas in which white settlers were pushing
into Indian territory. Before the beginning of the Second Seminole War in 1835,
the Florida militia was unprepared although on active duty. First to mobilize his
command, Brigadier General Joseph Hernandez issued the orders for his East
Florida Militia Brigade 26 October 1835. Short of serviceable guns and unaccus-
tomed to military discipline, the militia nevertheless revealed courage under fire
in their first campaign. 33 notes.   R. V. Calvert

1193. Bittle, George C. FLORIDA FRONTIER INCIDENTS DURING THE
1850'S. *Florida Hist. Q. 1970 49(2): 153-160.* Although no significant warfare
occurred on the Florida frontier at the beginning of the 1850's, the Indian
question was far from settled. The Florida militia was disorganized. Insisting that
the Constitution prohibited maintaining an army in peacetime, Governor Thomas
Brown vetoed a Seminole removal bill in January 1853 which provided for a
thousand-man militia, one-half to be infantry. The legislature overrode his veto
and his successor, James E. Broome, failed in 1853 to execute the law, because
not one company of the proposed infantry regiment could be raised. In January
1856, however, the services of several volunteer companies which offered to go
on active duty were rejected. As the Third Seminole War gradually ended, militia
units were removed individually from active duty until Governor Madison S.
Perry announced in November 1858 that no organized Florida militia existed,

except for one or two volunteer companies. From 1856 to 1858, about 24 companies had been called to active state and federal duty. Based partly on unpublished letters; 35 notes.   R. V. Calvert

1194. Buker, George E. LIEUTENANT LEVIN M. POWELL, U.S.N., PIONEER OF RIVERINE WARFARE. *Florida Hist. Q. 1969 47(3): 253-275.* Lineage of modern riverine warfare can be traced to the Second Seminole War of 1835-42 in Florida. Expeditions were begun from Tampa Bay in 1836 to perform a flanking and harassing action upon the Indians being driven southward along the Florida west coast by the army. In command of several amphibious expeditions against the Seminoles in the Florida coastal islands, inlets, rivers, and swamplands, Lieutenant Levin M. Powell, U.S. Navy, pioneered in the development of small boat assault tactics for shallow water and swamps. For greater mobility, supplies were cut to a minimun in the small boats while a larger ship, such as a Coast Guard cutter, provided a supply and operations base anchored in deep water. Powell participated in joint Army-Navy ventures against the Seminoles in the Everglades, where the Indians had boasted that white men could not go. While riverine warfare defies rigid tactical doctrine, 19th-century and modern practitioners would agree that it is not combat *on* the water but, rather, combat *from* the water. Based partly on unpublished letters and documents; 2 illus., map, 49 notes.   R. V. Calvert

1195. Covington, James W. AN EPISODE IN THE THIRD SEMINOLE WAR. *Florida Hist. Q. 1966 45(1): 45-59.* Skirmishes with small bands of disgruntled Seminole Indians in Florida, 1855 to 1858, generally overlooked by historians, retarded the growth of large sections of Florida and might well be called "The Third Seminole War." Based on secondary sources, memoirs, state papers, and newspapers.   G. L. Lycan

1196. Covington, James W. CUBAN BLOODHOUNDS AND THE SEMINOLES. *Florida Hist. Q. 1954 33(2): 111-119.* The effort to subdue the Seminoles in Florida, 1840, through the use of Cuban bloodhounds failed because of swamps and water and, possibly, improper training and handling of the dogs. Based on American military and territorial papers, newspapers, *Congressional Globe,* and a biography of Zachary Taylor.   G. L. Lycan

1197. Covington, James W. FEDERAL RELATIONS WITH THE APALACHICOLA INDIANS: 1823-1838. *Florida Hist. Q. 1963 42(2): 125-141.* A small band of Seminoles tried to live peaceably near the mouth of the Apalachicola River; but after years of harassment by the U.S. Government and frequent violence at the hands of criminal white men they gave up and moved westward, following the other tribes. Based on private papers, state papers, and secondary material.   G. L. Lycan

1198. Covington, James W. MIGRATION OF THE SEMINOLES INTO FLORIDA, 1700-1820. *Florida Hist. Q. 1968 46(4): 340-357.* The original Indian tribes of Florida, around 25 thousand Apalachee, Calusa, and Timucuan, were almost extinct when the Lower Creek began settlements on the peninsula. Relatively late arrivals to the Florida peninsula, the Seminole migrated in three distinct phases. In the first period, between 1700 and 1750, they made raids, as English allies, against the Spaniards and their Indian allies. In the second period, 1750-1812, several villages were settled in the northern part of Florida, while small groups explored the remainder of the peninsula. In the third period, 1812-20, pressure from white settlers in Georgia and Alabama pushed the Upper and Lower Creek tribes to move south into Florida. Available evidence indicates that prior to 1800, no Seminole villages were located south of Tampa Bay. As more of the Creek moved into Florida, where they were known as Seminole, they were welcomed by the Spanish. In the period 1812-20, around two thousand Upper and Lower Creek moved, seeking refuge in Spanish Florida following defeats in Alabama and Georgia. A compilation of Indian bands in Florida in 1822 listed only five (out of 35) bands at Tampa Bay or south of it. Within a short time after the signing of the 1823 Treaty of Moultrie Creek, a considerable number of Seminoles migrated into central and southern Florida. Partly based on unpublished English records; 69 notes. R. V. Calvert

1199. Covington, James W. THE ARMED OCCUPATION ACT OF 1842. *Florida Hist. Q. 1961 40(1): 41-52.* The Armed Occupation Act of 1842, giving 160 acres of land to actual settlers who moved into the area near the lands of the Seminole Indians, produced a rush of settlers and brought despair to the Indians. Based on U.S. state papers, newspapers, private papers, and secondary works. G. L. Lycan

1200. Cushman, Joseph D., Jr. THE INDIAN RIVER SETTLEMENT: 1842-1849. *Florida Hist. Q. 1964 43(1): 21-35.* Relates an unsuccessful attempt of some 50 families to establish an agricultural community in southeast Florida, 1842 to 1849, on lands donated by federal grant to attract settlers into an area near the home of the ferocious Seminole Indians. Based on official and personal papers and secondary works. G. L. Lycan

1201. Eby, Cecil D., Jr., ed. MEMOIR OF A WEST POINTER IN FLORIDA: 1825. *Florida Hist. Q. 1962/63 41(2): 154-164.* Semihumorous account by Lieutenant Alfred Beckley of a futile eight-day expedition in Florida swamps and wilderness to support a possible attack on Seminole Indians. The expedition was an irritant that probably helped bring on the Indian War 10 years later. Careful editorial comments and notes. G. L. Lycan

1202. Holmes, Jack D. L. THE SOUTHERN BOUNDARY COMMISSION, THE CHATTAHOOCHEE RIVER, AND THE FLORIDA SEMINOLES, 1799. *Florida Hist. Q. 1966 44(4): 312-341.* The American and Spanish surveying party commissioned to locate the boundary line of 31 degrees, as called for in the Treaty of San Lorenzo (Pinckney's Treaty) were molested and finally stopped by hostile Seminoles. Based on private papers, journals, Spanish and American state papers, secondary works, and newspapers. G. L. Lycan

1203. Kersey, Harry A., Jr. EDUCATING THE SEMINOLE INDIANS OF FLORIDA, 1879-1970. *Florida Hist. Q. 1970 49(1): 16-35.* Following the Seminole Wars, the few Seminole Indians still remaining in the interior swamplands of the southern Florida peninsula made few contacts with the white settlers who had taken their lands. Few federal or state efforts were made to bring public school education to the Indians between the 1870's and 1900. In 1875, however, Captain Richard Henry Pratt, founder of the Carlisle Indian Industrial School, took charge of 72 Indians from the Southwest, who were imprisoned at Fort Marion in St. Augustine. Pratt wanted to educate the Indians to enable them to learn the white man's culture, and to teach them a useful trade to prepare them for assimilation into white society. The first to be notably successful in educating small Seminole children was Ivy Julia Cromartie Stranahan, who shunned traditional school materials and taught informally for over 25 years, until the Dania Seminole Reservation federal day school was opened in 1927. Although the Dania School was closed in 1936, no Indian children actually attended any local public schools until the 1940's. Parental indifference toward education has gradually been changing among the Seminole, so more and more Seminole children are attending public schools. Based partly on taped interviews; 33 notes.

R. V. Calvert

1204. Laumer, Frank. ENCOUNTER BY THE RIVER. *Florida Hist. Q. 1968 46(4): 322-339.* About 250 regular army men under the leadership of Lieutenant Colonel Alexander C. W. Fanning and about 700 militia volunteers led by Richard Keith Call, ex-regular army captain and then territorial governor of Florida and general of Florida volunteers, all commanded by General Duncan Lamont Clinch, gathered at Fort Drane in mid-winter of 1835. Indian guides had brought word of a large force of warriors encamped beyond the Withlacoochee River, and General Clinch believed that a defeat in open battle would destroy Seminole resistance and secure the frontier for white settlers. Marching on 29 and 30 December, the troops arrived at the river on 31 December to discover there was no ford in the vicinity. Some 2 1/2 miles upstream at the nearest ford, Osceola, with 220 Seminole warriors and 30 armed Negroes waiting in ambush, quickly moved downriver to attack. Many of the volunteers whose enlistments would expire in 12 hours refused to cross the river and headed for home. A fierce, bloody battle was fought, with the Indians finally withdrawing. Osceola, recovering from a wound in his arm, sent word to General Clinch a month later that they would continue to fight until the last Seminole was killed. Based mainly on published works; 41 notes.

R. V. Calvert

1205. Laumer, Frank. THIS WAS FORT DADE. *Florida Hist. Q. 1966 45(1): 1-11.* Describes the purpose, erection, use, and decay of Fort Dade. The fort was an army outpost against the warring Seminoles in Florida. Based on secondary works, army reports, personal correspondence, state papers, and newspapers.

G. L. Lycan

1206. Mahon, John K. LETTERS FROM THE SECOND SEMINOLE WAR. *Florida Hist. Q. 1958 36(4): 331-352.* Letters from Lieutenant Joseph R. Smith with running editorial comments, forming a narrative of his experiences in the Second Seminole War in Florida, 1837-42.   G. L. Lycan

1207. Mahon, John K. TWO SEMINOLE TREATIES: PAYNE'S LANDING, 1832, AND FT. GIBSON, 1833. *Florida Hist. Q. 1962 41(1): 1-21.* These harsh treaties, probably obtained through "force and fraud," provided that the Florida Indians should move to Oklahoma and join their enemies, the Creeks. The Second Seminole War, 1835-42, resulted. Based on state papers, private correspondence, biographies, and other secondary works.   G. L. Lycan

1208. Neill, Wilfred T. SURVEYORS' FIELD NOTES AS A SOURCE OF HISTORICAL INFORMATION. *Florida Hist. Q. 1956 34(4): 329-333.* Recommends to historians engaged in research on the Seminole period in Florida the study of the field notes of government surveyors who mapped out parts of the state of Florida from 1830-40.   B. Waldstein

1209. Olsson, Nils W. ANDERS GARBERG AND TERTIUS OTTO BENGTSSON, INDIAN FIGHTERS. *Swedish Pioneer Hist. Q. 1964 15(3): 99-108.* Garberg (1809-52) was one of the many Swedish immigrants who enlisted in the U.S. Army for various reasons. He fought the Seminole Indians in Florida and did garrison duty throughout the Southeast. He never really enjoyed army life but served honorably. Garberg returned to Sweden to live after his discharge. In contrast, Bengtsson (1828-1911) adjusted well to army life. He served three enlistments, saw action in the Mexican War, and served in the Civil War. Finally discharged in 1866, he became a storekeeper in Mexico where he lived the remainder of his life. Based on recently located letters of the two men and on U.S. Army records.   E. P. Costello

1210. Porter, Kenneth W. [BILLY BOWLEGS.] *Florida Hist. Q. 1967 45.*
    BILLY BOWLEGS (HOLATA MICCO) IN THE SEMINOLE WARS: A STUDY IN RELATIONSHIPS AND IDENTITIES (PART I). (3): 219-242. Since Billy Bowlegs has been widely confused with three other prominent Seminoles, one purpose of the author is to disentangle those identities. Billy Bowlegs should not be confused with his kinsman, King Bowlegs, Seminole headchief (1813-18), nor did he die in 1859 as some claimed. The Billy Bowlegs who fought in the Florida wars was the same one who fought in the Civil War. Still at large at the end of the Second Seminole War in 1842, Holata Micco, nicknamed Billy Bowlegs, was acknowledged Seminole chief in Florida, refusing to agree to removal to Indian Territory until 1858. Deliberate destruction of his prize banana grove by soldiers, as a prank, set off the Third Seminole War in December 1855, but bribery, rather than victory, brought an end to the war with Billy Bowlegs' consent to moving in 1858. He was erroneously reported dead in 1859. Illus., 38 notes.
    BILLY BOWLEGS (HOLATA MICCO) IN THE CIVIL WAR (PART II). (4): 391-401. Billy Bowlegs was one of the principal chiefs of the Five Civilized Tribes who supported the Union in the Civil War. In general, the

conservative full-blood Indians were neutral at first and later pro-Union, since the little fair treatment they had received had come from Washington and the regular army, not from southern territorial and state governments. In May 1862, Billy Bowlegs was commissioned captain of Company A, First Indian Regiment, which participated in over 30 actions, mostly in Indian Territory and in northwestern Arkansas. After distinguishing himself in battle, Billy Bowlegs succumbed to smallpox in late 1863 or early 1864 and was buried in the National Cemetery near Fort Gibson, Oklahoma. 23 notes.   R. V. Calvert

1211. Porter, Kenneth W. NEGROES AND THE SEMINOLE WAR, 1835-1842. *J. of Southern Hist. 1964 30(4): 427-450.* The Second Seminole War resulted from the decision to move the Seminoles from Florida. This decision was influenced by the presence and position of several hundred Negroes among the Seminoles, some of them slaves of the Seminoles or nominally free, but some of them runaways from white masters. The Negroes, fearful of being turned over to whites, strongly influenced the general Seminole decision to resist removal. These Negroes were shrewd and farsighted in their plans for resistance and active and aggressive in carrying them out. Once convinced, however, that the government was inflexibly determined on Seminole removal—and persuaded, too, that if they and the Indians surrendered, their own freedom and the lives of both races would be respected—they were almost as influential in persuading the more recalcitrant Indians to surrender as they had previously been in rallying Seminole resistance.   S. E. Humphreys

1212. Rogers, George C. A DESCRIPTION OF OSCEOLA. *South Carolina Hist. Mag. 1964 65(2): 85-86.* Letters from a Providence, Rhode Island, woman to her brother concerning Osceola, a leader of the Seminoles, giving a general description and a report of his death. Based on eyewitness and newspaper reports.
                                        V. O. Bardsley

1213. Sturtevant, William C. SEMINOLE MYTHS OF THE ORIGIN OF RACES. *Ethnohist. 1963 10(1): 80-86.* Details Seminole myths.   S

1214. Upchurch, John C. ASPECTS OF THE DEVELOPMENT AND EXPLORATION OF THE FORBES PURCHASE. *Florida Hist. Q. 1969 48(2): 117-139.* The Forbes Purchase land tract in north-central Florida was an object of exploitation for 57 years, first under Panton, Leslie and Company, then under its successor John Forbes and Company, and later under the Apalachicola Land Company. Partners William Panton, Thomas Forbes, and John Leslie acquired title to the Forbes tract with Spanish government permission—as compensation for Indian debts to the trading firm. Total acreage was estimated at around one and one-half million acres. Since the Seminole Indians did not buy back the land, as was originally hoped, John Forbes decided to sell to settlers and speculators in order to reduce the company's loss. The War of 1812, coupled with Indian depredations and a decrease in trade, led to the partners' decision to sell the bulk of the tract to a Havana merchant and his partners. Uncertainty about the validity of the purchase continued until a Supreme Court ruling in 1835. Surveys showed that the land lacked valuable mineral resources and good agricultural lands, although that portion east of the Ochlockonee River had abundant timber. Formed in 1835, the Apalachicola Land Company became insolvent in 1858. By 1861, the entire Forbes Purchase had been sold—for only a few cents per acre. Based partly on unpublished maps; 57 notes.   R. V. Calvert

1215. Wallace, Fred W. THE STORY OF CAPTAIN JOHN C. CASEY. *Florida Hist. Q. 1962/63 41(2): 127-144.* Deals with Casey's able efforts to pacify the Seminoles and induce them to accept removal to Indian Territory (Oklahoma), and his diligent work in mapping the southeast Florida coastline, including Casey Key which was named in his honor. Based on private papers, secondary works, and newspapers.   G. L. Lycan

1216. White, Frank F., Jr., ed. MACOMB'S MISSION TO THE SEMINOLES. *Florida Hist. Q. 1956 35(2): 130-193.* The official diary of Lieutenant John T. Sprague with footnotes and annotations, describing the unsuccessful attempt of General Alexander Macomb to put an end to the Seminole War in 1835 by peaceful conferences with the Indians in Florida.   G. L. Lycan

1217. Wright, J. Leitch, Jr. A NOTE ON THE FIRST SEMINOLE WAR AS SEEN BY THE INDIANS, NEGROES, AND THEIR BRITISH ADVISERS. *J. of Southern Hist. 1968 34(4): 565-575.* Suggests that the causes of the First Seminole War in 1817-18 were more complex than the traditional U.S. explanation. The Indians considered that part of their lands lay in the United States above the Florida boundary, that the Americans were the aggressors, and that, rather than making unprovoked attacks across the U.S. border, they were merely defending their homeland. Moreover, it seems apparent from the diplomatic exchanges between the United States, Britain, and Spain, that the United States was determined to have all of Spanish Florida. 26 notes.   I. M. Leonard

1218. —. OSCEOLA. *Florida Hist. Q. 1955 33(3/4).*
        Goggin, John M. OSCEOLA: PORTRAITS, FEATURES, AND DRESS, pp. 161-192. The personal appearance and manner of dress of Osceola is established from available portraits, various personal memoirs, newspaper accounts, and personal objects that have been preserved.
        Ward, May McNeer. THE DISAPPEARANCE OF THE HEAD OF OSCEOLA, pp. 193-201. From medical reports, personal correspondence, museum records, and family traditions it is affirmed that Dr. Frederick Weedon, a "friend" of Osceola, removed the chief's head just before burial.
        Coe, Charles H. THE PARENTAGE OF OSCEOLA, pp. 202-205. Makes a fair case that Osceola was a full-blooded Indian—contrary to the general belief that his father was white. Based on U.S. Army records, contemporary statements and much secondary material.
        Sturtevant, William C. NOTES ON MODERN SEMINOLE TRADITIONS OF OSCEOLA, pp. 206-217. An attempt to determine Osceola's sib, his rank, the pronunciation of his name, and his descendants. Based on U.S. government publications, extensive interviews with Seminoles, and secondary works.
        Proter, Kenneth W. OSCEOLA AND THE NEGROES, pp. 235-246. Holds that the old tradition that Osceola's part-Negro wife was kidnapped and

subjected to slavery was fallacious, and was probably fabricated by the abolitionists. Based on American State Papers and other primary and secondary material.
   Boyd, Mark F. ASI-YAHOLO OR OSCEOLA, pp. 247-305. A brief history of the life and wars of Osceola. Little is actually known of this man, America's most famous Indian. Based on an immense array of primary sources, private and public.   G. L. Lycan

Westo

1219. Juricek, John T. THE WESTO INDIANS. *Ethnohist. 1964 11(2): 134-173.*
Analyzes and reconciles collated accounts of the hostile tribe most dreaded by colonists of South Carolina. Suggests that the Westos were not a single ethnic group but rather a federation of identifiable peoples formed in the late 16th and early 17th centuries. Spanish pressures in Florida and English settlement in Virginia are seen as having caused a great intermixing of Indian groups after 1607. "The Westos...were one product of this commingling." Presence and leadership of northern elements in the confederation also is indicated, the Rickohockans being definitely of Iroquoian ancestry. This tribe "acted as a magnet upon the alienated southern Indians." Reviews and updates earlier hypotheses of V. S. Crane and J. R. Swanton.   H. J. Graham

3

GENERAL INDIAN HISTORY
1492-1900

General

1220. Berkhofer, Robert F., Jr. PROTESTANTS, PAGANS, AND SE-QUENCES AMONG THE NORTH AMERICAN INDIANS, 1760-1860. *Ethnohist. 1963 10(3): 201-332.* Of all acculturative agents, Protestant missionaries who sought establishment of a "scriptural, self-propagating christianity [sic]," were most aggressive and demanded greatest change on the Indians' part. Efforts of six denominations (Quaker, Moravian, Baptist, Methodist, Presbyterian, Episcopalian) among six tribes (Oneida, Seneca, Cherokee, Choctaw, Ojibwa-Sioux, Nez Percé), all of which had lost substantial autonomy, are reviewed: four patterns of response are noted, and the degrees of cultural fragmentation discussed and analytically diagrammed.
H. J. Graham

1221. Carmichael, Leonard. THE SMITHSONIAN INSTITUTION AND THE AMERICAN PHILOSOPHICAL SOCIETY. *Pro. of the Am. Phil. Soc. 1957 101(5): 401-408.* The Englishman James Smithson (1765-1829) left his estate to the United States to found an institution "for the increase and diffusion of knowledge among men." The author gives a brief description of the administration of the institution, founded in 1846, followed by brief biographies of several of its secretaries, including Joseph Henry (1796-1878) and Spencer Baird (1823-88). Major John Wesley Powell (1834-1902) organized the study of the American Indian. The institute also has three art bureaus, including the National Gallery presented by Andrew Mellon (1855-1937) and the Freer Gallery of Art presented by Charles Freer (1856-1919). A rebuilding program is in progress.
N. Kurland

1222. Chaput, Donald. FROM INDIAN TO FRENCH: A FEMALE NAME CURIOSITY. *Names 1966 14(3): 143-149.* An examination of French names bestowed on Indian women who married Frenchmen in North America. The French made no attempt to translate the Indian name. Rather the Indian woman was simply given a saint's name for her first name. Her surname was usually entered in the records as "Sauvage," "Sauvagesse," or "Panis(e)" (the last stemming from Pawnee originally but having assumed the meaning of any person captured from another tribe), or with a tribal name such as "Huronne." Based on French-Canadian histories and genealogical works; 19 notes.

D. Lindsey

1223. Chaput, Donald E. A PLEA FOR MODERATION IN PLACE-NAME CONTROVERSIES. *Michigan Hist. 1965 49(1): 68-72.* Takes to task both "purists," who quibble ludicrously over authenticating Indian and French place-names, and "modernists," who would reject cultural and linguistic traditions for more "practical" designations.

J. K. Flack

1224. Courville, Cyril B. TRADE TOMAHAWKS. *Masterkey 1963 37(4): 124-136.* Discussion of the history of the tomahawk, developing from axes and war clubs to a pipe. The use of the tomahawk was encouraged by the French and English, and it was later converted to a combination pipe and tomahawk. Tomahawks were used as weapons of war by most North American Indians. However, after the Civil War, when the six-shooter and repeating rifle were developed, the tomahawk became less effective as a weapon and became a status symbol of rank among the Plains Indians. Based on primary and secondary sources; 6 illus., 3 notes, biblio.

C. N. Warren

1225. Cracroft, Richard H. THE AMERICAN WEST OF KARL MAY. *Am. Q. 1967 19(2 pt. 1): 249-258.* Discusses the American West as created in the nearly 40 volumes of the German adventure writer Karl May. May's Teutonic hero Old Shatterhand and the Indian chief Winnetou, the noble savage of Germanic imagination, held a powerful appeal for German readers. May's romanticism and his unvarnished nationalism shine through in the colorful adventures of Old Shatterhand, a sort of Christianized Siegfried. Old Shatterhand's overall superiority is contrasted against the vices and deficiencies of May's villains, the "half-breed, the Mormon, and the Yankee." While May never really visited the Wild West, his thrilling narratives presented an image which peculiarly suited the views of his largely Germanic audience. Based on German literary criticism, extensive quotation from May's works, and some citations from American critics; 15 notes.

R. S. Pickett

1226. Demikhovski, M. POLITIKA PRAVIASHCHIKH KRUGOV SSHA V OTNOSHENII INDEISKOGO NASELENIIA [The policy of U.S. ruling circles toward the Indian population]. *Voprosy Istorii [USSR] 1966 (2): 70-82.* Between 1817 and 1828, U.S. policy was based chiefly on "land-exchange" agreements with the Indians. This policy was based on mutual trust and ruled out any acts of violence or coercion. With the election of Andrew Jackson as president in 1829, the policy took on a completely different viewpoint. The Indian Removal Act of 28 May 1830 forced wholesale evictions of Indian tribes from certain territories which were coveted by land-owning capitalists. Only the large plantation owners of the deep South objected, fearing the loss of a cheap labor market.

Each successive government reflected the interests of one or another capitalistic group, but none of them really ever worked for the betterment of the Indian's position. 60 notes.   G. Tuscaeff

1227. Diket, A. L. THE NOBLE SAVAGE CONVENTION AS EPITOMIZED IN JOHN LAWSON'S "A NEW VOYAGE TO CAROLINA." *North Carolina Hist. R. 1966 43(4): 413-429.* John Lawson's book, *A New Voyage to Carolina* (1709), was important for the development of the concept of the noble savage. Literary conventions working toward this concept were: 1) the belief that all men were creatures of God and candidates for conversion, and 2) the constant depiction of the American wilderness as another paradise. Both of these ideas were present in Lawson's book. Moreover he expressed admiration for the Indian physique. To Lawson, as the "savage was in the body, so he was in mind." He compared the Indian favorably to the civilized man as being never idle, jealous, nor envious. Lawson, like others, blamed the lack of Christian example for the fact that so few Indians became Christians. He recommended that the English government subsidize intermarriage of white women and Indian men as a means of extending peacefully the British Empire. This advocacy of amalgamation of the races is the one essentially new element in Lawson's work which otherwise is an outstanding summation of similar previous works. 112 notes.
     E. P. Stickney

1228. Donnelly, Ralph W. PROCEEDINGS OF THE ORDER OF INDIAN WARS. *Military Affairs 1956 20(4): 229-230.* Lists addresses published in the *Proceedings* of the Order of Indian Wars, 1920-41, "since many are firsthand accounts not printed elsewhere."   K. J. Bauer

1229. Edwards, Clinton R. ABORIGINAL SAIL IN THE NEW WORLD. *Southwestern J. of Anthrop. 1965 21(4): 351-358.* Presents a synthesis of all known research on the use of sails in aboriginal watercraft in the New World, utilizing both modern anthropological and archaeological accounts as well as journals and other sources containing recorded observations on first contact. Based on primary and secondary sources; biblio.   C. N. Warren

1230. Ewers, John C. THE WHITE MAN'S STRONGEST MEDICINE. *Bull. of the Missouri Hist. Soc. 1967 24(1): 36-46.* A fundamental concept of primitive Indian religion was the belief that men, animals, and strange objects of unknown origin had supernatural powers superior to the natural powers of men. This concept of medicine, shared by all western tribes, conditioned their reactions toward early white traders and explorers. Horses and guns are prime examples of this, especially for the Indians of the Great Plains. Probably the strongest medicine, beyond the comprehension of the primitives, was the ability of the white man, through drawings, paintings, photographs, and writing, to record what he saw or experienced and to preserve these records for use by future generations. Without these powers, most of our records of Indian-white relations and of Indian life and customs of more than a century ago would be lost to us. Greater use must be made of the extensive records that are available. Areas and subjects for investigation are suggested. 18 notes.   D. L. Smith

1231. Ewers, John C. WHEN RED AND WHITE MEN MET. *Western Hist. Q. 1971 2(2): 133-150.* It is more accurate to study the history of the Indians in the American West in a context of Indian-white confrontation than it is to consider this history as background material for understanding of one of the minority group problems which plague the country today. The Indians have always been different from any other of the ethnic minorities. A large and complex body of laws gives Indians certain rights and privileges shared by no other groups, whether minority or majority. The collective label is misleading: there were scores of independent villages or tribes of Indians, and no political, cultural, or linguistic unity. Most Indian groups distrusted one another as much as they distrusted the first white invaders. In the Indian-white confrontation, both races made substantial contributions, positive and negative, to total world culture. Historians and anthropologists should not try to expiate any sense of guilt about present-day problems by rewriting the history of the American West so that all Indians become "red knights in breech-clouts" and all whites "pantalooned devils." Instead, all data should be weighed so that both sides can be given fair treatment. 19 notes. Banquet address, 10th Annual Western History Association Conference, 9 October 1970.   D. L. Smith

1232. Farb, Peter. GHOST DANCE AND CARGO CULT. *Horizon 1969 11(2): 58-65.* Analyzes millenarian cults, seeking to understand their rise and their effect. Such movements always originate in situations of social and cultural stress and are an effort on the part of the stress-laden to construct systems of dogma, myth, and ritual which will serve as guides to efficient action. Religious fervor is the driving force of the cult, and its end is the destruction of the cult or the evolution of a new social order. Examines the Ghost Dance cult of the Plains Indians, the cargo cults of the Melanesians, the Watch Tower Movement among certain African groups, the Code of Handsome Lake among the Iroquois, and the current Peyote cult among certain American Indian tribes. Includes an analysis of the stages involved made by Anthony F. C. Wallace, Professor of Anthropology at the University of Pennsylvania.   R. N. Alvis

1233. Farb, Peter. POVERTY, AFFLUENCE, AND CULTURE. *Am. West 1968 5(6): 18-23, 62-63.* The long unfashionable theory of cultural evolution, presently refined and considered the vogue, is applied to the extreme diversity of life-styles apparent in Indian societies of North America. The contention is made that these societies present an outline of human civilization, "an evolutionary spectrum" of the historical processes of the development of man from the stone age simple-extended family to the age of technology and the complex state. The author adapts the present study from his current volume *Man's Rise to Civilization as Shown by the Indians of North America from Primeval Times to the Coming of the Industrial State* (New York: Dutton, 1968). He compares the simple familial band societies of the Great Basin Shoshoni and the complex chiefdoms of the Pacific Northwest coast as a demonstration of how widely divergent societies construct the mechanics of a civilization appropriate to their time and location. 3 illus.   D. L. Smith

1234. Freeman, John F. THE INDIAN CONVERT: THEME AND VARIA-
TION. *Ethnohist. 1965 12(2): 113-128.* The theme is the Indian's overcoming a
burden of sin to reach a lasting happiness through conversion to a sect's norms
—all characteristic of the Great Awakening of the 1740's. The variation stems
from the differing views of the conversion experience—religion to support Western civilization, or religion to save the Indian's individual soul. 3 notes, biblio.
R. S. Burns

1235. Friedmann, Friedrich G. DIE INDIANER IN DEN USA [The Indian in
the United States]. *Stimmen der Zeit [West Germany] 1971 188(8): 106-121.*
Discusses 1) the first contacts between the Indians and European explorers and
settlers, 2) the part played by various Indian tribes in the European wars for the
control of the North American continent, 3) the fate of the Indians at the hands
of white settlers in the United States, especially as the frontier advanced, 4)
official American policies toward the Indians, and 5) the situation of the Indian
in modern industrial society. Provides a chronological factual framework but
emphasizes the attitude of white condescension observable from the time of the
earliest New England settlements, the basic conflict of cultures between the
competitive, individualistic, land-hungry white man and the group-minded, tribal
Indian, and the consequent ever-changing but never-ending mistreatment of the
Indian at the hands of the white man. Develops each of these themes by factual
examples and analyses of cultural factors, with greatest emphasis on the ill-
consequences to the Indians of the westward movement and on changing federal
policies. M. Faissler

1236. Goodwyn, Frank. THE FRONTIER IN AMERICAN FICTION. *Inter-
Am. R. of Biblio. 1960 10(4): 356-369.* Lists and comments on representative
novels dealing with frontier life at different times and places during the 19th
century in the United States. The Louisiana Purchase, the Lewis-Clark Expeditions, colonization of Texas, the fur trade, Oregon migration, missionary activities, the Mormon movement, the California Gold Rush, cowboy life, farming, and
the Indians: all these periods are background for frontier literature. In general,
the idealized frontiersman displayed peculiar traits setting him apart from other
popular fiction heroes: shrewdness, uncommunicativeness, aversion to people,
and claustrophobia. R. E. Wilson

1237. Gusinde, Martín. TROFEOS DE CABEZA EN AMERICA (KOPTRO-
PHAEEN IN AMERICA) [Head trophies in America]. *Aconcagua [Spain] 1967
3(3): 332-346.* A bilingual study in German and Spanish discussing the practice
of headhunting among the Indians of North and South America. The various
classes of trophies in the different tribes and the methods of preparing them,
especially among the Jivaro Indians, are discussed. Some authors, without indicating the titles of their works, are cited. T. G. (IHE 67322)

1238. Haines, Francis. WESTERN LIMITS OF THE BUFFALO RANGE.
Am. West 1967 4(4): 4-5, 8-9, 12, 66-67. The American bison (commonly called
buffalo) is associated with the plains and the culture of the Plains Indians. The
buffalo, nevertheless, ranged considerably westward from the rolling prairies.

There was a definite western limit, however, imposed by such natural barriers as deserts, canyons, forests, and mountains and the usual lack of suitable grazing which such features presented. In Canada, the northern limit can be roughly defined as the present Yukon-British Columbia boundary on the eastern side of the Rocky Mountains. From there south to Mexico the only passes to the Continental Divide penetrated by the buffalo were in southwestern Montana and South Pass in Wyoming. The foothills and sheltered valleys of the eastern slopes continued to mark the western limits southward to New Mexico. From here the Pecos River to its mouth and the Rio Grande from there to the Gulf of Mexico was the well-defined limit. Illus., map, biblio. note.   D. L. Smith

1239. Holway, Hope. THE AMERICAN INDIAN AND HIS NAME. *Chronicles of Oklahoma 1965 43(3): 340-344.* The origins of our names are very similar to those of Indians. In primitive society there was little need for names. Sometimes an individual would acquire a name related to a happening. Often not until puberty did a boy know his name, then he often changed it to indicate his prowess. Names were changed when the owners became ill to assure recovery. There were "nikie" names referring to some remote ancestor. "Great Walker," for example, might refer to an individual or to an ancestor. "Small Boiler" was a name for an Omaha woman who gave a feast but did not have enough food for her guests. There were dream names, color names, animal names, nature names, number names. Names presented a problem in signing legal papers, and names were a problem to census takers. Teachers sought to give children names of which they could be proud. Under the agency system an effort was made to introduce our own practical and useable name system. Wives and children had to be known by the husband's name. The preservation of dignified and easily handled Indian names is a custom to be followed. Note on sources.   I. W. Van Noppen

1240. Hultkrantz, Åke. NORTH AMERICAN INDIAN RELIGION IN THE HISTORY OF RESEARCH: A GENERAL SURVEY. PART I AND PART II. *Hist. of Religions 1966 6(2): 91-107, (3): 183-207, 1967 7(1): 13-34, and (2): 112-148.* A chronologically arranged review of European and American contributions to the study of North American religion, emphasizing their theoretical context. Europeans have stressed current ideas in the field of the history of religion; Americans have "interpreted religion within the framework of American anthropological theories." Part I. Surveys the earliest amateur observers—missionaries (Jesuits), travelers, early theoreticians; the beginning of professional anthropology with the Bureau of American Ethnology; and the impact of European evolutionism and the development of the new historicism (Franz Boas). 77 notes. Part II. Surveys the "Boas period," 1892-1925, during which Franz Boas and his students dominated American anthropology in general and specifically research on North American religions. While the research and the collection of data undertaken by Boas gave a "solid, factual, and empirical basis" to the study of Indian religions, his studies were nevertheless a by-product of his work. To his students fell the task of detailed analysis and theoretical formulation. Contributions of the principle disciples of Boas, such as Robert Lowie, Paul Radin, and Frank Speck, are summarized at some length. Less treatment is given to others, such as Kroeber, Sapir, Swanton, Parsons, and Wissler. 135 notes. Part III. Discusses research on North American Indian religion during the period of

Franz Boas and his immediate pupils and successors. American scholars of the period collected a great amount of data on religion, including the place of the Supreme Being, myths and legends, and totemism among American Indians. However, "the American approach suffered from the writers' behavioristic bias, and, usually, secondary interest for religion, but profited from their first-hand knowledge of aboriginal religion." The various schools of thought and points of view are distinguished and published research is catalogued. 113 notes. Part IV. Deals with the post-Boas period—1925 to the present. During this time, "two major changes occurred: the intense preoccupation with religion slackened in American anthropology at the same time as methods and approaches changed; and the professional interest of European ethnologists—later also European and American students of religion—in Indian religions was strengthened." The period of revival began about 1945. After discussing the reasons for decline and revival of interest, the author reviews the research material by subject and geographical-ethnic area. American and European studies are surveyed. 216 notes.

D. G. Davis

1241. Jagendorf, Moritz A. CHARLES GODFREY LELAND—NE-GLECTED FOLKLORIST. *New York Folklore Q. 1963 19(3): 211-219.* A biographical account of Charles Godfrey Leland (1824-1903), who first collected gypsy folklore. Besides various editing duties, he also made a comparison of Etruscan and Teutonic mythology, a comparative study of American Indian folklore, and studied the derivation of "Shelta," the tinker's language, from Gaelic. Partly based on Leland's own extensive published work. Illus.

M. A. Booth

1242. Jones, Louis T. INDIAN SPEECH ARTS. *Masterkey 1963 37(3): 91-97.* Discusses the oratorical ability of the American Indian with excerpts from some of the impressive public speeches made by American Indians. The point is made that in the Indians' unwritten literature is to be found a wealth of primary virtue that is worthy of preservation and aptly suitable to present-day speech art. Based on primary and secondary sources.   C. N. Warren

1243. Kell, Katherine T. FOLK NAMES FOR TOBACCO. *J. of Am. Folklore 1966 79(314): 590-599.* Begins with etymological conjecture about Central and South American Indian names for nicotine substances, and continues by tracing North American names for the plants, the varieties of ways in which they are used, and the sorts of people who used tobacco. Cites the first written use of certain terms, e.g., "smoking like a chimney" appeared in Ritt Barham's *In-goldsby Legends* (1845). The author considers pipes, snuff, chewing tobacco, cigars, and cigarettes, as well as their use. 51 notes.   M. W. Machan

1244. La Farge, Oliver. MYTHS THAT HIDE THE AMERICAN INDIAN. *Am. Heritage 1956 7(6): 5-19, 103-107.* Holds that the stereotypes of the American Indian, whether "noble savage," ruthless, bloodthirsty beast, or lazy, drunken lout, are all equally false oversimplifications. The Indians were of many tribes and vastly different cultures with differing traditions, beliefs and customs. Some were hunters, others agricultural, others can best be characterized as warlike. Some attained a high degree of cultural or political development, whereas others never progressed beyond a low state of development. The author maps out the main areas of Indian culture in the present bounds of the United States. Illus.

C. R. Allen, Jr.

1245. Manbeck, John B. AMERICAN INDIANS AND LAPPS: A COMPAR-ATIVE STUDY. *Am. Scandinavian R. 1971 59(4): 365-373.* While anthropological evidence quite firmly establishes that the American Indian crossed from Siberia to Alaska over a land bridge 10-25 thousand years ago, the origin of the Lapps remains a mystery. Both the Lapps and the American Indians settled around the time of extensive glaciation and, of necessity, had to adapt to nature. Originally, life was nomadic for both groups. In time, groups of Indians organized in communities. By 1492, some farming was conducted east of the Mississippi and in Arizona and New Mexico. The wealth of the nomad Lapps, even today, is based on the number of reindeer heads they own. "In order to salvage their existence, both the Lapps and the American Indians have, of necessity, turned outside their original interests. Civilizing influences have pressured both groups to accept the modern world. Whereas a self-supporting economy was possible to maintain when they were an isolated people, the invasion of the technological age has pushed them toward other goals....But the greatest external influences on contemporary Lapps and on the Indians, is education." 88 notes.

D. D. Cameron

1246. Mardock, Robert W. IRRESOLVABLE ENIGMA? *Montana 1957 7(1): 36-57.* Discusses the problem of the American Indian since the Civil War, making wide use of contemporary writings, either in the form of novels or of literature published by the various humanitarian groups sponsored by citizens in the East. Discusses the complexity of the Indian mind, soul, and culture, as well as the enigmatic characteristics which led to controversial concepts during the 19th century, varying from the sentimental pleas of the East for the "noble savage" to the often too harsh concept of the "murderous red devil" prevalent among western settlers. Outlines the official government policy in regard to Indians during this period and points to the many mistakes made by the administration in dealing with this problem, which has, in fact, not yet finally been solved.

B. Waldstein

1247. McCullen, J. T., Jr. INDIAN MYTHS CONCERNING THE ORIGIN OF TOBACCO. *New York Folklore Q. 1967 23(4): 264-273.* Tobacco is highly honored by the Indian and used reverently at religious ceremonies. Most Indian legends call the discovery of tobacco a precious gift from a greater power. Describes some of these ancient myths. 21 notes.

W. S. Rinaldo

1248. McKinley, Daniel L. THE WHITE MAN'S FLY ON THE FRONTIER. *Missouri Hist. R. 1964 58(4): 442-451.* Honey has been an item in mankind's diet since prehistoric times, but the bee did not make its appearance in America until relatively recently. Some records of De Soto's travels suggest they were here in 1540, but they apparently did not appear in significant numbers until a century later. To the Indians they were the "White Man's Fly." Records of travelers and explorers are used to trace the westward movement of the bee from the eastern coast to Missouri and to describe some of the practices of frontier honey seekers.

W. F. Zornow

1249. McNickle, D'Arcy. INDIAN AND EUROPEAN: INDIAN-WHITE RELATIONS FROM DISCOVERY TO 1887. *Ann. of the Am. Acad. of Pol. and Social Sci. 1957 (311): 1-11.* An exposition of the problem of Indian-white relations in the United States, in terms of the conflict of land use and tenure systems, 1450-1887. The author concludes with the Dawes Act of 1887.

J. S. Counelis

1250. Miller, Mary Rita. ATTESTATIONS OF AMERICAN INDIAN PIDGIN ENGLISH IN FICTION AND NONFICTION. *Am. Speech 1967 42(2): 142-147.* Because the Indians did not mix with the whites they retained their own languages, did not learn English, but developed a pidgin English for use in dealing with whites. The author has found that this Indian pidgin English is similar in structure to other types of pidgin English in such features as omitting verbs ("You fine?"), use of "no" for "not" ("No talk"), and the overuse of accusative case ("Him nice boy"). The author also suggests the linguistic steps necessary to provide the Indian today with a standard dialect of English. Based mainly on a study of Indian dialogue in 19th-century fiction; 49 notes.

R. W. Shoemaker

1251. Mitchell, Fredric and Skelton, James W. THE CHURCH-STATE CONFLICT IN EARLY INDIAN EDUCATION. *Hist. of Educ. Q. 1966 6(1): 41-51.* Beginning in 1819 annual sums of up to 500 thousand dollars were appropriated by Congress to churches for Indian education. When, in the 1890's, the government began to operate Indian schools, the Commissioner of Indian Affairs restricted the support of sectarian schools. While many Protestant churches acquiesced, the Catholic church opposed this policy, and conflict arose between the Bureau of Catholic Indian Missions and the U.S. commissioner. Relations were severed in 1895 when Congress cut off all federal funds for the support of sectarian schools. By 1906 the Supreme Court affirmed the "no-aid-or-no-hindrance" doctrine of the first amendment's separation of church and state.

J. Herbst

1252. Monical, David G. CHANGES IN AMERICAN ATTITUDES TOWARD THE INDIAN AS EVIDENCED BY CAPTIVE LITERATURE. *Plains Anthropologist 1969 14(44, pt. 1): 130-136.* "This study presents an analysis of the changes in the attitude of the American settler toward the Indian over a period of 120 years. Based upon a comparison of the narratives of the white captives of the Indians three significant periods are delineated: the colonial; transition; and, expansion."

J

1253. Moriarty, James Robert and Campbell, Walton. THE INDIANS SHALL HAVE NO WEAPONS OR HORSES. *Western Explorer 1966 4(2): 1-8.* A discussion of the beginnings of the horse-oriented culture of the Plains Indians of the southwest and of the reasons for the slow acceptance of the horse by southern California Indians. The authors challenge the conventional theory that the horses used by American Indians came from the natural increase of horses lost by early Spanish expeditions. They see the Indian acquisition of the horse as the product of the later Spanish colonial period when Pueblo Indians in the Santa Fe area drove out the Spaniards in 1680. As the Pueblo people traded horses taken from the vanquished Spanish colonists to tribes farther to the north, a distinctive horse-oriented culture was created on the Plains. Indians in southern California accepted the horse more slowly because their food-gathering and nonnomadic habits required little travel, and because they were either isolated from Spanish influence by being so far inland or they were so much under Spanish control at the presidios and missions that they had no opportunity to develop their own well-defined horse culture. Based on primary and secondary sources, 5 illus., biblio.	W. L. Bowers

1254. Noah, Mordecai Manuel. THE AMERICAN INDIAN AND THE LOST TRIBES OF ISRAEL. *Midstream 1971 17(5): 49-64.* Noah has been called by many the first Jewish intellectual that America produced. He is best known for his attempt to build a Jewish colony on Grand Island in the Niagara River, which he called "Ararat" in the early 19th century. In this article Noah argues that the American Indian is a descendant of the lost tribes of Israel. He comes to this conclusion by a study of their culture and compares it with that of the ancient Israelites.	R. J. Wechman

1255. Norwood, Frederick A. THE INVISIBLE AMERICAN—METHODISM AND THE INDIAN. *Methodist Hist. 1970 8(2): 3-24.* A study of the attitudes of the Methodist Church toward the American Indian. The author considers four major periods from the 1820's until the present: removal from the East, war, allotment of lands to the Indians, and reform. Using largely the various editions of the *Christian Advocate,* the author indicates what the Methodists had to say officially, as well as unofficially, during each phase of the history of the Indian. 71 notes.	H. L. Calkin

1256. Peterson, Helen L. AMERICAN INDIAN POLITICAL PARTICIPA-TION. *Ann. of the Am. Acad. of Pol. and Social Sci. 1957 (311): 116-126.* A social and historical survey of the political life of the American Indian, with special emphasis on the period after 1832.	J. S. Counelis

1257. Ricketts, MacLinscott. THE NORTH AMERICAN INDIAN TRICKSTER. *Hist. of Religions 1966 5(2): 327-350.* Discusses the problem of how the traits of trickster, transformer of the world, and heroic bringer-of-culture are combined within one mythical Indian character. Several theories are traced which have attempted to offer solutions, most of which isolate the various traits in some way. Attempts to "establish conclusively that the trickster-transformer-culture hero is in origin a unitary figure despite his complexity." After relating the trickster to several myths, concludes that "the trickster may best be understood as the personification of all the traits of man raised to the highest degree." Thus the trickster and his myths persist, because man may identify his own aspirations with him.   D. G. Davis

1258. Roberts, Warren E. STITH THOMPSON: HIS MAJOR WORKS AND A BIBLIOGRAPHY. *Arv [Sweden] 1965 21: 5-20.* Stith Thompson's pioneer work in collecting Indian legends with a European origin is described. His *Motif-Index* is also discussed as well as a number of his lesser contributions to folklore research. A thorough bibliography of all Thompson's publications is appended.
                                                                                    W. Mott

1259. Saum, Lewis O. FRENCHMEN, ENGLISHMEN, AND THE INDIAN. *Am. West 1964 1(4): 4-11, 87-89.* The accepted view of frontier Indian-French relationships is that the Frenchman understood the natives, humored and cajoled them, and, therefore, generally got along well with them. The Englishman, on the other hand, because of his cultural background, remained aloof from the Indians to a considerable extent, and was patronizing and condescending in his relations with them. The English attitude toward the aborigines was called intolerant; the French policy, enlightened. This traditional concept is subscribed to by historians and anthropologists as well as the layman. It is tested by close scrutiny of the literature of the fur trade and found to be wanting. The author contends that within this area at least there is little evidence of the validity to support the "tolerant" Frenchman-"bigoted" Anglo-Saxon dichotomy. Derived from a forthcoming book on the fur trade and the Indian. Illus., biblio.   D. L. Smith

1260. Stinson, Richard L. THE DEVELOPMENT OF INDIAN MISSION POLICY AND PRACTICE IN THE NATIONAL PERIOD. *Hist. Mag. of the Protestant Episcopal Church 1968 37(1): 51-65.* Examines the forces at work in the federal government, the American culture, and the Episcopal church during the first 50 years of the 19th century in an attempt to better understand the basis of subsequent missionary work with American Indians. The author admits that the Indian work of both the colonial and national periods had many shortcomings. 38 notes, mostly secondary; biblio.   E. G. Roddy

1261. Taylor, Dorothy Bright. INDIAN MEDICINAL HERBS AND THE WHITE MAN'S MEDICINE. *New York Folklore Q. 1967 23(4): 274-282.* Relates an Indian legend on the source of herbal medicines and gives an account of the author's talks with an elderly "medicine-man-philosopher." Speculates on the development of medicine among Indians and among white men. The Indians stayed with their traditional organic cures and the white man developed techniques to manufacture medicines inorganically.   W. S. Rinaldo

1262. Unsigned. INDIAN GAMES. *Wisconsin Then and Now 1965 11(8): 1-3.* In 1766 and in 1860 observers wrote accounts of the Indians playing lacrosse, a game named by the French in Canada. The Winnebago played the game at the site which is now La Crosse. Other games described are "bowl and dice," observed among 81 tribes belonging to 28 different linguistic stocks; "snow snake"; and "cat's cradle." Indian boys made tops out of acorns, nuts, and oval stones. Few of these games have survived. Illus.   E. P. Stickney

1263. Unsigned. NOTABLE ACCESSIONS TO THE LIBRARY, 1963. *Newberry Lib. Bull. 1965 6(5): 127-162.* Details richness of the library's growth in an exceptional year 1) by departments: English history and literature (stressing liturgy, manners, periodicals 1650-1730), American history, European history and literature (including Renaissance manuscripts and imprints); 2) by special collections: Wing (history of printing), Ayer (ethnology, American Indians, colonialism), Graff (western Americana), Greenlee (Portuguese history and literature).   H. J. Graham

1264. Washburn, Wilcomb E. SYMBOL, UTILITY AND AESTHETICS IN THE INDIAN FUR TRADE. *Minnesota Hist. 1966 40(4): 198-202.* Discusses one of the major problems of the fur trade—the different values that the two different cultures put on certain items. For instance, the Indians prized beads, mirrors, and bells, while the white man often was concerned primarily with gold, silver, and fur for their commercial value.   P. L. Simon

1265. Wechsberg, Joseph and Cracroft, Richard H., ed. and trans. WINNETOU OF DER WILD WEST. *Am. West 1964 1(3): 32-39.* Through the fictional characters of Old Shatterhand, "a German Natty Bumppo...a mixture of Tom Mix, Hopalong Cassidy, Siegfried, and Christ," and Winnetou, a noble Apache chief, who is "a cultured blend of the finest traits of the Indian and German nations," Karl May conjured up, without seeing it, a novelized portrayal of the American West in dozens of volumes that have thrilled generations of German males, including Einstein, Hitler, and Albert Schweitzer. Illus.
                                                                    D. L. Smith

1266. Wilhelm, Sidney M. RED MAN, BLACK MAN AND WHITE AMERICA: THE CONSTITUTIONAL APPROACH TO GENOCIDE. *Catalyst 1969 (4): 1-62.* "Racism is a basic component of American society, rising from the past, perpetuated in the present and assured for the future. The pattern of racism with its complementary myths now engulfs the Negro just as it foreclosed upon the Indians of yesterday. The white majority repudiates the black majority for the very qualities for which it must accept blame: poverty, ignorance, family disruption, filth, crime, disease, substandard housing. The white strategy reflects the nation's earlier history when the ingenious plan evolved of first maddening the Indians into war and falling upon them with exterminating punishment." Photo.
                                                                    P. A. Proett

1267. Wilson, Clifford P. BARK CANOES AND SKIN BOATS. *Beaver [Canada] 1965 296(Summer): 47-53.* A review article on Edwin Tappan Adney and Howard I. Chapelle's *The Bark Canoes and Skin Boats of North America,* Smithsonian Institution Bulletin No. 230(1964). Gives an account of the life of Adney (1868-1950). Objections are made to the identification of the north canoe

with the *canot de maître*. Two additional birch bark canoes preserved in Michigan are cited, and the present status of Eskimo skin boats is discussed. Illus.
L. F. S. Upton

1268. Wilson, Eddie W. THE MOON AND THE AMERICAN INDIAN. *Western Folklore 1965 24(2): 87-100.* A survey of the moon in the Indians' concepts of deity, ritual, and creation stories, including the particular beliefs of some tribes. Based on secondary works. J. M. Brady

1269. Winkler, A. M. DRINKING ON THE AMERICAN FRONTIER. *Q. J. of Studies on Alcohol 1968 29(2): 413-445.* "Many Americans inhabiting the western frontier during the 19th century drank whisky freely and frequently as they struggled to cope with a hostile environment. The trappers who opened each successive area in the movement toward the Pacific, the miners, the cattlemen and the pioneer farmers who followed later, all drank substantially greater quantities than did those who remained in the East. ...Whiskey, the most popular beverage after 1790 when distillation was found to be an economical way of transporting grain to market, became an expected part of all social intercourse and excessive drinking became a problem.... Even though intoxicated, drinkers were able to function fairly well. The drinking habits which developed among the various frontier groups were related to the patterns of daily activity. The trappers were unable to carry liquor with them and consequently drank explosively whenever they gathered together at the rendezvous for 1 month each year. The cowboys could not drink while they were on the trail, but they more than compensated for these dry periods when they reached the 'cow towns.' The western miners lived in crude communities where alcohol was readily available and they drank heavily throughout the year to help ease their loneliness for the families they had frequently left behind. Their habits became even more intemperate in the winter when the weather severely limited their activity. Western soldiers drank whisky so excessively that Congress in 1832 suspended their liquor ration; but the Indians were encouraged to drink by the fur traders and when drunk became violent and uncontrollable.... In the sparsely settled rural areas clergymen encouraged abstinence, but not until a territory was fairly well populated and reasonably structured communities had begun to develop could the reformers hope to make much progress. [Bibliography of 68 items.]" J

1270. Zolotarevskaia, I. A. SUD'BY INDEITSEV V SSHA [The fate of Indians in the United States]. *Novaia i Noveishaia Istoriia [USSR] 1966 10(4): 47-55, (5): 60-68.* Part I. History of the American Indian in the United States before the Civil War. Refutes the allegations concerning the backwardness of the Indians and treats such allegations as rationalizations to justify official U.S. policy aimed at depriving the Indians of their land and exterminating them. 17 notes. Part II. History of the Indians in the United States from the Civil War to the present. Emphasis is given administration policies toward the Indians stressing land robbery and physical annihilation as well as the confining of Indians to reservations. 33 notes. E. B. Richards

1271. —. OUR CONTACTS WITH AMERICAN INDIANS, POLYNE-
SIANS, AND AFRICANS. *Pro. of the Am. Phil. Soc. 1963 107(2): 83-111.*
Hanke, Lewis. THE DAWN OF CONSCIENCE IN AMERICA: SPAN-
ISH EXPERIMENTS AND EXPERIENCES WITH INDIANS IN THE NEW
WORLD, pp. 83-92. Considers the factors which influenced initial Spanish-
Indian relations, noting that some early Spaniards anticipated the approach of
modern anthropologists by giving serious attention to the nature of the various
Indian cultures and by considering Indians as men who were not inferior but who
were of equal ability with any other group of men. Many references to early
Spanish sources and to scholarly articles.
   Tolles, Frederick B. NONVIOLENT CONTACT: THE QUAKERS
AND THE INDIANS, pp. 93-101. Traces the long history of nonviolent contact
between Quakers and Indians, arguing that a theological concept, the Light
Within, best explains Quaker behavior. Documented.
   Washburn, Wilcomb E. DISCUSSION OF THE SYMPOSIUM ON OUR
CONTACTS WITH AMERICAN INDIANS, POLYNESIANS, AND AFRI-
CANS, pp. 110-111.   R. G. Comegys

1272. —. THE INDIAN AND THE WEST. *Montana 1964 14(2).*
   Andrews, Ralph W. HE KNEW THE RED MAN, pp. 2-12. Between 1900
and 1920 Edward S. Curtis induced many tribes to reenact traditional and ancient
ceremonies which he described and photographed for his 20-volume work, *The
North American Indian,* extensively quoted here.
   Conner, Stuart W. PRE-HISTORIC MAN IN THE YELLOWSTONE
VALLEY, pp. 14-21. Meager remains indicate the presence of human life in
southeastern Montana 12 thousand years ago.
   Greenfield, Charles D. LITTLE DOG, ONCE-FIERCE PIEGAN WAR-
RIOR, pp. 23-33. From 1840 to 1866 Little Dog led his people in war against
enemy tribes but was friendly to the whites.
   Gray, John S. WHAT MADE JOHNNIE BRUGUIER RUN?, pp. 34-39.
Adventures of a Sioux half-breed scout with General Nelson A. Miles in his
dealings with Sitting Bull from 1876 to 1890.
   Mueller, Oscar O. THE NEZ PERCE AT COW ISLAND, pp. 50-53.
Corrects the common belief that soldiers made no effort to protect goods seized
by the Indians during the Nez Percé retreat of 1877.
   Miller, David Humphreys. SITTING BULL'S WHITE SQUAW, pp.
55-71. In 1889 an eccentric Brooklyn artist, Mrs. Catherine Weldon, joined
Sitting Bull's household and influenced his negotiations with government author-
ities until his death in December 1890.
   Cheney, Roberta C. WHITE BEAR'S RENUNCIATION, pp. 72-73.
White Bear, whose family were the last Indian residents of Montana's Madison
Valley, resisted white intrusions stoutly, even putting to death his newborn grandson because the father was a white man.
   Mitchell, Jessie Lincoln. PORTAL TO THE PAST: THE BLACKFEET,
pp. 75-81. In 1932 General Hugh L. Scott visited the Blackfeet Reservation for
a reunion with old friends and a session of ceremony and sign-talking.
   Beeler, Joe. AN ARTIST LOOKS AT THE AMERICAN INDIAN, pp.
83-90. Compares various western tribes in regard to facial features, physique, and
personal characteristics.

Sterling, Everett W. THE INDIAN RESERVATION SYSTEM ON THE NORTH CENTRAL PLAINS, pp. 92-100. Traces the establishment of early reservations in Minnesota and the Dakotas, 1851-58, and discusses the philosophy of this approach to Indian problems. S. R. Davison

Discovery and Exploration
1492-1600

1273. Bullen, Ripley R. SOUTHERN LIMIT OF TIMUCUA TERRITORY. *Florida Hist Q. 1969 47(4): 414-419.* One significant factor to be considered in attempting to determine the landing place in Florida of Hernando de Soto is the southern limit of Timucua territory. If one assumes that common ceramic history usually indicates common culture history, consideration of the ceramics of the Timucua and those of the Calusa Indians from around 500 A.D. to the 16th century strongly implies that the Calusa were never occupants of any land north of the middle of Charlotte Harbor. That the division between the Timucua and Calusa territories occurred along the middle of Charlotte Harbor is supported by available archaeological evidence. Since de Soto apparently landed in Timucua territory, one would conclude that he landed no further south than Charlotte Harbor. Based on personal examination of archeological evidence and on published reports of excavations at various sites; 27 notes. R. V. Calvert

1274. Figueroa y Melgar, Alfonso de. LINAJES QUE FORJARON LA HISPANIDAD [Families who forged Spanish America]. *Hidalguía [Spain] 1967 15(83): 497-524.* Outlines a book, soon to be published, which gives the genealogical history of the illustrious families who seeded the lands of America from Tierra del Fuego to the Spanish regions of North America. Includes aborigines, colonizers, and discoverers. A. de F. (IHE 67424)

1275. Petersen, William J. THE JOLIET-MARQUETTE EXPEDITION. *Palimpsest 1968 49(10): 416-446.* The expedition of Louis Jolliet and Jacques Marquette, S.J., in 1673, is a significant episode in Iowa history, for the first recorded history of eastern Iowa begins with the advent of these two explorers. The author briefly describes the early life of the two explorers and the events leading up to the expedition. The major portion of the article discusses the events of the voyage, with emphasis on the visit to Iowa, and ends with Père Marquette's death. The later career of Jolliet is also discussed briefly. Père Marquette and Jolliet performed a valuable service for France, giving the country a strong claim to the interior of America. As for Iowa, the explorers were probably the first white men to set foot on its soil; they gave the first account of its Indians and they made the first map of its eastern shore. Documented with quotations from Père Marquette's journal; illus., map. E. M. Hade

1276. Simmons, Marc. TLASCALANS IN THE SPANISH BORDERLANDS. *New Mexico Hist. R. 1964 39(2): 101-110.* The Indians of Tlascala served the Spaniards in several capacities: 1) as formal colonizers clustered around mission centers where they functioned as teachers and exemplary farmers to Indian neophytes, 2) as free laborers in the new mining regions, 3) as auxiliary soldiers, and 4) as individual servants and assistants to Spanish explorers and friars going north. Tlascalans are mentioned at Zacatecas, San Luis Potosí, and Saltillo, Mexico; San Juan Bautista and the Seno Mexicano region of Texas; and Santa Fe and Analco, New Mexico.   D. F. Henderson

1277. Williams, Tennant S. THE DE SOTO EXPEDITION IN THE MISSISSIPPI VALLEY: ARMADA ON THE MISSISSIPPI, 1543. *Louisiana Studies 1968 7(3): 213-227.* An account of what happened to the De Soto expedition after his death 21 May 1542 at the Indian village of Guachoya on the Mississippi River. The new commander Luis de Moscoso de Alvarado decided to get the expedition out of North America as quickly as possible. On 5 June 1542, he led his men westward in an attempt to reach Vera Cruz. The expedition wandered through northwestern Louisiana and eastern Texas until he decided to retrace his steps in October. He reached Anilco, 10 miles west of Guachoya, in December and then traveled to Aminoya. Here they spent the winter, expropriating the food supply of the natives. Seven brigantines, each 50 feet long, were constructed and supplied with food for the 300 Spaniards on their voyage to Vera Cruz. Moscoso's armada set sail down the Mississippi 2 July 1543. A virtual day to day account of the journey until it reached the Panuco River 52 days later is given. Based on the report of the De Soto Expedition Commission; 34 notes, map.
                                                        G. W. McGinty

Canada

1278. Baillargeon, Noël. LA VOCATION ET LES REALISATIONS MISSIONNAIRES DU SEMINAIRE DES MISSIONS-ETRANGERES DE QUEBEC AUX XVII ET XVIII SIECLES [The vocation and the missionary accomplishments of the Foreign Missions Seminary at Quebec in the 17th and 18th centuries]. *Soc. Can. d'Hist. de l'Eglise Catholique. Rapport 1963 30: 35-52.* Founded in 1663, the seminary at Quebec in 1665 became the first branch of the Foreign Missions Seminary at Paris. The first missions to be established were in Acadia in 1676 and at Port-Royal. Msgr. Laval, first bishop of Quebec, considered its most important task the conversion of the Indians. The chapel dedicated to the Holy Family in Arkansas, founded in 1699, was important to maintain communication between Quebec and the missions of Louisiana. For 40 years from its founding the seminary carried the burden of the missionary work, saving the missions from total extinction. 58 notes.   E. P. Stickney

1279. Baptie, Sue. EDGAR DEWDNEY. *Alberta Hist. R. [Canada] 1968 16(4): 1-10.* An assessment of the role of Edgar Dewdney—trail blazer, Indian commissioner, lieutenant governor of the Northwest Territories, minister of the interior, and lieutenant governor of British Columbia—in the political affairs of western Canada. Emphasis is on his role in Indian affairs and in particular on his involvement with the Riel Rebellion of 1885. H. M. Burns

1280. Bartlett, Fred E. THE ORDEAL OF WILLIAM MACTAVISH. *Beaver [Canada] 1964 295(Autumn): 42-47.* William Mactavish (1815-70) was governor of Assiniboia and Rupert's Land, 1858-70. As such, he might have been expected to play a decisive part in the crises surrounding Riel's resistance of Canadian authority. The governor had considerable influence with the Métis, but showed little disposition to use it. He was critically ill in the winter of 1869-70 and could do nothing to stop Riel's usurpation of authority. He resigned, and died two days after arriving in England in July 1870. Illus. L. F. S. Upton

1281. Brochu, Michel. LES GRANDS PHASES DE L'HISTOIRE ECONO-MIQUE DU NOUVEAU-QUEBEC INDIEN ET ESQUIMAU [The major phases of the economic history of the Indian and Eskimo regions of New Quebec]. *Action Natl. [Canada] 1970 60(1): 27-41.* The economic history of New Quebec can be subdivided into three major periods: prehistoric (beginning with the arrival of Indian and Eskimo cultures, continuing until the arrival of the first white explorer-traders, and featuring isolated economic activity); historic (lasting until the turn of the 20th century, and featuring the activities of the fur trade companies and the eventual hegemony of the Hudson's Bay Company); and contemporary (from 1903 to the present, featuring the questioning of the dominance of the Hudson's Bay Company and the diversification of the area's economic life). Undocumented. A. E. LeBlanc

1282. Carrière, Gaston. LA PERE ALBERT LECOMBE, O.M.I., ET LE PACI-FIQUE CANADIEN [Father Albert Lacombe, O.M.I., and the Canadian Pacific Railroad]. *R. de l'U. d'Ottawa [Canada] 1967 37(2): 287-321, (3): 510-539.* It has been said that the two greatest influences on the making of the Canadian West were the Oblates of Mary Immaculate and the Canadian Pacific Railroad. These two organizations combined in the person of Father Albert Lacombe, who was appointed in 1880 as missionary on the Canadian Pacific Railroad line on behalf of the spiritual welfare of the Indians and the workingmen on the road. In recognition of his assistance in pacifying the Indians, he was feted by the officials of the Canadian Pacific Railroad in Calgary in 1883, and was made "president" of the railroad for the luncheon hour. He thereafter kept the title of honorary president. His assistance to the railroad continued in many ways. Based on unpublished papers of Lacombe, including lengthy selections from his journal. J. M. Bumsted

1283. Chabanier, J. HISTORIQUE DE L'ARMEE CANADIENNE DE 1627 A 1955 [Historical account of the Canadian army from 1627 to 1955], *R. Historique de l'Armée [France] 1956 12(2): 39-68.* A detailed survey of the development of the Canadian armed forces from the first regular (French) militia, 1651, through the integration of French and English units, 1760-1870, and the Indian and American wars, to World Wars I and II, with emphasis on unit movements in all theaters of war and Canada's economic contribution and present international commitments. Illus., biblio.   H. M. Adams

1284. Demers, George-Edouard, Msgr. DE TOURS A QUEBEC [From Tours to Quebec]. *R. de l'U. Laval [Canada] 1964 19(2): 99-104.* Relates the vision and the events leading to her journey to Canada of Mother Mary of the Incarnation (Marie Guyard Martin) who founded the first mission in French Canada, and who was accompanied by one nun from Tours and two from Paris and by Mme. de la Peltrie, a rich widow, who had vowed to devote her fortune to endow a seminary for Indian girls.   M. Petrie

1285. Dempsey, Hugh. THE "THIN RED LINE" IN THE CANADIAN WEST. *Am. West 1970 7(1): 24-30.* When, in 1870, the Canadian West was transferred from the Hudson's Bay Company to the newly-formed Dominion of Canada, no provision was made for legal jurisdiction. Montana-based traders, with whiskey as their main stock in trade, moved across the border. Prosperous and reasonably peaceful Indians were impoverished and victimized, and were even killed by the whiskey traders. American manifest destiny proponents proclaimed the traders as advance agents of northern expansion. In the summer of 1873, a troop of former British soldiers and young Canadians was raised, dubbed the North-West Mounted Police, and sent to Winnipeg, Manitoba, the gateway to the western prairies. A 900-mile trek (the Great March) to the Blackfoot country in southern Alberta had near disastrous consequences for the Mounties. By early 1875 intertribal warfare had been subdued, the whiskey trade was ended, and the area was safe for travelers. Unlike the American West, where settlement usually preceded law and where violence was a way of life, the Mounted Police arrived before large-scale settlement. By the time of the Klondike gold rush of 1897-98, the Mounted Police had not only a history but also a considerable body of legend. The fictional, stereotyped "Mountie" legend began with the poetic eulogies that members wrote to departed members of the force, and it was further romanticized in numerous novels written by ex-Mounties. Today the romantic image is firmly fixed. 9 illus.   D. L. Smith

1286. Dempsey, Hugh A. THE INDIANS OF ALBERTA. *Alberta Hist. R. [Canada] 1967 15(1): 1-5.* A discussion of the variety of the life and culture of the Indians of Alberta and of the transition necessitated by the advent of the white man.   H. M. Burns

1287. Dempsey, Hugh A., ed. THE LAST LETTERS OF REV. GEORGE MC DOUGALL. *Alberta Hist. R. [Canada] 1967 15(2): 20-30.* Collection of letters written by George McDougall, Wesleyan Methodist Church Superintendent of Missionary work in western Canada. The letters describe activities among the Cree, Assiniboin (Stony), and other Indian tribes in the area.
H. M. Burns

1288. Drouin, Emeric O. ST. PAUL DES METIS. *Alberta Hist. R. [Canada] 1963 11(4): 12-14.* The story of an attempt to found a farming colony for the Métis people and persuade them to abandon nomadic and adopt sedentary ways.
E. W. Hathaway

1289. Gaumond, Michel. of Cultural Affairs, Quebec). L'ARTILLERIE DE QUEBEC: ULTIMA RATION REGUM [The artillery of Quebec: the last resort of kings]. *Culture Vivante [Canada] 1969 14: 32-42.* None of the 160 guns in the citadel of Quebec in 1758 was fired against its conqueror, General James Wolfe; but the British, cannonading from Point Levis across the Saint Lawrence River during the previous summer, burned 180 houses in the lower part of the city. Cartier impressed the Indians with his cannon, Frontenac's guns held off Sir William Phips's expedition in 1690, and artillery was used throughout the colonial period, but no one knows what became of these early guns. The 183 now in the citadel are either short naval guns, introduced after 1779 and abandoned about 1860, or "trompettes" dating from the Napoleonic Wars. Colonial guns recoiled almost their full length and could be fired steadily almost once an hour. Their range, theoretically one or two miles, varied with the uneven quality of the powder and spherical balls. While their chained balls could break cables or dismast ships, their aim was poor. 20 illus., including citadel plan of 1720.
T. D. S. Bassett

1290. Grunfeld, Frederic V. RENDER UNTO CEDAR. *Horizon 1968 10(4): 64-69.* Discusses the totem carvings of British Columbia and their fate in the hands of missionaries, anthropologists, and museum curators. Evaluates the artistic qualities of the totem carvings, noting that they are unique in their realistic depictions of the human face.
R. N. Alvis

1291. Harrington, Lyn. PRAIRIE BATTLEFIELD. *Can. Geographical J. 1963 66(1): 28-37.* The story of the [Louis] Riel Rebellion and its suppression at Batoche, Saskatchewan. Photographs of the site on the occasion of the visit in 1962 of the Royal Regiment of Canada. Map.
A. H. Lawrance

1292. Heinrichs, Alfred. THE INDIAN AND THE CANADIAN MENNO-NITES. *Mennonite Life 1967 22(1): 27-28.* Criticizes the Canadian Mennonites for their failure to help underprivileged Canadian Indians. While exploiting the Indians economically, Mennonites have maintained Indian missions too narrowly concerned with the saving of souls. Greater emphasis should be placed on the social gospel. Mennonites should demonstrate their Christian love with practical job training and educational programs.
D. J. Abramoske

1293. Inderwick, Mary E. A LADY AND HER RANCH. *Alberta Hist. R. [Canada] 1967 15(4): 1-9.* Extracts from letters written by a cattle rancher's bride describing life in the Pincher Creek area of Alberta. Details are given of visits to the Indian reservations and to Fort McLeod.
H. M. Burns

1294. Kewley, Arthur E. JOHN STRACHAN VERSUS PETER JONES. *Bull. of the United Church of Can. 1963 16: 1-15.* Peter Jones was the first Indian to be ordained a Methodist preacher and the first Canadian-born Indian to have the ear of the government at home and in England. He came into conflict with Dr. Strachan who tried to make state aid to the Indians available only to those of the Anglican Church. A happier relationship resulted, partly from the interest of Sir John Colbourne, in education of Indians regardless of church affiliation and partly from the agreement of Anglicans and Methodists to print and distribute jointly Peter Jones' translation of the Bible. Quotes from his journal (Toronto, 1860).   E. P. Stickney

1295. Klaus, J. F. THE EARLY MISSIONS OF THE SWAN RIVER DISTRICT, 1821-69. *Saskatchewan Hist. [Canada] 1964 17(2): 60-76.* The story of the missionary activity in the Swan River District, which extended from Lakes Winnipegosis and Manitoba west to the 105th meridian, and from the International Boundary north to the Red Deer River. Map.   A. H. Lawrance

1296. Lagassé, Jean H. INDIANS OF CANADA. *Am. Indígena [Mexico] 1966 26(4): 387-394.* Of a population of more than 19 million in Canada (1965), there are more than 200 thousand Indians and 250 thousand people of mixed Indian-European ancestry. Ten main linguistic groups are found in the 560 Indian "bands" which occupy more than 2,200 reservations throughout Canada. Many Indians have abandoned the traditional occupations of hunting, fishing, and domestic crafts, though these still predominate among the Eskimos. Legislation has attempted to both protect the Indian and to increase his activity in national affairs, the most recent Indian Act that of 1951. Indians are subject to the same laws as all Canadian citizens, excepting areas covered by the Indian Act. They may be sued for contractual obligations and may vote in national elections. The Indian Affairs Branch of the government, established in 1880, administers reservations, tribal funds, welfare services, and treaty negotiations. A list of institutions working among Indians is given.   J. S. Buttrey

1297. Lee-Whiting, Brenda B. THE FORTUNES OF A TRADING-POST: FORT WILLIAM, QUEBEC, 1823-1869. *Can. Geographical J. 1968 77(1): 22-27.* To exclude competitors from the region, Hudson's Bay Company established a trading post on the Ottawa River in 1823, originally named Lac des Allumettes. As the lumber frontier advanced, furs declined; however, Fort William was useful as both a transport link and trading post for Indians and lumbermen. Transportation costs, competition, and settlement hurt profits. The advent of steamboats on the Ottawa River made many posts redundant after 1854. Fort William was sold in 1869 and was later used as a summer resort. Illus.
                                                                        R. D. Tallman

1298. Lewis, Maurice H. THE ANGLICAN CHURCH AND ITS MISSION SCHOOL DISPUTE. *Alberta Hist. R. [Canada] 1966 14(4): 7-13.* Discusses the Anglican church and its Indian education program. Consideration is given to the financial problems and to the role played by the Canadian government in support of the program.   H. M. Burns

1299. MacDonald, R. H. FORT BATTLEFORD, SASKATCHEWAN. *Can. Geographical J. 1963 67(2): 54-61.* Surveys the history of the fort and the settlement which was once the seat of government and the police headquarters at the junction of three Indian nations. The fort was significant at the time of the Riel Rebellion. Map, photos. A. H. Lawrance

1300. MacGregor, James G. WHO WAS YELLOWHEAD? *Alberta Hist. R. [Canada] 1969 17(4): 12-13.* Considers the identity of Tete Jaune of Tete Jaune Cache and Yellowhead Pass. The author indicates that this person was Pierre Haisination, an Iroquois Indian guide employed by the Hudson's Bay Company in Alberta, Canada. H. M. Burns

1301. Main, J. R. K. EARLY TRANSPORTATION IN CANADA. *Can. Geographical J. 1968 77(1): 14-21.* Discusses Indian fur trade transportation. The mode of transportation changed in the West from Indian travois, hauled by dogs, to use of the horse in the mid-18th century. The oldest commercial conveyance was the canoe: the Algonquin Indians made them from birch; the Iroquois made them from elm; and the West Coast Indians used dugout canoes. The birch canoe was replaced by the York boat about 1800, which was used for commercial purposes and allowed larger loads. The Red River cart of Métis, usually pulled by oxen, was the primitive mode of land transportation. Illus. R. D. Tallman

1302. Maurault, Olivier. APERÇU DE L'HISTOIRE DE L'EGLISE DU CANADA SOUS LE REGIME FRANÇAIS [Survey of the history of the church in Canada in the French colonial period]. *Cahiers des Dix [Canada] 1964 29: 9-23.* The church in New France began with the arrival of the Recollects in 1615. The trials of the missionaries, the hostility of the Iroquois, and the destruction of Huronia are described. The diocese of Quebec extended from the Gulf of St. Lawrence to the Gulf of Mexico, from the Alleghanies to the Rocky Mountains. 15 notes. L. F. S. Upton

1303. McGuinness, Robert. MISSIONARY JOURNEY OF FATHER DE SMET. *Alberta Hist. R. [Canada] 1967 15(2): 12-19.* An account of a journey made by a Jesuit priest, Pierre Jean De Smet, for the purpose of arranging a peace treaty between the Blackfoot and Plateau tribes. The portions reproduced refer to experiences in the province of Alberta. H. M. Burns

1304. McKay, W. A. THE STORY OF THE CANADIAN FUR TRADE. *Beaver [Canada] 1965 295(Spring): 20-25, (Summer): 24-29.* Part I. An account of the fur trade from the early 16th to the mid-18th centuries. The effect of European demand for beaver hats on Indian life is shown. International rivalry also played its part in the competition of English, French, and Dutch traders. Part II. Deals with the trade from the origins of the Hudson's Bay Company, through this company's contest with French and Scottish traders from Montreal, to its amalgamation with the North West Company. Illus. L. F. S. Upton

1305. McLeod, D. M. LIQUOR CONTROL IN THE NORTH-WEST TERRI-TORIES: THE PERMIT SYSTEM, 1870-91. *Saskatchewan Hist. [Canada] 1963 16(3): 81-89.* The system by which liquor could be obtained only by permission of the lieutenant-governor was intended, in 1873, to protect the Indians. It developed into a regular means of supplying the settlers but was fraught with administrative difficulties. Meanwhile the prohibitionists fought to restrict the issue of permits. In 1891 the system came to an end when the people of the territories were given the power to determine their own liquor policy.

A. H. Lawrance

1306. Meyer, Roy W. THE CANADIAN SIOUX: REFUGEES FROM MIN-NESOTA. *Minnesota Hist. 1968 41(1): 13-28.* Following the end of the Dakota (Sioux) uprising of 1862, several thousand of the defeated Indians fled to Canada seeking a refuge. At first they were treated as refugees and given temporary aid. Later, as the years passed, they were accepted as permanent residents and reservations were established for them at such places as Standing Buffalo and Wood Mountain in Saskatchewan and Turtle Mountain, Oak Lake, Long Plant and others in Manitoba. The author feels that the Canadian approach to its Indian problem, while similar to that of the United States, was more humane and, in the long run, more successful. The Parliamentary Sessional Papers provided the bulk of the source material.

P. L. Simon

1307. Montgomery, Malcolm. THE SIX NATIONS AND THE MAC DON-ALD FRANCHISE. *Ontario Hist. [Canada] 1965 57(1): 13-18.* Shows the politi-cal considerations underlying the enfranchisement of the Indians of eastern Canada by the Conservative federal government in 1885 and the subsequent disenfranchisement of the same Indians by the Liberal federal government in 1898. Gives particular attention to the 1896 election in Brant in which the votes of the Six Nations Indians helped to unseat the Liberal member for that riding. The Indian vote, a response to Liberal promises to repeal the 1885 act, in turn encouraged the new Liberal government to carry out those promises.

G. Emery

1308. Pearce, William. CAUSES OF THE RIEL REBELLION, A PERSONAL VIEW. *Alberta Hist. R. 1968 16(4): 19-25.* An analysis of troubles with Métis in western Canada which resulted in the rebellion led by Louis Riel in 1885. Included is an account of the capture, trial, and execution of Riel.

H. M. Burns

1309. Peel, Bruce. THE LAST BATTLE. *Beaver [Canada] 1966 297(Winter): 12-14.* The last battle between Indians in Canada was fought on 5 September 1880 on the trail to Moose Mountain. A band of Plains Cree Indians had gone on a friendly visit to the Mandans in Dakota Territory but on the way home had stolen a horse and killed a Mandan. A war party crossed into Canada in pursuit and attacked a small encampment of nine Assiniboine and two Chippewa (Saulteaux) Indians, apparently assuming that they were Crees. Illus.

L. F. S. Upton

1310. Poirier, Jean. PROBLEMES GENERAUX DE TOPONYMIE AU QUE-BEC [General problems facing toponymy in Quebec]. *Cahiers de Géographie de Québec [Canada] 1966 10(20): 219-233.* A comprehensive study of the toponymy of Quebec has not yet been prepared and to do so would involve the surmounting of innumerable obstacles. Many place-names have not yet been recorded. This occurs in both inhabited and uninhabited regions of the province. The same place-names have also been used several times. Different spelling resulting from the use of Amerindian nomenclature is another problem. And, finally, there is the problem resulting from the superimposing of English place-names over already existing French ones or vice versa. 27 notes citing published works on Quebec topography. A. E. LeBlanc

1311. Quinn, David B. and Rousseau, Jacques. LES TOPONYMES AMERIN-DIENS DU CANADA CHEZ LES ANCIENS VOYAGEURS ANGLAIS, 1591-1602 [Indian place-names of Canada as used by the early English explorers, 1591-1602]. *Cahiers de Géographie de Québec [Canada] 1966 10(20): 263-277.* Indian place-names of the Maritime and Gulf of St. Lawrence regions are studied. Such place-names as "Arambec," "Cibo," "Menay," "Menego," "Menequit," "Natiscotec," "Tadoac" or "Tadouac," and "Tadascu" are examined in depth. Makes extensive use of Richard Hakluyt's third volume of *The Principles of Navigation* and, to a certain degree, the writings of several of the early French explorers; 56 notes taken mainly from a variety of primary sources and concerned with toponymy. A. E. LeBlanc

1312. Rousseau, Jacques. LE CANADA ABORIGENE DANS LE CON-TEXTE HISTORIQUE [Aboriginal Canada in its historical context]. *R. d'Hist. de l'Amérique Française [Canada] 1964 18(1): 39-63.* The number of Indians in Canada when America was discovered is estimated at 220 thousand, but this number was greatly reduced by epidemics. The arrival of the whites radically modified their way of life: weapons, clothing, dwellings, and food. When scurvy broke out in Cartier's expedition (1535-36) a traveler described the decoction which got the remains of his followers on their feet in a few days. Contact with such conflicting types of whites as traders and missionaries retarded the native's integration into civilization and reduced his contribution to Canadian culture. Without the Indian snowshoe, toboggan, and canoe the whites could never have conquered the North. Biblio. E. P. Stickney

1313. Serven, James E. GUNS OF THE CANADIAN WEST. *Am. West 1967 4(1): 30-33, 71-74.* Citing the bow and arrow as an example, the author maintains that survival tools often became war weapons, and that the weapons of the past often become the toys of the future. The theme of this study is that the story of the guns that helped to conquer the Canadian West—Manitoba, Saskatchewan, Alberta, and British Columbia—is inseparable from the story of the development of that territory. Within this framework the evolution of the gun can be traced from tool to weapon to collector's item. The first firearms were items of trade, usually flintlocks from the Hudson's Bay Company for furs from the Indians. While the guns enabled the Indians and half-breeds to harvest greater fur crops, their complete dependence on the trading posts for guns and powder held abusive use in check. The 1858 British Columbia Fraser and Thompson Rivers gold rushers brought American caplock and breech-loading rifles, muskets, and pistols. In the mid-19th century, the Canadian Army carried back-East muskets, but soon replaced them with more up-to-date American rifles. Still other makes and types came with the Métis troubles, clashes with the Indians, creation of the Northwest Mounted Police, homesteaders, the rebellion, construction of the transcontinental railroad, and other developments that changed the role of the gun primarily from tool to weapon. The final stage has been reached and the author asserts that for the collector "a rich array of guns" is still to be found in Canada. Illus., biblio. note.   D. L. Smith

1314. Shave, Harry. JOHN WEST, PEGUIS, AND P. RINDISBACHER. *Beaver [Canada] 1957 (Summer): 14-19.* Commentary on five newly discovered watercolors of Indians and Eskimos by the Swiss artist, Peter Rindisbacher, relating to the Hudson's Bay Company's territory in the 1820's. Reproductions of the pictures are included.   R. W. Winks

1315. Spry, Irene M. ROUTES THROUGH THE ROCKIES. *Beaver [Canada] 1963 294(Autumn): 26-39.* Describes the known crossings of the Canadian Rockies by white men before Palliser's expedition surveyed the passes in 1857-60. Many of the actual routes used are difficult to identify from contemporary descriptions. Many Indians and halfbreeds undoubtedly knew the routes, which were used, for example, in the war of the Blackfoot Confederacy and the Kutenai. Illus.   L. F. S. Upton

1316. Spry, Irene M. THE TRANSITION FROM A NOMADIC TO A SETTLED ECONOMY IN WESTERN CANADA, 1856-1896. *Mémoires de la Soc. Royale du Can. 1968 6(4): 187-201.* The Hudson's Bay Company had maintained peace in Rupert's Land for the benefit of the fur trade; the Plains Indians had achieved a rough balance of power between themselves; the organization of the Métis provided internal security and a degree of external protection. This stable order broke down in the 1860's with the decline of the Hudson's Bay Company, the arrival of smallpox and trade-whiskey, and the disappearance of the buffalo. Anarchy was prevented by the creation of the North West Mounted Police. But the basic need was for capital to convert to a farming economy and this did not come until the railway opened the area to settlers.   L. F. S. Upton

1317. Stanley, George F. G. L'INVASION FENIENNE AU MANITOBA [The Fenian invasion of Manitoba]. *R. d'Hist. de l'Amérique Française [Canada] 1963 17(2): 258-268.* Prints a diary kept by Abbé Jean-Baptiste Proulx dit Clément at St. Boniface, Manitoba, 1-20 October 1970. William B. O'Donoghue (d. 1878), formerly treasurer of Riel's provisional government, hoped for a Fenian invasion of Manitoba to link up with the discontented Métis. Riel himself denounced such a plan and the invasion was a farce. With Métis support, however, such an attempt could have provoked a serious civil war.   L. F. S. Upton

1318. Stanley, George F. G. LOUIS RIEL. *R. d'Hist. de l'Amérique Française [Canada] 1964 18(1): 14-26.* Describes the career of Louis Riel (1844-85) and his organization of two resistance movements to the federal government. As the leader of the Métis nation he won special rights written into the Manitoba Act of 1870, but himself went into exile. Returning in 1884 to defend his people on the Saskatchewan, he was captured and executed in 1885. He became the symbol of the struggle between French and English Canada for the West, which in turn involved the issue of whether Canada was a dualistic federation or an English-dominated unitary state. Riel, French-speaking and Roman Catholic, came to stand for the maintenance of ethnic and cultural diversity with the Dominion.
L. F. S. Upton

1319. Turner, A. R. SASKATCHEWAN PLACE NAMES. *Saskatchewan Hist. [Canada] 1965 18(3): 81-88.* Considers the origins of many of the place-names in the province. Indians, missionaries, fur traders, pioneer settlers, and railway officials are among those responsible for choosing names, which often reflect phases or incidents in Canadian history.
A. H. Lawrance

1320. Unsigned. PAUL KANE: ARTIST AMONG THE INDIANS. *Gopher Historian 1968 22(3): 15-17.* Kane (1810-71) immigrated to Canada from Ireland as a boy in 1818. He lived in Toronto then a frontier town, and saw Indians daily. In 1846, after studying painting in Europe, Kane set out on a 2-year journey to make a pictorial record of the Indians. His canvases, many of which are now in the Royal Ontario Museum, show various aspects of Indian life. Based on Kane's book *Wanderings of an Artist among the Indians* (1859) recording his experiences and impressions; illus.
G. T. Sharrer

1321. Unsigned. THE FOREST IN CANADIAN LIFE: A BRIEF HISTORICAL ANTHOLOGY. *Forest Hist. 1967 11(3): 14-27.* Excerpts from various well-selected authors writing between 1613 (the date of Champlain's map of New France which is included) to 1906, when Judson F. Clark published an essay entitled "Canadian Forest Policy," rounding out the anthology. Life in the Canadian forest included the Indian culture, European settlers, and the voyageurs of New France: the making of masts, fur trading, clearing, felling, and forest conservation of British colonial Canada. 7 illus., map.
B. A. Vatter

1322. Wolfenden, Madge, ed. JOHN TOD: "CAREER OF A SCOTCH BOY." *British Columbia Hist. Q. [Canada] 1954 18(3/4): 133-238.* Autobiographical account, as originally told to Gilbert Malcolm Sproat, of the life of Tod during the early 1800's in northern Canada as an official of the Hudson's Bay Company, including his observations on historical developments, geography, Indians, animals, and climate. An introduction and notes by the editor are included.
C. C. Gorchels

1323. Woodcock, George. CARIBOO AND KLONDIKE: THE GOLD MINERS IN WESTERN CANADA. *Hist. Today [Great Britain] 1955 5(1): 33-42.* The beginnings of gold mining in the river valleys of British Columbia were organized by the Hudson's Bay Company under the pressure of miners from California, following rumors of easier prospecting in the North in the 1850's. By 1860, these valleys were depleted and were left to the Indians and Chinese, the whites moving north to the Fraser plateau and the Cariboo mountains. Life in the mining towns was never as violent as in California, due partly to administration by British colonial officials. Fur trading declined but other industries appeared. The Indians lost their land and tribal organization and were afflicted with the white man's diseases. The same pattern of events was repeated in the Klondike rush into the Yukon in the 1890's. But there, due to the climate, no other industries appeared, and the region became virtually deserted again once easy mining was no longer feasible.   W. M. Simon

United States

Colonial America

1324. Beaver, R. Pierce. METHODS IN AMERICAN MISSIONS TO THE INDIANS IN THE SEVENTEENTH AND EIGHTEENTH CENTURIES: CALVINIST MODELS FOR PROTESTANT FOREIGN MISSIONS. *J. of Presbyterian Hist. 1969 47(2): 124-148.* Believes that the Protestant missions established to convert American Indians may have been more successful as examples of methods which were later to be employed by missionaries to foreign countries than they were in their primary purpose—converting the Indians. These methods included a primary emphasis on preaching, the founding of churches, and the assumed unity of evangelization and civilization. Some settlements were founded and some schools opened for the training of an Indian ministry by New Englanders and then the "Presbyterian and Reformed of the Middle Colonies," but these declined appreciably in the mid-18th century. Based primarily on published writings by many missionaries from the 17th and 18th centuries; 57 notes.   D. M. Furman

1325. Chesterman, A. de M. THE JOURNALS OF DAVID BRAINERD AND OF WILLIAM CAREY. *Baptist Q. 1961 19(4): 147-156.* A discussion of the journals of the Baptist missionaries David Brainerd and William Carey. Brainerd's journal describes his experiences among the North American Indians from April 1742 to 1747. Carey's journal is devoted to his missionary efforts in Bengal from June 1793 to June 1795.   J. A. S. Grenville

1326. Gerlach, Don R. AFTER SARATOGA: THE GENERAL, HIS LADY, AND "GENTLEMAN JOHNNY" BURGOYNE. *New York Hist. 1971 52(1): 5-30.* Commander of the Northern Department, Philip Schuyler (1733-1804) was blamed for the evacuation of Fort Ticonderoga (5-6 July 1777) by General Arthur Saint Clair (1737-1818), and was stripped of his command by Congress. Not until

October 1778 did Congress clear Schuyler's name and restore his reputation. After the battle of Saratoga (1778), Schuyler used his personal credit to supply Continental troops, gathered intelligence information, and advised the expeditions against the Indians which avenged the Wyoming and Cherry Valley massacres. The British attempted to kidnap him in 1781. Although unjustly blamed for the loss of Fort Ticonderoga, Schuyler continued to work for the success of the Patriot cause. Based on primary and secondary sources; 7 illus., 64 notes.
G. Kurland

1327. Harper, Lawrence A. AMERICAN HISTORY TO 1789. *J. of Econ. Hist. 1959 19(1): 1-24.* Calls attention to about four hundred titles appearing since 1945. They range from problems of imperial planning, the Indian economy, the frontier and defense; through trade, industry, labor, agriculture, the professions, arts and education, money and banking; to accounts of population, immigration, travel and colonial diseases. The survey is supplemented by regional and bibliographical references and discussions of the era of the Articles of Confederation and the Constitution.
S

1328. Jordan, Albert F. THE MORAVIANS AND THE INDIANS DURING THE FRENCH AND INDIAN WAR. *Moravian Hist. Soc. Tr. 1969 22(1): 1-14.* A documented report given by Augustus Gottlieb Spangenberg and Andrew Anthony Lawatsch at Herrnhut, Germany, in 1763 at the end of the Seven Years War. Spangenberg, a Moravian clergyman from Prussia, spent the years 1735-62 working in America. The report discusses the attitude of the Moravians to the war as a result of Spangenberg's admonition to "Watch and Pray." The Mahony massacre demonstrated to the American colonists that the Moravians were not allied with the enemy. Includes a glossary of places.
J. G. Pennington

1329. Mahon, John K. ANGLO-AMERICAN METHODS OF INDIAN WARFARE, 1676-1794. *Mississippi Valley Hist. R. 1958 45(2): 254-275.* A review of tactics and weapons used by the Indians, and by American colonists, militia and British and American soldiers. The sharp-shooting frontiersmen were not as effective in fighting Indians as American folklore suggests. The soldiers in the ranks, well trained in the use of musket and bayonet, and applying tactics combining fire and movement, were most likely to win in encounters with the Indians. The Indians relied heavily on surprise and they usually succumbed when forced to make a stand. Based on published sources, among them contemporary diaries.
E. H. Boehm

1330. Pilling, Arnold R. A USE OF HISTORICAL SOURCES IN ARCHAEOLOGY: AN INDIAN EARTHWORKS NEAR MT. CLEMENS, MICHIGAN. *Ethnohist. 1968 15(2): 152-202.* Reports in the early history of European settlements in an area of the United States can lead to archaeological sites. Six reasons exist for pinpointing locations: 1) early European settlers sought the same ecological advantages that Indians sought in a location; 2) archaeological sites reported by early Europeans probably concentrated on the most conspicuous sites; 3) the uniqueness of the sites brought them to the attention of the Europeans; 4) sometimes early sites can be relocated and their surviving fragments

excavated; 5) detailed location of an archaeological site may allow descriptions
from various dates to be attributed to sites noted at an early period; 6) the
pinpointing of a site might allow the establishment of local ecological correlates.
14 notes, biblio.   R. S. Burns

1331. Sosin, Jack M. THE USE OF INDIANS IN THE WAR OF THE
AMERICAN REVOLUTION: A RE-ASSESSMENT OF RESPONSIBILITY.
Can. Hist. R. 1965 46(2): 101-121. Examines American and British actions
concerning the use of Indians. The decision to use them was precipitated on both
sides by local groups. Due to a distaste for savage warfare by certain British
officials, Indians were not used until relatively late and then with little effect.
Based primarily on unpublished manuscripts in the Clements Library and the
Public Archives of Canada.   A

1332. Sturtevant, William C. ETHNOGRAPHIC DETAILS IN THE AMERI-
CAN DRAWINGS OF JOHN WHITE, 1577-1590. *Ethnohist. 1965 12(1): 54-
63.* John White's drawings represent the major source on North American
aboriginal culture at the contact period. Though consummately reproduced and
edited, and "remarkably faithful to the originals," the collotype reproductions in
the British Museum (University of North Carolina Press, 1964) still fail to show
all ethnographic detail visible in the drawings and water colors of Indians and
Indian scenes as preserved in the originals in the British Museum. These discrepancies of detail are enumerated plate by plate by the ethnologist who prepared
the textual commentaries printed with the plates of the 1964 edition.
                                                                  H. J. Graham

1333. Willauer, G. J. PUBLIC FRIENDS REPORT TO LONDON YEARLY
MEETING ON THEIR MISSIONS TO AMERICA, 1693-1763. *J. of the
Friends' Hist. Soc. [Great Britain] 1968 52(2): 122-130.* An important source for
knowledge of English and Irish Quaker ministers who went to the American
colonies is the London Yearly Meeting Minutes, a source up to now largely
unexplored. In the period 1693-1763, 38 accounts of missions to America were
received, representing the activities of about 50 men. The most valuable of these
are 15 direct transcriptions of written statements. This source produced evidence
of growth of Societies of Friends not only in New England and Rhode Island (the
Puritan colonies) but also in the Episcopalian Southern colonies. A report of 1729
states that in Maryland and Virginia and North Carolina four, nine, and three
new meeting houses respectively were built, as well as 40 more in the other
colonies. In addition to the spiritual growth of the Quaker movement in the New
World and the missionary activities of the ministers, the minutes reveal the issues
which troubled the Quakers, such as the Ranters, who were particularly strong
in New England and Long Island. The Indians and later the Negroes also caused
concern to the Friends. That the accounts decreased in detail and number toward
the end of the period may have been due to the preoccupation of the London
Yearly Meeting with affairs at home rather than to any falling off of zeal in the
colonies. 24 notes.   L. Brown

1334. Witthoft, John. ARCHAEOLOGY AS A KEY TO THE COLONIAL FUR TRADE. *Minnesota Hist. 1966 40(4): 203-209.* By tracing the westward flow of certain items dug up through archaeological excavation, such as glass beads which were staples in the coastal trade between the Europeans and the Indians, it is possible for the historian to reconstruct the internal trade routes and markets of the Indians during the 16th and 17th centuries.   P. L. Simon

1335. —. CONFERENCE ON THE HISTORY OF RELIGION IN THE NEW WORLD DURING COLONIAL TIMES. *Americas 1958 14(4): 411-453, 485-488, 497-527.*

Jiménez Moreno, Wigberto. THE INDIANS OF AMERICA AND CHRISTIANITY, pp. 411-431.

Batllori, Miguel, S.J. SOME INTERNATIONAL ASPECTS OF THE ACTIVITY OF THE JESUITS IN THE NEW WORLD, pp. 432-436.

Maheux, Arthur. RELIGION IN FRENCH AMERICA, pp. 437-443.

Ricard, Robert. COMPARISON OF EVANGELIZATION IN POR-TUGUESE AND SPANISH AMERICA, pp. 444-453.

Gonsalves de Mello, José Antônio. THE DUTCH CALVINISTS AND RELIGIOUS TOLERATION IN PORTUGUESE AMERICA, pp. 485-488.

Lavengood, L. G. CONCERNING DR. ZAVALA'S CHAPTER ON RELIGION IN COLONIAL AMERICA, pp. 497-501.

Phelan, John L. THE INFLUENCE OF RELIGION ON THE HIS-TORY OF THE NEW WORLD, pp. 502-506.

Bishko, C. J. SOME REFLECTIONS UPON THE CHAPTER ON RE-LIGION IN THE COORDINATION OF THE COLONIAL PERIOD BY DR. S. ZAVALA, pp. 507-509.

Goveia, Elsa V. INFLUENCE OF RELIGION IN THE WEST INDIES, pp. 510-516.

Konetzke, Richard. POINTS OF DEPARTURE FOR THE HISTORY OF MISSIONS IN HISPANIC AMERICA, pp. 517-522.

Savelle, Max and Malagon-Barcelo, Javien. SUMMARY OF CONFER-ENCE ON RELIGION, pp. 523-527.

Specialists in religious and colonial American history examine both special historical problems and general issues of methodology and interpretation. The draft of a synthetic treatment of religion in the colonial Americas by Silvio Zavala served as the point of departure for the conference, held at Washington in December 1957, and many of the papers were designed to correct or enlarge upon Zavala's statements.   D. Bushnell

The Early Republic
1783-1830

1336. Boller, Paul F., Jr. GEORGE WASHINGTON AND THE QUAKERS. *Bull. of Friends Hist. Assoc. 1960 49(2): 67-83.* An account of the relations between Washington and the Quakers. Washington came gradually to respect, but not to share, the principles of the Friends. He did not sympathize with their pacifism during the Revolution: but he treated them with fairness and decency.

After the war his sympathy increased, although he objected to their vigorous agitation on the antislavery issue. He approved of their efforts on behalf of the Indians. On the issue of war with France, he had a disagreement with the Quaker George Logan. Documented.   N. Kurland

1337. Burns, Peter J. THE SHORT, INCREDIBLE LIFE OF JEDEDIAH SMITH. *Montana 1967 17(1): 44-55.* Biographical sketch of Jedediah Strong Smith, who at age 23 began trapping for the Ashley-Henry partnership in the northern Rocky Mountains. Soon entering the firm, he trapped and explored extensively, including two crossings of the Great Basin to the San Diego area, and a visit to the lower Columbia River. On an expedition to the Santa Fe country, he was ambushed and killed by Comanche Indians. Illus.   S. R. Davison

1338. Cutright, Paul Russell. LEWIS AND CLARK INDIAN PEACE MEDALS. *Bull. of the Missouri Hist. Soc. 1968 24(2): 160-167.* Giving medals to prominent Indians had been the practice from early colonial days. The Lewis and Clark expedition used them to promote peace and friendship. The Indians valued the medals highly. The circumstances of presentation and a description of the six medals and the one accompanying certificate which are known to have survived are included. 8 illus.   D. L. Smith

1339. Darnell, Donald. UNCAS AS HERO: THE "UBI SUNT" FORMULA IN "THE LAST OF THE MOHICANS." *Am. Literature 1965 37(3): 259-266.* In *The Last of the Mohicans,* Uncas, not Natty Bumppo, is the hero. The devices used to portray Uncas as a tragic hero are scenic positioning and increasing prominence in the action as a mythical and epic figure. 6 notes.
                                                              R. S. Burns

1340. Gale, Frederick C. JEDEDIAH SMITH MEETS INDIANS AND VICE VERSA. *Pacific Historian 1966 10(2): 34-38.* An account drawn from various western narratives of Jedediah S. Smith's early journeys among the western Indians from 1823 through 1824, including Smith's own account. Observations compare the various tribes with respect to their warlike, social, and moral traits, with some effort devoted to achieving a balanced judgement. The Crow, for example, are portrayed both as superb horsemen and petty thieves.
                                                              T. R. Cripps

1341. Hall, Joan Joffe. "NICK OF THE WOODS": AN INTERPRETATION OF THE AMERICAN WILDERNESS. *Am. Literature 1963 35(2): 173-182.* Comments on Robert Montgomery Bird's book dealing with American themes: settler vs. Indian, the American wilderness, the individual struggle to be a good Christian. Nathan Slaughter is a contrast to James Fenimore Cooper's Natty Bumppo, more akin to Herman Melville's Indian-hater in *The Confidence Man.* 12 notes.   R. S. Burns

1342. Havighurst, Walter. STEAMBOAT TO THE ROCKIES. *Am. West 1970 7(5): 4-11, 61-62.* Steamboats were introduced to the Missouri River in 1819.

Exploration, collection of scientific data, fur resources, Indian trade, the movement of troops, the transporting of military and civilian supplies, and the migration of settlers were all compelling incentives to make the Missouri River the principal transportation artery of the trans-Mississippi West. The author traces the history of the trials and errors of steamboat navigation on the Missouri to 1885, when the *Missouri* made the last trip through to Fort Benton, Montana. 7 illus., biblio. note. D. L. Smith

1343. Horsman, Reginald. AMERICAN INDIAN POLICY AND THE ORIGINS OF MANIFEST DESTINY. *U. of Birmingham Hist. J. [Great Britain] 1968 11(2): 128-140.* American attitudes toward the Indians are informative about American attitudes to other peoples and about the development of the ideology of expansion. An examination of the origins and development of "manifest destiny" as a concept and consequent relations with the Indians in the period between the Revolution and the Mexican War shows steady changes in attitudes. In the period 1790-1810 Americans assumed that Indians would adopt American civilization and thus would benefit by the expansion of the United States. By the 1820's this concept of improvability was under major attack; by the 1830's and 1840's it was commonly assumed that the Indians had succumbed because they were doomed by Providence and that their rights were less relevant than the expansion of American civilization. This doctrine began to assume racist overtones. 39 notes. D. H. Murdoch

1344. Jackman, S. W. A YOUNG ENGLISHMAN REPORTS ON THE NEW NATION: EDWARD THORNTON TO JAMES BLAND BURGES, 1791-1793. *William and Mary Q. 1961 18(1): 85-121.* Sixteen letters from Thornton, secretary to George Hammond from 1791 to 1793, to his mentor, Burges. The letters describe life in the United States, comment on the American reaction to the French Revolution, mention Indian relations, and discuss religion in America, with special reference to Thomas Jefferson's position and to Unitarianism. E. Oberholzer, Jr.

1345. Kunitz, Stephen J. BENJAMIN RUSH ON SAVAGISM AND PROGRESS. *Ethnohist. 1970 (1/2): 31-42.* "Benjamin Rush, one of the signers of the Declaration of Independence and the most influential physician of the revolutionary period, delivered a lengthy address concerning the natural history of medicine among North American Indians. The text of this lecture is analyzed to demonstrate how basic cultural assumptions and values affect our view of truth and, more specifically, how Rush's medical opinions were colored by the then-current notions of savagism and progress." J

1346. McCluggage, Robert W. THE SENATE AND INDIAN LAND TITLES, 1800-1825. *Western Hist. Q. 1970 1(4): 415-425.* To understand how Indian policy was defined in the early days of the Republic, examines the role played by the U.S. Senate. The Senate held ultimate control over this policy through its ratification of the treaties negotiated with the Indians. Central in this policy were the senatorial views on the nature of the legal title by which the Indians held the lands confirmed to them by treaties. Although it had been preached to the Indians that their salvation could only be assured through the private property concept, and although agents in the field had striven to convert them to the idea, senatorial decisions consistently denied the Indians the security of fee simple to the land, either as a group or as individuals. 22 notes.   D. L. Smith

1347. McDermott, John Francis. THE INDIAN AS HUMAN BEING. *Nebraska Hist. 1971 52(1): 45-49.* Recounts evidence, chiefly from the writings of Washington Irving, that catches a glimpse of common humanity in the Indian, indicating his sense of humor and his turn for satire closely bound to daily life.
R. Lowitt

1348. Muller, Paul Eugene. DAVID ZEISBERGER'S OFFICIAL DIARY, FAIRFIELD, 1791-1795. *Moravian Hist. Soc. Tr. 1963 19: 5-229.* David Zeisberger (1721-1808) was a Moravian missionary among the American Indians and was, along with Sir William Johnson, one of the most able and effective diplomats on the frontier during the revolutionary war period. Born in Zauchtenthal, Moravia, he first settled in Georgia and later in the Moravian settlements in Pennsylvania. A sympathetic friend of the Indians, he helped them establish settlements in New York, the Ohio area, Michigan, and at Fairfield, Ontario. The author gives a brief history of the *Unitas Fratrum* and patron Count Zinzendorf as well as details of the settlements. Biblio.   J. G. Pennington

1349. Murdoch, Richard K. THE CASE OF THE SPANISH DESERTERS, (1791-1793). *Georgia Hist. Q. 1960 44(3): 278-305.* Shows how an informal agreement between an American and Spanish officers on the Georgia frontier had repercussions in the case of three Spanish deserters that affected policy makers in both Madrid and Philadelphia. Involved also was tension between federal and Georgia officials regarding policy toward the Spanish and their Indian allies.
R. Lowitt

1350. Neil, William M. THE TERRITORIAL GOVERNOR AS INDIAN SUPERINTENDENT IN THE TRANS-MISSISSIPPI WEST. *Mississippi Valley Hist. R. 1956 43(2): 213-237.* After 1787, a territorial governor was automatically superintendent for Indian affairs. The governors had to report on Indian life in their respective territories, administer existing reservations, and, above all, negotiate treaties. They were handicapped in the realization of the principal aim of Indian policy—conversion of the Indians from a nomadic way of life to agriculture—by financial difficulties and by the delaying of ratification or the complete rejection of treaties by Congress. Public opinion was often opposed to treaty-making, since it was felt that treaties only encouraged the Indians to rape and murder and confirmed them in the belief that the land was theirs. Other problems with which the governors had to deal were the illegal Indian trade, encroachment upon Indian reservations, and friction with military or locally elected territorial authorities.   D. van Arkel

1351. Osuch, Joseph C. PATRIARCH OF THE AMERICAN JESUITS. *Polish Am. Studies 1960 27(3/4): 92-100.* Some facts concerning the life and works of

Father Francis Dzierozynski (1779-1850), based on recent research by Father Francis Domanski. Dzierozynski, one of the pioneers of American Catholicism, was patriarch of the American Society of Jesus and builder of the Jesuit educational system in the United States. A Pole, he entered the Society of Jesus at the age of 15. After the Society of Jesus was banished from Russia, he came to the United States to work with the resurrected Jesuit order there. In fact, the American Society of Jesus is a daughter of the Polish Society of Jesus. His three main accomplishments were: aiding the struggling Society of Jesus in the United States, promoting unity among brethren of diverse national origins, and missionary work among the Indians. He also saved Georgetown University, and founded St. Louis University and Holy Cross College.   R. E. Wilson

1352. Pattison, William D. THE SURVEY OF THE SEVEN RANGES. *Ohio Hist. Q. 1959 68(2): 115-140.* An account of the first subdivision of federal territory under the Land Act of 1785. Despite hope that at least 13 ranges (rows) of townships could be staked out in the summer of 1785, one each by a surveyor from one of the states, only seven ranges were complete by the summer of 1788. Progress was slowed principally by hostile Indians. Main immediate beneficiary of the surveying was the Ohio Company of Associates, whose representatives were allowed to reconnoiter lands and which gained a bridgehead to the lands finally chosen. As a trial of the American Rectangular Land Survey System, field work was a failure. Based on Hutchins Papers in Pennsylvania Historical Society, published collections, and records of the Continental Congress and of surveyors in the National Archives.   A

1353. Phillips, Edward Hake. TIMOTHY PICKERING AT HIS BEST: INDIAN COMMISSIONER, 1790-1794. *Essex Inst. Hist. Collections 1966 102(3): 163-202.* Although Pickering has been severely criticized by historians as an "intriguer, Anglophile, and arch-conservative," his services as an Indian commissioner from 1790 to 1794 should not be included in attacks upon his character and actions. As commissioner, Pickering evidenced courage and a willingness to endure personal discomfort. His lack of sophistication, his forthright honesty, and a genuine interest in Indian welfare made him respected by the Indians and enabled him to serve both the Indians and his country well in exceedingly difficult times. Some of the same characteristics which led to Pickering's diplomatic success with the Indians hampered him when he was later charged with planning and carrying out American foreign policy, but as an Indian negotiator he was an unqualified success. Documented largely from unpublished papers.   J. M. Bumsted

1354. Purcha, Francis Paul. THOMAS L. MC KENNEY AND THE NEW YORK INDIAN BOARD. *Mississippi Valley Hist. R. 1961/62 48(4): 635-655.* The Jacksonian policy in 1829 of forcible removal of the Indians to the West caused a storm of protest from humanitarian and religious groups. As an answer to the attacks, Thomas Loraine McKenney, a Jackson supporter and head of the office of Indian affairs, organized the New York Indian Board with the backing of the Dutch Reformed Church. McKenney issued three tenets: the states would have control over the Indians in their boundaries, the removal was in the best interest of the Indians, and no force would be used in their removal. A lack of motivation, internal dissension, and the use of force against the Indians combined to sterilize McKenney's plans.   G. M. Gressley

1355. Saum, Lewis O. THE FUR TRADER AND THE NOBLE SAVAGE. *Am. Q. 1963 15(4): 554-571.* The philosopher or intellectual expressed his dislike of civilization by comparing it invidiously with savagery. "Having seen the savage, the fur trader had fallen from innocence." Fur traders did utilize the noble savage theme, essentially in order to air their grievances but also to offer sincere warnings of the evils of our civilization. "In either case first-hand experience in the crude realities of wilderness existence provided no absolute immunity from that intriguing and perennial passion, the ennobling of the savage." Based largely on published early travels of fur traders.   E. P. Stickney

1356. Sheehan, Bernard W. THE QUEST FOR INDIAN ORIGINS IN THE THOUGHT OF THE JEFFERSONIAN ERA. *Midcontinent Am. Studies J. 1968 9(1): 34-51.* Discusses the interest of Jefferson and his contemporaries in the derivation of the American Indian. Varied theories expounded by numerous intellectuals of Jefferson's generation are cited, and the latter's investigation of Indian languages is surveyed at length, as are a number of weird explanations set forth by others. The majority of observers, however, manifested good judgment and a scientific approach and through their efforts helped to bring about a positive delineation of the Indian's place in the closed order of 18th-century society. Based on primary and secondary sources; 38 notes.   J

Ante-Bellum America
1830-1865

1357. Blackburn, Forrest R. ARMY FAMILIES IN FRONTIER FORTS. *Military R. 1969 49(10): 17-28.* Discusses the problems encountered by military dependents at frontier forts in the American West in the 1860's. Mentions high food prices, weather hazards, diseases and epidemics, Indians, and dugout homes. 4 photos, 8 notes.   G. E. Snow

1358. Brooks, George R., ed. THE PRIVATE JOURNAL OF ROBERT CAMPBELL. *Bull. of the Missouri Hist. Soc. 1963 20(1): 3-24, 1964 (2): 107-118.* Part I. A portion of the journal, with editorial introduction, of a prominent St. Louis fur trader and merchant, associated with William Sublette. Extensively footnoted by the editor, the journal covers the period of 21 September through 31 December 1833—a portion of Campbell's residence at Fort William on the upper Missouri—and is a significant new source for that critical phase of the western fur trade which found Campbell and Sublette attempting to challenge the large American Fur Company of the Astors and Chouteaus. The journal contains considerable detail about the life, personalities and problems of a fur post. Part II. The almost daily account—from 29 November through 31 December 1833—of the affairs of the firm of Sublette and Campbell at its trading post, Fort

William, on the upper Missouri River at its confluence with the Yellowstone River. The journal describes the difficult problems of construction, of supplies, of the Indians, and of employees—further complicated by constant and hostile competition from Kenneth McKenzie, chief clerk of the rival American Fur Company post at Fort Union. The last entry is a résumé of Campbell's activities in 1833.   R. J. Hanks

1359. Ewers, John C. WHEN THE LIGHT SHONE IN WASHINGTON. *Montana 1956 6(4): 2-11.* An experimental Indian policy was tried in 1831 when representative tribal leaders were invited to Washington for conferences with the president and other officials. The aim was to impress the Indians with the extent and power of the United States, and with the government's friendliness to those who would peaceably accept its control. Among the chiefs selected from the tribes of the upper Missouri was one known as "The Light," a translation of his Indian name. On his return, The Light antagonized many of his people by boasting about his eastern trip. His assassination by a disgruntled tribesman symbolized the failure of this attempt at integration. Based on contemporary press accounts and the published writings of Edwin T. Denig.   S. R. Davison

1360. Holzhueter, John O., ed. FROM WAUPUN TO SACRAMENTO IN 1849: THE GOLD RUSH JOURNAL OF EDWIN HILLYER. *Wisconsin Mag. of Hist. 1966 49(3): 210-244.* After a short introduction to Hillyer's life and the gold rush of 1849, the text of the journal is given with only repetitious portions deleted. It concludes with the author's arrival in Sacramento, California. The journal has several unique features: 1) it is one of the few journals chronicled by an 1849 immigrant that includes details of an Indian slaying; 2) it records a route taken by a minority of forty-niners (beginning at Council Bluffs, Iowa); and 3) because of Hillyer's education and interest in writing, it contains sufficient detail to make the journal "fresh and exciting." 3 photos, 13 drawings, map, 38 notes.
H. A. Negaard

1361. Levitin, Sonia. FIRST HISTORIC TREK ACROSS THE WILD LAND TO CALIFORNIA. *Smithsonian 1971 2(8): 68-73.* The story of the first party from the United States to reach California overland, in 1841. Organized by a Missouri schoolmaster, John Bidwell, the party had originally included 500 people. Finally 68 people gathered at Sapling Grove, Missouri, to make the trip. At that time no one knew the way to California. A fraudulent map and advice from a settler in California, John Marsh, however, seemed to indicate that the journey would be relatively easy. Before departing the California group joined with some missionaries (led by Father Pierre Jean De Smet) who were going to Oregon. Together they would follow the Oregon Trail to Soda Springs, where the groups would split. They crossed the plains, where they met a "prankish" Indian party and shot buffalo. When the group reached Soda Springs, 33 of the original 68 decided to go to California. They had no guide, and their map was in error. They found the Humboldt River and followed it to the Sierra Nevada. The mountains proved to be the most difficult obstacle to their journey. There they killed and ate their livestock. In November 1841 all 33 persons reached John Marsh's ranch. Based on diaries and memoirs; illus.   J. M. Hawes

1362. Nye, Russel B. PARKMAN, RED FATE, AND WHITE CIVILIZA-
TION. *Essays on Am. Literature in Honor of Jay B. Hubbell (Durham: Duke
U. Press, 1967), pp. 152-163.* Francis Parkman devoted his life to intensive study
of the American Indian. "In *The Oregon Trail* [1849] he drew the Indian as
savage; in *Pontiac* [1851] he concluded that the Indian's savagery insured his
ultimate extinction." *The Jesuits in North America* (1867) marks "the third and
final stage in Parkman's concept of the Indian." Because the Indian was "irre-
trievably savage," the Jesuits failed in their attempts to Christianize him; because
the Indian could not be civilized, "France could not hold the West; North America became English." 19 notes.   C. L. Eichelberger

1363. Prucha, Francis Paul. ANDREW JACKSON'S INDIAN POLICY: A
REASSESSMENT. *J. of Am. Hist. 1969 56(3): 527-539.* The usual historical
assessment of Andrew Jackson as Indian-fighter and "Indian-hater" is neither
accurate nor just. He was no believer in the Indian as a "noble savage" and he
could be ruthless to hostiles, but he tried to be fair to peaceful ones and protected
their rights. His policy of removal was dictated by a desire to allow the Indians
time to develop white civilization in an environment where they would be protected from white encroachment. The other alternatives of extermination, rapid
assimilation, or federal protection as sovereign enclaves within state boundaries
were inhumane, not feasible, or politically inexpedient. Based on Jackson's correspondence and messages; 40 notes.   K. B. West

1364. Prucha, Francis Paul. INDIAN REMOVAL AND THE GREAT
AMERICAN DESERT. *Indiana Mag. of Hist. 1963 59(4): 299-322.* Disputes a
widely accepted statement in American history textbooks that in the early 19th
century the U.S. government sought to solve the Indian problem by removing
Indians west of the Mississippi River into the area known as the "Great American
Desert." None of the official plans for Indian removal in the 1820's and 1830's
contemplated use of lands designated in maps of that time as part of this
"Desert," nor did even the critics of the government's plans mention such an idea.
The author concedes some Indians might have been settled there, but only "by
chance." Given present historical evidence, "the idea that the Indians were
deliberately disposed of in the desert loses all credibility."   J. Findlay

1365. Rogin, M. P. LIBERAL SOCIETY AND THE INDIAN QUESTION.
Pol. and Soc. 1971 1(3): 269-312. An investigation of the rhetoric used by
American statesmen to remove the Indian from the path of westward expansion.
Looks specifically at the Jacksonian era and shows that the father-children symbolism was constantly applied, but without allowing the Indian the possibility of
maturing as an Indian. He could either enter adult life accepting white civilization, or die as a child; i.e., as an Indian. Based on published material and
government documents.   G. L. Cole

1366. Shulman, Robert. PARKMAN'S INDIANS AND AMERICAN VIO-
LENCE. *Massachusetts R. 1971 12(2): 221-239.* Uses Parkman's *History of the
Conspiracy of Pontiac* (1851) to illustrate the American "myth" of violence.
Parkman stresses the violent acts of the Indians, as Americans play up the

atrocities of their current enemies, in order to dehumanize them. Thus, the Indians are a "murder-loving" race against which all white violence is justified in order to defend civilization. Whites, despite their technological superiority, are always portrayed as heroic underdogs who "kill" their howling Indian enemies (Indians never "kill," they always "murder"). No moral guilt attaches to the murder of an Indian, since he has already been dehumanized, and white violence is equated with masculinity. Parkman typifies the American attitude toward violence. Based on primary and secondary sources; 11 notes.   G. Kurland

1367. Slosser, Gaius Jackson. WALTER LOWRIE, MISSION ORGANIZER. *J. of the Presbyterian Hist. Soc. 1958 36(1): 3-18.* Born in Scotland in 1784, Walter Lowrie came with his family to Pennsylvania, eventually settling in Butler County. When only 27, he was elected to the Pennsylvania House of Representatives (1811-12), then to the state Senate (1813-19), and to the U.S. Senate (1819-25). From 1825 to 1836 he was secretary of the U.S. Senate, and in 1837 became the first corresponding secretary of the Presbyterian Board of Foreign Missions. For 28 years, until 1865, he provided, from his office in New York, statesmanlike guidance for the missionary enterprises of the church among the American Indians and in India, China and Africa.   W. D. Metz

1368. Taylor, P. A. M. EMIGRANTS' PROBLEMS IN CROSSING THE WEST, 1830-1870. *U. of Birmingham Hist. J. [Great Britain] 1955 5(1): 83-102.* Analyzes the problems facing emigrants crossing the American West. The "major problems were those of crossing rivers, finding forage and water, and deciding on the proper load for waggons," and not attacks by Indians, as is commonly supposed. The emigrants achieved "a fair degree of mastery over their purely technical problems," but they fared "much worse in dealing with problems of human organisation." The unity of emigrant groups sometimes broke down, and there was much discontent, even some bloodshed. The author examines the organization of emigrant companies in some detail and emphasizes that the larger Mormon groups, which acknowledged the authority of their leader ("His leadership was an institution with a spiritual sanction"), were most successful in organizing companies. Based on published sources, mainly diaries, journals, and reminiscences.   J. A. S. Grenville

1369. Willson, Lawrence. THOREAU ON EDUCATION. *Hist. of Educ. Q. 1962 2(1): 19-29.* From 1838 to 1841 Henry and John Thoreau kept a school in Concord, Massachusetts. Henry was concerned with vocational training for men, with using nature as a laboratory, and with education as an association with the most cultivated of one's contemporaries. As education was living, not learning how to get a living, Thoreau wanted adult education and wished "that villages were universities." He held the Indians, educated by and in nature, to be the most perfectly educated men. Thoreau's educational thought, appreciative of schools and civilization, nonetheless contained elements subversive of democratic institutions, as it was, at heart, aristocratic, intended to justify the training of independent, self-reliant individuals.   J. Herbst

1370. Willson, Lawrence. THOREAU'S MEDICAL VAGARIES. *J. of the Hist. of Medicine and Allied Sci. 1960 15(1): 64-74.* A compendium of Henry David Thoreau's opinions and knowledge of the medical practice of his contemporaries and of the American Indians. The author concludes that Thoreau believed disease to be eradicable, a consequence of man's failures to live in conformity with the laws of nature. Based on Thoreau's published and manuscript journals and notebooks, especially those kept for his projected study of the American Indian.

C. Rosenberg

Post-Civil War America
1865-1900

1371. Athearn, Robert G. THE FIREWAGON ROAD. *Montana 1970 20(2): 2-19.* Advances the thesis that the railroad was the primary force in subjugating western Indians—by bringing in overwhelming numbers of soldiers and giving them mobility, and by carrying in "hordes of settlers whose very numbers suffocated the Indian threat." It is shown that government assistance to the railroads, often pictured as a swindle, was really an excellent investment, which was repaid abundantly in reduced rates for shipments and fares, and still further by donations of services which had never been widely publicized. An additional dividend came from the railroads' role in shortening the Indian wars, which were always costly. Derived from official records and newspapers of the period 1865-85; illus., 58 notes.

S. R. Davison

1372. Beaver, R. Pierce. AMERICAN MISSIONARY EFFORTS TO INFLUENCE GOVERNMENT INDIAN POLICY. *J. of Church and State 1963 5(1): 77-94.* Under President Grant's "Peace Policy," American Indians were to be civilized and educated with the cooperation of the U.S. government and missionary organizations. This partnership was terminated at the end of the 19th century as a result of the evolution of the doctrine of separation of church and state. At the same time church concern for Indian affairs declined and was not revived until the 1950's. Biblio.

J (L. C. Brown)

1373. Berkhofer, Robert F., Jr. MODEL ZIONS FOR THE AMERICAN INDIAN. *Am. Q. 1963 15(2): 176-190.* Describes the frontier institution of the manual labor boarding school as an example of eastern preconceptions concerning Indian needs. Drawing upon plans suggested earlier by missionaries, the mission schools emerged as model microcosms of the larger society of "Christian Civilization" (American middle-class Protestantism). The red man, viewed simply as a type of man not as advanced as the whites, had only to be instructed in the ways of civilization. The boarding schools, consequently, became the device by which the missionaries removed Indian children from a culture which supposedly contaminated them. After removal, the child grew up in the utopian society of middle-class eastern white missionaries. Whatever virtues the Indian culture possessed were simply overlooked.

R. S. Pickett

1374. Bloom, Mary Geneva. SOLDIERS WESTWARD: WHERE ARE THEIR OWN STORIES? *Pacific Historian 1964 8(1): 39-41.* A plea for the need of historians to seek out the letters of the western pioneers and soldiers, for most of the literature of western history consists of memoirs and other works published from the distance of time. In three periods there was great excitement: 1) the California gold rush and the Mexican War, 2) the Civil War, and 3) the period of Indian warfare; but historians find a dearth of sources from the pens of common soldiers. "Did any of these men keep diaries of those decisive years of the seventies and eighties?"   T. R. Cripps

1375. Boeser, Linda. TWO COMSTOCK JOURNALISTS: SAMUEL L. CLEMENS AND WILLIAM L. WRIGHT AS REPORTERS AND AUTHORS. *Missouri Hist. R. 1965 59(4): 428-438.* The Virginia City *Territorial Enterprise* was an enterprising and unrestrained newspaper during the days of the Comstock Lode. Wright, who wrote under the pen name Dan De Quille, joined its staff in 1861 and remained for 31 years. The more famous Mark Twain joined the paper in 1862 and remained for two years. Wright had a greater respect for facts, which made him an excellent reporter but may have kept him from maturing into an audacious and popular writer like Twain. The attitudes of the two men toward such topics as Indians and outlaws are contrasted by referring to the treatment given such subjects in their literary efforts about the West, Wright's *The Big Bonanza* (1876) and Clemens' *Roughing It* (1871). 46 notes.
                                                                    W. F. Zornow

1376. Brown, D. Alexander. GALVANIZED YANKEES. *Civil War Times Illus. 1966 4(10): 12-21.* A summary of the service of the six regiments of U.S. volunteers formed by six thousand Confederate prisoners who had taken the oath of allegiance. Service was primarily in the West against hostile Indians. Illus., map.   W. R. Boedecker

1377. Brown, Lawrence L. THE EPISCOPAL CHURCH IN THE ARID WEST, 1865-1875: A STUDY IN ADAPTABILITY. *Hist. Mag. of the Protestant Episcopal Church 1961 30(3): 142-172.* Analyzes jurisdictional boundary changes and the missionary work of the Episcopal Church among prairie farmers, miners, Mormons, Indians, Latin Americans, and Orientals. Avowedly suggestive in nature, the article recommends further fields of inquiry.
                                                                 E. Oberholzer, Jr.

1378. Craighead, Alexander McC. MILITARY ART IN AMERICA, 1750-1914. *Military Collector and Historian 1965 17(2): 42-48.* Concerns such artists and their military works as Archibald M. Willard, *Yankee Doodle*, more commonly known as the Spirit of '76; Cassilly Adams, *Custer's Last Fight, the Battle of the Little Big Horn on June 25, 1876;* Charles Schreyvogel, *My Bunkie;* and Frederic Remington, *Cutting the Lemon, Indians Making Smoke Signals, Troops Guarding Train.* Illus.   C. L. Boyd

1379. D'Elia, Donald J. THE ARGUMENT OVER CIVILIAN OR MILITARY INDIAN CONTROL, 1865-1880. *Historian 1962 24(2): 207-225.* Depicts the sense of urgency that the issue of the transfer of the Indian Bureau aroused in the nation. By 1880 the seriousness of the movement waned, but friction between the army and the Department of the Interior persisted on into the 20th century. Based on Annual Reports of the Commission on Indian Affairs through the 1870's, on various other official records and reports, and on periodicals.   Sr. M. McAuley

1380. Dale, Edward E. A DEDICATION TO THE MEMORY OF GRANT FOREMAN, 1869-1953. *Arizona and the West 1964 6(4): 271-274.* Ill health and an employment opportunity motivated Ulysses Grant Foreman to quit his position in a midwestern law firm for legal fieldwork with the Commission to the Five Civilized Tribes (the Dawes Commission) in Indian Territory. Foreman gradually withdrew from the practice of law to devote his time to research and writing in Southwest history, particularly as it concerned the Indians of Oklahoma. His articles and books, largely a labor of love, compose a sizable bibliography. Appended with a selected list of his works relating to the American West, illus.
D. L. Smith

1381. Dippie, Brian W. THE SOUTHERN RESPONSE TO CUSTER'S LAST STAND. *Montana 1971 21(2): 18-31.* Southern newspapers presented the George Armstrong Custer incident (1876) as the result of Republican blunders, chiefly of keeping too many troops in the South while Indians slaughtered the outnumbered forces on the western frontier. Much was made of President Ulysses Simpson Grant's responsibility, and of the assignment of his son, Lieutenant (later Major General) Frederick Dent Grant, to safe military positions in the East. The journalists seemed willing to forgive Custer for his service in the Union Army during the Civil War, and to adopt him as a regional hero and martyr. Based on contemporary newspapers; illus., 61 notes.   S. R. Davison

1382. Eggan, Fred. LEWIS H. MORGAN AND THE FUTURE OF THE AMERICAN INDIAN. *Pro. of the Am. Phil. Soc. 1965 109(5): 272-276.* Analyzes ethnologist Lewis H. Morgan's (1818-81) attitude toward the American Indians and their future, noting also the environmental influences and experiences which helped to shape his evaluation. Having studied various tribes, Morgan concluded (unlike a large number of his contemporaries) that the Indian had a future. Though believing in white superiority, he urged a more enlightened and responsible government policy toward these American aborigines than was generally accepted in his day. He may be viewed as a harbinger of current theories which attempt to solve this problem. Based largely on Morgan's books; 17 notes.
W. G. Morgan

1383. Ellis, Richard N. THE HUMANITARIAN SOLDIERS. *J. of Arizona Hist. 1969 10(2): 53-66.* Agrees that in the 20 years after the Civil War, despite the detractions of civilian critics, many army officers actually favored a humanitarian policy toward the western Indians. Officers such as Major General George Armstrong Custer and Lieutenant General Nelson Appleton Miles sought glory and were not responsive to the legitimate needs of the Indians, but General George Crook, Major General Oliver Otis Howard, Brigadier General Benjamin Henry Grierson, and Major General John Pope did regard the Indians sympathetically. They fought the Indians as they had to, but felt compassion for a proud, conquered people. 4 photos, 24 notes.   R. J. Roske

1384. Ellis, Richard N., ed. GENERAL POPE'S REPORT ON THE WEST, 1866. *Kansas Hist. Q. 1969 35(4): 345-372.* Presents a report dated 25 February 1866 prepared by John Pope (commanding general of the Division of the Missouri) for his superior William T. Sherman (commanding general of the Division of the Mississippi). Pope described the geography, economy, and settlement of his vast command that reached from Texas to Canada and from Wisconsin to the Rockies. He also described the northern, central, and southern routes of transportation and commerce through his command. Pope's report contained elaborate recommendations on the placement of troops and revisions in the government's Indian policies. He favored transferring control of Indian affairs to the War Department, abandoning the unrealistic treaty system, and setting up new trade regulations. Based on books, articles, congressional reports, and the Official Records; illus., 2 maps, 25 notes.   W. F. Zornow

1385. Fowler, Don D. and Fowler, Catherine S. JOHN WESLEY POWELL, ANTHROPOLOGIST. *Utah Hist. Q. 1969 37(2): 152-172.* Review of Powell's activities in research on the origins, tribal organization, and culture of the American Indians of the West, concluding that he is a transitional figure in American anthropological studies, noteworthy mostly for the organization of investigations and contributing little to the literature or the theoretical conceptualizations of the field.   S. L. Jones

1386. Greenway, John. THE GHOST DANCE: SOME REFLECTIONS, WITH EVIDENCE, ON A CULT OF DESPAIR AMONG THE INDIANS OF NORTH AMERICA. *Am. West 1969 6(4): 42-47.* Religion is explained as the formulation and articulation of the unreasonable hope of a culture threatened with extinction that is manifested when all reasonable hope has vanished. A nativistic prophet or leader emerges who maintains that his credentials and charge to lead his people are divinely given. Natural selection determines whether his endeavor will succeed and survive the competition of other similar movements of the same time. This happened "scores" of times among American Indians. The most important, according to the author, was the Ghost Dance despair cult which first appeared briefly (1870-73) among the Ute in western Nevada. It resurfaced at the same place in 1889 under the leadership of a Paiute named Wovoka, otherwise known as Jack Wilson, who steadfastly maintained the divinity of his mission. The Ghost Dance cult combined primitive Indian beliefs and Christian conceptions. It spread rapidly from tribe to tribe, although its acceptance was not universal by all of the groups in the Plains and Rockies area. The cult is herein documented by accounts of competent white ethnographers on the scene. It came to an end in December 1890 with the massacre committed by the U.S. 7th Cavalry at Wounded Knee, South Dakota. 3 illus.   D. L. Smith

1387. Gressley, Gene M. A CATTLEMAN VIEWS INDIAN POLICY—1875. *Montana 1967 17(1): 2-11.* Discusses official and public attitudes toward western Indians in the 1870's, incorporating an essay, "The Nation's Wards," by William Sturgis, a Wyoming cattleman. Indian policies during Grant's administration are criticized. Illus.   S. R. Davison

1388. Hogarth, Paul. OFF TO THE PLAINS! *Am. West 1968 5(6): 4-17.* Victorian Englishmen were given glimpses of the rest of the world from elaborately drawn illustrations which appeared in London's weekly picture papers supplied by their traveling staff artists. The *London Graphic* was one of the outstanding examples. Its reputation for the superior quality, faithfulness to reality, and value as works of art of its illustrations was worldwide. They were reprinted extensively throughout Europe and the United States. Pre-eminent as a "Special Artist," as these artist-reporters were called, was Arthur Boyd Houghton. An 1869-70 assignment in the United States resulted in 72 published illustrations, 34 of which are western subjects—mainly confined to a visit to the Mormons in Utah, a buffalo hunt in Nebraska, and a Nebraska Pawnee agency. Usually they were accompanied by articles or short texts edited from Houghton's own descriptive notes. Their fidelity and realism are in contrast to the usual through-Victorian-eyes approach. 8 illus., biblio. note.   D. L. Smith

1389. Howell, Edgar M. THEODORE R. DAVIS: SPECIAL ARTIST IN THE INDIAN WARS. *Montana 1965 15(2): 2-23.* Davis is one of the few artists known to have witnessed personally the scenes he depicted for the sensational illustrated weeklies during the Indian wars of the mid-century. Examples of his work with the Hancock campaign of 1867 are here reproduced and discussed.   S. R. Davison

1390. Illick, Joseph E. "SOME OF OUR BEST FRIENDS ARE INDIANS...": QUAKER ATTITUDES AND ACTIONS REGARDING THE WESTERN INDIANS DURING THE GRANT ADMINISTRATION. *Western Hist. Q. 1971 2(3): 283-294.* Unlike federal efforts and the attitudes of much of the mainstream of the American people, the Society of Friends was motivated by high ideals and achieved considerable success in dealings with the Indians. Occasionally the Quakers worked with and through government agencies. After the Civil War their slavery abolition energies were rechanneled to improve the conditions of the Indians of the trans-Mississippi West. They became the principal instruments for the operation of President Ulysses Simpson Grant's peace policy. For over a decade, 1869-85, they served as appointed agents on the various western reservations and superintendencies in a program of moral uplift and manual training. Their efforts to achieve acculturation failed because of reasons external to the experiment: frontier land hunger and congressional patronage politics. With the collapse of government sponsorship, the Quakers quietly went to work outside the system. Biblio.   D. L. Smith

1391. Knight, Oliver. A REVISED CHECK LIST OF INDIAN WAR CORRE-
SPONDENTS, 1866-91. *Journalism Q. 1961 38(1): 81-82.* Reprints and adds to
the check list of accredited newspaper correspondents covering the Indian wars
published in 1940 by the late Professor Elmo Scott Watson.   L. Gara

1392. Lord, Francis A. DISPOSAL OF POST-WAR SURPLUS. *Civil War
Times Illus. 1968 6(10): 35-41.* Only 138 thousand muskets, rifles, and carbines
and 20 thousand pistols were paid for and taken home by veterans of the Civil
War. Many more were taken but not paid for. A large number were distributed
to the Indians in an effort to secure their friendship. In 1868 Congress passed a
law authorizing the Secretary of War to sell weapons without prior inspection and
condemnation. After that sales increased rapidly, particularly to foreign governments. The Turks managed to skim the cream. About a half million arms were
sold to France during the Franco-Prussian War. The price paid for a serviceable
rifle varied from five dollars to just over 12 dollars. Many pieces were sold for
the metal.   R. N. Alvis

1393. Lurie, Nancy Oestreich. LADY FROM BOSTON AND THE OMAHA
INDIANS. *Am. West 1966 3(4): 31-33, 80-85.* Alice Cunningham Fletcher was
a pioneer anthropologist of widely recognized scholarly achievements. Little
known is her role as an activist for Indian reform, resulting, in particular, in
federal legislation that established the earliest experiment in applied anthropology. In 1881, on her first field trip, she visited Indian reservations in
Nebraska and South Dakota. At once Miss Fletcher became an outspoken critic
of Indian policy and the injustices done to the Indians. She was the architect and
moving spirit behind the Omaha Allotment Act of 1882 which became the model
for the 1887 Dawes Severalty Act. By it, tribally held reservations were allotted
into individually owned tracts. Unallotted lands were sold on the assumption that
Indian population would continue to decrease. Within a decade, however, Indian
disdain for the responsibilities of farming, depleted resources, increase in population, and other problems negated much of the hoped for reform from the allotment program. The author analyzes and evaluates the reasons for Miss Fletcher's
misguided efforts. Based on a forthcoming essay on female American anthropologists; note, illus., biblio.   D. L. Smith

1394. Moore, N. Webster. JAMES MILTON TURNER, DIPLOMAT,
EDUCATOR, AND DEFENDER OF RIGHTS 1840-1915. *Bull. of the Missouri Hist. Soc. 1971 27(3): 194-201.* Turner attained prominence as the "cap-
stone of Negro leadership in the Middle West." First an educator in Missouri,
Turner subsequently took up preaching, oratory, and Republican politics in the
state. President Ulysses Simpson Grant appointed him ambassador to Liberia.
After Turner returned from Africa in 1878, he persuaded Grover Cleveland to
support certain Indian claims in Oklahoma. Turner represented the affected
Indian groups in reaching a claims settlement with the U.S. government. Based
on secondary sources; 24 notes.   H. T. Lovin

1395. Munn, Fred. MEMOIRS OF A CAVALRY VETERAN. *Montana 1966
16(2): 50-64.* Reminiscences recorded in 1937 by one of the last survivors of the

campaigns against the Dakota (Sioux) in 1876 and Nez Percés in 1877. He was among the first to view the scene of the Custer battle. The next year, under General O. O. Howard, he witnessed the Camas Prairie fight in Idaho. Illus.

S. R. Davison

1396. Pfaller, Louis. "ENEMIES IN '76, FRIENDS IN '85—SITTING BULL AND BUFFALO BILL. *Prologue: J. of the Natl. Archives 1969 1(2): 16-31.* Primarily discusses two episodes involving Sitting Bull and William F. Cody—the chief's highly successful participation in Buffalo Bill's "Wild West Show" in 1885, and Cody's attempts to restrain Sitting Bull from causing trouble and to deliver him to the army late in 1890 during the Indian "messiah craze." James McLaughlin, Indian agent, was deeply involved in both events. McLaughlin initially refused requests to exhibit Sitting Bull, fearing that publicity might make the chief unmanageable. However, he later relented, hoping that exposure to civilized life might induce Sitting Bull to persuade his followers to pursue both education and farming. Because of the Chief's obnoxious behavior, however, upon returning to the reservation after the 1885 tour during which he had befriended Annie Oakley and during which he had met President Grover Cleveland, McLaughlin refused to allow him to accompany later shows. During the 1890 craze, McLaughlin, fearing violence, was chiefly responsible for thwarting Cody's attempts to reach Sitting Bull. Based on records in the National Archives, the James McLaughlin Papers at Assumption Abbey Archives in Richardton, North Dakota, and some secondary sources; 8 illus., 43 notes.

W. R. Griffin

1397. Rickey, Dan, Jr. BULLETS BUZZING LIKE BEES. *Montana 1961 11(3): 2-10.* Relates facts about the regular and volunteer groups of the military in the Indian wars of the West. First hand experience of a few combatants illustrate some of the problems faced by Indian fighters. The differences between the regular soldiers and the volunteer soldiers are described. Based on a paper read at a Mississippi Valley Historical Association meeting.

L. G. Nelson

1398. Schulte, Marie Louise. CATHOLIC PRESS REACTION TO THE CUSTER DISASTER. *Mid-Am. 1955 37(4): 205-214.* A sampling of press opinion from "the most influential Catholic journals in the United States." Indicates no single reaction except for the tendency to attack the Indian policy of the Grant administration. Only one Catholic journal, The *San Francisco Monitor* reflected hatred for the Indians.

R. F. Campbell

1399. Smith, Duane A. GOLD, SILVER, AND THE RED MAN. *J. of the West 1966 5(1): 114-121.* Examines the impact of the mining frontier on the development of a systematic Indian policy and concludes that contemporary literature and journalism of that day contributed to the forming of adverse attitudes held toward the Indian by the pioneers, but that the polemics had little effect on government policy except as one facet of mounting general criticism. Thus, when the reaction of the miners toward the Indians is combined with other forces pressuring the national government, the indecision concerning the disposition of the Indian question in the 1860's and 1870's is more easily understood. Based on published sources, 12 notes.   D. N. Brown

1400. Sunder, John E., ed. THE REVEREND OCTAVIUS PARKER'S "JOURNEY FROM SAN FRANCISCO...TO ANVIK, ALASKA, TAKEN AT A TIME WHEN A DIRECT JOURNEY WAS IMPRACTICABLE" (1888). *Hist. Mag. of the Protestant Episcopal Church 1965 34(4): 333-348.* Journal entries of Octavius Parker (6 August to 24 October 1888), describing an 80-day sea and land journey from San Francisco to Anvik, Alaska, via the Bering Sea and the Kuskokwin and Yukon rivers. Interesting comments on geography, climate, Indian life, the dangers of travel by skin canoe and the missionary outposts of Moravians, Roman Catholics, Episcopalians and Russians. Lack of good food, illness, natural hazards and trouble with Indians made the journey a struggle for survival. The 27-page narrative is a part of the Alaska MSS collection of the Church Historical Society, Austin, Texas. Map, notes.   E. G. Roddy

1401. Walker, Henry P. GEORGE CROOK: THE "GRAY FOX," PRUDENT, COMPASSIONATE INDIAN FIGHTER. *Montana 1967 17(2): 2-13.* Summarizes the career of George Crook, with some details of his campaigns and battles in Arizona, Wyoming, and Montana. The author rejects accusations that Crook was timid, and defends his record. Derived from standard published accounts of the Indian wars, illus., 53 notes.   S. R. Davison

1402. Wallace, Edward S. BORDER WARRIOR. *Am. Heritage 1958 9(4): 22-25, 101-105.* Recounts the career of Ranald Slidell MacKenzie, Indian-fighting cavalryman of the American West in the 1870's. Illus.
                                                                           C. R. Allen, Jr.

1403. Wells, Merle W. CALEB LYON'S INDIAN POLICY. *Pacific Northwest Q. 1970 61(4): 193-200.* Working during the Civil War and the disruptive aftermath, a time of great difficulty for any territorial official, Caleb Lyon (1821-75), the governor of Idaho Territory, 1864-66, was a leader in trying to establish judicious Indian policies. Frustrated in his efforts to grant acceptable areas of land to the Indians for their reservations, Lyon also failed to gain government confirmation of his treaties with the Indians. The treaties, as proposed by Lyon, were considered benchmarks in attempts to treat the Indians with consideration and dignity.   C. C. Gorchels

4

THE INDIAN IN THE TWENTIETH CENTURY

General

1404. Berkhofer, Robert F., Jr. THE POLITICAL CONTEXT OF A NEW INDIAN HISTORY. *Pacific Hist. R. 1971 40(3): 357-382.* Analyzes the problems of producing an adequate new history of the American Indian which should be primarily a record of ethnic survival and cultural continuity and change despite white efforts toward assimilation and annihilation. The historian would thus make Indian-Indian relations the central theme rather than Indian-white relationships. Beyond the tribal studies of the anthropologist, the historian needs to explore the political dynamics of Indian life as evidenced in the important role of factionalism in both intratribal and intertribal relationships. Emphasizes the importance of the inclusion of political process as a major part of a new interpretation of the history of the Indian. 54 notes.　　　　　　　　　　　　E. C. Hyslop

1405. Berry, Brewton. THE MYTH OF THE VANISHING INDIAN. *Phylon 1960 21(1): 51-57.* Whether commentators have assumed the Indians to be brutish or noble, they were thought doomed to extinction. Time has not borne out these anticipations. The inhabitants of China, India, Ceylon, Java, Egypt, Algeria and the Philippines have increased in number, rather than diminished, following their contact with Westerners. The Indian population, too, has done more than merely survive. Today there are more South American Indians than before the arrival of Europeans. There were about 800 thousand North American Indians at the time of the discovery; there are now about 350 thousand Indians, a substantial gain over previous census figures. The figure varies according to definitions provided by the U.S. Bureau of Indian Affairs, Bureau of the Census, and Public Health Service. There are, in addition, many more individuals and whole communities with an Indian heritage. The Lumbee Indians of North Carolina, for example, caused a national sensation in the United States by dispersing in 1958 a gathering of members of the Ku Klux Klan who resented one of them "dating" a white man. Yet the 30 thousand Lumbee Indians are not noticed as such in the U.S. Census.　　　　　　　　　　　　L. Filler

1406. Boileau, Thornton I. and Boileau, Margot. JOE SCHEUERLE: MODEST MAN WITH FRIENDLY PALETTE. *Montana 1971 21(4): 39-58.* Presents 33 portraits of western Indians, painted by Scheuerle (1873-1948) between 1896 and 1938. Scheuerle was brought to America as a child and received early art training. He was a skilled commercial artist, and the Indian portraits reflect a personal hobby. He was a close friend and frequent companion of Charles M. Russell, Louis Hill (president of the Great Northern Railway), Buffalo Bill Cody, and many Indian notables including Red Cloud. Only genuine modesty and dislike of publicity kept him from greater fame during his lifetime.

S. R. Davison

1407. Brandon, William. AMERICAN INDIANS AND AMERICAN HISTORY. *Am. West 1965 2(2): 14-25, 91-93.* Traditionally in American history Indians are viewed as savages, deterrents to settlement, and colorful stereotypes for Hollywood productions. Even though there is overwhelming evidence to the contrary, very few have attempted to outline Indian history and to place it properly in American history. The significance of Indian participation in American history is suggested by several examples. It is tentatively argued that: the Indian "civilization" may have made a genuine and influential contribution to American history; it may have had so firm a commitment to itself as to have brought its own downfall; it may have been so incomprehensible that the Europeans could not recognize its existence; it may have affected not only our past but may also still have some influence on our future. At any rate, from the collision of the European and this New World civilization, modern America was born. American history is only half written without the Indian side of that story. Illus., biblio.

D. L. Smith

1408. Cawelti, John G. COWBOYS, INDIANS, OUTLAWS. *Am. West 1964 1(2): 28-35, 77-79.* The Western of today's movies, television, and novels elaborates the image of the West of the late 19th-century dime novels and William F. (Buffalo Bill) Cody's Wild West shows. These, with little concern for accuracy, dealt with the 1850-70 cowboy-Indian-outlaw phase of the history of the Great Plains. Collectively they portrayed the mythology of the West. Primarily the creation of "dudes" rather than Westerners, they remain apart from accounts of travelers and settlers and 20th-century serious historical novelists who present a more accurate and complete picture of the real West. This mythology evolves from earlier literature of the American frontier. The significance of the Western myth awaits the analysis of cultural historians.

D. L. Smith

1409. Chafe, Wallace L. ANOTHER LOOK AT SIOUAN AND IROQUOIAN. *Am. Anthropologist 1964 66(4, pt. 1): 852-862.* Vindicates Louis Allen's *Siouan and Iroquoian* (1931), which indicated evidence of a relationship between the two language families. Credits Allen as the first to publish tenable evidence of this proposed connection. Using the methods of comparative linguistics for the reconstruction of Proto-Siouan forms and restricting Iroquoian references to Seneca or, where pertinent, to internally reconstructed Pre-Seneca material, the author has drawn up a list of 67 suggested cognates followed by a list of phoneme correspondences in the material. He compares the phoneme inventories of Pre-Seneca,

Proto-Siouan, and Proto-Siouan-Iroquoian. He also notes some other similarities such as grammatical patterns, occurrence of a labial consonant, and lexical resemblances. Tables, biblio.   Sr. B. A. Barbato

1410. Chandler, Milford G. INDIAN ADAPTATIONS. *Masterkey 1968 42(2): 59-64.* Calls attention to aboriginal creativity in utilizing articles of non-Indian manufacture for purposes entirely different from those for which these articles were made. The many examples cited include: a drum frame made from the rim of an automobile wheel; empty brass cartridge cases and thimbles used as tiny bells on dance costumes; baking powder cans converted into rattles; tinfoil used as ornamental inlays; and a golf putter reworked into a fine, and deadly, tomahawk. Photo.   C. N. Warren

1411. Clark, J. Stanley. CAROLYN THOMAS FOREMAN. *Chronicles of Oklahoma 1968 45(4): 368-375.* Carolyn Thomas Foreman (1872-1967) was a historian of Oklahoma as well as an assistant to her husband Grant, a historian. She wrote and co-wrote numerous books and articles; her principal contributions were a history of prestatehood printing and a study of Indians abroad. Mrs. Foreman also inspired the Indian-Pioneer History project that resulted in the compilation of some 90 bound volumes. Illus., biblio., note.   D. L. Smith

1412. Collier, John. LA PERMANENCIA DEL DESCUBRIMIENTO SOCIAL [The permanence of social discovery]. *Am. Indígena [Mexico] 1955 15(3): 175-186.* Commenting on the contribution made by Dr. Manuel Gamio to the social sciences and to the welfare of the American Indian, briefly reviews the history and background of Indian policy in North and Latin America, with emphasis on reciprocal influences. The beneficial effects of the Indian Reorganization Act of 1934 on Indian communities in the United States are reviewed, and the advantages of group action and responsibility in Indian matters are indicated.   C. F. Latour

1413. Crow, John. SCHOOL FOR THE FIRST AMERICANS. *Am. Educ. 1965 1(8): 15-22.* Survey of the Bureau of Indian Affairs' program to develop the natural and human resources of the American Indian, especially to cope with problems faced by those who choose to leave the reservation and live among the general population and the majority who live on or near reservations. Reviews past policies and programs of the bureau. Concludes that the "growing attraction of education for the Indians has a certain ambivalence, a conflict between the hope of better income and a stronger voice in business affairs, and a desire to cling to the familiar past."   W. R. Boedecker

1414. Dundes, Alan. NORTH AMERICAN INDIAN FOLKLORE STUDIES. *J. de la Soc. des Américanistes [France] 1967 56(1): 53-79.* A survey of the state of North American Indian folklore studies, including only those folklorist genres actually studied as folklore by anthropologists and folklorists. These include riddles, proverbs, tongue-twisters, puns, metaphors, prayers, charms, speeches, poetry, song, dance, games, superstitions and folk narrative. Despite much work, the future of American Indian folklore studies is not bright. Fresh field-gathered materials are becoming more rare and unlikely and occasions for the observation of folklore in context are decreasing. Documented from printed sources.

R. Howell

1415. Dunstan, William. CANADIAN INDIANS TODAY. *Can. Geographical J. 1963 67(6): 182-193.* A survey of the extent to which Canada's 200 thousand Indians share in the general community's economic and social activities. Map, photos. A. H. Lawrance

1416. Fey, Harold E. HAUNTED BY HISTORY. *Christian Cent. 1956 73(12): 363-365.* Discusses the various historic causes of misunderstanding contributing to the unsatisfactory status of relations between American Indians and non-Indians. An adequate philosophy of the relations of people of different cultures has only begun to emerge in the 20th century. "Today we are moving beyond the blind determinism of history because we recognize Indians as persons, see in what remains of Indian culture that which is worthy of respect, accept the forms of association they choose for social organization as valid for themselves so long as they desire to maintain them." G. A. Mugge

1417. Fischer, Wolfram. NEUERE FORSCHUNGEN ZUR WIRTSCHAFTS- UND SOZIALGESCHICHTE DER USA [Recent research on the economic and social history of the United States]. *Vierteljahrschrift für Sozial-und Wirtschaftsgeschichte [West Germany] 1962 49(4): 459-538.* Discusses over 1,000 books and articles that have appeared since 1959, as well as some not previously listed in *Journal of Economic History* 1959 19(1): 1-121. Areas of research have included: the utilization of economic theory in historical work, capital accumulation in early America, use of official statistics, use of sociological concepts and methods, the robber baron tradition and entrepreneurial biographies, and statistical studies of business elites. The frontier and the Indians have received somewhat less emphasis than in the past. Complicating the writing of social history has been the diversified nature of American society with its heterogeneous ethnic background. Many writers fear the approaching "dehumanization" of social and economic historiography, since social historians increasingly use sociological techniques and economic historians increasingly use statistical analyses. European scholars have contributed little or nothing to this vast flood of research. H. C. Johnson

1418. Forbes, Jack D. EL HISTORIADOR Y LA POSICION SOCIAL DEL INDIO EN LOS ESTADOS UNIDOS [The historian and the social position of the Indian in the United States]. *Am. Indígena [Mexico] 1962 22(4): 355-358.* Reviews and deplores the treatment of the Indians in general history texts at all levels of education in the United States. Indian culture is generally ignored; texts ordinarily begin with European history rather than American origins, and when the natives are treated, the prejudices of the white frontiersmen prevail. The writer's views are supported by citing such texts as Avery Craven and Walter

Johnson, *The United States: Experiment in Democracy* (Boston: Ginn and Company, 1952) and John D. Hicks, *A Short History of American Democracy* (Boston: Houghton, Mifflin and Company, 1949).   R. J. Knowlton

1419. Forbes, Jack D. THE HISTORIAN AND THE INDIAN: RACIAL BIAS IN AMERICAN HISTORY. *The Americas 1962/63 19(4): 349-362.* An essay decrying the treatment of the Indians in U.S. historical writing, principally as reflected in textbooks. The vast sweep of American history before the arrival of the Europeans is largely ignored, while references to the Indian in later periods are scant and are written almost exclusively from the standpoint of "Anglo-European" settlers. Similar distortion and neglect can be seen, e.g., in the treatment of Spanish-Mexican settlement and contributions in the southwest.
D. Bushnell

1420. Forrest, James Taylor. ROBERT OTTOKAR LINDNEUX: LAST OF COWBOY ARTISTS. *Great Plains J. 1966 6(1): 32-35.* Biography of Lindneux who was born in New York in 1871, studied art in Europe and returned to the United States at the turn of the century. He went west, worked as a cowboy, and painted the western scene—Rocky Mountains, Indians, whites, and animals—with great technical ability and a strong sense of the dramatic. His paintings are found in many major museums and private collections. At 96 he now lives in Denver.   O. H. Zabel

1421. Grahl-Madsen, Atle. IDENTITY AND EQUALITY: LEGAL PROBLEMS OF NATIONAL MINORITIES. *Cooperation and Conflict [Norway] 1970 5(4): 275-281.* A critical review of Tore Modeen's *The International Protection of National Minorities in Europe* (Åbo Akademi: Åbo, 1969) and L. C. Green's *Canada's Indians—Federal Policy, International and Constitutional Law* (The Government of Alberta: Edmonton, 1970). Modeen, who has limited his study to national minorities in Europe, observes that actual equality will only be achieved when a minority enjoys special rights safeguarding it against assimilation. Tells of the treaty system up to World War II, notably the system created in the wake of World War I. "The text is all too often interspersed with irrelevancies; matters of principal interest are scattered throughout the book without any attempt being made to view them coherently; [but] he has definitely made the point that this problem is as worthy of serious legal study today as it has ever been." Green's book is a critique of the policy position paper which the Canadian government issued in 1969 on the status of the country's Indians. "Prof. Green concedes that the 'Indian Treaties' may not be treaties in the sense of international law, but he makes a very strong case for their being agreements having created legal obligations of a permanent character, which neither side can evade unilaterally....Prof. Green deserves commendation for placing the issue in a greater context, which in turn means that the problem of Canada's Indians also becomes meaningful for lawyers on distant shores."   D. D. Cameron

1422. Gurian, Jay. STYLE IN THE LITERARY DESERT: "LITTLE BIG MAN." *Western Am. Literature 1969 3(4): 285-296.* Asserting that realism is a limited principle, especially for a Western novel, the author shows how Thomas

L. Berger achieved a work of art in *Little Big Man* (New York: Dial, 1964) by using other methods. *Little Big Man* is first compared to Jack W. Schaefer's *Monte Walsh* (New York: Houghton Mifflin, 1963) to illustrate the limitations of realism. In language, for instance, Berger combined the coarse with the educated instead of continually relying on the "doggone it" phrases of *Monte Walsh*. Berger merged intuition and reason in language, characterization, and action, to such an extent that, for example, the Indians' superstition seemed sometimes credible. One of the most important facts about the novel is the point of view. Jack Crabb, the narrator, was white, but was brought up by the Indians, and thus he is able to speak from inside the Cheyenne culture. Berger said he read from 60 to 70 accounts of the West to give him a feel not only for facts about dates, places, and events, but also for the two world views expressed by whites and Indians. Berger's imagination was never sacrificed for realism, which is another key to the novel's literary success. And although Berger does not describe the West as traditional Western writers did, he does present it with genuine love and imagination. S. L. McNeel

1423. Haas, Theodore H. LEGAL ASPECTS OF INDIAN AFFAIRS FROM 1887 TO 1957. *Ann. of the Am. Acad. of Pol. and Social Sci. 1957 (311): 12-22.* A brief historical and legal discussion of the economic and social status of the American Indian through an examination of the legislation and application of federal and state laws. J. S. Counelis

1424. Hadley, J. Nixon. THE DEMOGRAPHY OF THE AMERICAN INDIANS. *Ann. of the Am. Acad. of Pol. and Social Sci. 1957 (311): 23-30.* A historical demographical survey of the American Indian population from pre-Columbian times to the present. J. S. Counelis

1425. Kroeber, Theodora. ABOUT HISTORY. *Pacific Hist. R. 1963 32(1): 1-6.* Personal account of how an anthropologist came to understand the meaning of history while writing a biography of an American Indian. J. McCutcheon

1426. Levine, Stuart. OUR INDIAN MINORITY. *Colorado Q. 1968 16(3): 297-320.* Discusses the Indians' role in modern American society and the whites' interpretation of that role. Indian groups obviously have assimilated much from American society, but they have continued to develop as independent cultural entities. Thus, the government's policy of complete assimilation does not coincide with Indian aspirations, and too many employees of the Bureau of Indian Affairs consider themselves missionaries who must teach assimilation. Because most Indians are poor and wish the financial and technical aid necessary to continue their lives as Indians, they generally want a program to establish means of adequate economic support on their reservations. One of the most serious problems is that the Indians cannot form a united front, and the only operating Pan-Indian movement seems to be the Native American Church, which varies widely from area to area. 5 notes. B. A. Storey

1427. Long, Paula. THE FORGOTTEN AMERICAN. *Radford R. 1971 25(1): 27-39.* Surveys federal policies toward the American Indian since the end of the 18th century; remarks critically on them all. Sees Indians' hope in Pan-Indianism, but finds basic material and psychological problems formidable in any attempt to bring Indians to equality with the American majority. 26 notes.

C. A. Newton

1428. Lurie, Nancy Oestreich. THE INDIANS CLAIMS COMMISSION ACT (1942). *Ann. of the Am. Acad. of Pol. and Social Sci. 1957 (311): 56-70.* Discusses the purpose, nature, importance and possible extent of usage of the Indians Claims Commission Act of 1942, as amended.

J. S. Counelis

1429. Lurie, Nancy Oestreich. THE WORLD'S OLDEST ONGOING PROTEST DEMONSTRATION: NORTH AMERICAN INDIAN DRINKING PATTERNS. *Pacific Hist. R. 1971 40(3): 311-332.* Challenges the idea that Indians drink because of an identity crisis and as an escape to a romanticized past. The drinking is a means of asserting and validating Indianness both to whites and within the Indian community. As an action which distresses whites, drinking has taught the Indian the "value of the negative stereotype as a form of communication and protest demonstration to register opposition and hold the line against what they do not want until they can get what they do want." Since nondrinking is likely to be in proportion to the availability of other effective means of validating Indianness, sees hope in the recent new ways of Indian expression of aggression and protest. 31 notes.

E. C. Hyslop

1430. Meyer, Roy W. HAMLIN GARLAND AND THE AMERICAN INDIAN. *Western Am. Literature 1967 2(2): 109-125.* Traces Garland's growing concern for the Indians and their fate. Garland, after several trips to the West, made a three-part literary portrayal of Indian life. *The Captain of the Gray-Horse Troop* (1902), a novel; *The Book of the American Indian* (1923), a collection of stories; and "The Silent Eaters," a prose poem, express Garland's fear that Indian culture was being changed by the coming of the white settlers. Although his attitude is touched by an unthinking paternalism, Garland sympathized with the complexities of Indian life. 29 notes.

R. N. Hudspeth

1431. Officer, James E. THE ROLE OF THE UNITED STATES GOVERNMENT IN INDIAN ACCULTURATION AND ASSIMILATION. *Anuario Indigenista [Mexico] 1965 25: 73-86.* A survey of the successes and failures of Federal policies toward the American Indian from 1776 to 1965, highlighting the legislative milestones and their effects on various aspects of Indian culture, e.g., family structure, language, religion, social and legal status. The author suggests that careful study of the Indian question in the United States can be of great value to Latin American leaders who are facing much greater problems of cultural unification. 11 notes, biblio.

R. L. Utt

1432. Parman, Donald L. THE INDIAN AND THE CIVILIAN CONSERVATION CORPS. *Pacific Hist. R. 1971 40(1): 39-56.* While the economic condition of the Indian paralleled that of Negroes in the Depression, his treatment in the CCC was different. The Bureau of Indian Affairs assumed the responsibility for supervision of the projects, the focus of which was the improvement and conservation of the reservations according to their particular needs. In addition to working for their own benefit, many of the workers were able to live at home or with their families. Special efforts were made to encourage the Enrollee Program for general educational training. While thousands of Indians increased their skills and education during these years, the long-range results are not conclusive since the same Indian problems still remain. 51 notes.   E. C. Hyslop

1433. Patterson, E. Palmer, II. ARTHUR E. O'MEARA, FRIEND OF THE INDIANS. *Pacific Northwest Q. 1967 58(2): 90-99.* Indians in British Columbia were in danger of losing most of their land as a consequence of the efforts of the provincial government to limit the land holdings of Indian families to no more than 20 acres, while the province was being settled by whites in the latter half of the 19th century. From 1909 to 1927 Arthur E. O'Meara devoted his energies to the fight on behalf of the Indians to gain more favorable terms. The author concludes that O'Meara's ultimate contribution was little more than acting as a catalyst in encouraging the Indians to voice their grievances and organize for action. 26 notes.   C. C. Gorchels

1434. Peri, David W. and Wharton, Robert W. [SAMUEL A. BARRETT]. *Kroeber Anthrop. Soc. Papers 1965 33: 1-35.*
TRIBUTES TO SAMUEL ALFRED BARRETT, pp. 1-2. The authors quote several tributes to Samuel A. Barrett given by various American Indians on the occasion of Barrett's death. Based on primary sources; note.
SAMUEL ALFRED BARRETT 1879-1965, pp. 3-28. Traces the professional life of Samuel A. Barrett. Some of the highlights of his life include: service as the curator and, later, director of the Milwaukee Public Museum; ethnographic work with American Indians; development of tactile models for cancer diagnosis training; and work with A. L. Kroeber in the establishment and production of American Indian films. Based on letters of Barrett, primary and secondary sources; 8 notes, biblio.
THE WORKS OF SAMUEL ALFRED BARRETT, pp. 29-35. A bibliography of 115 publications and 15 films by Samuel A. Barrett.
C. N. Warren

1435. Postal, Susan Koessler. BODY-IMAGE AND IDENTITY: A COMPARISON OF KWAKIUTL AND HOPI. *Am. Anthropologist 1965 67(2): 455-462.* A content analysis of the folklore of Kwakiutl and Hopi contrasting cultures identifying the recurrent motifs revealing attitudes toward body (self as an objective entity) boundaries. A table summarizes the contrasts in the folktales as the focus of concern, the desired goal; as a means of protection, manifestation themes; and as the affirmation of strength, manifestation themes. As expected, the contrasts of the cultures are paralleled in the folklores. 4 notes.
Sr. B. A. Barbato

1436. Povey, John F. AMERICAN EDUCATION AND FRENCH ASSIMI-LATION: A COMPARISON. *Midwest Q. 1970 11(3): 265-279.* A comparison of American educational policy with French educational policy in Africa. The author points out that American policy of the late 19th and early 20th centuries was the result of the necessity of Americanizing the great tide of immigration in what was called the "melting pot." The United States did not take advantage of the great cultural variety brought by immigration, but attempted to create a homogeneous society based on the assumption of the superiority of white Anglo-Saxon Protestantism. Immigrants were willing to change and accept this arrogant conception, but Negroes, Mexicans, and American Indians found it more difficult to reject their racial and cultural identity. French colonial administration in Africa printed instructions that it was essential to make the children understand the profound difference between the unstable and bloody past and the peaceful and fertile present due to a powerful and generous nation whose wars have been beneficial. The French emphasized that the native culture was abhorrent and obviously wrong. The author concludes that, when cultures meet, the interaction can move both ways and be a matter of mutual benefit rather than of conquest. Biblio. note.   G. H. G. Jones

1437. Rachlin, Carol. THE NATIVE AMERICAN CHURCH IN OKLA-HOMA. *Chronicles of Oklahoma 1964 42(3): 262-272.* The Native American Church of North America is an American Indian Christian nativistic religion. It is chartered in 12 states and in Canada and is the largest intertribal organization of American Indians. First chartered in Oklahoma 10 October 1918, its members are of the 57 tribes with about 22 thousand in Oklahoma. Its purpose is to "foster and promote religious believers in Almighty God" among the several tribes. The Indian sees the hand of God in the manifestations of nature. Services are per-formed for the sick and for thanksgiving, and each man communes with God in his own way. The four parts of the ritual ceremony are described. The priest passes the peyote cactus for each person to eat. Some critics say the peyote is a narcotic, but the author discusses its effects and says there are no inheritable effects from eating peyote. Eating of peyote can be compared with the taking of bread and wine in the Christian church. The red mescal bean, which is poisonous, is never used. People confuse peyote and mescal beans. The author contends that use of peyote in a service is justifiable for the Native Americans.
I. W. Van Noppen

1438. Rosen, Sanford J. MILITANCY IS GROWING AMONG RED INDI-ANS IN THE UNITED STATES. *Patterns of Prejudice [Great Britain] 1970 4(3): 13-16.* Describes the campaign of American Indians to maintain their cultural heritage and their civil rights. Reviews two books which prod the con-science of white America and urge Indians to control their own destinies: *Our Brother's Keeper: The Indian in White America* (Cleveland, Ohio: World Pub-lishing Co., 1969), edited by Edgar S. Cahn, and *Custer Died for Your Sins* (New York: Avon Books, 1970), by Vine Deloria, Jr.   G. O. Gagnon

1439. Roth, Barbara Williams. THE 101 RANCH WILD WEST SHOW, 1904-1932. *Chronicles of Oklahoma 1966 43(4): 416-431.* The rodeo developed in the

1890's; it was supplemented by 1900 with wild west shows. The Miller Brothers 101 Ranch Show fascinated Americans. They had thundering hooves, daring rescues, lots of gunfire, the pony express, stage holdups, and, of course, lots of Indians. After the show was originated in Oklahoma, the Miller Brothers took it all over the world. After World War I, the expense of maintaining the show increased until, plagued by the Depression and the movies, it broke up in 1932. 4 illus., 41 notes.   I. W. Van Noppen

1440. Roucek, Joseph S. THE AMERICAN INDIAN IN LITERATURE AND POLITICS. *Il Politico [Italy] 1962 27(3): 569-604.* Discusses white-Indian relations in America from early times to the present, the public image of the Indian, and government policies toward the Indian. The author concludes that today the welfare of the Indian is no longer ignored by the American public. The aim of enlightened Americans "has been recently to let him learn all the devices the white man has available to remain an Indian in the white man's industrialized world." Documented.   R. R. Mertz

1441. Smith, Michael T. THE HISTORY OF INDIAN CITIZENSHIP. *Great Plains J. 1970 10(1): 25-35.* Traces the legal landmarks by which all Indians finally achieved citizenship in 1924. In its early years the United States followed the precedent of European colonial powers in considering Indian tribes as independent nations and making treaties with them. Although Chief Justice John Marshall in *Cherokee Nation vs. Georgia* (U.S., 1831) considered tribes "domestic dependent nations," treatymaking continued until 1871. Legal jurisdiction of the federal government over reservation Indians remained vague until *United States vs. Kagama* (U.S., 1886) clarified the responsibility of Congress. The citizenship status of Indians was also vague. The case of *Ex Parte Crow Dog* (U.S., 1883) and Helen Hunt Jackson's book *A Century of Dishonor* (1881) resulted in the Dawes Act (1887). It provided for distributing land in severalty and for citizenship for Indians who received land. However, the Indians' political status still remained uncertain, as *Matter of Heft* (U.S., 1905), the Burke Amendment (1906), and *United States vs. Nice* (U.S., 1916) illustrated. Finally, in 1924, Congress conferred citizenship on all Indians. 48 notes.   O. H. Zabel

1442. Spicer, Edward H. INDIGENISMO IN THE UNITED STATES, 1870-1960. *Am. Indígena [Mexico] 1964 24(4): 349-363.* Asserts that indigenist movements everywhere in the Western Hemisphere are varieties of the same general phenomenon, that is, the reaction of dominant peoples against the process of domination. Variations are due to differences in national culture and to the role of Indians in each of the American nations. The first phase of the movement in the United States (1870-1920) was characterized by a minimum of objective knowledge, the second phase (1920-60) by greater knowledge of and contact with Indians and by a new concept of integration owing much to John Collier. References include John Collier's *Indians of the Americas: The Long Hope* and *From Every Zenith: A Memoir and Some Essays on Life and Thought* (1947). Biblio.   R. J. Knowlton

1443. Spicer, Edward H. THE ISSUES IN INDIAN AFFAIRS. *Arizona Q. 1965 21(4): 293-307.* The "Indian Question" has not been solved. Any solutions will have to be in response to the three central issues: 1) interference in Indian local government by the federal government, primarily through the Bureau of Indian Affairs; 2) the right of religious or cultural choice; and 3) protection for Indian lands. Emphasizes the contradiction in the government's official policy of laissez-faire while in reality it is working for assimilation.
J. D. Filipiak

1444. Steiner, Henry-York. ANOTHER NEW APPROACH TO INDIAN EDUCATION. *Organon 1971 2(2): 27-31.* The pattern of education for the Indian is set by the whites who control the process, and it reflects their attitudes about education and students in general and Indians in particular. Education for the Indian has usually meant educating the Indian to be un-Indian. This does violence to the identity and character of the Indian. What those in charge of educational institutions do not understand is how to organize educational opportunity without making rigid and insensitive demands for cultural conformity. The Indian must take pride in his history and culture, but not as lore or curiosity. All schools, as well as society at large, must develop means for understanding and enhancing cultural differences. We cannot go back but we can educate for a better future. Note.
P. W. Kennedy

1445. Stolpe, Herman. INDIANERNA I U.S.A. [The Indians in the United States]. *Svensk Tidskrift [Sweden] 1954 41(10): 505-514.* A survey of the different characteristics of Indian tribes in the United States from the post-Columbian era to the present, and the different approaches to this problem by the Spanish, Portuguese, British, French and Dutch until the end of the fighting in 1892. A radically new policy was adopted by the United States in 1933 when John Collier became chief of the Indian Affairs Office of the Department of Interior. Only then did the Indians achieve equality.
I. Luyken

1446. Szasz, Margaret Garretson. INDIAN REFORM IN A DECADE OF PROSPERITY. *Montana 1970 20(1): 16-27.* Examines the work of the Bureau of Indian Affairs under the administrations of Charles Burke (from 1921 to 1928) and his successor John Collier (from 1933 to 1945). The trend in the later years was away from the integration-absorption policy (in effect since the passage of the Dawes Act in 1887) and toward plans for preservation of the native culture and of the Indian's identity. Reformers are credited with some accomplishments and with the best of intentions, but "conditions on America's Indian Reservations have not improved a great deal in the last four decades...the battle for genuine improvement in the lot of the American Indian is yet to be won." Illus., 36 notes.
S. R. Davison

1447. Taber, Ronald W. SACAGAWEA AND THE SUFFRAGETTES. *Pacific Northwest Q. 1967 58(1): 7-13.* Sacagawea, the Indian woman who accompanied her husband as guide and interpreter on the Lewis and Clark expedition, was hailed as a heroine by the women's suffrage movement, especially in Oregon and

Wyoming from 1902 to 1921. Activities of some of the women who led the struggle for equal suffrage are related, including their efforts in fund raising and political campaigns.   C. C. Gorchels

1448. Tax, Sol. THE IMPORTANCE OF PRESERVING INDIAN CUL-TURE. *Am. Indígena [Mexico] 1966 26(1): 81-86.* A plea before the First Annual Meeting of the Foundation of North American Indian Culture at Bismarck, North Dakota, for the preservation of Indian culture. Help should not be limited to the preservation of art objects and their production on the basis of traditional forms; Indian culture is changing and creative and its preservation first requires helping "Indians to gain autonomous communities which will be their studios for the creation of a living culture in the spirit of the changing past."
                                                    R. J. Knowlton

1449. Thompson, Hildegard. EDUCATION AMONG AMERICAN IN-DIANS: INSTITUTIONAL ASPECTS. *Ann. of the Am. Acad. of Pol. and Social Sci. 1957 (311): 95-115.* A historical survey of American Indian education from 1568 to the present, with emphasis on the period from 1788 to the present.
                                                    J. S. Counelis

1450. Thompson, Laura. LA REORGANISACION INDIGENA DE LOS ES-TADOS UNIDOS CONSIDERADA COMO UN EXPERIMENTO EN LA INVESTIGACION DE ACCION SOCIAL [The Indian Reorganization Act of the United States considered as an experiment in social action research]. *Am. Indígena [Mexico] 1955 15(3): 187-198.* Reviews and analyzes the role of the Indian Reorganization Act of 1934 in the development and maturation of the social sciences. One key ingredient is missing in much current social science research: translating scientific hypothesis into administrative action. The princi-ples of IRA, which were applied not to, but by the Indians, have effectively bridged this gap by offering concrete democratic or integrative leadership. By testing and demonstrating the usefulness and applicability of various deductively formed hypotheses, the administration of IRA may help social scientists to trans-late human problems into scientific terms and solve them with scientific methods.
                                                    C. F. Latour

1451. Toelken, Barre. THE NATIVE AMERICAN: A REVIEW ARTICLE. *Western Folklore 1970 29(4): 268-278.* Reviews eight recent books dealing with the American Indian that indicate a new and intelligent approach to the Indian, and that recognize that the continuing Indian culture is creating its own folkloric values. The books are Navarre Scott Momaday's *The Way to Rainy Mountain* (Albuquerque: U. of New Mexico Press, 1969), Fulsom Charles Scrivner's *Mohave People* (San Antonio: Naylor), Louis Thomas Jones' *So Say the Indians* (San Antonio: Naylor, 1970), Earle R. Forrest's *With a Camera in Old Navaho-land* (Norman: U. of Oklahoma Press, 1970), Mary Shepardson and Blodwen Hammond's *The Navaho Mountain Community* (Berkeley: U. of California Press, 1970), Miguel León-Portilla's *Pre-Columbian Literatures of Mexico* (Nor-man: U. of Oklahoma Press, 1969), Grace Steele Woodward's *Pocahontas* (Nor-man: U. of Oklahoma Press, 1969), and Virgil J. Vogel's *American Indian*

Medicine (Norman: U. of Oklahoma Press, 1970). Also discusses some recent reprints of books on Indians. New books dealing with Indian folklore may be some of the most important works of modern times.   R. A. Trennert

1452. Tufts, Charlotte T. INDIANS ON POSTAGE STAMPS. *Masterkey 1967 41(3): 113-115.* Presents a description of seven recently-issued Czechoslovakian postage stamps which pay tribute to the American Indian and deplores the fact that the U. S. Government has yet to issue such stamps. These stamps have been added to the collection of the Southwest Museum in Los Angeles, California. An illustration shows the stamps.   C. N. Warren

1453. Unsigned. INDIAN HANDICRAFTS: THE TRUE AND THE FALSE. *Masterkey 1966 40(1): 33-37.* A report by the Indian Arts and Crafts Board, Department of the Interior, gives pointers on how to buy Indian handicrafts that are genuine, as opposed to those machine-made or otherwise produced.   C. N. Warren

1454. Unsigned. REPORT OF THE 1965 WORKSHOP ON AMERICAN INDIAN AFFAIRS. *Anuario Indigenista [Mexico] 1966 26: 237-249.* Discusses the successes and failures of the 6th annual Indian Affairs Workshop, a 6-week summer program offered by the Department of Anthropology at the University of Colorado and sponsored by the Colorado Chapter of American Indian Development, Inc. The author comments on student response to the structure and content of the workshop, with its heavy emphasis on civil rights and community development problems. Appendixes give names of participating students, a reading list and course outline, and a record of assignments and examinations.   R. L. Utt

1455. Vagts, Alfred. THE GERMANS AND THE RED MAN. *Am.-German R. 1957 24(1): 13-17.* An essay on the German concept of the American Indian and the place of the Indian in German literature.   G. H. Davis

1456. Wandruszka, Adam. GRUNDPROBLEME DER AMERIKANISCHEN GEISTESGESCHICHTE [Basic problems of American intellectual history]. *Mitteilungen des Instituts für Österreichische Geschichtsforschung [Austria] 1955 63(3/4): 650-658.* Investigates intellectual currents in the United States to test whether it has developed a "culture" or a "civilization." He concludes that the most prominent of these currents are: 1) the European heritage, as reinforced and modified by successive immigration; 2) the "American Dream," i.e., the experiment of the national and ethnic melting pot, which is reinforced by political and religious freedom; and 3) the influence of autochthonous factors such as the American Indian and the frontier, as expressed in Turner's thesis.   R. Mueller

1457. Washburn, Wilcomb. THE WRITING OF AMERICAN INDIAN HISTORY: A STATUS REPORT. *Pacific Hist. R. 1971 40(3): 261-281.* Evaluates the existing historical literature on the Indian by both historians and anthropologists. A successful general history has not yet been written, but much has been done in recent years in the comparatively new area of ethnohistory where the anthropologists are taking the lead. Discusses the contribution of the Indian writer and the possible increase in writing as a result of the establishment of Red Studies programs. It is now up to the historians to work together with the anthropologists and Indians to meet the challenge posed by the problems of writing Indian history. 19 notes.   E. C. Hyslop

1458. Washburn, Wilcomb E. PHILANTHROPY AND THE AMERICAN INDIAN: THE NEED FOR A MODEL. *Ethnohist. 1968 15(1): 43-56.* Suggests the necessity for constructing a theoretical framework to fully explore the many facets of American philanthropy in regard to the Indians. Elements of the model are time, place, cultural background, relative power of the participants in the philanthropic equation, and the functional roles of the individuals involved. Biblio.   R. S. Burns

1459. Waters, Frank. WORDS. *Western Am. Literature 1968 3(3): 227-234.* Discusses the Western concept of words, then gives African, Asian, and American Indian concepts of the same, illustrating the limitations of the English language and of Western thinking as a result, English words have not illuminated man but have enslaved him economically, rendering him inferior in his understanding of the universe to Africans and American Indians, whose languages are far superior in expressing local discrimination of causation, directness of experience and dynamic quality. The object of the paper is to challenge men in Western America to learn now from the great American Indian teachers whose language is much more magic and expressive than economic-centered English. Based on a paper delivered at the 1968 annual meeting of the Western Literature Association.   S. L. McNeel

1460. White, Gerald T. GOVERNMENT ARCHIVES AFIELD: THE FEDERAL RECORDS CENTERS AND THE HISTORIAN. *J. of Am. Hist. 1969 55(4): 833-842.* Since 1950, Federal Records Centers have been established in 14 localities throughout the nation. They provide economical storage for operational records of limited current use, records which increased greatly during the Great Depression and World War II. Relatively few scholars have made use of the records although archivists have been increasingly busy in publicizing accessions and conducting symposia with historians. The most important categories of federal records found in these centers include inferior federal courts papers of the Bureau of Customs, Indian affairs, public lands, and territorial governors of Alaska, and National Weather records, Selective Service records from World War I, Bureau of Budget records, and immigration records. Some solid historical works have been done with these records, but they need more careful investigation and research. 15 notes.   K. B. West

1461. Wiggins, Robert A. "WESTERN AMERICANA" AND ITS AUDIENCE. *Am. Q. 1966 18(4): 705-708.* Reviews five books which range from "a valid survey kind of approach" to the West to more restricted studies of specific subjects within narrower geographical limitations. The cumulative effect of the volumes tends to remind readers of past follies and raises the question of why so little of the knowledge learned of these follies has been applied. The books are: W. Eugene Hollon, *The Great American Desert* (New York: Oxford U. Press, 1966); Holway R. Jones, *John Muir and the Sierra Club: The Battle for Yosemite* (San Francisco: Sierra Club Books, 1965); William R. Goetzmann, *Exploration and Empire* (A. A. Knopf, 1966); Robert I. Burns, S.J., *The Jesuits and the Indian Wars of the Northwest* (New Haven: Yale U. Press, 1965), and Alvin M. Josephy, Jr., *The Nez Percé Indians and the Opening of the Northwest* (New Haven: Yale U. Press, 1965).   R. S. Pickett

1462. Wylder, Delbert E. THOMAS BERGER'S "LITTLE BIG MAN" AS LITERATURE. *Western Am. Literature 1969 3(4): 273-284.* Refutes former critics' appraisals of Berger's *Little Big Man* (Greenwich, Conn.: Fawcett Crest Books, 1965) as not being literature, emphasizing the importance of placing the novel in the correct frame of reference. The author insists that Berger's successful control of tonal change in the novel's narrative perspective is what makes it literature. The novel is Barthian in approach but Western in its attitude concerning human values and humanity. Its framework is absurd because of the character Ralph Fielding Snell. But Crabb's story, although beginning comically, ends with enough seriousness to convince the reader of the fact that Old Lodge Skins is equivalent to Oedipus, the mythical tragic hero. The novel is not merely a satire on westerns, but is a commentary on mankind's weaknesses. Therefore, it is not totally Barthian, because serious comment is made. The novel offers a general affirmation of what Max Westbrook terms "Western sacrality." 24 notes.
        S. L. McNeel

1463. Zimmerman, William, Jr. THE ROLE OF THE BUREAU OF INDIAN AFFAIRS SINCE 1933. *Ann. of the Am. Acad. of Pol. and Social Sci. 1957 (311): 31-40.* An exposition and evaluation by a former assistant commissioner of Indian affairs (1933-50) in the Bureau of Indian Affairs. He assesses the effect and value of the Bureau in terms of the Indian, and provides historical, legislative and administrative background for the period from 1857 to the present.
        J. S. Counelis

1464. —. THE INDIAN TODAY. *Midcontinent Am. Studies J. 1965 6(2): 3-21, 25-47, 51-72, 75-82, 84-99, 101-186.*
        Levine, Stuart. THE INDIAN AS AMERICAN: SOME OBSERVATIONS FROM THE EDITOR'S NOTEBOOK, pp. 3-21. Serves as an introduction to a series of essays regarding the "Indian as American," by discussing the various themes which are developed in this collection such as: the Indian's situation as a minority group, sociological aspects of Indian life and culture, problems of identification, and the movement toward Pan-Indianism.
        Lurie, Nancy Oestreich. AN AMERICAN INDIAN RENASCENCE? pp. 25-47. Reviews the contrasts between Indians and all other Americans, especially in light of the present concern for civil rights, and attempts to show how federal policy has long stressed programs geared to assimilate the Indian into the stream of American life and culture. The interesting fact noted here is that the Indian, unlike other minorities, has generally resisted these attempts at cultural

integration. By the same token, there appears to be a movement taking place on the contemporary Indian scene which the author has endeavored to identify by contacting experts on Indian affairs. Sample responses have shown that there is a definite emphasis by Indians on tribal loyalty within a larger "Pan-Indian" nationalist type of movement, and apparently a common concern for more education as the means to socioeconomic improvement. The term "renascence" signifying rebirth may not be suitable to explain current trends, due to the fact that Indian culture had not expired, but has simply evolved through time as cultures do.

Witt, Shirley Hill. NATIONALISTIC TRENDS AMONG AMERICAN INDIANS, pp. 51-72. Examines nationalistic trends in the world of the American Indian by tracing the historical background of nationalism in Indian life and by pointing to the fact that confederation among these Americans is not traditional despite the League of the Iroquois and the Creek Confederacy, to list two. Yet Indian nationalism did exist in the past, thus paving the way for future development. Late 19th- and contemporary 20th-century affairs are developed, especially in regard to the federal government's relation to the Indian. The Washington "fish-in" and the Kinzua Dam problem are noted as incidents that tended to unite various Indian groups. These incidents, coupled with federal programs and the Civil Rights Bill, which are leading to gradual economic stability, have motivated the individual and tribe to recognize the need for solidarity to promote Indian cultural identity, which in turn fosters nationalistic activity.

Thomas, Robert K. PAN-INDIANISM, pp. 75-82. An anthropological discussion of the complex factors regarding the social phenomenon referred to as Pan-Indianism. This movement, which finds expression as a new identity for the Indian, may be traced to the attractive, mobile life of the Plains Indians and the reservation system. Both factors fostered commonality, which in turn has led to pressure for tribal assimilation. The hypothesis is drawn that tribal societies cannot tolerate the forces of industrial civilization and hence tend to meet this stress by banding together, forming a new identity, yet retaining the solidarity of their social group.

Rachlin, Carol K. TIGHT SHOE NIGHT, pp. 84-99. Concerned with the general organization of Indian society in central and western Oklahoma. Observations regarding religion, rural and urban problems, economic status, and traditions are made which point to the quandary of trying to live by the conflicting codes of two societies.

Clifton, James A. CULTURE CHANGE, STRUCTURAL STABILITY AND FACTIONALISM IN THE PRAIRIE POTAWATOMI RESERVATION COMMUNITY, pp. 101-123. A sociological study of factionalism in the sociocultural process, using the Prairie Potawatomi community as a sample representative of all contemporary Indian reservations. Factionalism is defined here as the condition arising from the consequence of the stresses of culture contact situations. The historical development of the Potawatomi community is traced, showing the amplification of cultural change and its relation to the question of conflict over identification with family, clan, and tribe.

Kupferer, Harriet J. THE ISOLATED EASTERN CHEROKEE, pp. 124-134. This survey, encompassing the environment, economy, social and cultural grouping of the eastern Cherokee, attempts to explain why this group of American Indians, unlike most others, has not become a part of the general movement referred to as the "American Indian Renascence." It may be that due to geographic location, lack of major problems associated with the reservation, and a generally healthy economic situation, the Cherokee has had no need to join any nationalistic movement to improve his lot.

Walker, Deward. SOME LIMITATIONS OF THE RENASCENCE CONCEPT IN ACCULTURATION: THE NEZ PERCE CASE, pp. 135-148. Investigates the American Indian renascence in relation to past and contemporary Nez Percé culture. Demographic, religious, economic, and political structures are discussed showing that some areas within the culture have experienced renascence while others have declined. It was concluded that the term "renascence" does not uniformly apply to Nez Percé culture due to inconsistencies in decline and rebirth. The Nez Percé case demonstrates the complexities involved in studying cultural change among North American Indians.

Fischer, Ann. HISTORY AND CURRENT STATUS OF THE HOUMA INDIANS, pp. 149-163. A study of the Houma Indians of Louisiana, their ethnic derivation, socioeconomic status, and related problems, and the effect of the Civil Rights Bill in overcoming opposition from a prejudiced white community.

Wax, Murray and Wax, Rosalie S. INDIAN EDUCATION FOR WHAT? pp. 164-170. Questions the value of education in federal schools for Indians by pointing to the fact that the goals and motivations of school officials are not the same as those of Indian students. The social and cultural forces affecting the "drop out" problem, juvenile delinquency, etc., are based on a study of the Oglala Community High School of Pine Ridge Reservation.

Dobyns, Henry F. THERAPEUTIC EXPERIENCE OF RESPONSIBLE DEMOCRACY, pp. 171-186. Discusses the merit of extensive study of tribal cultures in regard to intergroup relations and the application of significant principles observed regarding international affairs. The development of self-determination by the Indian in modern industrial society is a necessary precondition to the reduction of psychological stress and racial discrimination.

B. M. Morrison

Urban

1465. Ablon, Joan. AMERICAN INDIAN RELOCATION: PROBLEMS OF DEPENDENCY AND MANAGEMENT IN THE CITY. *Phylon 1965 26(4): 362-371.* Discusses factors involved in the relocation experience based upon a two-year study (1961-63) of the general adjustment complex and the persistence of Indian values and tradition in the course of the relocation process among government-sponsored and self-relocated Indians in the San Francisco Bay area. Though more than sixty thousand Indians have migrated to large urban centers in the last decade, they differ from other immigrants in the persistence of tribal and folk values. A study of relocatees suggests a deeply entrenched dependency and widespread dislike of at least some aspects of city life. Those who succeed in the city generally conform to white economic standards by striving for employment stability and security; they acquire the ability to manage for themselves and to control their life situation.

S. C. Pearson, Jr.

1466. Coulter, E. J. INDIANS ON THE MOVE. *Beaver [Canada] 1966 297(Summer): 49-53.* Indians are leaving the reserves in Canada at the rate of 15 thousand a year. The first Friendship Centre to act as a referral agency and counseling service was established in Winnipeg in 1959. Since then many other centers have been set up, most, but not all, with federal, provincial, and community grants. Describes the work of the centers. Illus. L. F. S. Upton

1467. Davis, Arthur K. URBAN INDIANS IN WESTERN CANADA: IMPLICATIONS FOR SOCIAL THEORY AND SOCIAL POLICY. *Mémoires de la Soc. Royale du Can. 1968 217-228.* To understand the phenomenon of the urban-dwelling Indian in western Canada, it is necessary to draw upon all the social sciences, particularly history, and upon both orthodox and Marxian intellectual traditions of social philosophy and political economy. The author reports in detail on a study conducted in the early 1960's of Indians and Métis living in Prince Albert, North Battleford, and Meadow Lake, Saskatchewan. L. F. S. Upton

1468. Dowling, John H. A "RURAL" INDIAN COMMUNITY IN AN URBAN SETTING. *Human Organization 1968 27(3): 236-240.* An Oneida Indian community in the Green Bay metropolitan area is cited as having a demographic curve similar to that of rural areas, despite its urban location. The author hypothesizes that, for the community, social distance is the functional equivalent of territorial distance in remote rural settlements. The background and demographic characteristics of the community are presented. Evidence suggests that because the Oneida Indians perceive anti-Indian prejudice in Green Bay, many migrate to Milwaukee and Chicago for employment. The author concludes that the initial hypothesis is supported. Based on field work during the summer of 1966; 5 notes. E. S. Johnson

1469. Ervin, Alexander M. CONFLICTING STYLES OF LIFE IN A NORTHERN CANADIAN TOWN. *Arctic [Canada] 1969 22(2): 90-105.* A study of Inuvik, a settlement in the western Canadian Arctic. White civil servants now dominate the town's political and social life. The indigenous population, on the other hand, has experienced readjustment difficulties in changing from a trapping life to urban living. The result is a vacuum in native leadership, with concomitant features of individual alienation, excessive drinking, and reluctance to forego the mores associated with their former trapping culture. 2 tables, 2 figs., biblio. J. A. Casada

1470. Graves, Theodore D. PSYCHOLOGICAL ACCULTURATION IN A TRI-ETHNIC COMMUNITY. *Southwestern J. of Anthrop. 1967 23(4): 337-350.* Analyzes data derived from a survey interview conducted among adult members of a small Southwestern town and its environs in order to ascertain psychological acculturation of three ethnic groups (Indian, Anglo-American, and Spanish-American) in an integrated community. The author suggests that value orientations in the direction of Anglo norms occur from high exposure to the Anglo group, identification with them, and economic access to the resources and rewards of a mixed society. 5 tables, biblio. C. N. Warren

1471. Kunitz, Stephen J., Levy, Jerrold E., and Odoroff, Charles L. A ONE YEAR FOLLOW-UP OF NAVAJO MIGRANTS TO FLAGSTAFF, ARIZONA. *Plateau 1970 42(3): 92-106.* Analyzes factors determining the length of stay of Navaho migrants in Flagstaff. The study shows that the main forces affecting the migrants are economic. Those migrants who stay in Flagstaff for a prolonged period tend to be those who are protected from fluctuations of an unstable tourist economy by the civil service jobs. Those who leave tend more often than not to be from nearby areas, have smaller families, and live in the poorer area of town. Educational level and occupational skills, two of the standards commonly used by social scientists in determining degree of acculturation, are no help in determining which migrants will stay or which will leave. 15 tables, biblio.   W. A. Buckman

1472. Lubart, Joseph M. FIELD STUDY OF THE PROBLEMS OF ADAPTATION OF MACKENZIE DELTA ESKIMOS TO SOCIAL AND ECONOMIC CHANGE. *Psychiatry 1969 32(4): 447-458.* Disappearance of the food supply forced the Mackenzie Delta Eskimos to move into Canadian settlements. The culture that bound them together in cooperative survival groups was no longer viable. The Eskimos tried to adapt to a radically different culture, with profound effects on their personality. The Eskimo male, who once did the hunting, now is an unskilled failure in Western society. He has lost his sense of usefulness and as a result is radically depressed. Most males turn to alcohol as a means of regaining control of the situation. The Eskimo female has lost her respect for the male, as she compares him to the more successful white man. She tries to find acceptance through sexual activity with whites. She has an intense wish to be white, trying to imitate dress styles, hair styles, and even manners of the white woman. Whereas the male Eskimo dreams of returning to the land territory of the past, the Eskimo female repudiates her parents' values, looking for assimilation into white society. The situation is a classical description of denying possibilities of equality to a group with radically different cultural values, and then considering the psychological breakdown as evidence of inferiority. 7 notes, biblio.   M. A. Kaufman

1473. Marriott, Alice and Rachlin, Carol. INDIANS: 1966—FOUR CASE HISTORIES. *Southwest R. 1966 51(2): 149-160.* Sketches the problems faced by rural Indian families in moving into the urban environment of a southwestern city where they must adapt to mechanization and new surroundings besides losing at least part of their tribal identity.   D. F. Henderson

1474. Sorkin, Alan L. SOME ASPECTS OF AMERICAN INDIAN MIGRATION. *Social Forces 1969 48(2): 243-250.* "This paper is a study of federally assisted American Indian migration from the reservations to urban areas. The education of the migrants, their earnings before and after relocation, and the change in the degree of antisocial behavior after leaving the reservation are analyzed. It is found that while relocation can enhance the standard of living of those participating in federal programs, budget limitations prevent these programs from assisting enough applicants to markedly reduce the level of surplus labor on the reservations."   J

Arctic

General

1475. Brochu, Michel. ETUDE COMPARATIVE DE L'EVOLUTION DE LA VIE ECONOMIQUE ET SOCIALE AU NOUVEAU-QUEBEC ESQUIMAU ET INDIEN [Comparative study of the economic and social evolution of the Eskimo and Indian way of life in "New Quebec"]. *Actualité Econ. [Canada] 1966 42(2): 284-323, (4): 805-834.* Part I. Making use of the Eskimo settlement at Maricourt on Hudson Bay, the author examines such things as Eskimo hunting habits, means of transportation, type of clothing worn, types of food eaten, forms of dwellings used, occupations, and leisure activities to determine the impact of civilization on the economic and social life of "New Quebec" Eskimos. As a general conclusion, it is stated that all aspects of Eskimo life have been affected and modified and, in fact, some aspects are even being menaced. Based on the author's field observations; 4 charts. Part II. Continuing his analysis of evolutionary change in the economic and social habits of New Quebec, the author examines hunting, dress, means of transportation and dwellings of the Cree Indians of the James Bay region and comes to the same conclusions derived from his study of the region's Eskimo population. It is felt that either in the short or the long run this will mean the end of the Eskimo and the Indian as distinct entities. Reassuring, however, is the fact that the Quebec government is cognizant of the problem and that it is doing everything within its power—which, nevertheless, is quite limited—to respect the cultural integrity of the population. Based on the author's field observations; 4 notes.   A. E. LeBlanc

1476. Hartweg, Raoul. [THE DENTITION OF THE UNGAVA ESKIMOS AND OF THE WABEMAKUSTEWATSH INDIANS]. *J. de la Soc. des Américanistes [France] 1965 54(1): 117-126.*
L'IMPLANTATION DENTAIRE CHEZ LES ESQUIMAUX DE L'UNGAVA [The dental implantation of the Ungava Eskimos], pp. 117-122. The dentition of some 248 Labrador Eskimos was studied as to bone structure, spacing, and abnormalities of position (their nature and number). Tables, note.
LES MALPOSITIONS DENTAIRES DES INDIENS WABEMAKUS-TEWATSH DE LA CÔTE ORIENTALE DE LA BAIE D'HUDSON (COMPARIAISONS AVEC LES ESQUIMAUX DE L'UNGAVA) [The abnormalities of position in the dentition of the Wabemakustewatsh Indians of the eastern side of Hudson Bay (comparisons with the Ungava Eskimos)], pp. 123-126. Studied were some 60 Indians of this Algonquin group; multiple abnormalities of position were less frequent here than among the Eskimos and abnormally large gaps were nonexistent, but otherwise the dental structure of the two groups was found to be fairly similar. Tables, note.   M. E. Stoughton

1477. Hohn, E. O. RODERICK MAC FARLANE OF ANDERSON RIVER AND FORT. *Beaver [Canada] 1963 294(Winter): 22-29.* Describes the exploration of the Anderson River by Roderick MacFarlane (1833-1920) for the Hudson's Bay Company in 1857. He opened trade with the Anderson and Mackenzie Delta Eskimos and with the Hare Indians. A post was established on the Anderson River in 1859, but closed in 1865 when scarlet fever began to depopulate the area. MacFarlane was a naturalist who collected for both the Smithsonian Institution and the Geological Survey of Canada. Illus.   L. F. S. Upton

1478. Honigmann, John J. DANCE OF THE ANCIENT ONES. *Beaver [Canada] 1968 299(Autumn): 44-47.* Illustrates the drum-dancing distinctive of the western Arctic, especially northern Alaska. An ensemble dances to the accompaniment of an orchestra composed of several drummers who also sing. Some dance numbers mimic a story while others are "just dances." Singing can either be telling a story or chanting a collection of meaningless syllables. Illus.
L. F. S. Upton

1479. Sprudzs, Aleksandrs. DEVELOPMENT OF THE CO-OPERATIVE MOVEMENT IN NORTHERN CANADA SINCE 1963. *Polar Record [Great Britain] 1967 13(86): 597-599.* The Second Conference of the Arctic Co-operatives was held at Povungnituk, Quebec, 19-28 April 1966, three years after the initial conference. Earlier almost entirely Eskimo, now Indian and Métis settlements in the Northwest Territories have joined the movement. Invitations to the second conference were sent out to 22 cooperatives and eight developing groups. These are ordinarily multipurpose coops, involved in purchasing, in producing and marketing native crafts, fisheries, and lumbering, as appropriate. Annual business volume exceeded the million dollar mark. The conference worked out a broad plan of cooperation within a proposed federation, "Canadian Arctic Co-operatives, Limited," and called on the Co-operative Union of Canada for assistance.   J. E. Caswell

By Tribe

Aleut

1480. Berreman, Gerald D. ALEUT REFERENCE GROUP ALIENATION, MOBILITY, AND ACCULTURATION. *Am. Anthropologist 1964 66(2): 231-250.* A study of the traditional values maintained by the Aleuts of Nikolski on Umnak Island in the face of the positive valuation given many norms from the dominant white group. While dominant group values are adopted, many individuals remain loyal to their own social group so long as it remains a functional entity. Emphasizes the distinction between those who wholeheartedly embrace dominant values and those who value such concepts, but remain alienated from the dominant group.   A. Hopping

Eskimo

1481. Buchler, I. R. A FORMAL ACCOUNT OF THE HAWAIIAN AND ESKIMO-TYPE KINSHIP TERMINOLOGIES. *Southwestern J. of Anthrop. 1964 20(3): 286-318.* An application of generative grammar techniques to the analysis of Hawaiian- and Eskimo-type kinship systems. Based on secondary sources; 3 illus., 2 tables, biblio.   C. N. Warren

1482. Collins, Henry B. and Taylor, William E., Jr. DIAMOND JENNESS (1886-1969). *Arctic [Canada] 1970 23(2): 71-81.* A biographical sketch of Jenness, Canada's most distinguished anthropologist. Noted for his scholarly versatility, Jenness did most of his work on Eskimos, but he published significant articles and books in many fields. Outlines his scholarly life, primarily through a chronological discussion of his research and writing. Includes a complete listing of Jennessiana, covering 1916-70. Biblio.   J. A. Casada

1483. Denevi, Don. ESKIMO ART AND LANGUAGE AS POETRY. *U. of Windsor R. [Canada] 1968 4(1): 77-84.* Describes Eskimo art as an act of expressing life's innermost values and as a ritual revealing nature's patterns. The Eskimo world of cold and white is given form and meaning only through language and art. Language is viewed as the principal tool which the Eskimos employ to make their natural world a human one. Stonecut and sealskin-stencil artforms are described. 2 notes.   H. S. Shields

1484. Fidler, Vera. STRING FIGURES. *Beaver [Canada] 1963 294(Winter): 18-21.* Eskimo string games are highly developed versions of our old cat's cradles. Figures include caribou, dogs, and talking men. The art probably derives from the Bering Strait area. Chants accompany the making of the figures and there are taboos in some areas. Illus.   L. F. S. Upton

1485. Fitch, James Marston. NEW USES FOR THE ARTISTIC PATRIMONY. *J. of the Soc. of Architectural Historians 1971 30(1): 3-16.* "An appreciation of the material culture of preindustrial societies has grown in the Western world in almost exact proportion to the ever-intensifying industrialization of the West itself." The author traces the development of this interest. He finds that "progress" now threatens both the man-made and the natural past. He pleas for protection of the forms and intensive study of the theories and practices of the past, especially folk and primitive cultures. Examines the Eskimo igloo and the mud-walled houses of the American and African deserts as primitive examples from which modern architecture could profit. Also studies folk architectural forms representing different climatic and cultural conditions. The author feels that these forms, if they can be preserved, will be of immense value to future urbanists. Based on secondary sources; 17 illus., 24 notes.   J. K. Crane

1486. Godt, P. THE CANADIAN ESKIMO CO-OPERATIVE MOVEMENT. *Polar Record [Great Britain] 1964 12(77): 157-160.* Many Eskimos felt a need for cash wages after wartime construction in the Arctic ceased. To fill this gap, the Canadian government provided technical assistance and encouragement in establishing cooperatives. By 1963, 21 Eskimo cooperatives were in existence, producing sealskins, frozen fish, and objects of art, with an annual production valued at nearly 750 thousand dollars, and benefiting a fifth of the Eskimos.

J. E. Caswell

1487. Laughlin, William S. THE PURPOSE OF STUDYING ESKIMOS AND THEIR POPULATION SYSTEMS. *Arctic [Canada] 1970 23(1): 3-13.* Eskimos are among the most highly adaptable humans, and they need to be studied from various standpoints encompassing many disciplines in order to learn how they have developed. Discusses techniques and approaches which might be utilized in such research. Outlines cooperative efforts of the International Biological Program in this field, demonstrating how such research can be maximized with a minimum of expense and superstructure. Table, biblio.   J. A. Casada

1488. Martijn, Charles A. A RETROSPECTIVE GLANCE AT CANADIAN ESKIMO CARVING. *Beaver [Canada] 1967 298(Autumn): 4-19.* There are few art forms in the world about which more erroneous information has been disseminated. Arctic carvings of past centuries have had four main functions: decorative, magico-religious, toys and games, and self-entertainment. The present day concentration on carvings for sale has made carving a peripheral rather than an integral part of Eskimo life. The various categories, styles, and development of Eskimo carving are discussed. Illus.   L. F. S. Upton

1489. Milan, Frederick A. THE INTERNATIONAL STUDY OF ESKIMOS. *Arctic [Canada] 1968 21(3): 123-126.* The title applies to one section of the International Biological Program which involves scientists of 50 nations. Canada, Denmark, France, and the United States participate in the Eskimo Study. Methods will be strictly comparable to permit synthesis of results. General research categories are: General Health and Performance, Child Growth, Behavior, Ecology, and Prehistory. The United States program deals primarily with problems of human adaptability, and secondarily with environmental management. United States detailed categories include: General Health and Cardiology, Serum Epidemiology, Radiology, Work Physiology, Chronobiology, Anthropometry, Bone Mineral Content, Dentition, Demography, Salivary Amylase, and Population Genetics. Lists of investigations and principal investigators for Canada, Denmark, and France are also given.   J. E. Caswell

1490. Morrow, William G. JUSTICE IN THE CANADIAN ARCTIC. *Queen's Q. [Canada] 1965 72(1): 144-149.* An account of the administration of John Howard Sessions, the first justice to the new superior court of the Northwest Territories, established in 1955. He has devoted himself to studying the region, especially the Eskimos, and tempers "the whiteman's law to suit the local situation and to see justice done."   M. Abrash

1491. Timberlake, Harold D. ESKIMO SNOW HOUSES. *Can. Geographical J. 1968 76(3): 102-107.* Describes the building of the traditional Eskimo igloo. It is an art that is dying out as the Eskimo becomes dependent upon the luxuries of the modern age. Illus.   C. J. Allard

1492. Vastokas, Joan M. THE RELATION OF FORM TO ICONOGRAPHY IN ESKIMO MASKS. *Beaver [Canada] 1967 298(Autumn): 26-31.* The relationship of form to iconography is shown by establishing visual criteria, and testing against known ethnographic data on the subject matter and function of the mask in ritual and mythology. To the Eskimo, all things both animate and inanimate have an inner vitality of spirit, an *inua,* which is capable of assuming human shapes. The mask has to do with several levels of experience, the formal, the iconographic, the social, the religious, and the imaginative. Illus.
                                                          L. F. S. Upton

1493. Wattle, D. K. F. Ottawa). EDUCATION IN THE CANADIAN ARCTIC. *Polar Record [Great Britain] 1968 14(90): 293-304.* In 1968 over 8,500 Eskimo, Indian, white and Métis pupils were enrolled in 67 schools of the Northwest Territories and Arctic Quebec. Emphasis in the curriculum is determined by their cultural backgrounds. Specialized texts and curriculum guides have been developed with emphasis on learning English as a second language. For pupils living at a distance from the schools, 16 pupil residences are operated. Despite difficult teaching conditions, there is no shortage of teacher applicants. In 1953 the first vocational courses were established in the North; in 1967, 864 were enrolled. An apprenticeship program was established in 1964, the apprentice taking part of his training in a southern trade school. The first adult education program was introduced in 1966 to help Eskimos adjust to the shift into modern housing under the Eskimo Rental Housing Programme. In 1967-68, 71 northern university students, and 25 other advanced students were enrolled in southern schools. The federal government provided almost the entire financial support for these programs. By contrast, Yukon Territory has almost complete autonomy, as the federal government supports only one residential school to the territory's 22 public and Catholic schools.   J. E. Caswell

1494. Williamson, Robert. THE SPIRIT OF KEEWATIN. *Beaver [Canada] 1965 296(Summer): 4-13.* Describes certain aspects of Eskimo philosophy demonstrated in their carvings. Illus.   L. F. S. Upton

Eskimo, Alaskan

1495. Chance, Norman A. ACCULTURATION, SELF-IDENTIFICATION, AND PERSONALITY ADJUSTMENT. *Am. Anthropologist 1965 67(2): 372-393.* A study of acculturation of Barter Island Eskimos significantly interrelating three aspects of the process: cross-cultural contact, self-identification, and personality adjustment. The small size of the sample (91 percent of adult population—53 persons), reliance on a single questionnaire (culturally adapted Cornell Medical Index), and other limiting factors make the study only an admitted exploratory (but positive) test of the author's hypothesis that emotional disturbance occurs highest where culture-contact is low and identification with the other culture high, rather than in any other arrangement of these factors. Six charts and tables clarify the data drawn from the research as do 12 notes.

Sr. B. A. Barbato

1496. Connelly, Dolly. WALRUS SKIN BOAT. *Beaver [Canada] 1965 296(Autumn): 12-21.* A photographic article showing the construction of boats of split walrus skin fitted and lashed over the frame of an Eskimo umiak. The photographs were taken at Gambell, on the Saint Lawrence Island in the Bering Sea. Illus. L. F. S. Upton

1497. Hennigh, Lawrence. CONTROL OF INCEST IN ESKIMO FOLK-TALES. *J. of Am. Folklore 1966 79(312): 356-369.* Recounts and analyzes four Eskimo folktales chosen from among 100 tales collected along the Alaskan Arctic coast during the period 1961-62. At the end of the recital of each tale, the Eskimo informant was interviewed at some length about the story. "Examination of four folktales has resulted in three testable hypotheses: 1. A necessary condition for the expression of incest in folktales is the denial by the audience of at least one of these aspects: incestuous fact, incestuous motive, or identification with the incestuous person. 2. Incest may be directly expressed with pleasure to nonincestuous sources (i.e., when a means of denying identification is available). 3. No correlation exists between directness of expression of incest in folktales and conscious awareness by the audience of incest in folktales....The more interesting points are not the hypotheses but the type of data which produced them. The meaning of a folktale...exists not only in the text but also in the context in which it is told and the cultural interpretation which the audience brings to it." 8 notes.

D. D. Cameron

1498. Milan, Frederick A. A DEMOGRAPHIC STUDY OF AN ESKIMO VILLAGE ON THE NORTH SLOPE OF ALASKA. *Arctic [Canada] 1970 23(2): 82-99.* A demographic study of the Eskimo village of Wainwright. Examines data found by a 19-man study group sponsored by the U.S. International Biological Program. Utilizing graphs and tables, presents the birth, immigration, death, and dispersion rates of the Wainwright Eskimos as an interim report before publication of the complete findings of the study team. 3 tables, 12 graphs, biblio.

J. A. Casada

1499. Oswalt, Wendell H. GUIDING CULTURE CHANGE AMONG ALASKAN ESKIMOS. *Am. Indígena [Mexico] 1961 21(1): 65-83, (2): 151-170.* Part I. Serves as a guide to administration and field workers desiring to introduce change among western Alaska Indians. Summarizes and points out lasting influences from Russian and early U.S. possession and then indicates common pitfalls and problems in establishing programs of change among the Eskimos. One definite advantage is the general Eskimo susceptibility to change. Part II. Discusses the Kuskokwim River region and efforts of the U.S. government to terminate its guardianship. Eskimo susceptibility to change rather than a forceful, well-developed program accounted for changes effected in a short time. Because of the absence of village social unity, the success of innovation depends on its ability to penetrate the social system on the level of individual families. Based on secondary sources.   R. J. Knowlton

1500. Oswalt, Wendell H. TRADITIONAL STORYKNIFE TALES OF THE YUK GIRLS. *Pro. of the Am. Phil. Soc. 1964 108(4): 310-336.* An ethnographic analysis based on 41 stories told between 1956-60 by young Yuk girls at the Eskimo village of Napaskiak in Alaska. The stories, illustrated during narration by stylized drawings executed on a mud surface with a traditional "storyknife," a stick, or a table knife, usually have a grandmother and granddaughter as central characters and provide some clues to an earlier aboriginal life as well as the worldview of children in another society. The "storyknife complex" seems to be limited to the Eskimo girls of the Yuk or Yuit linguistic family in littoral southern Alaska. Illus., documented.   R. G. Comegys

1501. Ray, Dorothy Jean. LAND TENURE AND POLITY OF THE BERING STRAIT ESKIMOS. *J. of the West 1967 6(3): 371-394.* Writers often imply that Eskimos have no political organization, territorial concepts, boundaries, leadership, or law. The author contends that this is an oversimplification based on the interpretation of political organizations in terms of a complex, and usually large, state or nation. Examines 12 political units of Eskimos in the Bering Strait area of Alaska. Her political unit is a group of persons with a common residence and conceptual, if not hard and fast, boundary lines. After examining these people from the standpoint of land tenure, leadership, tribal alliances, and territorial separation, the conclusion is that each of these groups has specific and distinct political mechanisms of control, including leadership and traditional rules of behavior. While all recognize the superior political power of the United States, this has not erased their concepts of separate political organizations as tribes. Based largely on published sources; map, 39 notes.   D. N. Brown

1502. Rogers, George W. ESKIMO ADMINISTRATION IN ALASKA. *Arctic [Canada] 1967 20(4): 267-268.* The year 1966 may prove to have been a major watershed in the development of Eskimo administration in Alaska. In the political campaign the Eskimo voters were courted as they had never been before. This was in part due to the founding in 1962 of the *Tundra Times* by Eskimo Howard Rock, and the Eskimos' learning from the more politically experienced southeastern Indians the importance of union. Land was a cause common to all, and in October 1966 eight separate associations joined together in the united front of the Alaska Federation of Natives. By mid-1966 the new native groups had submitted title claims to public lands covering approximately 290 million of Alaska's 375 million acres. The economic and political impact of the resulting land freeze was immediate and far-reaching, threatening to put a damper on planned petroleum exploration. A threat has been posed to the fiscal base of the entire state. The nonnative community is on notice that the Eskimo, Indian, and Aleut are a political force with which to be reckoned.   J. E. Caswell

1503. Wright, Sam. A WAY OF LIFE CALLED ESKIMO: WITHSTANDING THE ELEMENTS IN NORTHERN ALASKA. *Am. West 1971 8(4): 36-39.*

The author and his wife spent a winter in the Arctic to study firsthand the inland Eskimo caribou hunters, of whom only 100 remain. They also wanted to experience the isolation of a small log dwelling in the fastness of the Brooks Range, 200 miles from Fairbanks and north of the Arctic Circle. 5 illus.   D. L. Smith

Eskimo, Central

1504. Baird, Irene. CAPE DORSET MAN. *Can. Geographical J. 1965 71(5): 171-176.* Describes Eskimo artists and their work in Cape Dorset, Baffin Island. Photographs.   A. H. Lawrance

1505. Baird, P. D. BAFFIN ISLAND. *Beaver [Canada] 1967 297(Spring): 20-32.* Baffin Island is one of the largest islands in the world; it is larger than any European country except France. The author surveys its prehistorical, historical, climatic, and wildlife aspects. Described are the people, their settlements, and the five principal regions of the island: the south shore, Cumberland Sound, Frobisher Bay, the northeast coast, and northwest Baffin. The impact of the European on the Eskimo and the future prospects for the island are considered. Illus., map.
                                                        L. F. S. Upton

1506. Bruemmer, Fred. HUNTER AT THE FLOE EDGE. *Can. Geographical J. 1968 76(5): 160-165.* The floe edge is the limit of the landfast or shorefast ice and a sinister place to all but the Eskimo. For him it is a source of food and life and an ideal place to hunt seal. The author describes the daily, except Sunday, trip to the floe edge by Pewatook, an Eskimo who lives with his family at Kapuyivik, a camp on Jens Munk Island in northern Foxe Basin. Every morning Pewatook makes the two hour trip to the floe edge and remains, always the patient hunter; from 10 in the morning until 10 at night. The seals are attracted by scraping a harpoon handle on the ice, and, when the curious animal comes into range, the hunter shoots. Dead seals are retrieved with a small plywood punt. Illus.   C. J. Allard

1507. Bruemmer, Fred. SUMMER CAMP. *Beaver [Canada] 1967 297(Spring): 40-49.* A photo-essay of the summer months of Etuguloopia, an Eskimo hunter from Frobisher Bay, Baffin Island, who spends the summer at Cormack Bay off Ward Inlet. Illus.   L. F. S. Upton

1508. Crisp, W. G. THE CASUAL KOGMOLIKS. *Beaver [Canada] 1963 294(Winter): 50-53.* An anecdotal account of a cruise in 1926 to the Hudson's Bay Company's post at Tree River. Here were the Copper Eskimo of Coronation Gulf, known to the Mackenzie Eskimos as Kogmoliks ("the people of the east"). Illus.   L. F. S. Upton

1509. Honigmann, John J. and Honigman, Irma. ESKIMOS LEARN TO RUN THEIR OWN AFFAIRS. *Dalhousie R. [Canada] 1965 45(3): 289-298.* Describes the formation and operation of an elected unpaid community council at Frobisher Bay, Northwest Territories, a town housing about 900 Eskimos. The authors carried out field work here for the Department of Northern Affairs, and jointly wrote *Eskimo Townsmen,* a report published by the department.

L. F. S. Upton

1510. Honigmann, John J. and Honigmann, Irma. HOW BAFFIN ISLAND ESKIMO HAVE LEARNED TO USE ALCOHOL. *Social Forces 1965 44(1): 73-82.* "Eskimo in Frobisher Bay, a new Baffin Island town, became legally entitled to drink alcoholic beverages in 1960. They embraced the opportunity with alacrity, one result being many arrests for drunkenness. To curb drinking, a law in 1962 limited alcohol sales. Public drunkenness has since declined and older Eskimo have begun to learn a drinking pattern resembling that of their Eurocanadian neighbors. Eskimo drinking shows few signs of being deficiency motivated. Men drink for the pleasure it gives them and consumption correlates with economic and social status, being one of the marks of a full-fledged townsman. Regular drinkers furnish only a small part of the trouble with which police must cope."   J

1511. Lentz, John W. INUIT KU: THE RIVER OF MEN. *Beaver [Canada] 1968 298(Spring): 4-11.* Describes a journey along the Kazan River, between Snowbird and Baker Lakes in the Northwest Territories, to visit abandoned Eskimo sites. When rifles replaced bows and arrows there were a few years of plenty along the river, followed by starvation as the caribou disappeared. After 1957 the Caribou Eskimos were resettled at Baker Lake and at ports along Hudson Bay. Illus.   L. F. S. Upton

1512. Mary-Rousselière, Guy. TOPONYMIE ESQUIMAUDE DE LA RE-GION DE POND INLET [Eskimo toponymy in the region of Pond Inlet]. *Cahiers de Géographie de Québec [Canada] 1966 10(20): 301-311.* After giving a brief description of that group of Eskimos known as the "Tununermiut" that inhabit the region of Pond Inlet, the author goes on to make brief observations on the 245 item listing of place-names that he has compiled. A map shows the location of the places named in the listing.   A. E. LeBlanc

1513. Unsigned. ARTISTS OF ARCTIC BAY. *Beaver [Canada] 1967 298(Autumn): 20-25.* A photo essay in items from the sculpture collection of Jerry F. Twomey of Winnipeg, and the carvers who made them. They are the work of two families living at Arctic Bay in northern Baffin Island, an area whose main economic support is the sealing industry, and where carving is not as important an occupation as it is further south. Individual carvers are identified.

L. F. S. Upton

1514. Unsigned. ESKIMO PAINTERS. *Beaver [Canada] 1967 298(Autumn): 48-53.* Illustrates the work of Nauja, Allukpik, and Pitseolak from Rankin Inlet, Coppermine, and southern Baffin Island respectively.   L. F. S. Upton

1515. Wemigwans, James. QUEST IN THE HUNTER. *Beaver [Canada] 1966 297(Autumn): 42-48.* Account of a 1963 voyage to islands in Frobisher Bay searching for soapstone to make Eskimo carvings. Illus., map.

L. F. S. Upton

1516. Whalley, George. COPPERMINE MARTYRDOM. *Queen's Q. [Canada] 1959 66(4): 591-610.* An account of the events leading to the death of two Oblate Fathers, Jean-Baptiste Rouvière and LeRoux, in October 1913 on the Coppermine River, while trying to establish a mission to the Coronation Gulf Eskimos. Based on a series of letters written by Rouvière covering a period of more than two years leading up to his murder at Bloody Falls by two Eskimos.

B. Waldstein

Eskimo, Labrador

1517. Brochu, Michel. L'HEURE DU NOUVEAU QUEBEC [The hour of New Quebec]. *Action Natl. [Canada] 1967 56.*
LA PRISE EN CHARGE DE L'AN I [The takeover of Year I], (5): 475-481. As of November 1962—the date that marks the beginning of Year I— the Province of Quebec announced its intention of gradually taking over the administration of its northern territories which had fallen under control of the federal government because of its concern with Eskimo affairs. Due largely to the efforts of René Lévesque, Minister of Natural Resources in the Lesage government, the Quebec government sent several functionaries to study the situation and from this came the first steps of the province in administration, education, and health. By the end of Year I no major responsibilities had been assumed by the province, but a positive start was apparent. Based upon the author's six trips to northern Quebec.
L'AN II, ANNEE DIPLOMATIQUE [Year II, the year of diplomacy], (6): 612-614. Year II was marked by an intense diplomatic activity between Quebec and Ottawa but due to the irreconcilable positions of Quebec's Minister of Natural Resources and Ottawa's Minister of Northern Affairs, little was achieved.
L'AN III, PREMIERE PHASE D'OCCUPATION [Year III, first phase of occupation], (7): 681-689. Year III, from November 1964 to October 1965, saw the most marked advance in the development of New Quebec. The government of Quebec civil servants started to distribute social allowances to the local inhabitants; the government also opened a teachers college that utilized Eskimo as the language of instruction and a program of adult education was also set up. Quebec's first steps toward improving the efficiency of the local bureaucracy were taken. Finally, power installations were constructed under government initiative thereby permitting the electrification of Eskimo households in five settlements.
LA POLITIQUE DE L'AN IV [Politics of Year IV], (8): 805-811. Year IV, due to a series of unfortunate political circumstances, saw active interest in New Quebec decline. On the other hand, it is of importance to note that during the provincial elections of that year (1966), all of the parties—with the exception

of the Liberals—took into account the growing importance of Quebec's northland; the Union Nationale went so far as to call for a separate provincial ministry for New Quebec.

MOUVEMENTS SCOLAIRES EN L'AN IV [Movements into education in Year IV], (9): 909-913. Examines the conflict between the Quebec and Ottawa governments in the realm of education in New Quebec. The author proposes a scheme for the education of Eskimo children that should have been employed—to the advantage of Quebec—during the period of conflict.

LE DOMAINE DE LA SANTE EN L'AN IV [The realm of health in Year IV], (10): 1004-1007. In 1965 the Quebec government finally interested itself in the health requirements of its northland inhabitants and immediately it came into conflict with the Dominion government. This frustrated Quebec's initiative. By 1966 the efforts of the Quebec government still remained miniscule.

A. E. LeBlanc

1518. Bruemmer, Fred. THE BELCHER ISLANDS. *Beaver [Canada] 1971 302(1): 4-13.* An account of Eskimos on the Belcher Islands in Hudson Bay past and present with an account of the religious hysteria that culminated in murder and suicide in 1941. Illus.

L. F. S. Upton

1519. Graburn, Nelson H. H. SOME ASPECTS OF LINGUISTIC ACCULTURATION IN NORTHERN UNGAVA ESKIMO. *Kroeber Anthrop. Soc. Papers 1965 (32): 11-46.* Discusses the linguistic result of Anglo-Eskimo contact during the 19th and 20th centuries in the Ungava Peninsula area. Included are lexicons of loanwords and lexical interpretations. The author discusses Ungava language and culture change in terms of lexical interference, loanshifts, and grammatical interference. By a comparison with the Dakota linguistic acculturation, he shows that the Ungava Eskimo language may be changing less rapidly than other American Indian languages have previously done, due to geographic location and the influence of the French language in the area. Based on secondary sources and field investigation; map, 8 tables, 28 notes, biblio.

C. N. Warren

1520. —. [CANADIAN REINDEER PROJECT]. *Polar Record [Great Britain] 1968 14(88): 15-24.*

Treude, Erhard. THE DEVELOPMENT OF REINDEER HUSBANDRY IN CANADA, pp. 15-19. The first reindeer were introduced into Canada in 1908 by Sir Wilfred Grenfell who hoped to develop a reindeer meat-and-dairy industry in Labrador. Grenfell's herd prospered until the Lapp herders returned to Norway. In 1919, at the suggestion of Arctic explorer Vilhjalmur Stefansson, Canada established a Royal Commission to investigate the possibility of reindeer and musk-ox husbandry. Meanwhile, Stefansson formed a company and shipped 627 reindeer to Baffin Island in the hope of establishing a large industry. As pasturage was not up to reports, the project failed. Meanwhile, the commission recommended the establishment of small native-owned herds for local use. Between 1935 and 1964 small herds were placed in the hands of Eskimos. None was successful for long due to "insufficient herding, over-exploitation of the herds, over-grazing...losses through disease, predation, and poaching."

Basic to these reasons was the impossibility of making responsible herders out of traditional hunters...." Based on journal articles, and Canadian government documents.

Hill, R. M. THE CANADIAN REINDEER PROJECT, pp. 21-24. The Canadian Reindeer Project is supported and controlled by the federal Department of Indian Affairs and Northern Development. Following an attempt to get Eskimos to own and operate herds, the reindeer remaining in government hands were turned over to a private contractor. "A successful reindeer industry in the Mackenzie District would unquestionably be of great benefit to the regional economy....Such risks as attach to the project are chiefly human and psychological, for biological and technical suitability have been amply demonstrated." Based on government reports; map, 2 photos.   J. E. Caswell

Eskimo, Mackenzie

1521. Bruemmer, Fred. SAMSON KOEENAGNAK: AN ESKIMO OF THE BARREN LAND. *Can. Geographical J. 1967 74(3): 84-91.* Of the three million caribou that migrated across the vast Barrens just 70 years ago it is estimated there are only about 278 thousand animals left today. The drastic decline in the number of caribou, upon which the inland Eskimos depended almost entirely for food, has caused almost all of the Eskimos to abandon the Barren Land, a region north of the treeline and west of Hudson Bay. From their permanent settlements many Eskimos go on long forays to hunt in autumn, but 46-year-old Samson Koeenagnak, his wife, and their three small sons chose to live on the Barrens all year. The author lived with the family when their camp was at the west end of the great Aberdeen Lake and he describes the difficult life they lead in their solitary existence. Illus., map.   C. J. Allard

1522. Flyger, Vagn. HUNTERS OF WHITE WHALES. *Beaver [Canada] 1965 296(Winter): 32-37.* Every summer thousands of beluga whales pass between the outer islands of the Mackenzie Delta. The whales are from 12 to 16 feet in length and weigh between 1,500 and 4,000 pounds. A hunting camp is formed early in July at Kendall Island by people from Aklavik, Inuvik, and Reindeer Station; it breaks up in mid-August. The whales are harpooned, shot, and hauled ashore to be cut up by the womenfolk. As other foods become increasingly available to the Eskimos, the importance of the whale hunt is rapidly diminishing. Illus.
                                          L. F. S. Upton

1523. Van Den Steenhoven, Geert. ENNADAI LAKE PEOPLE 1955. *Beaver [Canada] 1968 298(Spring): 12-18.* A diary kept in August and September 1955 when the author was living among the Ahiarmiut Eskimos on the Barren Grounds. These Eskimos were later moved to the region of Henik Lake, "which led to catastrophe." Illus.   L. F. S. Upton

Subarctic

General

1524. Douville, Raymond. LE PERE JOSEPH-ETIENNE GUINARD, MIS-SIONNAIRE CENTENAIRE (1864-1965) [Father Joseph Etienne Guinard, a centenarian missionary (1864-65)]. *Soc. Can. d'Hist. l'Eglise Catholique. Rapport 1965: 55-66.* Father Guinard worked among the James Bay Indians, 1892-98, and the Upper St. Maurice tribes, 1898-1942. He was a constant defender of the rights of the Indians. Retired since 1942, he has written his memoirs, but has refused to have them published.   C. Thibault

1525. Leitch, Adelaide. THE SNOWSHOE MAKERS OF LORETTEVILLE. *Can. Geographical J. 1965 70(2): 62-63.* Describes the present-day industry in the Indian village at Loretteville, near Quebec City. Illus.   A. H. Lawrance

1526. Littlejohn, B. M. and Staniforth, R. D. EDUCATIONAL EXPRESS TO THE BAY. *Beaver [Canada] 1968 299(Summer): 10-16.* Describes a train journey to James Bay by a party of schoolboys from Upper Canada College in 1967. The terminus was Moosonee, with a visit to Moose Factory, an old Hudson's Bay Company trading post. The Indian schoolchildren whom they met seemed sometimes to resent the visitors from the south. Illus.   L. F. S. Upton

1527. Searle, Ronald. RONALD SEARLE AT MALIOTENAM. *Beaver [Canada] 1964 295(Summer): 4-9.* Drawings by the British artist of life at Maliotenam, an Indian reservation near Sept-Iles on the north shore of the St. Lawrence. Illus.   L. F. S. Upton

1528. Vaughan, Frederick. THE CASE OF JOSEPH DRYBONES. LEGAL FORCE IN THE BILL OF RIGHTS. *Round Table [Great Britain] 1970 238: 214-216.* The Canadian Bill of Rights, passed in 1960, appeared to have little effect on Canadian law until the case of Joseph Drybones, an Indian convicted of intoxication, violating Section 94(b) of the Indian Act. On appeal, the Supreme Court held that Section 94(b) violates the Bill of Rights on the grounds of racial discrimination and is therefore inoperative. The Supreme Court thus for the first time faced the issue of the role of the courts toward the Bill of Rights. Undocumented.   D. H. Murdoch

By Tribe

Chipewyan

1529. Van Stone, James W. CHANGING PATTERNS OF INDIAN TRAP-PING IN THE CANADIAN SUBARCTIC. *Arctic [Canada] 1963 16(3): 159-174.* Field work at the Chipewyan village of Snowdrift on Great Slave Lake and reports from other areas indicate a growing preference for wage labor, welfare payments, and the comforts of village life. Fewer trappers seek remote regions or remain in the field for more than two weeks at a time. However, traditional trapping patterns, developed over three centuries, are still of considerable importance.   J. E. Caswell

Chippewa (Ojibwa)

1530. Foerster, John W. AN INDIAN SUMMER. *Can. Geographical J. 1964 68(5): 156-163.* Describes the life of the Fort Hope Band of the Ojibwa nation at Lansdowne House in northern Ontario and the evolution of the written language of the Ojibwa. Photos.   A. H. Lawrance

Cree

1531. Buck, Ruth M. LITTLE PINE: AN INDIAN DAY SCHOOL. *Saskatchewan Hist. [Canada] 1965 18(2): 55-62.* An account of the school on the Little Pine Reserve which was opened in 1923. Based on notes and an unfinished manuscript written by the late Reverend Canon Edward Ahenakew, 1885-1961.
                                                          A. H. Lawrance

1532. Buck, Ruth M., ed. THE STORY OF THE AHENAKEWS. *Saskatchewan Hist. [Canada] 1964 17(1): 12-23.* An account of the Ahenakew family of Cree Indians prepared from notes and an unfinished manuscript written by the Reverend Canon Edward Ahenakew (1885-1961). Photos.   A. H. Lawrance

1533. Cass, Elizabeth E. THE STORY OF EY-ASH-CHIS. *Beaver [Canada] 1964 295(Summer): 50-52.* A Cree Indian folktale.   L. F. S. Upton

1534. Macfie, John. THE COAST CREES. *Beaver [Canada] 1967 298(Winter): 13-21.* The Hudson's Bay Company had a post well established at New Severn on Hudson Bay by 1685. Today there are a small company store and 30 Cree families in the area. Drawing their livelihood from the coastal environment, these Cree have developed a way of life very different from that of the main body of eastern Canada's Algonkian tribes. Illus.   L. F. S. Upton

1535. Mitchell, Ross. *ACORUS CALAMUS. Beaver [Canada] 1968 298(Spring): 24-26.* Reminiscences of an interview with the Manitoba Icelandic poet Guttormur J. Guttormsson (1878-1966) about his early contacts with the

Cree Indians of the western shore of Lake Winnipeg. The author discusses the medicinal qualities of *acorus calamus*, "Indian root," the only medicine used by them. Illus. L. F. S. Upton

Kolchan

1536. Hosley, Edward. THE KOLCHAN: DELINEATION OF A NEW NORTHERN ATHAPASKAN INDIAN GROUP. *Arctic [Canada] 1968 21(1): 6-11.* "Archeological and ethnographic research in the region of the upper Kuskokwim River, interior Alaska, defines the territory and culture of a previously unstudied Alaskan Athapaskan Indian group. Cultural reconstruction indicates that the occupants of this region, earlier thought to be a subdivision of the Ingalik, are an independent geographical, cultural, and linguistic entity." The Kolchan have coalesced from six bands to one community of about 125 persons, Nikolai Village, and a satellite village, presently the residence of only one extended family. Originally caribou hunters, the Kolchan now depend upon fishing, trapping, and wage labor. Strongly Russian Orthodox in faith, they tend to be conservative, and remain one of the least acculturated groups in interior Alaska. 2 figs., 15 notes. J. E. Caswell

Montagnais-Naskapi

1537. Webber, Alika Podolinsky. THE NASKAPI CHILD. *Beaver [Canada] 1963 294(Winter): 14-17.* The Naskapi Indians of Labrador travel nine months of the year, searching for food from Ungava Bay to Seven Islands. Their children share in adult life from age seven. Illus. L. F. S. Upton

1538. Webber, Alika Podolinsky. DIVINATION RITES. *Beaver [Canada] 1964 295(Summer): 40-41.* Describes the divination of a burned caribou shoulder blade by Joe Rich, chief of the Davis Inlet band of Naskapi Indians. Illus. L. F. S. Upton

Nakotcho-kutchin (Loucheux)

1539. Harrington, Lyn. OLD CROW, YUKON VILLAGE. *Beaver [Canada] 1961 292: 4-10.* Old Crow village (Yukon, Canada) is an isolated settlement 75 miles north of the Arctic Circle, where a group of Loucheux Indians came in 1911 after three previous moves (they left the original village at Fort Yukon, Alaska in 1869). Contact with the white man has resulted in a high level of health, without loss of the basic way of life—an unusual case. The present population of 200 is noted for gaiety as well as for outstanding achievements in self-government. A. P. Tracy

Némiscau

1540. Rogers, E. S. THE NEMISCAU INDIANS. *Beaver [Canada] 1965 296(Summer): 30-35.* The Némiscau Indians on the Rupert River retain many of the traditional features of life in the eastern subarctic. They live by hunting, trapping, and fishing and depend largely on the fur trade. They spend the winter in camps of one or two lodges and still produce most of the tools necessary for their culture. In the summer they live in log cabins on Lake Némiscau. There are at present about 150 in the tribe. Illus.   L. F. S. Upton

Tatsanottine (Yellow-knife)

1541. Blanchet, Guy. EXPLORING WITH SOUSI AND BLACK BASILE. *Beaver [Canada] 1964 295(Autumn): 34-41.* Describes the author's exploration of the territory north of the east arm of Great Slave Lake in 1923-24. His guides were Sousi Beaulieu, descendant of the fur traders, and Black Basile, a Tatsanottine (Yellow-knife) Indian. Illus.   L. F. S. Upton

Tlingit

1542. Ingersoll, William T. LANDS OF CHANGE: FOUR PARKS IN ALASKA. *J. of the West 1968 7(2): 173-192.* Gives brief histories of the areas which later became national parks. Discusses Glacier Bay National Monument, Katmai National Monument, Mount McKinley National Park, and Sitka National Monument. The eruption and the effects of the eruption of Mount Katmai are given as well as a description of the relations between the Tlingit Indians and the white men. Photos.   R. N. Alvis

Tsattine (Beaver)

1543. Ridington, Robin. THE MEDICINE FIGHT: AN INSTRUMENT OF POLITICAL PROCESS AMONG THE BEAVER INDIANS. *Am. Anthropologist 1968 70(6): 1152-1160.* Describes the political process among the Tsattine (Beaver) of northeastern British Columbia, a representative society of North American hunters usually denoted in negative terms because of the simplicity of their institutions. Analyzes the medicine fight as a style of discourse among an intensely political people that defines the roles assumed in Tsattine competition for the validation of supernatural power. The medicine fight is related to the ecological imperatives that make success in hunting unpredictable and relatively infrequent. These are conditions opting for a projection of causation onto others rather than on acceptance of guilt. Complementary theories of explanation are held by members of the same society and the theory an individual will use is dependent on the needs of the political role he is playing. The roles played are in turn determined by an individual's failure or success relative to others; and success or failure is unpredictable and subject to chance. Notes.
Sr. B. A. Barbato

Northwest Coast Area

General

1544. Drew, Leslie. FOREST OF TOTEMS. *Beaver [Canada] 1964 295(Winter): 49-55.* An account of the last great stands of totem poles, located on the upper Skeena River in British Columbia. Illus.   L. F. S. Upton

1545. Hymes, Dell. SOME NORTH PACIFIC COAST POEMS: A PROBLEM IN ANTHROPOLOGICAL PHILOLOGY. *Am. Anthropologist 1965 67(2): 316-341.* A discussion of texts from Indian cultures (Haida, Kwakiutl) of the North Pacific Coast. The author analyzes six poems in relation to the disciplines of folklore, anthropology, linguistics, literary analysis, and poetry while placing the emphasis on linguistics as important in anthropological philology. He demonstrates the necessity for reanalyzing and reevaluating, especially from a linguistic basis, the heritage of American Indian poetry. The Indian-language texts, ethnological translations (literal and literary) of the six poems are included together with critical comment. 12 notes, biblio.   Sr. B. A. Barbato

1546. Wilson, Renate. BASKET MAKERS OF MOUNT CURRIE. *Beaver [Canada] 1964 296(Autumn): 26-33.* Describes life on the Mount Currie Indian Reserve in the heart of Pemberton Valley, a hundred miles north of Vancouver. Illus.   L. F. S. Upton

By Tribe

Gitsan

1547. Clemson, Donovan. SCENES ALONG THE SKEENA. *Can. Geographical J. 1966 72(5): 154-159.* Description of the Skeena Valley in British Columbia, famous for the totem poles of the Gitksan Indians. Photos., map.
A. H. Lawrance

Haida

1548. Hooper, Jacqueline. ARTISTS IN HAIDA-GWAI. *Beaver [Canada] 1969 300(Autumn): 42-46.* Describes the visit in 1968 of a photographer-artist team to the Haida country of the Queen Charlotte Islands, British Columbia, or Haida-Gwai. They recorded hand-carved canoes rotting on deserted beaches, magnificently worked storage boxes that had been abandoned, and toppling totem poles. A growing population and the influx of visitors will probably lead to destruction of these relics and will also change the way of life of the people beyond recognition. Illus.   L. F. S. Upton

Kitksan, Kispiox

1549. Hanna, Marion Woodside. KISPIOX LEGEND. *Beaver [Canada] 1963 294(Autumn): 40-41.* Indian story from the Skeena River country of northern British Columbia.   S

Kwakiutl

1550. DeLaguna, Frederica. MUNGO MARTIN. *Am. Anthropologist 1963 65(4): 894-895.* Mourned and honored by Canadians, Kwakiutl chief Mungo Martin was an internationally known artist and craftsman. He was particularly famous for his copying and restoring as well as designing of Kwakiutl totem poles. These stand today in Victoria's Thunderbird Park, Beacon Hill Park, and Windsor Great Park. The author, official representative of the American Anthropological Association, details the native funeral ceremonies in the Kwakiutl House, Thunderbird Park. Photo.   Sr. B. A. Barbato

1551. Hawthorn, Audrey. MUNGO MARTIN: ARTIST AND CRAFTSMAN. *Beaver [Canada] 1964 295(Summer): 18-23.* Describes the work of Mungo Martin, Chief NaKePenkim of the Kwakiutl Indians (1881-1963), sculptor of totem poles and artist. Illus.   L. F. S. Upton

Plateau Area

By Tribe

Nez Percé

1552. Haines, Francis. THE NEZ PERCE TRIBE VERSUS THE UNITED STATES. *Idaho Yesterdays 1964 8(1): 18-25.* Reviews the history of relations between white settlers and Indians in the United States from the first settlements, with particular emphasis on treaty negotiations with the Nez Percé Indians of north Idaho, dating from 1855. The author explains the problems of rights to Indian lands following the discovery of gold on Orofino Creek in 1860. He traces the negotiations with representatives of the Nez Percé tribe following the passage by Congress of the Indian Claims Commission Act of 1946 to the final settlement of the Nez Percé claims in 1957.   M. Small

1553. Lundsgaarde, Henry P. A STRUCTURAL ANALYSIS OF NEZ PERCE KINSHIP. *Res. Studies 1967 35(1): 48-77.* Studies the interpersonal relations of the Nez Percé Indians of Idaho centering on an analysis of marriage and kinship group alliance. The author outlines some of the influences of acculturative agents on traditional Nez Percé culture, the kinship terminology of which appears to have persisted from precontact times to the present in only slightly modified form. From data on Nez Percé kinship terminology and social behavior the contemporary reservation population largely follows customary modes of behavior, but changes of custom can be expected in the next generation. There is a strong emphasis on status allocation on the basis of advanced age and male sex evidenced in the kinship nomenclature in use today. By analyzing separate kin classes for major structural principles, it is possible to point to an area of field investigation which can aid in amplifying weaknesses in the data and predicting where subsequent investigation of related subsystems is likely to lead. Based on secondary sources and field investigation; 5 tables, biblio.   D. R. Picht

1554. Walker, Deward E., Jr. MEASURES OF NEZ PERCE OUTBREEDING AND THE ANALYSIS OF CULTURAL CHANGE. *Southwestern J. of Anthrop. 1967 23(2): 141-158.* An analysis of Nez Percé kinship "proportions" (e.g., one fourth Nez Percé, one fourth white, one half Mexican) and their relationship to cultural change. The author concludes that a positive inverse correspondence exists between low native kinship proportions and other acculturative variables such as English language proficiency and economic success. Based on field investigation, primary and secondary sources; 7 illus., 7 tables, biblio.
C. N. Warren

1555. Walker, Deward E., Jr. THE NEZ PERCE SWEAT BATH COMPLEX: AN ACCULTURATIONAL ANALYSIS. *Southwestern J. of Anthrop. 1966 22(2): 133-171.* Presents an analysis of the Nez Percé sweat bath complex (including hot water bath, cold water bath, emetic stick, and sweat bath), utilizing the Malinowskian or functional model for the analysis of culture change. The analysis includes both a description of the aboriginal sweat bath complex and the contemporary sweat bath complex. The author concludes that the functional approach to an analysis of culture change is not entirely adequate and suggests analysis based upon schemes such as those of K. L. Pike and P. K. Bock. Based on field investigation, primary and secondary sources; 7 illus., biblio.
C. N. Warren

Salish (Flathead)

1556. Aoki, Haruo. SALISHAN INDIAN LANGUAGES. *Idaho Yesterdays 1968 12(1): 8-11.* Fifteen Salishan languages are identified today, whereas John Wesley Powell (1834-1902) listed 64 without attempting any subdivisions. The Idaho Nez Percé formed an alliance with the Salish people, but no genetic relationship has been determined. Archaeology in Idaho has made spectacular progress recently; there may be a relationship between early north Idaho peoples with the Yakima, Umatilla, Chinook, and some California languages. Salishan researchers should now attempt to clarify the internal as well as the external relationship of the Salishan languages. Linguists interested in this research met in Seattle during the summers of 1966 and 1967. Based on secondary sources; 20 notes.   G. Barrett

1557. Elmendorf, William W. LINGUISTIC AND GEOGRAPHIC RELA-
TIONS IN THE NORTHERN PLATEAU AREA. *Southwestern J. of Anthrop.
1965 21(1): 63-78.* An investigation of the linguistic and geographic relations of
the Interior Salish speech communities of Indians in the northwestern United
States and southwestern Canada. Based on secondary sources; illus., map, table,
biblio.   C. N. Warren

Skitswish (Coeur d'Alêne)

1558. Dozier, Jack. THE COEUR D'ALENE LAND RUSH, 1909-10. *Pacific
Northwest Q. 1962 53(4): 145-150.* Events preceding, during, and following the
opening of the Skitswish (Coeur d'Alêne) Indian reservation to settlement of
pioneering farmers. Economic benefits to white settlers came in part at the
expense of Indians.   C. C. Gorchels

Great Basin

General

1559. Larson, Gustive O. WILLIAM R. PALMER. *Utah Hist. Q. 1963 31(1):
34-36.* Necrology of a scholar in local Indian history.   S

By Tribe

Ute

1560. Hartzell, Grace L. SIDELIGHTS ON THE UTE. *Masterkey 1963 37(1):
15-17.* Describes childhood experiences while living on the Ute reservation, as
well as describing some of the personalities of the Utes. 2 illus.
    C. N. Warren

1561. O'Neil, Floyd A. AN ANGUISHED ODYSSEY: THE FLIGHT OF THE
UTES, 1906-1908. *Utah Hist. Q. 1968 36(4): 315-327.* Traces the history of the
retreat of the Utes in the face of white advance into their territory and relates how
those members of the tribe who were forced to retreat to the Uintah Basin in Utah
reacted to invasion of that basin by fleeing in 1906 to South Dakota where they
hoped to ally with the Dakota (Sioux) to make a last stand against encroachment
on their lands. The Dakota (Sioux) rejected the offer of alliance, the federal
government refused to provide aid to the Utes at the South Dakota location, and

the army brought steady pressure to persuade them to return to Utah, which they did in 1908. Based in the main on Department of the Interior reports and newspaper accounts. S. L. Jones

California

General

1562. Brook, Richard. WHAT TRIBE? WHOSE ISLAND? *North Am. R. 1970 7(1): 51-56.* A photo-essay describing the Indian take-over of Alcatraz Island in late 1969 and some of the Indians' activities on the island. S. L. McNeel

1563. Fernandez, Ferdinand F. EXCEPT A CALIFORNIA INDIAN: A STUDY IN LEGAL DISCRIMINATION. *Southern California Q. 1968 50(2): 161-175.* An account of the legal discrimination practiced against California Indians. In the past, so-called "vagrancy laws" have bound Indians to forced labor for periods up to 15 years while other laws have denied them access to certain occupations. All California Indians were prohibited from buying and using liquor until 1953 and they could not legally possess firearms and ammunition between 1850 and 1913. California Indians were also the victims of social discrimination in the form of enforced segregation with respect to education. Moreover, they were denied citizenship and the concomitant rights to vote, hold office, and serve on juries until 1924. Only in the area of hunting and fishing have the laws been lenient. Here Indians have been exempted from the requirement of a license to hunt and fish, the prohibition upon the building of weirs in rivers to trap salmon, and other fish and game law provisions. The author closes on an optimistic note: while earlier legislation concerning California Indians was often oppressive, today it is friendly and more just. Based on California statutes, other public documents, and secondary sources; 96 notes. W. L. Bowers

1564. Gould, Richard A. and Furukawa, Theodore Paul. ASPECTS OF CERE-MONIAL LIFE AMONG THE INDIAN SHAKERS OF SMITH RIVER, CALIFORNIA. *Kroeber Anthrop. Soc. Papers 1964 31: 51-67.* Describes in detail Indian Shaker ceremonies among the Indians of Smith River, California, showing the gestures used in the curing ceremony. The Indian Shaker church was founded in 1881 and the community at Smith River in the 1930's. Commonly-held beliefs among the Shakers on curing, Bible usage, and language usage are examined. The Indian Shaker church may be a focus for Indian identity, despite and perhaps because no one tribe is represented in any numbers, and because of the common Indian elements which form such a large part of the services. Based on primary and secondary sources, and field investigation; 5 illus., biblio. C. N. Warren

1565. Steiner, Rodney. RESERVED LANDS AND THE SUPPLY OF SPACE FOR THE SOUTHERN CALIFORNIA METROPOLIS. *Geographical R. 1966 56(3): 344-362.* Discusses the ownership of land in the peripheral area of Los Angeles as a significant factor in urban development. The undeveloped land falls into the categories of public reserves, national forests, undedicated public domain, military installations, Indian reservations, other governmental reserves, and large private holdings. The author discusses the probable urban pressures on these lands and concludes the primary task of recreational planners will be for retention and suitable development of the existing open space. Illus., maps, tables.
R. McBane

1566. Valory, Dale. THE FOCUS OF INDIAN SHAKER HEALING. *Kroeber Anthrop. Soc. Papers 1966 (35): 67-111.* Discusses healing techniques and healing sessions among the Indian Shakers of the Smith River, California, area. There are three major techniques: brushing, rubbing, and push-and-pull; also examined is the relationship of these techniques to the concept of transference of sickness to the altar for cleansing. The order of a Shaker service, including songs, chants, and foot-stamping, is described and various Shaker beliefs on the subject of healing are examined. Based on primary and secondary sources, as well as field investigation; 2 illus., 9 notes, appendix, glossary, biblio.
C. N. Warren

By Tribe

Hupa

1567. Bushnell, John H. FROM AMERICAN INDIAN TO INDIAN AMERICAN: THE CHANGING IDENTITY OF THE HUPA. *Am. Anthropologist 1968 70(6): 1108-1116.* An examination of the cultural history of the Hupa of California. The traditional designation "American Indian" is most relevant when applied to the life-style developed as an accommodation to reservation living. Following World War II, rapid modernization and a changing status vis-à-vis the dominant society have placed the Hupa in a position parallel to many other U.S. minority groups which is more appropriately termed "Indian American." They now possess a culture largely American in content yet retain a sense of ethnic identity. Discusses this development and the viability of the Indian component of the Hupa identity in the context of cultural survivals and current interests and concerns within the tribe. Documented.
Sr. B. A. Barbato

Luiseño

1568. Dougan, Marjorie. THE MEMORIAL CEREMONY OF THE LUISEÑO INDIANS. *Masterkey 1964 38(4): 140-149.* Presents a straightforward account of a ceremony including initiation of a new chief and memorial services for a deceased chief, among the Luiseño Indians of Southern California. 3 illus.
C. N. Warren

Miwok

1569. Burrows, Jack. THE VANISHED MIWOKS OF CALIFORNIA. *Montana 1971 21(1): 28-39.* Boyhood memories and adult reconsideration of the last days of a small tribe in California's Mother Lode country. Neglect, if not outright persecution, hastened the deaths of the last few Miwoks in the early decades of this century. Derived from personal and family information; illus.

S. R. Davison

Paiute

1570. Roberts, Bertram L. DESCENDANTS OF THE NUMU. *Masterkey 1965 39(1): 13-22, (2): 66-76.* Part I. Examines current Paiute (Numu) customs, in the Owens Valley of California, comparing current attitudes with traditional ones in the areas of language, basketry, pine nuts, the sweat house, trade, the hand game, marriage, girls' puberty rites, the mother-in-law taboo, and death. Based on field investigation; 2 illus. Part II. Describes as of 1965 the Paiute (Numu) Indians of the Owens Valley in California. The author reports that they are being assimilated into white middle-class society, unfortunately at the expense of their own Indian customs. Based on field investigation, primary and secondary sources; illus., biblio.

C. N. Warren

Southwest Area

General

1571. Brugge, David M. A LINGUISTIC APPROACH TO DEMOGRAPHIC PROBLEMS: THE TONTO-YAVAPAI BOUNDARY. *Ethnohist. 1965 12(4): 355-372.* The boundary between the Western Apache and the Yavapai Indians is indicated in an analysis of proper names listed in the Navaho land claim investigations of 1962. Tables, 4 notes, biblio.

R. S. Burns

1572. Curtin, L. S. M. PREPARATION OF SACRED CORN MEAL IN THE RIO GRANDE PUEBLOS. *Masterkey 1967 41(4): 124-130, 1968 42(1): 10-16.* Presents information from interviews with inhabitants of the Rio Grande pueblos of New Mexico relating to the preparation of sacred corn meal. Based on field investigation and secondary sources; biblio.

C. N. Warren

1573. Fontana, Bernard L. THE HOPI-NAVAJO COLONY ON THE LOWER COLORADO RIVER: A PROBLEM IN ETHNOHISTORICAL INTERPRETATION. *Ethnohist. 1963 10(2): 162-185.* Breakdown and abandonment of efforts (made 1945-52) to resettle 148 needy families of the Hopi and Navajo tribes on surplus lands held by Mohave and Chemehuevi on the latter's Colorado River Reservation are traced to federal Indian policies and decisions in this Arizona-Southern California area, 1864-1945.   H. J. Graham

1574. Harvey, Byron, III. IS POTTERY MAKING A DYING ART? *Masterkey 1964 38(2): 55-65.* Examines the practice of pottery making among the Indians of Arizona and New Mexico, with special attention being given to descriptions of the pottery-making process as described by a Maricopa potter and an Isleta potter. The author concludes that while traditional pottery making is declining in some areas, it is strong in others, and that commercial pottery is increasing. Based on field investigation, primary and secondary sources; 3 illus., note.   C. N. Warren

1575. Hey, Nigel S. THE NOT-SO-VANISHING AMERICANS. *Interplay 1969 3(2): 20-24.* Concentrates on Indians in the southwestern United States. Traces their history before exploring their economic and cultural life. The Indian has held onto his culture with tenacity, though some changes have been made in terms of new industry and health services. After four centuries of exposure to Latin and Anglo-American cultures, the Indians are "coming to terms with the conceptual differences between the red and white worlds." 3 photos.
        J. A. Zabel

1576. Kunitz, Stephen J., Levy, Jerrold E., Odoroff, Charles L., and Bollinger, J. THE EPIDEMIOLOGY OF ALCOHOLIC CIRRHOSIS IN TWO SOUTHWESTERN INDIAN TRIBES. *Q. J. of Studies on Alcohol 1971 32(3): 706-720.* "Data on liver cirrhosis among the Hopi (population, 6000) and the Navaho (over 100,000) were obtained from the 1965-67 records of the U.S. Public Health Service hospitals and clinics in Phoenix and Window Rock, Ariz. Of 25 identified Hopi cirrhotics (10 women), 10 had died (4 women); of 91 Navaho cirrhotics (36 women) 17 had died (10 women). The average age of the Hopi cirrhotic men was 42, women 38; of the Navaho, 41 and 44. Their marital status was not significantly different from that of the rest of the population. Among the Hopi fewer of the cirrhotics came from traditional villages or from on-reservation wage-work communities than from off-reservation locations; none of the 9 on-reservation cirrhotics came from the more traditional villages that had refused to vote in the election of a tribal council. Among the Navaho fewer cases came from isolated areas and the incidence increased in areas closer to off-reservation communities. The cirrhosis mortality rate per 100,000 adults (20 years and over) was 13.0 (high-population estimate) or 17.0 (low estimate) among the Navaho and 104.0 among the Hopi, compared with the national adult rate of 19.9. It is suggested that the differences in cirrhosis rates reflect different drinking patterns. The Navaho tend to be abstainers or, as young men, heavy drinkers, many of whom stop drinking before their health is affected. The Hopi condemn drinking since it threatens the 'Hopi way' of peace and harmony. The heavy drinker is ejected from the community, continues to drink and is thus more likely to develop cirrhosis. The hypothesis that acculturation stress is the explanation of Indian problem drinking may hide many important cultural differences that exist between tribes."   J

By Tribe

Apache

1577. Basso, K. H. THE WESTERN APACHE CLASSIFICATORY VERB SYSTEM: A FORMAL ANALYSIS. *Southwestern J. of Anthrop. 1968 24(3): 252-266.* States that the study of classificatory verb systems can be of significant value in revealing the structure and content of "covert taxonomies" which refers to categories labelled by sub-lexical units such as numeral classifiers and classificatory verb systems. The author feels the problems encountered by the "definition by exemplification" method can be overcome by utilizing the "componential analysis" method. He describes this method as providing each member of a lexical set with a definition by signification, expressed as a "bundle" of distinctive attributes. Componential definitions are thus "unitary" or "conjunctive" in that they specify uniform criteria for membership in a category and do not contain alternative criteria. He then briefly describes the steps required to arrive at componential definitions and uses Western Apache examples as illustrations. The language data were collected from three male informants at Cibecue, Arizona. 2 graphs, 8 notes, biblio. C. N. Warren

1578. Martin, Douglas D., ed. AN APACHE'S EPITAPH: THE LAST LEGAL HANGING IN ARIZONA—1936 *Arizona and the West 1963 5(4): 352-360.* Earl Gardner, an Arizona Apache Indian, was a three-time killer. He was condemned by a federal court to die on the gallows, as provided for by a 1790 law of Congress. Rumor of a planned Apache armed protest brought federal agents to the San Carlos Reservation and precipitated the secret execution of Gardner. The grisly details of the bungled hanging on 13 July 1936, as reported later by the press, brought a change in the federal statute. Henceforth, federal executions were to be done in the manner prescribed by the legislation of the state wherein the crime was committed. Two articles from the *Phoenix Gazette,* excerpts from correspondence between the attorney general and the secretary of the interior, and the House Committee on the Judiciary report, which became the basis for the new federal statute, are reprinted here. 5 notes. D. L. Smith

1579. Uplegger, Francis J. A BRIEF REVIEW OF NEARLY NINETY YEARS OF LIFE BY THE GRACE OF GOD. *Concordia Hist. Inst. Q. 1965 38(3): 146-150.* Focuses on the author's training at Concordia Seminary in St. Louis and his ministry in the Midwest. In 1919 he began his long career as a missionary with an Apache Indian Mission in Arizona. D. J. Abramoske

Apache, Mescalero

1580. MacLachlan, Bruce B. THE MESCALERO APACHE QUEST FOR LAW AND ORDER. *J. of the West 1964 3(4): 441-458.* Traces the effort to get the Mescaleros to accept Euro-American concepts of law. It has been difficult to get the Apaches to abandon tribal customs but, due in large measure to the influence of the Indian agents, progress has been made. In 1936 a 10-man governing body called the Business Committee was organized in accordance with a new constitution and by-laws approved by the secretary of the interior. This committee had real powers available as positive sanctions in control over the Indian community. The committee established a new tribal court and, despite some difficulties, real progress is being made toward establishing a system of law and order. Documented from published sources, 50 notes.   D. N. Brown

Apache, White Mountain

1581. Levy, Jerrold E. and Kunitz, Stephen J. NOTES ON SOME WHITE MOUNTAIN APACHE SOCIAL PATHOLOGIES. *Plateau 1969 42(1): 11-19.* "Currently high death rates from homicide and, possibly, suicide found among the White Mountain Apache are interpreted as continuations of pre-reservation patterns rather than as recent responses to a stressful reservation life."   J

Havasupai

1582. Reilly, P. T. THE DISAPPEARING HAVASUPAI CORN-PLANTING CEREMONY. *Masterkey 1970 44(1): 30-34.* One of the old customs which has nearly disappeared from Havasupai life is the corn-planting ceremony. The process has changed considerably during recent years and the old planting ritual now is rarely practiced; in fact, few of the young people even know it, while others have no faith in its effectiveness. Dan Hanna, one of the tribesmen, recently agreed to go through the ceremony and to allow photographs. The author describes this ritual in detail, then compares it to that described by Spier in 1928. Discusses the present theories of the Havasupai's ancestral home and possible dates of entry into their present home in the western end of the Grand Canyon. 3 photos, biblio.   C. N. Warren

Mohave (Mojave)

1583. Robinson, W. W. SOUTHERN CALIFORNIA IN FIFTY VOLUMES. *Southern California Q. 1968 50(1): 1-4.* Comments on the occasion of the publication of the 50th volume of the *Southern California Quarterly.* Among the impressive contributions of the journal are: the story of the founding of Los Angeles which appeared in 1931; the 1836 census of Los Angeles which was published in 1936; the Mojave Indian studies which were seen in 1965-66 issues; biographies of Pío Pico, J. J. Warner, and Antonio María Lugo which appeared between 1894 and 1896; and account of old highways of the Los Angeles area which was published in 1905; and the story of Henry Dalton of Azusa which was in the 1917 volume. In 1958-59, a cumulative index for the preceding years was compiled, and since then annual indexes have been provided.   W. L. Bowers

1584. Sherer, Lorraine M. GREAT CHIEFTAINS OF THE MOJAVE INDIANS. *Southern California Q. 1966 48(1): 1-35.* Mojave Indians had a distinctive system of democratic tribal leadership, based on a line of hereditary and elected "great chieftains." The line ended with the death of Sukulai Homar (Pete Lambert) in 1947; in 1957 the tribe adopted a constitution providing for a tribal council headed by a chairman. Illus., 54 notes.   H. Kelsey

1585. Sherer, Lorraine M. THE CLAN SYSTEM OF THE FORT MOJAVE INDIANS: A CONTEMPORARY SURVEY. *Southern California Q. 1965 47(1): 1-72.* Between 1859 and 1890 the Mojave lived under military occupation, but retained their clan names, ancient stories, and songs through oral communication. From 1890 to 1931 boarding schools, intermarriage, and the assigning of English names by the Department of Interior broke down tribal ties and caused confusion. The shattering of the Mojave social system fragmented stories and songs and almost destroyed their oral tradition. With the aid of Mojave consultants and printed documents, the author gathered for the first time complete records of the old Mojave family clan names.   J. Jensen

Navaho (Navajo)

1586. Agogino, George and Martinez, June. ONE NAVAJO'S VIEW OF NAVAJO TRIBAL GOVERNMENT. *Masterkey 1970 44(1): 25-29.* Martinez, a Navajo and graduate anthropology student at Eastern New Mexico University, has written her views of her people's tribal government for Agogino, her professor. She feels that many of the shortcomings of this group stem from ancient Navajo traditions which the Navajo have not sufficiently adapted for today's needs. This situation has created feelings of resentment, hostility, and distrust that have undermined the group's effectiveness.   C. N. Warren

1587. Albrecht, Dorothy E. JOHN LORENZO HUBBELL, NAVAJO INDIAN TRADER. *Arizoniana 1963 4(3): 33-40.* Of Spanish and Vermont ancestry, Hubbell was born and educated in New Mexico. He had homesteaded at Ganado, Arizona, where he later bought the trading post. His work with the Navajo was performed with understanding—he spoke the language—and he was instrumental in improving their turquoise jewelry and rug crafts. The Department of the Interior in recent years selected the Hubbell post as the best illustration of an Indian trading post. Documented, illus.   E. P. Stickney

1588. Beatty, Willard W. HISTORY OF NAVAJO EDUCATION. *Am. Indígena [Mexico] 1961 21(1): 7-31.* Summarizes the development of government educational programs for the Navajo. Among problems faced were the language barrier, Navajo distrust and misunderstanding, and lack of a written language (overcome by the Harrington-LaFarge alphabet). The value of education has finally been impressed upon the Navajo largely by returning servicemen who recognize the need to know English. The rate of job placement of graduating Navajo has been high. Based on the author's past experience while director of education in the Bureau of Indian Affairs.   R. J. Knowlton

1589. Conklin, Paul. GOOD DAY AT ROUGH ROCK. *Am. Educ. 1967 3(2): 4-9.* Describes a demonstration Indian school in which a community control approach is applied in developing the educational program. The thesis for the experiment is that Indians ought to be able to be Americans and Indians. The program includes cultural identification units, teaching the Navaho language, and teaching standard subjects in Navaho. Illus.   W. R. Boedecker

1590. Downs, James F. THE COWBOY AND THE LADY: MODELS AS A DETERMINANT OF THE RATE OF ACCULTURATION AMONG THE PIÑON NAVAJO. *Kroeber Anthrop. Soc. Papers 1963 29: 53-67.* Many writers put forth the general assumption that conservatism is a general characteristic of all women, and that the Navajo are a good example in support of this assumption. This is based on the fact that Navajo men seem quite willing to adopt western ways in dress patterns (cowboy) and economic activities (cattle-herding is a major goal), while the women tend much more to fit into traditional Navajo patterns. It is more likely that these two patterns of behavior are traceable to the models of white society available and the possibility of emulation of those models. For the male, the model is the cowboy, as seen on television, in films, and throughout the Southwest; for the female, no one model is presented, other than perhaps the standard white middle-class mother-wife seen in television commercials. Since the model for the male is possible without total repudiation of Navajo life, he adopts it; for the female, however, it is impossible in the context of the reservation, and it is therefore rejected. Based on primary and secondary sources, as well as field investigation; 5 notes, biblio.   C. N. Warren

1591. Ferguson, F. N. A TREATMENT PROGRAM FOR NAVAHO ALCO-HOLICS: RESULTS AFTER FOUR YEARS. *Q. J. of Studies on Alcohol 1970 31(4): 898-919.* "Of a group of Navahos who had been arrested and jailed for drunkenness at least 10 times, 115 volunteered for alcoholism treatment. The program, conducted by McKinley County Family Consultation Service, Gallup, N. Mex., consisted of 5 days of detoxication, disulfiram treatment, counseling and psychotherapy, when indicated, 18-months' probation, and employment and welfare aid. Life histories, an attitude interview, psychological tests, daily nurse records, field notes and a treatment termination interview were collected. A comparison group of 60 untreated Navahos who also had had a minimum of 10 drunkenness arrests were matched by age and time of arrest. From these data 16 variables were selected in which an acculturation scale was embedded; chi-square analysis was done on each as it related to treatment results over four 6-month periods. Arrests for drunkenness and the patients' behavior were used to evaluate treatment outcome: 26 were considered successful for 24 months, 14 for 18, 10 for 12 and 22 for 6; 43 were failures. During the 18 months of treatment the 115 patients experienced a total of 258 arrests, compared with 1196 during 18 months prior to treatment; 31 [percent] had not been arrested at all. The average number of arrests of the treated groups dropped from 10.4 to 2.2 after treatment, that of the untreated group from 9.25 to 7.8 during the same period. Factors which correlated positively with treatment success were less facility with English (*p* [less than] .01), less than 4th-grade education (*p* .05), being in the age group 30 to 55 (*p* .01), taking disulfiram consistently for 12 months (*p* .001), and the opportunity to identify with a nonproblem-drinking peer group (*p* .05). A high arrest rate prior to treatment did not act as a deterrent to success: the 24-month success group had an average of 9.9 arrests before treatment, compared with 5.9

and 4.3 in the 18- and 12-month success groups. Few patients unsuccessful during their first 6 months moved into the successful group after resumption of treatment (p .001). Demographic characteristics of the 115 patients and results of an attitude interview given to 54 patients are detailed. Some other topics considered in the evaluation of results are the Navaho's response to authority in treatment, his participation after treatment in activities related to religion and witchcraft, and acculturation. Cultural differences and the language barrier made some of the psychological test results dubious and appeared to make psychotherapy difficult."   J

1592. Fonaroff, L. Schuyler. CONSERVATION AND STOCK REDUCTION ON THE NAVAJO TRIBAL RANGE. *Geographical R. 1963 53(2): 200-223.* Analyzes the livestock reduction program begun as a conservation measure by the federal government in the 1930's, with reference to some of the human problems involved in the Navajo country in northeastern Arizona. The first attempts to reduce the livestock met with resistance by the Indians who could not comprehend its purpose. The destructive native grazing techniques here described have still not been replaced by the agronomist's rational grazing pattern. In many areas where agriculture or seasonal wages might have produced more income, most Navajos still felt that the traditional sheep raising had a social value that outweighed the economic. The end of the reduction program in most districts was followed by a marked stock increase despite the fact that the range was continually deteriorating. Illus., map, table, 47 notes.
                                                              E. P. Stickney

1593. Fraser, James H. INDIAN MISSION PRINTING IN ARIZONA: AN HISTORICAL SKETCH AND BIBLIOGRAPHY. *J. of Arizona Hist. 1969 10(2): 67-102.* From the 18th to the early 20th century, the spread of printing to areas outside of Eastern Asia and Europe was closely tied to the Roman Catholic and Protestant missionary effort. The arrival of the printing press in the American West was directly related to missionary activity. The process was delayed longer in Arizona because of a lack of dictionaries of the Indian languages. In 1910 the Franciscan Fathers at Saint Michaels published a Navajo catechism and the *Ethnological Dictionary of the Navajo Language.* After that, few of the missionary translators did their own printing and most of the translations were printed outside the state. Since World War II the major translator and printer has been Wycliffe Bible Translators, Inc. Lists all Indian mission printing in the Apache, Cocopa, Hopi, Navajo, Pai, and Pima languages. The Roman Catholic center at Saint Michaels now prints in English. The demand for religious material in the Navajo language is strong. Indexes printers and presses, places of printing, and translators. Based on interviews and secondary sources; 6 illus., 39 notes, biblio.   R. J. Roske

1594. Hillery, George A., Jr., and Essene, Frank J. NAVAJO POPULATION: AN ANALYSIS OF THE 1960 CENSUS. *Southwestern J. of Anthrop. 1963 19(3): 297-313.* An analysis of population characteristics of the Navajo reservation in the southwestern United States. Based on secondary sources; 4 illus., 3 tables, biblio.   C. N. Warren

1595. Johnston, Philip. INDIAN JARGON WON OUR BATTLES. *Masterkey 1964 38(4): 130-137.* Recounts the use of Navahos and the Navaho language for secret military communications for the Marines in World War II. Based on personal experience; illus.   C. N. Warren

1596. Karam, A. H. MEDICINE MAN FROM THE EAST. *Southwest R. 1967 52(4): 393-403.* Tragic yet heartwarming recollections of a summer at the Indian Hospital on the Navaho Reservation at Crowpoint, New Mexico. In order to understand the people he was treating, the author spent three days with a Navaho family, eating their food—the dinner meal consisted of potato soup, a slice of fried bread, a celery stick, and a cup of coffee—sleeping in a damp, cold hogan, and helping to herd sheep.   D. F. Henderon

1597. Kelley, Lawrence C. THE NAVAHO INDIANS: LAND AND OIL. *New Mexico Hist. R. 1963 38(1): 1-28.* Traces the expansion of Navaho Indian Reservation land from 1868 to 1934. The discovery of oil in 1922 and a congressional decision in 1927 to uphold Indian title to the oil and to the land from which it came were the outstanding events of the 20th century. Although the oil revenues dwindled quickly, they proved enough to stimulate a reservation expansion program "which resulted in the present, apparently definitive boundaries of the reservation."   D. F. Henderson

1598. Kunitz, Stephen J. and Levy, Jerrold E. NAVAJO VOTING PATTERNS. *Plateau 1970 43(1): 1-8.* "The voting behavior of three contrasting groups in the tribal elections of 1966 and the national elections of 1968 is examined. Contrary to common belief, it was found that on-reservation Navajos tended to vote Republican. Long-term residents of Flagstaff voted Democratic, however. The proportion of Navajo voters participating in tribal elections far exceeded the proportion of voters participating in the national, state and county elections in Coconino County [Arizona]. The alienation of Navajos as measured by lack of involvement in political affairs is questioned."   J

1599. Luebben, Ralph A. ANGLO LAW AND NAVAHO BEHAVIOR. *Kiva 1964 29(3): 60-75.* "Since World War II, lead-zinc mines at 'Carbonate City,' Colorado, have presented an excellent opportunity for steady off-reservation employment. Navaho Indians residing off the reservation sometimes break laws and come into contact with the 'white man's' law enforcement agencies and concomitant legal system. Six hypotheses were tested, and three were verified: 1) A higher percentage of Navahos will be arrested for various offenses than Anglos. 2) Traditional Navaho patterns of social control will tend to disintegrate. 3) Some acculturated Navahos will attempt to manipulate other Navahos through the American legal system. Three other hypotheses were not verified: 4) Following arrests for similar charges, the percentage of convictions will tend to be greater for Navahos than Anglos. 5) The fines assessed under similar charges will tend to be greater for Navahos than for Anglos convicted. 6) As Navahos become increasingly familiar with American norms, fewer contacts with Anglo law can be expected."   J

1600. Luebben, Ralph A. PREJUDICE AND DISCRIMINATION AGAINST NAVAHOS IN A MINING COMMUNITY. *Kiva 1964 30(1): 1-17.* "Three hypotheses concerning the socio-cultural inter-relationships of Anglos and Navahos residing in 'Carbonate City,' Colorado, are tested using ethnographic data. It is concluded that Navahos experience discrimination, are a target of prejudice, and have become another American minority aggregate." J

1601. McKibbin, Davidson B. REVOLT OF THE NAVAHO, 1913.*New Mexico Hist. R. 1954 29(4): 259-289.* A closely documented account of the Navaho Indians' dissatisfaction with U.S. administration of the Navaho Indian Reservation of Southwestern United States climaxed in 1913 by open revolt, and the subsequent inaccurate reporting of the affair in the public press.
W. S. Wallace

1602. Patzman, Stephen N. HENRY CHEE DODGE: A MODERN CHIEF OF THE NAVAJOS. *Arizoniana 1964 5(1): 35-41.* Discusses a contemporary Navajo chief. Illus., biblio. S

1603. Savard, R. J. EFFECTS OF DISULFIRAM THERAPY ON RELATIONSHIPS WITHIN THE NAVAHO DRINKING GROUP. *Q. J. of Studies on Alcohol 1968 29(4): 909-916.* "To ascertain the effects of disulfiram therapy on relationships within the Navaho drinking group, more than 200 Navaho alcoholics who had undergone disulfiram therapy were observed for nearly 2 years. Two studies of portions of this population were also conducted: (1) the first 30 patients treated with disulfiram were studied; and (2) the relationship between cultural stress and alcoholism was compared in 62 alcoholics treated with disulfiram and 39 non-alcoholic patients also in the Fort Defiance (Ariz.) Indian Hospital. In the first group of 30, 16 had not drunk at all during the 6 months to 1.5 years since beginning treatment and 7 had resumed taking disulfiram after short drinking bouts. Prior to treatment, the 62 alcoholics of the second study had belonged to drinking groups which reinforced their commitment to continue drinking. By contrast, the nonalcoholics did much of their drinking at home and thus did not belong to the alcoholics' integrated system of drinking fellowships. By submitting to disulfiram therapy, the alcoholic made clear his desire to break with the drinking group. Since the group usually accepted this decision, the former alcoholic was then free to find an accepted position in the nonalcoholic community." J

1604. Shepardson, Mary and Hammond, Blowden. CHANGE AND PERSISTENCE IN AN ISOLATED NAVAJO COMMUNITY. *Am. Anthropologist 1964 66(5): 1029-1050.* A review of the population change in the small Navajo community of Rainbow Plateau on the Arizona-Utah border and of its adjustment to pressures imposed upon it by the outside world. Persistence of traditional patterns will resist change from within if there is "a value system and social structure sufficiently flexible to permit a selection and incorporation of new action systems as alternates" and from without if there is "a contact situation which in fact subsidizes the traditional economy and thus preserves the concomitant action systems which met the functional requisities of a little community as a distinct way of life." Biblio.   A. Hopping

1605. Spencer, Virginia E. and Jett, Stephen C. NAVAJO DWELLINGS OF RURAL BLACK CREEK VALLEY, ARIZONA-NEW MEXICO. *Plateau 1971 43(4): 159-175.* "In 1968, all rural dwellings in a twenty-mile-long section of Black Creek Valley, Navajo Indian Reservation, Arizona-New Mexico, were mapped, and classified by wall structure and materials. Dwellings were most frequent near farmed areas on floodplains of Black Creek and its right-bank tributaries. Houses comprised 80 [percent] of all permanent dwellings, hogans 20 [percent]. For every 13.5 permanent dwellings there was one temporary dwelling (shade). The most common house type was of frame construction, usually stuccoed. The most common hogan type was of cribbed-log construction. Horizontal-log houses and plank hogans were also common, and most major dwelling types recorded for the Navajo occurred in the area. The prevalence of frame structures reflects acculturation, availability of materials, and relative affluence."   J

1606. Thompson, Hildegard. EL USO DE LENGUAS INDIGENAS EN EL DESARROLLO DE LOS INDIOS AMERICANOS EN LOS ESTADOS UNIDOS [The use of Indian languages in the development of American Indians in the United States]. *Am. Indígena [Mexico] 1965 25(2): 229-237.* Summarizes the Bureau of Indian Affairs' use of Indian languages (especially Navaho) to promote Indian education and development. From the forced use of English, the program moved in the 1930's to a bilingual program and in the post-World War II era to other special programs which have been successful in the education of the Navahos for productive lives and for assimilation into the dominant culture.
R. J. Knowlton

Papago

1607. Jones, Richard D. THE WI'IGITA OF ACHI AND QUITOBAC. *Kiva 1971 36(4): 1-29.* "The *wi'igita (vi'ikita)* ceremonial is the most complex, and involves more participants, than any other in the Papago culture. It has been partially observed by several persons, but never in its entirety, and an attempt is made herein to correlate these various observations into a coherent whole and to describe the entire process of organizing and presenting the *wi'igita* ceremonial. The *wi'igita* at Achi [Arizona], once held at approximately four-year intervals, is much more elaborate than the smaller, annual *wi'igita* held at Quitobac in Sonora [Mexico]. The two ceremonies are compared."   J

1608. Padfield, Harland. and Van Willigen, John. WORK AND INCOME PATTERNS IN A TRANSITIONAL POPULATION: THE PAPAGO OF ARIZONA. *Human Organization 1969 28(3): 208-216.* To obtain data on occupational and economic changes among the American Indian population, a study was made of the Papago Indians of Arizona. The Indian population was defined on the basis of genealogies. A 10 percent sample of all males 14 and older was interviewed. The data was tabulated by age groups, educational achievement, work site (on-reservation, off-reservation, or both), type of work, and income. The on-reservation population was older, had a lower level of educational achievement, and earned a lower income than those who worked off the reservation for all or part of the year. 8 tables, 19 notes.   E. S. Johnson

1609. Wilson, C. Roderick. PAPAGO INDIAN POPULATION MOVEMENT: AN INDEX OF CULTURE CHANGE. *Rocky Mountain Social Sci. J. 1969 6(1): 23-32.* Delineates some of the dimensions of the population movement in one district of the Papago Indian Reservation (southern Arizona) and explores some of the social and cultural implications of this movement. Map, 5 tables, 6 notes.   R. F. Allen

Pima

1610. Dobyns, Henry F. TUBAC: WHERE SOME ENEMIES ROTTED. *Arizona Q. 1963 19(3): 229-232.* History of the contemporary place-name Tubac as an English borrowing of a Hispanicized form of an original northern Piman designation. Based on material from the Arizona State Museum. Notes.
                                                                      E. P. Stickney

Pueblo

1611. Harvey, Byron, III. NEW MEXICAN KACHINA DOLLS. *Masterkey 1963 37(1): 4-8.* Discusses form and function of New Mexican kachina dolls and compares the differences and similarities of the dolls in various pueblos. Based on field investigation; 3 illus.   C. N. Warren

1612. Ortiz, Alfonso. A UNIQUELY AMERICAN HERITAGE. *Princeton U. Lib. Chronicle 1969 30(3): 147-157.* To preserve the myths, songs, folk tales, prayers, and speeches, the author has made some 55 hours of tape recordings of the oral tradition of the Pueblo Indians. Examples of the material are given. Illus.
                                                                      D. Brockway

1613. Philp, Kenneth. ALBERT B. FALL AND THE PROTEST FROM THE PUEBLOS, 1921-23. *Arizona and the West 1970 12(3): 237-254.* Although the treaty of Guadalupe Hidalgo (1848) confirmed Pueblo Indian ownership of 700 thousand acres of Spanish land grants in New Mexico, and even though the federal Supreme Court had upheld Pueblo right to sell these lands as non-wards of the federal government, the 1910 enabling act for New Mexico statehood reversed this position. The Pueblo again became wards of the federal government. The validity of thousands of non-Indian claims to the lands within the Pueblo grants was at stake. At the request of Secretary of the Interior Albert Bacon Fall, Senator Holm O. Bursum from New Mexico sponsored a bill in Congress to confirm such titles as were held by non-Indians meeting certain conditions. The 1921 Bursum bill met determined opposition in a nationwide protest which resulted in its defeat and new laws to protect Indian rights. Although Fall's resignation in 1923 from his cabinet position is usually explained by his involvement in the Teapot Dome affair, the furor over his sponsorship of the Bursum bill was an important factor in his decision. 5 illus., map, 46 notes.

D. L. Smith

Pueblo, Hopi

1614. McIntire, Elliot G. CHANGING PATTERNS OF HOPI INDIAN SET-TLEMENT. *Ann. of the Assoc. of Am. Geographers 1971 61(3): 510-521.* "Because of their isolation, the Hopi Indians of northeastern Arizona escaped the disruption suffered by most tribes after the arrival of the white man, and they have been able to adapt slowly to American culture. Houses have changed gradually from the 'Southwestern pueblo' type to styles common in poorer parts of rural America. The densely nucleated villages with a clearly defined internal organization have given way to sprawling settlements with no noticeable pattern."   J

1615. Stanislawski, Michael B. THE ETHNOARCHAEOLOGY OF HOPI POTTERY MAKING. *Plateau 1969 42(1): 27-33.* Reports on a study in the summer of 1968 of the material culture of local peoples assumed to be the descendants of prehistoric groups in the area (Arizona). The purpose of the study was to collect information in order for archaeologists to understand well the artifacts, processes, systems, or social patterns of a prehistoric site. "The specific purposes of our 1968 study were to collect information concerning the traditional tools and techniques of Hopi and Hopi-Tewa pottery making; the modern uses of pottery and potsherds; the methods of teaching pottery making to children and adults and the social patterns of transmission; and the distribution of pots, potsherds, and pottery types within the Hopi and Tewa communities." A Hopi potter census was begun and the study is to be continued in succeeding summers.

W. A. Buckman

Pueblo, Keresan

1616. Hoebel, E. Adamson. THE CHARACTER OF KERESAN PUEBLO LAW. *Pro. of the Am. Phil. Soc. 1968 112(3): 127-130.* Examines the nature of the contemporary legal system of the Keresan Pueblo Indians who live in New Mexico, with considerable reference to their past laws and sociolegal heritage. The governor and war captain are the important officials in implementing the law. All legal authority centers in the bureaucracy, and every case must be handled through its auspices. Two rules are commonly applied to the settling of disputes: involve no more officials in deciding a case than necessary, and involve as few other people as well. The central concern of modern Keresan Pueblo law is the enforcement of performing required community work. Secondary sources; 7 notes.

W. G. Morgan

Pueblo, Taos

1617. Collins, Dabney Otis. BATTLE FOR BLUE LAKE: THE TAOS INDI-ANS FINALLY REGAIN THEIR SACRED LAND. *Am. West 1971 8(5): 32-37.* In 1906 Blue Lake became a part of the newly created Carson National Forest in New Mexico. A few miles from Taos, Blue Lake and nearly 50 thousand acres of surrounding forests and mountains are the ancestral sacred lands of the Taos Pueblo Indians. Symbolically, the sapphire waters of the lake are the source of all Taos life and the retreat of souls after death. Here occurs the annual secret ceremonial rites, witnessed by only two non-Indians. When they felt the implications of what had happened, the Taos Indians began a legal battle for restoration. A 1940 special federal use permit was substantial progress, but public recreation inroads and pressure from timber interests posed significant threats. After a 1965 Indian Claims Commission ruling the Taos rejected an offer of 300 thousand dollars for their claims. Soon Blue Lake became a national synonym for religious freedom with support from the press and communications media, congressmen, cabinet officers, and the National Council of Churches. After several bills were introduced in Congress and hearings produced determined opposition as well as support, a White House message broke the stalemate. After signature of a bill on 15 December 1970, 48 thousand acres of land surrounding Blue Lake were once again owned by the Taos. 3 illus. D. L. Smith

1618. Collins, John James. PEYOTISM AND RELIGIOUS MEMBERSHIP AT TAOS PUEBLO, NEW MEXICO. *Southwestern Social Sci. Q. 1967 48(2): 183-191.* There are three religious groupings of importance at Taos Pueblo: the Kiva religion group, adhered to by the older people; Catholics, supported by the younger individuals; and the Peyote members. Individuals can hold membership in all three groups, a majority are members of at least two. Peyotism is considered as a middle group of religious participation, and as such it is a mechanism for maintaining a common and vital religious and social identity for the Taos. 10 notes. D. F. Henderson

1619. Kelley, Dean M. GUEST EDITORIAL: THE IMPAIRMENT OF THE RELIGIOUS LIBERTY OF THE TAOS PUEBLO INDIANS BY THE UNITED STATES GOVERNMENT. *J. of Church and State 1967 9(2): 161-164.* Without compensation, sacred land held by the Indians of Taos Pueblo since the 14th century was incorporated in the Carson National Forest in 1906. The Indian Claims Commission was subsequently established for the Indians but it can only award compensation. The Indians want the sacred Blue Lake area returned. For the Indians there is a spiritual identification with the whole area, including all its flora and fauna. The Forest Service and lumber interests oppose a complete and unrestricted return to the Indians and a bill in Congress for the relief of the Indians has been stymied for the moment. G. W. Hull

Pueblo, Tiwa

1620. Houser, Nicholas P. THE TIGUA SETTLEMENT OF YSLETA DEL SUR. *Kiva 1970 36(2): 23-40.* "Ysleta del Sur, 15 miles south of El Paso, Texas, was established in 1682 for refugee Tigua [(Tiwa) Pueblo] Indians who abandoned the old Isleta pueblo, near Albuquerque, New Mexico, during the Pueblo Revolt of 1680. Despite loss of pueblo lands, intermarriage with non-Indians, and the acculturative influences of a dominant Mexican population, the Tigua of Ysleta del Sur have retained an Indian identity and tribal organization. Officially recognized by the federal government in the spring of 1968 as a surviving tribe of American Indians, they are presently active in reinterpreting and revitalizing their Indian heritage."   J

Yaqui

1621. Wharfield, H. B. A FIGHT WITH THE YAQUIS AT BEAR VALLEY, 1918. *Arizoniana 1963 4(3): 1-8.* Escaping notice because of World War I struggles at the time, the skirmish of 9 January 1918, west of Nogales, Arizona, involved Troop "E" of the Negro 10th U.S. Cavalry under Captain Frederick H. L. Ryder and a band of some 30 Yaquis. Text of a letter of reminiscence by Ryder is included. Documented, illus.   E. P. Stickney

Great Plains Area

General

1622. *Arizona and the West 1965 7(2): 91-104.* Berthrong, Donald J. WALTER STANLEY CAMPBELL: PLAINSMAN. Except for the years at Oxford, service in World War I, and a few years as a high school English teacher in Kentucky, Walter Stanley Campbell spent most of his life among the Plains Indians and as an English professor at the University of Oklahoma. In his writing he drew upon his intimate knowledge of the Indians to correct the warped and distorted image of them held by most writers. His most successful books were concerned with the Dakota (Sioux) and their resistance to white advance in the northern Plains. Present- day historians value Campbell's writings not as sources in Western history, but for apt characterizations and incidents in Western history. Based on the Campbell Papers in the University of Oklahoma Library and Campbell's published works; 3 illus., 25 notes.   D. L. Smith

1623. Braroe, Niels W. RECIPROCAL EXPLOITATION IN AN INDIAN-WHITE COMMUNITY. *Southwestern J. of Anthrop. 1965 21(2): 166-178.* Describes what appears to be a system of reciprocal exploitation between Indians and whites in a small unidentified community in Saskatchewan during 1963. A complex system of reward within each subgroup serves to perpetuate stereotypical images of Indian and white. Based on field investigation, primary and secondary sources; biblio.　　　　　　　　　　　　　　　　　　C. N. Warren

1624. Dundes, Alan and Porter, C. Fayne. AMERICAN INDIAN STUDENT SLANG. *Am. Speech 1963 38(4): 270-277.* A study of English slang used by one thousand Indian students from 80 tribes at the vocational Haskell Institute in Kansas. With English as the lingua franca of Indians from diverse linguistic backgrounds, a particular type of slang has developed among the Indians at this school. It has not yet been determined whether this slang is either used or known in any of the Indian reservation cultures. Some of the slang is general American, other is peculiar to Haskell. Indians from Alaska are called "polar bears" or "Alaskamos," those from Oklahoma are "ditch diggers" or "dust bowlers," and those from North Carolina are "moonshiners." All these terms are acceptable, yet most students resent being called "redskins." This slang reveals Indian student attitudes such as "Indian time" meaning "indefinite" and "white man's time" meaning "punctual." Based on the authors' experience with Indians at the Haskell Institute; 7 notes.　　　　　　　　　　　　　R. W. Shoemaker

1625. Ewers, John C. CYRUS E. DALLIN, MASTER SCULPTOR OF THE PLAINS INDIAN. *Montana 1968 18(1): 35-43.* Biography of a versatile sculptor whose work ranged from notable figures of western Indians to the angel Maroni atop the Mormon Temple in Salt Lake City. Coming from the Utah village of Springville, he met difficulty in finding acceptance in the East, but in his lifetime was recognized abroad as well as in America. Much of his work was done in Europe and New England on a variety of historical subjects; he is best known for his statues of Indians.　　　　　　　　　　　　　　　　　S. R. Davison

1626. Franklin, J. L. THE FIGHT FOR PROHIBITION IN OKLAHOMA TERRITORY. *Social Sci. Q. 1969 49(4): 876-885.* Through the efforts of the Women's Christian Temperance Union and the Anti-Saloon League, the well-entrenched liquor interests were defeated in 1907 when prohibition was included in the first Oklahoma constitution. The struggle began in 1888. Local option grew to the point that, by 1906, statewide prohibition seemed possible. By the Oklahoma Enabling Act (1907), Congress linked the Indian Territory and Oklahoma Territory and required continuation of prohibition in the Indian portion as a condition of statehood for the whole. Based chiefly on newspapers and public documents; 45 notes.　　　　　　　　　　　　　　　　　M. Hough

1627. Gilles, George. THREE INDIAN TALES. *Alberta Hist. R. [Canada] 1967 15(1): 25-28.* Stories written by an educated Métis in the late 1890's relating commonplace events in the Blackfoot and Cree camps.　　　　　H. M. Burns

1628. Gleason, Ruth, compiler. RECENT ADDITIONS TO THE LIBRARY. *Kansas Hist. Q. 1968 34(2): 201-228.* A partial list of books received by the Kansas State Historical Society from 1 October 1966 to 30 September 1967. These additions, by purchase, gift or exchange, are grouped under the following general headings: books by Kansans and about Kansas, books on American Indians and the West, genealogy and local history, and books on United States history, biography, and allied subjects.   W. F. Zornow

1629. Johnson, John L. ALBERT ANDREW EXENDINE: CARLISLE COACH AND TEACHER. *Chronicles of Oklahoma 1965 43(3): 319-331.* Exendine made football history as a player in 1907, on the second-team All-American. The Carlisle Indian School had been established in 1879 on the theory that Indians should continue many of the activities that they engaged in at home. They excelled in football under Coach "Pop" Warner. In 1908 Exendine became an assistant coach and developed the forward passing game, although it was not used widely until 1913. The Carlisle Indians had used it in 1907. Exendine coached Jim Thorpe and became his friend. In 1909 "Ex" became head coach at Otterbein, and from 1914 to 1922, coach at Georgetown. He coached also at Washington State, Occidental, Northeastern, Oklahoma, and Oklahoma State. As a coach, educator, lawyer, and Indian agent he devoted a lifetime to the education of youth. 20 notes.   I. W. Van Noppen

1630. Jones, Douglas C. MEDICINE LODGE REVISITED. *Kansas Hist. Q. 1969 35(2): 130-142.* In 1867 an Indian peace commission concluded a treaty at Medicine Lodge, Kansas, with the Comanche, Kiowa, Cheyenne, Arapaho, and Plains Apache, the wild tribes south of the Arkansas River. Since 1926 the residents of the area have often reenacted the incident. The ceremony in 1967 marking the centennial of the original event was conducted on such a grand scale that it may well be the last time that the incident will be commemorated. This account is both a description of the reenactment in 1967 and an effort to add supporting detail and to correct some factual errors appearing in the reports of the original participants and the 9 journalists who accompanied them to the site. Based on newspaper reports, government records and monographs; illus., photo, 18 notes.   W. F. Zornow

1631. Jones, William K. GENERAL GUIDE TO DOCUMENTS ON THE FIVE CIVILIZED TRIBES IN THE UNIVERSITY OF OKLAHOMA LIBRARY DIVISION OF MANUSCRIPTS. *Ethnohist. 1967 14(1/2): 47-76.* An alphabetically annotated bibliography of maps, microfilm, and manuscript holdings in the collection totaling about 145 items.   R. S. Burns

1632. Kehoe, Alice B. THE GHOST DANCE RELIGION IN SASKATCHEWAN, CANADA. *Plains Anthropologist 1968 13(42, pt. 1): 296-304.* "The 'Ghost Dance' religion taught by the Paiute Jack Wilson (Wovoka) was carried to Saskatchewan at the beginning of this century. Its most successful proselytizer was an Assiniboine who inspired the most northern Dakota Sioux community in the province to become a congregation. Surviving members of this congregation profess a creed that closely follows Wilson's later teachings, recorded by James Mooney, but that differs significantly from the more militant versions Mooney heard from some United States Dakota. The Saskatchewan creed appears to have been a viable accommodation to early reservation-period conditions."   J

1633. Martin, Harry W., Sutker, Sara S., Leon, Robert L., and Hales, William M. MENTAL HEALTH OF EASTERN OKLAHOMA INDIANS: AN EXPLORATION. *Human Organization 1968 27(4): 308-315.* In order to test the validity of a psychiatric screening device, standardized on a non-Indian population with an Indian population, and to compare the results with other racial groups of similar socioeconomic status, the Cornell Index (N2) was administered to 640 out-patients and the Division of Indian Health, U.S. Health Service clinics in Shawnee and Claremore, Oklahoma. An additional 278 non-Indians were tested at the University Medical Center in Oklahoma City. The test results were checked by selective interviews eight months after the initial examination. The results are tabulated and compared on the basis of age, sex, and race. The authors conclude that the Cornell Index is a valid instrument for use on an Indian population and that the prevalence of psychiatric problems does not differ significantly between Indians and non-Indians. 5 tables, 36 notes.

E. S. Johnson

1634. McCown, Robert A. A COMPARISON OF THE HOLDINGS OF FOUR LIBRARIES ON GREAT PLAINS HISTORY. *Great Plains J. 1970 9(2): 91-99.* Describes and compares the holdings of four libraries which have outstanding collections on the Great Plains. The Yale University Library has the Beinecke and Coe Collections. The DeGolyer Foundation Library at Southern Methodist University has comprehensive holdings in the cattle trade, the Dakotas, frontier and pioneer life, Indians, Kansas, Nebraska, railroads, western travel, and exploration. The Newberry Library of Chicago has a "good deal of material on statemaking," the Edward E. Ayer Collection on American Indians, and the Edward D. Graff Collection of western Americana. The Minnesota Historical Society Library is not limited to Minnesota history and has important manuscript collections including the Pond and Neill Papers. 19 notes.

O. H. Zabel

1635. Merriam, Harold G. SIGN TALKER WITH STRAIGHT TONGUE: FRANK BIRD LINDERMAN. *Montana 1962 12(3): 2-20.* An account of Linderman's life in Montana, emphasizing his accurate portrayal of the Indian and reporting the existence of Linderman stories still unpublished. The author utilized papers from the Linderman estate, items from Volumes 11 and 19 of *Frontier and Midland Magazine,* and the author's personal acquaintance with Linderman.

L. G. Nelson

1636. Meyer, Roy W. FORT BERTHOLD AND THE GARRISON DAM. *North Dakota Hist. 1968 35(3/4): 216-335.* The Fort Berthold Indian Reservation was created in 1851 as the home of the Hidatsa, Mandan, and Arikara. Here the Indians concentrated principally on agriculture in the bottomlands of the Missouri River that traversed the reservation. The Garrison Dam, erected by the government as a flood control project, brought their relocation in the late 1940's and early 1950's and disrupted their way of life. The Indians were thus presented with what they regarded as another example of white persistency in forcing Indian adoption of white middle-class ways. Resettled in new homes with comforts and amenities they neither coveted nor needed, the Indians could not find employment to maintain themselves properly in their new situations. Whatever white intentions were, Indian-white relations were given a setback. 18 illus., 2 maps, 324 notes.   D. L. Smith

1637. Oates, Stephen B. BOOM OIL! OKLAHOMA STRIKES IT RICH! *Am. West 1968 5(1): 11-15, 64-66.* The gold rush towns with their lawlessness and unrestrained individualism did not constitute the last American wild west frontier. All of the drama which attended the mining frontier was recast in the opening quarter of the present century and replayed on the red plains of Oklahoma. A series of spectacular oil discoveries, 1904-23, stirred the nation as nothing else had since the discovery of gold in California in 1848. The earlier "boomer" and "sooner" human stampedes into Oklahoma when the territory was opened paled in comparison. The author illustrates his generalizations with accounts of Drumright, the hub of the great oil field; Ragtown, the bloodiest boomtown in the state's history; Burbank, where the unlucky Osage Indians became the wealthiest, per capita, people in the world and the victims of "hordes of white flies"; and Seminole City and Bowlegs, where the new hosts for oil field parasites were illiterate Seminole farmers. 4 illus., biblio. note.
                                                                      D. L. Smith

1638. Quinten, B. T. OKLAHOMA TRIBES, THE GREAT DEPRESSION AND THE INDIAN BUREAU. *Mid-Am. 1967 49(1): 29-43.* American leaders only slowly recognized the grave effects of the depression years of 1929-33 on the nation's Indians. Not until the autumn of 1931 did the Bureau of Indian Affairs organize a relief program and call for support from Congress. Even this help did not suffice, and the Indians had to await the New Deal for satisfactory economic assistance. An analysis of the experience of over a hundred thousand Indians in Oklahoma during 1929-31 reveals the causes and consequences of this prolonged aid delay. Based primarily on government documents; 74 notes.
                                                                      L. D. Silveri

1639. Steinmetz, Paul B., S.J. THE RELATIONSHIP BETWEEN PLAINS INDIAN RELIGION AND CHRISTIANITY: A PRIEST'S VIEWPOINT. *Plains Anthropologist 1970 15(48): 83-86.* "The American Indian who is dedicated to his own religious tradition and to Christianity has the same identity crisis that the Jewish convert did in the early church. The Jews discovered that their religious tradition was the foreshadowing of Christianity, containing the types of Christ, and that Christ fulfilled and did not destroy their Jewish tradition. The Christian Indian today can do the same by discovering that his Sacred Pipe and the tradition for which it stands is also a foreshadowing of Christ in his office of mediator, and the type of the whole plan of salvation. The Christian Indian can understand that Christ is the Living and Eternal Pipe who fulfills and does not destroy their sacred pipe. Without this fundamental insight all blending of the two traditions will be superficial."   J

1640. Sue, Mary and Schusky, Ernest L. A CENTER OF PRIMARY SOURCES FOR PLAINS INDIAN HISTORY. *Plains Anthropologist 1970 15(48): 104-108.* "Preservation of the nation's Indian records is recognized as a task of

national importance. Public access to government documents and data is now possible at 10 regional record centers across the country. The material stored provides detailed and analytic accounts of daily activity and business at Indian agencies. The nature and content of the data relevant to Plains Indian agencies is described in this paper."
J

1641. Yeast, William E. THE MESQUAKIE MEMORIAL FEAST. *Ann. of Iowa 1963 36(8): 591-598.* In researching for material on Indians in and around Iowa for his book *Mesquakie, the Red Earth People,* Yeast had the honor of attending a Mesquakie Memorial Feast. This feast is usually taboo to outsiders and the author is one of two exceptions to this rule in the last hundred years. The feast is an ancient Sac and Fox ritual held in observance of the dead.
W. F. Peterson

By Tribe

Assiniboin (Stoney)

1642. Pocaterra, George W. AMONG THE NOMADIC STONEYS. *Alberta Hist. R. [Canada] 1963 11(3): 12-19.* Reminiscences of an immigrant, his arrival in Canada and his many years of association with the Assiniboin (Stoney) Indians during which he often shared their lives for weeks or months at a time. Some comments on their customs.
E. W. Hathaway

1643. Wenzel, Johanna. WALKING BUFFALO: WISE MAN OF THE WEST. *Beaver [Canada] 1968 (Spring): 19-23.* The life of Tatunga Mani, Walking Buffalo (1871-1967), who rose to chief of the Alberta Assiniboines, now commonly called Stonies. As Moral Rearmament's representative of the natives of North America, he traveled around the world several times. Illus.
L. F. S. Upton

Blackfoot (Siksika)

1644. Ewers, John C. WINOLD REISS: HIS PORTRAITS AND PROTEGES. *Montana 1971 21(3): 44-55.* Describes the work of Reiss (1888-1953), a leading painter of Blackfeet (Siksika) portraits between 1919 and 1953, emphasizing his dedication to accuracy and his humane interest in the Blackfeet. Reiss' help and encouragement to young Indians led several into careers in art. Illus.
S. R. Davison

1645. Willcomb, Roland H. BIRD RATTLE AND THE MEDICINE PRAYER. *Montana 1970 20(2): 42-49.* Between 1923 and 1937, the author visited periodically with Bird Rattle and other elderly Blackfeet tribesmen in their homeland east of Glacier National Park. He often joined in their ceremony of smoking the Medicine Pipe, which he came to understand was a mingling of social and religious elements. The ritual involved a prayer, uttered in the native language. A translation, which is supplied, expresses a wish for harmony with the Creator and all creation. Illus.   S. R. Davison

Cherokee

1646. Wahrhaftig, Albert L. and Thomas, Robert K. RENAISSANCE AND REPRESSION: THE OKLAHOMA CHEROKEE. *Trans-action 1969 6(4): 42-48.* Examines the historical and sociological factors that have created the present relationship of the Cherokee people with the dominant white society of Oklahoma. Due to their differences toward assimilation in the 19th century, the Cherokee divided into two parties. One has tried to retain the status and ways of an autonomous group, while the other has seen full assimilation into white society as the way to survival. White society has called those Cherokee who have assimilated good, successful, and acceptable, and called those who have maintained autonomy and separateness, shiftless and failures. The myth of assimilation has suited the ends of those who created it. This in turn has led to the disguise of the social system of the entire state. Even many contemporary sociologists have been wedded to these myths in their description of Cherokee society. That is another type of racism. Illus., biblio.   A. Erlebacher

Cheyenne

1647. Frink, Maurice. DONALD HOLLOWBREST: FIGHTING CHEYENNE EDITOR. *Montana 1964 14(4): 27-30.* A full-blooded Cheyenne edits and prints the *Birney Arrow,* at Birney, Montana, devoted to publishing intimate local news of the Tongue River Reservation.   S. R. Davison

1648. Liberty, Margot. THE NORTHERN CHEYENNE SUN DANCE AND THE OPENING OF THE SACRED MEDICINE HAT 1959. *Plains Anthropologist 1967 12(38): 367-385.* A day-to-day account of the 1959 Sun Dance of the Northern Cheyenne Indians at Lame Deer, Montana, as observed by the author. The purpose of the Sun Dance has nothing to do with the sun. It is held to regenerate the earth. A lodge and altar are built by priests and dancers. Flexibility combined with adherence to the essential elements of the ceremony is the impression the author got of the modern Sun Dance. After the week of dancing and singing the "Sacred Medicine Hat Bundle" (an ancient religious object) was opened to see if its contents were safe. Little was remembered since the last opening in 1934. The opening revealed a bundle of braided sweetgrass, five scalps, a fur skin, a package of old-time tobacco, a bundle of fluffy white material, and the Sacred Hat itself. 2 plates, biblio.   K. Adelfang

1649. Poteet, Chrystabel Berrong. THE ENDING OF A CHEYENNE LEGEND. *Chronicles of Oklahoma 1963 41(1): 9-13.* Geary, Oklahoma, and the surrounding countryside were struck by a tornado in 1961, thus dispelling the old legend of the Cheyenne and Arapaho Indians that this valley, their spring camping spot for centuries, would never be destroyed by a tornado. Oklahoma City's radio and television stations warned the residents, who sought shelter in storm caves. Only one life was lost. Based on an account by a participant.

I. W. Van Noppen

1650. Powell, Peter J. JOURNEY TO SE'HAN. *Montana 1968 18(1): 70-75.* An account of the last years, death, and funeral of John Stands In Timber, a venerable leader among Montana's Northern Cheyenne Indians. The author, his friend for 11 years, took part in the burial service. He reports on the non-Christian aspect of the ceremony, which preserved many of the ancient ways. Se'han is the Cheyenne hereafter, "a pleasant land, one where the Cheyennes of the past are living above just as they did upon earth."

S. R. Davison

1651. Powell, Peter John. ISSIWUN: SACRED BUFFALO HAT OF THE NORTHERN CHEYENNE. *Montana 1960 10(1): 24-40.* The history of the Sacred Buffalo Hat of the Northern Cheyenne Indians. The author describes the influence of the rites connected with the sacred object on the life and development of the tribe. He was present at the performance of the ancient rites of the unveiling of the Hat in July 1959.

B. Waldstein

1652. Richard, Bertha Maxham. MOURNING ENDS IN SPRING. *Montana 1970 20(1): 86-89.* Tells how the death of an infant brother resulted in a close and comforting relationship with the neighboring Cheyenne Indians of southern Montana, who had themselves been through a long period of grief and mourning.

S. R. Davison

Chippewa (Ojibwa)

1653. Dusenberry, Verne. WAITING FOR A DAY THAT NEVER COMES: THE TRAGIC STORY OF THE DISPOSSESSED METIS OF MONTANA. *Montana 1958 8(2): 26-39.* Descendants of French fur traders and Chippewa women live in Montana and North Dakota as dispossessed, landless Indians. Rights to government assistance were lost through the terms of the McComber Commission of 1893. Their history is one of injustice.

A

1654. LaBlanc, Rosella. THE DEVELOPMENT OF TURTLE MOUNTAIN INDIAN RESERVATION. *Am. Benedictine R. 1970 21(3): 407-420.* Created in 1884, the Turtle Mountain Indian Reservation in North Dakota was badly underdeveloped until the 1930's when new schools and a hospital were built. In 1933 Benedictine missionaries established a school which has since expanded. In recent years such government efforts as the Poverty Program, Operation Main Stream and Housing Development, Neighborhood Youth Corps, Head Start, and other programs have greatly improved reservation conditions. Indian radicalism helped spur these developments. This same radicalism, however, has also disrupted Indian efforts at self-government through tribal organization. Further development of the reservation depends on better self-government and more enlightened federal government policies. 35 notes.

E. J. O'Brien

Cree, Plains

1655. Woodward, John A. PLAINS CREE BEADWORK. *Masterkey 1969 43(4): 144-150.* In the summer of 1969 the author and his wife spent several weeks with an Alberta Plains Cree band. Discusses the contemporary practice of making and using the decorative beadwork of these people. Mentions motifs, style, techniques, materials, and the commercial aspects of their craft. 3 photos, biblio.
C. N. Warren

1656. Wuttunee, William I. C. PEYOTE CEREMONY. *Beaver [Canada] 1968 299(Summer): 22-25.* Describes taking part in the peyote ceremony at the Red Pheasant Indian Reserve of the Plains Cree in Saskatchewan in July 1964. The dried top or button of the peyote plant is used in the ceremony and chewed during an all-night session of prayer and meditation. Illus.
L. F. S. Upton

Crow

1657. Castles, Jean I. "BOXPOTAPESH" OF CROW AGENCY. *Montana 1971 21(3): 84-93.* During the first third of this century, Fred E. Miller (1868-1936) lived in the region of the Crow Reservation in southern Montana, recording anecdotes of the people and making photographs of them and their land. After his death, his 500 glass-plate negatives drifted into unsympathetic hands and were thrown onto the city dump; only a few, which had been made into prints, are preserved. His nickname, "High Kicker" (Boxpotapesh), he earned through his skill with a football while he was working with his Indian friends to interest them in sports. Undocumented, 13 photos.
S. R. Davison

Dakota (Sioux)

1658. McCone, R. Clyde. BASIC PERSONALITY STRUCTURE AMONG THE LAKOTA. *Plains Anthropologist 1968 13(42, pt. 1): 305-309.* "A brief field survey among the Dakota (Lakota) on the Cheyenne River, Rosebud, and Pine Ridge reservations was made possible by a grant from the Long Beach California State College Research Foundation. The purpose of the survey was to decide whether further in-depth studies were warranted of the psychological dimension of acculturation among these people. Hallowell's hypothesis regarding the persistence of the modal personality structure seemed to be at least a relevant working hypothesis among the Lakota. Since cultural understandings of death have been shown to be integrally related to the modal personality structure, overt expressions relating to death were chosen as one possible clue to the continuance of the covert aspects of the typical personality. Observations made support Hallowell's hypothesis, and suggest that further study is warranted."
J

1659. McCone, R. Clyde. CULTURAL FACTORS IN CRIME AMONG THE DAKOTA INDIANS. *Plains Anthropologist 1966 11(32): 144-151.* Charts show crime rate patterns among Dakota Indians and rural and urban Americans. Indian crime rate against property is about half that against the person. Discussed is the breakdown of the Indian form of social control through the kinship system which results in a loss of close interpersonal relations, producing misunderstanding and tension. The author shows the large crime rate against property in the United States is due to the fact that success and status are determined by profit, possessions, and wealth. In Indian culture, possessions and wealth are not symbols of prestige as is reflected in the low crime rate against property. Illus., biblio.

K. Adelfang

1660. Richardson, Ernest M. BATTLE OF LIGHTNING CREEK. *Montana 1960 10(3): 42-52.* Describes the last known battle between Indians and whites in Wyoming. In 1903 a small party of Sioux from the Pine Ridge Agency defied a sheriff's posse which tried to arrest them for taking game animals out of season and killing livestock. In the resulting gunfire two whites and at least one Indian died. The site, near Lance Creek, is marked by a monument. Derived from government reports and from family records of the white participants.

S. R. Davison

1661. Ruby, Robert H. YUWIPI: ANCIENT RITE OF THE SIOUX. *Montana 1966 16(4): 74-79.* An eyewitness account of a ceremony conducted by Dakota (Sioux) medicine men in the mid-20th century. Describes the ritual as "a pure, native form of Indian worship being practiced today, unaffected by 'foreign' influence."

S. R. Davison

Dakota, Oglala

1662. Collins, Dabney Otis. A HAPPENING AT OGLALA. *Am. West 1969 6(2): 15-19.* A Jesuit who had spent summers teaching on the Pine Ridge Reservation in South Dakota was assigned to the nearby Oglala parish when he completed studies for the priesthood in 1961. He moved an unused church building to the parish and established Our Lady of the Sioux Catholic Church. Believing that the success of Christian culture among the Indians must come through the increase of Indian identity within the religion, the church was rebuilt and decorated to establish the proper relationship between altar and people and to make the entire church a natural expression of its worshipers. The accommodation of the liturgy and the ceremonial ritual are not regarded as a return to paganism any more than the accommodations of early Christianity to the traditions of Judaism. 6 illus.

D. L. Smith

Dakota, Teton

1663. Smith, J. L. THE SACRED CALF PIPE BUNDLE: ITS EFFECT ON THE PRESENT TETON DAKOTA. *Plains Anthropologist 1970 15(48): 87-93.* "In the legends of the Teton Dakota the White Buffalo Calf Maiden, as a messenger from Wakan Tanka, gave the people the Sacred Calf Pipe Bundle. This bundle became the center of the Teton's religious beliefs, for with the bundle the Calf Maiden also gave the people certain religious ceremonies. Chief among these were the Sun Dance, the Hunkalowanpi and the Spirit-keeping ritual. From the old days to the present this bundle has been held in great reverence. To date there have been 11 keepers of the bundle, the present keeper being a 15 year old boy. To some extent the attitudes and views toward the old religion have been modified by the present generation. However, through the efforts of certain individuals a reawakening of the people towards things 'Indian' is taking place. One example is a new course of studies in some Indian schools on 'How to be a Modern Indian.' A second is the proposed building of a new Catholic church at Pine Ridge, South Dakota, in the image of a tipi decorated with the symbols and meanings of the old Teton religion, and a third is the use of the 'peace pipe' in Catholic services."

J

Kickapoo

1664. Hurley, William M. THE KICKAPOO WHISTLE SYSTEM: A SPEECH SURROGATE. *Plains Anthropologist 1968 13(41): 242-247.* "The Mexican and Oklahoma whistle and Ilute languages are presented as dual surrogates which have been maintained and utilized as communications systems for over 100 years."

J

1665. Wallace, Ben J. OKLAHOMA KICKAPOO CULTURE CHANGE. *Plains Anthropologist 1969 14(44, pt. 1): 107-112.* "The Kickapoo are one of the more traditionally oriented Indian tribes in the state of Oklahoma. This is not only a view held by the writer, it has been expressed by another anthropologist (Pope 1958-59), a historian (Gibson 1963), a social worker (Saeger 1957), and a public health service employee (Goodman 1960). The merchants, farmers, and educators of the Kickapoo area also ascribe to this belief. The purpose of this paper is to briefly examine the Oklahoma Kickapoo in historical perspective, noting some of the salient factors which led them to resist cultural change. Before dealing specifically with this problem, however, some of the changes that have occurred in Kickapoo culture since their arrival in Indian Territory (Oklahoma) in 1873 are reviewed."

J

Osage

1666. Burchardt, Bill. OSAGE OIL. *Chronicles of Oklahoma 1963 41(3): 253-269.* Discusses the murders of some oil-rich Osage Indians and the sensational trial of wealthy rancher W. R. Hale and his nephew Ernest Burkhart for these murders. Henry Roan, Anna Brown, and the Smith family had been murdered. Ernest Burkhart's wife was to inherit all their holdings. The U.S. Bureau of Investigation solved the murders and secured convictions in federal court of Hale and Burkhart. These events serve as a springboard for the author to relate the history of the Osage Indians. In 1906 the reservation was broken up into 160-acre tracts. Each Osage received a "headright," meaning that he or she would receive an equal share of all mineral rights. After 1906 public lease auctions were held with oil companies bidding nearly two million dollars for each 160-acre tract. Oilmen and geologists came on special trains. Bootleggers, whiskey dealers, and criminals of all kinds flourished. Many Osage were murdered. Finally, after the U.S. Bureau of Investigation obtained convictions of Hale and Burkhart, the murders ceased. Documented, illus., biblio.   D. L. Smith

Potawatomi (Fire Nation)

1667. Bee, Robert L. POTAWATOMI PEYOTISM: THE INFLUENCE OF TRADITIONAL PATTERNS. *Southwestern J. of Anthrop. 1966 22(2): 194-205.* Shows the influence of traditional patterns of behavior on leaders and members of the Potawatomi Peyotist group and points out that, although the group is split, with two leaders, those leaders follow traditional patterns of avoidance of direct confrontation and utilize gossip for combat. Membership is not split into factions but attends both leaders' services. Points out that some members of the Peyotist group also belong to the Sacred Drum and to Bundle sodalities, which can be seen as a continuation of traditional Potawatomi overlapping memberships in groups. Based on field investigation, primary and secondary sources; biblio.   C. N. Warren

Northeast Area

General

1668. Edgerton, Robert B. SOME DIMENSIONS OF DISILLUSIONMENT IN CULTURE CONTACT. *Southwestern J. of Anthrop. 1965 21(3): 231-243.* An analysis of the general patterns of relationship development involved in cultural contact between individual Europeans and natives. Fieldwork with Indians in Wisconsin in 1959 and with four East African tribes in 1961-62 shows that the essential features of this special type of interpersonal conflict are composed of the following elements: a differential in status, a history of antagonism between status superiors and status inferiors, distrust of each other, an offer of friendship by the status superior, and indirect probing by the status inferior to determine the extent to which the offer can be trusted. The testing often causes the termination of the friendship and resultant disillusionment of both parties, coupled with a reinforcement of traditional stereotypes of the "native" and the European. Based on field investigation, primary and secondary sources; biblio.   C. N. Warren

By Tribe

Chippewa (Ojibwa)

1669. Rogers, E. S. and Updike, Lee. THE OJIBWAY. *Beaver [Canada] 1969 300(Summer): 46-49.* A general survey of the life and social organization of the Ojibwa, known in some areas as Chippewa, Saulteaux, Bungi, or Mississauga Indians. They live in the region of the upper Great Lakes and have been in contact with Europeans for more than 300 years. Confined to treaty reserves by the British now begun to move out into the industrial world. Illus.

L. F. S. Upton

1670. Schneider, Kathryn J. MUTE TESTIMONY TO NEGLECT. *Wisconsin Then and Now 1964 11(3): 4.* On Madeline Island, in the Apostle Islands of Lake Superior, is a French cemetery which contains the graves of Michel Cadot, an early French trader, of the supreme chief of the Chippewa (Ojibwa) of Lake Superior, and of many others who settled and developed these lands. A plea is here made to the citizens of Wisconsin to include this cemetery in the American Landmarks celebration, part of UNESCO'S International Campaign for Monuments, and to take the needed concerted action to keep the record of those who came before. Illus.

E. P. Stickney

Delaware

1671. Bruemmer, Fred. THE DELAWARES OF MORAVIANTOWN. *Can. Geographical J. 1964 68(3): 94-97.* The story of the only exclusively Delaware Indian settlement left. For a time the Delawares were led by Moravian missionaries. Photos.

A. H. Lawrance

Fox

1672. —. THE TAMA POWWOW. *Palimpsest 1967 48(7): 289-320.*

Gallaher, Ruth A. THE TAMA INDIANS, pp. 289-299. When the Sauk and Fox Indians were moved from Iowa in 1845 to lands in Kansas, a small group refused to obey the government order and remained in Tama County. The Indians came to be called the Tama or Meskwaki (Mesquaki). Over the next few years others returned to Iowa from Kansas and ultimately the federal government recognized their right to remain. Over the years they purchased land and now own over three thousand acres. In a report of 1925, there were 363 Indians living in Tama County.

Spencer, Dick, III. POWWOW TIME, pp. 300-319. Describes the annual autumn or "leaf-falling" powwow of the Meskwaki Indians in Tama County. In 1957, when the article was written, the Indians were donning their regalia to perform tribal dances and ceremonies for visitors for the 42d time.

Petersen, William J. TAMA INDIANS IN 1967, p. 320. A brief survey of the Tama Indians in 1967. While only 415 live in the county, 780 are still on the tribal rolls. Although they own 3,800 acres of land, many have jobs in Marshalltown, Cedar Rapids, and Waterloo. Attending school are 151 children. Illus.   D. W. Curl

Iroquois (Five Nations, Six Nations)

1673. Montgomery, Malcolm. HISTORIOGRAPHY OF THE IROQUOIS IN-DIANS 1925-1963. *Ontario Hist. [Canada] 1963 55(4): 247-257.* An evaluation of three recent works. Edmund Wilson's *Apologies to the Iroquois* (New York: Random) analyzes the resurgence of the Iroquois and the impact of the emergence of the nonwhite nations of Africa. The focus of concern is recent encroachments on Indian lands by state authorities. Although Ella Cork, in *The Worst of the Bargain,* makes recommendations inimical to the conservatism of the Six Nations she has made an important contribution to their political history. The *Caughnawaga Indians and the St. Lawrence Seaway* (Grenwich, Conn.: Devin-Adair) by Omar Z. Ghobashi attempts to show the independence of the Mohawks but is marred by "glaring omissions and errors."   J. M. E. Usher

1674. Montgomery, Malcolm. THE LEGAL STATUS OF THE SIX NATIONS INDIANS IN CANADA. *Ontario Hist. [Canada] 1963 55(2): 93-105.* In their efforts to secure a legal judgment on their claim the Indians put their case to the League of Nations and brought test cases before the Canadian courts. By 1961 the Indians were also concerned because the Indian Act discriminated against Canadians classed as Indians. This was a possible violation of the Canadian Bill of Rights. The author argues, however, that the Indian Act is a protection to Indians, preserving their land and preventing its sale by individuals.
J. M. E. Usher

Iroquois, Onondaga

1675. Blau, Harold. DREAM GUESSING: A COMPARATIVE ANALYSIS. *Ethnohist. 1963 10(3): 233-249.* Described in the Jesuit *Relations,* and still performed as a part of the Onondaga midwinter ceremony, the Dream Guessing Rite is characterized as "a method of satisfying the underlying Iroquois need to have their desires fulfilled, and to act as agents in fulfilling the desires of others."
H. J. Graham

1676. Blau, Harold. FUNCTION AND THE FALSE FACES. *J. of Am. Folklore 1966 79(314): 564-580.* Subtitled "A Classification of the Onondaga Masked Rituals and Themes," traces the history of Onondaga masks from written sources and categorizes rituals which the author personally witnessed. Eight rites and 16 rules outlining human dependency on masks are described. Illus., 35 notes.
M. W. Machan

1677. Blau, Harold. HISTORICAL FACTORS IN ONONDAGA IROQUOIS CULTURAL STABILITY. *Ethnohist. 1965 12(3): 250-258.* In addition to the stability of the Iroquois language, religion, music, and soc al and political culture, the Onondaga possess prestige and territorial security. Note, biblio.

R. S. Burns

1678. Blau, Harold. ONONDAGA FALSE FACE RITUALS. *New York Folklore Q. 1967 23(4): 253-264.* Describes rites that have been performed for over 300 years and are still being carried out by Indians in New York State. Mentions every detail of the masks, from the wood used to the distorted features represented on the mask. The masks are designed to conceal the individual's identity and to present a frightening figure. The masks are used in various ceremonies in the Mid-Winter Festival and are said to have powers to cure illness and purify homes. 2 photos, 7 notes.

W. S. Rinaldo

1679. Blau, Harold. THE IROQUOIS WHITE DOG SACRIFICE: ITS EVOLUTION AND SYMBOLISM. *Ethnohist. 1964 11(2): 97-119.* Traces and describes a ceremony still practiced by the Onondaga on the ninth day of their Midwinter Rites. During the 17th and 18th centuries "one or two dogs of a 'pure white breed' were strangled, hung up and ceremonially burned with prayers to the Creator." Present-day survivals and modifications are interpreted in the light of the Iroquois tribal organization, Dream Guessing, and religious symbolism generally.

H. J. Graham

Iroquois, Tuscarora

1680. Graymont, Barbara. THE TUSCARORA NEW YEAR FESTIVAL. *New York Hist. 1969 50(2): 143-163.* The most sacred event in the traditional Iroquois ritual calendar is the midwinter festival occurring late in January or early in February. It is a time of thanksgiving, feasting, and hunting, and a time to commune with the good spirit forces in nature. It is still celebrated by all the Iroquois tribes save the Tuscarora who, being predominantly Baptist, have modified the midwinter festival to make it more acceptable to Christian doctrine. The Tuscarora New Year festival takes place over the three days prior to January 1st. While the feasting and hunting features of the traditional festival have been retained, the Tuscarora no longer engage in the sacrifice of the "white dog," or the "stirring of the ashes." Based on oral interviews, primary and secondary sources; 9 illus., 26 notes.

G. Kurland

Wyandot (Huron)

1681. Morisonneau, Christian. DEVELOPPEMENT ET POPULATION DE LA RESERVE INDIENNE DU VILLAGE-HURON, LORETTEVILLE [The development and population of the Huron Village Indian Reserve, Loretteville]. *Cahiers de Géographie de Québec [Canada] 1970 14(33): 339-357.* Examines the historical development of the Lorette Wyandot (Huron) reservation. Analyzes the process of the reservation's economic growth as well as its spatial problems. The demographic profile of the reserve and its physical layout is similar to a small suburban town in Quebec. Its proximity to Quebec City has promoted its economic growth. For the past half century the manufacture of canoes, snowshoes, and snowboots has been the basis of the economic activity of the reserve. The social psychology of the inhabitants is healthy and the growing role played by Indians in the administration of their reserve is considered to be a factor of positive integration. Based on secondary sources; 5 photos, 9 tables, 2 charts, 11 notes.   A. E. LeBlanc

Southeast Area

General

1682. Howell, Elmo. WILLIAM FAULKNER AND THE MISSISSIPPI INDI-ANS. *Georgia R. 1967 21(3): 386-396.* An analysis of four Indian stories—"Red Leaves" (1920), "A Justice" (1931), "Lo!" (1934), and "A Courtship" (1948)—by William Faulkner (1897-1962) which occupy a special place in the chronicles of "Yoknapatawpha County" in the wilderness of North Mississippi. "They are pre-history, and consequently the works of the imagination in a way that the other Mississippi stories are not, since there were no Indians in the country in Faulkner's lifetime, nor had been for almost a hundred years....With no experience to draw from and with his aversion to research, Faulkner makes no pretensions to accuracy in his treatment of Indian life. He is careless with details, often confusing the customs of the two Mississippi tribes and, in his early work, labelling his Indians indiscriminately as Chickasaws or Choctaws....'A Justice,' like 'Red Leaves,' is about the horror immanent in the principle of life itself, which civilization tries to ignore but which is common acceptance in the Chickasaw wilderness-....The moral earnestness of the two earlier Indian stories gives way in 'Lo!' to the comic....If 'Lo!' represents a lessening of the tension in the earlier Indian stories, 'A Courtship'...reflects an altogether different concept of Indian life.... Though a lively story with a pleasant surprise at the end, it lacks dramatic seriousness, like much of Faulkner's last work." All quotations from Faulkner are from the 1950 edition of *Collected Stories of William Faulkner* (New York: Random House).   D. D. Cameron

By Tribe

Catawba

1683. Hicks, George L. CULTURAL PERSISTENCE VERSUS LOCAL AD-APTATIONS: FRANK G. SPECK'S CATAWBA INDIANS. *Ethnohist. 1965 12(4): 343-354.* Speck's view of the Catawba's closed culture ignored the influence of the matrix of southern white culture. Even the so-called aboriginal traits which have survived are aspects of social adaptation to a specific environment. 5 notes.   R. S. Burns

Cherokee

1684. Kilpatrick, Jack Frederick and Kilpatrick, Anna Gritts. CHEROKEE RITUALS PERTAINING TO MEDICINAL ROOTS. *Southern Indian Studies 1964 16: 24-28.* Provides interesting comments on the practice of the Cherokee medicine man and his gathering of medicinal herbs and roots with which to practice his art. Translations of three chants used by medicine men while collecting medicinal roots are given. 9 notes, biblio.   K. P. Davis

Chickasaw

1685. Howell, Elmo. WILLIAM FAULKNER AND THE CHICKASAW FUNERAL. *Am. Literature 1965 36(4): 523-525.* William Faulkner was indifferent to historical accuracy in his description of Indian customs. 4 notes.
                                                                        R. S. Burns

Choctaw

1686. Coker, William Sidney. PAT HARRISON'S EFFORTS TO REOPEN THE CHOCTAW CITIZENSHIP ROLLS. *Southern Q. 1964 3(1): 36-61.* Beginning in 1887, inducements were held forth to the Indian tribes of the United States to divide their lands and other wealth among their members. The Choctaws as a tribe controlled property worth many millions of dollars in 1907 when the time granted for proving membership in the tribe expired. Byron Patton Harrison, Mississippi congressman, led the fight to renew the period for proving up. Much of the argument hinged on whether or not the Mississippi Choctaws, most of whom had dropped their connections with the tribe in Oklahoma, had forfeited their right to share in the estate by not moving west when their fellows were relocated. Harrison fought a valiant fight but he and the Mississippi Choctaws were finally defeated.   D. A. Stokes

1687. Howell, Elmo. PRESIDENT JACKSON AND WILLIAM FAULKNER'S CHOCTAWS. *Chronicles of Oklahoma 1967 45(3): 252-258.* In *The Collected Stories of William Faulkner* (New York: Random, 1950) the visit of a Choctaw Indian to Washington to obtain the President's affirmation of the innocence of a nephew accused of murder is related. This critique calls Faulkner's knowledge of history erratic and completely subjective. His Indian stories are "a curious jumble of fantasy, history, and unassimilated lore." Two visits by two different Choctaw in 1824 to President James Monroe and in 1831 to President Andrew Jackson, are the factual basis for the Faulkner story. 16 notes.
                                                                        D. L. Smith

REFERENCE MATTER

INDEX

This is a combined index of author, biographical, geographical, and subject entries. Biographical entries are followed by an asterisk. Autobiographical entries are followed by two asterisks. Personal names without asterisks are authors of articles.

Index

LIST OF PERIODICALS

This list contains the titles of the periodicals surveyed for abstracts in INDIANS OF THE UNITED STATES AND CANADA. The titles are arranged in alphabetical order by journal title.

The frequency of publication, years of coverage, and the code of the country of publication follow the title of the periodical.

Example:

Alabama Historical Quarterly	Q	1963-	US
Deutsche Aussenpolitik	BM	1961-	EG
History Today	M	1954-	GB
Revue de Defense Nationale	M	1955-	FR

Abbreviations and explanation:

A	annual		Q	quarterly
B	biennial		SA	semiannual
BM	bimonthly		SM	semimonthly
BW	biweekly		3	3 times a year
I	irregular		T	triennial
M	monthly		W	weekly

Other frequencies of publication are indicated by a number such as "3."

Persons interested in further information concerning the journals are referred to HISTORICAL PERIODICALS (Santa Barbara: Clio Press, 1961) and ULRICH'S INTERNATIONAL PERIODICALS DIRECTORY 1969/70, thirteenth edition (New York: R. R. Bowker, 1969).

Alphabetical list of country codes and countries:

AA	Austria	NO	Norway
CA	Canada	SP	Spain
FR	France	SU	Union of Soviet Socialist Republics
GB	Great Britain	SW	Sweden
IT	Italy	US	United States
MX	Mexico	WG	German Federal Republic
NE	Netherlands		

A

Aconcagua	Q	1965-	SP
Action Nationale	10	1963-	CA
Actualité Economique	Q	1963-	CA
Agricultural History	Q	1954-	US
Alabama Historical Quarterly	Q	1963-	US
Alabama Review	Q	1963-	US
Alberta Historical Review	Q	1963-	CA
América Indígena	Q	1954-	MX
American Anthropologist	BM	1963-	US
American Archivist	Q	1954-	US
American Benedictine Review	Q	1967-	US
American Book Collector	8	1963-	US
American Education	10	1965-	US
American-German Review	5	1955-	US
American Heritage	BM	1955-	US
American Historical Review	5	1954-	US
American History Illustrated	10	1966-	US
American Journal of Legal History	Q	1957-	US
American Literature	Q	1963-	US
American Quarterly	Q	1954-	US
American-Scandinavian Review	Q	1954-	US
American Slavic and East European Review (old title, see Slavic Review)			US
American Speech	Q	1963-	US
American West	BM	1964-	US
Américas	M	1969-	US
Americas, The	Q	1954-	US
Annals of Iowa	Q	1963-	US
Annals of the American Academy of Political and Social Science	BM	1954-	US
Annals of the Association of American Geographers	Q	1963-	US
Annals of Wyoming	SA	1963-	US
Anthropological Papers of the American Museum of Natural History	I	1963-	US

Anuario Indigenista	A	1963-	MX
Arctic	Q	1963-	CA
Arizona and the West	Q	1963-	US
Arizona Quarterly	Q	1963-	US
Arizoniana (old title, see Journal of Arizona History)			US
Arkansas Archaeologist	Q	1970-	US
Arkansas Historical Quarterly	Q	1963-	US
Army Quarterly and Defence Journal	Q	1963-	GB
Arv	A	1964-	SW

B

Baptist Quarterly	Q	1955-	GB
Beaver	Q	1955-	CA
Bijdragen en Mededelingen Betreffende de Geshiedenis der Nederlanden	A	1958-	NE
Bijdragen en Mededelingen van het Historisch Genootschap (old title, see Bijdragen en Mededelingen Betreffende de Geschiedenis der Nederlanden)			NE
British Columbia Historical Quarterly (ceased pub)		1954-63	CA
Bulletin of the Friends Historical Association (old title, see Quaker History)			US
Bulletin of the History of Medicine	BM	1963-	US
Bulletin of the Missouri Historical Society	Q	1962-	US
Bulletin of the United Church of Canada	I	1963-	CA

C

Cahiers de Géographie de Québec	3	1966-	CA
Cahiers des Dix (ceased pub)		1963-	CA
California Historical Quarterly	Q	1954-	US
California Historical Society Quarterly (old title, see California Historical Quarterly)			US
Canadian Army Journal (old title, see Canadian Forces Sentinel)			CA
Canadian Forces Sentinel	10	1963-	CA
Canadian Geographical Journal	M	1963-	CA
Canadian Historic Sites	I	1970-	CA
Canadian Historical Review	Q	1954-	CA
Catalyst	SA	1969-	US
Catholic Historical Review	Q	1954-	US

Chicago History	Q	1963-	US
Christian Century		1954-59	US
Chronicles of Oklahoma	Q	1963-	US
Church History	Q	1954-	US
Civil War History	Q	1955-	US
Civil War Times Illustrated	10	1962-	US
Colorado Magazine	Q	1964-	US
Colorado Quarterly	Q	1963-	US
Concordia Historical Institute Quarterly	Q	1962-	US
Cooperation and Conflict	Q	1968-	NO
Culture Vivante	Q	1968-	CA

D

Dalhousie Review	Q	1954-	CA

E

Essex Institute Historical Collections	Q	1963-	US
Ethnohistory	Q	1963-	US

F

Florida Historical Quarterly	Q	1954-	US
Forest History	Q	1963-	US

G

Geographical Review	Q	1963-	US
Georgia Historical Quarterly	Q	1955-	US
Georgia Review	Q	1963-	US
Gopher Historian	3	1968-	US
Great Plains Journal	SA	1963-	US

H

Halve Maen	Q	1963-	US
Hidalguía	BM	1955-	SP
Hispanic American Historical Review	Q	1954-	SP
Historian	Q	1953-	US
Historic Preservation	BM	1963-	US
Historical and Scientific Society of Manitoba Papers (old title, see Transactions of the Historical and Scientific Society of Manitoba)			CA
Historical Magazine of the Protestant Episcopal Church	Q	1954-	US
Historical New Hampshire	Q	1963-	US

History of Education Quarterly	Q	1954-	US
History of Religions	Q	1962-	US
History Today	M	1954-	GB
Horizon	Q	1958-	US
Human Organization	Q	1963-	US
Huntington Library Quarterly	Q	1954-	US

I

Idaho Yesterdays	Q	1963-	US
Indiana Magazine of History	Q	1958-	US
Inland Seas	Q	1963-	US
Inter-American Review of Bibliography	Q	1955-	US
Interplay	M	1967-	US

J

Jahrbuch für Amerikastudien	A	1959-	WG
Journal de la Société de Américanistes	SA	1963-	FR
Journal of American Folklore	Q	1965-	US
Journal of American History	Q	1964-	US
Journal of American Studies	3	1960-	GB
Journal of Arizona History	Q	1963-	US
Journal of Church and State	3	1963-	US
Journal of Economic History	Q	1954-	US
Journal of Mississippi History	Q	1963-	US
Journal of Negro History	Q	1954-	US
Journal of Presbyterian History	Q	1954-	US
Journal of Southern History	Q	1954-	US
Journal of the Folklore Institute	3	1964-	US
Journal of the Friends' Historical Society	3	1957-	GB
Journal of the History of Medicine and Allied Sciences	Q	1954-	US
Journal of the Illinois State Historical Society	Q	1963-	US
Journal of the Presbyterian Historical Society (old title, see Journal of Presbyterian History)			US
Journal of the Society of Architectural Historians	Q	1963-	US
Journal of the West	Q	1963-	US
Journalism Quarterly	Q	1954-	US

K

Kansas Historical Quarterly	Q	1963-	US
Kiva	Q	1963-	US

Kroeber Anthropological Society Papers	Q	1963-	US

L

Library of Congress Quarterly Journal	Q	1963-	US
Lincoln Herald	Q	1955-	US
Long Island Forum	M	1969-	US
Louisiana History	Q	1955-	US
Louisiana Studies	Q	1963-	US

M

Mankind	BM	1967-	US
Manuscripta	3	1954-	US
Maryland Historian	SA	1970-	US
Massachusetts Review	Q	1968-	US
Masterkey	Q	1963-	US
Memoires de la Société Royale du Canada (old title, see Transactions of the Royal Society of Canada)			CA
Mennonite Life	Q	1963-	US
Methodist History	Q	1962-	US
Michigan Archaeologist	I	1968-	US
Michigan History	Q	1963-	US
Mid-American	Q	1954-	US
Midcontinent American Studies Journal	SA	1963-	US
Midstream	M	1971-	US
Midwest Quarterly	Q	1963-	US
Military Affairs	Q	1955-	US
Military Collector and Historian	Q	1963-	US
Military Review	M	1963-	US
Minnesota History	Q	1963-	US
Mississippi Valley Historical Review (old title, see Journal of American History)			US
Missouri Historical Review	Q	1963-	US
Missouri Historical Society Bulletin	Q	1962-	US
Mitteilungen des Instituts für Österreichische Geschichtsforschung	A	1954-	AA
Montana	Q	1955-	US
Moravian Historical Society Transactions	A	1963-	US

N

Names	Q	1965-	US
National Genealogical Society Quarterly	Q	1963-	US
Nebraska History	Q	1963-	US
Nevada Historical Society Quarterly	Q	1963-	US
New-England Galaxy	Q	1963-	US
New England Quarterly	Q	1954-	US
New Jersey History	Q	1963-	US
New Mexico Historical Review	Q	1954-	US
New York Folklore Quarterly	Q	1963-	US
New York Historical Society Quarterly	Q	1963-	US
New York History	Q	1955-	US
Newberry Library Bulletin	3	1963-	US
Newfoundland Quarterly	Q	1963-	CA
North American Review	Q	1968-	US
North Carolina Historical Review	Q	1963-	US
North Dakota History	Q	1963-	US
North Dakota Quarterly	Q	1963-	US
Northwest Ohio Quarterly	Q	1963-	US
Northwestern Report	Q	1967-	US
Noticias	Q	1963-	US
Nova Scotia Historical Society Collections	I	1963-	CA
Novaia i Noveishaia Istoriia	BM	1957-	SU
Now and Then	Q	1962-	US

O

Ohio History	Q	1958-	US
Ontario History	Q	1963-	CA
Oregon Historical Quarterly	Q	1955-	US
Organon	3	1969-	US

P

Pacific Historian	Q	1964-	US
Pacific Historical Review	Q	1954-	US
Pacific Northwest Quarterly	Q	1955-	US
Palimpsest	BM	1964-	US
Patterns of Prejudice	BM	1970-	GB
Pennsylvania History	Q	1963-	US
Pennsylvania Magazine of History and Biography	Q	1955-	US
Phylon	Q	1954-	US
Plains Anthropologist	Q	1963-	US
Plateau	Q	1969-	US
Polar Record	3	1964-	GB

Polish American Studies	SA	1959-	US
Political Science Quarterly	Q	1954-	US
Il Politico	Q	1954-	IT
Politics and Society	Q	1970-	US
Princeton University Library Chronicle	3	1963-	US
Proceedings and Collections of the Wyoming Historical and Geological Society	I	1970-	US
Proceedings of the American Antiquarian Society	SA	1954-	US
Proceedings of the American Philosophical Society	BM	1955-	US
Proceedings of the Massachusetts Historical Society	A	1953-	US
Proceedings of the New Jersey Historical Society Quarterly (old title, see New Jersey History)			US
Prologue: Journal of the National Archives	3	1969-	US
Psychiatry	Q	1969-	US

Q

Quaker History	SA	1954-	US
Quarterly Journal of Studies on Alcohol	Q	1968-	US
Queen's Quarterly	Q	1954-	CA

R

Radford Review	Q	1966-	US
Records of the American Catholic Historical Society of Philadelphia	Q	1954-	US
Register of the Kentucky Society	Q	1963-	US
Rendezvous	SA	1968-	US
Research Studies	Q	1964-	US
Revista de Indias	Q	1953-	SP
Revista de la Universidad de Madrid	Q	1955-	SP
Revue d'Histoire de l'Amérique Française	Q	1954-	CA
Revue de l'Université d'Ottawa	Q	1963-	CA
Revue Historique de l'Armée	Q	1954-	FR
Revue Maritime	M	1963-	FR
Rocky Mountain Society Science Journal	SA	1966-	US
Round Table	Q	1955-	GB

S

Saeculum	Q	1954-	WG
Saskatchewan History	3	1963-	CA
Sessions d'Étude: La Société Canadienne d'Histoire de l'Englise Catholique	A	1963-	CA
Slavic Review	Q	1954-	US
Smithsonian	M	1970-	US
Smithsonian Journal of History (ceased pub)	Q	1966-68	US
Social Forces	Q	1963-	US
Social Science Quarterly	Q	1963-	US
Societe Canadienne d'Histoire de l'Eglise Catholique Rapport	A	1963-	CA
Sociology and Social Research	Q	1966-	US
South Carolina Historical Magazine	Q	1963-	US
South California Quarterly	Q	1962-	US
Southern Folklore Quarterly	Q	1959-	US
Southern Indian Studies	A	1959-	US
Southern Quarterly	Q	1963-	US
Southwest Review	Q	1963-	US
Southwestern Historical Quarterly	Q	1955-	US
Southwestern Journal of Anthropology	Q	1963-	US
Stimmen der Zeit	M	1954-	WG
Svensk Tidskrift	10	1954-	SW
Swedish Pioneer Historical	Q	1963-	US

T

Tennessee Historical Quarterly	Q	1963-	US
Texana	Q	1964-	US
Trans-Action	11	1967-	US
Transactions of the Historical and Scientific Society of Manitoba	A	1964-	CA
Transactions of the Royal Society of Canada	A	1954-	CA

U

University of Birmingham Historical Journal	A	1955-	GB
University of Windsor Review	SA	1965-	CA
University of Wyoming Publications	A	1966-	US
Utah Historical Quarterly	Q	1963-	US

V

Vermont History	Q	1963-	US
Vierteljahrschrift für Sozial- und Wirtschaftsgeschichte	Q	1955-	WG

Virginia Cavalcade	Q	1963-	US
Virginia Magazine of History and Biography	Q	1955-	US
Voprosy Istorii	M	1954-	SU

W

West Virginia History	Q	1963-	US
Western American Literature	Q	1966-	US
Western Explorer	I	1964-	US
Western Folklore	Q	1963-	US
Western Historical Quarterly	Q	1970-	US
William and Mary Quarterly	Q	1954-	US
Wisconsin Magazine of History	Q	1963-	US
Wisconsin Then and Now	M	1963-	US

Y

Yonkers Historical Bulletin	SA	1963-	US

FESTSCHRIFTS

Essays on American Literature in Honor of Jay B. Hubbell (Durham: Duke U. Press, 1967).

Essays on the American Civil War (Austin: U. of Texas Press, 1968).

The Old Dominion: Essays for Thomas Perkins Abernethy (Charlottesville: The U. Press of Virginia, 1964).

LIST OF ABSTRACTERS

A

D. J. Abramoske
M. Abrash
G. R. Adams
H. M. Adams
K. Adelfang
C. J. Allard
C. R. Allen, Jr.
R. F. Allen
R. N. Alvis
H. Aptheker
D. van Arkel
C. W. Arnade

B

Sr. B. A. Barbato
V. O. Bardsley
G. Barrett
T. D. S. Bassett
G. Bassler
K. J. Bauer
L. Beckom
H. F. Bedford
D. I. Blanchard
W. R. Boedecker
E. H. Boehm
J. B. Boles
M. A. Booth
W. L. Bowers
C. L. Boyd
J. M. Brady

N. C. Brockman
D. Brockway
W. J. Brooks
D. N. Brown
E. Brown
L. Brown
W. A. Buckman
J. M. Bumsted
R. S. Burke
H. M. Burns
R. S. Burns
D. Bushnell
J. S. Buttrey

C

H. L. Calkin
R. V. Clavert
D. D. Cameron
R. F. Campbell
J. A. Casada
J. E. Caswell
G. L. Cole
R. G. Comegys
T. M. Condon
J. F. Cook
E. P. Costello
J. S. Counelis
H. E. Cox
J. K. Crane
T. R. Cripps
J. C. Crowe
D. W. Curl

D

D. G. Davis
G. H. Davis
K. P. Davis
S. R. Davison
R. W. Delaney
D. B. Dodd
G. B. Dodds
B. A. Drummond
J. B. Duff

E

H. G. Earnhart
C. L. Eichelberger
W. Elkins
G. Emery
E. E. Eminhizer
E. A. Erickson
A. Erlebacher
H. Ershkowitz

F

M. Faissler
T. J. Farnham
J. D. Filipiak
L. Filler
J. Findlay
J. K. Flack

R. J. C. Ford
W. L. Fox
D. M. Furman

G

G. O. Gagnon
D. P. Gallagher
L. Gara
J. S. Gassner
C. C. Gorchels
H. J. Graham
C. L. Grant
J. A. S. Grenville
G. M. Gressley
W. R. Griffin

H

E. M. Hade
R. J. Hanks
L. R. Harlan
E. W. Hathaway
J. M. Hawes
D. F. Henderson
J. Herbst
J. W. Hillje
A. Hoffman
A. Hopping
M. Hough
D. Houston
R. Howell
J. A. Hudson
R. N. Hudspeth
J. K. Huhta
G. W. Hull
S. E. Humphreys
E. C. Hyslop

J

D. C. James
K. James
J. Jensen
E. S. Johnson
H. C. Johnson
P. Johnson

G. H. G. Jones
S. L. Jones
H. D. Jordan

K

M. Kanin
L. D. Kasparian
M. A. Kaufman
G. H. Kelsey
H. Kelsey
P. W. Kennedy
L. A. Knafla
R. J. Knowlton
G. Kurland
N. Kurland

L

R. B. Lange
C. F. Latour
A. H. Lawrance
A. E. LeBlanc
I. M. Leonard
D. Lindsey
H. T. Lovin
R. Lowitt
I. Luyken
G. L. Lycan
J. L. Lycan

M

M. W. Machan
J. F. Mahoney
H. F. Malyon
R. J. Marion
Sr. M. McAuley
M. J. McBaine
R. McBane
P. M. McCain
J. M. McCarthy
J. J. McCusker
J. McCutcheon
G. W. McGinty
D. McIntyre

S. L. McNeel
R. S. Melamed
R. R. Mertz
W. D. Metz
R. A. Mohl
T. L. Moir
W. G. Morgan
B. M. Morrison
W. Mott
R. Mueller
G. A. Mugge
D. H. Murdoch
E. C. Murdock

N

H. A. Negaard
L. G. Nelson
C. A. Newton
R. L. Nichols
I. W. Van Noppen

O

E. J. O'Brien
E. Oberholzer, Jr.
C. F. Ogilvie
G. L. Owen

P

S. C. Pearson, Jr.
D. P. Peltier
J. G. Pennington
N. L. Peterson
W. F. Peterson
M. Petrie
D. R. Picht
R. S. Pickett
S. R. Pliska
H. B. Powell
P. A. Proett

Q

B. T. Quinten